# Motivation

Third Edition

# MOTIVATION
## Theories and Principles

### ROBERT C. BECK
*Wake Forest University*

Prentice Hall, Englewood Cliffs, New Jersey 07632

Library of Congress Cataloging-in-Publication Data

Beck, Robert C. (Robert Clarence).
    Motivation : theories and principles / Robert C. Beck. -- 3rd ed.
      p.   cm.
    Includes bibliographical references.
    ISBN 0-13-603077-7
    1. Motivation (Psychology)   I. Title.
BF503.B38  1990
  153.8--dc20                                        89-37529
                                                        CIP

Editorial/production supervision
  and interior design: *Mary Kathryn Leclercq*
Cover design: *Joel Beck*
Manufacturing buyer: *Robert Anderson*

 © 1990, 1983, 1978 by Prentice-Hall, Inc.
A Division of Simon & Schuster
Englewood Cliffs, New Jersey 07632

Printed in the United States of America
10  9  8  7  6  5  4  3  2

ISBN   0-13-603077-7

Prentice-Hall International (UK) Limited, *London*
Prentice-Hall of Australia Pty. Limited, *Sydney*
Prentice-Hall Canada Inc., *Toronto*
Prentice-Hall Hispanoamericana, S.A., *Mexico*
Prentice-Hall of India Private Limited, *New Delhi*
Prentice-Hall of Japan, Inc., *Tokyo*
Simon & Schuster Asia Pte. Ltd., *Singapore*
Editora Prentice-Hall do Brasil, Ltda., *Rio de Janeiro*

*To Terra Anne Hines and Justyna Kristine Rominger,
the two newest members of the clan.*

# Contents

# Preface

This third edition of *Motivation: Theories and Principles* expresses the same orientation toward motivation as that in earlier editions. It is an experimentally-oriented survey of research and theory on animal and human motivation. In the first edition I noted that it is difficult to maintain a completely logical and consistent conceptualization of motivation without sacrificing a large amount of material which many people consider important to the topic. This is still true. Motivation theorists and researchers are still fragmented in their efforts to understand motivation. Much of the reason for this, it seems to me, is that *evolution* has not been a completely logical and consistent process. Consequently, principles developed in the context of, say, animal appetitive behaviors may not be applicable to a different set of motivational problems, or in different species. The end result is a great diversity of approaches to motivation, none of which can probably be considered *the* correct approach.

*Motivation, 3/e* therefore continues to reflect the above diversity while still trying to provide an umbrella approach to motivation which sets motivation off as a distinct area of psychology. Motivation is much more than a series of questions about why organisms behave as they do. It is a distinctly definable and useful concept for understanding behavior.

Given the same ambitions as the previous editions, there are numerous changes in the structure and content in this edition, which reflect the changing face of the science. Almost a third of the references are new to this edition, updating old topics and adding new ones. Chapter 2 updates research on emotion, especially on facial expression and effects of mood. Emotion in one way or another has been given greater emphasis throughout. Chapters 7 (pain, fear, avoidance, punishment), 8 (frustration, conflict, anger, aggression) and 9 (anxiety, stress, coping) have been designed to provide a smooth transition from basic research and theory on aversive conditions to human stress and coping. Instinct, drive, and activation have been combined (Ch. 3). Chapters 4 (hunger, thirst, taste) and 6 (rewards) take a more ecological approach by discussing optimal foraging theory and behavioral economics. A new chapter (Ch. 5) covers temperature regulation, ESSB, and sex. More detailed discussions of power and interpersonal attraction have been added in Chapters 11 and 12. New sections on motivation in advertising and sports have been combined with job motivation in Chapter 13.

I would like to thank a number of people for their assistance. Foremost among these are Jane Reade, Teresa Hill, and Joan Worth, whose patience and good will in getting text and references in and out of the computer were exemplary. Also, I give my thanks to David Berger, SUNY at Cortland, and Alan Randich, University of Iowa, for their reviews of the third edition, and to Susan Finnemore and Katy Leclercq of Prentice Hall for their efforts. Finally, once again, I express my appreciation to my family for enduring the whole writing/production process with me.

R.C.B.

# Motivation

# 1

# The Nature of Motivation Theory

Introduction

Mind and Body: One or Two?

> *Dualisms*
> *Monisms*

Freedom of Choice: Illusion or Reality?

> *The Problem of Freedom*
> *Determinism: Hard, Soft, and Probabilistic*

Philosophy and Language of Science

> *Syntactics: Putting Words Together*
> *Semantics: The Problem of Definitions*

Scientific Theory

> *Nature of Scientific Theory*
> *Criteria for Goodness of a Theory*

Objectivity, Explanation, and Causation

> *Objectivity: Intersubjective Reliability*
> *Explanation*
> *Causation*
> *Levels of Analysis*

The Problem of Defining Motivation

> *Regulatory versus Purposive Approaches*
> *Learning and Motivation*
> *Motivation as an Intervening Variable*
> *Desire and Aversion as Intervening Variables*

Summary

## INTRODUCTION

On August 1, 1966, Charles Whitman, twenty-five years of age, climbed to the observation deck of the Tower Building at the University of Texas. In two hours, he killed fourteen people and wounded twenty-four others before he himself was slain by the police. The question raised for all psychology, and especially for motivation theory, is *why?* By any common meaning of the term, Whitman was not rational, even though his actions seemed carefully planned. There were numerous interesting little twists in the accounts that followed.[1] Many people thought him a fine young man. He liked children, worked hard, and had been an Eagle Scout at the age of twelve. He had a good sense of humor, and most of his friends and acquaintances seemed to regard him highly.

There are many possible explanations for Whitman's two-hour spree. He had a need for achievement, particularly to surpass his father, but was frustrated by not doing as well as he hoped in school. He was continually stressed by overwork; he carried heavy academic loads and part-time jobs. His family had an abiding interest in guns, which reporters saw in every room of his parents' house after the incident. And there was possibly a specific biological disorder: He was reported (upon autopsy) to have a brain tumor in an area known to be related to aggressive behaviors. Any of these factors, as well as others not considered here, might have led to the final tragic outcome. We cannot really know the answer to this particular drama, because the central character is gone. This much we do know: The answer is not simple. But it is the kind of mystery psychologists are supposed to help unravel. Its very irrationality seems to demand a "motivational" account.

To explore and analyze motivational concepts, as in the macabre drama of Charles Whitman, we must go into the seemingly more prosaic world of scientific theory and research. Motivational concepts are supposed to help explain the fact that *under virtually identical external circumstances there are great variations in individual behavior.* Someone else in Charles Whitman's situation might have behaved quite differently than he did.

Sometimes a *single* motivational concept seems to provide adequate explanation, such as "I eat when I am 'hungry' but do not eat otherwise." Many motivational concepts might be needed to explain a situation as complex as Charles Whitman's, however, and we might find ourselves discussing instincts, needs, drives, goals, incentives, conflict, needs for achievement or power, frustration, and aggression. We shall look at many such ideas *critically,* becoming wary of the easy answer but gaining insight into motivation theory and concepts.

---

[1] I am indebted to the late Dr. James Steintrager, a Texas faculty member who was on the Texas campus that day, for detailed descriptions of the unfolding events.

Some psychologists have argued that motivational concepts are too vague to be useful. But many real-life problems seem to demand motivational explanations: Why do some children steal? Why do some people take drugs? Why do some kids do well in school when equally talented ones fail? How can we get people to work harder? Why do we have wars and killings? Why do people create? The individual variations in these activities highlight the need for motivational explanations and the possibility of producing change for the better.

*Outline of this chapter.*   This chapter lays the groundwork for our study of motivation: it encompasses a number of ideas fundamental to the understanding of scientific explanation in general and motivation theory in particular. First, we consider two *philosophical* questions uniquely important to psychology: the nature of the relationship between mind and body, and whether our behavior is *free or determined.* Second, we look at the *language of science.* Third, we explore the nature of *scientific theory,* because motivational concepts cannot be understood except in the context of theory and in relation to other concepts. Fourth, we examine the meaning of such commonly used terms as *objectivity, explanation, and causation.* Finally, we tackle the problem of *defining motivation objectively* and consider which factors determine our choice of a definition.

In subsequent chapters we explore the relation of *emotion* to motivation (chapter two), *biological* analyses of motivation (chapters two to five), *behavior theory* analyses (chapters six to nine) and *social-cognitive* analyses (chapters ten to thirteen). In reading these chapters, it is good to keep in mind the main points of chapter one, which represent the guiding orientation for the book as a whole.

## MIND AND BODY: ONE OR TWO?

Psychology is the science that uniquely studies both mind and body. There is a long history of thought probing the relationship between the two and we need to be familiar with the issues involved. For the average person the relationship of mind to body probably is clear. The "official doctrine" (Ryle, 1949) is that "body" is physical, material, limited in space, time, and size, and objectively observable. "Mind," on the other hand, bears the opposite of all these qualities. It is subjective, directly known only to the individual possessing it, unlimited in physical dimensions, and, perhaps, everlasting. This distinction is essentially the same doctrine generally accepted in Western theology to maintain the separation of "body" and "soul." It goes back to the Greek philosopher Plato, came into Christianity with St. Augustine, and reemerged in modern philosophy with the French philosopher René Descartes.

As a "person on the street" might view it, then, we are aware of our circumstances, feelings, and ideas. Faced with several possible actions, we *consciously* and *freely will* ourselves to take this or that action. This brief statement assumes that Descartes's view of mind and body is correct, and that we really are free to make any choice. Since psychologists generally look at mind-body and freedom-determinism issues differently from the person on the street, however, we need to scrutinize these assumptions.

There are two general classes of opinion regarding mind and body. The proponents of *dualism* assume that mind and body are qualitatively different. The *monism* camp assumes that the mind and body really are qualitatively the same.

### Dualisms

*Interactionistic dualism.*   This is the view developed by Descartes, commonly called *Cartesian dualism.* Mind and body are considered qualitatively different categories, immaterial and material, and what the body does depends on the mind. That is, there is a causal relation. Where and how do the two interact, however? Descartes ([1650] 1892) suggested the pineal gland in the brain as the point of interaction and developed a physical model based on reflected light rays to include this idea. He proposed that light energy comes into the eyes and activates "spirits" that are reflected one way or another by the pineal gland, which he saw as something like a pivoting mirror. Depending on where the spirits were reflected, different movements of the body occurred. The term *reflex*, referring to an automatic movement following a particular stimulus (such as a knee jerk when the patellar tendon is struck), comes from Descartes's description of the "reflection of spirits." We would now call these "spirits" *neural impulses.* According to Descartes, animal behavior consisted entirely of reflexes; humans were said to have reflexes, but also the human mind could *will* various behaviors.

The logical problems with such a theory are very difficult. If our minds and bodies really are so unlike each other, how could they interact? Factually, we now know that the pineal gland serves no function such as Descartes speculated.

*Parallelistic dualism.*   Suppose we set two atomic clocks to exactly the same time, then leave them to run out their separate existences. Whenever we look at one clock we will be able to tell what the other says. The German philosopher Gottfried Wilhelm Leibniz proposed such a view of mind and body (Duncan, 1890). Just as one clock does not cause the other to tell a particular time, so the mind does not cause the body to do a particular thing. There is a high *correlation* between the two events in question, however. This view recognizes the obvious existence of mental life, as well as the body, and the correlation between experience and behavior, but it does not raise the problem of how they could interact.

Parallelism may indeed simply make a *practical* distinction between mind and body. The *methods* for studying mental activity (such as recording what people *say* about their experiences) are sufficiently different from the methods of studying bodily action (such as physical recordings) that the mind-body distinction is worth maintaining for this reason alone.

### Monisms

*Mentalistic monism.*   How do we know about the existence of a world outside our own minds? It seems obvious that we know about it through our consciousness of it, through our minds. But, what *proof* could we offer that things exist outside our minds? Our dreams in all their terror or sensuousness seem real at the time, but we know they are not "real." Neither are hallucinations. Mentalistic monism is the view that we do not *have* to assume any external world if our only knowledge of it is from our experience. This was proposed by the British philosopher Bishop George Berkeley ([1710] 1939). If we know the world only from experiences, perhaps experience is *all* there is.

Another British philosopher, David Hume ([1748] 1939), proposed an even more extreme view, called *solipsism*. Hume's logical extension of Berkeley is the possibility that there is but a *single mind* and that any other apparent minds are only the experience of this mind, just as apparent objects are the experience of this mind. There are no physical objects, no bodies, no other minds. The logic is undeniable. Now someone may cry, "Why do thorns pain me unless thorns exist?" The answer is that the existence of thorns has to be *assumed* first. The assumption is built into the question. The solipsistic argument assumes the opposite, that such things do *not* exist. The burden of proof falls on "you" to show that they *do* exist as separate entities. If the experience of pain accompanies the experience of thorns, that is just the way experiences are. "But," may come the reply, "surely a mind would not produce pain for itself." This is irrelevant. One does not pick and choose experiences, they just happen. Indeed, even the objections to my argument do not exist outside my own mind because there is no separate "you" outside my own mind. The mind-body problem disappears since there is only the mind. Right or wrong, this argument has a practical implication about how we look at the causes of events, an issue to which we turn later.

*Materialistic monism.*   This view holds that the single underlying reality is material. The mind represents the functioning of the brain. Let us use the analogy of a dump truck. The truck moves about, picks up and drops things, generally acting as a dump truck should. We do not, however, talk about these functions of the truck as *causing* the truck to behave in its ordained manner, or as existing separately from the truck. From this point of view, the body, especially the nervous system, is so constructed that one of its functions is consciousness. This *function* does not cause behaviors to occur, however; the nervous system causes them to occur.

The *neural identity theory* says that the material brain can be viewed in two different ways, just as we view two sides of a coin differently. The physiologist's description of the brain and a person's report of his or her own experience are both *symbolic* statements about the same thing (Pepper, 1959). Both describe the activity of the brain, but from different points of view and with different languages. For example, the person talks about seeing the color red, whereas the physiologist talks about certain neurons firing under certain stimulus conditions.

For every conscious mental event, there is a corresponding brain event. The converse is not necessarily true, however; we are not necessarily aware of everything that goes on in our nervous systems. We are not aware of the neural activities that control breathing, for example. Nor are we aware at a given time of most of the things we remember. Many neural processes involved in motivation, emotion, and memory may influence our behavior without our being aware of them at the moment. Neural activities of which we *are* aware may be especially important for such activities as learning, but this is speculation and its validity must be determined by research. (Considerable research shows, for example, that we do not learn while sleeping.)

The close identity of conscious experience and brain function is increasingly shown in neurophysiological research. For example:

1.  Some individual neurons in the visual part of the brain respond only to lines with vertical orientations, others to horizontal lines, and some to both orientations. Other neurons respond only to moving stimuli, not to stationary ones. Such relationships have been found in frogs, cats, and monkeys, and it is reasonable to assume they also exist in humans.
2.  If the two hemispheres of the brain are surgically separated, there are two independent "minds" where before there was one. Each half of the brain is now an independent unit, and things learned in one half are unknown to the other half (e.g., Gazzaniga, 1967). Reason or logic never would have predicted that splitting the brain into two hemispheres would produce two minds.

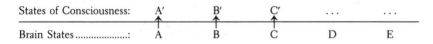

FIGURE 1-1.   Neural Identity Theory. For every distinguishable state of consciousness (A', B', C', etc.) there is a corresponding distinguishable state of the brain (A, B, C,). Consciousness *reflects* particular states of the brain. Every state of the brain, however, (such as D and E) does not necessarily have a corresponding state of awareness. We are not aware of the neural activity controlling our heart rate or breathing, nor are we continuously aware of all the things we have learned in the past. The brain states reflecting our past learning nevertheless influence us.

3.  Various drugs have mind-altering effects, such as producing hallucinations or reducing anxiety.

Many other lines of evidence also indicate the close relationship of mind and body: studies based on injury to the nervous system and diseases affecting the nervous system; the extensive study of drugs affecting the mind; and electrical stimulation and recording from the brain.

One final point on the mind-body problem. By nature and definition, science deals with *observable events*. For psychology, these observable events are *behaviors*, body activities ranging from filling out attitude survey questionnaires to throwing baseballs to describing drug experiences. Do we need to infer something behind those behaviors that is uniquely different from what the nervous system can reasonably be expected to do? The answer would seem to be no. This is not to say that all experience is, or can be, *expressed* in behavior, or that behavior tells us everything about a person. It simply says that, from a scientific point of view, the minds of *other* people are inferred from their behavior, including the things they say. We do not really question the existence of consciousness, but the immediate experience of consciousness is not usable scientific data, open to observers other than the self.

In summary, the popular view that mind and body are different and that mind controls body is but one of several logical possibilities. The particular belief anyone has in this matter may have important practical consequences — deciding how to go about studying and treating "mental" disorders, for example. (What meaning would drug therapy have if the nervous system were not related to the mind?) But there is no way to know which view is "really" correct.

## FREEDOM OF CHOICE: ILLUSION OR REALITY?

### The Problem of Freedom

Our second philosophical issue related to the mind-body problem is freedom to act versus determinism. This problem has powerful implications for life in general, as well as for psychological science. We all like to feel free to act as we choose, and an unkept resolution is a failure of our will in keeping it. The concepts of freedom and will are among our most precious intellectual commodities. From a scientific point of view, however, we see that freedom to choose poses a problem: If we can do anything we wish at any time, then how can we predict behavior? Furthermore, if we could not predict the behavior of others, and thus could not know how to act toward other people, would not utter social chaos arise?

Society deals inconsistently with the question of freedom. A person may be imprisoned because he or she "chose" to commit a crime. But if we assume complete freedom of choice of behavior, then punishment should not deter future crimes. Punishment would then be nothing more than a retributive "eye for an eye." Punishment makes sense only if we expect it to alter (determine) future behavior. Even the argument that punishment sets an example for others assumes that the threat of punishment will partly determine their behavior. Because of such inconsistencies in the free-will argument, as well as because of the impossibility of having a science of behavior without assuming determinism, determinism has been accepted as necessary for the behavioral sciences, just as it is for the physical sciences.

### Determinism

Stated simply, determinism means that if Cause A occurs, the Effect B will follow. If I suddenly make a loud sound behind you, you will jump. If I am hungry, I will eat. In the psychology laboratory we can repeatedly do experiments with human subjects and obtain the same results under the same conditions. Indeed, most undergraduate experimental psychology laboratories use at least some "tried and true" demonstration experiments that almost always work, such as simple experiments in human learning or perception. We depend on the predictability of behavior to make such demonstrations reliable.

Behavior is affected by many different conditions, however, and to the extent that we do not know what conditions are prevailing at a given time, our predictions are less reliable. A psychologist is unwilling to predict the behavior of a person at a party for the same reason that a physicist balks at predicting the behavior of a handful of confetti thrown at that party: In neither case are known all the conditions bearing on the behaviors. Prediction in psychology is also made more difficult because some of the variables influencing behavior are *internal* variables, not open to direct observation by outsiders. The "impressions" of past experiences are obviously important, but we can neither recall all our own past experiences nor know all those of other people.

"Freedom," then, often comes down to *lack of predictability*. Freedom of behavior is perceived differently according to where the cause(s) of a particular behavior are located. If a particular behavior is *mainly* controlled by external, observable events, we tend to say it is *determined*. If the behavior is primarily controlled by internal, unobservable events, we might call it *free*. As Tomkins (1981) also points out, the more choices we have, the "freer" we seem. Failure to predict behavior with perfect accuracy is not the same thing as freedom.

There are several different meanings of determinism, however, If we knew enough, perhaps we could predict all the behavior of a person with mathematical precision. This is an untestable hypothesis, however, since we never have this much information. Such precise prediction, called *hard determinism*, is thus possible only as an ideal, not an immediate, practical goal.

A different view, called *soft determinism*, is that some behaviors are determined and others are not. This is perhaps the worst approach to the problem because it provides no rules for saying whether an inaccurate prediction about behavior means the behavior is "free" or whether we are simply ignorant of important variables which tomorrow we might understand. Predictions of behavior can go wrong for many reasons. We may have poor measurement procedures, use sloppy research technique, or simply be studying the wrong variable for predicting a behavior of interest.

*Probabilistic determinism* approaches prediction as insurance companies do (Vorsteg, 1974). If we can predict with a respectable level of probability that people will perform a certain way under certain conditions, we believe we have predicted rather successfully. We have statistical techniques (inferential statistics) to help evaluate our success in such probabilistic situations. Probabilistic prediction, then, is no denial of determinism; it is just a realistic recognition of the fallibility of science and scientists.

The question of social freedom or control is not the issue here. Belief in freedom does not change the laws of behavior, and belief in determinism does not imply any particular kind of social control. A *belief* in freedom, however, could be an internal determinant of behavior with different effects than those following a belief in determinism. Political leaders who believe in determinism may try to exert different social controls than the leaders who believe in freedom. By the same token, anyone asking for improved teaching methods, cures for mental illness, or less violence is asking, "What can we do to *produce* those ends?" These questions assume determinism since they imply that if we had the answers we could *make* things happen the way we want.

## PHILOSOPHY AND LANGUAGE OF SCIENCE

We now turn to the general features of scientific theory, the larger enterprise of which psychological theory is a part. What is a scientific explanation of behavior? It is far more than a recitation of dull statistics; it involves a complex set of relationships among concepts, and the possibility that the explanation can be supported or disproven by evidence.

Knowledge is communicated by language, but there are different uses of language. If we wanted an emotional or poetic description of behavior or thought, we could use poetic language to produce the desired effect, without concern for detailed accuracy. If we wanted a chronology of events such as those preceding the Whitman killings, we would have to be *historically* precise in our language. If we wanted to be scientifically accurate, we would have to be more mathematically and logically precise. In each case we use language, but with somewhat different purposes.

The philosopher Charles Morris (1938) has given us a system for understanding *scientific* language, called *semiotic*. The three subareas, illustrated in Figure 1-2, are *syntactics* (the relations of different signs to each other), *semantics* (the relations of signs to the objects to which they refer), and *pragmatics* (the relations of signs to their users). Signs are any linguistic conventions, words, or numbers. We are interested here in syntactics and semantics.

### Syntactics: Putting Words Together

Syntactics refers to formal rules for manipulating signs (or words). Every language, including logic and mathematics, has such formal rules. For example, by applying the basic rules of arithmetic and algebra, we can manipulate the formula $M = \Sigma X/N$ in various ways, including $NM = \Sigma X$ or $N = \Sigma X/M$. As any psychology student would recognize, this is the formula for the arithmetic mean, in which M equals the mean, $\Sigma X$ is the sum of the individual scores, and N is the number of scores. However, we can move the signs around into different combinations, following the rules, even if the signs do not actually refer to anything. Whatever the symbols' meaning, all that is required to manipulate them is to know the rules.

As another example, consider the elementary syllogism:

Dogs bark.
Fred is a dog.
Therefore Fred barks.

Now, we can determine the *validity* but not the *truth* of the conclusion that "Fred barks" by *logically* analyzing the two premises and the conclusion. If these are in the proper form, as described in any introductory logic book, the conclusion is *valid,* which means that the conclusion follows from the premises according to the rules. In order for the conclusion to be *true,* however, the premises would have to be true in *fact* as well as being logically sound. If it *is* true that all dogs *do* bark, and if there *is* a Fred who *is* a dog, then the conclusion that "Fred barks" is both valid and true. The syllogism, as well as the more sophisticated forms of symbolic logic, is important because the validity of an argument can be determined in symbolic form, separately from

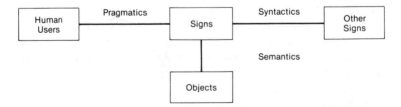

**FIGURE 1-2.** The three areas of semiotic: Syntactics, Semantics, and Pragmatics.

the specific content of the argument. Thus we can evaluate the argument that

All A's are B's.
C is a B.
Therefore C is an A.

The conclusion in this case is clearly wrong: C might or might not be an A, because there may be some B's that are not A's. In summary, syntactics is concerned with the establishment and use of agreed-on rules by which we can relate signs (symbols or words) to each other. This greatly helps reduce ambiguity in our use of language.

### Semantics: The Problem of Definitions

*Semantics* refers to the rules by which we assign a symbol to an object or event; these are the rules for *defining* terms. The simplest definition is the ostensive, or pointing, definition. For example, we may say *"That* is what I mean by *dog,"* while pointing to a dog. All definitions eventually have to appeal to sense observations. We might read that a "dog" is "a four-legged animal that barks and is commonly used as a house pet," but we have the problem of knowing what is meant by "four," "legged," "animal," "barks," and so on. The individual reading the definition must know the meaning of these more *primitive terms,* based on observation, before the definition makes sense. We usually assume that everybody knows what we mean by color names, simple numbers, and so on, and we progress from there to build more complex definitions via language.

*Operational definitions.*    Scientific definitions can be very complicated, in order to be accurate. Thus, P. W. Bridgman argued that we define the *meaning* of something in terms of how we *measure* it. The procedures for *measuring* length are what we mean by the term *length.* "In general," he said, "we mean by any concept nothing more than a set of operations; the concept is synonymous with the corresponding set of [measurement] operations" (Bridgman, 1927, p. 5). Length, weight, and time are defined in terms of how we measure them.

Without measurement procedures such concepts are *empirically* meaningless words, not related to the "real world." Length, for example, can be measured by laying down a standard rod repeatedly and counting the number of times it takes to go from one end of an object to the other. This gives us a common definition and meaning for "length." But what about situations where we cannot perform this operation? We cannot measure the diameter of the sun, the diameter of an atom, or the distance of the stars by "laying down a rod." Neither can we measure the length of an object moving at high speed (such as a photon) in this manner. When we use new measurement procedures, we may be led to changes in fundamental concepts, either in physics or in psychology. The development of psychological tests, for example, has had a profound impact on our understanding of human personality and intellect.

*Operationism and psychological concepts.* There is a saying that "intelligence is what intelligence tests measure." In a trivial sense, this remark denies any understanding of intelligence. Operationally, however, it means that our understanding of intelligence depends on measurement operations. If we define intelligence in terms of such hypothetical properties as "problem-solving ability," we do little to understand it and nothing to measure it. But if we set up a series of problems, and measure the ability to solve them, we have taken a step in the right direction. Alfred Binet did just this. He defined mental age in terms of successful completion of various tasks. The concept of intelligence quotient, $IQ = (MA/CA) \times 100$ gives a *series* of operations by which to define the concept. We define mental age (MA) and chronological age (CA) and divide to get IQ.

*A loosening of operationism.* An operationally defined concept is not necessarily useful since it might be too specific to relate to anything else. Conversely, a concept not fully defined operationally might still be useful. Most theorists have backed off from the notion that we can only work with operationally defined concepts, but the problem needs to be considered at two levels: operationism in *research* and operationism in *theory construction.* In a specific experiment, for example, if we talk about "hunger" affecting some behavior, we have to define in exact *operational terms* what we mean by hunger. We might define hunger in terms of hours of food deprivation prior to testing. In a broader theory, however, we might find it useful to theorize about hunger under conditions different from deprivation but operationally still undefined.

*Converging operations.* A *single* set of operations seldom isolates a single concept as an account of a behavior. Rather, we *converge* on a concept by using different operations (Garner, Hake, & Eriksen, 1956). For example, an experiment by McCleary and Lazarus (1949) showed that emotion-arousing words had to be flashed in front of a subject for longer periods of time to be accurately recognized than did neutral words. One interpretation was that emotional arousal "blocked" *perception* of the words (McGinnies, 1949). On the other hand, it is possible that a *response bias* was involved, lesser willingness to report the "emotion-arousing" words. Thus, college students of the 1950's might have hesitated to *say* out loud such "dirty words" as *bitch,* flashed at them in a psychology laboratory, unless they were certain of what the words were. Recognition of more neutral words would not be held back, however. Experiments involving other operations were conducted to converge on this response-bias interpretation. Postman, Bronson, and Gropper (1953) told different groups of subjects that it was a sign of good or poor mental health to recognize such words readily. The "good health" group was quicker to "recognize" (report) the words than a group given no instructions, and the "poor health" group was slowest. The results did converge on the response-bias interpretation as the correct one. Converging operations have also been used in experiments attempting to distinguish between learning and motivational influences on behavior.

## SCIENTIFIC THEORY

We have seen how we define terms and how we put them together with syntax. Now we see the way we put all this together in scientific theory.

### Nature of Scientific Theory

A scientific theory is like a model. However, just as a model airplane is not exactly like a real airplane, but contains the main features, so a scientific theory does not represent all the world, but only certain features. We use the word *model* in a broad sense, referring to an actual physical model, to a set of diagrams, or to a set of mathematical equations.

Similarly, Toulmin (1953) likened a scientific theory to a map, the map being a kind of model. There is a domain of reality, such as the geographical terrain, which can be described by a map, but only imperfectly. The map also includes lines for longitude and latitude, which, although useful, are not found on the terrain itself. As part of the map, they do not have to have an actual correspondence to reality to be good or useful. Furthermore, we may have an entire set of maps for the same geographic area, such as maps for sewer lines, power lines, water lines, streets, topography, and population density. Which one is the *real* city? None of them is the "real" or complete city, but each is a model, or theory, useful to describe particular things. Similarly, no scientific theory tries to encompass everything, but each theory is intended to be useful for some events.

In a scientific theory, concepts are defined in terms of observable events (semantics), and the theory states how the concepts are related to each other (syntactics). Predictions about the real world are made on the basis of the syntax of the theory. For example, in Figure 1-3, A, B, and C are theoretical concepts defined by specific experimental control procedures (operations) a, b, and c. Concept D, however, is defined by the syntax of the theory $D = (A \times B) + C$. If we know the values for A, B, and C (the independent variables in the experimental situation), then we can predict the value for D, which is measured as the *dependent* variable in the situation. If we hold A and B constant, changing only the value of C, the measured outcome tells us how C affects the dependent variable. If the theory does not

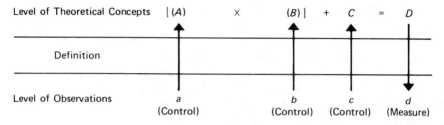

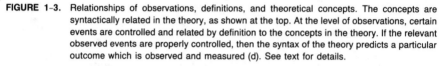

FIGURE 1-3. Relationships of observations, definitions, and theoretical concepts. The concepts are syntactically related in the theory, as shown at the top. At the level of observations, certain events are controlled and related by definition to the concepts in the theory. If the relevant observed events are properly controlled, then the syntax of the theory predicts a particular outcome which is observed and measured (d). See text for details.

predict accurately, we will change its syntax, add new concepts, or eliminate old ones. We may have to scrap the theory if it never works right.

As a specific example, Hull (1943) proposed that learning multiplies with motivation to determine performance. He symbolized learning as H (for habit), motivation as D (for drive), and performance potential as E (for excitatory potential). His theoretical statement was:

Excitatory Potential = Habit × Drive, or
$E = H \times D$

He defined the magnitude of H operationally in terms of number of previous learning trials, magnitude of D in terms of hours of food deprivation, and E as H × D. In Figure 3-1, we have another illustration of the principles embodied in Figure 1-4.

Given the concepts and the syntax, we can make many specific predictions about experimental outcomes. For example, the theory says that running speed depends on the *multiplication* of habit and drive. If a particular response has not been learned (H = O), or if there is no drive (D = O), then E = O and there would be no performance. To make exact predictions, we would need *exact numerical values* for our concepts, such as numerical values for habit and drive. In psychological research we seldom have such high precision, and therefore we usually deal with *inequalities.* Thus, we might say that 22 hours of food deprivation produces *more* "drive" than 2 hours, and performance should be "better" (running faster to food) at 22 hours. We cannot predict exact speeds, however.

### Criteria for Goodness of a Theory

How do we distinguish a good scientific theory from a bad one, or from a theory which claims to be scientific but is not? Four criteria distinguish a good theory: testability, fruitfulness, simplicity, and comprehensiveness.

(1) *Testability.* The most important characteristic of a good theory is that it can be shown to be *wrong* (Popper, 1959). Its predictions are specific enough to be "risky," and some outcome other than the predicted outcome

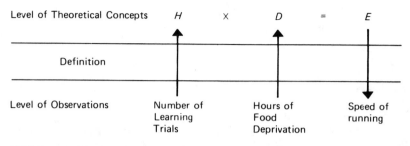

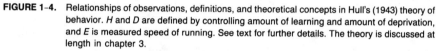

FIGURE 1-4.  Relationships of observations, definitions, and theoretical concepts in Hull's (1943) theory of behavior. *H* and *D* are defined by controlling amount of learning and amount of deprivation, and *E* is measured speed of running. See text for further details. The theory is discussed at length in chapter 3.

can *disconfirm (falsify)* the theory. A theory that cannot be falsified is not a good theory, because it cannot be tested.

(2) *Fruitfulness.* A fruitful theory generates research so that more knowledge is gained than that from the initial attempts to test the theory. Hull's (1943) theory generated a great deal of research, much of which falsified the theory! Such built-in obsolescence is characteristic of a fruitful, falsifiable theory.

(3) *Simplicity.* If there are two explanations for an event, the simpler of the two is preferable. This principle of *parsimony* is commonly called "Occam's razor." The term *simplicity* may refer to the *number* of concepts in a theory (the fewer the better if they are adequate) or to the *complexity* of the relationships among them.

(4) *Comprehensiveness.* The better theory explains the greater number of observations. Einstein's theory was more complicated than Newton's, but Einstein's theory also explained more. A less comprehensive theory may be more practical for some situations, however. Newton's theory is quite adequate to work out bullet trajectories, for example, and the additional complications of Einstein's theory would hinder more than help.

## OBJECTIVITY, EXPLANATION, AND CAUSATION

### Objectivity: Intersubjective Reliability

We often think of objectivity as involving "perfect" observation, free from any bias on the part of the researcher. Less-than-perfect observations are "subjective" and hence "nonscientific." Yet, all observations are subject to some kind of error, and *objective* and *subjective* are relative terms, not absolute. We try to keep errors to a minimum by recognizing that they may occur and by using techniques that tend to be relatively error-free. For instance, we use automatic counters and timers other than counting in our heads. We also try to estimate the size of error, so that we can take the error in our results into account. Amount of error can be estimated by taking repeated measurements, such as the accounts of several observers observing the same events simultaneously. If such observers are in high agreement (have high intersub-jective reliability), then the measurement is relatively objective. With low agreement, the measurement is relatively subjective (low intersubjective reliability).

### Explanation

We have used the term "explain," but what does it mean to "explain" an event? Turner (1967) distinguishes between explanations that are *psychologically* satisfying and those that are *logically* satisfying. A psychologically satisfying explanation may be pleasing to hear, familiar, or even mystifying, but not necessarily accurate. To say that "aggression wells up in a person until it spills into behavior like water overflowing a tank" may be appealing (both Sigmund Freud and Konrad Lorenz have used such an analogy), but the appeal is based on our familiarity with water tanks and has little to do with the facts of behavior or of the nervous system. Witchcraft, astrology, and magic might also be psychologically satisfying explanations to some people, but not to scientists.

One kind of scientific explanation is to identify a specific event as an *instance* of a more general principle or law. One principle in psychology is the *serial position effect* in verbal learning. Words in the middle of a list are harder to learn than words at the beginning or end of the list. If someone were having trouble learning the middle of a list we could explain his or her difficulty as an *instance* of the serial position effect. Such an explanation is, however, said to be a "low level explanation." A higher level explanation would explain the serial position effect itself, as well as other facts of verbal learning. Hull, Hovland, Ross, Hall, Perkins, and Fitch (1940) proposed such a theory, using the concepts of "excitatory" and "inhibitory" response tendencies to derive the serial position effect and other learning phenomena.

### Causation

Explanations often involve statements of causation. "Why did George's knee jerk?" "Because the doctor struck him below the knee with a rubber hammer." The blow caused the knee jerk. Or, if a child started crying when a dog approached we might say the dog caused the child to cry. Psychologists often phrase cause-and-effect relations in terms of stimuli and responses; a stimulus causes a response. Such statements may be put in *functional* terms, such as "responses are a function of the stimuli and the organism" or, $R = f(S,O)$. Or, "behavior is a function of the person and the environment," $B = f(P,E)$.

But what is a cause? Recalling our earlier discussion of David Hume and the mind-body problem, all we can be sure of is a series of *sense impressions*. We perceive that some events occur closely in time and space (the dog appeared and the child cried), and arrive at a *verbal statement of causality*: The dog caused the child to cry. But, even though we perceived that certain things happened together, can we be absolutely sure that a particular effect had the cause we attributed to it? Perhaps the child's parent said something to the child that made the child cry, and the dog just happened to appear at that time. Hume concluded, in agreement with later philosophers, that causes are what we perceive or think them to be, and nothing more. Scientists do not find ultimate truths or ultimate causes. Rather, they make formal statements, called *laws*, about observed events. The causality is in the statements, the language of science, rather than directly in the physical world.

### Levels of Analysis

Depending on one's interests, a problem may be attacked at a number of levels of complexity of behavior. Consider eating. A social psychologist might study cultural development of eating patterns and preferences (such as for chili peppers). Another researcher may be interested in the neurological aspects and study some small part of the brain. A third may study the taste preferences of animals or humans.

In studying particular problems, some behaviors are more informative than others. When an animal moves, some muscles contract and other extend. But psychologists interested in the effects of food reward on lever pressing probably would be unconcerned with which muscles are used to press the lever. They would be concerned that the lever got pressed with a certain frequency under certain conditions. Similarly, a social psychologist interested in how people form groups would not care which muscles or neurons are involved. Specific muscle movements are of great interest in other situations, however. Electrical activity from particular muscles might be recorded to assess the effectiveness of relaxation therapy. Or we might record activities from facial muscles to see how the activity pattern changes with different emotions. Our choice of simple or complex activities to study depends on what is relevant to the problem concerning us. This book deals with motivation at three major levels of analysis: biological, individual, and social.

## THE PROBLEM OF DEFINING MOTIVATION

### Regulatory versus Purposive Approaches

The most difficult task for a motivation theorist is to define motivation, particularly because there are two fundamentally different approaches to motivation. The *regulatory approach* emphasizes the body's responses to such disruptive forces as hunger and pain, while the *purposive approach* emphasizes the goal-directed nature of behavior. The regulatory theorists tend to work in animal laboratories and study physiological aspects of motivation. The purposive theorists fall into the ranks of behavioral/personality/social psychologists, and their laboratories are bloodless. Attempts at reconciliation have not been notably satisfactory, and indeed, often it is not even attempted.[2] Thus, a recent volume on the physiological mechanisms of motivation (Pfaff, 1982) has excellent surveys of research on hunger, thirst, temperature regulation, and brain mechanisms of reward and punishment. But there is no mention of achievement, power, or affiliation. The reason, of course, is that at present there is little to be said about the physiological mechanisms, especially in the brain, for these motives. Unfortunately, the two approaches share a common terminology, such as *need*, which may refer to different concepts. To the regulatory theorist, need refers to a life-threatening physiological deficit or excess. To the purposive theorist, needs account for many social behaviors, such as striving for affiliation, power, or achievement, that are hardly lethal. These equally legitimate approaches to motivation are deeply rooted in different historical traditions.

*Background of the regulatory approach.*    The regulatory approach has a biological tradition, traceable to Darwin's theory of evolution and to experimental medicine. At the turn of the century the *functional school* of psychology was formed, led by such intellectual luminaries as William James and John Dewey. The question they raised was, How does mental activity help organisms adapt to their environment? The functionalists viewed psychology as one approach to understanding how evolution works. The "continuity of organisms" emphasized by evolutionary theory was extended to the study of mind and behavior.

Under the influence of Pavlov in Russia and Sherrington in England, the study of *reflexes* became popular. Such reflex responses as salivating were behaviors simple enough to be analyzed in detail. Complex behaviors were interpreted as "strings" of reflexes and so, it was theorized, understanding reflexes would lead us to understand complex social behaviors. John B. Watson's *behaviorism* used the concept of the stimulus-response reflex as the smallest unit of behavior which could be objectively observed. Watson denied any role for "mental" events in the determination of behavior and had little use for the notion of purpose. More sophisticated modern forms of *methodological behaviorism* say that we *infer* mental activities from behavioral observations. Contemporary psychologists who might deny any strong allegiance to a behavioristic point of view would generally admit to this methodological limitation on how we go about studying internal events.

---

[2]There have been some major exceptions. Ross Stagner (e.g., 1980) tried for many years to bring all motivated behavior under the umbrella of homeostasis but mostly has been ignored. Other theorists, such as Hull (1943) and Mowrer (1960) tried to show how social motives were learned in the context of such "primary" motives as hunger and thirst. Also, there is research and theory on brain mechanisms and cognition and there is physiological research and theory on goal-oriented behavior. At the same time, however, there are wide differences of opinion about what a psychology of motivation *ought* to be.

At their inceptions, the functionalist and behaviorist approaches relied solely on stimuli as causes of behavior, without a separate motivational concept. Behavior was said to flow from one stimulus to the next. Some stimuli were *motivating stimuli,* however. In 1918, Robert S. Woodworth added the term *drive* to psychology's dictionary. He argued that, like an automobile, behavior had a *driving* mechanism and a *steering* mechanism. The driving mechanism provided the power or energy to make an otherwise motionless organism run. Environmental stimuli helped to guide or steer the organism in one direction or another. A *biologically adaptive act,* then, consisted of the following sequence:

Internal Need → Drive → Activity → Goal → Quiescence

Need for food drives an organism to be active until it finds and consumes food, after which it is quiet until some new need re-arouses drive. The motivational emphasis of the regulatory approach is on the need/drive aspect of the process and the underlying physiology of need/drive. Goals come into play in the service of internal disturbances.

*Background of the purposive approach.*     The origins of the purposive approach are found in ancient philosophical views about *choices* of goals and behaviors. At a high philosophical level is the dilemma of choosing between good and evil. Scientifically, we phrase the question in terms of what makes a person choose any kind of goal over some alternative. Why choose steak rather than fish for supper? Why this person for a spouse and not that?

At least two elements are necessary for an answer. First, we look to the *future,* at the potential outcomes of choosing a particular course of action. Time does not run backward to influence us, but our anticipation of future events does influence us. Second, we strive towards goals which we anticipate will be of the greatest *value* to us. Given the choice between two spouses, we choose the one we anticipate will provide the greater satisfaction. There is no *necessary* concept of internal need or drive from the purposive point of view. The closest concept is the *will,* a mental mechanism for making choices. William James (1890) described will in terms of what we now call *conflict,* and said the greatest strength of will was required when we make choices between two very similar goals.

The problem for the modern motivation theorist is to bring the regulatory and purposive approaches together under a common definition. In effect, this means that the definition has to be rather "loose," including a large number of specific concepts under the umbrella of motivation.

*Freud and the Psychoanalytic Approach.*     The emphasis in this book is on experimental approaches to motivation, but we cannot ignore the contributions of Sigmund Freud and the psychoanalytic movement. The details of

Freud's contributions are often controversial, but three of his major contributions are at the foundations of psychology. First, Freud emphasized that all behavior is *determined*. His concept of *psychic determinism* runs throughout his analyses of what he called the psychopathology of everyday life, of dreams, and of neurosis (Freud, 1938). Second, Freud's analysis of how *unconscious* mental activities influence us is even now a part of our general culture. We may not always be *aware* of our sexual and aggressive motives, for example, but they nevertheless exert their influences on us. Third, Freud emphasized the *development* of mental life and behavior from earliest infancy through adulthood. The importance of early infantile experiences on later behavior has been verified many times over in laboratory research.

Freud would align more with the regulatory approach than the purposive approach. He believed that when there is internal tension, often produced by sex, aggression, or anxiety, a person engages in activities to reduce the tension. Dreams, for example, were said to reduce anxiety so we can sleep better. Neurotic behavior reduces anxiety so an individual can go about his daily business more effectively. In terms of his own theoretical concepts, Freud emphasized unconscious *id* (basic biological) functions and their control by *ego* (rational thought) functions and *superego* (social influences). Later psychoanalytic theorists began to place more emphasis on ego functions than did Freud.

Our definition of motivation emphasizes *choices* of goals and behaviors, but it does not hinge on the issue of conscious versus unconscious determinants, for surely there are mixtures of both in many of our choices. For example, we may agonize a long time over some choice without being aware of the sources of some of our likes and dislikes which go into making our final decision.

### Learning and Motivation

How we approach motivation also depends partly on how we approach *learning*. We distinguish between *mechanistic* and *cognitive* views of learning (Bitterman, 1967), which are historically associated with the regulatory and purposive approaches, respectively.

*Mechanistic view.*    According to this view, organisms learn specific responses to specific stimuli, the classic stimulus-response (S-R) analysis of behaviorism. As noted earlier, some versions (e.g., Watson, 1924; Thorndike, 1932; Guthrie, 1952; Estes, 1958) held that simply presenting the appropriate stimulus was sufficient to arouse the response associated with that stimulus. Later versions, building on Woodworth (e.g., Hull, 1943; Spence, 1956), held that the learning component ("habit," an S-R connection) has to be "energized" by the motivational component.

The S-R view has had great appeal because it seemed to make sense physiologically. The notion that stimuli enter the nervous system, go to the sensory parts of the brain, and then are connected to the motor parts of the brain via the "association" areas (e.g., frontal lobes) seemed to be compatible with nervous system concepts prevailing in the early part of the century. Karl Lashley (e.g., see 1950) and many other researchers demonstrated convincingly that such connections were not formed in the neocortex. More recent findings (e.g., McCormick & Thompson, 1984) indicate that such conditioning may take place in the cerebellum, but there is no indication yet that such connections are motivationally "energized."

*Cognitive view.*   According to this view, organisms learn *relationships* among environmental events, or between responses and their outcomes. The organism is said to learn *expectancies,* rather than learning automatic responses to specific stimuli. The organism learns to expect that "in this situation, *if* I do such and such, there will be a particular result." The learned expectancy is not tied to any specific muscular movements, however, in the way that a reflex is tied to a stimulus. This point of view, championed most strongly by E. C. Tolman during the many years that the S-R theorists held sway, assumes a much more active role for central brain processes.

On the motivational side, the organism performs a particular act if it expects an outcome which has some *value.* Value is a motivational concept, and something that has value is an *incentive.* Since the concepts of anticipation and purpose are so important to this viewpoint, Tolman called his approach *purposive behaviorism.*

A cognitive view of learning is just as physiological and mechanistic as a mechanistic (or S-R) view, however, in that all learning has a physiological basis in the nervous system. Human thought processes now seem as physiologically explicable, in principle, as classical conditioning once did. We know what modern computers can do in terms of decision-making, so it no longer seems that thought processes are necessarily too complex to be accounted for in neural terms. Our preference for one *psychological* concept of learning over another should be determined by how well that learning concept helps explain the facts of behavior and not by some physiological preconception of what the psychology of learning *ought* to be.

These distinctions between regulatory versus purposive approaches to motivation, and mechanistic versus cognitive approaches to learning, are of necessity oversimplified in order to highlight the issues and thereby clarify the reasons for approaching motivation as this book does.

### Motivation as an Intervening Variable

*Motivation refers to a set of concepts which are best defined as intervening variables.* This is generally true even with reference to physiological approaches to motivation. The reason is that motivation has *many* behavioral and physiological manifestations and often these are not correlated with one another. Until we can say that one measure is unquestionably the "true" measure of motivation against which all others should be judged, then all we can say is that different measures are tapping into some *conceptually common* processes. The processes will remain conceptual ones until the physiological mechanisms are fully understood.

*Desire and aversion as motivational concepts.*   We consider the *choice* of behaviors to be the primary motivational question, because we do *not* assume that organisms are inert unless jump started into action by a physiological imbalance. The nervous system is continually active, sometimes violently even as we sleep. The motivational problem then is how to account for fluctuations in the choice of activities.

Our basic premise is that organisms *approach* goals, or engage in activities which are expected to have *desirable outcomes,* and *avoid* activities that are expected to have unpleasant or *aversive outcomes.* We must use this premise with caution, however, in two regards. First, we must define desire and aversion *objectively,* and not rely on impressionistic accounts of what is, or ought to be, desirable or aversive. Secondly, we must not define desire and aversion *circularly.* To say that "George went to the ball game because it was desirable" tells us nothing if we know only that it was desirable because he went. This is a *circular definition;* we would be saying that "he went because he went." We gain objectivity and avoid circularity by defining desire and aversion as intervening variables. There are many *specific* motivational intervening variables, such as fear or need for achievement, however, so we shall use desire and aversion as *superordinate* concepts which include concepts tied more closely to specific situations.

Let us now see more exactly what intervening variables are, and then go on to define desire and aversion operationally as intervening variables.

*Motivational intervening variables.   An example.* Let us begin with what Tolman (1938) called the *defining operations* for an intervening variable. Suppose we have a pair of rats which we let run a number of times in a T-maze having water in one arm of the T but not in the other. One of the animals consistently runs to the water and consumes it, while the other runs randomly to either side and does not consume the water. We might believe that the one animal prefers to go to the water because it is thirsty, but we cannot use this explanation unless we have defined thirst. Doing a little detective work, we find that the rat going to water had been without water for a day, but the other animal had water in its home cage right up to the time of testing. We might then say that a day without water produced a change in the animal which led to a preference for water. We could then control water deprivation and study behavioral changes more precisely in an experiment to see if we were correct that the preceding water deprivation affected behavior toward water.

The elements of the intervening variable then are (1) an *antecedent condition* controlled or measured by the experimenter (such as hours of deprivation) and (2) a *consequent condition* measured by the experimenter (preference for water). Keeping all other conditions constant (such as amount of prior experience in the apparatus) we define an intervening variable on the basis of these antecedent and consequent conditions. We can diagram this as follows:

| Antecedent Condition | Intervening Variable | Consequent Condition |
|---|---|---|

Water Depriviation ---------------------------------X --------------------------------Water Preference

The longer the deprivation period, the greater X is, and the greater the preference for water. If there were no systematic relationship between antecedent and consequent conditions, we would have no reason to talk about an intervening variable. In this example, no name is attached to X, because X really says all there is to say thus far. Another name might give *additional meaning* to X. This example is so simple that hesitation in talking about "thirst" may not make sense. In other situations, hesitation makes more sense. Suppose that we frustrate a person and she acts aggressively. Can we argue that frustration produces anger, which leads to an aggressive act? We might be better off to stick with X, instead of naming it "anger." We need to be *careful* in assigning names to intervening variables to avoid implying something more or different than what we have defined operationally.

You may ask, Why bother with the intervening variable? Wouldn't it be easier just to relate hours of deprivation to water preference? Indeed, the water-deprivation story *was* made more complicated by the intervening variable. Suppose, however, there are several antecedent conditions (such as water deprivation, salt injections, and eating dry food) and several consequent behaviors (preference for water, amount drunk, speed of running to water, and pressing a lever for water). An intervening variable that relates *all* of the antecedents to *all* of the consequent conditions *does* simplify our thinking (Miller, 1959). Indeed, a theoretical concept must generalize across a number of situations to be of use.

*Two ways of defining intervening variables.*   The example of water deprivation used a **stimulus-response (S-R) relation.** The experimenter controls some condition (S) and measures some response (R). As another example, the experimenter might vary the intensity of electric shock (S) and observe speed of escape from shock (R). This would define a different intervening variable;

we would probably talk about pain or fear, which are aversive. Once we have defined pain (or fear), we are reasonably confident that future manipulations of the antecedent condition will change the level of pain/fear, and we can then relate this to behaviors besides those used in the defining experiment. We might study pain aroused by electric shock as a punisher.

In **response-response (R-R) relations,** one set of responses defines the intervening variable on the antecedent side and a different set of responses defines it on the consequent side. For example, David McClelland and his colleagues (McClelland, Atkinson, Clark, & Lowell, 1953) developed a procedure for scoring imaginative stories written about certain pictures. From such stories, a person is given a score on *need for achievement* (a motivational concept). The stories constitute the first set of responses, $R_1$. The individuals are then measured on a second set of responses, $R_2$, such as speed of doing simple arithmetic problems. If the two response measures are correlated, then speed of doing the problems is related to achievement motivation measured by the test. We would want to have several response measures related to achievement stories, of course, just as we wanted several responses related to water deprivation. The R-R approach is widely used in personality research, because often we must depend on existing differences between people for comparison rather than experimentally producing differences. It is more difficult to establish *causal* relationships with the R-R (correlational) approach than with the S-R approach, however. A person scoring high on need achievement might also differ from a low-scoring person in ways which affect performance but are not related to achievement motivation. Such questions can only be answered by research.

We could also define intervening variables in other ways, such as by measuring a physiological variable like blood sugar level and relating that to performance. The point, however, is that the intervening variable can be defined by any two independent operations. We just have to be careful in specifying what our operations are.

*Criteria for calling an intervening variable motivational.*    At what point do we say that an intervening variable is *motivational* rather than, say, learning? When we identified the intervening variable between water deprivation and drinking as X, we were not being abstract (or obscure) without reason. Our problem is this: If we have reliably defined some intervening variable, X, how do we decide if it is a *motivational* intervening variable and give it a "motivational" name? We shall say that: *If a difference in the level of an intervening variable is related to a difference in preference, persistence, or vigor of behavior, the intervening variable is motivational.* Depending on the nature of the difference, we might classify the variable as *desire* or *aversion.* The following discussion is based on the logic most fully developed by Irwin (1971).

### Desire and Aversion as Intervening Variables

*The hedonic axiom.*  All concepts start from some assumption. We assume the following *Hedonic Axiom: Organisms direct their behaviors to minimize aversive outcomes and maximize desirable outcomes.* This axiom has been held by all hedonic theorists, from Jeremy Bentham ([1789] 1936) to P. T. Young (1961), as well as by Irwin. At any given time, there is assumed to be an *ordering* of events along a continuum ranging from very aversive, through neutral, through very desirable. This is called the *hedonic continuum.* It is assumed, according to the hedonic axiom, that organisms make choices in favor of the direction of the arrow, as shown in the diagram below.

| $-5$ | $-4$ | $-3$ | $-2$ | $-1$ | $0$ | $+1$ | $+2$ | $+3$ | $+4$ | $+5$ |
|---|---|---|---|---|---|---|---|---|---|---|

| Very Aversive | Neutral Range (Affective Zero) | Very Desirable |
|---|---|---|

Objects may shift location on the hedonic continuum, however. If I am not hungry, a steak may seem neutral, but if I have not eaten all day it may be very desirable. If I have overeaten, the very thought of a steak may be aversive. The concepts of desire and aversion both hinge on the idea of *neutrality,* or *affective zero. If a behavioral outcome, A, is preferred to a neutral outcome, then A is desirable. If a neutral outcome is preferred to A, then A is aversive.*
Symbolically, where $>$ means "is preferred to":

If $A > neutral$, then A is *desirable*
But, if $neutral > A$, then A is *aversive*

Obviously, an objectively observed preference does not necessarily mean that an outcome is either desirable or aversive. Suppose we have made preference tests for six outcomes and found the order of preference from A to F, with A the most preferred and F the least preferred. Which of the outcomes are desirable and which are aversive? We can answer this question only with reference to a neutral point. In the illustration below, D, E, and F are aversive, and A, B, and C are desirable.

| Preference Test: | | F | E | D | | C | B | A | | | |
|---|---|---|---|---|---|---|---|---|---|---|---|
| $-5$ | $-4$ | $-3$ | $-2$ | $-1$ | $0$ | $+1$ | $+2$ | $+3$ | $+4$ | $+5$ |

| Very Aversive | Neutral Range (Affective Zero) | Very Desirable |
|---|---|---|

Consider how we might be misled if we uncritically equate preference with desire. An instructor teaches a course which every semester has a high enrollment. He concludes that he is a superb instructor teaching a fascinating course—his course is obviously desirable because students flock to it in preference to all the other courses they might take. Then the college requirements are changed and his course enrollment plunges, and he faces a harsher reality: His course had not really been very desirable to most students, it was simply *less aversive* than the alternatives. With reference to the diagram, his course might have been E, taken in preference to F. With the new requirements, even a mildly aversive course D is preferable.

The question remains, How do we *find* a neutral point or *zone* of neutrality? In many situations, including the example just given, perhaps we cannot. Technical difficulty in determining a neutral point is not a fatal flaw in the *definitions* of desire and aversion, however, and in research we can overcome the difficulty, as in the following example.

*Operationally defining desire and aversion.*     *Desire.* Consider the following situation. We have a small child and two identical opaque jars, A and B, both empty. We ask the child to put a hand in each jar several times, and she does so. She has only a random, 50-50, preference. The child is indifferent between them, so the two jars provide *common outcomes* for either choice. Now we put a piece of candy in Jar B. The child puts her hand in the jar, finds the candy, and now regularly chooses Jar B over the otherwise equal Jar A. Because the child prefers the candy jar (B) to the neutral alternative (A) we say that the outcome of choosing that jar is *desirable*. If putting candy in Jar A did *not* change the child's preference, we would say the candy was *neutral. An outcome is desirable if it is preferred to a neutral outcome or some other already-known desirable outcome.*

The above definitions apply only if we have controlled for nonmotivational effects, however. Suppose the child were consistently choosing the candy jar, but without her noticing it, we put something possibly more desirable in the other jar. The child might keep choosing Jar B simply because she never discovered there was anything in Jar A. We could be fooled into believing that the candy was preferred to the alternative. In this example, the need to control for such experience is clear. But less obviously, a woman might have a job that she continues in because she does not perceive any better alternative. To the outsider, it might seem that her present job is the most desirable to her when it really is not.

*Aversion.* Suppose that instead of food we put a squirmy, crawly caterpillar into Jar B, and made no change in Jar A. Assume that the child chooses Jar A with great regularity. We would say that Jar B is aversive because the otherwise neutral Jar A is preferred to it. *An outcome is aversive if a neutral or less aversive outcome is preferred to it.*

If we had simultaneously put candy in one jar and a caterpillar in the other, we could not specify *from this alone* whether the candy was desirable, the caterpillar was aversive, or both. Preference alone does not define desire or aversion. Preference *over* a neutral outcome defines desire and preference *for* a neutral outcome defines aversion.

*Other measures of motivation.* We have taken *preference* as the behavioral measure for *defining* desire and aversion. For practical purposes, however, other *correlated* measures may be more useful, such as *speed, vigor,* or *persistence* in responding. The different measures are not always highly correlated, however, because more than one variable can influence a measure. For example, if an animal were already responding as quickly as possible, giving it a more desirable reward could not increase its response speed even though the new reward could be demonstrably preferable to the old one.

As Atkinson and Birch (1978) have argued, we cannot take *any* single behavior in isolation from other behaviors. A child washing dishes is easily tempted away by ice cream, but a child playing a favorite game is harder to lure away. Much motivational research, especially with animals, has not been approached with such multiple responses in mind. This perhaps is because arousal and vigor of behavior have been considered *the* important motivational problems. Such responses as running in an alleyway provide little opportunity for shifts in activity or preference, since they offer little opportunity for alternative behaviors. Multiple response measures have been elegantly discussed by Atkinson and Birch (1978), as well as by Premack (1971).

Vigor of response (such as speed or force) may also be difficult to interpret because it can be part of what is learned. Even the rat will run or lever-press fast or slow if it is *selectively rewarded* for responding fast or slow (Logan, 1960). Capaldi and Davidson (1979) even got rats to run more rapidly with a short period of food deprivation than with a long period. They just did not reward the rats with food if they ran too vigorously when very hungry. The rats learned to take it easy when they were most hungry.

*Desire and aversion as classes of variables.* Many different operationally defined concepts can be put under the broad headings of desire or aversion. But this is not to say that they are all the same concepts or subject to manipulations of the same variables. For example, sweet food, sex objects, and good music may all be desirable and approached, but are hardly the same thing otherwise. Similarly, pain, fear, and foul odors are aversive, but not otherwise identical. The following list illustrates some motivational concepts which fit under the umbrellas of desire and aversion:

| *Desire* | *Aversion* |
|---|---|
| need for achievement | fear of failure |
| positive incentives | negative incentives |
| rewards | punishers |
| cognitive consistency | cognitive dissonance |
| love | fear |
| hope for power | fear of power |
| relaxation | stress |

*Motives are hierarchical.* Each of us strives towards some goals more persistently than towards others. If we rank such goals in order of importance, we have a *hierarchy of motives.* The concept of a motivational hierarchy was popularized by Abraham Maslow (1970), who argued that motives are ordered from more to less basic as follows: (1) *Physiological* (hunger, etc.), (2) *Safety,* (3) *Belongingness and love,* (4) *Esteem* (e.g., achievement), and (5) *Self-actualization* (fulfilling one's unique potential, whatever it may be). The concept of a hierarchy is precisely what the hedonic continuum represents: The ordering of outcomes from left to right is a hierarchy of desirability. Harder to accept are Maslow's stipulations that (a) higher level needs do not come into play until lower needs are satisfied, and (b) the same hierarchy applies to all individuals. There is little evidence for either of these assertions. Instead, it is arguable that each individual has his or her own hierarchy of motives. For example, a student wishing strongly to graduate from college would choose activities which lead to this goal, or at least do not conflict with it. Similarly, a presidential candidate may select every behavior for years with the goal of the presidency always in mind. Such goals can change, and rearrangement of hierarchies occurs, but for some people there are long-persistent, highly dominant goals.

## SUMMARY

1. *Motivation* is that aspect of psychology concerned with explaining variations in behavior, among different individuals and within the same individual from time to time.

2. Our ideas about motivation are influenced by our views on two broad *philosophical issues:* (1) the *relation of mind to body,* and (2) whether behavior is *free* or *determined.*

3. Among the various possible views, psychologists assume that mind and body are closely related, if not identical, and that behavior has *causes and is predictable.*

4. *Scientific theories* are *linguistic analyses* in which symbols are used to represent such events as the occurrence of behaviors.

5. *Semiotic,* one type of linguistic analysis, involves *syntactics* (the rules for relating signs to each other, as in *grammar*), *semantics* (the relations of signs to objects, the definitions of signs), and *pragmatics* (relations of signs to their users).

6. *Operational definitions* define concepts in terms of the *procedures* (operations) used to *measure* the concepts. For example, aggression may be defined as the number of times one child pushes another on the playground.

7. Scientific theories are like *maps* of geographic areas, relating *selected aspects of an area* (such as roads) to each other. Theories are "good" to the extent that they are *testable, fruitful (productive), simple,* and *comprehensive.*

8. *Objectivity* is the extent to which different observers *agree* about observations of the same events. *Explanation* is the application of general principles to account for specific events. A *cause* is a *verbal statement of what we perceive* to be a unique set of conditions preceding some observed event.

9. We can *analyze* behavior at many *levels*, depending on our interest. At one time we may be interested in simple reflex actions and at another time in complex social interactions.

10. Defining motivation is made more complicated by the fact that there are different approaches to motivation. Two of these are the *regulatory* approach (emphasizing the body's physiological reactions to such disruptive forces as hunger) and the *purposive* approach (emphasizing the goal-directed nature of behavior). These different approaches are rooted in different historical backgrounds. Freud's *psychoanalytic theory* is more closely related to the regulatory approach.

11. A definition of motivation also depends partly on the definitions of *other concepts* in the same theoretical context, especially *learning*. In this text we view learning as a *complex cognitive process*, not as an association between stimuli and responses. We assume that living organisms are *always active* and that the *main* problem for motivation theory is to account for the *choice* of behaviors, not for the initiation or vigor of behavior.

12. Motivation is considered as *an intervening variable*, defined by the relationship of conditions which are *antecedent* to a particular behavior, and the behavior itself. This avoids *circular definitions*, which only give behavior a different name.

13. Two major *classes* of motivational variables are *desire and aversion*. Desire is defined as a preference for a behavior whose outcome is *more preferred* than a neutral outcome. Aversion is defined as a preference for a behavior whose outcome is *less preferred* than a neutral outcome. Many different *specifically defined* motivational intervening variables may fall within these two classes.

14. The *hedonic axiom* states that organisms work to *minimize aversive outcomes* and *to maximize desirable outcomes*. It is an objective and empirical question whether an outcome is desirable or aversive, however, not a subjective decision on the part of an observer.

15. Motives are *hierarchical*. For any given individual, some motives are more important and enduring than others.

16. *Preference* is considered the most basic motivational index, but *persistence* and *vigor* of behavior are often correlated with preference and, under particular conditions, may be better measures.

# 2

# Emotional Foundations of Motivation

Introduction and Historical Background

> *Wundt and Titchener*
> *James and Lange*
> *Cannon and Bard*
> *Elizabeth Duffy*
> *The Papez Circuit and the Kluver-Bucy Syndrome*

The Study of Emotion

> *Verbal Behavior*
> *Nonverbal Behavior*
> *Physiology*
> *Right-Left Hemispheric Differences and Emotion*

Contemporary Theories of Emotion

> *Discrete Emotion Theories*
> *Dimensional Approaches to Emotion*
> *Cognitive Approaches to Emotion*

Mood, Memory, and Behavior

> *Background*
> *Research on Mood Effects*

Relation of Emotion and Motivation

Summary

## INTRODUCTION AND HISTORICAL BACKGROUND

Chapter One *operationally* defined *desire* and *aversion* as motivational concepts. It described how we would use these terms and concepts in a preference situation, based on direct observations of behavior. The very selection of these words *desire* and *aversion*, however, adds what the philosophers call *surplus meaning* to the concepts. The words desire and aversion imply some kind of relationship between motivation and emotion. This chapter clarifies this relationship by first examining emotion broadly and then incorporating aspects of emotion theory into a discussion of motivation.

### Wundt and Titchener

Early scientific psychologists looked at emotion as a *content* of experience, to be studied by introspection. Research subjects, often the experimenters themselves, "looked into their own minds" and reported what they were aware of. From such research, Wilhelm Wundt proposed a tridimensional theory of emotion. He said that all emotional experiences could be produced by some appropriate combination of pleasant-unpleasant, tension-relaxation, and excitement-depression. More than a hundred years later, Wundt still has support in contemporary research.

Edward B. Titchener, the Englishman who carried Wundt's psychology to the United States, argued that the single dimension of pleasant-unpleasant was sufficient to describe the totality of emotional experience. Affections (emotions) had several attributes in common with sensory experiences, such as *quality, intensity,* and *duration.* The affects were vague, however, whereas sensations could be sharp and clear. Titchener's student, Paul Thomas Young (e.g., 1961), carried the concept of emotion into the developing realm of motivation theory. Young did research with rats almost exclusively, but his basic concepts were *delight* and *distress*. Organisms work to "maximize delight and minimize distress." The James-Lange and Cannon-Bard theories were the classical beginnings of the modern era of emotion theory, however.

### James and Lange

Common experience seems to suggest that emotion is first aroused by some event and then we act in accordance with the emotion aroused. For example, we run because we are afraid. William James (1884) turned this view upside down by proposing that *emotion is the perception of bodily changes which occur in response to an event.* That is, our response (such as running) to an emotion-arousing situation comes *before* the emotional experience. The emotional experience is the perception of the response to the situation.

James especially emphasized the sympathetic nervous system and the visceral responses it controls, such as heart rate, blood pressure, perspiration, and gastrointestinal functions. James did *not* deny the importance of skeletal muscular movements and the perception of them, but over a period of time his theory became identified almost solely with visceral activity. About the same time, a Swedish physiologist named Carl Lange (1885) proposed a similar theory, restricted to vascular system changes. The theory has since been known as the James-Lange theory.

The immediate importance of the James-Lange theory was that, since it made emotion dependent on specific identifiable portions of the body, it seemed to be testable by use of the surgical techniques available at the time. One could cut the sympathetic nervous system, which lies largely outside the spinal cord and brain, with a scalpel and then observe whether animals still behaved emotionally. Figure 2-1 shows the brain, sympathetic nervous system, and viscera.

It also followed from James's theory that each emotional experience had its own unique physiological counterpart; otherwise, emotions would be indistinguishable. This has been referred to as the *identity theory of emotion*; there is a one-to-one relation between experienced emotion and physiology. In one sense, this is axiomatic. If two events are discriminated, there is something different in the brain about the two events. At another level, the theory had problems because James was referring mostly to *peripheral* physiological differences, activity of the organs innervated by the autonomic nervous system.

### Cannon and Bard

The inevitable attack on the theory came from Walter Cannon (1927), who proposed the following five arguments against James:

1. Separating the viscera from the nervous system does not change emotional behavior.
2. The same visceral changes occur in different emotional states as well as in such nonemotional states as violent activity.
3. The viscera are relatively insensitive structures.
4. Visceral changes occur too slowly (a matter of seconds) to be the source of sudden emotional changes.
5. Artificial induction of the visceral changes typical of strong emotions does not produce these same strong emotions.

Cannon's alternative proposal was a *central neural theory*, supported by research in Philip Bard's laboratory. He suggested that neural impulses flowing into the thalamus (not at that time clearly distinguished from the hypothalamus) were experienced as emotion as they were routed "upstream" to the cortex, and slightly later produced visceral changes as they were routed "downstream" to the autonomic nervous system and viscera. This contrasts with James's view that such impulses first excited the viscera and feedback from the viscera to the cortex was experienced as emotion.

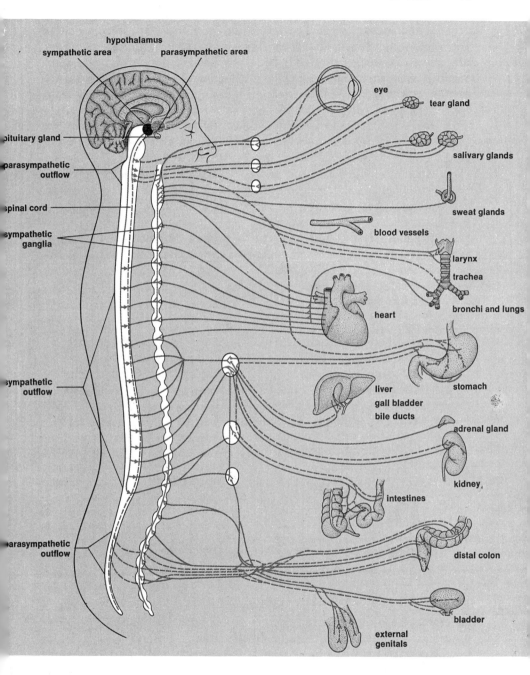

**FIGURE 2-1.** The autonomic nervous system and the body organs it controls. The limbic system is a set of brain structures surrounding the hypothalamus. (Reprinted from Krech, Crutchfield & Livson, 1970. Copyright 1970 by Alfred A. Knopf. Used by permission.)

Cannon's own arguments have since been criticized. In some of the experiments he cited, it is not clear that all the connections between viscera and nervous system had actually been severed. Furthermore, these experiments were with animals, usually dogs. But James had said that emotional *experience* was produced by feedback from the viscera, not necessarily emotional *behavior*. This made the relevance of the animal research questionable.

Two relevant studies of humans with spinal cord injuries have produced contradictory results. In the first (Hohmann, 1966), amount of spinal cord damage did seem to be correlated with amount of loss of emotional experience. In a more recent and more detailed study, however, patients with severe cord damage and very limited body feeling often reported experiencing emotions even *more* intensely than they had prior to their injuries (Chwalisz, Diener, & Gallagher, 1988). This lends more support to Cannon than to James, since it indicates that the many different body responses which typically occur during emotion-arousing situations are not absolutely necessary for experienced emotion.

### Elizabeth Duffy

Elizabeth Duffy (1934) argued that emotion consisted of *energy mobilization* of the body for strong activity. Emotion *is* this energy mobilization. This is similar to what Cannon called the *emergency theory of emotion,* preparation of the body for fight or flight. Duffy's premises were that behavior can be described in terms of its *direction* (approaching or avoiding objects or situations) and *intensity* (fast or slow, vigorous or sluggish). The most important departure from previous theories was that Duffy did not deal with "desire" and "aversion" or "pleasantness-unpleasantness," but only with the direction and intensity of *behavior*. This approach was subsequently picked up by the *activation theorists* in the 1950's, who argued that the amount of neural activity in the brainstem determined emotion (e.g., Lindsley, 1951). Chapter 3 discusses activation theory in more detail because it has been widely applied to motivational phenomena.

### The Papez Circuit and the Kluver-Bucy Syndrome

In 1937 two monumental publications changed our way of looking at the neuroanatomy of emotion (Kluver & Bucy, 1937; Papez, 1937). James Papez, in a masterful integration of much seemingly unrelated evidence, proposed that in the core of the brain is a set of pathways running from one location to another, constituting a circuit underlying emotional experience and behavior. This *Papez circuit* (Figure 2–2) runs from the *hippocampus* via the *fornix* to the *anterior thalamus,* then to the *cingulate cortex,* the *amygdala,* and back to the hippocampus. We now know much more about this circuit and its connections to other parts of the brain under its more modern name, the *limbic system*. This system, essential to emotion, is buried deep inside all

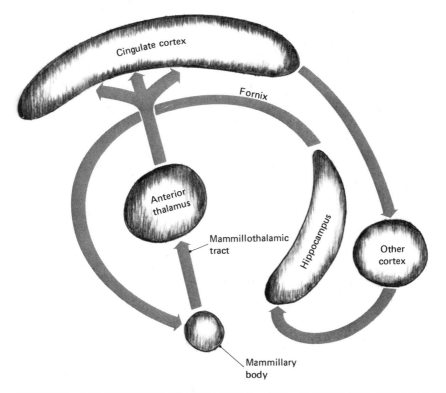

**FIGURE 2-2.** A schematic drawing of the Papez circuit for emotion. All of these structures lie deep in the brain, underneath the cerebral hemispheres. (From Carlson, *Physiology of Behavior* (2nd ed.), 1980. Figure 19.30, p. 659. Reprinted with permission of Allyn and Bacon, Inc.)

mammalian brains and accounts for most of the brain mass of reptiles. More recently evolved brain structures, such as the neocortex, may exert control over the primitive limbic systems, but the Papez circuit may still not be fully adapted to life in modern civilization, as indicated by the occurrence of emotional disorder (e.g., Malmo, 1975).

About the same time as Papez's work became known, Heinrich Kluver and Paul Bucy described the effects of experimentally removing the temporal lobes of rhesus monkeys. In particular, after damage to the hippocampus and amygdala, they found the following bizarre pattern of behavior now known as the *Kluver-Bucy Syndrome:*

1. A "psychic blindness"; the animals apparently could not remember things visually, although there was no apparent damage to the primary visual system.
2. Heightened orality, which consisted of licking, biting, chewing, or touching with the lips almost everything with which they came into contact.
3. A strong tendency to respond to all visual stimuli indiscriminately and compulsively.

4. A disappearance or great reduction of reactions usually associated with fear and anger.

5. A great increase in sexual activity, including masturbation and attempts to mate with members of other species.

This syndrome was unexpected because no one had any idea that the temporal lobes were involved in such a diversity of motivational, emotional, and perceptual functions. This experiment provided the foundation for fertile research ideas for half a century. Whereas earlier emotion research had been predominantly concerned with the autonomic nervous system, the groundwork was now laid for study of the role of the "reptilian brain" in the control of emotion.

## THE STUDY OF EMOTION

Emotion, like other topics in psychology, requires several different approaches for an understanding. These include studying verbal and nonverbal behavior and physiology.

### Verbal behavior

We cannot feel other people's feelings, but we can record what they say about their emotional experiences. Freud used this approach extensively in psychotherapy, as did early scientific psychologists in their laboratories and as later therapists have done. Modern researchers also use psychological tests and scales as somewhat more quantifiable indicators of emotional experience. Verbal behavior is subject to many biases, however, and has to be assessed cautiously. The research subject, the clinical patient, and the person-on-the-street often may say what they think is expected or is socially desirable, rather than just what is felt.

### Nonverbal behavior

This is any behavior, besides talking, that a person or animal might do which can readily be seen by the naked eye, such as changing facial expression or making particular body movements. If I clench my fist, someone watching me could infer that I am angry. There is the possibility of error, though; I might have clenched my fist for emphasis while speaking. We have to be just as careful in interpreting behaviors as we are with speech.

The study of escape and avoidance in animals is particularly useful because these are analogous to many human "neurotic" behaviors. Animals can, for example, learn to avoid electric shock and may do so for hundreds of trials. We would surely be astounded by seeing an animal compulsively moving back and forth in an experimental apparatus, were we to come upon it without knowing its previous history. If we know how a behavior came to be learned, however, it makes sense and we can form ideas about how to change it. Psychologists have long been concerned with giving accounts of adult neurosis so that the "strange" behavior of humans could be as understandable as the behavior of persistently avoiding rats. Classical conditioning of "emotional" physiological responses has also been extensively studied.

### Physiology

The nervous system is divided into *central* (brain and spinal cord) and *peripheral* portions (everything else). It is also divided into *somatic* and *autonomic* portions. The somatic nervous system regulates interactions with the environment: sensory inputs and muscle movements.

The autonomic nervous system (ANS) is particularly important for emotion. It regulates internal body activities involved in maintaining and replenishing the body. It controls *heart muscle*, the *smooth muscle* of the body cavity, such as stomach and intestines, and the release of hormones from *glands* such as the pituitary and adrenal glands.

The *parasympathetic* portion of the ANS is concerned with digestive activity. The *sympathetic* portion of the ANS is concerned with *emergency functions*, such as preparation of the body for *fight* or *flight* (Cannon, 1939). The intense activity we feel in our bodies when we are very active, angry, or frightened reflects the activity of the sympathetic nervous system and the arousal of the internal organs.

In the brain, the *limbic system* and the *brainstem* are particularly important for emotion. These systems are summarized in Table 2-1 and Figure 2-3.

The parasympathetic and sympathetic systems affect every visceral organ and are generally *antagonistic* to each other. When the sympathetic system is strongly aroused, the parasympathetic system is relatively suppressed, and vice versa. We thus understand why we have indigestion when we are upset: The sympathetic system partly suppresses the parasympathetic system, which controls digestion.

We commonly speak of "adrenaline flowing" during excitement. This

**TABLE 2-1   Divisions of the Nervous System. The Somatic Nervous System is Involved in Interactions with the External Environment. The Autonomic System is More Involved with the Regulation of the Internal Activity and Chemistry of the Body.**

|  | SOMATIC | AUTONOMIC |
|---|---|---|
| CENTRAL | Brain and Spinal Cord | Limbic system, hypothalamus and brain stem |
| PERIPHERAL | Nerves to Skeletal muscles and from sense organs | Sympathetic, Parasympathetic |

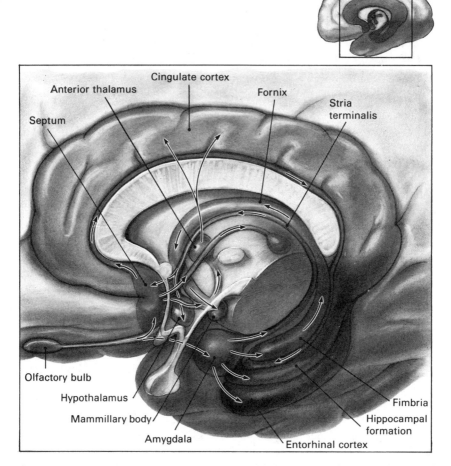

**FIGURE 2-3.** Schematic and simplified representation of the limbic system. (From Carlson, *Physiology of Behavior* (3rd ed.), 1987. Copyright ©1987 by Allyn and Bacon, Inc. Used by permission.

hormone is circulated through the body via the bloodstream and is also released from nerve endings in the sympathetic system. This double-barrelled action produces both quick and widespread arousal, which prepares the body for emergency activity. This preparation includes the release of blood sugar into the body, more rapid breathing, quicker circulation of oxygen, and perspiration for cooling. Continued emotional arousal over a long time may produce the so-called *psychosomatic* or *stress diseases* discussed in chapter 9.

Most of the body changes described above are impossible to observe with the naked eye but are observable with the aid of electronic amplification. The most common measures of emotion are: (1) *heart rate*; (2) *blood pressure;* (3) *galvanic skin response,* an increase in the electrical conductivity of the skin during emotional arousal; (4) *respiration (breathing) rate;* (5) *blood volume change,* easily recorded at the tips of the fingers; (6) *perspiration;* (7) *muscle tension,* measured by means of electrodes placed over specific muscles; and (8) *skin temperature,* an indirect measure of blood flow, through the fingers, for example. Much has been written about change in *pupil size* as an index of emotion, but such change is awkward to measure and gives little information that could not be found with simpler measures.

Other useful measures, such as of hormone levels, can be obtained from blood and urine samples. With animals, experimental surgery is also possible. Moreover, human brain damage from accidents or disease occurs with such frequency that we can learn a great deal about emotion from clinical cases. One new and exciting area of research is on hemispheric differences in function, including emotion.

### Right-Left Hemispheric Differences and Emotion

It is well established that there are reliable differences in the functioning of the right and left cerebral hemispheres of humans. Neural structures required for speech, for example, are located in the left hemisphere. As a generalization, the left hemisphere is concerned with such sequential, analytic activities as we associate with language. The right hemisphere is relatively more concerned with "holistic impressions," a more immediate grasp of a spatial situation. More important in the present context is evidence that the right hemisphere controls emotion recognition and expression better than the left (Kalat, 1988; Rinn, 1984). If a humorous visual stimulus is presented to the right hemisphere but not to the left, a research subject may smile but will not be able to say *why.* The emotional quality of the stimulus has been detected by the right hemisphere but cannot be put into language since the left hemisphere has not gotten the information. Lesions in the right hemisphere but not the left, impair the ability of the affected person to detect emotion in other people. There is still some controversy about such generalizations, however (Leventhal & Tomarken, 1986).

Another possibility is that both hemispheres contribute to emotion, but in different ways. This is suggested by evidence that there is right hemisphere dominance for *negative* emotions and left hemisphere dominance for *positive* emotions. Thus, left hemisphere damage or sedation (by a drug injected into the hemisphere) is associated with excessive worry, pessimism, and crying. Conversely, right hemisphere damage or suppression is associated with euphoria or laughing (Tucker, 1981). There are reported to be right-left hemisphere differences in brain waves during happiness and sadness, but not all investigators have found these (e.g., Collet and Duclaux, 1986). The evidence seems clear that there are hemispheric differences in emotion, but the details of these differences are still being worked out.

## CONTEMPORARY THEORIES OF EMOTION

### Discrete Emotion Theories

Discrete emotion theories assume there is some small number of specific, biologically determined emotional responses, whose expression and recognition is considered to be fundamentally the same for all individuals and peoples. The number of such emotions is in the range of 7 to 10, depending on the particular theory (e.g., Ekman & Oster, 1979; Izard, 1977; Plutchik, 1980; Russell, 1980; Tomkins, 1981). We might think there would be agreement among theorists as to the number of basic emotions, but it is difficult to demonstrate that *any* psychological function has entirely genetic origins.

Table 2–2 shows the discrete emotions identified by various theorists. There is a large degree of overlap, determined by the fact they are working with the same kinds of data, such as facial expressions.

*Plutchik.* Plutchik's (1980) approach to the problem was somewhat unique. He noted that most "definitions" of emotion depend on the reader's having already known what is to be "defined." That is, if the reader's emotional experience corresponds to some particular emotion description the emotion is said to be defined. Plutchik considered emotions from a broad biological perspective, in terms of what he believed to be universal adaptive behaviors necessary for survival. He proposed that there are eight such adaptive behaviors common to *all* organisms, but that in higher mammals there are corresponding emotional states. The specific terms for these activities, such as *protection* and *destruction*, are *functional* and do not necessarily refer to any specific behavior. A number of behaviors might serve the same purpose. Running, for example, might serve both approach and avoidance functions at different times.

**TABLE 2–2   Discrete Emotions According to Several Theorists**

|  | IZARD | TOMPKINS | EKMAN | PLUTCHIK |
|---|---|---|---|---|
| 1. | Interest-excitement | Interest | — | Expectancy |
| 2. | Joy | Joy | Happiness | Joy |
| 3. | Surprise | Startle | Surprise | Surprise |
| 4. | Distress-Anguish | Distress | Sadness | Sadness |
| 5. | Anger-Rage | — | Anger | Anger |
| 6. | Disgust | — | Disgust | Disgust |
| 7. | Contempt-Scorn | — | Contempt | — |
| 8. | Fear-Terror | Fear | Fear | Fear |
| 9. | Shame-Shyness | — | — | — |
| 10. | Guilt | — | — | — |
| 11. | — | Laughter | — | — |
| 12. | — | — | — | Acceptance |

Plutchik described each of the adaptive acts in terms of four different kinds of languages that psychologists use:

- *Subjective language* is the language of human introspection. For example, "I feel afraid" or "I am angry."
- *Behavioral language* refers to the behaviors we might observe in humans or other animals, from which we might infer a particular emotion.
- *Functional language* refers to the life-sustaining functions on which the theory is based, such as reproduction or protection.
- *Trait language* is that commonly used to describe personality characteristics, such as "He is timid" or "She is gregarious."

Many words either are *synonyms* of the emotion terms or represent different *degrees* of a particular emotion. For example, "distracted," "surprised," and "amazed" are different degrees of surprise. These can be represented as a cone, as shown in Figure 2–4.

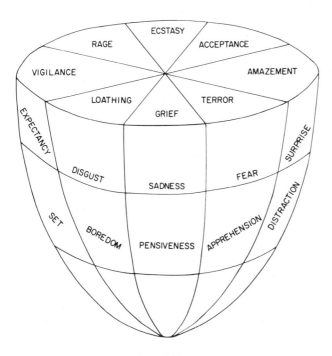

**FIGURE 2–4.** Plutchik's multidimensional model of emotion. Across the top of the inverted cone are the eight primary emotions, with lesser degrees of intensity of each as one reads downward within each "slice." (From Plutchik, Emotions, evolution, and adaptative processes, Figure 1, p. 10, in M. Arnold (ed.) *Feelings and Emotions*, 1970. Reprinted by permission of Academic Press.)

**TABLE 2-3    Four Languages Used to Describe Emotional States in Plutchik's Theory**

| SUBJECTIVE LANGUAGE | BEHAVIORAL LANGUAGE | FUNCTIONAL LANGUAGE | TRAIT LANGUAGE |
|---|---|---|---|
| Fear | Escaping | Protection | Timid |
| Anger | Attacking | Destruction | Aggressive |
| Joy | Cooperating | Reproduction | Gregarious |
| Sadness | Crying for help | Reintegration | Depressed |
| Acceptance | Affiliating | Incorporation | Trustful |
| Disgust | Repulsing | Rejection | Distrustful |
| Expectancy | Exploring | Exploration | Controlled |
| Surprise | Stopping | Orientation | Dyscontrolled |

From Plutchik, R. *Emotion: A Psychoevolutionary Synthesis.* New York: Harper & Row, Publishers, 1980. Table 13.6, p. 217. Reprinted by permission of Harper & Row, Pub.

*Tomkins.*    Sylvan Tomkins (1981), to whom most contemporary discrete emotion theorists owe an intellectual debt, argues that the genetically programmed emotional responses serve to amplify biological need states. He says, for example, that an animal or person may *detect* hunger or thirst, but this recognition is just a cue to produce emotion, and it is the emotion which "energizes" behaviors for getting food or water. Need states do not directly energize behavior, Tomkins says, except insofar as they are amplified by emotions. He also suggests that different emotions can be described biologically in terms of change in rate and level of neural firing, as shown in Figure 2-5 (from Tomkins, 1981, p. 318). This seems to be a simplistic view of neural functioning in relation to emotion. It does not, for example, identify any specific neural structures underlying emotions. However, and more importantly, it is an attempt to tie emotion to some specific neural activity.

*Evidence for discrete emotions.*    Discrete emotion theories have leaned heavily on evolutionary principles to account for emotional development. Darwin himself (1965/1872), observed that many species show similar expressions of emotion. Dogs, cats, and monkeys draw back their lips and bare their teeth when angry, much as people do, and such emotional *displays* may replace actual fighting. In humans, such displays are often pale reflections of those shown by lower animals, but the evolutionary relationship to our animal ancestors seems clear enough.

*Facial expression in humans.* Three general lines of research on the facial expression support the genetic-programming concept of discrete emotions: (1) A small number of facial expressions are universally displayed and recognized. (2) Children around the world seem to show the same progression of emotional development. (3) Children blind from birth, who could not have learned facial expressions by observing others, show the same expressions.

Research on facial expressions goes back to the 19th century but in recent years has been dominated by the work of Paul Ekman and his col-

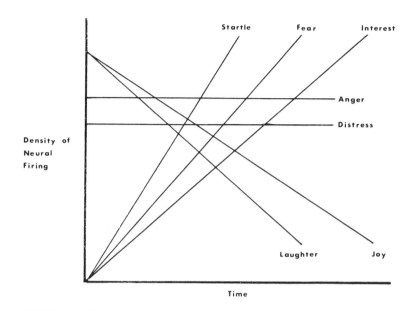

**FIGURE 2-5.** Changes in density of neural firing over time as related to basic emotions. From Tomkins (1981, Figure 1). Copyright 1981 by the American Psychological Association. Reprinted by permission.

leagues (e.g., Ekman & Friesen, 1975; Ekman & Friesen, 1986). Research from such diverse cultures as preliterate mountain natives of New Guinea and tribespeople of Iran, as well as more developed cultures, indicate universal recognition of expressions of *happiness, anger, sadness, disgust, surprise, fear,* and *contempt.* People who have never seen Caucasians, nor been exposed to photographs or television, correctly identify specific facial expressions as indicative of the emotions a person in a story would express (Ekman & Friesen, 1971). Deaf and blind children also show the typical facial expressions for these emotions (Ekman & Oster, 1979). Emotional expressions may be universal because they are biologically valuable forms of communication, arousing caretaking activity by adults. Infants who can express emotions are more likely to survive than those who cannot.

*Anatomy of facial expression.* Facial expressions are determined by contractions of muscles in the face which contort the skin to form the visible expression. It is possible to catalog the specific muscles which contract during different facial expressions. Once these are known it is possible to distinguish spontaneous expressions from faked ones and to learn more about the details of emotion. Such a catalog has been developed by Ekman & Friesen (1978), in what they call the *Facial Action Coding System.* Figure 2-6 shows a simplified diagram of some of the muscles which are important for the facial expression of emotion. The *frontalis* muscles produce wrinkles in the forehead; the *corrugator* muscles produce frowning eyebrows; the *or-*

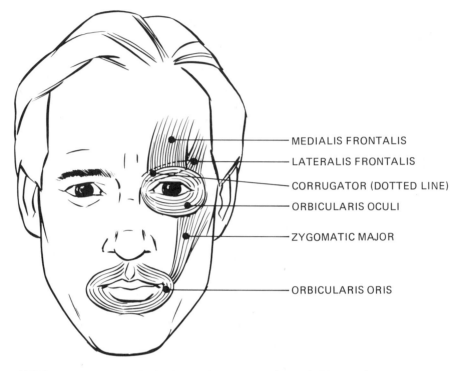

MEDIALIS FRONTALIS

LATERALIS FRONTALIS

CORRUGATOR (DOTTED LINE)

ORBICULARIS OCULI

ZYGOMATIC MAJOR

ORBICULARIS ORIS

**FIGURE 2-6.** Important muscles involved in pleasant and unpleasant facial expressions.

*bicularis oculi* muscles produce the "crow's-feet" which characterize smiling; and the *zygomatic major* and *orbicularis orbis* muscles around the cheeks and mouth produce smiling. When we change moods from negative to positive, activity of the *corrugators* decreases and activity of the *zygomatic* and *orbicularis orbis* increases (Cacioppo, Petty, Losch, & Kim, 1986). Not surprisingly, then, *zygomatic* activity is also greater during the presentation of sexual stimuli than of nonsexual stimuli (Sullivan & Bender, 1986). The extent to which facial expression is a *determinant* of experienced emotion has been a question of some interest. Can we make ourselves feel better by "putting on a happy face"?

    *The facial feedback hypothesis.* William James's theory of emotion stated that the experience of emotion is the perception of one's responses to some kind of stimulation. This led him (1890) to consider whether actors, for example, actually *felt* the emotions which they were mimicking with their faces. He concluded that the evidence on the question was ambiguous, probably because the actors could not easily produce the appropriate *visceral* changes to go along with the facial expressions. Tomkins (1962) and Izard (1971) argued, however, that the facial musculature is complex enough that the feedback produced is adequate to produce the experience of different emotions. If this is true, then *artificial* manipulation of facial expressions should modify emotional experience.

Artificial manipulation of facial reactions has been studied by *directly manipulating* facial muscles, and by *instructing* subjects to express or hide a particular emotion (Leventhal & Tomarkan, 1986). Indirect manipulation has also been done by using such cues as "canned laughter" to facilitate such humorous responses as smiling and laughing. Laird (1974) reported that subjects instructed to frown also reported feeling aggressive in response to photographs, but smiles induced more positive feelings toward the same photos. The evidence is ambiguous, however. Tourangeau and Ellsworth (1979) produced appropriate facial expressions of fear or sadness in their subjects, but these expressions did not affect the subjects' reports of their *feelings* while watching fearful or sad movies, and did not produce any other physiological changes in the subject.

Leventhal and Tomarkan (1986, p. 580) conclude that expressive changes can alter subjective states, but that such effects are very small. Matsumoto (1987), analyzing 16 experiments on manipulation of facial expression, found that facial feedback accounts for only about 12% of the variation of reported emotional change. This 12% is equivalent to a correlation of .35, however, which is typically what researchers find as meaningful correlations in personality research. Artificially manipulated facial feedback may not produce large changes in experienced emotion, then, but the effect seems to be as large as is found with many other variables in personality research.

*Emotional expression as social communication: Display rules.* Facial expression of emotion may be genetically programmed, but cultural "display rules" tell us when and how we *ought* to express grief, joy, and other emotions and may therefore interfere with "basic" emotional expressions. Thus, if I win a lottery I will feel happy and communicate that happiness. If I were to feel happy at someone else's misfortune, however, I probably would *not* want to communicate that joy and would try to mask it. Ekman and Oster (1979) reported that Japanese people watching a movie controlled their facial expressions if they knew they were being observed more than Americans in the same situation did. The stereotypes of the "stoic" Britisher, the "inscrutable" Oriental, or the "excitable" Latin may have arisen because of such specific cultural influences on the expression of emotion. Overt expressions of emotion may be aroused more readily by social cues than by other events. Bowlers, hockey fans, and people strolling down the street were more likely to smile in response to other people than to cues regarding sports results which should have made them happy, such as good bowling scores (Kraut & Johnston, 1979).

*Moderator variables* also affect social communication. One such variable is the degree of *spontaneity* of expression. Spontaneous reactions to stimuli are stronger, in terms of both facial expression and reported feelings than are artificial reactions. In fact, voluntary and involuntary (spontaneous) emotional responses appear to "originate" in different motor systems in the brain (Rinn, 1984). Involuntary emotional responses operate through the *extrapyramidal motor system* and voluntary responses through the *pyramidal motor system*. A person with damage to the extrapyramidal system may laugh or cry uncontrollably, expressing emotion inappropriate to the situation. Voluntary expression of emotion, however, is not affected. Conversely, a person with pyramidal damage has difficulty making *voluntary* expressions of emotion, but shows appropriate involuntary responses. This dual control system would account for the fact that there is sometimes *emotional leakage*. Sometimes when people try to disguise their emotions (pyramidal control) their "true" emotion still "leaks" through in facial expression (extrapyramidal control). An angry person may try to hide his anger, but some component of the involuntary emotional response cannot be inhibited and leaks through so that the anger can be detected by others.

*Development of facial expression.* The facial muscles of newborn humans are fully operative, and adultlike expressions occur early. In the first few hours of life infants show expressions of distress, disgust, and startle. Imitation of adult facial expressions may occur as early as two or three weeks of age. At about three months, smiling begins to occur reliably, and infants begin to distinguish adult facial expressions and respond differently to them (Ekman & Oster, 1979). Preschool children know most of the common facial expressions and what elicits them, although this knowledge continues to grow until at least age ten.

In summary, there appears to be a handful of biologically determined emotions, whose functions may be to amplify need states and whose expression conveys information about such internal states to others. (For a lengthy discussion of communication see Buck, 1985.)

### Dimensional Approaches to Emotion

In contrast to the discrete emotion approach is the *dimensional* approach, exemplified by Wundt's theory. Wundt, recall, said that all emotional experiences could be considered as combinations of *pleasant-unpleasant, tense-relaxed*, and *excitement-depression* (see Table 2-4). "Very unpleasant-tense" is a very different experience from "pleasant-relaxed." Since Wundt's time, virtually every study of emotional expression or recognition which has looked for dimensions has found *pleasant-unpleasant* as the most important and *level of arousal* as second most important.

Figure 2-7 (from Russell, 1980) shows a number of different emotions placed along these two dimensions. Russell and Bullock (1985) have found

**TABLE 2-4    Dimensions of Emotion Found by a Number of Different Researchers**

| NAME | DIMENSIONS | | |
|---|---|---|---|
| | FIRST | SECOND | THIRD |
| Wundt (1902) | Pleasant-Unpleasant | Tense-Relaxed | Excitement-Depression |
| Titchner (1910) | Pleasant-Unpleasant | — | — |
| Schlosberg (1954) | Pleasant-Unpleasant | Tense-Relaxed | Acceptance-Rejection |
| Osgood, Suci | Evaluative | Activity | Potency |
| & Tannenbaum (1957) | (Good-Bad) | (Fast-Slow) | (Strong-Weak) |
| Davitz (1970)* | Hedonic Tone | Activation | Competence |
| | (comfort-discomfort) | | |
| Russell and Mehrebian | Pleasure- | Degree of | Dominance- |
| (1977) | Displeasure | Arousal | Submission |

*Davitz also identified a fourth dimension which he termed "relatedness."

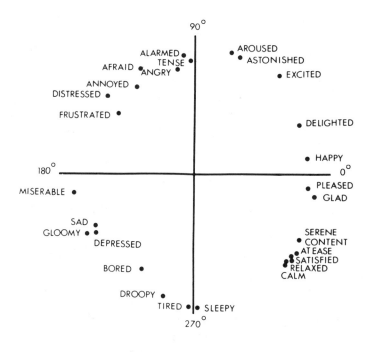

**FIGURE 2-7.** Russell's circumplex model of emotion. A representation of 28 emotion-related words on the two dimensions of pleasant-unpleasant and level of arousal. From Russell (1980, Figure 2). Copyright 1980 by the American Psychological Association. Reprinted by permission.

similar results for both adults and preschool children, and argue that dimensions of emotion may represent a developmentally more primitive differentiation of emotion than discrete emotions represent.

Dimensions of emotion are discovered by studying similarities and differences in *recognition* of different *facial expressions* or by studying similarities and differences in *emotion words*. Starting with many words or pictures representing emotions the problem has been to find a smaller number of threads running through these. For example, if the word *joy* is used similarly to the word *euphoria*, there is overlap in the *meaning* of the two words and they do not represent entirely different emotions. When appropriate statistical analyses (such as *factor analysis*) are applied to such data, we obtain sets of words which vary *qualitatively* (such as *good* versus *bad*, *pleasant* versus *unpleasant*, or *happy* versus *sad*). Other sets of words vary *quantitatively* (such as *irritation*, *anger*, and *rage*, which represent progressively stronger degrees of the same emotion). The richness of poetic description depends partly on the use of emotional words which differ in sound, number of syllables, or other linguistic characteristics but do not necessarily represent different emotions.

Whether or not there are important emotional dimensions beyond pleasant-unpleasant and level of arousal is still unanswered. Thayer (1978) has distinguished two dimensions of arousal, not just one: *tense-relaxed* and *energetic-sleepy*. The former is characterized by the tension which builds up during a day full of hassles, following which a person may just want to relax. The latter is characteristic of hard work or play, following which a person is sleepy. Other researchers have reported other dimensions as the third. One, which may be called *control-lack of control*, has appeared under such names as *competence* (Davitz, 1970), *dominance-submission* (Russell & Mehrabian, 1977), and *potency* (Osgood, Suci, & Tannenbaum, 1957). Russell (1979) suggests that a feeling of control is not a separate dimension, but only a determinant of whether an event is experienced as pleasant. The feeling of control has been extensively studied in research on motivation, emotion, stress, and anxiety in recent years. It is discussed in more detail in chapter 9.

The most remarkable fact is that the same small number of dimensions have been repeatedly found over the years, regardless of method. This is important for a number of reasons.

First, if dimensional models of emotion are more accurate descriptions of emotional experiences than discrete-emotion accounts of emotion, then we would look for *physiological* bases of emotion in different ways. Routtenberg (1968), for example, argued that there are two types of neural systems for arousal. The *limbic system* underlies *reward* and *punishment*, which corresponds to pleasant-unpleasant experience, whereas the *reticular activating system* underlies *level of arousal*. If all emotions consist of combinations of these two dimensions, we have a clue to the great difficulty in finding physiological bases for *discrete emotions*. That is, what *appear* to be discrete emotions share a common physiological basis (combinations of activity in the two neural systems) so that discrete emotions cannot be distinguished very well physiologically.

Second, *in practice* many types of emotional research are based on a dimensional approach. Research on *mood,* for example, generally assumes that people have *good* and *bad* moods which affect how they think and behave (e.g., Isen, 1984).

Third, if there is in fact only a small physiological range for different experienced emotions, *cognition* may be accorded a greater role in emotion. Our *experienced emotions* might depend on our *appraisal* or *interpretation* of the situation we are in, as well as differences in internal arousal. However, *cognitive activities are also physiological events.* It is easy to fall into the trap of mind-body dualism (recall chapter 1) and to look at cognition and arousal as two distinct categories, mental and physical.

### Cognitive Approaches to Emotion

*Background.*     The essence of cognitive approaches to emotion is that emotion depends on how we *appraise* or *evaluate* situations. If I hear footsteps in the dark, I may appraise them as bad (a burglar) and be anxious, or I may appraise them as good (a friend or loved one) and be relieved or happy. The "objective situation" may be the same in either case, but my responses entirely different. Magda Arnold (1970) has long argued that a detailed *psychology* of emotion is needed to provide clues to understanding the *physiology* of emotion. What neural structures are involved in appraisal, and how are these related to emotional arousal? Workers in *cognitive psychology* and *neuroscience* are actively engaged in research to understand neural bases of thought processes, but we still know very little.

A recent debate has arisen on whether cognitive activity is *necessary* for emotion. Robert Zajonc (1980, 1984) argues that *preferences* for stimuli can be *immediate* responses and do not require previous cognitive appraisal. For example, people report *liking* stimuli more if they have previously been exposed to the stimuli, even though they *do not remember* the earlier exposure. This is called the *Mere Exposure Effect.* Since the preference occurs without awareness, Zajonc concludes that cognitive appraisal is not a necessary condition for all emotional responses. Richard Lazarus (1982) responds by pointing to extensive research showing that appraisal *is* often involved in emotion, and then argues that appraisal is not necessarily *conscious.* The argument then seems to hinge on the question of how we are to define appraisal. If appraisal, *by definition,* is a *conscious* process, then appraisal may *not* be necessary. But if appraisal, by definition, can sometimes be *unconscious,* then appraisal may be necessary. Suffice it to say that the role of cognition in emotion is still unsettled because we do not have an exact definition of cognition, because we do not clearly understand what roles "conscious" and "unconscious" factors play in cognition, and because we are not certain which neurological structures and processes are involved in cognition. Whether or not cognition is a *necessary* condition for emotion, there is little question that psychologists have considered cognitive processes to be *important* to emotion.

*Attribution theory and emotion.* *Cognitive-arousal theory.* The failure to find specific physiological correlates of experienced emotions does not mean that such correlates do not exist, but by the 1960's psychology was ripe for a new approach to emotion. Activation theory did not require much specificity, but most psychologists found it difficult to believe that differences in level of activation alone could account for all the perceived differences in emotional experience. The new approach grew out of the developing *attribution theory* in social psychology. Attribution theory is concerned with how people seek and find *causes* for behavior. It was a short step to propose that people also seek causes to account for how they *feel*, and to interpret their feelings in terms of the *situation(s)* in which they find themselves. For example, if I feel myself becoming aroused I might interpret this arousal in any of several ways. If a large, unfriendly dog is approaching I might interpret my arousal as *fear*. If someone has just insulted me, I might interpret my arousal as *anger*. If a friend is approaching, I might interpret my arousal as *joy*. Mandler (1962) and Schachter and Singer (1962) simultaneously proposed that such interpretations are crucial to emotional experience. The latter were more influential, however, because they also presented an experiment purporting to show that the same state of internal arousal could be interpreted as either happiness or anger, depending on environmental circumstances. The theory was compelling, not because of the data, but because the theory filled a theoretical vacuum in which psychologists had been foundering for half a century.

Schachter and Singer proposed that perceived emotion is a *joint* function of internal arousal *and* an appropriate cognition with which to *label* the arousal. The labeling, such as referring to the arousal as fear, is a cognitive activity (in this case, an attribution). *The arousal and the cognition are both necessary for the experienced emotion.* If either the arousal or the cognition is not present, a particular emotion is not experienced. Schachter and Singer tested this hypothesis by giving subjects injections of adrenaline (to produce general arousal) and then putting them into different situations calculated to produce different cognitive labeling of the arousal.

*The Schachter-Singer Experiment.* The experimental outline is summarized in Table 2-5. The subjects were given the cover story that the experiment concerned the effect on vision of a new vitamin compound called *suproxin.* The drug was actually epinephrine (adrenalin), which produces many symptoms of autonomic nervous system arousal, such as increased blood pressure, heart rate, skin conductance, respiration, and muscle tremor.

**TABLE 2-5    Summary of Experimental Procedures and Happiness-Angry Ratings of All Groups in The Schacter-Singer (1962) Experiment. Positive Numbers Mean More Happy than Angry, and Negative Numbers Mean More Angry than Happy. Numbers of Subjects per Group Ranged from 22 to 26.**

| TREATMENTS | MOOD SCORES (HAPPY-ANGRY) |
|---|---|
| Happy conditions. Subjects wait with playful stooge | |
| *Epinephrine Informed.* Subjects injected with epinephrine and told of drug effects. Should *not* feel happy. | .98 |
| *Epinephrine Ignorant.* Subjects not told of drug effects. Should attribute arousal to situation and be happy. | 1.78[a] |
| *Epinephrine Misinformed.* Subjects told wrong effects of drug injection. Should be happy, like ignorant group. | 1.90 |
| *Placebo.* Saline injection should not produce arousal; Subjects should *not* feel happy. | 1.61 |
| Angry Conditions. Subjects fill out tedious and insulting forms | |
| *Epinephrine Informed.* Subjects told of drug effects. Should *not* feel angry. | 1.91 |
| *Epinephrine Ignorant.* Subjects not told of drug effects. Should feel angry. | 1.39[b] |
| *Placebo.* Should not be aroused and should *not* feel angry. | 1.63 |

From Schaeter, S. and Singer, J. (1962). Cognitive Social and physiological determinants of emotional state. *Psychology Review*, 69, 379–399. Copyright © 1962 by the American Psychological Association. Used by permission.

[a]The informed group was significantly different below the ignorant and misinformed groups, but there were no other significant differences.

[b]The informed group was significantly "less happy" than the ignorant group but there were no other significant differences. All angry groups reported being more happy than angry.

The subjects' *cognitions* were manipulated by (1) giving them different information about the effects of the drug, and (2) putting them in different situations.

The *informed* subjects were told there would be transitory side effects of *suproxin,* and were given the actual symptoms to be expected from adrenalin. They should then attribute their arousal to the *drug.* The *ignorant* subjects were not told about any side effects, and therefore should attribute their arousal to the situation, not to the injected drug. *Misinformed* subjects were given false information about side effects, such as that there might be numbing of the feet or itching. This was a control for whatever *experimenter demand* effects might occur in the experiment, and subjects should act like subjects in the ignorant condition. Subjects in the *placebo* condition got saline injections, which should not produce arousal, and did not get any other information. Half the subjects in the informed, ignorant, and placebo groups were then subjected to conditions intended to arouse *happiness,* and half

were subjected to conditions intended to provoke anger. Misinformed subjects were only in the happy condition.

In the *happy* condition, subjects were asked to wait a few minutes with
"another subject," actually an experimental stooge, until the drug had time to
take effect. During a 20-minute waiting period, the stooge performed such
frivolous acts as flying a paper airplane and shooting paper-wad basketballs
into a trash can. Following a prearranged script, the stooge also tried to
engage the real subject in these activities. In the *angry* condition, the subjects
were asked to fill out a five-page questionnaire containing progressively more
personal and irksome questions, to which the stooge loudly objected.

The subjects then filled out various self-reports concerning physiological symptoms and mood. There were separate 5-point scales (0 to 4) for
happiness and anger. The data presented by the experimenters, summarized
in Table 2-5, are the mean *differences* between happiness and anger: Happy
Score — Anger Score. "Happy" subjects (more happy than angry) should have
*positive* scores and "angry" subjects (more angry than happy) should have
*negative* scores.

There are several noteworthy aspects of the Schachter-Singer data.
First, under the happy conditions (which the experimenters now called
*euphoria*, instead of *happiness*), the *informed* group scored significantly below
the *ignorant* group. The standard interpretation is that the informed group,
having been told of the "side effects" of the injection, attributed their arousal
to the injection. Therefore, they did not interpret their arousal as happiness.
The *ignorant* group, not knowing the drug effects, searched for a cause of
their arousal when asked to make ratings. Since the apparent cause is the
preceding gamelike situation, they labeled their arousal as happiness. The
results for these two groups follow the theoretical predictions. Unfortunately,
the *placebo* group was just about as "happy" as the ignorant group, and indeed
not significantly different from any of the groups in the happy condition.
This does *not* fit the prediction.

Second, the *angry* groups should all have *negative* scores (happy —
angry), but the average scores for all groups were positive; they were all more
happy than angry. Indeed, if we take results reported to the second decimal
place seriously, the angry-informed group is the most "euphoric" group in the
experiment. The authors suggest that the subjects, students in the experiment for course credit, were not about to endanger their grade by getting
angry at the experimenter. Perhaps, perhaps not. The *ignorant* group did
report less happiness than the informed group, which is at least in the right
direction, but once again the placebo group falls between the ignorant and
informed groups. The authors duly note that the results with the placebo
condition made it impossible "to evaluate unequivocally the effects of the
state of physiological arousal and indeed raises questions about our entire
theoretical structure" (Schachter & Singer, 1962, p. 393). The authors were,
thus, initially modest about the import of their research — a level of humility
suppressed in later writing about the same experiment.

The above experiment is described in considerable detail because, in spite of the weak support for the theory, the experiment has been extremely influential both in generating other experiments and in providing theoretical explanations for many phenomena. Unfortunately, twenty years of research has not supported the theory very well. Reisenzein (1983) concluded that the only adequate support is from research involving *misattributed* arousal from an irrelevant source, such as attributing exercise-induced arousal to sexual arousal in the presence of sexual cues. He further concluded that there is no evidence that unexplained arousal instigates a search for the cause of such arousal. Leventhal and Tomarken (1986, p. 574) agree that research testing predictions from cognitive-arousal theory "has yielded disappointing results."

In addition to the above difficulties, in two experiments (Maslach, 1979; Marshall & Zimbardo, 1979), unexplained arousal was described by subjects as unpleasant, and not described as "happiness" even under the happy experimental condition used by Schachter and Singer. Indeed, it makes clinical sense that unexplained arousal should be unpleasant; it sounds suspiciously like free-floating anxiety, a very unpleasant experience.

*Excitation Transfer Theory.* The one area of support, noted above, involves what is called *excitation transfer* (Zillman, 1978). According to this theory, when sympathetic arousal has occurred, it takes some period of time for the arousal to decay. While arousal is still decaying, a person may incorrectly identify the source of arousal. *Already-existing feelings* of anger, aggression, or sexual arousal may be *intensified* by irrelevant arousal.

Excitation transfer theory differs from cognitive-arousal theory in several ways (Leventhal & Tomarken, 1986). First, excitation transfer theory does not assume any causal search for the source of unexplained arousal. Misattributions occur *by accident*, not as a result of logical thinking. Second, excitation-transfer theory assumes that misattribution is most likely to occur when people are actually becoming *less aware* of their arousal. For example, Cantor, Zillman, and Bryant (1975) studied the effect of prior physical exercise on self-reports of sexual arousal from erotic films.

They had separate groups of subjects view a film entitled *Naked Under Leather* at either zero, five, or nine minutes after exercising, when the exercise-induced arousal is high, imperceptible, or back to preexercise baseline. Subjects rated their level of sexual arousal on a 100-point scale. Mean arousal ratings at the three times were 28, 52, and 28, respectively. Only subjects in the five-minute group, who still had residual arousal but *did not perceive* the arousal, rated their level of sexual arousal higher. Presumably, the zero-delay group recognized that much of their arousal was attributable to exercise and the nine-minute group was no longer aroused by the exercise and so had no excitation to transfer. Results from this line of research seem robust.

*Valins's Attribution Theory.* Valins (1966, 1970) extended the Schachter-Singer approach by suggesting that the *perception of physiological change is a sufficient condition for experienced emotion, whether or not the perception is accurate.* If we only *think* we have been aroused, we can *interpret* this as emotion. Valins (1966) tested his hypothesis by giving subjects false information about their heart rates as they viewed slides of *Playboy* centerfolds. Three groups of subjects had microphones taped to their chests. In Group 1, subjects heard sounds that the experimenter said were their heart beats. While viewing half the ten slides, the subjects heard an initial *increase* in heart rate, then a return to normal, but there was no heart rate change during the other five slides. Group 2 was treated the same except that their supposed heart rates *decreased* during some slides. Group 3 subjects were treated the same as Groups 1 and 2 except that they were told the noises they heard were just extraneous sounds. During a second viewing each slide was rated on a 100-point scale of attractiveness. Subjects also selected the five slides they would like to keep and several weeks later rated the slides again in apparently unrelated circumstances. It was predicted subjects would attribute the apparent heart rate changes to the slides and rate the heart-rate-change slides higher than the no-change slides. The results seemed clear. Table 2–6 compares Valins's findings with data from an experiment that simulated Valins's, conducted in the author's laboratory.

The slides associated with heart rate change (increase or decrease) were rated more attractive than those not associated with change. This did not occur in the unrelated-sound condition. Furthermore, 29 out of the 40

**TABLE 2-6   Mean Attractiveness Ratings of Slides of Valins's (1966) Experiment Compared With Paper-Pencil Simulations Based On Precisely Written Descriptions of the Valins Experiment. Subjects in the Simulations Saw No Slides. (HR = Heart Rate; R = "Reinforced", Slides Said To Show A Change in HR; NR = "Non-Reinforced", Slides Not Said to Show a Change.)**

|  | HR INCREASE | | | HR DECREASE | | | SOUND | | |
|---|---|---|---|---|---|---|---|---|---|
|  | R | NR | DIFF | R | NR | DIFF | R | NR | DIFF |
| Valins | 72.4 | 54.1 | 18.3 | 69.3 | 62.6 | 6.7 | 60.9 | 63.8 | −2.9 |
| Male Simulation[1] | 72.0 | 35.0 | 37.0 | 63.0 | 37.5 | 25.5 | 69.7 | 56.4 | 13.3 |
| Female Simulation | 68.1 | 25.5 | 42.6 | 54.3 | 42.3 | 12.0 | 57.0 | 45.1 | 11.9 |

**Number of 20 Subjects in Each Condition Selecting Three or More "Reinforced" Slides to Keep When Offered Five**

|  | HR INCREASE | HR DECREASE | HR INCREASE DECREASE | SOUND |
|---|---|---|---|---|
| Valins | 17 | 15 | 32 | 9[2] |
| Male Simulation | 18 | 16 | 34 | 15 |
| Female Simulation | 20 | 14 | 34 | 15 |

[1] The data for the male and female simulations are from unpublished research conducted in the author's laboratory by Charles Gibson and Wendy Elliott, respectively.

[2] All percentages of reinforced slides "kept" were significantly greater than 50% except Valins's sound group.

subjects in Groups 1 and 2 chose at least three of the "reinforced" slides to keep, whereas only 6 of 20 subjects in Group 3 chose three or more. The preferences still held up a month later. These results strongly supported Valins's hypothesis: When subjects heard the fake heart rate changes they searched the slides for characteristics of the models (such as parts of the anatomy) that might have caused the cardiac changes and then attributed the changes to these "attractive" features. In short, subjects reached the attribution that they had made emotional responses to slides which were more attractive.

There are problems with Valins's hypothesis, however. Consider that a typical false-feedback experiment contains the following elements: (1) male subjects who are instructed that the experiment is about emotional arousal, (2) female nude slides, (3) heart rate, popularly understood as an emotional response, said to be recorded, (4) false feedback about heart rate, and (5) subjects rating the slides for attractiveness. "Reinforced' slides, said to be associated with heart rate change, are rated more attractive than "nonreinforced" slides. Given these circumstances, there are a number of possible interpretations of how the experimental procedures lead to higher attractiveness ratings.

First, there is Valins's original *attribution search* hypothesis, which is in question. Second, false heart rate feedback may induce *real* heart rate changes. There is some evidence for this possibility, but a number of studies have found the false feedback effect *without* changes in real heart rate (see Parkinson, 1985, for a recent critical review). Third, merely bringing a subject's *attention* to some slides may lead to higher attractiveness ratings. Valins's extraneous-sound condition was meant to control for this possibility, and in it he did not get the feedback effect. Several experiments have shown, however, that when subjects pay close attention to "extraneous sounds" as they view slides, there are higher attractiveness ratings (Stern, Botto, & Herrick, 1972; Parkinson & Manstead, 1981; Parkinson, 1985).

Fourth, there is the possibility of an *expectancy-demand* effect. Given the experimental conditions described above, a subject might say to himself: "What am I expected to do here? I am a subject in an experiment on emotional arousal, looking at pictures of naked women; they tell me my heart rate is higher for some pictures than others, and I am supposed to rate the pictures. Maybe they want me to give higher ratings to pictures where my heart rate changes." Quite apart from emotional arousal, the situation may set up a *demand* to rate repeated slides as more attractive. Data from the author's laboratory support this hypothesis. Thus:

1. Male subjects were given a written description of the Valins procedure (but not the results) and asked to rate *blank squares as if* the squares were pictures, and as if they were the subjects in such an experiment. The ratings were very much like those reported in Valins's experiment. Furthermore, female subjects asked

to pretend they were males gave virtually the same ratings as males. Table 2–6 summarizes the numerical ratings from Valins's experiment and our simulation. It also shows the number of subjects in both experiments who would choose at least three of the "reinforced slides" to keep if offered five. Our results were identical to Valins's, but were obtained without slides, without real arousal, and without false feedback. There seem to be sufficient "demand cues" to tell the subjects what to do.

2. If the above simulation is modified for females, by saying the imaginary slides are from *Playgirl*, the females rate the blank squares much like the males in the original experiment did. And, males pretending to be females give the same general ratings.

In other research we used the Barefoot and Straub (1971) variation of Valins's procedure. Instead of getting feedback slide by slide, subjects were shown all ten slides, then five of these, said to be the ones which showed the greatest heart rate change, were shown a second time. The second showing was actually the false feedback. Subjects almost universally rated the "change" slides higher than the no-change slides. Barefoot and Straub argued that if the subjects saw the feedback slides only briefly (5 seconds) they would not have enough time to search the slides for the source of arousal and thus would rate all slides about the same. With a longer showing (20 seconds), however, subjects would have time to make an attribution and therefore give higher ratings to the feedback slides. Their data supported these predictions. However, in a series of experiments we found the following:

1. In a simulation of the Barefoot-Straub study, along the lines described above, the results were similar to those found by Barefoot and Straub for the 20-second feedback group (Table 2–7). Knowledge of the procedure appears to provide adequate information to produce the effect.

2. In *replications* of the Barefoot-Straub study (not simulations) we obtained the feedback effect with the five-second feedback time, with significant differences between heart-rate-change slides and no-change slides in two of three experiments and in the right direction in the third, using both male and female subjects (Beck et al., 1988, Exps. 1 and 2).

3. In experiments involving emotional versus nonemotional feedback (heart rate versus eyeblink), emotional versus nonemotional slides (male slides with female subjects versus tourist slides of Rome, Italy), and varying instructions (e.g., the experiment is about emotional arousal versus no mention of what the experiment is about), we found the feedback effect under virtually all conditions. A group predicted from the attribution search hypothesis to *not* show the effect (having gotten eyeblink feedback, nonemotional instructions, and tourist slides) showed virtually the same mean difference between change and no-change slides (3.5) as did a group expected to show a very large difference (having gotten heart rate feedback, emotional instructions, and male slides), with a mean of 3.6.

4. In an experiment with eight different conditions (Beck et al., Experiment 5), the only significant determinant of the feedback effect was whether, after the experiment was completed, subjects said *they thought they should rate the repeated slides higher*. For those who did, the difference was 10.0; for those who did not, the difference was 1.5.

TABLE 2-7   Comparison of Simulation Data and Exact Replications of the Barefoot-Straub Experiment with Male and Female Subjects. Subjects (1) Saw Ten Slides for 30 Second Each, (2) Saw Half for Either 20 Seconds (High Search) or 5 Seconds (Low Search), and (3) Then Saw All Slides for 5 Seconds While Rating Them on 50-Point Attractiveness Scale. The Simulation Used Only Written Materials and No Slides.

| | HIGH SEARCH (20 SECONDS EXPOSURE FOR "REINFORCED" SLIDES) | | |
| --- | --- | --- | --- |
| | "REINFORCED" SLIDES | "NON-REINF." SLIDES | DIFFERENCE |
| Barefoot-Straub | 31.3 | 26.0 | 5.3 |
| Simulation (males) | 34.4 | 30.3 | 4.1 |
| *Replication 1 (M)[1] | 35.5 | 28.9 | 6.6 |
| *Replication 2 (F) | 33.7 | 29.4 | 4.3 |
| *Replication 3 (F) | 33.2 | 27.5 | 5.7 |
| | LOW SEARCH (5 SECONDS EXPOSURE FOR "REINFORCED" SLIDES) | | |
| Barefoot-Straub | 29.6 | 29.5 | 0.1 |
| Simulation (males) | 37.5 | 29.7 | 7.8 |
| Replication 1 (M) | 34.4 | 30.2 | 4.2 |
| Replication 2 (F) | 35.0 | 32.9 | 2.1[2] |
| Replication 3 (F) | 34.3 | 30.2 | 4.1 |

[1]M = male subjects: F = female subjects.

[2]Not significantly different from the high search groups in the same experiment.

*From Beck et al (1988). False physiological feedback and emotion: Experimenter demand and salience effects. *Motivation and Emotion,* 12, 217–236. Copyright 1988 Plenum Publishing Corporation. Used by permission.

The literature as a whole (Parkinson, 1985) lends little support to the attribution search hypothesis but seems to support an expectancy-demand hypothesis. Subjects take in all the situational cues they can and then respond as each deems most appropriate for the perceived situation. It is still necessary to identify the factors producing the demand in the Valins situation, however. It appears that the necessary condition is to make some stimuli more *salient* than others. That is, if attention is drawn to some stimuli the demand begins to operate. Taylor and Fiske (1978) proposed that if stimuli are highly noticeable, people tend to overattribute causality or preference to them. For example, a person singled out from a group was better liked than when he was an anonymous member. The Valins effect is obtained when some slides are singled out and made more salient than others. If the subject has the hypothesis that the salient slides are to be rated higher, this is done *without any attribution search.*

We conclude that cognitive factors, including attributions, *can* affect emotional responses. However, the evidence does not support cognitive-arousal theory as a general theory of emotion; nor does it support the attribution-search hypothesis very well. The false-feedback experiments seem to indicate more about conditions under which a person will make particular ratings about any stimulus than about what might be truly emotional responses.

In summary, then, *different kinds of real arousal seem to be necessary for different emotions.* It is not clear what "real arousal" consists of, but it does *not* seem to be the same as cognition, or attribution. The thought of a burglar triggers one kind of emotional response and the thought of a loved one triggers a *different* kind of response. It does *not* appear that the *same kind of arousal* is triggered in both cases and that the emotion is different only because the after-the-fact interpretation is different. There may be some *ambiguity* about the source of arousal, as emphasized by excitation transfer theory. For example, exercise-induced arousal may add to (or be confused with) sexual arousal, but the sexual arousal *already* has been elicited. It is not just a general arousal which has been interpreted as sexual.

## MOOD, MEMORY, AND BEHAVIOR

### Background

We have been examining the nature of emotion thus far. An equally interesting question is, what *effect* does emotional arousal have on us? We explore this in a number of later chapters. An area of recent research explored here concerns the effects of *moods* on cognitive and behavioral activity. We may define mood as a *relatively pervasive and long-lasting emotional response.* Thus, I may be specifically angry at someone for a brief period of time, but may "get up on the wrong side of bed" and generally be grouchy all day. This "bad mood" may affect how I work, how I interact with other people, and how I think about problems. This section considers some effects of mood on helping behavior, learning, and memory.

### Research on Mood Effects

*Effects of mood on helping.* Politicians and salespeople have long capitalized on the belief that people are more willing to help you if you get them in a good mood first. And, in a number of studies (see Clark & Isen, 1982), randomly selected pedestrians in shopping malls have been given small gifts (ballpoint pens, candy) by one experimenter. Then, a little further down the mall walkway another experimenter has a problem, such as dropping some bags, which obviously calls for help. As expected, shoppers who have just received a gift are more likely to give help. Such results may seem so commonplace that it is easy to overlook the question of *why* being in a good mood promotes helping behavior.

One theoretical possibility is that altruistic behavior helps *maintain* the positive mood which has been established by the gift. After such positive mood induction, people have a brighter, more optimistic outlook on life (Clark & Isen, 1982). If in the past I felt good for helping someone, my present good mood may remind me of my earlier helping behavior. My present mood may be a *cue* for me to be helpful again. This account of helping behavior is strengthened by research showing that a person in a good mood is *less likely* to help someone if the helping might reduce the good mood. A subject in a good mood is less likely to do something unkind to another person, for example (Clark & Isen, 1982).

*Mood-congruent memory.* Mood-congruent memory means that a person can better remember materials which are emotionally similar (congruent) with the person's mood at the time of recall. For example, Bower, Gilligan & Monteiro (1981) asked subjects in a neutral mood to read a narrative containing specific happy and sad incidents. Subsequently, subjects in an experimentally induced happy mood remembered relatively more of the happy incidents, and subjects in a sad mood remembered relatively more of the sad incidents. Since all subjects were in the same neutral mood at the time of the learning, differences in learning could not account for the difference in memory. One interpretation of mood-congruent memory is *associative network theory* (Bower, 1981).

In associative network theory, illustrated in Figure 2–8, memories are represented by specific locations, called *nodes*. Each specific memory, for an emotion, event, behavior, or word, has its own node. The strength of association between any two nodes is represented by the distance between the nodes: the closer the nodes, the stronger the association. Events that occur when a person is happy are closely associated with the node for a happy mood, and events which occur when a person is sad are closely associated with the node for a sad mood. When a *retrieval* cue is present, a particular node is *activated*. This activation *spreads* to other nodes, but progressively more weakly to more distant nodes. The activated node for a mood, such as happy, would therefore activate most strongly the memories for words or events which are most strongly associated with it. A happy mood would activate more memories of happy events, and a sad mood would activate more memories of sad events. Research has provided only ambiguous support for this account of mood-congruent effects (Leventhal & Tomarkan, 1986), but there is at present no better theory.

*Mood-dependent memory. State-dependent memory* is frequently illustrated with this story from the Charlie Chaplin movie, *City Lights*. During a night on the town Charlie is befriended by a rich albeit very drunk gentleman, who takes Charlie home for the night. The next morning, when sober, Charlie's new friend does not remember him and throws him out of the house. That evening the rich man gets drunk again and remembers Charlie. Being drunk facilitated the memory of something learned while previously drunk. It is well documented that such drug-induced states show state-

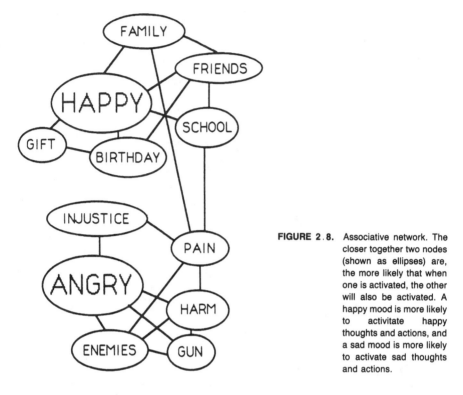

**FIGURE 2.8.** Associative network. The closer together two nodes (shown as ellipses) are, the more likely that when one is activated, the other will also be activated. A happy mood is more likely to activitate happy thoughts and actions, and a sad mood is more likely to activate sad thoughts and actions.

dependent memory effects: Material learned in a particular state is better recalled in the same state. It is a short step, then, to suppose that mood states also might serve as cues for memories. Such mood-dependent memory (MDM) might account for the oft-expressed complaints about memory by depressed individuals. Much of what a depressed person knows was learned when he or she was *not* depressed. In the depressed state there is a different set of internal cues which are not associated with very many earlier events, so memory suffers. Both the theoretical and practical aspects of the problem have stirred interest in MDM.

The basic paradigm for studying mood-dependent memory is this:

| Group | Mood During Learning | Mood During Memory Test |
|---|---|---|
| 1 | Elated | Elated |
| 2 | Elated | Depressed |
| 3 | Depressed | Depressed |
| 4 | Depressed | Elated |

Groups 1 and 3 (same mood during learning as during memory test) should show better memory than Groups 2 and 4 (different moods during learning and testing). The four-group *crossover design* is important because, for example, poorer performance by Group 2 than by Group 1 might mean only that depressed persons generally show poor cognitive performance. This finding would be important in its own right, but it does not necessarily support a mood-dependent memory effect. However, if Group 4 (depressed while learning but elated during testing) remembers more poorly than Group 3 (depressed in both situations), then we are more convinced the effect is due to specific memory loss. Poorer memory by subjects elated during testing could not reasonably be interpreted as the result of poorer cognitive capability.

In spite of initial bursts of optimism (e.g., Bower et al., 1981) subsequent research has lent only modest support to the MDM hypothesis (Blaney, 1986). The disappointing results to date are matched by the equally poor results of research on *context-dependent memory* (e.g., Fernandez & Glenberg, 1985). In this research, learning takes place in one environment (such as a green room) and testing takes place in the same or a different (e.g., pink) room. Conceptually, such a *nonspecific external* stimulus as room color seems like a *nonspecific internal* stimulus (mood). Therefore, failure to find support for a dependent effect in this research area weakens one's faith that it will be strongly found in the other. The more robust effect found with drugs and in animal research is still a cause for optimism for MDM theory, however, as is a modest amount of human research (e.g., Ellis, Thomas, MacFarland, & Lane, 1985).

It is also possible that research has not shown an MDM effect because of weaknesses in method. First, have experimenters induced moods strong enough to provide distinctive differences in learning and testing? Manipulation checks (self reports by subjects) usually indicate *statistically* significant differences between reported moods, but such manipulations may be subject to strong *experimenter demand effects*. For example, the *Velton mood induction procedure* calls for the subject to read and dwell upon a series of elating (or depressing) statements. The manipulation check then asks the subject to indicate whether he or she feels elated or depressed. The induction procedure may set up a demand to answer such questions in accordance with the induction procedure, and the manipulation check may therefore indicate bigger mood differences than actually exist. Any potential MDM effects are diluted, however.

A second weakness is that the degree of memory may be attributable to learning, not mood (Eich, 1980). If a subject learns the experimental material very poorly or very well, there may be little room for differences in mood cues to facilitate memory, because of floor or ceiling effects for recall, which are not related to mood.

Third, MDM effects may be demonstrable only when other cues are weak or absent. For this reason we might expect MDM effects to be clearer with *recall* tests than with *recognition* tests. In a recall task (like an essay test), the subject may be asked to write down as many items as possible from a previously studied list. There are few external cues to expedite memory, so mood might be a relatively powerful cue. At the same time, demand effects may be strong. In a recognition task (like a multiple-choice test), the subject is to pick out from a larger list those items which were in the original learning list. This reduces demand, but the actual items may be much more powerful cues than any mood cue, and so mood may not be an important factor. Research does support this prediction (Eich, 1980).

In summary, then, research on the effects of mood on behavioral and cognitive activities is exciting for both theoretical and practical reasons, but the data are often inconsistent. It is hoped that the methodological problems will soon be worked out so that phenomena of real interest may be clarified.

## RELATION OF EMOTION AND MOTIVATION

This chapter has covered many theories of emotion, ranging from those which argue for a number of discrete, biologically determined emotions, through emotional dimensions and nonspecific arousal and its interpretation, to purely cognitive (attributional) interpretations. Lacking any "standard" theory of emotion, it is difficult to integrate emotion and motivation. In view of the majority of the motivational concepts explored throughout this book, the author finds it most congenial to relate emotion and motivation as follows. The motivational concept of desire corresponds to *the anticipation of a pleasant situation or a medium level of arousal.* Conversely, the motivational concept of aversion corresponds to *the anticipation of an unpleasant situation or very low or high levels of arousal.*

These anticipations, of course, are based on prior experiences where these emotional events produced *unconditioned* emotional arousals. Emotions are initially processes aroused under certain conditions. Motivationally, we can try to re-create those conditions in anticipation of the same arousals happening again (or *not* happening, in the case of unpleasant events). Such anticipations are *motives*. Subsequent chapters deal with many motivational concepts and theories, and most of them can be accommodated comfortably (if not completely) within the framework just described.[1]

## SUMMARY

1. Most contemporary motivation theorists consider *motivation* and *emotion to be intimately related.* This chapter examines theories and data from emotion research in order to define this relationship more thoroughly.
2. Early psychologists considered emotion a *content of mind*, like perception or

---

[1]Buck (1985), in his *prime* theory of emotion, has attempted an ambitious integration which is beyond our scope here.

thought. Emotion was studied by *introspection,* or "looking into one's own mind" and reporting the contents thereof. The primary emotional characteristics were reported to be feelings of *pleasantness* and *unpleasantness.*

3. The *James-Lange theory* proposed that emotion is the *perception of bodily activity* which is aroused as a response to some environmental situation. This theory emphasized the visceral activity controlled by the *autonomic nervous system.* The *Cannon-Bard theory* emphasized activity in the *thalamic area* of the brain as the core of emotion. This led to extensive research on the brain and emotion. It has been found that the right hemisphere of the brain seems to be more actively involved in emotion than the left hemisphere.

4. Contemporary research on emotion combines research on *verbal behavior, nonverbal behavior,* and *physiology.* A large number of theories of emotion have been developed in the last quarter-century.

5. *Discrete emotion theories* assume there is some fixed number of genetically programmed emotional reactions to specific kinds of situations. Six have been reliably identified across many cultures: *happiness, anger, sadness, disgust, surprise,* and *fear.* Others have been reported less consistently. *Facial expressions* are among the most reliable indicators of emotion, but many expressions are also *blends* of the "basic" emotions, and expression of even these basic emotions can be modified by experience. The *facial feedback hypothesis* proposes that a person's *felt emotion* is partly due to facial expression.

6. *Dimensional theories* of emotion assume that all emotional experience can be accounted for by combinations of different intensities of some small number of emotional dimensions. Much research shows that the most important dimension is *pleasant-unpleasant,* followed by *level of arousal* (tension). It may be that these basic dimensions represent a simpler level of development than do discrete emotions.

7. *Cognitive theories* emphasize that emotional responses are largely determined by how we *evaluate* or *appraise* situations. A controversial issue is whether such evaluations are *necessary* for emotional experience, and whether evaluations are necessarily *conscious.*

8. *Cognitive-arousal* theory proposes that both *visceral arousal* and an *attribution* of the *cause* of the arousal are necessary for emotional experience. Different interpretations of the *same* arousal are said to produce different emotional experiences. Research has not supported this theory very well, but it has supported a limited variation called *excitation transfer theory.* Another variation has proposed that just *thinking* we are aroused may lead to emotional experience. This is not well supported by evidence, either.

9. There may be *several qualitatively different kinds of arousal.* These may be modified by appraisals but not easily changed completely.

10. Much recent research and theory has focused on the effects of *moods* (pervasive, long-lasting emotions) on thought and behavior. A "good" mood is consistently found to facilitate helping behavior, and thoughts tend to be *congruent* with whatever mood a person is in. A controversial issue is whether we can better remember things if we are in the same mood as when we learned them (*mood-dependent memory*).

11. It is suggested that *desire* (as a motivation concept, defined in chapter 1) corresponds to the *anticipation* of pleasantness and a medium level of arousal. Conversely, *aversion* corresponds to the anticipation of unpleasantness and a very low or very high level of arousal. This approach integrates large bodies of theory and research on emotion and motivation.

# 3

# Instinct, Drive, and Activation

Introduction

## INTRODUCTION

Biological approaches to motivation have largely grown out of Darwin's theory of evolution by natural selection. If complex organisms are to reproduce, they must survive. To survive, they must monitor the status of their *internal environments* so they can make corrections when necessary, such as getting food or water. Some preliminary comments about this approach are in order.

### Open Systems and Homeostasis

*Closed systems versus open systems.* A closed physical system is one which does not have energy *inputs*. The fate of such a system is to eventually deteriorate and dissipate randomly until it reaches a state of *equilibrium*. This principle of deterioration is called *entropy*. Any system approaching equilibrium loses whatever *form* or *structure* it may have had. If a beautiful piece of furniture burns, all that remains is a randomly organized pile of ashes, and these also scatter randomly. The closed system concept posed a dilemma for biologists, for if *all* systems deteriorate in this fashion, how can there be the increased growth and complexity which characterizes living things? Some nonphysical or metaphysical life-force seemed to be necessary to account for growth, and even for life itself.

In this century, however, the concept of a physical system which does *not* aim toward equilibrium was developed. This is the *open system*, which has energy *inputs* as well as outputs. Excess energy input is used for growth. Therefore, rather than moving inexorably toward deterioration and equilibrium, an open system maintains a *steady state* of its constituent parts. *A living organism is an open system with mechanisms for maintaining a steady state.* Energy lost through work is replaced by additional energy input. If these steady-state mechanisms break down, through disease, injury, or lack of input, the system breaks down and the organism dies. At death, the organism becomes a closed system which decays until it too reaches equilibrium. Ashes to ashes. Maintaining steady states is the basic motivational problem of regulating the internal environment. Understanding how regulation works is a basic problem for the psychology of motivation.

*Constancy of the internal environment.* Claude Bernard (1865), often called the father of experimental medicine, developed the dictum that *the necessary condition for a free life is constancy of the internal environment.* The internal environment (*milieu interieur*) consists of the body fluids which bathe our body cells, bringing nutrients to the cells and carrying metabolic waste products away. Individual body cells can therefore survive, and the integrity of the entire body is maintained. The skin is the spacesuit of the earthbound organism, protecting the internal environment from the hazards of the external environment. An animal is "free" when it carries its internal environment around, without undue threat of cell destruction by air and temperature.

*Homeostasis.*    Walter Cannon (in *The Wisdom of the Body,* 1939) built on Bernard's ideas to develop the concept of *homeostasis.* This refers to the capacity of organisms to maintain their internal environments within very close tolerances of temperature, acidity, glucose concentration, salt and water balance, and so on, which are necessary for life. Cannon described homeostasis as the *automatic* adjustments the body makes to restore stability when there is a departure from a narrow tolerance range. Homeostatic mechanisms are under the control of the autonomic nervous system, but this system can do only so much until behavior becomes necessary. When the body becomes overheated, perspiration promotes evaporative cooling, but at the cost of losing body water. Mechanisms come into play to conserve water, but eventually the organism must *do* something. It must take action to get water or to cool without evaporation. The study of such actions is part of the study of *motivated behavior.*

*Nonhomeostatic regulatory mechanisms.*    Across different species, and even within the same species, there are multiple "solutions" to the question of how to maintain homeostasis. So-called *emergency mechanisms* for regulating internal states come into play when there is a severe departure from homeostatic balance, but *nonregulatory* mechanisms also help maintain homeostasis. For example, we often eat or drink before we are "really" hungry or thirsty. We may drink so many glasses of water a day because we have learned to, or eat three meals a day because our culture tells us to, and thus go for long periods without invoking the emergency mechanisms. Our study of regulation, then, shall examine homeostatic mechanisms and regulatory behaviors, as well as nonregulatory behaviors which help us survive.

## INSTINCT

In some animals it appears that survival behaviors are unlearned and unique to a species. Spiders spin webs, birds build nests, salmon migrate upstream to a spawning area, and green turtles shuttle back and forth between South America and Africa to play out their dance of life. Such behaviors, seemingly as automatic as internal physiological mechanisms, may be called *instinctive.* William James (1890, p. 393) captured such behaviors as the above in his definition of instinct, the *faculty of acting in such a way as to produce a certain end without foresight of that end, and without the individual's having previous education in that performance.* Our concern here is whether the concept of instinct is useful in explaining behavior, and if so, what is the relation of instinct to motivation? Unfortunately, the term *instinct* has been used in so many ways as to defy simple analysis.

## Common Uses of the Term Instinct

*Universality versus individual differences.*   Sometimes instinct refers to behavior common to a species. Maternal behavior is sometimes called instinctive because most mothers engage in so-called maternal activities. William James (1884) thought that no woman could resist the charm of a small, naked baby. John B. Watson (1924), on the other hand, pointed out that new mothers tend to be awkward with their first child and do not necessarily do all those tender, loving things said to characterize "maternal instinct." It is, in fact, very difficult to demonstrate that any behavior, especially of humans, is genetically determined and universal. Higher-order animals learn early and learn fast, and even prenatal events can affect later behavior.

In contrast to the above, instinct is sometimes used to refer to *differences* in behavior within a species. In practice, this use of the term is just another way of saying "well learned" or "automatic." For example, a prize-fighter quick to dodge his opponent's jabs may be said to "duck instinctively." The term is applied as if some people have the instinct and others do not. Among scientists, the term instinct is not used in this way.

*Instinct as urge versus instinct as behavior.*   Rather than referring to such specific behaviors as nest building, instinct is sometimes considered a general *urge* toward some activity, without reference to specific behaviors. For example, the urge to eat may be considered instinctive, but not refer to specific eating behaviors. In this use of the term, Freud was one of the foremost instinct theorists, especially with reference to sex and aggression. He spoke of instincts as having a *source, impetus, aim,* and *object.* Internal or external stimulation (source) arouses an "instinct"; the instinct carries some degree of force (impetus) that is related to the intensity of behavior. The person tries to reduce the tension (aim) and this process is brought to completion by some object. The instinct is an urge which has neither fixed behaviors nor invariant objects.

Most serious theorists have argued that, when applied to higher animals, the term *instinct* should be limited to very small segments of behavior, almost at the level of reflexes, or to general urges. Obviously, there have to be *some* inborn tendencies, else an organism could not survive at birth, but these are quickly overshadowed by learning. James said that on its first occurrence an instinct was without foresight of its end, but thereafter there would be foresight. Anticipation of pleasant or unpleasant consequences would facilitate or block the expression of the instinct. He even called the idea of invariable instincts "mystical" and observed (James, 1890, p. 395) that "The minuter study of recent years has found continuity, transition, variation and mistake wherever it has looked for them, and decided that what is called an instinct is usually only a tendency to act in a way of which the *average* is pretty constant, but which need not be mathematically 'true.'"

### Status of the Instinct Concept

Psychologists and biologists agree that behavior is in part genetically determined, but the actual term *instinct* rarely appears in the biological literature on behavior, except perhaps to put it into historical perspective (e.g., Eibl-Eibesfeld, 1975).[1] Instead, it is argued that genes establish the *potential* for *species-specific behaviors* and that this potential is fulfilled to greater or lesser degree under different environmental conditions. The problem then is to determine what specific mechanisms are inherited and what environmental conditions bring them into play. This kind of analysis proceeds quite nicely without mentioning instinct.

A sophisticated differentiation of the concepts of *instinct* and *motivation* has been proposed by Epstein (1982), however, who argues that a large amount of animal behavior *is* unlearned. If we look at a wide spectrum of animal life, we find that most of the earth's animal population is far less complicated than primates, or even vertebrates, and it is among the masses of insects, mollusks, and arachnids that instinctive *behaviors* are most likely to occur. Epstein distinguishes instinctive and motivated behaviors in terms of the behavioral characteristics summarized in Table 3-1 (Epstein, 1982, p. 49). Briefly stated, instinctive behaviors lack *variability, foresight,* or *emotion,* but motivated behaviors are characterized by these features. There are *species-specific behaviors* at all levels of complexity, however. Species vary genetically in their behavioral capabilities, which shall be referred to upon numerous occasions.

### Stimulus Control of Species-Specific Behaviors

*Stimulus sensitivity.* Of the many energy forms in the environment, living organisms are *sensitive* to only a few, and these vary even from species to species. An animal's sensory systems operate as filters that let some energies "pass" into the nervous system but keep out others. An animal is *sensitive* to those energy forms for which it has receptors to convert the stimulus energy into neural activity. The perceptual world of an animal then depends on the kinds of receptors it has and the organization of its nervous system. The animals that occupy the earth do not all live in the same perceptual world. Bats and porpoises hear sounds (up to 80 kHz, or 80,000 cycles per second) which are far beyond the range of a dog's hearing (up to 40

---

[1] After much thought on the subject I have decided not to discuss the Lorenz-Tinbergen hydraulic model, on the grounds that virtually no scientist has accepted this model for 20 years and there is no point to setting up a straw man. Some instructors may feel otherwise.

**TABLE 3-1   A Comparison of Instinct and Motivation (Adapted from Epstein, 1982)**

I. COMMON CHARACTERISTICS

1. Both employ innate mechanisms for behavior.
2. Both employ acquired (learned) components.
3. Both are organized sequentially into highly variable goal-seeking behavior, followed by more specific consummatory responses.[1]
4. Both are drive induced (i.e. induced by some physiological imbalance).
5. Both contribute to homeostasis.

II. DIFFERENCES

  A. INSTINCT

1. Species-specific in terms of the kinds of stimuli which *release* the behavior and the specific organizations of behaviors.
2. Goal-seeking (appetitive) behavior not changed by expectancy (i.e. is not changed by learning.)
3. Nonemotional
4. Biologically common, occurring across many different phyla and orders.

  B. MOTIVATION

1. Goal-seeking behavior can be modified by learning.
2. Anticipates goals.
3. Accompanied by expression of emotion.
4. Biologically rare (very few animals show it.)

From Epstein, A. (1982). Instinct and motivation as explanations for complex behavior. In D.W. Pfaff (ed.) *The physiological mechanisms of motivation.* New York: Springer-Verlag. Copyright © 1982 Springer-Verlag. Used by permission.

[1]These are commonly referred to as *appetitive* and *consummatory* phases.

kHz), which is double that of the best human hearing (20 kHz). Migrating birds are sensitive to the earth's magnetic fields, and bees are sensitive to polarized light. Most mammals are color-blind, but birds enjoy excellent color vision. Sea animals often do not have particularly good vision, but have highly developed smell, which is essential to them for the location of food. The moral of this story is that we cannot make assumptions about what nonhumans are perceiving on the basis of our own perceptions.

Given that an animal is *sensitive* to a particular range of stimuli, it has to *respond* appropriately to *stimulus configurations* within that range. Configurations are the patterns or shapes formed by different stimuli. Such responding may be based on inherited neural mechanisms for responding in relatively specific ways or may depend on prior experience. We may refer to these respectively as *releasing stimulus control* and *acquired stimulus control.*

*Releasing stimuli.*   Releasing stimuli are any stimuli which evoke specific response patterns, based on some prewired perceptual motor organization. Many species may be *sensitive* to a particular response pattern, but only some are uniquely *responsive* to them. For example, many animals are sensitive to other animals looking them in the eye, but primates are especially *aggressive* in response to being stared in the eye. Rhesus monkeys respond by baring their teeth, screaming, and perhaps attacking. Male squirrel monkeys make penile displays as a ritualistic response that has apparently replaced fighting. Releasing stimuli also help regulate parent-child interactions. Baby birds gape (open their mouths wide) in response to particular stimuli from the parents, and the gaping, in turn, is a releasing stimulus for the parents to feed the baby.

"Instinctive" mother love and love for mother both suffer, however, because it turns out that the *effective* stimuli for releasing many social behaviors are only small fractions of the total stimulus input from another animal. We determine what the effective stimuli are by making model stimuli (which vary in similarity to living organisms) and finding what *minimal* aspect of the natural stimulus is effective. We then discover that the gaping behavior of hungry baby birds can be released by a stick with a spot on it (in some cases, a ring around it) similar to the bill of the parent. For the stickleback fish, a piece of wood which looks vaguely like the swollen belly of a female with eggs will release male sexual behavior. Male turkeys get excited by a turkey head (or a model thereof), even if the head is not attached to a body. And the squirrel monkey's penile display can be released by letting the animal look into a mirror so small that it can see nothing more than the reflection of its own eyeball. Finally, there are some *supernormal stimuli*. Gulls will take care of oversize artificial eggs in preference to their own.

*Interaction of internal states and releasers.* Releasing stimuli, such as for sexual activity, are not equally effective at all times. Responsiveness also depends on *internal conditions*, often hormonal, which may fluctuate from month to month or season to season. In seasonal mating, sex hormone changes are initiated by the pituitary gland, which is itself under the control of dark-light cycles. Sexual arousability by members of the opposite sex is therefore under the control of complex organismic and environmental interactions. Even sexually mature human females are more sensitive to musk odors (as in perfumes) during their childbearing years, and males are sensitive to such odors only if injected with estrogen prior to the odor test.

*Acquired stimulus control.* Many organisms, of course, *learn* to use stimuli as cues. We learn that particular foods are good or bad, that particular events are painful, or that certain words portend good things to come. But there appears to be greater ease of learning some things than others, which is referred to as *preparedness* (Seligman, 1970). In one early study, for example, it was reported that a child could readily learn to be afraid of caterpillars but not of opera glasses or a bottle (Valentine, 1930). There may be "latent fears" of certain things, genetic predispositions which make some fears easier to learn than others (Hebb, 1949). Fear of creepy, crawly things (spiders, snakes, lizards, and insects) are easier to condition than are fears of flowers and trees (Öhman, 1985).

Research on poison avoidance, important for any species, shows that in rats there is a greater readiness to associate a *taste* stimulus than visual stimulus with illness, but for the quail this is reversed (Wilcoxin, Dragoin, & Kral, 1971). Since the rat has highly developed taste and olfactory systems, as compared to its vision, and the reverse is true for the quail, it all makes good biological sense.

*Imprinting.* Imprinting is a particular kind of learning which occurs most reliably with precocial birds, such as chickens and ducks, which are born with down and are active immediately after hatching. The behavior usually studied is the *following response.* Newborn birds follow any object that moves in front of them on the first day or so of life, but there is a *critical period* of time after hatching during which a permanent attachment to the moving object occurs. This is imprinting. Mallard ducklings follow a duck-mother model or a ball or a box that moves and are imprinted most strongly at about 16 hours after hatching (Hess, 1962). In the normal course of duckling events, fortunately, the most likely moving stimulus is the real mother.

For different species, there are different critical periods for imprinting, but there is always variability. Hinde, Thorpe, and Vince (1956) found imprinting in coots as late as six days after hatching and were able to correlate the end of the imprinting period with the onset of a *flight period.* The birds would imprint until they reached an age where they became afraid of strange objects and refused to follow them. This suggests that imprinting is not a unique kind of learning. Rather, the birds imprint until they reach an age when they become afraid of strange objects and will not follow them, hence they do not become "attached." The approach-flight view of the critical period is given support in research showing that the imprinting period can be extended by delaying the onset of the flight period. This is done by giving the birds tranquilizers (Moltz, 1960). According to this view, then, during the critical period for imprinting the animal is in a state of "low anxiety," as shown by behavioral observations. Stimuli present during this time become conditioned to low-anxiety responses by association. Later, when the organism is fearful, it approaches or follows those stimuli previously associated with low anxiety, usually the parent.

Gallagher and Ash (1978), studying Japanese quail, have also reported that imprinting to an albino hen during the first 10 days of life is strong, as shown in sexual preferences as adults for albino hens. Post-imprinting experience with hens different than the imprinted hen can change this preference. But lacking later experience, the early establishment of a social bond does last into adulthood.

## DRIVE THEORY

Drive theory comes out of the regulatory approach and emphasizes a general energization of behavior. It has expanded so far beyond its biological origins into personality theory and social psychology, however, that the student of motivation needs to be conversant with drive theory in order to understand its use in many different areas of psychology.

### Background

*Homeostasis and psychoanalysis.*  As noted, if hunger is so severe that the body cannot compensate for lost energy by using its own stores, we must actively do something to restore nutrition and return to a homeostatic balance. We also saw Freud's conception of instinct as an "urge" to relieve internal tensions. Stripped to their essentials, the principles stated by homeostatic theory and psychoanalytic theory are very similar: when an organism is internally aroused by a state of imbalance it will do whatever it can to restore balance. The critical question is, how do internal imbalances result in the *particular* behavioral adjustments which restore balance?

*Adaptive acts.*  As discussed in chapter 1, the functional school of psychology emphasized the *adaptation* and *adjustment* of organisms to the environment. Harvey Carr (1925) argued that the basic animal behavior was the *adaptive act.* When an organism needs food or water there is a persistent internal stimulus that arouses adaptive activity until the need is satisfied. A number of key concepts emerged from this view.

1. *Need.* Need is an excess or deficiency of some product related to survival. As an intervening variable, need is defined on the antecedent side in terms of deprivation (such as food) and on the consequent side in terms of health or survival. Needs frequently lead to activity which restores the appropriate balance, but not necessarily. Some needs, such as some vitamin deficiencies or oxygen deficit, do *not* stimulate compensatory activity. Therefore, the concept of drive is introduced.
2. *Drive.* Drive is not directly observed; it is inferred from the behaviors of an animal. Its antecedents could be the same as for need (e.g., deprivation), but its consequent conditions are behaviors. It is drive, not need, that goads the animal to activity; drive provides the persistent stimulus to behavior. Miller (1951b) suggested that any persistent and strong stimulus can have drive properties. Need and drive may be correlated, but the fact that they are not always correlated is why there are two concepts and not just one.
3. *Goal.* A goal is some commodity that will reduce the drive that initiated the activity. A hungry animal consumes food and for awhile thereafter is inactive as far as food is concerned.

The whole sequence then is: need leads to drive, drive energizes activity, achievement of a goal reduces drive and goal-oriented activity. Clark Hull produced one of the most systematic theories attempting to deal with such questions as how drive energizes behavior, and why one behavior rather than another occurs.

### Hull's Theory

One of America's most prestigious psychologists, Hull was noted early in his career for work on aptitude testing and hypnosis. About 1930, however, he began to develop a general theory of behavior, culminating in the *Principles of Behavior* (1943). Research related to the *Principles*, both supportive and contradictory, dominated the fields of motivation and learning for 20 years. Many aspects of the theory have not stood the test of time well, but some aspects are still considered to be useful. The *Principles* was intended as the beginning of a more complete theory of behavior, but we shall consider only those parts most relevant to motivation.

*Drive as an intervening variable.*    Hull distinguished between *performance* and the variables that *determine* performance. The two main variables were *habit strength* (sHr), which is the strength of association between a given stimulus and response,[2] and *drive* (D), which "activates" habit into performance. Hull argued that drive does not direct, guide, steer, or select responses. Instead, Hull proposed, drive equally energizes *all* learned responses. In a specific situation, the response which has the strongest association (or habit strength, sHr) to the stimuli present would be the response most likely to occur.

In the more precise language of the theory, drive *multiplies* habit to produce the *excitatory potential* for a particular response. Thus:

Excitatory Potential = habit × drive,
or, symbolically: sEr = sHr × D,
or,                E = H × D.

E, H, and D *are intervening variables*, with different antecedent conditions. The strength of Variable H is defined in terms of number of learning trials, increasing with the number of S-R associations. The strength of D is defined, for example, in terms of number of hours of food deprivation or strength of a noxious stimulus. Variable E is defined according to the *syntax of the theory* (see page 10, chapter 1), as a relation between H and D. On the consequent side, these intervening variables are *measured* in terms of amplitude, frequency, probability, or latency of responding. This is illustrated in Figure 3-1, a variation on Figure 1-4 in chapter 1. Observable events are outside the box, intervening variables are inside the box.

---

[2] The assumption that learning involves only S-R associations is one of the major flaws of Hull's theory overall, but this does not necessarily negate everything Hull has to say about the relation between learning and motivation.

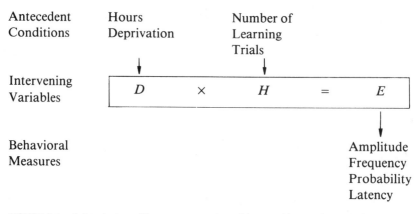

**FIGURE 3-1.** Antecedent conditions, consequent conditions, and intervening variables in Hull's (1943) theory.

The multiplicative relationship between H and D was arrived at partly by logical considerations and partly by research. Logically, it would make little sense to propose that $E = H - D$ or that $E = H/D$, since either of these statements says that performance (E) would get *weaker* with increasing drive. Either $E = H + D$ or $E = H \times D$ makes more sense, since either of these formulations says that performance will improve with increasing drive. On the basis of data from previous experiments, Hull selected the $H \times D$ formulation. The general prediction from the multiplicative formulation is illustrated in Figure 3-2. Many subsequent researchers have used such diverging curves as illustrated in Figure 3-2 as evidence for the operation of motivational variables (e.g., Zajonc & Sales, 1966; Cooper & Fazio, 1984).

We make different predictions from the theory depending on whether the responses to be made are simple or complex. A *simple* response is a *clearly dominant response,* and the theory predicts that such a response will become even more dominant with a higher level of drive as Figure 3-2 indicates. If an animal has learned the simple response of running down a straight alleyway to get to food, the animal should run faster with longer deprivation (higher drive).

In a *complex* situation, however, there are several habits of near-equal strength. These produce *competing responses.* If such competing responses are simultaneously activated we would expect error and confusion. Suppose a machine operator has several similar levers to pull in order to perform different job functions. If he is not careful, the operator might "accidentally" pull a wrong lever at any time. If his drive is very high, such as during an emergency, the chances of making an error are even greater because all the responses are more strongly energized. In short, the theory says that at high levels of drive, dominant responses become even more dominant, but competing responses interfere with each other even more and performance gets worse.

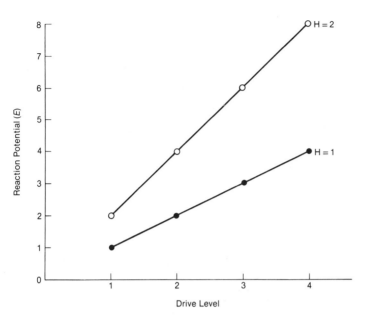

**FIGURE 3-2.** Habit and drive interaction in Hullian theory (E = H × D).

*Criteria for calling a variable "drive."*  In Hull's theory, what criteria distinguish drive from other variables? The following criteria have commonly been used to identify drive:

1. *An increase in the level of the variable energizes a wide range of responses.* This distinguishes drive from a specific stimulus which evokes a specific response, such as a reflex response. Food deprivation energizes eating, running to food, pressing a level to get food, and so on. When such a variety of responses is energized, a specific S-R connection is ruled out and a more general "motivating" variable is indicated.

2. *A decrease in the level of the variable is reinforcing.* If pain is reduced following a particular response, and that same response occurs more frequently in the future under similar circumstances, the variable (pain) may be said to be drive. Reduction of pain drive reinforces (strengthens) the association between the situation and the response. The criterion of *reinforcement of responses by drive reduction* best applies to noxious situations because it is very difficult to determine, for example, that very small amounts of food which reinforce responding also reduce hunger. Furthermore, other properties of food, such as taste, may be what makes them reinforcing (rewarding), not hunger reduction.

3. *An increase in the level of the variable is punishing.* If a response is followed by increased pain, the response is less likely to occur; it has been punished. Pain meets this criterion for drive, but hunger and thirst have never clearly met this criterion, at least in the laboratory. Starvation has been used as punishment for humans, but has not formally been related to Hull's theory.

### Evaluating Drive Theory

If drive theory predicts stronger responding with higher drive, we should expect that hungrier animals should respond more for food, thirstier animals should respond more for water, and so on. Research going back to the 1930's clearly shows this to happen. Warden (1934), for example, used an *obstruction box* to study the strength of drive. In this apparatus, an animal has to cross an electrified floor to reach food, water, or whatever is the appropriate goal. The more hours of deprivation, the more times an animal would cross, or would tolerate stronger shocks to get to food. The problem for a nice, clean drive theory interpretation is that the animals were running *to* some goal. The effect of deprivation could therefore be on *responsiveness to the goal*, not just an energization of behavior. A less ambiguous demonstration of a drive effect would be on behavior where there is no clear goal. One drive theory notion is that drive energizes "random" activity, which should facilitate *finding* an appropriate goal. If a hungry animal is active, for example, its chances of getting food should be greater if it is more active. Activity studies, then, have been one way to test drive theory ideas.

*Drive and activity.*    In 1925, John F. Dashiell reported that hungry rats explored a "checkerboard" maze more than satiated rats. This was confirmed in many subsequent experiments and was taken by a generation of psychologists to mean that drive energizes activity. But does drive energize all kinds of activity, as Hull said it should? There are many equally "good" ways to measure activity. For example, the *activity wheel*, commonly used for pet mice or hamsters, can be rigged so that each revolution of the wheel is counted and activity thereby measured. A *jiggle cage (stabilimeter)* is mounted on springs so that when an animal in the cage shifts its weight the cage moves and electrical contacts open and close. Or, we can automatically record the number of times an animal moves across the midline of a cage, or count the number of squares on the floor that an animal crosses in an "open field." Each of these measurement procedures, and others not mentioned, provides an operational definition of "activity." Do higher levels of deprivation increase activity by all these measures?

The answer, in a nutshell, is no, deprivation does not affect all kinds of activity equally. Consider a study reported by Campbell (1964), summarized in Figure 3-3. Using albino laboratory rats as subjects, Campbell compared food and water deprivation in three different apparatuses (activity wheels, stabilimeters, and mazes). The animals were continuously in their respective apparatuses for several days. As Figure 3-3 shows, food-deprived rats in activity wheels increased their activity to a peak of about 1200% of the baseline measure, but increased only about 500% in the other two apparatuses. Water-deprived rats increased about 500% in the activity wheels, but not at all in the other apparatuses. The broad generalization that drive

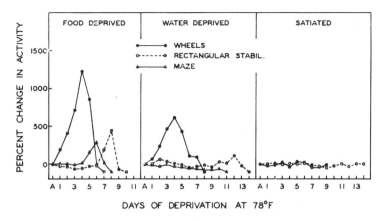

**FIGURE 3-3.** Percent changes in activity of food-deprived, water-deprived and satiated rats in activity wheels, rectangular stabilimeter cages, and an automatic Dashiell maze at 78°F. (From Campbell, 1964, p. 330. Copyright ©1964 by Pergamon Press. Reprinted by permission.)

energizes activity simply does not hold. The amount of activity depends on the kind of deprivation (food or water) and the particular measure of activity used.

Bolles (1967) made a similar observation regarding female rats in estrus at the peak of sexual receptivity. In activity cages, female rats show a sharp increase in running when they are in estrus, but animals in the home cage do not show any such increases. Bolles concluded that the activity wheel itself is a critical factor; estrus alone does not "drive" an animal to activity. Finally, Campbell, Smith, Misanin, and Jaynes (1966) found that deprivation affected the activity of chicks, guinea pigs, hamsters, and rabbits differently. The exact effects depended on the species, the type of deprivation, and the type of measure. For example, hungry hamsters were more active in the wheel than satiated hamsters, but thirsty hamsters were less active.

As if the above were not enough, animals also *learn* to become more active. If rats are fed immediately after they have been running in an activity wheel they become more active in the wheel than if their food is delayed an hour (Finger, Reid, & Weasner, 1957; Hall, 1958). The general conclusion from the activity studies is that activity is to a large extent learned and to some extent unlearned (e.g., Campbell & Cicala, 1962; Finger, 1965). Even when unlearned, however, activity depends on type of deprivation, type of measure, and species. The generalization that "drive increases activity" is subject to so many qualifications as to be almost useless.

*Irrelevant Drive.* According to Hull's theory, *any source of drive should energize any response tendency.* For example, thirst should energize a habit originally learned with food deprivation and food reward. In such a case, hunger is called a *relevant* drive because it is relevant to the food which reduces the drive. Thirst is called an *irrelevant drive* because it is not relevant to the hunger and food used to establish the response. In general, irrelevant drive refers to internal motivational states which are not relevant to the goal available at the moment. Hull's equation for excitatory potential is then expanded as follows:

$$E = sHr \times (Dr + Di)$$
where   $Dr$ = relevant drive
and     $Di$ = irrelevant drive

The concept is, of course, not limited to hunger and thirst. Pain, fear, or any other source of drive could serve as either relevant or irrelevant drive. The concept was originally developed by Hull (1943) to explain why animals satiated for food made a large number of responses during extinction of the food-getting response (Perin, 1942). They responded many times with no reinforcement and no apparent drive. Hull felt that this could only mean that some source of drive other than hunger must have been present since, according to the theory, the animals should not respond without some drive. Two major strategies have been used to study irrelevant drive with animals. In *drive substitution* experiments, animals are trained to respond while in one deprivation state (such as, to get food while hungry) and then are satiated for that state and tested while in another state (such as thirsty). Thirsty animals should respond more than satiated control animals because of the irrelevant thirst drive. In *drive summation* experiments, animals are trained while in one deprivation state (such as hungry) and then tested while both hungry *and* thirsty. They should respond more with double drive than with the single drive. The results of such hunger and thirst experiments give little support to the irrelevant drive concept: Neither substitution nor summation improves responding much above control levels (see Bolles, 1975; or Beck, 1983, for summary). The problem for such studies became obvious in experiments by Verplanck and Hayes (1953) and Grice and Davis (1957): When animals are food-deprived they *drink less* and when water-deprived they *eat less*. Hunger and thirst do *not* summate or substitute in the simple way Hull's theory said they should.

*Adjunctive Behavior.*   Falk (1961) reported a curious drinking phenomenon. Hungry rats pressing a lever to get a food pellet an average of once a minute over a three-hour period also drank about a third of their body weight in water during this same time. This was three to four times their normal *daily* intake. Subsequent research showed that the main requirements for getting such drinking are that the animal be hungry and that the food pellets be small and spaced fairly widely in time. Falk (1969) suggested that this unusual drinking might be considered *adjunctive behavior*, which occurs when some other goal-directed behavior is thwarted. Eating and drinking normally occur closely together, and come under the control of similar environmental stimuli. When eating is thwarted, by spacing out the delivery of small food pellets, the animals drink.

It also turns out, however, that a large number of different behaviors can be elicited by *nonspecific arousal*. For example, Valenstein and Kakolewski (1970) reported that electrical stimulation of the *same* brain area produced different behaviors on different days, partly depending on the environment. If food was available the animals would eat; if water was available they would drink. Even a pinch to the tail of the animal elicited such adjunctive behaviors as eating, drinking, or attacking another animal. In short, when an animal is aroused by any of a large number of stimuli it may engage in whatever behavior the environment "supports" at the moment (Carlson, 1987). This could be interpreted in terms of a nonspecific drive which energizes a wide variety of responses, lending some support to a general drive theory.

### Human Applications

Although drive theory has not worked as well with animals as its proponents had hoped (Miller, 1959; Spence, 1956), it has provided useful predictions and explanations in human research.

*Eyeblink conditioning.*    In eyeblink conditioning, we may sound a soft tone as the conditioned stimulus (CS), followed by a brief puff of air to the cornea of the eye as the unconditioned stimulus (UCS). The eye normally blinks in response to the airpuff. Conditioned responses are those eyeblinks to the CS that occur before the airpuff. The conditioned eyeblink becomes a dominant response to the CS. It is presumed that higher intensities of airpuff produce higher levels of drive, and many experiments have shown that the level of conditioning is higher with stronger airpuffs (Spence, 1956). Taylor (1953) assumed that the level of anxiety (considered an irrelevant drive) varies from person to person and that this level can be measured by a self-report scale of anxiety symptoms, such as "I am often sick to my stomach" and "My sleep is restless and disturbed." By manipulating intensity of airpuff we can *produce* high or low levels of drive, and by measuring anxiety (using the Taylor Manifest Anxiety Scale) we can *select* subjects who are high or low in irrelevant drive. Spence and Taylor combined these procedures in a single experiment, with the results shown in Figure 3-4.

As predicted, subjects getting 2 pounds of pressure per square inch (psi) in the airpuff conditioned better than subjects getting 0.6 psi. In addition, high-anxious subjects conditioned better than low-anxious subjects. Both of these results follow directly from drive theory predictions for dominant responses. The data also showed that the *two sources of drive add together*, so that the 2 psi/high-anxious subjects conditioned the best and the 0.6 psi/low-

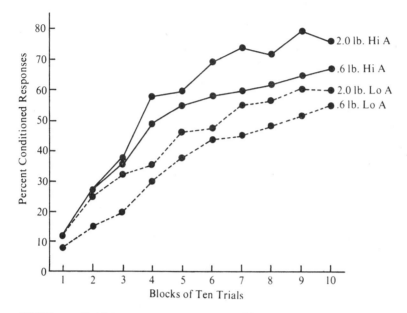

**FIGURE 3-4.** Eyeblink conditioning as a function of UCS intensity (pounds of pressure per square inch of the airpuff) and level of anxiety (measured by the Taylor Manifest Anxiety Scale). (Originally from Spence and Taylor, 1951, adapted from Spence, 1958. Copyright 1951 by the American Psychological Association. Reprinted by permission.)

anxious subjects conditioned the poorest, with the other groups in between. If the airpuff produces relevant drive (relevant to the defensive reaction of protecting the eye) and anxiety is irrelevant drive (not specifically relevant to the eyeblink reaction), then we have a combination of relevant and irrelevant drive (the drive summation procedure). This experiment is very good support for drive theory.

*Paired associates learning.* In paired associates learning, a person views a series of word pairs. The first member of a pair is the stimulus word, the second is the response word. The task on successive presentations is to give the correct response word when only the stimulus word is shown. The experimenter can set up word pairs that have very strong initial associations (such as dog-cat) or very weak ones (like zov-dax). Drive theory predicts that high-anxious subjects should perform better than low-anxious subjects on lists with strong associations (highly *dominant* responses to the stimuli) and worse on lists with weak associations (where there are competing responses). The results have been positive often enough to be provocative, although far from conclusive (see Bolles, 1967; or Byrne, 1974).

*Social facilitation.* *Social facilitation* refers to the fact that the presence of observers influences individual performance (Triplett, 1897). Robert Zajonc (1965) proposed that an *audience* arouses an irrelevant drive in an *actor*. He then predicted that dominant responses should be facilitated by an audience and performance of non-dominant responses should become poorer, which was supported in his experiment. The theory can be extended to explain a wide range of social phenomena (Weiss & Miller, 1971; Guerin & Innes, 1984). A highly trained professional athlete, whose responses to virtually every situation in his sport are well practiced, performs better in a stadium full of fans. A young child, just learning the same sport and having few well-learned (dominant) responses may perform more poorly in front of an audience.

The effects of an audience also vary according to audience characteristics, not just size. For example, a student's performance may be worse if she thinks she is being *evaluated* by a relatively high status person, such as one having a PhD, as compared to evaluation by another student. If high- and low-status persons are put together in an audience, however, the social facilitation effect is weakened because the low-status person averages out with the high-status person (Seta, Crisson, Seta, & Wang, 1989; in press).

*Aggression.*   A number of experiments have shown that pornographic movies (sexually arousing stimuli), loud sounds, and the presence of weapons all seem to raise the level of aggressive behavior shown by laboratory subjects. Leonard Berkowitz (1974) argued that this is because these conditions produce a higher level of irrelevant drive.

### Drive Stimulus Theory

Since specific drive-producing conditions, such as food or water deprivation, seem to have fairly specific effects on behavior, how can a drive theorist cling to general drive theory? One solution to the dilemma is to say that, in addition to arousing general drive, *specific drive-producing procedures also arouse specific stimuli in the organism.* These internal stimuli, called *drive stimuli* (Sd), could arouse specific responses just as external stimuli arouse specific responses. The need for such a concept in Hull's theory is seen in the facts that we eat when hungry and drink when thirsty. As obvious as these differences are, they are *not* predicted by general drive theory, because according to the theory the "same" drive is aroused by all drive-producing operations. Diagrammatically, we may view the situation on following page.

Sd is a specific internal stimulus, such as invoked by food deprivation (Sd Hunger) or by water deprivation (Sd Thirst), and D is general drive which would be aroused by either food or water deprivation. Such internal stimuli are presumed to have the same properties as external stimuli: They can be *discriminated* (we can tell them apart), they can serve as *cues,* and they can be *conditioned* to responses.

Considerable animal research indicates that drive stimuli do have these

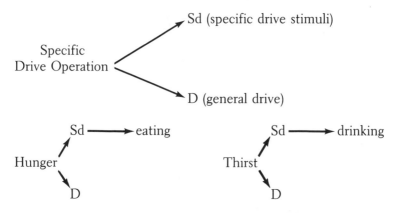

properties. For example, if an animal gets food in the right arm of a T-maze and water in the left arm, it learns to go left or right according to whether it is hungry or thirsty on a given day. On the very *first trial* on a day when the animal is thirsty, for example, it turns left to the water. Since all aspects of the apparatus are the same every day, the animal appears to be using its own hunger or thirst to guide its behavior (Bailey, 1955; Leeper, 1935). Capaldi and Davidson (1979) found that rats easily discriminated among different *levels* of deprivation. Capaldi, Viveiros, and Davidson (1981) had rats run in a straight alleyway, with *kind* of deprivation (food versus water) or *amount* of deprivation (short versus long) signalling the *presence* or *absence* of reward on a given day's trials. For example, a particular animal might get food reward on days when it had short deprivation but not get food on days when it had long deprivation. This is a particularly interesting combination because it directly pits the "higher drive" against the internal cue for no reward, and vice versa. Animals *ran faster under low deprivation than high deprivation if low deprivation signalled reward and high deprivation signalled no reward.* Capaldi's research indicates that drive stimuli can arouse reward expectancies very reliably and influence behavior strongly, especially if there are no obvious external cues to help the animal decide how to respond. The data also indicate that the expectancy is a more influential determinant of running speed than is deprivation level.

### Learned Drives

Hunger, thirst, and pain commonly have been called *primary drives*, to indicate their biological primacy and to indicate there is little learning involved in their arousal. But, much of the behavior of complex animals, especially humans, is *not* directed toward reducing hunger, thirst, or pain. Consequently, in order to "save the concept" of drive, drive theorists have postulated that behavior is motivated by *learned drives* (also called *secondary* or *acquired* drives). A learned drive is one which is aroused by stimuli associated with a primary drive. We need to distinguish clearly between learned *drives* and learned *goals* (*incentives, rewards*), however. "Drive" refers to an internal state of arousal in the organism; "goal" refers to some external stimulus toward which behavior is directed. The distinction is important because drives and goals are separable; all goals do not involve drive reduction. Incentives are discussed in more detail in chapter 6. The most widely examined learned drive, however, has been *fear*.

*Fear as an acquired drive.*     Once again, we credit Freud with giving direction to a long line of research. O. H. Mowrer (1939), a leader in the study of acquired drives, said:

> Freud ... posited that *all* anxiety (fear) reactions are probably learned; his hypothesis when recast in stimulus-response terminology runs as follows. A so-called traumatic ("painful") stimulus (arising either from external injury, of whatever kind, or from severe organic need) impinges upon the organism and produces a more or less violent defense (striving) reaction. Furthermore, such a stimulus-response sequence is usually preceded or accompanied by originally "indifferent" stimuli which, however, after one or more temporally contiguous associations with the traumatic stimulus, begin to be perceived as "danger signals," i.e., acquire the capacity to elicit an "anxiety" reaction.... In short, *anxiety (fear) is the conditioned form of the pain reaction*, which has the highly useful function of motivating and reinforcing behavior that tends to avoid or prevent the occurrence of the pain-producing (unconditioned) stimulus.

We may say that *fear is an aversive state of the organism aroused by stimuli that signal a future threatening event*. Mowrer's analysis was the foundation for a generation of laboratory work on fear conditioning and avoidance learning. Many psychologists believed that analogs for human anxiety and neurotic behavior could be applied to clinical problems and that we needed to develop experimental procedures for producing animal equivalents of human conflicts, frustration, anxiety, and even love and affection, so that we could develop principles applicable to clinical situations.

*What is necessary for fear learning?*     If fear can be conditioned, we can think of it as a conditioned response which also has drive properties. As a conditioned response it should follow the same laws as other conditioned responses, showing acquisition, extinction, generalization, and discrimination. Fear does follow these laws, but the details are more properly the subject matter of learning theory (e.g., see Gordon, 1989). Two points should be made here, however.

First, *overt skeletal muscular responses to either the conditioned stimulus or unconditioned stimulus are not necessary for fear learning*. Some kind of response is necessary to demonstrate that learning has occurred, but overt responding is not necessary for the learning per se. Animals paralyzed by the "blowgun poison" curare cannot move during conditioning, but they show appropriate "fearful" responses when tested after the drug wears off. A long history of research leads to the conclusion that specific overt responses are not necessary for conditioning (Bitterman, 1967; Bolles, 1972).

Second, contemporary theory (e.g., Rescorla, 1967, 1987) says that *conditioning occurs reliably only when a conditioned stimulus (CS) informs the subject that an unconditioned stimulus (UCS) is forthcoming.* For example, a tone (CS) signals that a painful UCS is imminent. Rescorla (1967) argued that there must be a *contingency* (correlation) between CS and UCS, so that a CS means that UCS is coming, and no CS means that no UCS is coming. This produces *excitatory conditioning;* the CS produces an arousal similar to that excited by the UCS. *Inhibitory conditioning* is produced if a CS signals that a UCS is not coming and no CS means that a UCS *is* coming. For example, a light means no shock, and no light means shock. The inhibitory CS light has a *calming* effect, opposite the excitatory effect produced by the UCS.

*Measurement of fear.* As with any *emotion* (see chapter 2) we may index fear by *verbal reports, nonverbal behaviors,* or *physiological responses.* All these different indices are necessary because they do not always correlate well and there is no agreement that one type of measure is necessarily a better measure of fear than the others. Physiological measures like heart rate or galvanic skin response might seem the most direct measures of fear, but the exclusive use of such measures would assume that fear is entirely reducible to such responses. In fact, physiological responses do not correlate very well among themselves, so they are not perfect indices of fear. The behavior of the whole animal is then often the best index of fear, such as observing the animal's escape or avoidance behavior in an aversive situation (McAllister & McAllister, 1971).

We may then think of fear as an intervening variable which has learning (aversive conditioning) as the antecedent condition, and physiological responses, verbal behavior, or nonverbal behavior as the consequent condition. If we think of fear as a learned drive, then we expect it to meet the criteria which define any other drive. That is, fear should *energize* a range of response, fear reduction should be *reinforcing,* and fear increase should be *punishing.*

*Fear as an energizer.* Fear-drive should energize a variety of responses, either reflexive or voluntary. A reflex response ought to be advantageous for study, however, because it ought to be inherently less variable than a learned response. Brown, Kalish, and Farber (1951) used the startle reflex as a measure of fear conditioning in the rat. They reasoned that as fear is conditioned it should get stronger and energize the reflex response more. To test this hypothesis, they placed rats in a small apparatus mounted on a postage scale, so that when the animal was startled by the sharp sound of a cap pistol it jumped. The magnitude of this startle-jump was recorded by the pressure against the scale. Over a series of trials, a tone was paired with footshock, and periodically the animals were tested for startle when the fear-arousing tone was on. As predicted (Figure 3-5), the magnitude of startle response increased with the number of fear-conditioning trials. Control animals, on the other hand, did not show any change in the startle response, which suggests that fear was indeed energizing the startle response. Meryman (1952, in Brown, 1961, p. 152–154) also found that food deprivation added to fear produced a further increase in startle magnitude — just as irrelevant drive theory predicts. This research has been challenged (e.g., Kurtz & Siegel, 1966), but many subsequent studies (with much more sophisticated apparatus!) have found the same results as Brown et al. (e.g., Davis & Astrachan, 1978; Davis, 1986).

*Fear reduction as reinforcement.*    The reference experiment for fear reduction was conducted by Neal Miller (1948). Rats were shocked in one compartment of a two-compartment apparatus and escaped into the other compartment. After this training, the escape route was blocked but no more shock was given. A wheel was made available to the animals, and when they turned it, the door blocking escape was opened and the animals ran to the "safe" side of the apparatus. After wheel turning had been learned, the wheel

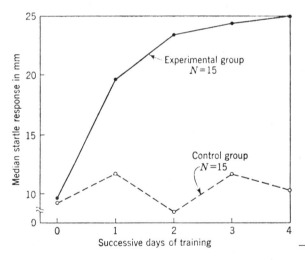

**FIGURE 3-5.** Median Amplitude of startle responses of fearful and nonfearful rats to a loud, sharp sound. The upper curve shows that experimental animals presumed to be fearful jumped more and more vigorously to the sound as the number of fear-conditioning trials increased. The responses of control (nonfearful) subjects, however, did not change progressively or significantly during the same period. (From Brown, Kalish, and Farber, 1951, p. 321. Copyright © 1951 by the American Psychological Association. Reprinted by permission.)

was made inoperative and pressing a lever became reinforced by escape. Wheel turning extinguished and lever pressing increased. The conclusion was that escape into the safe compartment was fear reducing, and this fear reduction reinforced the learning of the two instrumental responses. Many, many experiments conducted by Miller and others (see Mowrer, 1960, for a review) point to the interpretation that fear reduction is reinforcing. Davis and Miller (1963) even found that fearful rats would press a lever more for an intravenous injection of sodium amytal, a nervous system depressant, than would non-shocked control animals. They argued that the drug reduced the fearfulness of the previously shocked animals but did not reinforce the control animals because the control animals were not fearful in the first place.

*Fear as a punisher.*   Stimuli associated with pain clearly can suppress ongoing behavior, but punishment is a broad topic and is addressed in chapter 7.

*An application of secondary drive theory to humans.*   As noted, much of the research and theory related to secondary drives grew out of attempts to translate clinical problems into stimulus-response language and theory (e.g., Miller & Dollard's (1950) *Personality and Psychotherapy*). An example from Brown (1961) is particularly interesting, however. Brown described how mi-

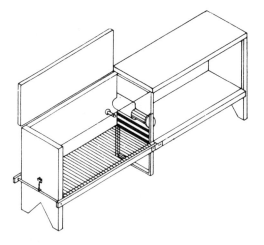

**FIGURE 3-6.**   Acquired drive apparatus. The left compartment is painted white, the right one black. A shock may be administered through the grid that is on the floor of the white compartment. When the animal is placed on the grid that is pivoted at the inside end, it moves down slightly making a contact that starts an electric timer. When the animal performs the correct response, turning the wheel or pressing the bar as the case may be, he stops the clock and actuates a solenoid that allows the door, painted with a horizontal black and white stripes, to drop. The experimenter can also cause the door to drop by pressing a button. The dimensions of each compartment are 18 x 6 x 8½ inches. (From Miller, 1948, p. 90. Copyright © 1948 by the American Psychological Association. Reprinted by permission.)

serliness, or "desire for money," could be interpreted in terms of anxiety and anxiety reduction. He proposed that at some point in life the stimulus of *not having money* becomes a conditioned stimulus for fear. The child may hear the parents argue about not having money, expressing anxiety over where money for food and rent is going to come from, and so on. The arguments and fears expressed by the parents may be considered unconditioned stimuli for fear on the part of the child, and such words as "We have no money," and other stimuli indicating lack of money, become conditioned stimuli for arousing this fear. The child or young adult may then learn that *this fear is reduced by getting and having money.* Therefore, whenever the cues for *not* having money are presented the adult does what he has learned as the means of reducing this fear (eliminating the cues): He gets money. This kind of fear, and a conspicuous consumption which serves to hold down the anxiety cues of poverty, has been described poignantly by the great American playwright Moss Hart in his autobiography *Act One.*

Other kinds of compulsions may have the same or similar bases. Excessive sexual activity is frequently interpreted in this fashion: Not being loved may serve as an anxiety-arousing cue which is temporarily removed by the sex act. Clinically, this kind of interpretation helps account for behaviors that otherwise seem to have no common explanation.

Other applications of drive or drive-like theories are covered in later chapters. Suffice it here to say that other motivational accounts of behavior are now more in vogue than drive theory, but drive theory, or something like it, is still found useful by some theorists.

## ACTIVATION THEORY

Chapter 2 discussed activation as a dimension of emotion, but activation theory has broader motivational implications. Like drive theory, activation theory has been used to account for the *energization* of behavior, but not its *direction* or form. Elizabeth Duffy (1934), who originally proposed activation theory under the name of *energy mobilization,* emphasized the autonomic arousal which characterizes Cannon's *fight-flight,* or *emergency reaction.* Subsequently, the role of the *reticular activating system* (RAS) of the midbrain (e.g., Berlyne, 1960; Duffy, 1962; Hebb, 1955; Lindsley, 1951; Malmo, 1959; Woodworth & Schlosberg, 1954) was emphasized. Much of the early enthusiasm for the theory was because it seemed to provide a physiological account of drive while at the same time solving many problems faced by drive theory.

### The Reticular Activating System

The basic activation (or arousal) mechanism in the brain was considered to be the RAS, a complex tangle of neurons in the brainstem, illustrated in Figure 3–7. It receives inputs from all sensory systems except smell and then

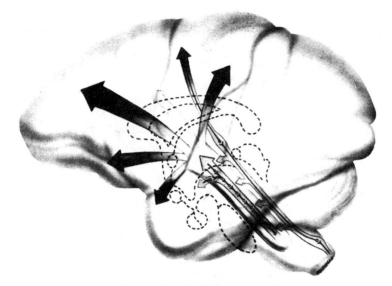

**FIGURE 3-7.** Schema projected upon monkey brain showing ARAS, including reticular formation in central core of lower brain stem with multisynaptic relays and its upward diffuse projections to all parts of cortex. To right a single afferent pathway with a relay in thalamus proceeds to postcentral cortex, but gives off collaterals (arrows) to reticular formation. These are respectively the unspecific and specific sensory systems. (From H. W. Magoun, The ascending reticular system and the wakefulness. In J. F. Delafresnaye (ed.) *Brain Mechanisms and Consciousness*, 1954, p. 13.) Used by permission of the publisher.

distributes these diffusely to all parts of the cerebrum via the *ascending* RAS. Specific sensory information is lost in the RAS, but the widespread distribution of RAS output "tones up" the cortex in preparation for further input and attention to the environment. At the same time, impulses sent to motor neurons via the *descending* RAS serve to maintain muscle tonus over long periods of time.

Increased RAS activity is seen in the electroencephalogram (EEG — brainwaves recorded from various locations on the scalp) as a shift from a "resting" alpha wave pattern (8 to 12 Hz; Hz is the abbreviation for hertz, or cycles per second) to an "activated" beta pattern (15 Hz and up, with lower amplitude and greater irregularity). This shift in EEG pattern, illustrated in Figure 3-8, is widely spread over the cortex and may be conceptualized as something like a fire alarm that gets people into action but does not really say where the fire is. To determine the direction in which to go, or what responses to make, more specific environmental information must be gained via the sensory channels that run more directly to specific areas of sensory cortex.

The alpha pattern, which has a relatively high amplitude and low frequency, is said to be "synchronized." The beta pattern, of higher frequency and lower amplitude, is "desynchronized." Such desynchronization is

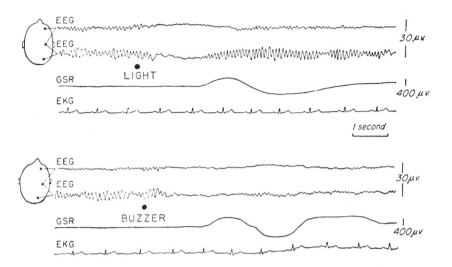

**FIGURE 3-8.** Arousal effects of unexpected light and sound stimuli on the electroencephalogram (EEG), galvanic skin response (GSR), and heart rate (EKG). Electrode placements for the EEG are indicated from the top of the head. Note that the posterior electrodes show a large-amplitude, low-frequency alpha wave before the presentation of light or buzzer. This is a typical, relaxed, waking record. After the light or buzzer, there is a transition to a low-amplitude, high-frequency beta wave that is typical of more alert or excited subject. The alpha is "blocked" by activity from the brain stem reticular system following presentation of the light and buzzer. The buzzer in this illustration was obviously a more "exciting" stimulus, since the alpha blocking lasted longer and there was a larger GSR change as well. HR is not obviously faster after stimulation, but the naked eye is not a good indicator of HR records shown in this manner. (From D. B. Lindsley, Emotions and the electroencephalogram. In M. L. Reymert (ed.), *The Second International Symposium in Feelings and Emotions*, p. 241. Copyright © 1950 McGraw-Hill Book Company. Used with permission of McGraw-Hill Book Company.)

readily seen in EEG records from the occipital cortex at the back of the head, the primary receiving area for visual input. If a normal human EEG is recorded with eyes closed, the occipital alpha pattern is very pronounced, but when the eyes are opened there is immediate desynchronization as the light input is carried through the RAS. Alpha and beta normally fluctuate as we go about our daily activities. Moruzzi and Magoun (1949) showed that direct electrical stimulation of the RAS through permanently implanted electrodes produces this same desynchronization.

Early research of the 1950's indicated that destruction of the RAS had effects opposite to those of stimulation. Severe RAS damage left animals comatose, unresponsive to stimulation, with a continuous highly synchronized EEG. Electrical records showed that stimuli reached the sensory cortex but that no overall desynchronization of the EEG appeared and there was no overt response to the stimulation. Energizing drugs like amphetamines increase RAS activity and alertness, and central nervous system depressants like barbiturates decrease activity and alertness. Such data supported the idea that the RAS is an important, if not completely critical, area of the brain for attention and consciousness.

Although EEG activity is heavily emphasized in activation theory, other measures are more commonly used for practical reasons. These include the usual measures of emotion: heart rate, blood pressure, muscle tension, galvanic skin response, and so on (see chapter 2). It is presumed that all such physiological activity should increase or decrease in unison under conditions of stress or relaxation, reflecting greater or lesser energy expenditure by the organism. Figure 3–8 also shows the effect of a sudden stimulus on some of these other measures.

### The Optimal Level of Arousal Hypothesis

The primary motivational proposition of activation theory has been that there is an optimal level of arousal for behavior, an inverted-U function, as shown in Figure 3–9. Some intermediate level of RAS activity is said to be better than either lower or higher levels. It is also generally implicit that such a medium level of arousal is also *desirable* and sought (Hebb, 1955; Malmo, 1959).

A major impetus for this view came from studies of sensory isolation which indicated that after many hours of severely reduced sensory input, normal college-age subjects had difficulty in concentrating and solving problems. After hours in an unchanging environment, they even showed abnormalities in their ordinary perceptions. Printed lines refused to stay in place, walls bowed outward, and objects seemed to retreat as one looked away from

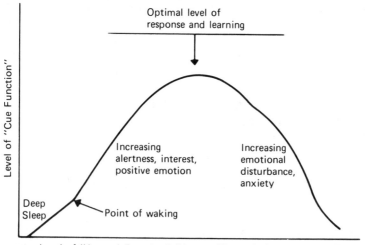

FIGURE 3-9. Relationship between level of arousal (in the ascending reticular activating system) and effectiveness of responses to cues in the environment. (From Hebb, 1955, p. 250. Copyright © 1955 by the American Psychological Association. Reprinted by permission.)

them (e.g., Bexton, Heron, & Scott, 1954). Such data suggested that insufficient sensory input had a detrimental effect on perception, which Hebb thought to be due to reduced RAS activity. Later experiments with *stabilized retinal images* gave further support to this conjecture (e.g., Pritchard, 1961). A tiny, high-frequency vibration of the eyes normally produces constantly changing retinal stimulation. By various mechanical means, such as mounting a miniature slide project on a contact lens, the visual stimulus can be made to vibrate right along with the eye. With reference to the visual stimulus, then, the eye is not moving and the image is stabilized. Such stabilized images *disappear* within a minute or so, and it is clear that *stimulus change* is important for normal visual perception. And, in fact, this is true for all sensory systems: Unchanging stimulation leads to adaptation and reduced sensory activity (see also Reisen, 1961). Stimulus change is necessary for proper functioning of perceptual and cognitive systems. What all this says is that the lowest possible level of arousal is not a viable biological goal; complex organisms cannot thrive on minimal stimulation.

Neither can organisms thrive on *maximal*-intensity stimulation. In such highly stressful situations as fires, floods, and auto accidents, only about one person in four responds rationally. This same percentage has been reported for trained soldiers under enemy fire. Even in situations which would not be characterized as "life-or-death," for example when simply asked to speak before a crowd, many people "fall apart."

*Why are extremes of arousal detrimental?* Hebb (1955) suggested that extremes of RAS activity impede the smooth flow of neural activity. (In the technical terms of his theory, *phase sequences* are interrupted; Hebb, 1955, 1972.) An intermediate level of RAS activity is simply optimal for integrated neural functioning.

Actually, Hull's drive theory also accounts rather well for an optimal level. If there are two habits, H1 and H2, of similar strength, both will be equally multiplied by drive. If drive is very low, the *reaction potentials* for H1 and H2 will not be great enough for either response to occur. At a somewhat higher drive level, the reaction potential for the stronger habit will be great enough for a response to occur, but not for the weaker habit. If the stronger habit is the "correct" response, we have good performance. If drive is very high, reaction potential for both responses is strong, and the responses interfere with each other. A distinct *advantage* of Hull's theory is that it says something fairly specific about *when* a strong drive will produce inferior performance: Performance will be poorer when there are closely competing (nondominant) responses involved.

Activation theory and drive theory both deal with an intensity dimension of motivation, but whereas drive theory assumes that the lowest possible level of drive is the "ideal" state of the organism, activation theory assumes nirvana to be at some intermediate level of stimulation. To reach this intermediate level, we may have to either increase or decrease stimulation, depending on our momentary level. Table 3-2 illustrates this point in simplified form. If the momentary level of arousal is low, an even lower level would be aversive. Therefore, a higher level is sought — pushing toward the optimum. Conversely, if the momentary level is very high, an even higher level would be aversive, and a lower level is sought.

*Sensation-seeking behavior.* The fact that extremely high levels of arousal are ever sought is troublesome for activation theory, as well as for drive theory, but people do jump out of airplanes for recreation and pursue other such activities to increase arousal. Berlyne (1971) suggested that high arousal may be *temporarily* enjoyable *if* the arousal is reduced fairly quickly, what he termed an *arousal jag.* A mountain climber might find it briefly enjoyable to dangle in space, but not for too long.

There are wide individual differences in "fearlessness," based on some combination of genetics and experience (Farley, 1986; Zuckerman, 1984). Farley, for example, describes a *Big T* (Big Thrillseeker) personality as a person who actively seeks excitement, stimulation, and risk. A *Little t* personality, on the other hand, clings more to certainty and predictability. Zuckerman (1979) distinguishes four different kinds of *sensation seeking,* which are defined by his *Sensation Seeking Scale,* shown in Table 3-3. The point is that there are wide *individual differences* in the extent to which people seek arousal, and a situation which may be terrifying to one person may be merely exciting to another. Figure 3-10 illustrates hypothetical individual differences in arousal-seeking.

Piet (1987), however, found that thrill seeking was *not* the motivation of professional stunt performers, whose lives are regularly at stake in dangerous situations. They displayed the same kind of strong motivation for achievement which characterizes leaders in any field, but emphasized that because of their ability and training the dangers they faced were relatively small. The hazards of stunting were perceived as *controllable* by skill and preparation. Hazards of everyday life, in contrast, are not controllable because they depend on other people. The stuntmen interviewed by Piet were in agreement that they could not afford to be afraid if they were to survive.

We can probably generalize this to a great many professions, including window washers, iron workers, race car drivers, and parachutists.

*Intermediate stimulation as low arousal.* Berlyne (1960) and Hunt (1965) both voiced opposition to drive theory but were more comfortable with

TABLE 3-2    Desirable (+) and Aversive (−) Outcomes of Stimulus Change in Terms of the Optimal Level of Arousal Hypothesis

| | | PRESENT STATE OF AROUSAL | |
| --- | --- | --- | --- |
| | | LOW | HIGH |
| ANTICIPATED | Lower | − | + |
| STATE OF AROUSAL | Higher | + | − |

something like drive theory than with Hebb's position. They argued that either low or high levels of *stimulation* produce strong *arousal*, but that intermediate levels of stimulation lead to *low arousal*. An organism seeking moderate stimulation, then, is really seeking *minimal arousal*. This differs from traditional drive theory in that minimal arousal is *not* zero arousal, it is something greater than zero. It is not clear, however, that this restatement of arousal theory adds to its theoretical value. The main virtue of any version of arousal theory is to account for facts which give pause to drive theory and all versions of arousal theory account for stimulus-increasing behavior.

**TABLE 3-3   Items From the Sub-Scales of Zuckerman's Sensation-Seeking Scale.**

THRILL AND ADVENTURE SEEKING

I often wish I could be a mountain climber.
I sometimes like to do things that are a little frightening.
I would like to take up the sport of water skiing.
I would like to try surfboard riding.
I would like to learn to fly an airplane.
I would like to go scuba diving.
I would like to try parachute jumping.
I like to dive off the high board.
I would like to sail a long distance in a small but seaworthy sailing craft.
I think I would enjoy the sensations of skiing very fast down a high mountain slope.

EXPERIENCE SEEKING

I like some of the earthy body smells.
I like to explore a strange city or section of town myself, even if it means getting lost.
I have tried marijuana or would like to.
I would like to try some of the new drugs that produce hallucinations.
I like to try new foods that I have never tasted before.
I would like to take off on a trip with no preplanned or definite routes or timetables.
I would like to make friends in some of the the "far-out" groups like artists or "hippies."
I would like to meet some people who are homosexual (men or women).
I often find beauty in the "clashing" colors and irregular form of modern painting.
People should dress in individual ways even if the effects are sometimes strange.

DISINHIBITION

I like wild, "uninhibited" parties.
I enjoy the company of real "swingers."
I often like to get high (drinking liquor or smoking marijuana).
I like to have new and exciting experiences and sensations, even if they are a little uncon-
    ventional or illegal.
I like to date members of the opposite sex who are physically exciting.
Keeping the drinks full is the key to a good party.
A person should have considerable sexual experience before marriage.
I could conceive of myself seeking pleasures around the world with the "jet set."
I enjoy watching many of the "sexy" scenes in movies.
I feel best after taking a couple of drinks.

**TABLE 3-3   Cont.**

BOREDOM SUSCEPTIBILITY

I can't stand watching a movie that I've seen before.
I get bored seeing the same old faces.
When you can predict almost everything a person will do and say, he or she must be a
   bore.
I usually don't enjoy a movie or play where I can predict what will happen in advance.
Looking at someone's home movies or travel slides bores me tremendously.
I prefer friends who are excitingly unpredictable.
I get very restless if I have to stay around home for any length of time.
The worst social sin is to be a bore.
I like people who are sharp and witty even if they do sometimes insult others.
I have no patience with dull or boring parties.

From M. Zuckerman, S. Eysenck, and H. Eysenck. (1978). Sensation-seeking in England and
   America: Cross-cultural, age, and sex comparisons. *Journal of Consulting and Clinical Psy-
   chology, 46*, pp. 139–149. Copyright © 1978 by the American Psychological Association.
   Used by permission.

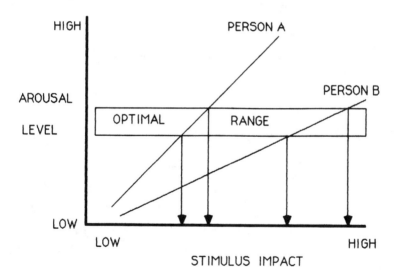

**FIGURE 3-10.**   Individual differences in arousal level as a function of stimulus impact. Stimulus impact
refers to any stimulus characteristic which might produce arousal, such as intensity,
variation, or meaning (e.g. a fearful stimulus). As stimulus impact increases, Person A is
quickly aroused to his or her optimal range of arousal and therefore does not have to seek
out arousal very much. Person A is also more likely to avoid situations with high stimulus
impact. Person B is more difficult to be aroused to the optimum range and therefore is more
likely to seek stimulus situations which produce greater arousal in order to reach his or her
optimal range. Person A is a low level sensation seeker (or small t) and Person B is a high
level sensation seeker (or Big T).

### Arousal Theory and Animal Appetitive Behavior

If arousal theory were to be a viable alternative to drive theory, then its predictions should apply to appetitive situations, supposedly the stronghold of drive theory. Physiological measures of arousal should increase with deprivation and there should be an inverted-U function relating deprivation and performance. The data have been less than compelling and the problems are illustrated in the use of heart rate.

*Heart rate and appetitive behavior.*   In an early study, Belanger and Feldman (1962) reported that heart rate increased steadily with hours of water deprivation (presumably reflecting activation), but bar pressing measured simultaneously with heart rate showed an inverted-U function, as illustrated in Figure 3–11. Unfortunately, this was found only with sequentially decreasing levels. Furthermore, Mathieu (1973) reported that different training procedures eliminated the inverted-U altogether, casting further doubt on the activation interpretation of the Belanger and Feldman results.

In a perverse way, heart rate data have been "reliably inconsistent": Heart rate has been found to increase with water deprivation up to 96 hours (Ashida, 1969), not to change at all (Eisman, 1966), and to decrease with deprivation (O'Kelly, Hatton, Tucker, & Westall, 1965). One explanation for

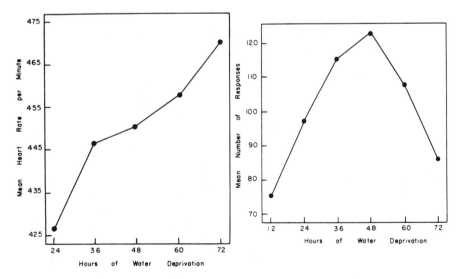

**FIGURE 3-11.**   Heart rate and bar pressing as a function of water deprivation. (From Belanger & Feldman, 1962, p. 222–23. Copyright © 1962 by the American Psychological Association. Reprinted by permission.)

such inconsistencies is that there might be different amounts of body movement by the animals in the different experiments.

Correlations between heart rate and *instrumental activity*, such as lever pressing, are inconsistent (e.g., Hahn, Stern, & McDonald, 1962; Ducharme, 1966; Brillhart, 1975). Correlations between *overall body movement* and heart rate are high, however. With either water deprivation (Elliott, 1975) or food deprivation (Brillhart, 1975) there are correlations of .75 between heart rate and movement of *individual animals* measured at different times. Low correlations between heart rate and lever pressing, measured across *different animals*, might be due to different response styles of different animals. Some animals pounce vigorously on the lever, while other animals depress the lever with only a delicate touch of a paw. Therefore, a fast-responding animal expending little energy might have a low heart rate while a slower-responding animal could work harder and have a high heart rate. Obrist (1976) termed the relationship between effort and heart rate *cardiac-somatic coupling*, which means that the heart has to work harder to supply energy to a body at work than to a body at rest. Even in aversive conditioning with dogs or rats there is a high correlation between activity and heart rate (Roberts, 1974). If the animal has to remain immobile to avoid shock, its heart rate goes down while it is making the avoidance response. But, if the required response is an active one, heart rate goes up.

*Heart rate and incentives.*   There is also evidence, however, that heart rate is correlated with the "goodness" of incentives, independent of the effort required to obtain them. Rats drinking sucrose (Brillhart, 1975), and human infants sucking at a nipple to obtain sucrose (Lipsett, Reilly, Butcher, & Greenwood, 1976), show *higher* heart rate and *lower* activity with increasing sucrose concentrations. Sucrose may directly activate the sympathetic nervous system, and hence the heart. Under normal circumstances, positive incentives may produce more activity and a higher heart rate, but heart rate differences do not depend entirely on activity differences (Obrist, 1981).

Fowles (1983) studied heart rate and incentives in a different manner. He used money as a reward for human subjects pressing a button, analogous to the rat pressing a lever for food. The rewarded subjects showed higher heart rates than control subjects engaged in the same amount of activity. And, analogous to the sucrose results, the greater the reward the higher the heart rate. Fowles's data further indicate that there are incentive motivational effects on heart rate arousal separate from the metabolic requirements of greater activity. His data generalize this phenomenon considerably.

*Attention-rejection model of cardiac function.*   Lacey and Lacey (1970) proposed that heart rate is not just a correlate of behavioral activity, nor even an index of autonomic arousal. Rather, they suggest that cardiac activity is a physiological *coping mechanism*, an attempt on the part of the body to reduce the level of arousal by reducing sensory input. Increased heart rate produces greater pressure on baroreceptors in the carotid sinus and aortic arch of the heart. Pressure on these receptors is known to produce a shift in EEG activity from an activated beta wave pattern (low voltage, fast activity) to a resting alpha wave pattern (higher voltage, slower activity). Heart rate thus is actively involved in regulating EEG arousal.

Conversely, a decrease in heart rate makes the organism *more receptive* to external stimulation, shown in many experiments. For example, in aversive conditioning, the *conditioned* heart rate response is a decrease in heart rate when the conditioned stimulus comes on, not the acceleration that occurs when the unconditioned stimulus (e.g., a painful stimulus) comes on. Tasks involving mental activity, such as doing arithmetic problems in the head, are associated with increased heart rate, as if the heart were blocking out extraneous stimuli which might interfere with the task. On the other hand, tasks involving close attention to the environment lead to lower heart rate (Lacey, Kagan, Lacey, & Moss, 1963). This includes waiting for an aversive signal, as in avoidance learning. It makes sense that the body can attend to external stimuli better without interference from its own activity.

### The Yerkes-Dodson Law

The notion of an *optimal level of arousal* for performance dates back in psychological research to 1908, when Yerkes and Dodson reported that, as a brightness discrimination problem was made more difficult the optimal level of punishment for errors was lower. The Yerkes-Dodson Law gained great currency and has subsequently been referred to in the context of any inverted-U function relating motivation to behavior. It has gained further support in animal research. For example, Broadhurst (1957) deprived rats of different amounts of air by holding them under water for different periods of time. When released to swim to safety, there was indeed an inverted-U function for a difficult brightness discrimination problem, but an optimal level was not clearly shown with problems of simple or moderate difficulty.

More recent research shows it possible to obtain an inverted-U function with a *potentiated startle response* (Davis & Astrachan, 1978). This is the startle response elicited while a fear stimulus is present. At the highest levels of fear conditioning, Davis and Astrachan found, the startle response was *inhibited*. Furthermore, this inhibition was reduced after partial *extinction* of the fear response. The conclusion seems to be that almost *any* response can potentially be inhibited at a high enough level of arousal. It is not just nondominant, competing responses or difficult task behaviors which deteriorate. An individual may simply freeze, as with stage fright. There is evidence from sleep research that there is a brainstem inhibiting mechanism which paralyzes motor activity when there is a high level of arousal (Morrison, 1983).

*Human motor performance.*    Much research on optimal level of arousal in recent years has involved athletic performance. It is a common observation that either an individual or a team can be "too psyched up" to perform well. In terms of the above lines of theorizing we might expect that some sports would be more sensitive to overarousal than others. Oxendine (1970) ranked different sports in terms of the amount of fine muscular control and judgment involved. Bowling, field goal kicking, skating, and tournament-level golfing require very delicate control, whereas weightlifting, sprinting, and football blocking and tackling do not require as much control. Weinburg and Genuchi (1980) reported that golfers performed better with low levels of anxiety, as expected. For basketball, however, it has been reported that medium anxiety levels are more effective (Sonstroem & Bernardo, 1982). Klavora (1978) assessed the pregame anxiety levels of 95 boys during a high school basketball season. Performance level was determined by having coaches rate the players in terms of their customary levels of ability. Performance was again found to be better with medium levels of anxiety.

Sonstroem (1984) and Neiss (1988) have both made the point, however, that a simple inverted-U function relating arousal and performance may indeed be too simple. There are several problems in applying the optimal level notion. First, it is difficult to quantify arousal levels. Psychologists often must resort to looking at motivation levels in terms of *greater than* or *less than*, and we may not be able to define arousal levels precisely enough to test the inverted-U hypothesis well. Second, even if we could define levels of arousal accurately, there are ethical sanctions against experimentally inducing extreme levels of arousal in experimental situations. Third, we must ask whether there is more than one kind of arousal. In sports psychology, being "anxious" and being "psyched up" refer to two different kinds of arousal. Indeed, these two kinds of arousal sound like Thayer's energetic-sleepy and tense-relaxed dimensions of arousal (see chapter 2), and there is some physiological evidence for such a distinction. Exercise-induced arousal produces an increase in epinephrine output, but not cortisol (an adrenal cortex stress hormone). Exercise plus fear produces an increase in both (Neiss, 1988). This being the case, we would then have to ask in any particular situation *which* arousal dimension we are referring to if we say that arousal is low, medium, or high. Furthermore, suppose that an athlete also gets angry. Is anger a third type of arousal? And, for each of these types of arousal is the optimal level of arousal the same?

A final consideration in evaluating the inverted-U function hypothesis concerns the methods used to produce arousal. Again, drive operations may have both *drive* and *stimulus* effects. This is generally true of any experimental manipulation. Thus, if we think of the crowd at an athletic event as a "social facilitator," raising the level of irrelevant drive, we would have to keep in mind that a screaming crowd might be a distracting stimulus as well. If performance were worse with such a crowd, we would have no certain way of knowing whether the motivational element (irrelevant drive) or the stimulus element (distracting noise) were the important determinant of performance. Both might be important.

In the face of such difficulties, Neiss (1988) argues that the inverted-U hypothesis is given only weak support in the motor performance literature. High arousal on one dimension (such as energetic-sleepy, or psyched up) might facilitate performance, but on another dimension (such as tensed-relaxed, or anxious) it might inhibit performance. John Lacey (e.g., 1962) distinguished among behavioral, EEG, and autonomic arousals. These kinds of arousal may covary in some circumstances and not in others. For example, the drug *atropine* produces sleeplike EEG wave forms in either dogs or cats, but the animals remain behaviorally active and alert. Conversely, other drugs (*physostigmine, chlorpromazine*) produce "alert" brain waves (beta waves), but make an animal drowsy. Chlorpromazine, recall, is a tranquilizer. We need to specify which kind of arousal is related to performance and an inverted-U.

### Mutlidimension Activation Theory

The hope that the RAS might underlie a unitary arousal dimension was in fact crushed soon after intense research on the RAS was begun. It was found that:

1. If an animal survives RAS destruction it may recover its normal sleeping/waking pattern and be responsive to external stimulation (Lindsey, Schreiner, Knowles, & Magoun, 1950);
2. If RAS destruction is done in a series of small steps, with recovery time between steps, even a temporary comatose state is forestalled (Adametz, 1959);
3. If the RAS is removed by suction rather than electrolytic lesions (burning), sleep/waking cycles are undisturbed; and finally
4. Massive lesions of sensory pathways, without direct damage to the RAS, produce many of the same overt behavioral effects as do RAS lesions (Sprague, Chambers, & Stellar, 1961).

Other areas of the brain, including the posterior hypothalamus, may be more important for arousal than the RAS. RAS lesions that *spare* the posterior hypothalamus do not eliminate behavioral arousal, but lesions *restricted* to the posterior hypothalamus *do* eliminate behavioral arousal. All this suggests that there may be *multiple* systems for arousal.

*Routtenberg's two-arousal system theory.* Routtenberg (1968) proposed that there is an RAS arousal system and a limbic arousal system. The RAS system produces neocortical desynchronization, but the limbic system can do this if the RAS system is damaged. Routtenberg suggests that the RAS system is primarily concerned with *drive-like* phenomena and the limbic system with *reward-punishment* phenomena. Mild RAS stimulation makes responding more likely (in a drive-like fashion) but limbic arousal is necessary for reward and punishment (changing the likelihood that a particular response will occur again). Routtenberg's account also applies to the two primary *dimensions* of emotion: *pleasant-unpleasant* and *level of arousal*. Pleasant-unpleasant corresponds to reward-punishment and level of arousal corresponds to drive.


## SLEEP AND WAKING

### Rapid Eye Movement Sleep (REM)

Early activation theories assumed that sleep represents a low state of arousal, supported by the early research indicating that RAS destruction produced a sleeplike state. In the mid-1950's, however, the discovery of rapid eye movement (REM) sleep changed our entire view of sleep and dreaming (Aserinksy & Kletiman, 1953; Dement & Kleitman, 1957). Sleep, it turns out, can be a very active brain process, contrary to early activation theory.

As the individual goes to sleep, there is progressive change in EEG activity, as illustrated in Figure 3.12. The amplitude of alpha waves decreases, then the record becomes relatively flat and irregular, possibly interspersed with *theta* waves (4.8 Hz) in some parts of the brain. In very deep sleep, *delta* waves (1.3 Hz) are prominent. Respiration is deep and regular, heart rate is slow and regular, the eyes are relatively still, and there is some muscle tension. This is *nonrapid eye movement* (NREM) sleep.

After about 90 minutes there is a dramatic change. The EEG becomes active, showing the *beta* waves of an alert waking person. There is pronounced movement of the eyes, breathing becomes shallow and irregular, heart rate is faster and more irregular, muscle movement is inhibited, and in males there is penile erection. This is *rapid eye movement* (REM) sleep, also called *paradoxical sleep*. If human subjects are awakened during REM sleep, they report dreaming most of the time, but they are not likely to report dreaming when awakened from NREM sleep. As the night goes on, REM and NREM sleep fluctuate, with REM periods becoming gradually longer, culminating with a REM period of about 90 minutes in early morning. The dream most likely to be remembered in the morning is this last one. Jouvet (1958) coined the phrase *paradoxical sleep* to describe REM periods because there is so much violent internal activity (EEG and autonomic) during this phase of sleep. Also, paradoxically, it is harder to waken a person from REM sleep even though the brain appears alert.

Individuals who are selectively deprived of REM sleep by being awakened just as they go into this phase for several nights subsequently show a rebound effect. They spend more time in REM sleep on undisturbed nights immediately following. This is as if a person deprived of REM sleep tries to make up for the deficit, just as an animal drinks more if deprived of water. A

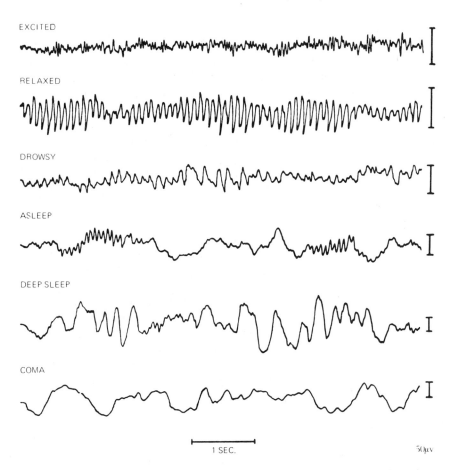

EXCITED

RELAXED

DROWSY

ASLEEP

DEEP SLEEP

COMA

1 SEC.                                            50μv

**FIGURE 3-12.** Typical EEG records from normal subjects in different states of arousal and from a comatose subject. (From Penfield and Jasper, 1954, p. 188. Copyright © 1954 by Little, Brown, Co. Reprinted by permission.)

rebound effect for NREM sleep also occurs following selective NREM deprivation.

Virtually all animals with brains more complicated than reptiles show REM and NREM sleep, with about 22% of a normal adult's sleep in REM. Newborn infants spend about half their sleeping time in REM, and premature infants even more than that. So a consistent pattern in humans is that, with longer sleep or with developing brains, there is more REM. Such evidence suggests that REM sleep might be important for the development and maintenance of normal brain function.

Vertes (1986) has recently proposed a new version of this theory. He maintains that *slow wave sleep* (NREM) is primarily for rest and recuperation. Thus, brain neurons discharge more slowly, protein synthesis is increased, and strenuous activity increases the duration of such sleep. The distinguishing features of REM sleep are that the person sleeps in spite of increased EEG and autonomic arousal even though the body moves very little. Vertes's theory, then, is that *the brain requires periodic reactivation from slow wave sleep* in order to maintain its normal functioning, as well as to ensure that the unconsciousness of sleep does not drift into a comatose state from which the individual may not recover.

Vertes relates his theory to two fatal, sleep associated syndromes, the *Sudden Infant Death Syndrome* and the *Oriental Nocturnal Death Syndrome*. In the former, infants die during sleep for no apparent reason. Vertes suggests that they simply do not have sufficient REM sleep to reactivate them from slow wave sleep. In the latter, apparently healthy males of Oriental descent suddenly die in their sleep, also from no discernible cause. There is evidence that the death results from ventricular fibrillation (an arrhythmic pattern of heart beat which keeps the heart from pumping blood properly) during the first three hours of sleep. This may be *before* REM sleep appears during a night, and the cause of death may therefore be the same as for infant death.

Early in the century, Freud (1935) argued that dreams are the "guardians of sleep," lowering the level of anxiety so we can sleep better. Just the reverse seems to happen, however. Dreams occur concurrently with the greatest arousal found during sleep, and they may represent part of the brain's self-excitation to keep itself alive and well. In any event, it is abundantly clear that sleep is *not* just a low level of activation, even though NREM sleep might be described this way.

## SUMMARY

1. Biological approaches to motivation are largely concerned with how organisms maintain their *internal environments* within narrow biochemical tolerances. Organisms may be conceived as open energy systems having *steady states* which must be maintained.

2. The concept of *homeostasis* refers to the automatic adjustments a body makes to restore stability when the internal environment is unbalanced. Homeostasis is maintained by means of *regulatory* mechanisms, some of which work to *restore* balance and some of which help *prevent* imbalance.

3. The concept of *instinct* is sometimes used to account for apparently unlearned behaviors which aid survival. In higher organisms, unlearned behaviors are limited, but among such simple species as insects they are much more common.

4. *Species-specific behaviors* are genetically determined, but their expression is also determined by environmental factors. *Releasing stimuli* are genetically determined stimulus configurations which trigger species-specific behaviors. The *effective* releasing stimuli may be only a small fraction of the total stimulus. The effectiveness of releasing stimuli varies with the internal state (e.g., hormonal) of the organism.

5. Organisms *learn* to respond to new situations, but *biological limits* to learning are set genetically. Some things (e.g., fears) are more readily learned than others.

*Imprinting* is a particular kind of early learning of social attachments which carries over into adulthood.

6. According to *drive theory*, disruptions of internal balance *energize* an organism into action. The most influential drive theory (Hull's) holds that drive is a *general* energizer and that particular responses are determined by learning. Responses are said to be learned if they are *reinforced* (rewarded) by *drive reduction*.

7. The effect of drive on behavior depends on the kind of response involved. If a response is a *simple, dominant* response, a high level of drive *facilitates* the response. If the response is *complex* or not the dominant response in a particular situation, high drive may make performance *worse*.

8. Tests of predictions from drive theory have met with variable success. Hunger and thirst do not generally produce an increase in "random" activity, as suggested by the theory. *Nonspecific arousal* does seem to produce an increase in so-called *adjunctive behaviors*, however. With humans, high anxiety does facilitate eyeblink conditioning but interferes with more complex tasks.

9. In Hull's theory, drive cannot *direct* or *select* behavior, but internal stimuli called *drive stimuli* can do so. Drive stimuli are specific stimuli accompanying particular drive-producing operations. Hunger and thirst have unique stimuli which can help direct behavior to appropriate goals.

10. *Learned drives*, such as *fear*, are drives which are aroused by stimuli previously associated with such *primary drives as* pain. Fear is the best example of a learned drive. Fear has been shown to *energize* responses, fear-reduction is *reinforcing*, and increased fear is *punishing*.

11. *Activation theory*, like drive theory, is concerned with the energization of behavior, not the direction of behavior. Activation theory is more concerned with *physiological arousal*, however, in either the brain or the autonomic nervous system.

12. The major *behavioral prediction* of activation theory is that behavior is less efficient at either very low or very high levels of arousal than at some medium level of arousal. This is the *optimal level of arousal hypothesis*, which has been influential in motivation theory. The hypothesis has received only limited support in research, perhaps because it is difficult to accurately control or measure arousal levels and because there seem to be several kinds of arousal.

13. Attempts to relate arousal to appetitive behavior have met with some success. *Positive incentives*, such as the sweet taste of sugars, produce higher heart rates for both animals and human infants. Monetary incentives trigger higher heart rates for adult humans.

14. Lacey and Lacey have argued that heart rate acceleration is a mechanism for limiting sensory input, thereby helping to regulate the internal level of arousal. Higher heart rate is associated with such mental tasks as working math problems in the head; lower heart rate is associated with tasks requiring close attention to the external environment.

15. *Sleep* is not just a lower level of arousal. In *rapid eye movement (REM) sleep* there is a high level of brain and autonomic nervous system activity, including dreams. In non-REM (or NREM) sleep the brain and viscera are less aroused and dream is infrequent.

16. One theory of sleep is that sleep is a recuperative process, but that the brain requires periodic activation (REM sleep) in order to maintain its normal function and to ensure that the individual does not drift off into a coma. Two lethal sleep disorders, *Sudden Infant Death Syndrome* and *Oriental Nocturnal Death Syndrome*, have been associated with NREM sleep.

# 4

# Hunger, Thirst, and Taste

Hunger

Thirst

Taste

Summary

# HUNGER

## Background

Chapter 3 discussed homeostasis in relation to open systems on the one hand, and to regulatory physiology on the other. This approach to motivation is predominantly concerned with the mechanics of maintaining a constant internal environment. The question now is: What *actual* regulatory activities occur in the body when an animal runs short of food, water, or air, or when body temperature gets out of its proper range?

Further, we distinguish mechanisms which are specifically homeostatic (such as mechanisms which come into play to counteract a dwindling supply of water in the body) from those which are nonhomeostatic, such as taste. If we eat or drink because food or fluid tastes good, we forestall the shortages which would activate the homeostatic *emergency mechanisms.* There are also nonhomeostatic motivational mechanisms which aid survival without regard to homeostatic mechanisms, such as when we seek novel stimulation.

*Peripheral versus central theories.* In the 1930's, Walter Cannon (e.g., 1934) argued for a peripheral theory of motivation. Peripheral theories emphasize body structures and functions outside the central nervous system. Cannon argued that the stimuli for hunger and eating were contractions of the stomach and that drinking was stimulated by a dry mouth. Peripheral mechanisms cannot be the whole story, however. Animals without stomachs still eat relatively normal amounts of food, as do humans whose diseased or injured stomachs have been surgically removed. Similarly, a man without salivary glands drank normal amounts of water, although wetting his mouth more often to keep it comfortable (Steggerda, 1941).

Other investigators stressed the importance of central (nervous system) factors in motivation. Karly Lashley (1938) said that mechanisms controlling instinctive behaviors were in the brain, and Frank Beach (1942) argued the same point for the excitation of sexual behavior. Nevertheless, peripheral theories were still dominant until the 1950's.

*Central motive state.* Clifford Morgan (1943, 1959) proposed the concept of a central motive state (CMS), a hypothetical system of brain centers and pathways concerned with particular kinds of motives. A specific CMS was defined in terms of the kinds of environmental stimuli to which an animal is responsive. Responsiveness to food indicates a hunger CMS; responsiveness to water indicates a thirst CMS. Morgan attributed three properties to a CMS. First, once it is triggered the CMS *persists* for some time without further stimulation — it is self-maintaining. Second, a CMS *predisposes* an organism to act in a certain way to particular stimuli (e.g., to approach them) but not to other stimuli. Third, the CMS may also *directly emit* certain behaviors. Such "instinctive behavior" as that of a female rat in heat making sexual movements might occur as a direct response to a CMS.

Morgan held that hormones were probably more important than external stimuli in arousing and maintaining CMSs. This seems fairly obvious in the case of sexual arousal. One reason for emphasizing hormones is that a hormone circulating in the blood could maintain a state of excitability over a long period of time. Morgan suggested (1) that the CMS could be "turned off" by eliminating the stimulus or hormone factor which initially triggered the CMS, or by stimulating inhibitory receptors, such as the inhibitory effect of a sweet taste on hunger, and (2) that the behavior resulting from the CMS might directly turn off the CMS that aroused the behavior of the CMS in the first place. There is evidence, as we shall see, for all these "cutoff" mechanisms.

Elliot Stellar (1954) proposed more specifically that motivated behavior resulted from arousal of excitatory centers in the hypothalamus of the brain. The activity of these centers, in turn, was a function of (1) *inhibitory centers* that depress the excitatory centers; (2) *sensory stimuli;* (3) *humoral factors;* and (4) *cortical and thalamic centers* that can produce either excitatory or inhibitory effects on the hypothalamus. These various factors do affect hypothalamic activity, but research also indicates that the hypothalamus is motivationally important mainly because neural pathways to and from other areas of the brain funnel compactly through the hypothalamus as they cross the brain.

Dalbir Bindra (1969, 1978) expanded the CMS concept by arguing that such rewards as food and water are effective because they produce *motivational excitement.* This is different than the S-R reinforcement theory of learning discussed in chapter 1, which argues that rewards (reinforcers) somehow serve to "glue" together or "hook up" stimuli and responses. In Bindra's view, the "rewarded response" in any particular situation is important because it is the only response the experimenter (or, the teacher, the parent, or the environment) allows to be reinforced. Like its predecessors, Bindra's CMS approach is "correct" as far as it goes, but peripheral events are still important. The brain is not the only organ of motivation.

### The Regulation of Body Weight

From the point of view of *systems theory,* body weight is *regulated* by equalizing energy inputs and outputs. Living animals need an almost continuous supply of energy, which is used for several purposes (Keesey & Powley, 1986): (a) for carrying on life functions (basal, or resting, energy); (b) for converting newly-acquired food into body energy; (c) for muscular activity; and (d) in warm-blooded animals, for regulating internal body temperature. Corbett and Keesey (1982) found that about 75% of a laboratory-rat diet was converted to usable energy. Of this, about 73% was used for basal metabolism, 11% for digestive activity, and only the remaining 16% for behavior. Some animals maintain an energy balance by eating more or less continuously, such as cows and hummingbirds. Others, including predatory animals, eat more sporadically and may go for days without food. With such erratic feeding, energy must be stored so that enough is available when needed, but is compact enough to be portable. Body fat meets these requirements nicely, and is the primary form of energy storage.

If regulation of homeostasis is precise, and energy inputs equal outputs, a mature organism should have a relatively constant body weight. Many people show large weight fluctuations, however, which suggests that energy inputs and outputs are not equivalent and that body weight is *not* being regulated. Keesey and Powley (1986) point out that body weight would not have to stay *exactly* the same, however, any more than blood pressure has to be exactly constant in order to demonstrate blood pressure regulation. Furthermore, energy *output* is adjusted in ways other than just activity. For example, weight gain is held down by increased metabolic rate, burning off some of the excess energy. Conversely, a person who loses weight has a lower metabolic rate and burns less energy. Since metabolic activity is one of the major uses of energy (73%), adjustments in metabolic activity are more important for regulating weight than are changes in overall body activity (accounting for 16% of energy use). *Brown adipose tissue* stores energy as fat but quickly releases surplus energy in the form of heat. If an organism does not have this tissue (some species do not, and some individuals are so lean that they do not), energy loss is controlled in other ways. For example, highly trained female athletes or dancers, who have minimal body fat, may save body energy by not having menstrual cycles.

### Neural Mechanisms in Hunger

*The dual hypothalamic theory of hunger.*   The dual hypothalamic theory of hunger guided research for many years. The theory says that neural activity in the *lateral hypothalamus* (LH) excites eating behavior and that activity in the *ventromedial nucleus* (VMN or VMH) inhibits eating. When the body has a fuel shortage, the LH becomes more active. When sufficient food has become consumed the VMN is said to inhibit the activity of the LH. The primary evidence is that (a) direct stimulation of the LH via implanted electrodes produces eating as long as the stimulation is turned on, but (b) destruction of the LH leads to self-starvation. Conversely, (a) electrical stimulation of the VMN while an animal is eating will inhibit eating, but (b) destruction of the VMN produces an animal which eats itself into the equivalent of an 800-pound person.

*Lateral hypothalamic lesions.*   Extensive bilateral lesions of the lateral hypothalamus produce predictable changes in both eating and drinking, called the *lateral hypothalamic syndrome* (e.g., see Epstein, 1971; Teitelbaum, 1971). There are four identifiable stages of recovery from the lesions, but the amount of recovery time ranges from days to months depending on the specific location and size of the LH damage. These stages are:

*Stage 1.* The animal neither eats nor drinks and must be tube fed or it dies.

*Stage 2.* The animal begins to eat, but only wet and palatable foods, such as chocolate chip cookies soaked in milk. The animal does not eat enough to survive, however, and requires supplementary tube feeding.

*Stage 3.* The animal now begins to *regulate* its food intake so that it can survive by eating on its own. It will not drink water, but will drink enough of a sweet solution (such as sugar or saccharin flavored water) to survive.

*Stage 4.* The animal begins to drink water and *appears* to have recovered because it eats and drinks enough by itself to maintain normal body weight. The animal does not in fact fully recover, however. For example, it does not drink normally after having water withheld for several hours. Such an animal gets enough water only because it drinks when it eats, called *prandial drinking.* Even slight changes in the taste of water, such as adding a bitter substance (quinine) in such small amounts that it does not affect the drinking of a normal animal, will completely keep the "recovered lateral" animal from drinking. The recovered lateral does not salivate nearly as much as normal (Kissileff, 1973) and the eating and drinking of the recovered lateral can be mimicked by tying off the salivary glands of a normal animal. The recovered lateral apparently drinks plain water only to wet its mouth when eating. It accidentally survives because of nonhomeostatic mechanisms, taste factors, and prandial drinking.

Teitelbaum and Cytawa (1965) reported that temporarily anesthetizing the cortex of the recovered lateral with potassium chloride immediately reinstated the feeding and drinking deficits for several days, but only affected a normal animal for a few hours. The newborn rat shows a developmental pattern of change in eating and drinking which parallels the recovery stages of the LH-lesioned rat (Teitelbaum, 1971). This suggests that cortical tissue is important for normal feeding and drinking.

### Lateral Hypothalamic Stimulation

*Electrical stimulation.*   Electrical stimulation of the lateral hypothalamus produces stimulus-bound eating, drinking, or other motivational effects, persisting only when stimulation is applied. This is more than excitation of specific consummatory activity, however, because lever pressing for food is also aroused. (See Hoebel, 1971, for a review of this literature.)

Valenstein, Cox, and Kakolewski (1970) report, however, that electrical stimulation with the *same* electrode may arouse eating one day, drinking the next, and gnawing at a block of wood on the third. This raises the intriguing possibility that brain areas are not entirely fixed and immutable in their function, perhaps changing daily. If this were so, considerable re-evaluation of brain function in general would be called for.

*Chemical stimulation.*    Grossman (1962) placed small amounts of various crystalline chemicals directly into the lateral hypothalamus by means of permanently implanted hypodermic needles. Noradrenaline produced eating in satiated animals, but depressed drinking. Conversely, carbacol (which is like acetylcholine) stimulated drinking but inhibited eating. These chemicals also influenced bar pressing for food and water in the same manner. Control chemicals had no effects, showing that the eating and drinking were not due to simple irritation of the stimulation sites. These effects were, overall, very much like those with normal hunger and thirst.

Chemical stimulation is effective in many brain areas, however. Fisher (1964) suggests that the whole limbic system is important to many motivational systems because chemical stimulation throughout it influences eating and drinking, reproductive, and aggressive behaviors.

The experiments of Valenstein et al. are intriguing, but it does appear that the feeding and drinking areas of the brain are both anatomically and chemically separated. Chemical stimulation seems specific to the chemicals used, since different chemicals in the same location have different effects. Chemicals may spread from one location to another, but this spreading is minimized by using minute crystals. The existence of different kinds of adrenaline-sensitive neurons in the hypothalamus is also well documented.

### Role of Nonhypothalamic Areas in Hunger

The evidence now strongly indicates that the hypothalamus is primarily a way station where fiber tracts from many widely separated areas of the brain funnel together very compactly, then spread out again. Lesions in such a compact area can disrupt many different pathways and hence are highly dramatic in their effects. The same devastating effects found with hypothalamic lesions can be duplicated with lesions at other locations along the pathways winding through the hypothalamus (Grossman, 1975). Implicated areas range from the frontal lobes to the brainstem, the entire length of the brain. Many areas are serially connected, like extension cords strung together, so that a disconnection (lesion) at any point along the line will interfere with the function. As an example, Gold (1967) showed that if the hypothalamus was lesioned on *one* side of the brain and the brainstem tegmentum (roof) was damaged on the *other* side, the effects on feeding were the same as with *bilateral* hypothalamic lesions. The brainstem lesion apparently cut into the same system as the hypothalamic lesion, indicating that the two areas are "wired" in series.

*Sensorimotor deficits and hypothalamic lesions.*    The neural link between food deficit and making movements to get food is not well understood. A variety of evidence, however, shows that the lateral hypothalamic rat has both motivational and motor deficits (cannot make eating movements well), and Morgane (1964) showed that lesions of the *globus pallidus,* a forebrain area involved in control of movement, produced more severe effects than the usual LH lesions. Pathways from the globus pallidus run through the *far lateral* hypothalamic area, so it is also interesting to note that lesions of the far lateral area are also more severe than more medial LH lesions. Such animals are inactive, fail to groom themselves, and do not respond well to sensory

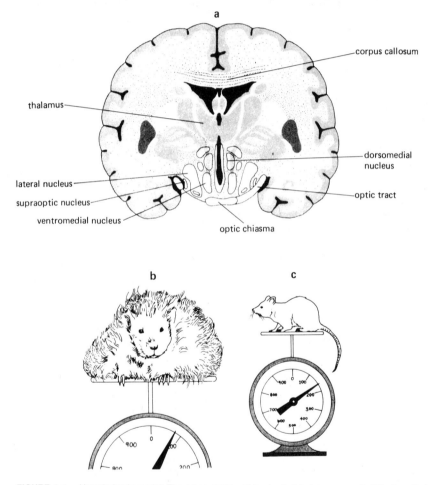

**FIGURE 4-1.**  Hypothalamic nuclei. The cross-section of the brain (a) shows several of the hypothalamic nuclei. The obese rat (b) has lesions in the ventromedial nuclei. A normal rat (c) is shown for comparison. A rat with lesions in the lateral nuclei starves itself. From Schneider & Tarshis, *An Introduction to Physiological Psychology,* 1975, p. 278. Reprinted with permission of Random House, Inc.

stimuli (Grossman, 1975). Since recovering LH animals *can* eat palatable foods even when they *will not* eat lab chow, and there is a deficit in bar pressing for food (an arbitrary response which also "recovers" along with feeding), there appears to be a strong motivational component in the LH syndrome (Rodgers, Epstein, & Teitelbaum, 1965).

White (1986) has recently summarized evidence relating motivational and motor deficits to dopamine transmitters in a brain area called the *nigro-striatal bundle*. Dopamine in this area very clearly has been related to the experience of pleasure. White concludes that the LH syndrome is caused by two factors: First, there is reduced responsiveness to the *sensory* properties of food and water because dopamine pathways have been damaged, a sensory/motivational loss. Second, greater effort is required to eat and drink because of damage to pathways from the globus pallidus. White suggests that the dopamine neurons in the nigro-striatal area may carry a feedback signal based on blood glucose levels, and this signal influences eating.

### Ventromedial Hypothalamic Effects

Ventromedial hypothalamic lesions produce extensive overeating (hypothalamic hyperphagia) and very fat rats or cats. Rats may gain as much as 10 grams a day, as compared to 1 to 3 for normal animals, and may double or triple their adult body weights (moving from 400–500 up to 1,000–1,200 grams). Figure 4–2 shows weight changes and food intake of lesioned and control rats. There are two stages of hyperphagia. In the first (*dynamic* hyperphagia), there is much eating and rapid weight gain. In the second (*static* hyperphagia), there is a leveling off of weight at a very high level.

The ventromedial-lesioned animal is typically, although not always, characterized by a finickiness of eating (Graff and Stellar, 1962). It tends to overeat highly palatable foods and undereat unpalatable ones. The animals do not eat more frequently but eat larger meals than normal. This suggests that they are not hungrier but are slower to stop because the "stop mechanism" for feeding is defective. Electrical stimulation of the ventromedial area will stop eating in progress, and simultaneous stimulation of lateral and ventromedial areas results in no eating (Wyrwicka & Dobrzecka, 1960). Neural activity in the two areas is also reciprocal; when one is increased, the other is decreased (Oomura, Kimura, Ooyama, Maeno, Iki, & Kuniyoshi, 1964). This kind of evidence has been the support for the satiety center hypothesis, but we already have seen the story is not this simple. Surgical separation of medial and lateral areas does not produce hyperphagia, and electrical stimulation of the medial area will stop many kinds of ongoing activities. Grossman (1966) proposed that the ventromedial area is a "center" for a range of affective responses. (Ventromedial-lesioned animals are also vicious, and their escape and avoidance behavior is enhanced.)

Powley and Keesey (1970) suggested that there is a *set point* for body

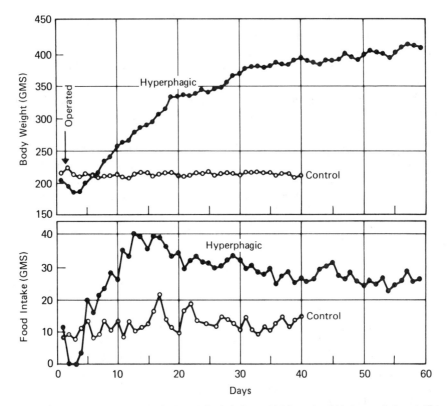

**FIGURE 4–2.** Effects of ventromedial hypothalamic lesions on intake and weight changes in the rat. (From Teitelbaum, Disturbances in feeding and drinking behavior after hypothalamic lesions. Reprinted from 1961 *Nebraska Symposium on Motivation*, by permission of University of Nebraska Press. Copyright © 1961 by University of Nebraska Press.)

weight that is established by a balance of activities represented by the ventromedial and lateral areas. If the ventromedial area is damaged, the set point goes up, and animals eat more readily; if the lateral area is damaged, the set point goes down, and they eat less readily. The animal tries to maintain whatever body weight its set point is adjusted for. They showed that lateral hypothalamic animals reduced to 80% of their normal body weight *before* lesioning did not show severe disruption of feeding and drinking after lesioning. As already noted, ventromedial animals eventually do level off their body weight and intake in the static phase, just as normal animals eventually stop growing.

### Start Cues for Eating

Common observation shows that many different cues will signal us to eat. Sometimes we do so just because other people are eating. Other times we eat because we "feel hungry." Other times still, we think we are not hungry, taste something (an appetizer) and then eat as if we were very hungry. It seems clear, then, that we are not going to find any simple principle to account for all the reasons we eat. In terms of eating-when-hungry, however, there are considered to be a number of possible peripheral body events which influence brain areas involved in eating. Most commonly there are glucostatic, lipostatic, and animostatic theories. The suffix -static refers to some hypothesized internal mechanisms for detecting when the quantity of the relevant substance goes below some point (glucose, fat, or amino acids, respectively). There is some evidence for each of these, but no one principle—nor indeed all three together—account for all the data.

*Glucostatic theory.* This says that feeding is initiated by a drop in blood sugar level and is stopped by an increase. Direct measures of blood sugar level do not correlate well with amount of food consumed, however, and do not account for the fact that diabetics (who have a very high blood sugar level) are hungry. It is generally believed that some more subtle detection is involved, such as the difference between amount of sugar in the arteries and veins. A large arterio-venous difference means that the body is absorbing more through the capillaries, whereas a small difference would mean the body is not absorbing sugar. Some of the most compelling evidence, however, is that (1) insulin injections increase glucose intake; (2) glucose injections into the blood reduce lateral hypothalamic neural activity; and (3) glucose injections increase ventromedial activity (e.g., Anand, Chhina, & Singh, 1962; Oomura et al., 1964). There is no brain area known, however, where glucose injections will stop eating, including the VMH.

*Lipostatic theory.* Animals made diabetic by experimental means cannot utilize glucose because it cannot be absorbed into the cells without insulin. Such animals do not increase their intake if the amount of sugar in their diet is reduced, but they do increase their intake if fat in the experimental diet is diluted. They therefore seem to be responding to a lowered amount of fat (Friedman, 1978). It thus appears that there may be a lipostatic mechanism for the short-term regulation of food intake, as well as for the long-term regulation that sets the upper limit of body weight.

*Aminostatic theory.* The primary evidence in favor of some kind of amino acid receptor is that foods high in amino acids are very satiating. This is in spite of the fact that an amino-acid-rich diet also results in a relatively low blood sugar level. Research manipulating amino acids in the manner of Friedman's experiment with lipid content of the diet apparently waits to be done.

*Set point theory.* Nisbett (1972), arguing in support of the set point theory, says the fat person is probably not gluttonous, probably not emotionally disturbed, and probably not out of order physiologically. He or she probably has a set point that is different from that of the average person and therefore eats because he or she is, in fact, hungry. The degree of fat one can attain is determined by the number of fat cells (adipocytes) a person has. This number, if not hereditary, is established very early in life and is supposedly constant thereafter. The size of these cells can vary, however. A person with a lot of fat cells has a higher set point than a person with few fat cells. It is easier for this person to get below the individual set point; so he or she eats more readily.

Studies of starved people or animals show they eat more, eat faster, prefer more palatable foods, are less active, and have less interest in sex. The same is true of hypothalamic hyperphagic rats and of many fat people. But why should a fat person act like a starving person? Because, says Nisbett, our society pushes people to keep their weight down and therefore the fat person is continually below his or her set point even though above average weight. Left to his or her own devices, the "normally fat" person eats more and does not necessarily show the characteristics of a hungry person.

### Stop Cues for Eating

*Satiation Hormone.*   A perennial problem in accounting for satiation has been that feeding seems to stop before anything metabolically very important can happen. This has suggested that some quick-acting effect produced by food in stomach or small intestine temporarily cuts off feeding until a slower-acting metabolic effect has time to occur. A "satiation hormone" could do this. Three different peptides produced by the gut have been implicated in satiation: *glucagon, cholecystokinin (CCK),* and *bombesin* (Carlson, 1987). When animals are given injections of glucagon, which is normally produced in both the pancreas and the gut, they eat less. This appears to be due to the glucagon breaking down liver glycogen into glucose, which in turn sends a signal to the brain via the vagus nerve from the stomach. Cholecystokinin also inhibits eating, but there is some controversy over whether it instigates a satiation signal or whether it produces an aversion. It is known that CCK can be used as a UCS in establishing aversions to flavors (e.g., Deutsch & Hardy, 1977). It appears, however, that CCK changes the *palatability* of food as the animal eats, and this reduced palatability may be the reason that animals slow down their eating (Ettinger, Thompson, & Staddon, 1986).

*Stomach Distention.*   Mechanical receptors in the stomach and intestine may signal the brain to stop eating whether the stomach and/or intestine are extended by food. Distention of the stomach with a water-filled balloon increases neural activity in the ventromedial area, but not in the lateral hypothalamic area (Sharma, Anand, Dua, & Singh, 1961). Other research suggests that the site of distention feedback is in the upper part of the small intestine.

*Osmotic dehydration.*   When an animal eats solid food, which is more concentrated than body fluids, the food pulls fluid from surrounding tissue into the stomach and intestine. This increases gastrointestinal volume and reduces the water supply in the rest of the body. This suggests that an animal may stop consuming *hypertonic* food or drink (more concentrated than body fluids) when the ingested substance makes it thirsty (McCleary, 1953). Mook (1963) tested this by putting tubes into animals so that a fluid drunk by an animal would not reach the stomach, and the experimenter could inject a different fluid directly into the stomach. The results showed, for example, that if an animal were drinking glucose and getting glucose put into the stomach it stopped drinking much sooner than if water were put into the stomach instead of glucose. Several different combinations of substances drunk and injected into the stomach supported the idea that the osmotic properties of the fluid were important in cutting off drinking. Measurement of the *amount* of dehydration produced by different concentrations of ingested sucrose also indicate that dehydration plays a role in the cessation of eating (Beck, 1967).

*Specificity of satiation.*   Common experience tells us that even when we feel "full" from eating one food, we may immediately eat something which tastes different. A number of experiments convincingly demonstrate that only minor changes in the color, taste, or texture of food can stimulate animals to eat again after they have apparently been "satiated" for eating (e.g., Rolls, Rolls, & Rowe, 1983; Brala & Hagen, 1983; Treit, Spetch, & Deutsch, 1983). This suggests that just as we respond to specific kinds of need (e.g., sugar versus protein) by eating more of particular foods, satiation itself can be specific to certain kinds of foods. There is good evidence that the upper intestinal tract is sensitive to specific kinds of nutrients, not just to total amount of food (Pureto, Deutsch, Molina, & Roll, 1976). In fact, there may be several different kinds of satiation, with different characteristics depending on the particular food in question (Mook, Brane, Gonder-Frederick, and Whitt, 1986).

### Specific Hungers

*Specific hunger* means deprivation of a specific food substance which leads to an increased preference for that substance. The best researched example is sodium appetite.

*Sodium appetite.*   If a rat has its adrenal glands removed, it promptly begins to increase its salt intake (Richter, 1936). Adrenal hormones are necessary for the regulation of the body's salt content, and without them too much salt is lost and must be replaced by consumption. Given a choice between water and salt solutions at various concentrations, normal rats show a peak preference for drinking salt solutions of about 0.9%. Adrenalectomized rats show peak preferences at higher salt concentrations. What signals the animal to respond differently?

Richter suggested that adrenalectomized animals are more *sensitive* to saline. The threshold concentration of NaCl sufficient to produce neural firing when applied directly to the tongue, however, is the *same* for normal and adrenalectomized animals (Pfaffman & Bare, 1950). Furthermore, if a normal rat is *forced* to discriminate between water and saline by being punished if it does not, it can detect the same low concentrations that produce neural firing. It is now generally accepted that the effect of salt depletion is on *preference* for salt, not upon sensitivity to salt. Salt-deprived humans report that salt tastes better, and apparently a taste change occurs for the rat without having previously experienced salt deprivation. Immediately after an animal is made salt deficient, sometimes literally overnight, it shows increased salt preference upon first post-depletion exposure to salt (Krieckhaus & Wolf, 1968; A. N. Epstein, 1967; Falk, 1961).

*Other specific hungers.*    A number of other specific hungers have been documented, as for calcium, some vitamins, fat, protein, carbohydrate, and water. There are so many demonstrated specific hungers that we may ask whether it is even reasonable to suspect that *every* dietary deficiency has a mechanism to make some substance more preferred. Or, is there a more generalized mechanism? Convincing research shows that animals can indeed learn specific food preferences or aversions in relation to their health.

*The learning of specific hungers.*    When an animal is on a deficient diet it becomes ill, and the foods it is eating become aversive through association with the illness. The animal then chooses novel foods because they have not been associated with illness. A new food that eliminates the deficiency makes the animal feel better and becomes preferred because its taste is associated with well-being. This would not account for the rapid preference changes that occur with salt depletion, but it may well account for preferences that take more time to develop. The learning hypothesis mainly requires that the animal be able to discriminate between the "good" food and the "bad" in order to show a preference. Harris, Clay, Hargreaves, and Ward (1933) indeed found that vitamin B deficiency was corrected by dietary choice if the vitamin were tagged with a distinctive flavor (licorice) so the animal could discriminate it, but not otherwise.

Many studies (see reviews by Rozin & Kalat, 1971; Revusky & Garcia, 1970) show that rats avoid foods associated with illness produced by X-rays or drugs (apomorphine for instance). Furthermore, the food (conditioned stimulus) is presented several *hours* before the radiation or drug (unconditioned stimulus). This upsets any simple notions about the necessity of close contiguity between conditioned and unconditioned stimuli. It has been proposed that the aftertaste of food in the mouth when animals are made ill is the actual CS, and hence there really is a short CS-UCS interval. This is pretty clearly disproven by the fact that animals can differentiate between dry lab chow (paired with illness) and wet mash made from the same lab chow (but not paired with illness). After several hours, there should be no difference in aftertaste, but the animals show avoidance of the appropriate food modes. Apparently, the animals remember what they ate.

*Poison avoidance: interference and learned safety.* According to *interference theory* (Revusky & Garcia, 1970), the CS-UCS interval can span hours because there are no *interfering* taste stimuli between CS and UCS. This is experimentally necessary because a taste stimulus closer to the UCS would be the one conditioned. With external stimuli, however, many new stimuli inevitably come between CS and UCS if the interval is long. Such later stimuli would interfere with the intended CS-UCS association.

According to *learned safety theory* (e.g., Rozin & Kalat, 1971), animals avoid dangerous tastes but accept safe ones. All rats taste new stimuli very tentatively and wild rats are especially "neophobic"—fearful of new stimuli. But after a while, if nothing happens, the new stimulus (including food) is considered safe and the animal returns to it. A new food associated with illness is dangerous, however, and avoided. The theory, then, is that animals avoid foods that are associated with illness and tentatively try out new foods until they find one that is safe, and this becomes associated with well-being. The great biological advantage of this kind of mechanism is that it allows for "specific hunger" for practically anything.

There may be different laws of learning (due to different types of neural connections) for taste in relation to illness than for the typical classical conditioning experiment. Garcia and Ervin (1968) did not get differential aversion to one of two external stimulus characteristics of food (two sizes of food pellet) with X-rays as a UCS. There was a discrimination, however, if electric shock followed one size but not the other. They hypothesized that it is easy to develop external (size)-external (shock) associations or internal (taste)-internal (illness) pairings, but difficult to develop external-internal associations.

*Early experience.* Young rats just weaning prefer foods that their mothers eat, and even further back, prefer foods their mothers ate while pregnant. In the latter instance, we presume that the food taste worked its way into the amniotic fluid to affect the unborn infant. In either case, the young rats become familiar with particular "safe" tastes and subsequently prefer them (Galef, 1971; Galef & Henderson, 1972). These learning mechanisms help account for food preferences of entire cultures (for example, hot Mexican food versus bland English food).

In summary, two different mechanisms seem related to specific hungers. First, there are *automatic* changes in taste preference due to deprivation, as with saline. This may also apply to sugars for species that have sugar preferences. Sweet substances are consumed in greater quantity and preferred at higher concentrations by animals that are food deprived (e.g., Collier & Myers, 1961; Beck & Ellis, 1966; Jacobs & Sharma, 1969). Malfunction of the mechanism underlying normal taste preferences may partly explain the finickiness of hypothalamus-lesioned animals. Second, there is a change in preference due to *learning*. Tastes (and related stimuli) may be avoided or approached depending on whether they are associated with danger (illness) or safety (well-being), or whether they were familiarized during early development.

### Ecological Approaches to Feeding Behavior

It has generally been implied here that a *depletion-repletion* model accounts for much feeding behavior. A reduction of energy supplies (depletion) sets various mechanisms into operation to trigger feeding until there is a recovery of the lost energy supplies (repletion). We also noted counterexamples, however — palatability and social factors in particular.

*Collier's Approach.*     Collier and his associates (e.g., Collier, Kanarek, Hirsch, & Marwine, 1976; Collier, Hirsch, & Hamlin, 1972) have taken the opposite tack. They argue that either animals or people *rarely* eat because they are depleted. Rather, they eat to *prevent* depletion. We can readily show that laboratory eating or drinking increases with deprivation, but we seldom see or hear of this in nature. In fact, laboratory animals in their home cages are not normally food depleted when they initiate eating. The depletion-repletion model predicts that feeding should be correlated with amount of time since the last meal (or until the next one), but such correlations are rarely found. Laboratory animals do not starve themselves to the extent that we usually deprive them to get them to press levers or run mazes. Each kind of animal in its own particular ecological niche comes to know (whether by nature, nurture, or a combination) what to do to keep itself from getting overly hungry most of the time.

Collier and his colleagues (1976) conclude there are two different sets of factors important for feeding. The first is that a particular kind of animal in a particular environmental niche adjusts its feeding capabilities to the situation. This is an interaction between species and situation. The various strategies tend to keep animals from getting depleted. The second set of factors is based on body weight loss and is an emergency system that comes into play when the preventive mechanisms do not work. A third set of factors about which Collier has also importantly increased our understanding over the years is taste and palatability of foods. These factors also operate to induce eating or drinking in nondeprived animals or people.

*Optimal foraging theory.*   The basic assumption of optimal foraging theory is as follows: *Organisms search for and eat food so as to get the maximum caloric input for the least amount of work.* This is an oversimplification but catches the flavor of the approach (but see Kamil, Krebs, & Pulliam, 1987). The *net energy* to be gained from pursuing a particular type of prey (or nuts, or whatever) will depend on the *expected energy* to be gained by searching for and "handling" a particular prey, divided by the amount of *time and energy used* to capture and eat that prey. The theoretical details, derived largely from economic theory, are more complicated than this, cast in terms of probabilities of finding prey of particular energy values.

The theory assumes that animals are in some sense aware of the probability of obtaining a given kind of prey with a particular caloric value, and can also take into account the amount of energy expended in hunting down and consuming the prey. Given these capabilities, animals are said to choose foods in an *optimal* way. That is, they will engage in *optimal foraging.* A point of contention among theorists is what specifically is *meant* by optimum? If we *assume* that animals are engaging in optimal foraging, then *whatever* a surviving animal does may be considered optimal. This, of course, is a circular argument. A number of specific predictions from the theory have been proposed, however, and these help to break out of the circularity (Gray, 1987):

1. *Select profitable prey*, the prey which produces the most energy per amount of work involved.
2. *Be more selective when profitable prey are abundant.* If there are many prey one can become choosy, but if there are few, take what you can get.
3. *As long as a better food is available, it should be chosen.*
4. *There are no "partial preferences"*; the optimal food should always be chosen if it is available.

How well do the available data support these assumptions? According to Gray (1987), the data do *not* offer very good support. For example, the assumption that there are no-partial-preferences is contradicted by much evidence showing that organisms *do* change food preferences from time to time, although some species are more rigid than others in their food preferences. One prediction which has received some support concerns *risk-aversive* behavior. The prediction is that, as organisms are better fed they will take fewer risks in their food search. For example, a well-fed animal might prefer a food which has a 100% chance of providing 3 grams of energy over a food for which there is a 50% chance at 6 g. The *expected value* (3 g) is the same in both cases ($1.00 \times 3$ g $= .50 \times 6$ g). A hungrier animal, however, is predicted to engage in riskier behavior, to gamble for the bigger meal. There is good data to support this notion (see Fantino, 1987; Stephens & Krebs, 1986). In an experiment with *yellow-eyed juncos,* Caraco, Martindale, and Whittam (1980) compared various combinations of fixed and variable numbers of seeds. When the birds were in a state of *positive energy balance* (not needing food), they were risk aversive, choosing the fixed number of seeds. But when they were in a state of *negative energy balance* the birds were risk prone (choosing the variable numbers of seeds). Thus, even birds shift from being more liberal while hungry to more conservative when well fed. In general, however, Gray argues that animals show considerable flexibility in the way they hunt and eat. This is further illustrated in a study by Johnson and Collier (1987), who had rats press levers for access to either of two diets which varied in number of calories provided and in the number of lever presses required to get the food. The rats always included *both* kinds of food in their diets (thus failing to support the partial-preference assumption) and were influenced by the amount of work and the number of calories provided by the alternative food available (thus denying the assumption of staying with the best food).

Fantino (1987) has proposed, on the basis of operant conditioning research, what he calls the *delay reduction hypothesis.* This hypothesis says that a stimulus becomes a (secondary) reinforcer if it correlates with a reduction in the amount of time to receive food. The greater the reduction, the more reinforcing the stimulus. For example, a pigeon pecking at either of two keys prefers the key with the short delay. This seems to fit into optimal foraging theory by suggesting a principle by which organisms can maximize their energy gain. A shorter delay means more reinforcement, hence more energy, in a fixed amount of time.

It is still too early to say whether optimal foraging theory is a better account of feeding behavior than more psychologically oriented approaches, but the theory is interesting and does provide a broader picture of feeding behavior than that gleaned from the more typical laboratory experiments.

### Hunger and Obesity in Humans

Although a widely recognized health problem, little solid psychological research has been devoted to obesity until recently. Some of the most influential research, by Stanley Schachter and his associates, has compared eating by obese humans as closely as possible with that of hypothalamic hyperphagic rats (e.g., Schachter, 1971a, b). The two species are remarkably similar. Both eat faster, are more finicky, and are influenced to eat more in the presence of food than are normal-weight subjects, but will not work more for food. One particularly ingenious experiment is described by Schachter (1971b, p. 135) as follows: "When a subject arrived he was asked simply to sit at the experimenter's desk and fill out a variety of personality tests and questionnaires. Besides the usual student litter, there was a bag of almonds on the desk. The experimenter helped herself to a nut, invited the subject to do the same, and then left him alone with his questionnaires and nuts for 15 minutes. There were two sets of conditions. In one, the nuts had shells on them; in the other the nuts had no shells. I assume we agree that eating nuts with shells is considerably more work than eating nuts with no shells."

The striking result was that 10 of 20 normal-weight subjects ate nuts with shells and 11 of 20 ate them without shells. Of the overweight subjects, however, only 1 of 20 ate them with shells, while 19 of 20 ate them without shells. Similarly, 22% of normal-weight patrons of Chinese and Japanese restaurants were observed to engage in eating with chopsticks, which is presumably more work (for Americans) than using a knife and fork. Only about 5% of obese patrons used chopsticks, however.

Schachter relates the eating of obese subjects to emotionality, arguing that the obese person is more reactive to external stimuli than the normal-weight person, who is more reactive to internal cues for eating. An extensive series of experiments has supported this hypothesis. The whole approach has somewhat fallen on hard times, however. First, hypothalamic hyperphagic rats do not always show the characteristics on which this line of research was based. Secondly, Rodin (1981) has reviewed the human obesity research and repudiated the idea that obese individuals are either more or less responsive to environmental stimuli than are normal-weight individuals. Nevertheless, Schachter's hypothesis was one of the most research-stimulating ideas to appear in the study of obesity.

## THIRST

### Background

People may survive for weeks without food, with relatively little subjective discomfort. In a hot, dry environment, however, a person without water may die a most unpleasant death in a matter of hours. We cannot store water in our bodies as we store food (in fat), and there is continual water loss through evaporation during breathing and perspiration, and by urination. Without sufficient water, our bodies become a hostile environment to the individual cells within. The problem of water regulation has been "solved" in different ways by different species. Some desert animals, such as the kangaroo rat, can survive *without drinking at all*. They metabolize water from dry seeds. Neither laboratory rat nor human, who are very close cousins when it comes to thirst, can do this, and must rely on water consumption. We shall limit our discussion here to domesticated mammals, with the understanding that there are differences among even these.

Two sets of mechanisms control drinking, regulatory and nonregulatory. Regulatory drinking is done to offset a water deficit, to maintain homeostatic balance. Nonregulatory drinking is done for reasons besides maintaining homeostasis, social drinking for example. In sufficient amount, nonregulatory drinking alone could compensate for water loss. Regulatory drinking at some point is generally a necessity, however.

### Regulatory Drinking

*The stimulus to water drinking.*   Animals can be induced to drink, or to work for water, by water deprivation, eating dry food, working in a hot environment, consuming excess salt, or losing blood. Each of these conditions might be used to define thirst. As with hunger, however, it would seem that there must be some smaller number of internal mechanisms activated by these various conditions. Walter Cannon, for example, thought that a dry mouth was the common element which excites drinking. As noted earlier, this has been disproven as the sole factor in drinking, but the search for other stimuli to drinking has continued.

*The double depletion hypothesis.*   Two well-defined systems for the initiation of regulatory drinking have been identified. The first system, depending on relative concentrations of salts, is an *osmotic gradient* between intracellular and extracellular fluid spaces. The second system is sensitive to the volume of fluid in the body. These two factors must be teased apart experimentally in order to see how the mechanisms work.

*The osmotic gradient: an intracellular mechanism.* If saline solution more concentrated than about 0.9% (the normal concentration of body fluids) is injected into an animal, drinking is stimulated. This occurs without any change in fluid volume. Two things do happen. In Figure 4-3 we see a body cell and its *intracellular fluid* surrounded by *extracellular fluid,* which is all

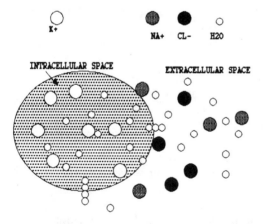

**FIGURE 4-3.**   Water readily passes through the cell membrane, moving in the direction of greater concentration. Sodium, chloride, and potassium do not cross the cell membrane readily. Therefore, if water is lost for the extracellular space, water leaves the intracellular space, shrinking the cell and stimulating drinking.

body fluids not found inside cells. When salt is put into the extracellular fluid, water is pulled from the less concentrated fluid inside the cell. Water easily passes through the cell membrane, but salt does not. Gilman (1937) demonstrated that the difference in concentration inside and outside the cell was critical. He injected dogs with urea, a substance which readily passes into the cell so that there is an equal increase in concentration both inside the cell and out. In contrast to saline, urea produced very little drinking. Specialized cells, called *osmoreceptors*, detect the concentration difference and signal the brain to initiate appropriate action.

Any mechanical distortion of the "osmoreceptors" may be sufficient, however. If salts are *removed* from the extracellular space, water moves *into* the cell and makes it swell (osmosis working in the opposite direction). This also stimulates drinking. Indeed, it may lead to a condition called *water intoxication*, characterized by excessive drinking and urination, and mental aberration. The treatment, paradoxically, is to give the patient *more* salt. The water then leaves the cells, which return to normal size, and excessive drinking is no longer stimulated.

*The site of the osmoreceptor.* The hypothalamus and surrounding areas are crucial to water regulation, which involves *conservation* of water as well as increased intake. When the *supraoptic nucleus* of the hypothalamus is damaged, animals engage in excessive drinking and urination (known clinically as *diabetes insipidus*). In the normal animal, the supraoptic nucleus manufactures *antidiuretic hormone* (ADH), which is released when the animal is water deprived. This hormone increases the rate of reabsorption of water from the kidneys, so that not as much is lost by excretion. Without ADH, the animal urinates excessively and has to drink excessively to make up the loss (Ranson, Fischer, & Ingram, 1938). Injection of saline into the carotid artery, which supplies the hypothalamus with blood, stimulates drinking and decreases urine output. Direct injections of very small quantities of saline into the hypothalamus also induce drinking (Andersson, 1952). Drinking can also be elicited by electrical stimulation of the hypothalamus and limbic system, and by various drugs placed in small quantity into the limbic system (e.g., Fisher, 1964).

*Fluid volume: the extracellular mechanism.* Thirst often accompanies blood loss, vomiting, or diarrhea, even though these do not change osmotic pressure (Wolf, 1958). Fitzsimmons (1972) and others have shown that if the blood supply to the kidneys is reduced, drinking increases. For example, if the aorta is tied off above the renal arteries (which carry blood to the kidneys), drinking increases, as it does if the vena cava (going directly to the heart) is blocked. There appear to be independent sets of *pressure receptors* in the heart and in the renal blood supplies (Carlson, 1980). These receptors may send direct signals to the brain, but they also initiate a major chemical mechanism. When the venous pressure drops, the kidneys release *renin* into the bloodstream, which is in effect a "thirst hormone." The renin reacts with another substance to form *angiotensin,* which acts on brain receptors to incite drinking. Injected directly into the brain, angiotensin is the most powerful stimulus to drinking yet found. The location of the brain receptors for angiotensin has provided a lively dispute among those interested in the problem, but the two prime candidates (the *subfornical organ* and the *organum vascularis of the lamina terminalis*) both lie near the *ventricles* of the brain, in the vicinity of the hypothalamus.

### Drinking elicited by eating

In the normal animal, as well as the hypothalamus-lesioned animals, there is a positive correlation between eating and drinking. While LH-lesioned animals may drink to lubricate their mouths when they eat, other factors also affect the prandial drinking of the normal animal. Drinking occurs when *histamine* receptors in the intestines are activated by food in the stomach (Kraly, 1984). It appears that insulin is released upon eating, and the insulin, in turn, stimulates the release of histamine from endocrine-like cells in the gastric lining. The animal then drinks. Serotonin, another neurotransmitter, may also be released when the rat eats and stimulates drinking in its own right. Histamine and serotonin effects on drinking are due to two independent mechanisms whose effects are synergistic: Together they produce greater drinking than either by itself (Kraly, Simansky, Coogan, & Trattner, 1985). The histamine and serotonin effects are eliminated if the vagus nerve from the stomach is cut, so there is no signal from the stomach to the brain via the autonomic nervous system.

### Taste factors

If thirsty animals have their drinking water adulterated with a small amount of quinine (a bitter taste), they drink less. When the animals are made thirstier by further deprivation, they drink more of the adulterated fluid. Miller (1959) made this the basis of his "quinine test" for thirst: The thirstier an animal is, the more quinine it will tolerate in its drinking water. We might conjecture, then, that when an animal is thirsty water tastes better. The "good" taste balances out the "bad' taste of quinine. Conversely, non-hungry or hungry rats prefer water with sugar in it to plain water. Indeed, water by itself is not a very attractive substance to such animals. If forced to lap water from a tube to avoid shock, rats let the water dribble out of their mouths without really drinking it (Williams & Teitelbaum, 1956). If they are deprived of water, however, the same animals readily consume water, and also show a greater relative preference for water as compared to sugar water. For example, the lowest concentration at which the rat shows a preference for sucrose solution over water is higher when animals are water deprived (Beck, Self, & Carter, 1964; Sclafani & Nissenbaum, 1987). In fact, if the animal can obtain only small amounts of solution at a time, there is no apparent preference for sugar water over plain water (Beck & Bidwell, 1974; Beck, Nash, Viernstein, & Gordon, 1972). Under extreme conditions, water may be preferred to sugar solution (Cohen & Tokieda, 1972). Recall, also, that LH-lesioned animals early in recovery drink only sweet solutions, as if a mechanism for making water taste good to the normal animal had been impaired. From such data as the above, we begin to piece together the picture of an animal which finds water not very palatable unless thirsty. When thirsty, however, water palatability increases to the extent that it overrides the bitterness of quinine and competes with the sweetness of sugar. In short, water is more palatable when an animal is water-deprived, just as salt is more palatable when an animal is salt-deprived.

A number of experiments suggest another explanation, however. Increased palatability might be due to cooling of the mouth and throat. Mendelsohn and Chillag (1970), for example, reported that thirsty rats would lick at a drinking spout which delivered a stream of cool air instead of water. To study the cooling effect in humans, Boulze, Montastruc, and Cabanac (1983) studied the relation between water temperature, affective ratings of water, and amount consumed by humans dehydrated by profuse sweating or mountain climbing. As water temperature increased from about 32° F to about 56° F, the amount drunk increased. Beyond 56° F the amount drunk declined as temperature increased. Pleasantness of water taste, however, never increased with increasing temperature, and taste became unpleasant at higher temperatures. Both rat and human data thus suggest that mouth cooling is a major factor in the "liking" for water. In sum, as Toates (1979) pointed out, drinking is under the control of many different factors, not just some homeostatically determined need for a certain amount of water.

### Stop cues

According to the regulatory model, when an animal has drunk an amount of water sufficient to offset its deficit, it should stop drinking. Indeed, there is rather nice evidence that after injections of saline, rats accurately consume enough water to restore proper concentrations of body fluids—that is, to dilute the salt to body-fluid concentration (Corbit, 1969). There must be some kind of "meter" running, however, to tell the animal when it has had "enough." There are several possible cues, but there is no specific brain area known to be a satiety area for drinking.

*Mouth metering.* If a fistula (a tube) is inserted into the esophagus of a dog so that ingested fluid does not reach the stomach, the dog will drink an amount of water proportional to the number of hours it has been without water. In absolute terms, it may drink twice as much as it actually needs, but the intake is still proportional to the need (Bellows, 1939). Since a normal dog offsets its water deficit with nearly 100% accuracy, mouth metering cannot be the only cutoff mechanism. It does seem a useful one, however. There is also evidence for osmoreceptors in the mouth (Nicholaidis, 1968), so water passing through the mouth may also "turn off" the stimuli to drinking.

*Stomach distention.*   To determine if a "full" (distended) stomach might be a cutoff cue for drinking, Towbin (1949) put balloons into the stomachs of thirsty dogs, and found that as more air was pumped into the balloon the dogs drank less. On the other hand, if a thirsty dog has tubed directly into its stomach enough water to offset its deficit, it will immediately drink the same amount of water all over again, as if it did not know it had been tube-filled with water. If drinking is delayed for just a few minutes after tubing water into the stomach, however, the animal does *not* drink. This whole sequence is just the opposite of how stomach distention should work (the animal should not drink just after tubing, but should drink after a delay). It therefore does not seem that stomach distention is a potent cue for cutting off drinking in normal animals. Water may not be effective in producing distention because water drains through the stomach very quickly as the animal drinks. Substances with more bulk (like solid food) or with greater concentration (like sugars), which do not clear the stomach as quickly as water, may produce more stomach distention and thus cut off consumption. This, however, is not the same as distention by consumed water.

*Reversal of the initiating stimulus.*   Water ingestion has often been thought to cease before there is time to reverse the stimulus that triggered drinking. In fact, however, about 25% of water tubed into the stomach of the rat is absorbed within 15 minutes (e.g., O'Kelly & Beck, 1960). Novin (1962), recording changes in electrical resistance of fluids in the region of the hypothalamus, found them to change within 10 minutes of the onset of drinking by the rat. In other words, water was getting from the intestine to the brain within 10 minutes, several minutes before the rats voluntarily stopped drinking. Reversal of the initiating stimulus, then, may be another cutoff cue.

### Nonregulatory Factors in Drinking

*Ecology, effort, and satiation.*   In the natural environment of animals, where food and water are more or less easy to come by, we might expect ease of availability to influence the amount consumed. A simple regulatory theory would say that the animal should drink until it offsets its imbalance, but a more ecologically oriented argument would take availability factors into account. A number of experiments (e.g., see Toates, 1979) show that, even with an unlimited supply of water available, rats consistently drink less when more effort is required to obtain water. For example, if animals have to press a lever to obtain water, they take less water when more presses are required.

Similarly, when rats were required to run six feet to obtain each sip of water they stopped running after obtaining far less water than animals running only two feet (O'Kelly & Beck, 1960). The amount of water required to "satiate" an animal therefore depends on factors other than just the amount of water needed to offset a deficit, including amount of water drunk, effort to get the water, taste, and perhaps other variables.

*Taste.* The rat *can* regulate its water balance without smelling or tasting water, by pressing a lever which produces a squirt of water directly into its stomach (Teitelbaum & Epstein, 1963). A normal animal, however, *does* have taste and smell to guide it, and behavioral studies show that these are important in water-regulatory behavior. As mentioned, animals do show an increased preference for water when thirsty, although they drink tastier fluids when these are available. Humans drink great quantities of soft drinks for taste alone (e.g., sugar- and caffeine-free drinks), which reduces the need to drink water at other times. Thus, taste may indirectly be part of the regulatory mechanism for drinking.

### Learning of Hunger or Thirst?

There is little evidence that hunger or thirst can be directly conditioned to external stimuli in the way that fear can be conditioned (Mowrer, 1960; Wright, 1965; Enscore, Monk, Kozub, & Blick, 1976). A different question is whether animals have to *learn to be hungry in the first place.* Ghent (1957) argued that they do. For example, if a rat is restricted to eating only one hour a day, it eats less than in 24 hours, but over a period of days it eats progressively more. Ghent argued that the animals are learning to be hungry (or thirsty, in the case of similar results with water deprivation). Other authors have agreed with this position (e.g., Wong, 1976, 1979).

Such deprivation-schedule effects seem likely to be due to a cumulative physiological deficit, however (Beck, 1962, 1964, 1979). Animals on repeated water-deprivation-and-recovery cycles drink the same amount on each cycle. This has also been shown for food deprivation and eating (Williams, 1968), as well as lever pressing for food (Tang & Collier, 1971). These experiments, as well as research on recovery from deprivation (Kutscher, 1964), are contrary to the learning hypothesis. If animals have experience with a deprivation schedule, they begin eating or drinking more quickly when given food or water (Hatton & Almli, 1967; Schmidt, Stewart, & Perez, 1967; Bolles, 1962), but this may be the instrumental learning of approach to food or water, not learning to be hungry or thirsty. Quicker consummatory activity also might occur with experience because the animals have become adjusted to the situation and do not spend any time exploring the environment. Finally, Fitzsimmons and LeMagnen (1969) reported data suggesting that rats learn to *anticipate* the osmotic water deficit which results from eating hypertonic food. Specifically, they shifted rats from a high-carbohydrate (low thirst-arousal) diet to a high-protein (high thirst-arousal) diet. In the first few days, the animals drank more *after* the meal, but gradually began to drink more *during* the meal, as if anticipating thirst. This is useful to the rat, as well as to people, but learning to *anticipate* being thirsty is not exactly the same as learning to *be* thirsty.

## TASTE

As a physiological model for motivation, the taste system is nearly ideal in several regards. Taste is important. It involves approach and avoidance behaviors and is related to the regulation of hunger; some aspects of taste stimuli can be quantitatively manipulated; and there are some correlates of taste and neural activity. Few motivational systems can make such claims.

### Taste Qualities and Their Stimuli

In humans, there are four commonly accepted taste qualities: sweet, bitter, salty, and sour. The prototype stimuli for the four taste qualities are sucrose, quinine, sodium chloride, and hydrochloric acid. Other taste qualities seem to be either a combination of these four or a mixture of taste and smell. Stimuli entering the mouth can be detected in the nose, and vice versa. A fifth taste quality, *umami*, is referred to in Japanese taste research. Represented by the taste of *monosodium glutamate*, umami may be roughly translated as "delicious taste." It appears to be a combination of the four primary qualities, however, and is not reported in research outside Japan (Lawless, 1987).

Chemically, salty taste is produced by water-soluble salts, with both positive and negative ions contributing to the salt taste. With sour, the degree of acid taste is correlated with the concentration of hydrogen (H+) ions, with a number of different acids having the same taste. Sweet taste is produced by a variety of organic compounds, including sugars, glycols, and alcohols, with no specific chemical similarities among them yet known. Similarly, there is no known specific chemical structure for all stimuli having a bitter taste.

### Taste and Motivation

As discussed, taste is a powerful determinant of what foods are preferred and ingested (Mattes & Mela, 1986). In fact, taste (and smell) have a variety of effects on motivation-related activities. For example, taste may actually affect the absorption of nutrients from the intestine and stimulate salivary and gastric secretions important for digestion (Mattes, 1987).

All the details of the sensory-motivational link are not yet known, but they involve "sensory" inputs splitting off to go into "motivational" neural structures. At some point, the taste pathways must branch off into the limbic system and hypothalamus, for example; otherwise damage to these structures would not affect an animal's taste preferences, as with lateral hypothalamic lesions.

Having defined motivation in terms of preference and aversion, we may consider taste stimuli as motivational since they affect preference and aversion. Of particular significance is the quantitative relationship between preference *behavior* and specific taste qualities. Figure 4–4 shows the relationship between taste preferences for the four prototype stimuli and the magnitude of neural responses, recorded from appropriate nerves running from the tongue. For sucrose and salt, increasing rates of neural firing are related to inverted-U functions for preference and aversion. For bitter and sour, however, increasing rates of neural firing are related only to declining preference, from a baseline of 50% preference for distilled water. Most food tastes are combinations, such as for lemonade, which is both sweet and sour, so the

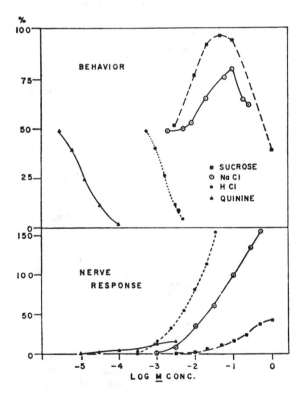

**FIGURE 4–4.**  Composite graph of behavioral and afferent neural responses in the rat. Upper figure shows the preference-aversion responses as percentage intake as a function of stimulus concentration. Lower figure shows neural responses in arbitrary units. (From Pfaffmann, The pleasures of sensation. *Psychological Review*, 1960, *67*, p. 257. Copyright © 1960 by the American Psychological Association. Reprinted by permission.)

taste preference story is much more complicated than Figure 4–4 indicates. But we can immediately see in Figure 4–4 that by itself rate of firing does not define the degree of desirability of a particular taste stimulus, nor indicate the effort to approach or avoid the taste. The role of taste in everyday life and behavior is sorely underestimated in much of psychology and needs to be looked at a great deal more.

## SUMMARY

1. Physiological approaches to motivation can be divided into *broad theories* (attempting to account for many behaviors with a few common principles) and *specific system theories* (dealing with such specific motives as hunger or thirst).
2. *Peripheral theories* have emphasized events outside the central nervous system, whereas *central theories* have emphasized the role of the brain in regulating internal states. The hypothalamus and limbic system are especially important.
3. From the point of view of systems theory, body weight is *regulated* by equalizing energy inputs and outputs.
4. The *dual hypothalamic theory* of hunger says that the *lateral hypothalamus* is *excitatory* for feeding activity and the *ventromedial nucleus* of the hypothalamus is *inhibitory* for feeding. The theory is partly correct, but many more brain areas are involved in feeding.
5. Lesions of the lateral hypothalamus produce self-starvation, which has been related to changes in the *taste* of food and to impairment of *movement*. Both deficits may be related to destruction of nerve cells manufacturing the neurotransmitter *dopamine*.
6. *Start mechanisms* for feeding involve structures sensitive to changes in blood levels of *glucose, fat,* and *amino acids.*
7. *Stop mechanisms* for feeding involve the release of peptides in the gut (*glucagon, cholecystokinin, bombesin*). These may reduce the palatability of food. Other mechanisms involve *volume* of food in the stomach or intestine, and dehydration from ingested food. Satiation may be specific to certain foods, which suggests other chemical mechanisms.
8. Many organisms have *specific* hungers for particular foods or tastes. These may be biologically programmed (such as with salt) or based on the association of particular foods with good or ill health. Early experience with particular foods modifies taste preferences of individuals and even of entire cultures.
9. The above approaches to eating involve *depletion* of body stores. Many animals eat *before* they are hungry, however, and *avoid* getting very hungry. Different species handle this in different ways. *Optimal foraging theory* is an economics theory approach to how organisms go about choosing foods.
10. According to the *double-depletion theory*, the stimuli to drinking are *increased concentration of body fluid* due to water loss and *reduced volume of body water*. The former is detected by osmoreceptors in the hypothalamus and the latter by *pressure receptors* in the vascular system. Reduced pressure triggers a chemical reaction, which leads to stimulation of hypothalamic cells by a chemical called

*angiotensin*, which elicits drinking behavior. Drinking is also stimulated by *histamine* and *serotonin*, which are released when food is ingested.

11.  The *palatability* of fluid is an important factor in water regulation. This involves *taste* but also seems to involve the *cooling* effects of water.

12.  Drinking is *terminated* by cues from the *mouth* and *stomach*, and by rapid absorption of water, which turns off the cues which initiated drinking. Termination of drinking is also determined by such behavioral factors as the amount of effort required to get water, so satiation is not determined by some fixed quantity of water consumed.

13.  *Taste* underlies important motivational systems, either approach or avoidance. The four "standard" human taste qualities are sweet, bitter, salty, and sour, with many tastes being combinations of these and also involving *smell*. The importance of taste and smell is well known experimentally but is also reflected in the sale of "junk" foods whose attractiveness is based on palatability.

# 5

# Thermoregulation, Brain Stimulation, Sex, and Addictions

## THERMOREGULATION

Extremes of temperature, high or low, are aversive, and we work hard to escape or avoid them. The largest energy use of the year comes during summer heat waves when air conditioning is at its peak. The second largest is in winter cold spells. In the extreme, we all know of the failures of temperature regulation, death by freezing or heatstroke. In fact, however, these are rare events and animals and people survive very well in extreme environments. Polar land animals survive in subzero temperatures, and sea animals survive in subfreezing waters (because of its salt content sea water freezes below 32° F). A combination of anatomical characteristics (such as fat and fur insulation), homeostatic mechanisms, and behaviors combine to keep body temperature within the range required for survival. Temperature regulation is important because temperature is one of the major variables in the chemical reactions necessary for life. The proper utilization and transfer of substances within the body, including nerve transmission, involve chemical reactions which must occur within an appropriate temperature range if they are to occur at all.

Cold-blooded animals, such as fish, amphibians, and reptiles, are *poikilothermic*, which is to say that their body temperature is usually slightly higher than that of the surrounding environment. Warm-blooded animals, such as mammals and birds, are *homeothermic*, maintaining a nearly constant internal temperature in spite of changing environmental temperature. The "constant" temperature actually fluctuates regularly with the time of day in accordance with the *circadian rhythm* of the animal, the so-called *biological clock*. Many of our body processes wax and wane with approximately a 24-hour cycle. The "normal" temperature for humans is slightly higher in the afternoon (about 37° C) than during the night (about 36° C) (Kalat, 1988). A constant body temperature also permits animals to be equally active at many different environmental temperatures. Cold-blooded animals are more sluggish when the temperature is low.

### Mechanisms of Temperature Regulation

One of the body's first rules of temperature regulation is to protect the brain and vital organs at the expense of peripheral parts. When the temperature goes down, peripheral blood vessels contract so that less blood is exposed to cold air and less heat is lost. We are all aware that our fingers and hands get cold before our bodies do, sometimes with frostbite resulting. About half of our body cooling occurs from exposure of the head and neck to the environment; hence, the admonishment, if your hands get cold put on a hat. That is, cold hands are a signal that body temperature is going down, and by covering the head, you slow down the loss of body heat. Other responses of the body include generation of heat by shivering and fluffing of the fur (with furry animals).

When we get too hot, the opposite reactions occur. Peripheral blood vessels expand so that more blood passes under the surface of the skin and is cooled, and we perspire so that we are cooled even more when the perspiration evaporates. Cats lick their fur and cool themselves by evaporation of the saliva. Dogs cool primarily by evaporation from the mouth and tongue when they pant.

*Brain mechanisms of thermoregulation.* The hypothalamus plays a major role in thermoregulation, just as it does in hunger and thirst. The *preoptic area* of the hypothalamus monitors body temperature and activates homeostatic mechanisms for raising or lowering temperature. If a device called a *thermode* is inserted into the preoptic nucleus, thermoregulatory mechanisms can be manipulated experimentally. The thermode can be warmed or cooled, thereby fooling the preoptic nucleus into believing the body is warming or cooling. If the thermode is cooled, an animal shivers; if the thermode is warmed, the animal pants or perspires. These effects occur within a constant laboratory environment. If the preoptic nucleus is damaged, animals do not show appropriate thermoregulation and have large fluctuations (e.g., 10° C) in body temperature. However, the preoptic nucleus is not the only part of the brain or body involved in temperature regulation. There are also temperature receptors in the skin and spinal cord, and areas of the brain other than the hypothalamus are involved.

Eating and drinking are also affected by temperature regulatory systems. When the preoptic nucleus is cooled, animals eat more and drink less, but when it is warmed they drink more and eat less. Reduced food intake in warm environments may occur because the increased specific dynamic action of food ingestion may generate an uncomfortable increase in body temperature.

The preoptic nucleus seemed for a number of years to fit the ideal model of a thermostat. It is set at 37° C. If the temperature goes down, the preoptic nucleus instigates warming activities; if temperature goes up, cooling activities are instigated. A problem for this notion (Satinoff, 1983) is that, when there is preoptic damage so severe that shivering or sweating, or other automatic mechanisms do not go into action, animals will still thermoregulate behaviorally, such as by pressing a lever to warm or cool themselves. This means that thermoregulation is not destroyed, only that one aspect of it is changed (Satinoff, 1983).

*Thermoregulatory behavior.* Within limits, warm-blooded animals can maintain constant body temperature with homeostatic mechanisms, but what happens with cold-blooded animals or warm-blooded ones in more extreme environments? Poikilothermic animals have only their behavior to fall back on, and what they do is move to warmer or cooler environments. Fish can move to shallower or deeper water to warm or cool, and desert reptiles can move about seeking sunnier or shadier spots. Some desert animals, having to face extreme temperature differences between night and day, burrow into the ground at night and slowly come out into the sun in the morning. As the day heats up they burrow again to keep cool.

Satinoff (1983) points out that psychologists generally think of behavior as being more complicated than homeostatic regulatory mechanisms, but that physiologists often think of behavior as being simpler. In the case of thermoregulation, Satinoff says (1983, pp. 461–462): "The responses to thermal stress are many and varied, but in the beginning was behavior ... all species tested, from insects through humans, show behavioral temperature selection." Even single-celled organisms show *thermotaxis,* moving toward or away from areas of extreme water temperatures to areas of more moderate temperatures. There is no simpler response.

### Organization of Thermoregulatory Responses

Satinoff (1983) argues against the notion that there is a single "thermostat" in the preoptic nucleus; there is simply too much evidence to the contrary. In particular, destruction of the preoptic nucleus does not lead to complete failure of temperature regulation. What the preoptic nucleus seems to do in the normal course of events is *organize* or *integrate* the activities of a number of different thermoregulatory responses, including behavioral. If the preoptic nucleus is made inoperative, these specific thermoregulatory responses are still available and thermoregulation can still occur. For example, shivering may not occur, but moving to a warmer location may.

Satinoff also points out that thermoregulatory mechanisms did not evolve only as thermoregulatory mechanisms. Panting in dogs, for example, cools a dog which has been running, but also increases the amount of oxygen consumed. With alligators, there is greater heat loss if their mouths are open than if they are closed, a variation on dog panting. Such variation suggests that there is no reason to believe that there should have evolved a single thermoregulatory center in the brain. Rather, various specific responses evolved which individually may operate at the level of the spinal cord, but which also gradually came under the control of higher brain centers, such as the hypothalamus. Destruction of the higher control centers does not destroy the responses and thermoregulation still occurs. It does not occur as a single response which is turned on by a hypothalamic thermostat, however.

### Fever

When someone feels sick, the first thing we do is take his or her temperature to determine how serious the illness is. If oral temperature is much above 98.6° F (37° C), we consider taking some action. With infants, one of the first things we do is try to reduce the body temperature, by washing the baby with lukewarm water, for example. But why does temperature go up at all when we are sick? Fever is not the illness, but a symptom of the body's response to infections by viruses or bacteria. When foreign substances enter the body, white blood cells are mobilized to fight those substances. The white blood cells (*leukocytes*) release a protein called *leukocytic pyrogen*, which causes production of *prostaglandin E*, which, in a yet unknown manner, acts on the preoptic nucleus to increase body temperature.

Does a fever in itself do us any good? Again, temperature is an important variable in chemical reactions, and some bacteria grow less well at elevated body temperatures (Kluger & Rottenberg, 1979). Therefore, fever may have direct value in fighting disease. From a strictly motivational point of view, however, fevers (or the conditions with which they are associated) are usually unpleasant and we do all we can to get rid of them.

## SEXUAL MOTIVATION

Sex is as much a survival motive as hunger or thirst, and sexual motivation can be more powerful than either of these. Much of the early psychology of motivation, beginning with the work of Freud, was related to sex. Freud's work was more concerned with the clinical manifestations of sexual problems than with an understanding of the nature of sex itself, however.

Animal researchers studied sexual motivation in rodents in the 1930's. For example, Warden (1931) compared the number of times that rats would cross an electrified floor to reach various goal objects. He found that one day without sex was a more compelling motive than a day without food or water; male rats made more crossings to reach a female than to get to food or drink. After several days of deprivation, however, hunger and thirst were more powerful. Warden hoped, in these early studies of animal drive, to be able to determine what drives were strongest. As noted in chapter 4, however, the story is more complicated, since specific goal characteristics are also important determinants of goal-directed behavior. This is true of sex. Sexual behavior is not entirely "driven" by internal states any more than eating or drinking are entirely driven by internal states.

Sex differs from other biological motives as hunger and thirst in a very important way: Sex is not a homeostatic motive. Sexual deprivation is not a life-threatening departure from homeostatic balance. Total abstinence from sex by all members of a bisexual species would be a biological disaster for the species, however, since the species would die out in a generation. One religious extremist group, the Shakers, did die out because it required total sexual abstinence by its adherents. We may presume, however, that sex evolved into such a powerful motive because animals with this motivation did reproduce more and hence were favored by natural selection.

Sexual arousal very much depends on an interaction between internal states and external stimuli. Some species, deer for example, will mate only when their hormone levels are high, which may be for only a few weeks a year for either males or females. But when they do mate, it still is only with appropriate members of their own species, determined by stimulus factors.

### Stimulus Factors in Sex

*Visual and auditory signals.*   Many different stimulus elements determine sexual attraction. Among birds, for example, there are complex courtship rituals. Male birds are usually more flamboyant in plumage and coloration than are females, and they use these characteristics to attract females. Different species also have their own specific mating signals. Crickets have their calls, frogs have theirs, and mockingbirds have theirs. Obviously, these animals do not respond to calls of the other species. Mockingbirds are an unusual case of signalling. They have about five *hundred* different calls during mating season and a different 500 calls during the "off" season. It is not clear just what they do with all the information-sending capacity, but it would seem to be sex-related.

*Chemical stimuli.*   Some animals, such as moths, have powerful airborne chemical sex attractants called *pheromones* to entice potential mates. These chemical stimuli have direct effects on the physiology or behavior of their recipients. The effects of pheromones may depend on hormones in the recipient. For example, castration decreases a male hamster's interest in female odors (Gregory, Engle, & Pfaff, 1975). It appears that male sex hormones excite neural circuits in the amygdala so that these brain circuits respond to the odor of vaginal secretions (Carlson, 1987).

Smell plays a role in primate sexual behaviors, but there do not seem to be any pheromones which excite specific unlearned sexual behaviors in either humans or other primates (Carlson, 1987). Swabbing a female monkey with strange odors increases the interest of a male, even when the odors bear little conceivable relation to normal sexual attraction (such as chemicals that smell like green peppers!). Such novel odors probably just arouse curiosity. Familiar odors may also play a role in sexual attraction because they are associated with a particular individual and produce sexual arousal because of this association.

*Individual differences in attraction.*   Within a species, some members have particular attractiveness to others. This obviously applies to people, but it also applies to dogs. Frank Beach (1969) found that male beagles had reliable but different preferences for particular females. Females also had their own preferences, however, and some females rejected the amorous advances of particular males even though other females accepted the advances of those males. It is not clear why such preferences occurred, but it is clear that a mutual attraction between male and female had to be present before things progressed any further.

Stimulus variation also plays a role in sexual attraction. Male animals which have copulated to the point of exhaustion with a particular female partner will immediately resume their activity if a new partner is presented. In fact, Beamer, Bermant, and Clegg (1969) provided a ram with a new female after each ejaculation and found the animal able to ejaculate in less than two minutes with each of twelve different females. This is not typical, even for a ram. The "exhaustion" found with repeated intercourse is not just a physical inability to perform. It involves a "psychological" factor, perhaps akin to boredom. Among humans, it is not uncommon to find that stimulus variation produces an increase in sexual activity.

### Internal Factors: Arousal versus Arousability

When we discuss internal factors in sex we need to distinguish between sexual *arousal* and sexual *arousability* (Whalen, 1966). Arousability refers to the ease or rapidity with which sexual arousal occurs. An animal or person may not be aroused at a particular moment, but may be aroused with greater or lesser ease. An animal with a new partner may be easily aroused by appropriate stimulation. We would conclude that the animal was previously arousable, even though not aroused by the previous partner. Our heroic ram, described above, was highly arousable.

Among such "lower" mammals as rodents, arousability is largely determined by sex hormones, the *androgens* (primarily *testosterone*) in males and *estrogens* in females. Castrated farm animals lose their interest in sex and do not engage in sexual activity, and laboratory experiments clearly show the role of sex hormones in this activity. If castrated animals are given hormone replacement therapy (injections of testosterone) they resume sexual activity as long as the hormone lasts. Interest again wanes until further injections. Human males, on the other hand, may be sexually aroused and display sexual interest long after castration. Similarly, some men show considerable sexual activity at advanced ages when testosterone levels are very low. Human females are also sexually aroused and engage in sexual behavior after hormones have been reduced to very low levels, after menopause for example. Such observations of humans indicate that sexual arousal is under neural control more for humans than for other animals. This may be due to greater cognitive abilities, such as engaging in sexual fantasies, which presumably requires a complex brain. Since we know little of the fantasies of nonverbal species, however, we cannot be sure that fantasizing is uniquely human. We do know from such surveys as the Kinsey reports (Kinsey et al., 1948, 1953), from sales of popular magazines, and from videotape rentals, that humans do actively engage in sexual fantasies.

## Human Sexual Behavior

*Hormone effects.*   Human sexual behavior is influenced by hormones but is not fully determined by them. For example, if a male had female hormone replacement therapy he would not act like a female just because of this. Conversely, testosterone treatment will not cause a woman to lose sexual interest in men (Carlson, 1987). Excessive exposure to androgens during the prenatal period has been associated with somewhat different social characteristics in adult females. For example, they consider themselves more "tomboyish" and are more athletic. At the same time, however, they show the same level of satisfaction with a female sex role and various activities associated with this role as do non-androgenized control subjects (Money & Ehrhardt, 1972). The interpretation of the androgen effects is another matter, however. For example, androgens may lead to greater physical activity and hence to more male-like behaviors (Carlson, 1986). None of these are "abnormal" behaviors, however, and may be worthy of comment only because they are different from the "feminine" stereotype. Women may engage in many nonstereotypical activities if given opportunities to do so.

*The human sexual response.*   The most dramatic breakthrough in human sexual research came with the pioneering studies by Masters and Johnson (1966). Using direct observation as well as color cinematography and physiological recordings, they arrived at some general characteristics of both male and female sexual responses. Both male and female responses are divided into the following four phases, characterized by general body changes as well as reactions of sex organs. Not all of these occur with every individual, and some may be so brief that they are not noticed without the aid of recording instruments.

1.  *Excitement.* Sexual excitement may be produced by fantasy, looking at pictures, physical contact, or a variety of other stimuli. Nipple erection is common in females but also occurs in some males. There is sometimes a reddening of the skin of the chest and head, called a "sex tension flush." In females this may spread to lower parts of the body. Males show penile erection, which may occur in seconds (and reverse just as fast), and females have vaginal lubrication and thickening of the vaginal walls. Female breast size may also begin to increase.
2.  *Plateau.* Arousal increases with sustained stimulation. There is an increased frequency of sex tension flush, general muscular tension, spasmodic movements of wrists and ankles, hyperventilation, and increased heart rate (100–160 beats per minute). Female breast size may increase as much as 25% above prestimulation baseline, along with other changes in the sex organs. The circumference of the corona of the penis may increase twofold, change to a purplish color, and emit from the Cowper's gland a fluid which deacidifies the interior of the penis and provides lubrication.
3.  *Orgasm.* At the peak of sexual excitement there are specific muscle contractions, related to pelvic thrusting as well as abdominal and facial muscles. In

males there is contraction of the various accessory organs necessary for ejaculation. The female shows corresponding contractions of the uterus and genital area. The actual climax, expulsion of semen by the male and vaginal contraction by the female, takes only a few seconds and once started is not under voluntary control.

4. *Resolution.* After climax there is often a sweating reaction by both male and female, but this is not related to actual exertion. There is also hyperventilation and high heart rate, which may be largely due to physical exertion. Males show a "refractory period," with reduced penile erection. During this refractory period, which may last from minutes to hours, the male cannot readily be rearoused. Females, clearly showing the greater durability of their half of the species, can maintain continuously high levels of sexual arousal, with no refractory period. A female may reach climax many times during a sexual episode where the male climaxes only once.

The Masters and Johnson type of research has been criticized on the grounds that it deals only with the mechanical aspects of sex, ignoring the roles of love and affection. This is true, and the reason is simple: Any research can deal with only a limited number of questions at a time. The Masters and Johnson research was not intended to answer all possible questions about sexual responses. Later chapters in this text deal more with love and affection, the more social side of sex.

### Sexual Orientation

Most people experience sexual attraction and arousal toward members of the opposite sex, but a significant minority (about 4% of males and 1% of females) are exclusively attracted to persons of the same sex. The percentages are higher if we include people who have a bisexual orientation. Homosexuality has long been a hotly debated topic. It has been viewed as sinful, deviant, an illness, and as perfectly normal activity. What is clear is that the male homosexual population, for example, has a wide range of members whose only common characteristic seems to be homosexuality. The male homosexual is not necessarily effeminate. Alexander the Great of Macedonia, conqueror of the ancient world, was homosexual, as have been some stars of the National Football League. Similarly, female homosexuals are not necessarily masculine in appearance or behavior.

The biological, psychological, and social factors which might affect sexual orientation have all been explored extensively, but thus far there is no single factor, or even a set of factors, known to produce heterosexuality or homosexuality. It should be pointed out that it is just as reasonable a question to ask why someone is heterosexual as to ask why someone is homosexual. If heterosexuality is explained, so probably will be homosexuality. It helps little to say that heterosexuality is "natural," since all that tells us is that most people are heterosexual; it does not tell us why. Supposed biblical exhortations are not useful biological or psychological accounts, although such dogma may give some insight into social explanations.

What is most clear, perhaps, is that homosexuality is not due to just a preponderance of a particular hormone. A castrated male who is injected with female hormones does not become homosexual, nor does a female who is ovariectomized and given male hormones. Present evidence indicates that homosexual males have normal levels of androgens (Carlson, 1987), although two lines of evidence suggest the possibility of a biological factor. First, many homosexual men show a female type of hormonal response if injected with estrogen (Gladue, Green, & Hellman, 1984). Second, abnormally high levels of testosterone injected into a pregnant sheep at a critical time during gestation may produce a lesbian offspring (Money, 1987). An interesting bit of evidence comes from studies of twins, where we have identical genetic composition. If one identical (monozygotic) twin is homosexual, the other is likely to be homosexual as well (Zuger, 1976). This suggests, but certainly does not prove, that a biological factor is involved in homosexuality, since identical twins are likely to have similar environments. In a family which had three pairs of identical twins, two pairs were homosexual but the third pair was heterosexual. This would seem to eliminate environmental factors as sole determinants of homosexuality, since all the twins might be expected to be of the same sexual orientation if reared in the same family. The reason for searching for such biological factors is that social factors do not seem to account for homosexual orientation (Storms, 1983 a, b). There simply is no strong evidence that interpersonal relationships within a family, such as a domineering mother and a weak father, lead to male homosexuality.

## ELECTRICAL SELF-STIMULATION OF THE BRAIN (ESSB)

### Background

Suppose you were to accidentally walk into a psychology laboratory one day and spy a rat furiously pressing a lever in a Skinner box. You might think to yourself, that must be one hungry rat. As you look closer, however, you observe that there is no food or water or any other visible reward for this vigorous activity. You also note that the animal has a small contraption connected to the top of its head. You ask someone what is going on and discover that when the animal presses the lever it gets a brief surge of weak electrical current passed into its brain, and that animals will forgo eating, drinking, or sex just for the thrill of brain stimulation. This stimulation is one of the most powerful motivating forces known for dogs, cats, rats, and monkeys.

Research on electrical stimulation burst upon the scene in 1954 when Olds and Milner (1954) reported that electrical stimulation of areas deep in the rat brain is a powerful reward, and Delgado, Roberts, and Miller (1954) found that such electrical stimulation could be punishing. The relevance to motivation is dramatic: We may have the neural mechanisms for positive and negative emotions, or rewards and punishments, pinpointed. There had been stimulation research before this, of course, but this had dealt with more specific behaviors rather than the generalized reward/punishment phenomena.

Olds and Milner first noticed that their animals continually returned to a part of an open field apparatus where they happened to have been when briefly shocked by a tiny electrical current through the brain electrodes. It was as if the rats found the shocks pleasant. Guessing that the effect was rewarding, they tested rats in a different situation, the T-maze, and found the animals would go to the side where the stimulation was obtained. Finally, they reasoned that if the current were rewarding the animals would turn it on repeatedly by pressing a lever in a Skinner box arrangement like that diagrammed in Figure 5-1. The stimulation had rewarding effects on three

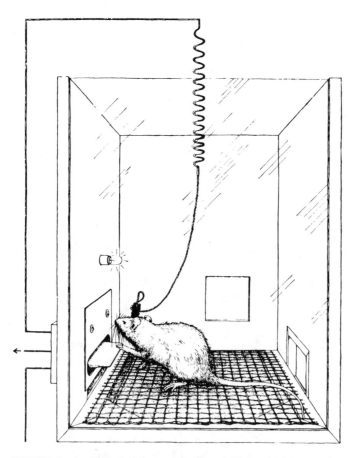

FIGURE 5-1.    A self-stimulation circuit is diagrammed here. When the rat presses on the treadle, it triggers an electric stimulus to its brain and simultaneously records action via wire at left. (From Olds, Pleasure centers in the brain. *Scientific American,* 1956, *195,* p. 108. Copyright ©1956 by Scientific American, Inc. Reprinted by permission.)

arbitrarily defined behaviors, so it clearly is a general effect, not specific to a particular behavior.

Figure 5–2 shows a cumulative lever-pressing curve for a single animal tested over thirteen hours. The animal pressed steadily when rewarded by brain stimulation, but stopped pressing when the current was eliminated.

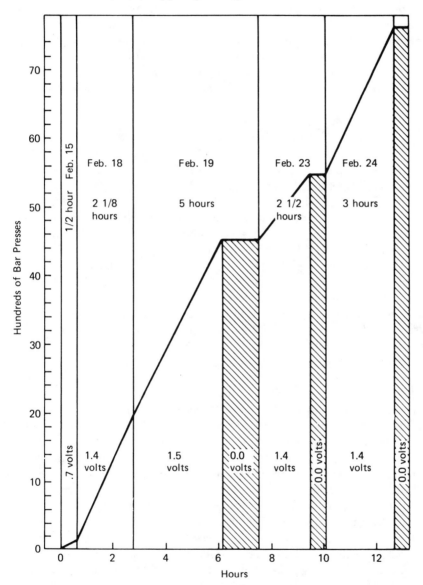

**FIGURE 5–2.**   Smoothed cumulative response curve for a rat. (From Olds & Milner, Positive reinforcement produced by electrical stimulation of the septal area and other regions of the rat brain. *Journal of Comparative and Physiological Psychology,* 1954, *47,* p. 424. Copyright © 1954 by the American Psychological Association. Reprinted by permission.)

Olds (1958) showed data from an animal that responded about 2,000 times an hour for twenty-four consecutive hours before collapsing from fatigue. Since the animals were neither deprived nor in pain, it seemed they were seeking the stimulation; the phrase "pleasure centers" was coined to describe the phenomenon. This phrase, of course, says only that brain stimulation is a strong reward. An immediate implication of the discovery was that it was incompatible with the then-influential drive reduction theory of reinforcement, and many further questions have been raised. What parts of the brain are involved in reward and what parts in punishment? Do conventional reinforcers like food and water have their effects via these same brain areas? Does brain stimulation function like conventional reinforcers such as food or electric shock?

### Loci of Positive and Negative Effects

The first step in determining effective stimulation sites is to put an electrode into some specific brain area which is located by reference to a brain atlas. The electrode is constructed of fine wire insulated everywhere but at the tip. An anesthetized animal is fixed rigidly into a *stereotaxic instrument* so that its head is immobile, and on the basis of standard "landmarks" on the skull, the stereotaxic instrument is used to put the electrode into the brain very precisely. After placement, the electrode is permanently attached to the skull with screws and cement, exposed leads sticking through the scalp for attachment of wires from the source of stimulation. (It is now possible to have radio-controlled stimulation so that wires are not necessary.) The shock duration is controlled by a timer turned on by either the experimenter or the animal pressing a lever. The animal suffers no ill effects from the procedure and lives normally in its home cage.

The exact electrode placement must be verified post mortem. On completion of the experiment, the animal is sacrificed by an overdose of anesthesia and its brain is perfused with formalin and removed from the skull. The area around the electrode site is cut into thin slices, and stained slices are mounted on microscope slides. From these slides, the exact location of the electrode tip is determined. Just prior to sacrificing the animal, a current strong enough to burn an area around the tip is passed through the electrode, leaving a hole in the brain that is easily seen in the slide. Referring back to the brain atlas, the electrode site is then determined. Figure 5-3 shows such a slide, magnified several times.

Olds (1961) examined over 200 electrode placements. About 60% of these, including all of the neocortex and most of the thalamus, were neither rewarding nor punishing. About 35% of the placements showed positive reinforcing effects, and only about 5% were punishing. Reward sites are found throughout the limbic system, but the most effective are in the lateral hypothalamic feeding area, followed by preoptic and septal areas, just in front

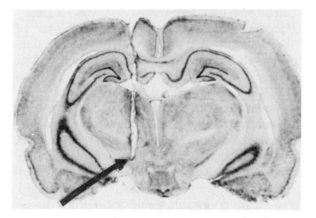

FIGURE 5-3.  Cross-section of the rat brain showing electrode track. The tip of the electrode (dark arrow) had been in the posterolateral hypothalamus, an area which produces high rates of electrical self-stimulation. The slide was stained with cresyl echt violet, which shows nerve cell bodies in a dark color. (Photograph courtesy of Drs. G. F. Koob, G. R. Sessions, G. E. Martin, and S. L. Meyerhoff of the Walter Reed Army Medical Center, Washington, D.C.)

of the hypothalamus. Pure negative reinforcement areas are scattered through the thalamus, dorsal tegmentum, and periventricular areas of the brain, generally closer to the midline of the brain than are the positive areas. These aversive areas do *not* correspond to the sensory pathways for pain. In several different mammalian species, equivalent brain areas are rewarding and punishing.

Recent anatomical and biochemical studies have revealed that locations ranging from the neocortex and frontal lobes all the way down to the brain stem can be rewarding with ESSB. These locations turn out to be those parts of the brain which utilize dopamine as a neurotransmitter (Stellar & Stellar, 1985), predominantly in the hypothalamus and limbic system. Stimulation of the dopamine system is very pleasurable to the animals, if the rate at which they work to get the stimulation is any indication of pleasure-seeking. This same dopamine system is considered by many researchers to be the brain location where addictive drugs have their pleasurable effects. This belief is bolstered by the fact that cocaine affects the brain in a manner similar to the effects of dopamine. Activation of the dopamine system by such natural causes as pleasant environmental stimulation, by such unnatural causes as drug ingestion, or by direct electrical activation, produces what can only be described as a pleasurable result.

Another kind of evidence relating the dopamine system to pleasure is found with schizophrenia. One characteristic of this disorder is lack of affect. One hypothesis to account for this is that dopaminergic neurons are destroyed by an inherited defect in the breakdown of dopamine in the synapse. A substance called 6-hydroxydopamine (6-HD) is formed and reabsorbed by the dopamine neuron. This substance is toxic to the neuron and, over a period of time, destroys the neuron so that dopamine transmission is greatly reduced. This presumably produces the reduced affect characteristic of schizophrenia. If given before neurons are too badly destroyed, the tranquilizing drug *chlorpromazine* protects the neurons from 6-HD and is a major treatment for schizophrenia.

All available evidence does not support the dopamine hypothesis for ESSB effects, however (Kalat, 1988). Research on the details of the neuron systems activated by ESSB do not match the known characteristics of dopamine neurons (Gallistel, Shizgal, & Yeomans, 1981). It seems that the brain stimulation electrode must be placed in a dopamine-rich area of the brain, but that release of dopamine is not the critical element. An alternative hypothesis is that endorphins are the key neurotransmitters for reward. Given the addictive effects of opiate drugs, this would not be surprising.

In humans, where electrodes have been inserted in a few severe clinical cases, behavior for positive reinforcing effects is far less "urgent" than the all-powerful effect seen with lower animals. The human reaction seems to be more of curiosity than pleasure.

### Similarities of ESSB to Other Rewards

An early question raised about ESSB was whether it functions like conventional rewards. Since some of the most effective sites for positive ESSB are the same areas that lead to "stimulus-bound" eating or drinking, consummatory behavior that persists only when the stimulus is turned on, is there some stimulus-bound behavior involved in ESSB reward? The answer is no, animals learn a maze for ESSB at the same rate as they learn it for food, and there is no possibility of stimulus-bound behavior in the maze. Positive ESSB is a motivational phenomenon, and many different responses can be learned to obtain ESSB.

Hoebel (1969) related food deprivation and satiation to electrical stimulation: Deprivation increases responding for ESSB and satiation reduces responding. Conversely, satiation increases responding to *turn off* stimulation of the lateral hypothalamus. Obese rats do not respond as much for lateral stimulation but increase their responding when they return to normal weights. All this suggests that ESSB works the way we would think it should if it were a neurological basis of more conventional rewards.

Olds argued, correctly it seems, that ESSB taps directly into generalized systems underlying all positive and negative reinforcers. It has also been pointed out (Trowill, Panksepp, & Gandelman, 1969) that, with nondeprived animals ESSB is a "pure" incentive, much like nutritionless but tasty saccharin. They showed that shifts in the intensity of ESSB produced corresponding behavioral changes. If various procedures for increasing incentive motivation are added to brain stimulation, animals respond more for ESSB (Hoebel, 1969). For example, allowing animals to eat during self-stimulation, wafting odor of peppermint by them, or dripping sucrose directly into the animals's mouths by tube when they are self-stimulating, all increase rate of responding for ESSB. In short, ESSB acts like an incentive whose effects can be modulated by other stimuli or by internal states (such as hunger).

## ADDICTIONS

Study of brain areas involved in what appear to be very high levels of pleasure leads us to look at addictions. A drug addict has an overwhelming craving for the drug to which he or she is addicted and this craving is a two-headed motivational monster. The addict first seeks the pleasure produced by the drug, then must seek relief from the pain and torment of not having the drug. These tandem motivational factors make it difficult to break away from even a life-threatening addiction. Drug addictions are hardly new, but the need to study and treat them has assumed a new importance as use of cocaine and crack has dramatically increased. Addictions to opiate drugs, including opium, morphine, and heroin, and to alcohol have been with us longer and are still major problems. But cocaine and crack seem to be even more addictive and life-threatening.

The two major classes of addicting drugs are the central nervous system depressants and excitants. The major types of depressants commonly used are alcohol, the barbiturates, the tranquilizers, and the opiates. The major excitants are the amphetamines and their close cousin, cocaine. Caffeine and nicotine are also addictive excitatory drugs.

### Addiction Characteristics

Addiction is generally defined by two major symptoms. First, the addict becomes increasingly tolerant of a drug. Tolerance means that more of the drug must be taken to produce the same effect, usually a pleasant or exciting experience. Second, the addict has withdrawal symptoms if the substance is withheld. These symptoms are feelings and physiological effects essentially the opposite of whatever the addicting substance produces. If a person is addicted to a drug which excites the central nervous system, such as amphetamine, the withdrawal symptoms are related to a depression of central nervous system activity.

One of the most addictive classes of drugs is the barbiturates, commonly used as sleeping pills. A person who had never taken the drug before would normally become sleepy with a single tablet. If the drug were taken frequently and repeatedly, however, many tablets would be required to produce the same degree of sleepiness, the addiction. A person taking many tablets is also at greater risk for an accidental overdose, passing over the line between sleepiness and life-threatening central nervous system depression. If the drug is suddenly withheld, the addicted individual shows symptoms of extreme agitation, and possible seizures and death. Drugs also show *cross-tolerance.* This means that if a person becomes tolerant to one type of drug, such as a central nervous system depressant like barbiturates, he or she is also tolerant in some degree to other central nervous system depressants, such as tranquilizers. In practical terms, mixing drugs is a very bad idea since two drugs may interact in some way unknown to the drug consumer.

### Theories of Addiction

*Opponent process theory.*    This theory is covered in more detail in chapter 6, but the basic principle of the theory (Solomon & Corbit, 1974; Solomon, 1980), in brief, is that when the circumstances producing a strong emotion are removed, you do not just feel neutral, you strongly feel the opposite emotion. This same principle can be used to account for drug addictions.

Suppose a friend of yours has been taking a "recreational" drug which makes him feel euphoric. He gradually requires more of the drug to get the same good feeling, and then the drug supply is cut off. Without the drug he feels very bad, very depressed, and very ill. His new experience is just the opposite of that which he felt while taking the drug, but is just as much determined by the drug as the earlier good experiences were. Both his addiction and the withdrawal experience are determined by the drug. According to opponent process theory, with successive drug experiences the negative effect of the drug becomes stronger and stronger until it begins to cancel out the positive emotional experience. This is the opponent process beginning to work. A stronger stimulus (more drug) is needed to produce the same level of positive emotion or excitement previously experienced. This is the addiction. When the positive effect of the drug wears off, the opponent process, the negative effect, lingers and is so strong that the addicted person feels he must have the drug to relieve this unpleasant experience. This develops into a vicious cycle. The more the drug is taken, the greater the tolerance, and the more unpleasant the opponent process when the drug wears off. When the addict goes off the drug, the system gradually comes back into "balance," unless the withdrawal symptoms are so severe that serious illness or death ensue. This may happen, for example, with barbiturate addictions.

*The dopamine depletion hypothesis.*    We have seen that the dopamine system in the brain is closely related to pleasure. Cocaine addiction is also hypothesized to occur in relation to dopamine depletion (Dackis & Gold, 1985). Cocaine addiction is somewhat different from that which occurs with sedative drugs in that the withdrawal symptoms for cocaine are less severe. The craving for cocaine is very strong, however. Dackis and Gold outline the following sequence of events as a possible explanation for cocaine addiction. If cocaine is put into the body, it quickly migrates to neuron areas where dopamine is the neurotransmitter, those areas underlying the pleasurable effects of reward. The cocaine triggers the release of dopamine (producing the pleasurable experience) but also blocks the normal re-uptake of dopamine into the neuron from the synapse. As the drug wears off, the brain has a shortage of the dopamine neurotransmitter and there are some withdrawal effects because the brain cannot respond pleasurably to the stimuli which are normally effective. Consequently, there is a great craving for more of the drug in order to re-create the euphoric experience. The addict may progress from "snorting" the drug up the nose to "freebasing," dissolving the drug and injecting it. The euphoric "rush" from freebasing occurs literally within a few seconds of injection.

If the very strong craving of the addict is to be reduced, the brain must start manufacturing its own dopamine again while the addict is not using the drug. This may be difficult, since the craving for the drug is so intense. The addict must have considerable social support for abstaining, and certainly no temptations to use the drug lest immediate relapse occur. All sorts of stimuli (such as social situations in which the drug has been taken) may become conditioned stimuli to increase the craving and lead to relapse. The power of the drug is evidenced by several highly publicized examples of million-dollar-a-year athletes whose careers have been ruined or jeopardized by cocaine addiction.

It is also likely that endorphins, the brain's own opiate-like transmitters, are involved in some addictions (Kalat, 1988). Therefore, in terms of brain chemistry, there may be multiple forms of addiction, but possibly with the same general principle. Opiate drugs could reduce the normal release of endorphins, just as cocaine reduces the availability of dopamine as a transmitter. Tolerance and withdrawal symptoms would then occur, but are more severe for opiates than for cocaine.

## SUMMARY

1. In order for animals to survive, their body temperatures must be protected, sometimes in the face of extreme shifts in environmental temperature. Cold-blooded animals have the same temperature as the surrounding environment and regulate temperature by selecting environments. Warm-blooded animals keep the same temperature in spite of changes in environment, utilizing a combination of behavioral and homeostatic mechanisms.

2.  When temperature drops, heat is first conserved for the internal organs of warm-blooded animals by constriction of peripheral blood vessels. When temperature rises, these vessels expand, producing evaporative cooling through perspiration.

3.  The *preoptic* area of the hypothalamus monitors body temperature and activates homeostatic mechanisms for raising or lowering temperature. If this area is damaged there are large fluctuations of body temperature. Even without the preoptic nucleus, however, warm-blooded animals can still regulate temperature behaviorally.

4.  The preoptic nucleus seems to organize a number of different thermoregulatory responses, homeostatic and behavioral. If there is damage to part of the system, other parts can still function. Most thermoregulatory responses (e.g., panting in dogs) are also parts of other functions (getting more oxygen), so thermoregulation can be maintained in the normal course of other events.

5.  *Fever* occurs when white blood cells stimulate the release of *prostaglandin E*, which acts on the hypothalamus to increase body temperature. Increased temperature may directly help fight disease by altering the body's chemical reactions to viruses or bacteria.

6.  Sex is a powerful biological motive for survival of the species, but it does not involve homeostatic mechanisms like hunger, thirst, or temperature regulation. Sexual deprivation is not life-threatening, but does involve complex interactions between environmental stimuli and internal states.

7.  Many kinds of visual, auditory, chemical, and tactile stimuli affect sexual arousal, depending on the particular species. Chemical substances called *pheromones* are released by many species and serve as olfactory sexual attractants, as perfumes are said to do. It is not clear that pheromones function among primates as they do among lower animals, however. Simple stimulus variation appears to be an important factor in sexual arousal.

8.  Internal factors, mainly sex hormones, affect sexual *arousal* and *arousability*. Arousal refers to the level of sexual motivation at the moment; arousability refers to the ease or rapidity of arousal. Two animals may be equally unaroused at the moment, but one may be much more easily aroused than the other.

9.  Human sexual behavior is influenced by hormones, but not fully determined by them. Thus, males or females injected with hormones of the opposite sex still behave much as they did before. The main effect of androgens (male sex hormones) on women may simply be to increase the amount of physical activity and hence give the appearance of male-like behavior.

10. The human sexual response has been divided by Masters and Johnson into four phases, said to characterize both males and females: (1) excitement, (2) plateau, (3) orgasm, and (4) resolution. Each phase is described in terms of specific physiological changes.

11. Sexual preferences, especially homosexuality, have engendered a great deal of heated debate, but the basis of homosexuality is not known. These two facts seem to stand clear: (1) Homosexuality is not caused by a dominance of one or another sex hormone, and (2) It is not related to any specific family constellation, such as a weak father and a domineering mother.

12. *Electrical stimulation* of the brains of many animals is powerfully rewarding or punishing, depending on the location of the electrode. The brain areas which

are rewarding have neurons with *dopamine* as the neurotransmitter. For many species, electrical stimulation of these areas is the most powerful reward known.

13.  There is evidence that the stimulating electrode must be in a dopamine area, but that release of some other substance, such as the brain-opiates (*endorphins*) may be the critical rewarding factor.

14.  *Drug addictions* involve overwhelming cravings for a specific drug for two reasons. First, the addict seeks the pleasure produced by the drug. Second, the addict seeks relief from the pain and torment of not having the drug because he or she has developed a *tolerance* for the drug and has *withdrawal symptoms*.

15.  According to *opponent process theory*, any event which has pleasurable physiological effects also arouses the opposite (unpleasant) effects, which are manifest when the pleasant effects wear off. These opposite effects (the opponent process in action) are the negative feelings which drive the addict to seek more drugs.

16.  A more directly physiological account of cocaine addiction is that cocaine triggers the release of dopamine (producing the pleasurable experience) but blocks the reabsorption of dopamine into the neuron so that there is less dopamine available for future pleasurable experience. More cocaine is then required to produce normal feelings of well-being.

# 6

# Positive Outcomes: Rewards as Reinforcers and Incentives

Rewards are behavioral outcomes that are desirable and worked for. In this chapter we look at rewards in two different ways: (1) as *reinforcers* for learning new behaviors, and (2) as incentive stimuli which motivate approach behaviors. Both these reward characteristics have received a great deal of attention.

## REWARDS AS REINFORCERS

Rewards are commonly called reinforcers because a response followed by a reward is "strengthened," or more likely to recur. Thorndike (1932) coined the phrase *Law of Effect* to say that the effect of a behavior (its consequences) determines whether the behavior will be repeated. A *weak* law of effect says just that reinforcers change behavior, without concern for *how* they work. Skinner's (1938) approach to operant conditioning represents this view. We can study *schedules of reinforcement,* for example, without having a theory of how reinforcers work. A *strong* law of effect says something about the *necessary* conditions of reinforcement. Hull (1943), for example argued that *drive reduction* was necessary for reinforcement. There is little argument that reinforcers "strengthen" behavior in the sense that reinforced behaviors are more likely to be repeated, but the theoretical accounts have been more disputable.[1] The various theories on rewards as reinforcers are classed as *response, motivational,* or *stimulus* theories.

### Response Theories

*Functional analysis.* Skinner and his followers have defined reinforcers *functionally,* saying that *any stimulus following a response which increases the probability of that response recurring is a reinforcer.* You just keep trying things until you find a stimulus which will do this. The functional approach has considerable practical utility, because it is often difficult to say *in advance* what will be a good reinforcer for a given person in a given situation. Years of experience may tell us that money or praise will be a good reinforcer, but even these tried-and-true stimuli sometimes fail to modify human behavior in the way we expect them to.

*The Premack principle.* Premack (1959) proposed a more systematic functional analysis, saying (p. 220) that *any Response A will reinforce any other Response B, if A has a higher response rate than B.* If a rat licks at a water tube at a higher rate than it presses a lever, then licking can reinforce lever

---

[1]Some authors (e.g., Postman, 1947) have argued that the concept of reinforcement is *circular,* that a reinforcer is known only by its effects on behavior. This would only be true, however, if the concept were applied to a single response in a single situation. If a stimulus such as food is reinforcing in many different situations for many different responses, as food is, then there is no circularity (Meehl, 1950).

pressing, but lever pressing cannot reinforce licking. This example seems trivially obvious, so Premack performed a number of other experiments, including the following: Schoolchildren were given their choice of operating a candy machine or a pinball machine, and according to their choices were designated as "eaters" or "manipulators." Subsequently, getting candy reinforced playing pinball for the eaters. and playing pinball reinforced getting candy for the manipulators. Premack himself (1971) eventually concluded that the *hedonic* properties of stimuli provided a simpler account of reinforcers than did the response rate theory. Nevertheless, Premack's original analysis was highly influential among workers in applied behavior modification. It follows, for example, that the sequencing of activities during a daily classroom routine can be arranged to advantage. Unpopular academic activities can be scheduled earlier and reinforced by popular activities which come later. Arithmetic might be followed by reading, which in turn might be followed by drawing.

*Elicitation theories.*    Denny and Adelman (1955) proposed that all that is required for reinforcement is that a response be repeatedly *elicited* by some stimulus. For example, if an animal gets food following lever pressing, it goes to the food and eats it. Going to the food reinforces lever pressing, eating reinforces going to the food. Thus:

LEVER PRESSING→ RUNNING TO FOOD → EATING FOOD

*Each response reinforces the preceding response.* The only relevance of food is that *food reliably elicits eating.* The main weakness with the theory is that stimuli can be reinforcing even when no reliable responses are elicited by the stimuli.

Sheffield (1966) proposed a similar theory, but limited to *consummatory* responses. Keeping in mind that this theory was mainly pitted against drive reduction theory, a number of provocative experiments supported Sheffield's position. For example, Sheffield, Wulff, and Backer (1951) showed that male rats would learn responses reinforced by copulation (a consummatory response) without ejaculation (drive reduction). The consummatory response interpretation is less convincing if we consider sexual arousal reinforcing in itself, but the experiment was in fact another nail in the coffin of drive reduction theory. Sheffield and Roby (1950) also reported that rats would work hard for nonnutritive (and non-drive-reducing) saccharin solution. This is also better interpreted in terms of taste, however, because the reinforcing effect is correlated with the concentration of the reinforcer, but not with the rate of licking at the reinforcer (Kraeling, 1961).

*The Glickman-Schiff biological theory.*    The above theories require that "reinforcing responses" actually occur. Glickman and Schiff (1967) suggested that a stimulus would be reinforcing if it just *activated the neural systems underlying responses even if an overt response did not occur.* Thus, for example, animals will normally eat if the lateral hypothalamus is electrically stimulated and food is available. Stimulation to the lateral hypothalamus is also a powerful reinforcer for lever pressing even when food is *not* available, however. This suggests that stimulation of the response system in the brain is adequate for reinforcement. Since we now know that reinforcing brain stimulation triggers the release of dopamine, it is less clear that stimulation of a *response* system is critical to reinforcement. The dopamine may produce positive affect, which is reinforcing.

### Motivational Theories

*Drive reduction theory.*   Drive reduction theory directly ties reinforcement to motivation by saying that drive reduction is a *necessary condition* for reinforcement (Hull, 1943). Without drive there can be no drive reduction. It is necessary to distinguish between *need reduction* and *drive stimulus reduction,* however. Thus, Miller (1951a, 1959) argued that *any strong stimulus has drive properties, but all need states do not produce stimuli.* For example. oxygen deficit is not discomforting and by itself has no identifiable drive properties. By this analysis, *drive stimulus reduction* is the reinforcing event, whether the drive stimulus is generated by some internal need such as hunger, or comes from an unpleasant external stimulus. Miller and Kessen (1952) supported this view by showing that milk *drunk* by a hungry rat was a better reinforcer in a T-maze than milk tubed directly into the stomach. Tubed milk was more reinforcing than tubed saline solution. They argued that if *need reduction* were the critical factor, the milk should be equally reinforcing whether drunk normally or tubed into the stomach. Therefore, drinking was reducing both drive stimulus intensity *and* need, whereas tubing reduced only need. Saline reduced neither. Such analytical experiments as this are important because the observation that food or water reinforce hungry or thirsty animals does not *necessarily* support the drive reduction theory. The palatability of ingested food might be the critical reinforcing factor, and the trick is to separate palatability from need/drive reduction.

*Evidence for drive reduction.*   Drive-reduction theory is supported by research on pain reduction, fear reduction, and reward-by-fistula (as in the Miller-Kessen experiment). Pain reduction is the clearest example of drive reduction. Pain (as from electric shock) is easy to control, and its termination, like getting rid of a toothache, is a powerful reinforcer. Since there is no observable incentive corresponding to food or water, shock reduction is often considered a "pure" case of drive reduction. Termination of almost any uncomfortably intense stimulus is demonstrably reinforcing.

Animals will learn new responses if reinforced by opportunity to escape from a fear-arousing environment (Miller, 1948). Escape from a fear-arousing compartment increases with such variables as the intensity of the shock used to condition the fear and the number of fear-conditioning trials given before testing the escape response (Kalish, 1954).

The sensory qualities of foods (taste, texture, etc.) can be eliminated as possible reinforcers by inserting a plastic tube (a fistula) directly into the stomach or bloodstream so that nutritive material bypasses the mouth and nose. Such injected foods are reinforcing, but there is also evidence that the *temperature* of fluids passing through the tube may be critical for reinforcement (Holman, 1969; Mendelson & Chillag, 1970). The fistula experiments therefore may not be "pure" tests of drive reduction.

*Evidence against drive reduction.*    The above evidence suggests that drive reduction may be a *sufficient* condition for reinforcement, but not that drive reduction is the *only* or *necessary* condition. Research shows that *neutral* or *exciting* events are also reinforcing. We have already seen that Sheffield's sex and saccharin studies challenge drive reduction theory, so let us look at what has been called the *pain-fear paradox* (Mowrer, 1960).

The paradox is that *whereas pain reinforces the learning of fear, pain punishes other responses.* Furthermore, a drive reduction theorist would have to say that it is the *end of pain* which reinforces fear learning. The paradox is resolved by experiments showing that the *onset of pain*, not the termination, reinforces fear learning (Mowrer & Aiken, 1954; Davitz, 1955). This led to the development of *two-factor theory,* which says that some responses are reinforced by *drive induction* (increase) and others by drive reduction.

*Arousal theory.*    Since arousal theory is discussed in detail in chapter 3, suffice it here to say that either *increases* or *decreases* in internal arousal can be reinforcing as long as they lead to a more optimal level of arousal.

### Stimulus Theories

*Hedonic reinforcers.*    Animals not under any known dietary deficiency, and never deprived of food or water, will press levers or run through mazes for sweet-tasting substances (e.g., Young, 1959). Taste, not drive reduction, seems to account for this. Drive reduction theorists have argued, however, that the sweet-tasting substances used in such experiments have been drive reducing. This is a weak argument, however, since it must make the unsupported assumption that the animals in such experiments were under some level of drive. It has also been argued that sweet tastes may have become *conditioned reinforcers* through their previous association with drive (hunger) reduction, especially during nursing. In fact, however, sweet substances *are preferred by newborn infants* before there is association of the sweet substances with hunger reduction (Jacobs, 1964; Lipsett, et. al., 1976). Newborn rats and newborn humans lick at and swallow sugar solutions placed on the lips almost immediately after birth, but they reject bitter solutions. Furthermore, even months of exposure to a bitter taste from birth on does not change the preference for sweet substances with guinea pigs (Warren & Pfaffman, 1958). Direct evidence for genetic differences in taste preference also argues against the learning interpretation (e.g., Ramirez & Fuller, 1976). Also the ability to taste phenylthiocarbamide (PTC) is genetic: It is tasteless to some people and bitter to others. In short, not all reinforcing taste preferences are based on association with drive reduction.

Learning *can* be involved in taste preferences, as shown in chapter 4. Galef and Henderson (1972) even found that weanling rats showed taste preferences similar to their mothers', possibly because the mother's diet was reflected in the taste of her milk and the infants thus became familiar with it. With humans, there is the interesting question of how different cultures manage to get their children to eat certain foods — such as hot chili peppers. Rozin and Schiller (1980) concluded from their research that chili burns just as much after years of exposure to it, but people come to *like* the burning sensation. Some reasons people find such masochistic meals pleasant are that peppery food may be associated with pleasant events (parties), that there are social rewards for eating it (praise), and there may be a kind of *constrained risk* of sensation-seeking (constrained because there is no real danger). Pepper-eating is not just "macho," either, since women like peppers as much as men do.

*Sex and brain stimulation.*  We shall only put some previous commentary into context here. First, sexual *arousal* appears to be very reinforcing. Second, electrical stimulation of the brain produces excitement in animals and is highly reinforcing.

*Stimulus change and information.*  Harry Harlow (1953) said: "It is my belief that the theory which describes learning as dependent upon drive reduction is false, that internal drive as such is a variable of little importance to learning, and that this small importance steadily decreases as we investigate learning problems of progressive complexity." He then went on to point out that he usually fed his laboratory monkeys *before* the experiment session. The monkeys stored food in their cheek pouches and then proceeded to swallow a little food after every response they made, whether the response was right or wrong. But the animals learned the correct responses. "It would seem" said Harlow, "that the Lord was simply unaware of drive reduction learning theory when he created, or permitted the gradual evolution of, the rhesus monkey." In general, Harlow made the point that external stimuli are more important sources of motivation than are internal drive states and suggested that the "main role of the primary drive seems to be one of altering the threshold for precurrent responses." That is, already available responses are simply made more likely to occur when an animal is deprived.

Monkeys will work for hours on puzzle-type problems without deprivation or external reinforcement. They will also work inside a dark box at a task which permits no more than a window opening so they can see out of the box. And, they are very active in exploring their environments. Indeed, even rats will choose the arm of a T-maze which leads to an explorable checkerboard-type maze rather than a plain box, and food deprivation actually reduces this tendency to explore (Montgomery, 1953).

When rats are run in a T-maze with no reward at all, they tend to alternate running to one side or the other on successive trials. That is, they tend *not* to go to the goal box they entered on the previous trial. This is called *spontaneous alternation behavior*. Two explanations proposed to account for alternation behavior are *response inhibition* and *stimulus satiation*. Response inhibition theory says the animal tends *not to repeat the same response*. Stimulus satiation theory says the animal tends *not to go to the same stimulus*. The animal becomes satiated for the stimulus just experienced and so goes to the alternate stimulus on the next trial because it is more novel, or informational. Both theories account equally well for simple alternation, so the following critical test of the theories has been conducted.

Animals are run without reinforcement in a T-maze where the left goal arm is white and the right goal arm is black (with appropriate controls for brightness in various groups). Assume that on Trial 1 the animals run to the *right*, choosing the *black* goal arm. On Trial 2, the animals are run in the maze with the colors of the goal boxes reversed. In which direction should they turn? According to response inhibition theory they should go to the *left* since they went to the right on the previous trial. According to stimulus satiation theory they should repeat the same response and go to the *right* because that is now where the alternate stimulus is. And a large number of experiments indicates they do go to the alternate stimulus: They alternate with reference to stimuli, not responses. Interestingly, it has also been found that animals alternate with reference to *absolute direction* (such as east versus west), not just light versus dark. This is still alternation with reference to stimuli, however.

Like most research stories, even such an apparently simple phenomenon as spontaneous alternation quickly becomes more complicated (Dember & Richman, 1989; Richman, Dember, & Kim, 1986–87). First, if the choices are side-by-side and readily visible from the same position, animals alternate with reference to *goal box brightness*. But if the choices are more discrete, alleys going in different directions in a T-maze, animals alternate with reference to *direction* (e.g., east versus west). And, under some conditions, it also appears that animals *do* alternate with reference to responses (Dember & Richman, 1989; Richman, Dember, & Kim, 1876–87). If animals under *low drive* (e.g., four hours' food deprivation) can obtain a food pellet following the choice of *either* arm in a T-maze, they alternate with reference to stimuli in early trials of "training." After many trials in the apparatus, however, they switch to alternating responses. It is as if the animals "switched off" environmental information which was useless to them and let their bodies run on automatic pilot. Indeed, most of us do this with such highly routine tasks as driving—until something goes wrong to attract our attention again.

A number of authors have proposed that *exposure to complex, changing stimuli is reinforcing*— (Dember & Richman, 1989). Dember and Earl (1957) proposed that there is an optimal level of stimulus complexity which is reinforcing and which varies from one individual to another. They further argued that organisms tend to respond to stimuli which are just a little more complex than the optimum. These are called *pacer stimuli.* Once an individual's preferred complexity level is established, any change in preference will be in the direction of greater complexity, not less. The capacity to deal with progressively more complex stimuli—psychological growth—is thus built into the theory.

The informational approach says that stimuli can be reinforcing simply by virtue of telling an organism, human or otherwise, something it did not already know. An experiment by Bower, McLean, and Meacham (1966) exemplifies this. Bower and colleagues asked whether *information* about the delay of reward would be reinforcing to pigeons even though this information could not change the delay. Given their choice of either of two keys to peck at, birds pecked over 90% of the time at a key which signaled whether a short or long delay was coming (by red or green light) and less than 10% at a key which turned on a white light whether the delay was long or short. The birds clearly preferred to know what was going on. There is undoubtedly considerable survival value to knowing what is happening in the environment.

*The "need for cognition."*     Are informational stimuli equally reinforcing for all people? Cacioppo and Petty (1982) devised a scale to assess the "need for cognition," which they defined as "the tendency for an individual to engage in and enjoy thinking." The scale has such items as "I really enjoy a task that involves coming up with new solutions to problems" and "When something I read confuses me, I just put it down and forget it" (scored negatively). They then had high- and low-scoring subjects do a simple or complex number-circling task for ten minutes. In the simple task, subjects were told to circle as many 1's, 5's, and 7's as they could from a list of 3,500 random digits. In the complex task, the subjects circled all 3's, any 6 that preceded a 7, and every other 4. The reported enjoyment of the task for each of the four conditions is summarized in Table 6–1, where a higher number on a 7-point scale means more enjoyable. Obviously, nobody was terribly thrilled by such a boring task, but the subjects with a high need for cognition did enjoy the complex task more than the simple one, and the low-need subjects

**TABLE 6-1    Reported Enjoyment from Performing the Number Circling Task by Subjects High and Low on Need for Cognition Scores. A 7-Point Scale was Used, With "1" Representing Low Enjoyment and "7" High Enjoyment.**

| GROUP | TASK | |
| --- | --- | --- |
| NEED FOR COGNITION | SIMPLE | COMPLEX |
| Low | 2.00 | 1.15 |
| High | 1.29 | 2.17 |

From Cacioppo, J.T. & Petty, R.E. The need for cognition. *Journal of personality and social psychology,* 1982, 42, 116–131, Table 4, p. 127. © Copyright 1982 by the American Psychological Association. Reprinted by permission.

enjoyed the simple task more. It thus appears there are individual differences in the degree to which information processing activities are found pleasant and, presumably, reinforcing.

### Secondary Reinforcement

*Background.*    Just as such "primary" biological drives as hunger and thirst do not influence our behavior much of the time, neither do their corresponding primary reinforcers, food and water. As a consequence, the concept of *secondary (acquired, conditioned) reinforcement* was devised. A secondary reinforcer is *a formerly neutral stimulus which, through association with a primary reinforcer, takes on some of the same functions as a primary reinforcer.* A primary reinforcer may be any established reinforcer, but we usually think of things like food and water as primary reinforcers. A buzzer previously associated with food may reinforce lever pressing. Secondary reinforcement has been used to account for much human behavior. Money, for example, is one of the most general secondary reinforcers, useful only in relation to some other commodity.

Four different *functions* are ascribed to secondary reinforcers: (1) reinforcing the learning of *new responses;* (2) *maintaining behavior during extinction;* (3) mediating *delay of reinforcement* by presenting a secondary reinforcer between the time a response is made and the delivery of a primary reinforcer; and (4) establishing and maintaining *schedules of reinforcement.* (See Wike, 1966; Hendry, 1969; Mowrer, 1960, for classic book-length discussions of secondary reinforcement.) Secondary reinforcers are supposed to do the things that primary reinforcers do, and then some (span a delay between responding and primary reinforcement). If a secondary reinforcer is periodically "reconditioned" (associated with its primary reinforcer) it may retain its potency almost indefinitely (Wike, 1966; Zimmerman, 1957; 1959).

The power of a secondary reinforcer depends on variables similar to those that affect the strength of classical conditioning (Wike, 1966). These include *number* of associations with a primary reinforcer, the *amount of* primary reinforcement, close *temporal* association with primary reinforcement, and *probability* that the secondary reinforcer will be followed by the primary reinforcer.

*Theories of secondary reinforcement.*  Theories of secondary reinforcement also fall into response, motivation, and stimulus categories.

*Response theories* say that a secondary reinforcer is just another stimulus which comes to elicit a response. If a clicking sound *elicits the response* of running to get food, it is an effective secondary reinforcer (Denny & Adelman, 1955; Bugelski, 1956).

*Motivational theories* are stretched, however, because secondary reinforcers *cannot reduce need* the way the primary reinforcers can (the sound of a buzzer is not likely to make us less hungry). A secondary reinforcer *might* reduce drive stimulus intensity, however (Mowrer, 1960). A somewhat critical test is whether a stimulus paired with shock termination can become a secondary reinforcer. There is virtually no evidence demonstrating that this can occur (Beck, 1961; LoLordo, 1969; Siegel & Milby, 1969). However, a stimulus which *signals a shock-free period of time* can become a secondary reinforcer (Moscovitch & LoLordo, 1969; Rescorla, 1969). The signalling property of the stimulus is apparently reinforcing, however, not drive stimulus reduction. Such a reinforcer may signal a period of *relaxation*. Denny (1971) argued that *relief* (decreased tension) occurs immediately after shock ends, but a *qualitatively different relaxation response* starts about fifteen to thirty seconds later. Denny suggested that a stimulus paired with relaxation can be reinforcing, but a stimulus paired with relief cannot.

*Stimulus theories* say that a stimulus becomes a secondary reinforcer if it provides *reliable and unique information* about a forthcoming primary reinforcer, such as a buzzer signalling that food is coming. A *redundant stimulus*, coming after another signal has already informed an animal that food is coming, is *not* a good secondary reinforcer (Egger & Miller, 1962, 1963). The most widely accepted theoretical view now is that a secondary reinforcer is a stimulus which is *positively correlated* with the occurrence of a primary reinforcer (Rescorla, 1987).

Several lines of evidence suggest that secondary reinforcers may be doing something other than reinforcing responses. For example, secondary reinforcers might be *energizing* behavior and not just *selectively reinforcing* certain responses. Animals become more active when a secondary reinforcer is presented; a response like lever pressing occurs more frequently even though the supposed reinforcer does not *follow* the response (e.g., Wyckoff, Sidowski, & Chambliss, 1958). This might be due to *frustration*, the secondary reinforcer exciting the animal as it signals food which does not come (see Lott, 1967; Amsel, 1968). It might also be another example of *adjunctive behavior*, which occurs when there is any kind of motivational arousal. In any case, interest has shifted towards thinking of secondary reinforcing stimuli as *incentives*, stimuli which arouse the anticipation of reward (e.g., Bindra, 1978).

## REWARDS AS INCENTIVES

### The Concept of Incentive

Having examined the idea that rewards work "backward" to reinforce responses, let us now explore the alternative notion that the *anticipation* of rewarding stimuli (incentives) is what affects behavior. Incentives, like drives, are said to "motivate" behavior, but drives differ from incentives in that (1) primary drives are biologically *inevitable*, such as getting hungry, and are *cyclic*, automatically occurring at periodic intervals. Incentive *motivation* is not so inevitable, because it develops through experience and can be aroused whenever the appropriate stimuli are present, not depending on a cyclic process.

### Importance of the Incentive Concept

Laboratory evidence favoring the importance of incentives in the motivation of behavior has been developing for well over half a century, providing data which are not easily accounted for by even the most strident drive theorist or the most liberal interpretation of drive theory. The following five different kinds of data are especially compelling.

1. *Amount of reward and reward shifts.* Animals reliably perform better (faster, more vigorously, more accurately) for large rewards than for small ones (see Black, 1969, for a review). This could mean either that the animals are more motivated or that they have learned better with large rewards. When animals are *shifted* from small to large rewards, however, their performance improves much more quickly than we would expect on the basis of response learning principles. The sudden changes are not accounted for by a change in drive, either, because drive (amount of deprivation) is held constant. This leaves incentive motivation the most viable alternative account.

The classic incentive shift study was by Crespi (1942). Rats received 1, 4, 16, or 256 small food pellets as reward at the end of a straight runway. The more pellets received, the faster the animals ran. When the number of pellets was increased or decreased the animals ran faster or slower, respectively. Figure 6-1 shows the shift effect resulting from an experiment patterned after Crespi's. Following the shift upward is an *overshooting* effect, known as the *elation effect*. The upshifted animals perform *better* at the new reward level than do animals which have been at the same large-reward level continuously. Conversely, there was an *undershooting* effect for downshifted animals, known as the *depression effect*. These exaggerated shift effects are theoretically important because they cannot be accounted for by changes in drive level or by response learning (the animals already know the response). Crespi (1944) suggested that the animals developed different amounts of anticipatory excitement, which he called *eagerness*, and said that this was related to learning only to the extent that the animal had to find out how much incentive it was getting before it exhibited the appropriate amount of eagerness. Many experiments (e.g., Zeaman, 1949) have replicated Crespi's general results.

   2. *Incentive contrast effects.* By *contrast effect* we mean that if different incentives are presented simultaneously or successively to the same animal, the animal will respond differently to them than if they were presented alone. This is exemplified by the elation and depression effects in the Crespi experiment. Animals respond more positively to the "better" of two stimuli and more negatively to the "worse" of two stimuli when the stimuli are contrasted. This holds true for either consummatory or instrumental responses (Flaherty, 1982; Flaherty & Rowan, 1986).

   3. *Quality of reward.* Different kinds of rewards have different incentive motivational properties. In 1924 Simmons showed that rodents performed better in a maze if rewarded with bread and milk than they did for rewards of sunflower seeds. In general, preferred substances are also better incentives. Guttman (1953; 1954) separated quality from quantity of reward by giving animals fixed amounts of different concentrations of sucrose or glucose

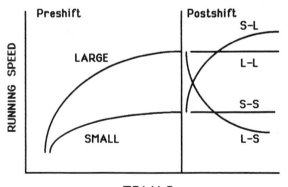

TRIALS

**FIGURE 6-1.**   Idealized presentation of the Crespi shift effect. During original training (preshift) animals run faster to large rewards than to small ones. After the shift, animals switched from small to large rewards (S-L) quickly increase their speed to a level even higher than that of animals continuously trained with large rewards (L-L). Conversely, animals shifted from large to small rewards (L-S) drop below the level of animals continuing to get small rewards (S-S).

solution when they pressed a lever. Response rate was highly correlated with concentration of reward, as shown in Figure 6-2.

4. *Deprivation effects*. Incentive theorists argue that deprivation does not directly energize behavior. Rather, deprivation enhances incentives. Hunger makes food a better incentive, and so on. Such enhancement is illustrated by the fact that preference for a specific flavor food increases if that food has been eaten when the animal is very hungry (Revusky, 1967; 1968). Curiously, one report found that animals tended to *avoid* foods consumed while very hungry, as if they did not want to be reminded of the long deprivation (Capaldi & Myers, 1982). Positive enhancement is the more frequently reported effect, however.

Deprivation effects are sometimes more spectacular when we compare

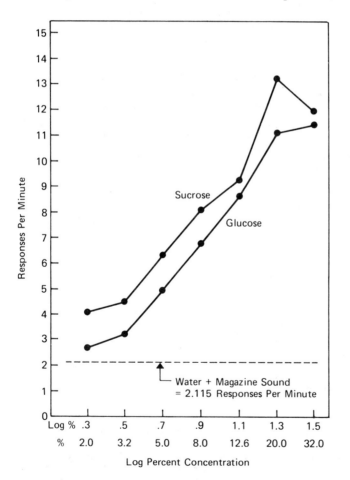

FIGURE 6-2.   Rate of bar pressing as a function of concentration of reinforcing agent. (From Guttman, 1954, p. 359. Copyright © 1954 by the American Psychological Association. Reprinted by permission.)

different *kinds* of deprivation rather than different amounts. For example, given the choice between 6% sucrose and water, hungry rats virtually always choose the sucrose but thirsty rats are almost indifferent between the two choices. Preferences are reversed simply by making the thirsty rats hungry and the hungry rats thirsty, as shown in Figure 6-3 (from Beck & Bidwell, 1974).

5. *Latent learning and latent extinction.* In a truly classic experiment, Tolman and Honzik (1930) demonstrated that learning and performance are not the same thing. They had three different groups of rats learn a complex maze. One group was rewarded with food in the goal box after each run, and showed progressively fewer errors. A second group was never rewarded and showed no improvement. A third group ran the maze for several days without reward and did not improve during this time. Reward was then introduced and the performance of this group improved almost immediately to the level of the first group (See Figure 6-4). This showed that reward was not necessary for *learning* the maze, but was necessary to get the animals to *perform* better. The learning was *latent*, not demonstrated in performance until reward was introduced. Many subsequent experiments validated the principle of latent learning (Thistlethwaite, 1951).

In the latent learning experiment, learning occurs without reward. In the *latent extinction* experiment, extinction occurs (at least partly) without the animal performing the response to be extinguished. Thus, two groups of animals are trained to run in a straight runway with food reward. One group

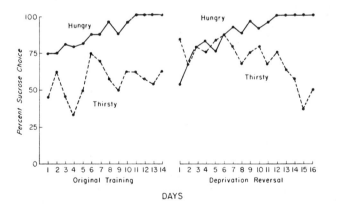

**FIGURE 6-3.** Preferences for eight percent sucrose over water by hungry or thirsty rats in a maze choice situation. The animals were run six trials a day and were forced to go to the nonpreferred side, if necessary, in order to equalize number of trials to each side. Equal experience with each incentive each day was thus guaranteed. After fourteen days of original training, each group was switched to the opposite deprivation condition (deprivation reversal) for the next sixteen days of training. In each case, the animals adjusted to the new deprivation condition by responding similarly to the behavior of the other group in the original deprived condition (sucrose preference increased quickly for the now-hungry animals and declined for the now-thirsty animals). (From Beck and Bidwell, Incentive properties of sucrose and saccharin under different deprivation conditions. *Learning and Motivation*, 1954, p. 331.)

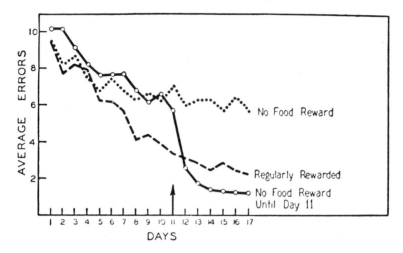

**FIGURE 6-4.** Evidence for the latent learning in the maze. With no food reward, there is some reduction in errors, but not as great a reduction as with regular food reward. Despite the higher error scores prior to the introduction of food, the group rewarded only from the 11th trial immediately begins to do as well as the group that had been regularly rewarded. The interpretation is that some learning went on within the first 10 trials, which did not show in performance until the food incentive activated it. (After Tolman and Honzik, published in 1930 by The Regents of the University of California; reprinted by permission of the University of California Press.)

is then placed in the goal box a number of times without food, the other is not. The running response is then extinguished in both groups by having the animals run to the empty goal box, the normal extinction procedure. The result is that the placement group extinguishes faster than the control group. Since drive was the same for the two groups, and the placement animals did not actually do any running during latent extinction (goal box placement) trials, the results are attributed to a lower level of incentive motivation. The placement group learned not to expect reward.

These five lines of evidence converge on the idea that incentive motivation is very important, perhaps the most important motivational determinant of performance. Incentive motivation is in turn influenced both by *experience* and by *internal states* of the organism. We now turn to theories which attempt to explain how incentive motivation works. One type of theory assumes that incentive motivation develops out of *responses*, the other assumes that incentive motivation is a *central nervous system process* which does *not* depend on responses.

### Response Theory: The Anticipatory Goal Response ($r_g$)

On the basis of the Crespi data, Hull (1952) added an intervening variable for incentive motivation to his system, symbolized as the letter K.

The new formulation then read:

$$E = H \times D \times K$$

The antecedent conditions for manipulating the strength of K were the amount, quality, and delay of reinforcement (longer delays produce weaker incentive motivation). Black (1965) later suggested deprivation level as an additional antecedent. The details of the syntax have been a matter of debate (should it be $D \times K$ or $D + K$?), but this is no longer a matter of great concern.

Spence (1956) suggested that K itself might be *derived* from one of Hull's own earlier concepts, the *fractional anticipatory goal response*. Hull (1933a) had used this concept to account for purpose and expectation in terms of stimulus-response theory. The details of the establishment of the fractional goal response are given in Box 6–1, modified from Hull (1933a). We may describe the mechanism more briefly as follows: When an animal is rewarded with food after making a response, it *eats* the food. Eating is the *goal response* ($R_G$), and occurs only when there is food. When the animal eats, however, there are also *fractional goal responses* ($r_g$'s) which may occur with or without food, such as small chewing or licking movements. These fractional responses are considered to be *conditionable* just like other responses. For example, maze stimuli preceding the goal response ($R_g$, eating) could become conditioned stimuli for the fractional goal responses ($r_g$'s.). The $r_g$'s could then be aroused by stimuli in the maze *before* the animal reaches the goal box and the food. Similarly, *internal stimuli* (drive stimuli accompanying deprivation) could also be conditioned to the $r_g$'s. After a number of training trials, the maze cues and internal stimuli could arouse conditioned $r_g$'s at the *beginning* of the maze. The $r_g$'s have become *anticipatory* goal responses, occurring in anticipation of the goal response of eating.

The anticipatory $r_g$'s become motivational by virtue of the fact that they have *stimulus consequences*. Any response which we can "feel," for example, has stimulus consequences which feed information about the response back to the brain. The stimulus consequences of $r_g$'s are $s_g$'s. The $s_g$'s in turn can become conditioned to overt responses. We then have the following sequence:

$$S \rightarrow (r_g\text{-}s_g) \rightarrow R$$

where S is an environmental stimulus, R is an overt response, and $r_g\text{-}s_g$ is the anticipatory goal response and its stimulus. If S is a maze stimulus and R is running in the maze, then $r_g\text{-}s_g$ is conditioned to running in the maze. The stronger the $r_g$, the stronger the $s_g$, and hence the stronger the effect of $s_g$ on behavior.

BOX 6-1   DETAILED DESCRIPTION OF THE DEVELOPMENT OF THE ANTICIPATORY
GOAL RESPONSE MECHANISM. (MODIFIED FROM HULL, 1931, PP. 489–496.
COPYRIGHT © 1931 BY THE AMERICAN PSYCHOLOGICAL ASSOCIATION.
REPRINTED BY PERMISSION.)

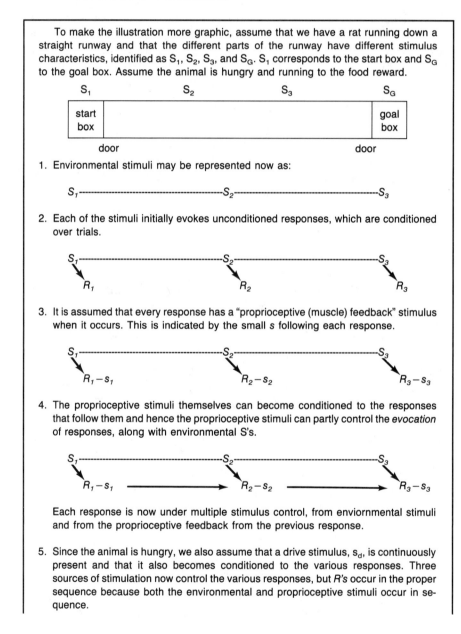

To make the illustration more graphic, assume that we have a rat running down a straight runway and that the different parts of the runway have different stimulus characteristics, identified as $S_1$, $S_2$, $S_3$, and $S_G$. $S_1$ corresponds to the start box and $S_G$ to the goal box. Assume the animal is hungry and running to the food reward.

1. Environmental stimuli may be represented now as:

$$S_1\text{------------------------}S_2\text{------------------------}S_3$$

2. Each of the stimuli initially evokes unconditioned responses, which are conditioned over trials.

3. It is assumed that every response has a "proprioceptive (muscle) feedback" stimulus when it occurs. This is indicated by the small $s$ following each response.

4. The proprioceptive stimuli themselves can become conditioned to the responses that follow them and hence the proprioceptive stimuli can partly control the *evocation* of responses, along with environmental S's.

Each response is now under multiple stimulus control, from enviornmental stimuli and from the proprioceptive feedback from the previous response.

5. Since the animal is hungry, we also assume that a drive stimulus, $s_d$, is continuously present and that it also becomes conditioned to the various responses. Three sources of stimulation now control the various responses, but *R's* occur in the proper sequence because both the environmental and proprioceptive stimuli occur in sequence.

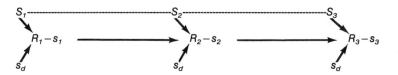

6. At this point, we introduce a crucial element in the diagram: the goal response itself. (It has been present all along, of course, as far as the animal is concerned. It is just that now we explicitly introduce it to the diagram.) When the animal eats the food, it makes the overt goal response ($R_G$). At the same time, there is a covert or *fractional goal response* ($r_g$) which occurs along with eating but which can also occur without actual eating. This $r_g$ is also conditionable. Furthermore, like other responses, it has its own stimulus feedback ($s_g$).

We abbreviate the diagram to show this part of the sequence:

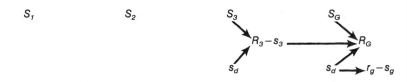

7. $R_g$ is conditioned directly to $s_d$ and to $S_G$ (the goal box stimuli) since both of these are present when it occurs. $r_g$ is somewhat less strongly conditioned to $S_1$, $S_2$, and $S_3$ by two means: (1) delay of reinforcement, and (2) stimulus generalization, the earlier stimuli having characteristics something like the later stimuli.

Since $r_g$ is aroused early in the sequence, $s_g$ is also aroused and can become conditioned to the overt responses, just as was $s_d$. We finally have the following diagram, which shows the overt responses being evoked by environmental stimuli ($S$'s), feedback stimuli from responses ($s$'s) drive stimuli ($s_d$'s), and feedback stimuli from anticipatory goal responses ($s_g$'s).

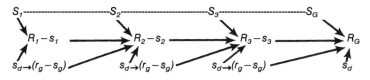

To the extent that $r_g$ is strongly aroused by the food (or other appropriate incentive) then $s_g$ will be strongly aroused and will play a relatively bigger role in the evocation of responses.

*Applications of $r_g$ theory to incentive phenomena.*    The $r_g$-$s_g$ mechanism accounts for some of the major incentive phenomena as follows.

1. *Incentive shifts.* When rewards are shifted from small to large, there is a larger $R_G$, and therefore a larger $r_g$-$s_g$. Since $r_g$-$s_g$ was already conditioned to

responses in earlier training, a sudden increase in the intensity of $r_g$-$s_g$ could produce a sudden "improvement" in behavior.

2. *Latent learning.* Incentive motivation could not develop in non-rewarded animals because there is no $R_G$ (eating) and hence no $r_g$-$s_g$ related to eating. When food is introduced, $r_g$-$s_g$ occurs and can be conditioned to various maze stimuli, and performance improves. Hull (1933a) explained the elimination of maze errors in these terms. He argued that $r_g$-$s_g$ is most strongly conditioned to responses that get the animal to the reward faster. Correct responses do this and hence are more strongly conditioned to $r_g$-$s_g$ than are errors. The errors are therefore eliminated.

3. *Latent extinction.* During training, the $r_g$-$s_g$ is conditioned to goal-box stimuli, as well as other apparatus cues. When the animal is placed into the goal box without food, $r_g$ is aroused but not reinforced by the presentation of food. Therefore, $r_g$ extinguishes to the goal box cues and to some extent to other apparatus cues. During regular extinction which follows, these animals stop running sooner because stimulation for running ($r_g$-$s_g$) has already been partly extinguished.

4. *Quality of reward.* A more-preferred reward arouses a strong $R_G$ and hence a strong $r_g$-$s_g$. The stronger $r_g$-$s_g$ stimulates more vigorous performance.

**Problems with $r_g$ theory.**    (1) *Theoretical ambiguity about what $r_g$-$s_g$ does.* The apparent simplicity of the $r_g$-$s_g$ mechanism is somewhat deceptive. On the one hand, $s_g$ might facilitate responses because it is an *intense stimulus* and therefore has drive properties like any other intense stimulus. This would quite nicely account for situations where *vigor* of response is measured, such as running speeds in the Crespi experiment. On the other hand, $s_g$ might facilitate responding because it is just another stimulus to which responses are conditioned. This is an associative (learning) interpretation, however, not a motivational interpretation.

Some theorists have argued for the associative interpretation for incentive effects on the grounds that there is little direct evidence that positive incentives are internally arousing. As shown in chapter 3, there is some evidence indicating positive incentive arousal. For example, Beck and Meinrath (1978) and Lipsett and colleagues (1978) found that both rodents and human infants had higher heart rates when drinking higher-concentration sucrose solutions. This is in line with a motivational interpretation. After considerable experience with the solutions, however, the animals in the Beck and Meinrath research did not show such a differential heart rate even though they continued to press a lever more for higher concentrations. It may be that the "motivational" (arousal) effect dropped out, leaving only an associative effect for the different incentives. There is little research along these lines, however. Finally, $r_g$ is supposed to account for very rapid behavioral changes, following incentive shifts. Supposedly this negates a learning interpretation for the shift effects. But since $r_g$ itself is learned (conditioned), how can it be evidence against learning? One answer is that $r_g$'s are learned more rapidly than other responses. Within the context of Hull-Spence theory, this is a weak answer. The best that can be said is that there are *two kinds of learning*, incentive learning and response learning (Logan, 1968; Young, 1959).

(2) *Empirical* problems with $r_g$-$s_g$. $R_g$ theory had a seductive appeal for S-R theorists because it seemed to account for incentive motivation while still relying on observable stimuli and responses rather than mentalistic concepts. The empirical problem is the lack of tangible evidence that such fractional responses either occur or are conditioned to environmental cues. Three specific problems are illustrative. First, the vigor of consummatory and instrumental responses should be *highly correlated* if strong $r_g$'s stimulate stronger responses. Such correlations are small at best, however (e.g., Black, 1969; Robbins, 1969). Second, $r_g$'s should be conditioned to start-box cues if the theory is to account for the well-documented fact that larger rewards produce quicker starting. This simply has not been observed (e.g., see Sheffield, 1966).

In conclusion, $r_g$ theory was ingenious, but seems inadequate because of lack of evidence that $r_g$'s either occur or function as the theory says. We are therefore pushed back into the central nervous system and a more cognitive account of incentive theory. In fairness to Hull's theory, however, his addition of incentive motivation to his basic formulation ($E = H \times D \times K$) does not require the $r_g$-$s_g$ formulation. The $r_g$ interpretation was added by other theorists.

### Central State Theories

Central state theories assume that *incentive motivation is a central brain process directly aroused by positive or negative stimuli.* Some stimuli produce *unconditioned* arousal of a central motive state while other stimuli can be *conditioned* to evoke arousal. Such theories agree that instrumental responses are learned by some process which does not require reward for learning. Incentive motivation involves a *different* learning process. Incentive stimuli provide the motivation for selecting one response over another but do not reinforce behavior in the sense of an "S-R gluing" process, as discussed earlier.

*Tolman's purposive behaviorism.*    E. C. Tolman championed the incentive view before it was generally popular among American psychologists. We examine Tolman in some detail because of his historical priority, the generality of his concepts to many areas of psychology, and the contemporary usage of many of his concepts.

For many years Tolman and his followers at the University of California were the primary antagonists to the Hull and Spence groups at Yale and Iowa. The active controversy often clouded the fact that Tolman's approach was every bit as behavioral as Hull's. In fact, Tolman (1938) introduced intervening variables into psychological theory, insisting on the importance of tying theoretical concepts to observable events. However, Tolman was concerned with what he called *molar behavior*, not with specific "muscle twitches." Thus, if an animal turns to the right in a maze, "turning right" is the response. It makes little difference which exact muscles do the job. Tolman was a strict behaviorist, but not an S-R theorist in the sense of believing that learning consists of S-R connections, as Hull believed (Tolman, 1932; 1938).

Tolman, like Hull, was concerned with *purposive*, or *goal-oriented* behavior, but Tolman's theoretical concepts had more mentalistic-sounding names than Hull's, and these words grated on the ears of S-R theorists. For example, two of Tolman's early concepts were *expectancy* and *demand*. An expectancy is the anticipation that under given circumstances a particular behavior will lead to a particular outcome. Going to the store will result in getting food. A demand is the motivation *for* food. Whereas Hull had an S-R concept of learning (habit is the association between an S and an R), Tolman had an $S_1R_1$-$S_2$ theory. *An expectancy included a response* (if I do this, then such and such will happen). For Tolman, the S's were environmental places or events, and behavior was how a person or animal got from one place or event to another.

Demand, the motivation component, is related to the outcome of behavior. I might *expect* that if I go to the refrigerator there will be a piece of chicken to eat, but unless I have a *demand* for food I will not go to the refrigerator. Demands are determined jointly by internal and external events, such as being hungry and liking the taste of chicken. There are demands both for and against events. We have demands *for* desirable outcomes and *against* aversive outcomes.

*Cognition in Tolman's theorizing.*    Tolman believed that expectancies were central brain processes, not requiring overt responses, What distinguished his approach from the "mentalistic" approach of some earlier psychologists was that he worked only with observable events and *inferred* underlying expectancies and demands from his objective observations. Studying laboratory rats, he showed that it was possible to discuss purpose, foresight, and expectation, using objective events as the primary data rather than depending on human introspective reports. Purpose, foresight, and expectation were intervening variables. Much contemporary cognitive research takes a similar approach.

*Cognitive maps.*    If a person or animal has expectancies about "getting from here to there," he must have some notion about where "here" and "there" are. Tolman (1948) argued that animals have environmental "maps" in their heads, which they follow. He likened the brain to a map room, in contrast to the telephone switchboard analogy used by S-R theorists. The telephone analogy says that incoming sensory information is automatically switched to outgoing motor lines, with little information processing in the head. Modern information processing theorists emphasize to a much greater extent what goes on in the head. The cognitive map concept has turned out to be important to modern *environmental psychologists,* who are much concerned with how people perceive, learn about, and locomote through their environments.

*Tolman's systematic theory.*   We shall use Tolman's own final presentation of his theory (1959) for our remaining discussion. but MacCorquodale and Meehl (1954) have the most detailed presentation of his system available.

The following formula is modified from Tolman (1959, p. 134). We do not use his symbolism or the entire formula.

Performance Tendency =
f (Expectancy, Drive Stimulation, Incentive Valence)

Each of these is an intervening variable which has a rough equivalent in Hull's theory. *Performance tendency* corresponds to excitatory potential; *expectancy* is a learning concept corresponding to habit; *drive stimulation* refers to internal stimulation, as does drive; and *incentive valence* corresponds to Hull's K. Tolman defines his concepts differently, of course, and attributes different characteristics to them.

*Performance tendency* is the strength of the tendency for an expectancy $S_1R_1$-$S_2$ to be expressed in behavior, just as sEr in Hull's theory is the tendency for sHr to be expressed in behavior. Performance tendency is a function of many variables, as is sEr.

*Expectancies* were of two kinds. Tolman considered the $S_1R_1$-$S_2$ expectancy more important, since it involves behavior. The second kind was an $S_1$-$S_2$ expectancy, that one stimulus event will follow from another. This is the general form of classical conditioning, where $S_1$ and $S_2$ correspond to CS and UCS.

A concept closely related to expectancy is *means-end-readiness,* or *belief.* When a particular $S_1$ occurs, there is "released" an expectancy that a particular response will lead to a particular outcome, or that an $S_2$ will follow. A belief is more enduring than an expectancy. Thus, I may have an enduring *belief* that with certain temperature and cloud conditions it will snow. But only when these conditions actually prevail will I *expect* it to snow.

*Incentive valence* refers to the *value* of $S_2$ to the organism. If a tasty food has a high positive value now, I expect it to have a high value in the future. This *expected value* is the *valence* of the food. Valences are learned from experiences with objects of particular values. The combination of drive stimulation and valence is what Tolman had earlier called *demand.*

*Evidence for Tolman's system.* Tolman (1959) saw evidence for the correctness of his theory throughout all experiments in instrumental learning. His approach simply looks at everything differently from an S-R approach like Hull's. Problems which nagged at Hull's theory simply dissipated in Tolman's. Such issues as drive reduction reinforcement and whether learning can take place without responding simply did not bother Tolman. Tolman also believed that his view was more likely to be a fruitful approach to human cognition than was S-R theory, a view vindicated in modern cognitive theory.

*Young and Logan.*    P. T. Young long held to an hedonic theory of motivation (e.g., 1968). He assumed that incentive objects produce *primary affective arousals* (incentive values). Stimuli *associated* with these primary arousals elicited *conditioned affective arousal* (incentive motivation). Behavior is then *regulated* by these conditioned affective arousals, which determine the direction and intensity of behavior, but not its specific form. Incentives determine whether an organism *will* approach or avoid a goal, but do not determine the specific muscle movements involved. Affective processes can be positive or negative in many degrees and are ordered along an hedonic continuum. Organisms engage in behaviors which, in Young's words, "minimize distress and maximize delight."

Frank Logan (e.g., 1968) used the intervening variable approach of Hull and Spence. He assumed that each quantitative value of reward has a particular *incentive value* when the organism is exposed to the reward. Over successive experiences with a specific reward, *incentive motivation* increases up to a maximum value as great as the incentive value. His concepts of incentive value and incentive motivation are like Tolman's value and valence, or Young's primary and conditioned affective arousals. Logan also believes that response learning and incentive learning involve two different processes.

### Central Motive State

As discussed in chapter 4, Morgan (1943; 1959) proposed that a variety of circumstances lead to a central nervous system change that he called the *central motive state* (CMS). The CMS has the following properties: It persists for some time without outside sensory support; it predisposes the organism to react in certain ways to some stimuli, but not others; and it may directly cause certain responses to be emitted. Morgan intended the CMS to apply to drive states, such as hunger and thirst. Its theoretical importance at the time Morgan developed it was that it departed from the prevailing views that such drive states are aroused by peripheral events: hunger by stomach contractions, thirst by a dry mouth, and so on.

Bindra (e.g., 1969, 1978) has further elaborated the CMS concept, saying that the CMS is generated by the interactions of "neural representations of organismic state and incentive object" (1969, p. 12). A "reinforcing" stimulus does not produce any specific response selection, but arouses a motivational state that influences *many* subsequent behaviors. The supporting arguments are the same as for incentive theories: Response occurrence can be changed without the "reinforcing" stimulus directly following the response in question. The CMS alters the value of incentive objects and changes the likelihood of appropriate approach and consummatory responses. Stimuli associated with incentives control approach responses, but not consummatory responses (for example, food controls eating responses, not stimuli paired with food).

An experiment by Bindra and Palfai (1967) illustrates the theory. Thirsty rats had the click of a metronome paired with water while they were confined in a small cage where locomotor activity was impossible. The animals were then divided into three groups (low, medium, and high water deprivation) and, in a larger cage, the activities of perambulation (locomotion), sitting, and grooming were recorded before, while, and after the metronome was turned on. Perambulation was generally higher under medium or high deprivation, but presence of the metronome, the conditioned stimulus signalling water, further increased perambulation only under medium or high deprivation.

### The Solomon-Corbit Opponent Process Theory

Hedonic theories generally assume that particular environmental events arouse certain internal states in the same way, either positive or negative. The effects of experience are usually assumed to be caused by conditioning such processes to other stimuli, in an associative manner. The theory of opponent processes (Solomon & Corbit, 1974; Solomon, 1980) postulates a *non-associative effect of experience on hedonic processes.*

Consider this illustration. A woman discovers a lump in her breast and is immediately fearful of cancer. She makes an appointment with her doctor but frets about it until he reports the tumor is benign. Her strong anxiety is then replaced by great elation. An opposite example would be the sudden loss of something or someone that has brought us great pleasure; we are then depressed. The crux of the opponent process theory, then, is this: *Every affective state, whether pleasurable or aversive, tends to arouse the opponent state.* Extreme fear arouses the opponent process, which is pleasure, and when the source of the fear is removed the pleasure process becomes dominant and lingers for a while. At any given time, the affective state of the individual is the algebraic sum of the two processes. The process directly aroused by a stimulus situation is *dominant* while the situation lasts, but the opponent process becomes dominant when the situation changes.

The initial process aroused is called an *A-state*, whether positive or negative, joy or terror. The opponent process, which is aroused by the A-state and not directly by the situation, is called the *B-state*. The person who does something very frightening, such as jumping out of an airplane, initially has a fearful A-state aroused and the joyful B-state automatically follows. The A-state is dominant until the person lands safely on the ground, the danger is over, and the joyful B-state is very strong for a while.

The degree to which the B-state is aroused depends on (1) the magnitude of the A-state, B increasing with A, and (2) the number of times the A-state has occurred, B again increasing with A. With successive A-state arousals the effectiveness of the A-state stimulus *decreases* because the A-state effect is being diminished by the opponent B-state. Over a period of time, then, a stronger arousal of the A-state is necessary just to get the same degree of pleasure from the positive A-state that was initially obtained. Figures 6–5 and 6–6 illustrate the temporal course of events with the A and B states as a function of the number of times the A-state has occurred.

### Predictive Stimuli and the Transfer of Control

Earlier we saw that a secondary reinforcer may be a stimulus that reliably informs the individual about some important forthcoming event, such as food, or, unpleasant events, such as shock. We can think of incentive stimuli also as stimuli which predict the occurrence of good or bad events. The organism, human or otherwise, can then act upon these predictions to approach or avoid the predicted events. This is a cognitive view of the role of incentive stimuli, much along the lines of Tolman's theorizing, but developed in more detail in recent years.

If incentive stimuli are predictive, and cognitive, we might expect they

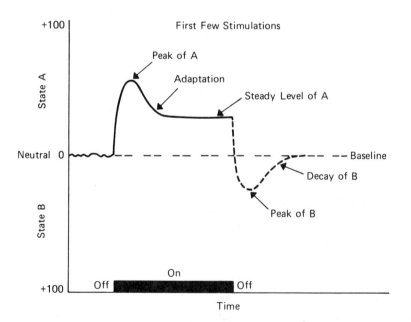

**FIGURE 6-5.** The manifest temporal dynamics generated by the opponent process system during the first few stimulations. (The five features of the affective response are labeled.) The curves are the algebraic summation of the opponent processes. Note the high level of *A* relative to *B*. (Solomon and Corbit, 1974, p. 128. Copyright © 1974 by the American Psychological Association. Reprinted by permission.)

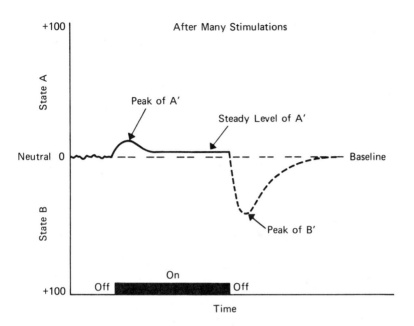

FIGURE 6-6.    The manifest temporal dynamics generated by the opponent process system after many repeated stimulations. (The major features of the modified patterns are labeled.) Compared to the curves in Figure 6–5, note the low level of A, and the relatively high level of B.

could readily *transfer their predictive properties to new situations without requiring specific learning in the new situations.* This is different from simple stimulus generalization, where we are talking about the *same* response being made to a somewhat modified stimulus from that used in training. Predictive relations may develop in either classical conditioning or instrumental conditioning situations.

The concept of response *contingency* is useful here. By contingent we refer to whether the predicted outcome of an event hinges on the organism's behavior. If it is not dependent, it is a *noncontingent* stimulus. Contingency may be involved in either classical or instrumental conditioning. We usually think of classical conditioning as noncontingent, since the unconditioned stimulus (such as food) follows the conditioned stimulus (a tone, for example) regardless of what the animal does. The animal may, however, make some *unnecessary response* which it associates with food presentation, so that there is an element of response contingency involved, from the animal's point of view. Conversely, in a maze certain stimuli (like goal-box shape, color, and brightness), invariably precede the reward so there is in instrumental learning an element of noncontingency which corresponds to classical conditioning.

*Classification of predictors.*    A straightforward classification for predictive stimuli is according to whether the predicted outcomes are positive (desirable) or negative (aversive). We may further subdivide the stimuli ac-

cording to whether they predict the occurrence (S +) or nonoccurrence
(S −) of a following event. We then have the following possibilities:[2]

1.  S+ for a positive event (food) predicts a desirable outcome.
2.  S− for a positive event (for example, no food) predicts an aversive event.
3.  S+ for a negative event (like shock) predicts an aversive event.
4.  S− for a negative event (no shock, for instance) predicts a desirable outcome.

The following research examples illustrate what is meant by this classification.

1.  A stimulus paired with food (S+ ) or absence of food (S− ) in one situation,
    independently of the animals' behavior, later facilitated or retarded perfor-
    mance when presented in the start box of a runway (Bolles, Grossen, Hargrave,
    & Duncan, 1970).
2.  Dogs trained in a shuttle box to avoid shock shuttled faster if S+ for shock in
    another situation was presented during shuttling, but shuttled slower if S− for
    shock was presented (Rescorla & Lolordo, 1965).

There are many possibilities for such transfer experiments, depending
on (1) whether outcomes are positive or negative; (2) whether S + or S − are
used; (3) whether initial training is contingent or noncontingent; and (4)
whether the transfer tests are contingent or noncontingent. It appears that
transfer is effective if it is from one appetitive situation to another, or from
one shock situation to another. If the transfer is from shock to food situations, or from food to shock situations, the theory works less well—except
that an S + for shock inhibits performance in many different situations (e.g.,
see Bolles & Moot, 1972).

**What is the mechanism of transfer?**  Overmeir and Lawry (1979) have
discussed the issues involved in the interpretation of transfer of control in
some detail. We can safely say that we are dealing with a mediation process or
processes, but we need to ask what the nature of the mediation is. For
example, is the mediation *associative* or *motivational?* This was the question
asked earlier of the $r_g$-$s_g$ mechanism, which was a mediational mechanism.
Second, is the mediational mechanism sequential or parallel? That is, must
an external event occur, followed by the mediating response which then cues
the overt response, or might the two run parallel? Symbolically, might we
have S-M-R or S⟋^M⟍R? The answer to the first question seems to be that

---

[2]We use the terms desirable and aversive in this context a little uncertainly, because the
predicted events may be situation-specific. For example, there is virtually no evidence that a
stimulus which predicts the end of electric shock will be sought after in a neutral (nonshock)
situation. We are thus in at least temporary violation of the definitions of desire and aversion
developed in chapter 1.

there are *both* associative and motivational functions of mediating events. The internal (cognitive) representation of an external event can both cue and motivate. The answer to the second question is much more complex, but Overmeir and Lawry suggest that there are two kinds of mediational links, which can be independent but usually run in sequence. These are (1) a stimulus-mediator link, and (2) a mediator-response link. *In practice,* the stimulus-mediator-response sequence usually has the same mediator attached to both stimulus and response, but this is not theoretically necessary. Furthermore, Overmeir and Lawry have shown how it is possible to "break" the link between a mediator (such as fear) and a response, while still leaving the original stimulus-mediator link intact. This line of research is new, however, and much remains to be discovered.

### Incentives and Fantasy

The final approach to incentives we review is that developed by Eric Klinger (1975, 1977). Klinger's basic concepts are *commitment to goals and current concerns* about achieving goals. Current concerns are considered to persist over time, even when there are numerous interruptions in striving for a particular goal. For example, as I write I am interrupted by the telephone, then return to the typewriter. Then there is a meeting, a different concern, after which I again resume typing. This behavior persists intermittently for perhaps a year or two, at which time I become *disengaged* from the particular writing goal, and have a different set of concerns. Once there is commitment to a goal, Klinger suggests, there are at least four kinds of consequences, affecting (1) actions, (2) content of thoughts and dreams, (3) sensitization to goal-related cues, and (4) perceptual qualities of goal-related stimuli (Klinger, 1975, p. 4).

First, the anticipation of obtaining incentives (commitment to goals) is vital in instigating, directing, and maintaining action. Second, " . . . a person is most likely to think or dream about something while it is related to one of his current concerns" (1975, p. 5). These thoughts, dreams, or fantasies may involve achievement, power, affiliation, fear, sex, aggression, and so on. If you know what a person's current concerns are, you can likely predict rather well his or her fantasy life. Third, without speculating on all the possible details of explaining the phenomena, it does appear that people are more sensitive to stimuli associated with current concerns. Among other things, people hear their own names when they do not detect other stimuli. Granted other interpretations, it is not unreasonable that a major current concern is related to oneself. And fourth, it appears that stimuli related to current concerns are more prominent or noticeable.

*Disengagement from incentives.* The value of incentives and commitment to them is, of course, not permanently fixed. The value of a graduate degree may change with the economy, and our commitment stops after a goal has been achieved. But what *happens* when commitment to a goal ends? First of all, even if a goal is achieved we may feel let down, and perhaps even somewhat depressed, unless we have other ongoing concerns and incentives. Indeed, this is said to be a major problem with retirement.

The more devastating instances, however, may come when we *fail* to achieve the incentive we are committed to. Klinger sees five phases of the incentive disengagement cycle. First, there is *invigoration*, a stronger attempt to achieve the goal. This happens in frustrating situations (see chapter 8). Second, there may be *aggressive* behavior, as when aggression follows frustration. Third, there is a *downswing into depression*, a giving up when an important incentive or incentives, remain(s) unachieved. Fourth, there is *depression*, characterized by apathy toward a great many normally attractive incentives. Fifth, there is *recovery*, which seems to occur commonly after *reactive* depressions (those related to specific life events). One may find other concepts to explain this cycle, the opponent process theory being a prime candidate to explain many of these phenomena (such as depression following the pursuit of exhilarating goals). Our main concern at this point, however, is to emphasize the role given to cognitive processes, including fantasy and perception, in relation to incentive motivation. The kind of cognitive theory proposed by Tolman, applied to rats, can be considerably expanded when applied to humans.

## INTERACTION OF EXTRINSIC REWARDS AND INTRINSIC MOTIVATION

Industrial psychologists commonly distinguish between *intrinsic motivation* and *external rewards*. Intrinsic motivation refers to factors that make certain activities rewarding in themselves, such as hobbies, games, puzzles, creative endeavors, and so on. Extrinsic rewards refer to those rewards given us by other people for our behavior. This is the standard approach of operant conditioning and behavior modification. We might expect the two forms of motivation/reward would be *additive*, that a person would perform an activity he or she likes even better if also paid for the activity. This does not always seem to happen, however. In some situations external rewards for an already interesting task may actually *reduce* performance on the task, or even liking for the task.

As an example of this phenomenon, in a study of nursery school children, Anderson, Manoogian, and Reznick (1976) compared the effects of money, a "good player" award, and verbal praise as reinforcers. The children were first pretested for the amount of time spent drawing with magic markers. They were then rewarded for drawing. Finally they were posttested, without reward, for drawing. Both the money (pennies) and the good-player award produced a drop in amount of time spent drawing, but the praise produced a slight increase. Similar results have been produced in a variety of experiments, with both children and adults (Notz, 1985; Deci, 1975; Lepper & Greene, 1978; Deci, 1980). Given the importance generally attached to external rewards in the control of behavior, such "hidden costs of reward" call for clarification.

This line of research was stimulated by deCharm's (1968) suggestion that there should be an *interaction* of intrinsic motivation and external motivation, not just an additive effect. DeCharms believed this interaction would be based on a person's perception of whether he or she was the controlling agent in getting rewards or was at the mercy of outside agents. If the person sees himself or herself as the causal factor in getting desirable outcomes, then the behavior producing those outcomes is intrinsically motivating and desirable. The individual will continue to do things over which there is personal control. On the other hand, if the person sees rewards as depending on someone else, the activities necessary to get those rewards will be less intrinsically motivating. A person may continue to work at his or her job because money is needed to live, but the work is likely to be of little intrinsic interest.

Deci (1978) concluded that intrinsic motivation and external rewards interact in the following way:

> External rewards *facilitate* behavior when (1) they primarily convey information that a person is competent and the rewards are not perceived as controlling behavior; and (2) they are given for routine, well-learned activities. The first instance fits the "praise condition" in the Anderson et al. experiment with nursery school children, and the second fits an assembly-line type of job.
>
> External rewards tend to *impair* performance when (1) they are obvious and given for activities already of high interest; and (2) they are related to such open-ended activities as problem solving. The first instance is like the use of money in the Anderson et al. experiment. The second instance is closer to the creative activities of managers, artists, musicians, or others who do not know in advance just what they are going to do or how they are going to do it.

People often are not even striving for predetermined rewards, but *discover* the rewards as they go along. Highly creative artists, for example, do not have preset notions about what a picture *should* look like before they start. Rather, they change their ideas as the work progresses. Much the same holds for writing; a book begins to take on a "form of its own" as it develops, often very different from the form initially projected by its author. Similarly, small children may pile blocks on top of each other with no idea of what they are trying to build, but they are reinforced at various steps by characteristics of the block tower that appeal to them. The motivation (reward) is not only intrinsic, it is actually discovered moment by moment (Csikszentmihalyi, 1978).

Deci's theory of *cognitive evaluation* (Deci, 1980; Deci & Ryan, 1985) says that rewards have a *controlling* aspect and an *informational* aspect. If the controlling aspect is more salient, a person will perceive control as external. If the informational aspect is more salient, control will be perceived as internal, and feelings of competence and self-determination will emerge. It should follow, then, that external reward can in fact facilitate *any* behavior if the reward informs a person that he or she is doing well. As a character in a movie once said, business is a game and money is how you keep score. Money is not *always* controlling.

Other theorists have looked at the problem somewhat differently. Kruglanski (1978), for example, distinguished between activities that are ends unto themselves and activities that are the means to some other goal. In this view, an activity is perceived more favorably if it is an end rather than a (perhaps unpleasant) means to something else. It has also been argued from an operant conditioning point of view, that the performance decrement that occurs after reward is simply because *reward has been omitted.* In other words, it is an *extinction* effect. Considerable research is still needed in this area to sort out many problems.

*Control and desire for control.* If the perception of self-control (or personal causation) is truly important, we might ask whether external rewards would be more detrimental to the intrinsic motivation of people with a high desire for control. People not concerned about control would presumably be less affected by low perceived control than would those with high concern for control. Burger (1980) tested this hypothesis by paying or not paying subjects who were either high or low in need for control according to a scale devised by him. The results are shown in Figure 6–7. Payment of $2.00 for doing a

FIGURE 6-7.    Effect of paying subjects with high and low desire for control on intrinsic interest in the task. (From Burger, 1980, doctoral dissertation.)

task reduced the intrinsic motivation of the task in high-desire-for-control subjects but not in low-desire-for-control subjects.

## EXPANDED REINFORCEMENT THEORY: BEHAVIORAL ECONOMICS

Psychologists have traditionally developed their theories of reinforcement in laboratory settings, with tight experimental control, and then extrapolated their findings to non-laboratory settings. This has been done most elegantly within the framework of Skinner's operant conditioning approach, where practical applications abound. Skinner's novel *Walden II* (1948) described a Utopian society based upon operant conditioning principles, and small-scale "token economies" of the kind Skinner described in his novel have actually been established in such institutional settings as psychiatric hospitals, prisons, and classrooms. These economies use tokens for reinforcers, and these tokens can later be traded for food, special privileges, or other commodities.

A very different approach comes from viewing reinforcers as commodities or money in *open* economies where there are many choices, as contrasted with the *closed economy* of the traditional laboratory experiment, where subjects seldom have choices about what reinforcers they get or what it takes to get them.

Over the past two decades, psychologists have begun to explore reinforcers in broader contexts than the usual Skinner box or T-maze environments. One reason is the recognition of the possibility that the "standard" laboratory methods for studying reinforcers have an artificiality about them, so that the *concepts* derived from such research may be too specific to those situations. A number of psychologists have become interested in *economic theory* in relation to reinforcement. The Skinner box provides a nice analogy. An animal gets *paid* (reinforced) a certain amount for a given amount of work (lever presses, key pecks). How does an animal adjust its behavior as the *price* (work required) for a commodity changes?

The mathematical curve which relates the *amount* of a commodity to the *price* of the commodity is called a *demand curve*. For example, the number of food pellets a rat will "buy" (work for) varies with the price, such as the number of lever presses required for a reinforcer. The number of presses required per pellet is one characteristic of a *schedule of reinforcement*. A reinforcer requiring ten presses is more expensive (greater cost) than one requiring only five responses. The demand for a commodity is said to be *elastic* if the animal works *less* as the cost increases. Conversely, a commodity is *inelastic* if the demand remains relatively constant in spite of increasing cost. This is illustrated in Figure 6–8. "Luxury" items tend to be more elastic than such necessities as food, but such "luxuries" as coffee are very inelastic.

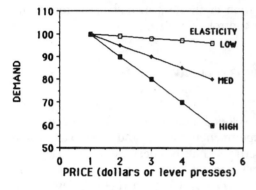

FIGURE 6-8
Demand curves varying in elasticity. A demand curve with low elasticity shows little change in demand (sales) with increasing price. A demand curve with high elasticity shows a large drop in sales when there is increasing price. In economics, cost is typically measured in monetary units, such as dollars. In animal research, cost is given by the amount of work, such as the number of lever presses required to obtain a fixed amount of food. Arbitrary units are used on both axes.

Governments also tax "sin" (such as alcohol and cigarettes) with foreknowledge that these commodities are very inelastic; they sell at nearly the same volume even at the higher prices resulting from the tax.

The effect of a price change can be divided into two parts, however: the *income effect* and the *substitutability effect*. The income effect is the extent to which a price change affects the real income of a person, the total amount of goods a person can buy with his or her money. If an increase in price is balanced by an increase in income (inflation), there may be no effect of price on demand. Conversely, if price goes up while income goes down, the unhappy situation with high inflation and low employment, there may be a greatly reduced demand with higher price. The substitutability effect refers to the availability of a *similar* commodity at a lower price. If there is no substitute, as with oil for automobiles, there is a smaller effect of price increase on consumption than if there were a substitute. The demand for butter, however, changes with price because a number of good substitutes are available (margarine, cooking oils). In like manner, with the influx of foreign products selling at lower prices than American-made products, there is great substitutability, therefore great elasticity in demand for American goods.

Another principle, called the *complementarity effect*, works opposite the substitutability effect. Complementarity means that an increase in the demand for one product also produces an increased demand for another. A rise in the sale of pretzels increases the sale of beer, and increased air travel increases the sales of flight insurance.

These principles have been shown to work to some extent in the animal laboratory. For example, in one study rats either pressed one lever for food and another for water, or one lever for Tom Collins mix and another for root beer. As the price (number of presses) required for a morsel of food increased, the animals did not switch to pressing for water (no substitutability); they paid more (pressed more) for food. When the price of Tom Collins mix went up, however, the rats readily switched their allegiance to root beer. The two commodities were substitutable (Lea, 1978).

If animals have *free access* to food for a certain amount of time daily, they will press a lever in a Skinner box for food anyway—until the cost becomes too high. When this happens, the animals simply stop "eating out," no longer pressing the lever if free food is available. The free food is substitutable for the food bought with lever presses. If, however, the only food available has to be bought by lever pressing, the demand for the food is much less elastic than if there is free food. The animals keep responding until they spend virtually all their time working to get food (e.g., Collier and colleagues, 1976).

It is not yet clear whether the application of human economic principles will further our understanding of reinforcers, or whether there is simply a new set of words for already established principles. Further research will decide that question. Meanwhile, it is worth considering that human economic principles may have developed as they have *because they do in fact represent broad biological principles of reinforcement.*

## SUMMARY

1. *Rewards* (reinforcers) are desirable outcomes of behavior, and organisms work to get them. An *empirical law of effect* simply states that rewards have an effect on behavior. A *theoretical law of effect* makes some statement about why rewards are effective (such as reducing drive).

2. Rewards apparently are not necessary for *response learning,* but organisms do learn *about* rewards as outcomes that can be expected if one behaves a certain way under certain circumstances.

3. A *functional analysis of behavior* involves determining what rewards are effective for a given individual. No theory of reinforcement is necessary beyond this.

4. *Response theories* of reinforcement say that the effective rewarding events are the responses made, not the subsequent stimuli. Food is effective because it elicits the response of eating. Actual responses may not be necessary; activation of brain processes underlying responses may be adequate. *Motivational theories* emphasize increases or decreases of drive or arousal as reinforcing events. *Stimulus theories* say that stimuli which produce positive emotion or provide information are reinforcing.

5. *Secondary reinforcers* are formerly neutral stimuli which, through association with such primary reinforcers as food, have gained reinforcing capacity of their own. A good secondary reinforcer provides reliable information about a forthcoming primary reinforcer.

6. The concept of *incentive motivation* is based on the idea that rewards do not necessarily affect *specific responses.* Rather, the *anticipation* of rewards arouses whatever responses might be effective in obtaining the rewards. A variety of experiments shows that changes in *incentive value* produce changes in performance even though not associated with particular responses.

7. Hull added incentive motivation (K) to his theory, so that his expanded formula now reads : $E = H \times D \times K$. Spence proposed that incentive motivation grows out of *goal responses.* A fraction of the eating response, for example, is condi-

tioned to eating. This fractional goal response, rg-sg, is conditioned to environmental cues and has drive-like properties. The rg-sg mechanism then has incentive motivational properties. There is little evidence for the existence of such responses, however.

8.  *Tolman's purposive behaviorism* is much like the approach we took in defining motivation in chapter 1. In Tolman's system, organisms are said to learn *expectancies* about incentives. Incentives have positive or negative *valence*, which is their motivational power.

9.  Other theories of incentive motivation have used concepts similar to Tolman's.

10. Solomon and Corbit's *opponent-process theory* postulates that every positively or negatively experienced situation also arouses an opponent process. Pleasant situations arouse an underlying negative process, and vice versa. When the events maintaining pleasant experiences are removed, the underlying opponent process (negative) becomes dominant. Thus, depression may follow the loss of a loved one. The theory accounts for many motivationally important phenomena.

11. *Central motive state* (CMS) theory proposes that incentive stimuli, in conjunction with internal states, produce a central motivational state that influences many behaviors. Since the central state may persist for some time, it seems likely to have a neurochemical or hormonal basis.

12. Incentive-related stimuli have *predictive value*, such as a tone which predicts the coming of food. This predictive power is *transferable* from one situation to another, even to responses not previously associated with the predictive stimulus.

13. *Human incentives* are also related to *fantasy*. Klinger has proposed that we have *commitment to goals* and this commitment is reflected in our *current concerns* which persist over time. Current concerns are shown in fantasy, dreams, and thoughts.

14. External rewards for behavior sometimes *reduce intrinsic motivation* to engage in those behaviors. Deci's theory of cognitive evaluation says that rewards have *controlling* and *informational* aspects. When rewards are perceived as controlling behavior, intrinsic motivation is said to decrease.

15. External rewards are more detrimental to the intrinsic motivation of people with a *high desire for control*, presumably because external rewards are perceived as *not* being under the individual's control.

16. *Behavioral economics* is the application of economic principles to laboratory research on rewards. *Demand curves* (effects of increasing cost for commodities) have been studied, using the number of lever presses required to obtain a reward as a definition of cost. This approach has made some verifiable predictions in the animal laboratory.

# 7

# Aversive States and Outcomes: Escape, Fear, Avoidance, and Punishment

In the previous chapter we looked at environmental events which are desirable and sought. In this chapter we look at events which are aversive conditions: events which are escaped, feared, avoided, and punishing.

## INSTRUMENTAL ESCAPE LEARNING

Instrumental escape learning refers to any response that is reinforced by a reduction of aversive stimulation. An obvious escape response is running away; it is also escape if we terminate a conversation which is unpleasant, even though we do not physically leave the situation. Electric shock has been the most-used aversive stimulus in the animal laboratory, but cold water, loud noises, and bright lights have also been used. The most commonly used aversive stimuli with humans now are loud noises and threats of various kinds, such as of shock or some kind of evaluation.

### Variables Affecting Animal Escape Learning

*Amount of reinforcement.* Amount of reinforcement is an important variable in escape learning just as it is in reward learning. Campbell and Kraeling (1953) had rats run in a straight alley to escape from 200, 300, or 400 volts of grid shock to some lower level of shock. Early in training, higher shock produced faster running, although all groups eventually converged to the same maximal performance. It was also found that early running speed depended on the *proportion* of shock reduction, not the absolute amount of reduction in the goal box. For example, a 100-volt reduction was very effective if the change was from 100 volts to no shock, but less effective going from 200 to 100 volts, and still less effective going from 400 to 300 volts. The data were an approximation to Weber's law in perception:[1] Amount of reinforcement depends on percentage change, not just absolute change. The psychophysics of reinforcement have been discussed in detail by Campbell and Masterton (1969). There is an even more important implication of these data from our point of view, however. If animals are running faster from 400 volts to 100 volts than from 400 volts to 300 volts, then they must be anticipating the amount of shock reduction to come. If their running speed were determined only by the shock in the alleyway, they would have run at the same speed. Thus, there seems to be an incentive effect with escape learning.

"Drive" and "incentive" effects have been studied in some detail with rats swimming to escape cold water (Woods, Davidson, & Peters, 1964). Drive

---

[1]According to Weber's law, the minimum amount of stimulus intensity change, in any stimulus dimension, is some constant proportion of the reference stimulus. For example, if the value of the proportion were .10, it would take a change from 10 to 11, or from 100 to 110, to be noticed.

was manipulated by varying temperature in a "runway" tank, and incentive was manipulated by adjusting temperature in the "goal" tank. The results were that goal tank temperature was much more important than runway tank temperature in affecting swimming speed to escape. This lends further emphasis to the incentive aspects of escape learning. Other investigators have reported similar results (Stavely, 1966).

*Delay of reinforcement.*     Immediacy of reinforcement after a response is made is also important for escape learning, as it is for reward learning. Fowler and Trapold (1962) had rats running from a 250-volt runway shock to a goal box where shock termination was delayed between 0 and 16 seconds for different groups. Running speed was faster with shorter delays of reinforcement (Figure 7–1). When shock levels are high, however, long delays are less detrimental to running than short delays (Bell, Noah & Davis, 1965).

*Incentive shifts.*     The *pièce de résistance* for an incentive interpretation for shock reduction reinforcement would be to show incentive shift effects like those found by Crespi for positive incentives. Bower, Fowler, and Trapold (1959) did exactly this. They had rats running from a 250-volt alleyway shock to a goal box where shocks of 200, 150, or 50 volts were continued for 20 seconds after the animal entered. The animals escaped faster with greater shock reduction, and when the goal-box shock level was adjusted upward or downward, and the animals rapidly adjusted their running speeds accordingly. The results (Figure 7–2) look very much like those found in other incentive shift experiments. Woods (1967) reported similar results when goal-tank water temperatures were lowered or raised for escape from a cold-water alley tank.

**FIGURE 7–1**
Running speed (100/time in seconds) as a function of the delay (in seconds) of shock termination in the goal box. (From Fowler and Trapold, 1962, p. 465. Copyright ©1962 by the American Psychological Association. Reprinted by permission.).

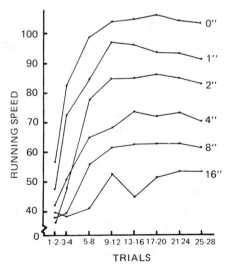

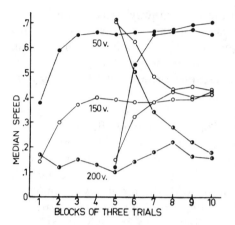

**FIGURE 7-2**
Group median speed (1/time in seconds) as a function of goal-shock voltage. (From Bower, Fowler, and Trapold, 1959, p. 483. Copyright © 1959 by the American Psychological Association. Reprinted by permission.).    fc;7-3

Unlike results with positive incentive shifts, however, the elation and depression effects were not found. Animals going from a lower amount of reinforcement to a larger one did not run faster than animals continuously on larger reinforcement, for example. In general, contrast effects have not been reported for escape learning.

### Theories for Escape Learning

*Drive Theory.* For a long time, drive theory seemed such an obvious interpretation for escape learning that alternatives were not seriously considered. An intense stimulus produces drive; the more intense the stimulus the harder an animal will work to escape, and the greater is the reinforcement when the animal does escape. Thus, shock produces a drive and shock reduction (drive reduction) is the reinforcer. In the experiments just reviewed, however, where animals ran to different amounts of shock in the goal box, the animals were clearly responding to *anticipated* shock levels in the goal box, as well as to the shock they encountered in the alleyway. At the very least, then, we need to supplement a drive interpretation with an incentive interpretation.

*Incentive theory.* *Hope* and *relaxation* are similar concepts to explain escape learning in incentive terms (Mowrer, 1960; Denny, 1971). When a painful stimulus ends, there is an *internal change* which can be conditioned to stimuli preceding the end of the stimulus. We shall simply denote this conditioned change as *anticipatory relaxation*. When an animal learns to escape from shock, for example, it also learns anticipatory relaxation. When an animal finds its way to the shock-free goal box, the "goal response" is relaxation and the conditioned component of the goal response is anticipatory relaxation. Anticipatory relaxation is stronger as the animal gets closer to the goal box, and the animal makes responses which increasingly maximize anticipatory relaxation and finally lead to "real" relaxation.

What is the role of shock intensity in an incentive theory of escape learning? Just as deprivation increases the incentive value of food, intense stimulation should increase the amount of anticipatory relaxation. The stronger the shock, the greater the anticipatory relaxation. Without shock, there should be no anticipatory relaxation, so "poor" performance should result. Why should the animal run down the alleyway to the goal box if there were no shock in the alleyway? Increasing or decreasing either alley shock or goal shock changes the amount of anticipated relaxation and behavior changes appropriately: the incentive shift effect.

An expected exception to the above predictions can occur due to fear learning. The alleyway stimuli could become conditioned stimuli for fear because they have been paired with shock. Even without shock in the alleyway the animal would be fearful, and anticipatory relaxation would still occur as long as this fear persists. The fearful subject would continue to escape at least until the fear extinguished to a low enough level that anticipatory relaxation was too weak an incentive to arouse behavior.

## CONDITIONED AVERSION: FEAR

### Historical Background and Clinical Importance

In 1920 Watson and Raynor reported their classic experiment with Little Albert. An eleven-month-old child, Albert, was initially exposed to a series of objects, including a white rat, a rabbit, a dog, a monkey, masks with and without hair, cotton, wool, and so on. "Manipulation was the most usual reaction called out. At no time did this infant ever show fear in any situation" (Watson & Raynor, 1920, p.2). Albert was then shown a white rat while a steel bar behind him was struck with a hammer. The rat was the conditioned stimulus (CS) and the loud noise the unconditioned stimulus (UCS). After seven trials, spread over several days, "The instant the rat was shown the baby began to cry" and to try to get away. Five days later, Albert was not only fearful of the rat but also of the rabbit, the dog, a seal-fur coat, and a Santa Claus mask. A fear response had been classically conditioned and generalized to other stimuli. Watson pointed out that the results demonstrated that not *all* anxiety was related to sex, as Freud had claimed.

Shortly thereafter, another student of Watson's (Mary Cover Jones, 1924) studied the elimination of children's preexisting, not experimentally induced, fears. Describing her most effective technique for doing this, she said: "By the method of direct conditioning, we associated the fear object with a craving object and replaced the fear by a positive response" (p. 390). In contemporary terminology, this is *counterconditioning*.

In these two experiments, the foundations of contemporary behavior therapy could well have been laid, and we might have expected an outpouring of further research of this type. Instead, the Freudians held the day and it remained for Mowrer (1939), 15 years later, to focus on the problem of aversive conditioning and neurosis in a way that was to have real impact on psychological research and theory. We have already seen part of this development in the study of learned drives (Chapter 3), but the study of fear has not been limited to such a drive concept. Because of the clinical importance of fear, anxiety, and phobias (intense fears of specific objects), fear has been approached from many different directions.

### Sources of Fear

*Genetic/Maturational.*     Intense or pain-producing stimuli are not the only sources of fear (Hebb, 1946; Gray, 1971). A common phobia, for example, is fear of snakes. Jones and Jones (1928) reported that young city children who had never encountered snakes in the wild did not have a fear of snakes, but that a large percentage of adults reared in the city did have this fear. Hebb concluded that snake phobia is the result of maturation and does not require specific experience with snakes for its occurrence.

Not only are snake phobias common in adults, but they are also a common theme in visions produced by hallucinogenic drugs throughout the world. It is possible that fear of snakes (as well as insects, lizards, and other "slimy, crawling" animals) is a kind of species-specific reaction left over from a period of evolutionary development when it was adaptive to avoid snakes without having to be bitten first. Ancestors who ran first and "asked questions later" may have lived to love more frequently than those who waited around for attack. This genetically determined fear might indeed account for the evil attributed to the serpent, and the worldwide use of dragon and serpent symbols in mythology.

One line of research concerned with such genetic bias has studied the ease of conditioning, say, pictures of snakes or lizards, to aversive stimuli, as compared to pictures of flowers (Öhman, 1986). Galvanic skin responses conditioned to such animal stimuli are more resistant to extinction than are responses to neutral stimuli. Hebb argued that "psychologically" there is little in common among the many events that arouse fear. For example, loud noises arouse fear, but so does darkness. We may conjecture, however, that these are all stimulus conditions in which emotional responses have enhanced survival (Gray, 1971). Loud noises call for attention and make us wary. We may also need to be more attentive in the dark because we do not have the use of vision, our major source of information about the environment.

Hebb (1946) also noted that fears could occur due to direct changes to the nervous system. For example, people affected by the nutrition-deficit disease pellagra show psychotic fears that disappear on treatment with nicotinic acid. The individual may recall the fears that he had while sick and be at a loss to explain them. Hormones can also produce unexpected emotional responsiveness. For example, pregnant women or women getting injections of estrogens may inexplicably break into tears. Such responses disappear after the pregnancy is completed or hormone treatment is discontinued.

*Learning of Fears.    Classical Conditioning.* Fear can be readily conditioned in the general manner described by Watson and Raynor, but more subtle factors than those indicated in that experiment are involved. Recall that, according to Rescorla's theory of conditioninng (see Chapter 3), a stimulus becomes an effective CS if it reliably and uniquely predicts the occurrence of some other stimulus, the UCS. The theory does not say that an organism has to be consciously aware of such a relationship, but there is good evidence with human subjects that often this may be the case. For example, Fuhrer and Baer (1967) presented one stimulus as a CS+ (followed by shock) to human subjects and a different stimulus as CS− (not followed by shock). This is a *differential conditioning* paradigm, which controls for such factors as sensitization to all stimuli as a result of a UCS being presented. If the response being measured is elicited by CS+ but not by CS−, we have evidence of conditioning. In the Fuhrer and Baer experiment, differential conditioning of the galvanic skin response occurred only with those subjects who reported that the CS+ meant that shock was coming on. If they were not aware of this relationship, differential conditioning did not occur. Other experiments have reported similar results. This does not mean that classical conditioning can never occur without awareness, but it does throw a different light on how we look at classical conditioning.

*Fear of the unfamiliar.* At about three months of age, human infants begin to make positive responses to people, smiling and cooing. But at six months, they may show a strong negative reaction to strangers (or even to people to whom they have previously shown positive responses, such as grandparents). The child may cry and withdraw, for example. Hebb (1946) suggested that this is based on experience, but not on classical conditioning. Rather, the child becomes familiar with certain people and when an unfamiliar face appears, the child is afraid. This kind of fear involves the violation of an expectation. As an example of such a violation with an adult, the author was violently startled early one morning, when getting off the elevator at his accustomed floor, to find that the hallway was not there! It took a few troubled seconds to realize that earlier in the morning physical plant employees had moved in a number of tall metal cabinets and for temporary storage had placed them in the middle of the hall where they blocked off all the usual signs of the hallway. Had this been my first trip ever to this floor there would have been no startle.

### Phobias

Phobias are intense fears of specific stimuli, such as a fear of high places, open or closed spaces, flying, or such objects as snakes or insects. Phobias are resistant to change and may have debilitating effects, such as keeping a person from going outside or always having to avoid animals. According to classical psychoanalytic theory, a phobia is anxiety attached to some specific object. Anxiety is vague and difficult to deal with, whereas a phobia can be dealt with, for example by avoiding the situation which arouses the phobia. The psychoanalytic treatment would be to try to find the underlying conflict, or source of anxiety, leading to the phobia and then to reduce that anxiety.

Behavior theorists have taken a different approach, namely that phobias are acquired through classical conditioning (Wolpe & Rachman, 1960; McNally, 1987). Behaviors that reduce the phobic responses are reinforced by fear reduction (discussed in the next section). An important question, however, is whether phobias presented to clinicians by their patients really are the same kinds of fear as those established by laboratory conditioning. Seligman (1971) pointed out that phobias differ from conventional conditioned fears in that they (1) are acquired very quickly, (2) persist in spite of the patient's "objective knowledge" that the phobic object is harmless, (3) relate to objects (such as animals) that rarely pose a threat in modern life, and finally, (4) are resistant to extinction by normal Pavlovian procedures.

Seligman's *preparedness* theory (Seligman, 1970; 1971) maintains that organisms are "prepared" or "predisposed" to learn associations which have had survival value in the past, although perhaps are outmoded. The common phobias of snakes, lizards, cats, insects, and the like represent stimuli whose forms are readily conditionable to humans. McNally (1987) concludes that there is not a great deal of empirical support for the preparedness theory of phobias. Some experiments have shown faster GSR conditioning with "phobic" stimuli as CS's than to such neutral stimuli as triangles (e.g., see Öhman, 1986), but many experiments have not. The best evidence for preparedness theory is that *extinction* of the GSR conditioned to such prepared phobic stimuli as snakes is consistently much slower than extinction to neutral stimuli. Evidence for other aspects of preparedness theory and phobias is, at best, ambiguous albeit intriguing.

### Modifying Fears

Several approaches to modifying fears (or phobias) have been utilized in *behavior therapy*, the application of learning principles to therapeutic problems.

*Extinction.*   One treatment, called systematic desensitization, is to present a phobic stimulus repeatedly to a patient, showing that it has no ill effects and, it is hoped, producing extinction. This is often done in conjunction with a *fear hierarchy*, gradually presenting a client with stimuli which are progressively more similar to the phobic stimuli. When the client's fear of the generalized stimulus has extinguished, another stimulus more like the phobic stimulus is presented until fear to that stimulus extinguishes, and so on. For example, the word "snake" may be presented first, followed in progression by a picture of a snake, a model of a snake, a real snake at a distance, and finally a real snake to be touched and held. This kind of treatment has been found to be quite effective (Rimm & Masters, 1979).

*Counterconditioning.*   A phobic stimulus, which arouses a fearful response, is presented in conjunction with a stimulus which arouses an incompatible response. For example, a phobic stimulus might be presented along with food which arouses a pleasant response, so that the phobic stimulus becomes associated with the food. This has also been reported for pleasant music (Eifert, Craill, Carey, & O'Connor, 1988). It is also common practice to do extinction in conjunction with relaxation exercises, the relaxation presumably being incompatible with fear-related tension.

*Flooding.*   Flooding refers to presenting a fear-arousing stimulus repeatedly or intensely to a client. Thus, a person with a snake phobia might be "bombarded" with pictures of snakes. Fear responses may extinguish when no harm follows the stimuli.

*Cognitive changes.*   Foa and Kozak (1986) argue that emotional changes, such as reduction of phobic responses, result from exposure to emotional stimuli because of changed *meanings* of the phobic stimuli. They argue that "fear is represented in memory structures that serve as blueprints for fear behavior (p. 21)." The therapeutic tactic then is to (1) activate the fear structure, by facing the client with those stimuli/situations which arouse fear, and (2) incorporate information about a stimulus which is incompatible with the fear-arousing elements. The phobic stimuli may be presented imaginally or live. Just presenting a phobic stimulus repeatedly may not in itself be sufficient to produce change (because adequate new information may not be conveyed) and just giving new information may be inadequate (if the "fear structure" is not aroused at the time). The new information may be cognitive (such as a different interpretation of the stimulus which arouses the fear) and emotional (fear-reducing, pleasure-arousing) at the same time.

## AVOIDANCE LEARNING

Most of us tend not to stick metal objects into electrical outlets or walk in front of speeding automobiles indiscriminately. We are careful to avoid doing things which lead us into too-threatening situations, including social situations which we anticipate to be unpleasant. Such avoidance behavior has been studied intensely in animals because of its clinical relevance; unnecessary avoidance of many situations or people can be socially debilitating.

### Laboratory Avoidance

If we put a rat into a grid-floor apparatus and sound a buzzer, the animal will make little noticeable response. If we electrify the grid sufficiently five seconds later, however, the response is immediate. The rat may jump about and perhaps urinate or defecate, strong signs of emotional arousal. In a few seconds the animal crosses the midline of the box to the other side, where there is no shock. The animal has *escaped* the shock. We repeat the buzzer-shock sequence a number of times, with a minute delay after the animal has successfully responded. The escape response becomes swift and precise.

After about 30 trials or so, however, something new happens. The animal crosses the midline of the box in less than five seconds, and therefore does not get shocked. It has made its first *avoidance* response. On an increasing percentage of trials the animal responds before the shock comes on, becoming a proficient avoider. Figure 7–3 illustrates the performance of a single animal during the course of avoidance training. Two important elements seem to be involved in this situation: The animal learns to become afraid when the buzzer sounds, and the animal learns to run to the other side of the box before it gets shocked. These events have been quantified in a number of experiments (e.g., Hoffman and Fleshler, 1962).

Many factors related to stimulus presentation and response requirements determine how fast an animal learns to avoid and how proficient it becomes. But the main question has always been, *What keeps the animal avoiding?* Fear seems to be involved. But if the animal successfully avoids getting shocked, should it not become less afraid because of extinction? And if it is less afraid, should it not stop avoiding? Yet, dogs in such a situation have been found to avoid for literally hundreds of trials without getting

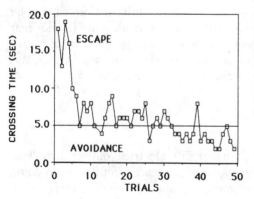

**FIGURE 7–3**

The course of avoidance learning. A five-second signal forewarns the animal of impending shock. Early in learning, the animal escapes from shock, taking more than five seconds to make the appropriate response. Later, it avoids shock by responding in less than five seconds after the signal is presented..

shocked; the experimenters wore down, not the dogs (Solomon & Wynne, 1954b).

### Interpretations of Avoidance Behavior

The most popular interpretation of active avoidance has been two-process (also called two-factor) learning theory. The processes are (1) classical conditioning of fear to the CS as a result of shock coming on after a buzzer sounds, and (2) instrumental conditioning of the escape and avoidance behaviors. A two-process theory seems to be demanded because neither classical nor instrumental conditioning alone provide adequate explanation of avoidance (Mowrer, 1960; Rescorla & Solomon, 1967). Let us see why.

*Avoidance as classical conditioning.* Brogden, Lipman, and Culler (1938) showed why classical conditioning could not account for avoidance. Using guinea pigs in a revolving cage, they used a buzzer as the CS and shock as the UCS. For a classical conditioning group, the buzzer was always followed by shock. The shock typically evoked running. For an avoidance conditioning group, however, shock was delivered only if an animal failed to run when the buzzer sounded. According to Pavlovian conditioning principles, the classical conditioning group should have run more reliably when the buzzer sounded. In fact, however, its best performance (Figure 7–4) was only about 50%. The avoidance group, on the other hand, quickly learned to run on every trial when the buzzer sounded. The reason for the poor performance by the classical conditioning group was clarified by Sheffield (1948). The animals in that condition are sometimes *already moving* when the shock comes on. The shock is *punishment for their moving,* therefore they run inconsistently. The death knell to the classical conditioning interpretation was sounded in an experiment by Mowrer and Lamoreaux (1946). They trained rats to *run* to escape shock and to *jump off the floor* to avoid shock in the same situation. The escape and avoidance responses were very different, and the avoidance

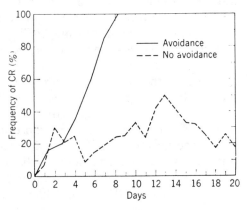

**FIGURE 7–4**
Learning curves showing the performance of animals for whom the response to the CS was not followed by shock (avoidance) and those for whom the CS was always followed by shock (no avoidance). These results show that avoidance learning is not just classical conditioning. (From Brogden, W. J., Culler, H. and Lipman, E. A. The role of incentive in conditioning and learning. *American Journal of Psychology*, 1938, *51*, p. 110. Reprinted by permission of The University of Illinois Press.).

response was not even the same as the unconditioned response to shock. The animals nevertheless learned the problem without difficulty, and the classical conditioning interpretation for avoidance was put to rest.

*Avoidance as instrumental conditioning.*    The inadequacy of the instrumental conditioning explanation is brought out in the question "What is the reinforcer if the animal is successfully avoiding the shock?" It cannot be shock reduction, since the animal is not getting shocked. But if fear reduction is the reinforcement, we have to postulate that fear was learned. This leads us back to the two-process theory of avoidance.

*Two-process interpretation of avoidance.*    According to two-process theory, an animal first learns to become afraid of the buzzer through classical conditioning (buzzer paired with shock). Simultaneously, the animal learns to escape from shock. The animal then transfers the running responses from the shock stimulus to the fear stimulus. This transfer can occur because the shock aroused both fear and pain in earlier training, and thus the fear also was a stimulus for running at that time. The animal is reinforced on successful avoidance trials because the fear-arousing buzzer is turned off when the avoidance response is made. The fear in this case functions as both a drive and a cue, and fear reduction is the reinforcer. This theory solves many problems, but it also raises many questions about the role of fear and the CS.

All available evidence would indicate that fear plays some role in the learning of avoidance; avoidance learning does not seem to occur without some measurable amount of fear (Mineka, 1979). Beyond this, the evidence on the role of fear is much less certain. If the role of fear is questionable, then any theory requiring fear (such as two-factor theory) is equally in doubt.

### Evidence for Fear in Avoidance

*Cutting the sympathetic nervous system.*    If we reduce the autonomic aspects of the fear response by cutting the sympathetic nervous system we would expect avoidance behavior to be disrupted. The results of such an experiment (Solomon & Wynne, 1950a) are even more intriguing than this, however. If the operation is done *before* avoidance training, avoidance learning is much poorer. This supports the theory that fear is important to avoidance. If the operation is performed *after* the animal has already learned to avoid, however, performance is not affected; the animals continue to avoid quite adequately. This suggests that once the behavior is well-learned, the CS may only be a *cue* to make the response, and not arouse fear the same way it does in the early training. This is also supported by research showing that fear is in fact greatly reduced in animals that have learned an avoidance response well. In this research, fear and avoidance responding are measured independently of each other (Hoffman & Fleshler, 1962). Solomon and Wynne (1954) proposed, however, that even slight amounts of fear might be aroused by the CS and avoidance occurs so quickly that a large amount of fear is not necessary. In this case, cutting the sympathetic nervous system might greatly reduce fear, but not completely eliminate it, so the animals can still avoid.

*Curare experiments.*    Suppose we conditioned fear when no overt response could be made. If later the fear arousal facilitated avoidance we would have to conclude that fear was important to avoidance. In such an experiment dogs were first given standard avoidance training with a light as the CS. Then, while immobilized by the paralyzing drug curare, the animals were given differential classical conditioning with one tone as CS + and a different tone as CS −, and shock as the UCS. Subsequently, the tones (not the light) were used as CS's for avoidance. The animals made avoidance responses to CS + but not to CS −. Since CS + had never before been paired with the avoidance response, only with shock, we conclude that the fear response aroused by CS + is important to avoidance (A. H. Black, Carlson, & Solomon, 1962; Solomon & Turner, 1962; Leaf, 1964). At the very least, fear seems to increase the likelihood of avoidance responding.

*Tranquilizing drugs.*    Tranquilizing drugs, such as Valium (*diazepam*) operate selectively to suppress avoidance, and other fear-related behaviors, but have relatively little effect on positively motivated behaviors (Ray, 1963; Gray, 1982). This indicates that fear is involved in avoidance.

### Dissociation of Fear and Avoidance

*Fear declines during avoidance learning.*    As avoidance learning progresses, animals become less fearful, as shown by various measures of fear (Mineka, 1979). This decline has something to do with *responding,* because control animals getting the same shocks (but not avoiding) do not show the fear decrement (Starr & Mineka, 1977). The importance of declining fear is the theoretical problem it poses, namely, Why is avoidance response getting better when fear is declining?

If fear were critical to avoidance, we would also expect that, during extinction of avoidance responding, fear would decline as avoidance decreases. This does not happen reliably, either. Animals that show significant extinction of avoidance responding have been shown to be just as fearful as animals without extinction trials at all (Kamin, Brimer, & Black, 1963). Why then do animals extinguish at all, if fear is not being reduced during extinction? This leads us to look at *response prevention* and *flooding.*

*Response prevention and flooding techniques.*    Two-factor theory would predict that, if animals had extensive nonreinforced exposure to the CS, fear should extinguish and avoidance responding decline. Flooding refers to exposure to fear stimuli, without any effective response for getting rid of the stimuli. The fear stimuli may be naturally occurring ones or, as in our present discussion, CS's in a fear situation. Page (1955) however, showed that after animals had been prevented from responding in the avoidance situation (response prevention), and subsequently showed extinction of avoidance due to this prevention, the animals refused to go back into the avoidance apparatus when given the opportunity to do so. Presumably, they were still afraid, even though no longer avoiding. The continued presence of fear in such situations is shown in an experiment where rats had undergone a flooding procedure, and stopped avoiding, but their heart rates were still as elevated as when they were avoiding (Werboff, Duane, & Cohen, 1964).

Flooding results are further complicated by the fact that confining animals in novel places, or fear-provoking places not related to the avoidance learning, can also hasten later extinction of avoidance. Crawford (1977) suggested that this result was due to the emergence of a new response. Specifically, during the course of confinement, when an animal is fearful, it may engage in what Bolles (1972) called a *species-specific defense reaction* (SSDR). In this case, freezing would be a typical rat response. Placed back into the avoidance apparatus the animal might now show the new dominant response, freezing.

The most we can say at this point is that fear seems to be involved in the learning of avoidance behaviors, and that fear can facilitate the occurrence of avoidance responding. There are many conditions, however, where fear and avoidance responding seem to be unrelated to each other.

### The Role of the CS in Avoidance

We have seen that fear is involved in avoidance learning, but what does the CS do? In the early avoidance learning experiments, the CS was left on until the animal made an avoidance response, at which time the CS was terminated. It was argued that avoidance was reinforced by CS termination. The animal was said to respond because it was afraid (the CS aroused fear) and to respond because it was reinforced by CS termination (CS termination produced fear reduction). With this experimental procedure, however, shock avoidance and CS termination were confounded, since both occurred. Kamin (1956) tried to separate the effects of CS termination and UCS avoidance, and concluded that both were important.

A variation on the CS-arouses-fear theme is the notion of fear as *Pavlovian conditioned excitation* (Rescorla & Solomon, 1967). A CS signalling the onset of shock will increase the rate of avoidance responses even though it has never been specifically paired with those responses, as in the case of the curare experiments. The CS presumably increases fear. Conversely, a signal that indicates that no shock is forthcoming produces *conditioned inhibition* of fear, and reduces the rate of avoidance responding.

A third idea is that the CS for avoidance is a *discriminative stimulus,* or cue, for responding (Herrnstein, 1969). Herrnstein argued that a CS is not necessary for avoidance learning at all; all that is required is that the animal learn that when it makes an avoidance response there is less shock than if it does not make the avoidance response. The CS just tells the animal when to respond to keep down the amount of shock. In the usual avoidance experiment responding is followed by shock avoidance only after the CS has come on. Therefore, the CS may seem to be more important than it really is. If this view is correct, then it should be possible for an animal to learn avoidance without an external stimulus as a CS.

*Unsignalled avoidance.*     Avoidance learning without an external signal is learned in the following manner (Sidman, 1966). Animals in a Skinner box with a grid floor are given brief shocks (e.g., 0.5 second) which cannot be escaped. These shocks are programmed according to two different schedules. If the animal never responds at all, it is automatically shocked every so often (say, 20 seconds). This is the *shock-shock interval.* If, however, the animal presses the lever during the shock-shock interval, the next shock is *postponed* for a set length of time (say, also, 20 seconds). This is the response-shock interval.

If the animal were to press the lever just once every 20 seconds, it would never get shocked. But, pity to say, it never works quite this way.

If the shock-shock and response-shock intervals are the same duration, there is considerable variability in how rapidly and well animals learn the avoidance response. Figure 7-5 shows the performance of one "typical" learner and one "fast" learner. Note that the sessions are eight and six *hours* long respectively, and each blip represents a shock. Even the fast learner gets many, many more shocks than is typical for the shuttlebox situation. The animals never seem to just "wait out" an interval, responding just before the next shock is to come. To the contrary, the animals are as likely to respond in the first half of the shock-shock interval as in the last half. By special training procedures animals can be taught to wait until the last part of the shock-shock interval to respond, but they do not seem to learn this spontaneously. Animals will learn spontaneously that if the response-shock interval is much shorter than the shock-shock interval, they are better off not to respond. They are, in effect, punished for responding.

Since there is no external CS in Sidman's situation, the role of the CS in avoidance is questioned. It has been argued (Anger, 1963; Mowrer, 1960) that the CS for responding is some internal "stimulus trace" from the previous avoidance response. That is, when the animal makes an avoidance response this produces a feedback stimulus which gradually gets weaker after the response is made. A strong feedback trace is associated with no shock, since the animal is never shocked immediately after responding. As the trace weakens, however, shock becomes more likely and the trace gradually be-

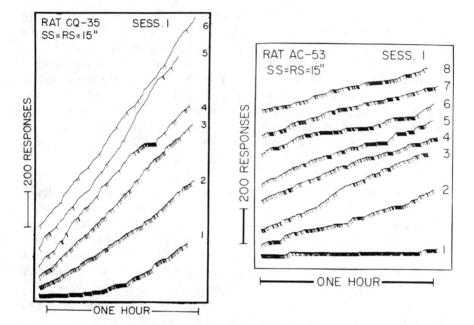

**FIGURE 7-5.**  Cumulative records for two rats in their first sessions of Sidman avoidance learning, about six and eight hours long, respectively. To condense the figures, the records have been cut into segments of approximately one hour each, and are numbered in temporal order. The oblique "pips" on the record indicate shocks. Rat CQ-35 learned more rapidly than did Rat AC-53, but CQ-35 had a few minutes in the fourth hour when it got a large number of shocks. (Murray Sidman, "Avoidance Behavior," in OPERANT BEHAVIOR: Areas of Research and Application, W. K. Honig, ed., ©1966, pp. 451, 452, 453. Reprinted by permission of Prentice Hall, Inc., Englewood Cliffs, New Jersey).

comes a CS for fear. At some point the fear builds up to a level where it triggers the animal to respond. This response is followed by fear reduction, and the whole cycle starts up again. In the Sidman situation a Pavlovian conditioned excitation CS (never previously associated with the avoidance response) will increase the rate of responding and a conditioned inhibitor will reduce the rate of responding. This indicates that fear is playing some role in unsignalled avoidance.

### Cognitive interpretations of avoidance.

At the time research on avoidance learning was undertaken the primary researchers were strongly behavioristic and wary of cognitive concepts. Therefore, they emphasized classical and instrumental conditioning. Quite early, however, Osgood (1950) proposed a cognitive interpretation based on Tolman's theory. Osgood said the buzzer becomes a signal of shock, and that the animals do whatever is required to avoid shock. A problem for cognitive theory is why avoidance should ever decline. Unless the animal fails to make the avoidance response, how will if find out that shock will not follow the buzzer? Osgood simply assumed that the *demand* against shock declines with successful avoidance. Occasionally, the animal will fail to respond in time to avoid shock. Then, either (1) It will get shocked, its expectation of shock will be reconfirmed, and it will start avoiding again; or (2) It will not get shocked, (as with extinction), a new expectation of no-shock will be established, and avoidance will cease.

More recently, Seligman and Johnston (1973) proposed a theory based on Irwin's (1971) theory of intentional behavior, as follows. At the peak of avoidance learning, an animal acquires two expectancies: (1) If it responds in a given time after CS onset, it will *not* get shocked; and (2) If it does not respond fast enough it *will* get shocked. The animal prefers not getting shocked and therefore makes the avoidance response.

Even with cognitive interpretations for the *learning* of avoidance, however, we would still have to consider the effects of protracted aversive stimulation, pain or fear, on an animal or person. A cognitive interpretation of avoidance does not eliminate stress and aversion from the situation; all it does is say that drive reduction (i.e., fear reduction) is not a necessary condition for learning avoidance.

## PUNISHMENT

Punishment takes such varied guises as physical pain or its threat, social sanctions, isolation, and withdrawal of privileges. All of these are supposed to suppress "undesirable" behavior. Events that are supposed to be punishing are often ineffective, however. Supposed punishment sometimes increases the very behavior it is expected to eliminate and sometimes suppresses behaviors indiscriminately. Thus, while it is true that "punishment suppresses behavior," our understanding of exactly what is involved requires more detailed study (Campbell & Church, 1969; Dunham, 1971).

### Definition

According to a *stimulus definition* of punishment, *punishment is the delivery of an aversive stimulus to an organism following a response.* The organism is expected to suppress the response as a means of avoiding punishment.[2] This definition requires that in the study of punishment we must use stimuli which are demonstrably aversive, otherwise we are simply assuming that the definition is good.

---

[2]Punishment has therefore sometimes been referred to as *passive avoidance*. The animal learns *not* to respond as a means of avoiding punishment, as compared to the *active avoidance* which we have just discussed, where the animal must learn to make some defined response to avoid an aversive stimulus.

A *response definition* of punishment, on the other hand, says that *punishment is the delivery of a stimulus that suppresses the preceding behavior,* whether or not the stimulus is demonstrably aversive otherwise. This does not predict for us what stimuli will be punishers, but it does encourage us to look for effective punishers. For example, a retarded child who stuck out her tongue several times a minute was resistant to all kinds of attempted punishment until the therapist hit upon putting lemon juice on her tongue whenever she stuck it out. This was an effective punisher. A response definition also helps clarify such situations as when a fixed stimulus, such as a specific shock intensity, suppresses one response but not a different response. That stimulus was not a punisher in the second situation. This tells us that punishers are not invariant, that the effectiveness of any stimulus as a punisher depends on other factors. For the sake of consistency, we will hereafter assume a response definition of punishment unless otherwise indicated.

### Suppressive Effects

It is clear from much research and practical experience that punishment does *not eliminate* behaviors, it suppresses behaviors in certain situations. According to the *alternative response theory,* punished behaviors are less likely to occur because they have been replaced at least temporarily by other behaviors. Skinner (1938), in one of the earliest reports of punishment of free operant behavior (lever pressing) in the laboratory, slapped the rat's paw when it touched the lever. Lever pressing was suppressed for a while but came back because there was no alternative response by which the animal could get reinforced. Estes and Skinner (1941) went on to show that even electric shock suppressed lever pressing only temporarily. Dunham (1971) tested the alternative response hypothesis directly, with Mongolian gerbils as subjects. Given the opportunity, isolated gerbils will spend most of their waking time doing just three things: shredding paper, eating food pellets, and drinking water. Each of these is easily measured (amount of paper pulled from a roll can be recorded automatically), so it is possible to get normal baseline measures for each and then see how the responses change when punished. Dunham found that a punished response did decline and that one of the other responses would increase, thus supporting the alternative response hypothesis.

### Response Factors

The nature of the response elicited by punishment is very important, since the elicited response may either interfere with or facilitate the punished response, as we saw with the guinea pigs in avoidance learning. If an animal is punished while running, the automatic response is to stop. If an animal is punished while standing still, the response may be to run. In order to predict the effects of punishment, then, we should have to know what response the punishment evokes. To indicate the importance of this, Fowler and Miller (1963) showed that animals that had their *hind paws* shocked just as they entered the goal box at the end of a straight alley (thereby facilitating forward movement) ran *faster* with higher shock levels. On the other hand, animals that had their forepaws shocked, ran *slower* with higher shock levels. Therefore, it was not shock intensity per se which determined how fast the animals responded, but the response elicited by the shock.

### Stimulus Factors

*Immediacy of punishment.*    Given that one has an effective punisher at his disposal, the single most basic rule for effective punishment is that the punisher should immediately follow the punished response. The longer the delay between response and punishment, the less effective the punishment is. Figure 7–6 shows the results of an experiment in which punishment of lever pressing by electric shock was delayed from zero to 30 seconds (Camp, Raymond, & Church, 1967). The zero-delay group was most suppressed and the 30-seond delay the least. Note also in Figure 7–6 that a noncontingent punishment group (NC), which received the shocks but not in relation to lever pressing, showed less suppression than the 30-second delay group.

What is meant to be response-contingent punishment often ends up being either *noncontingent* or *stimulus-contingent*. By stimulus-contingent we mean that the punishment is associated with a particular stimulus (as in classical conditioning) rather than with a particular response. For example, instead of punishing a child immediately for some indiscretion, a parent waits until the spouse comes home to have the spouse punish the child. In this case, the punishment may become stimulus-contingent: the punishing parent becomes associated with the punishment. The result may be fear of the punishing parent but little suppression of the undesired behavior. Punishment must be clearly associated with the undesirable behavior to be effective. With older children or adults this may be accomplished over long delays by "verbal mediation," such as discussing the behavior to be punished and the reason.

*Effects of noncontingent punishment.*    A noncontingent punishment procedure called *conditioned emotional response* (CER) procedure has been used to study punishment of free operant behavior. The punishing stimulus follows some signal, rather than a response, but such behavior as lever pressing is suppressed when the signal is turned on. The CER procedure has a number of different effects than does response-contingent punishment, however (Hunt & Brady, 1955; Church, 1969). For example, the CER procedure suppresses many different behaviors, is slower to extinguish, and is

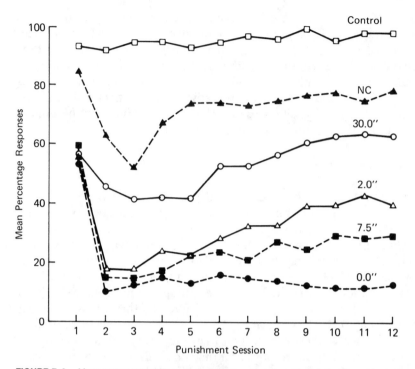

FIGURE 7-6.    Mean percentages of responses as a function of sessions for groups with .0, 2.0, 7.5, 30.0 seconds delay of punishment, noncontingent shock, and unpunished control group. (Failure to press the lever within 10 seconds of stimulus onset was defined as a nonresponse.) (From Camp, Raymond, and Church, 197, p. 121. Copyright ©1967 by the American Psychological Association. Reprinted by permission.)

harder to countercondition with positive reinforcement. And, as we have seen, even delayed response-contingent punishment is more effective in suppressing specific responses than is noncontingent punishment.

*Stimulus intensity and adaptation.* More intense stimuli do have greater suppressive effects (Azrin & Holz, 1966), and if the punishing stimulus is strong enough the effects may be nearly irreversible. For example, cats which had received strong punishment for eating refused thereafter to eat in the experimental apparatus (Masserman, 1943).

If experimental animals gradually adapt to increasingly strong shocks, however, the suppressive effect is considerably weakened (Miller, 1960). It is especially interesting that this weakening is not due to simple sensory adaptation to the shocks. Animals which were exposed to the same intensities of shock outside the apparatus did not show the effects of this adaptation when they were in the apparatus. The adaptation in some sense was psychological rather than physical. When shock was increased gradually in the apparatus the animals may have learned to cope with it by responding in particular ways. Increasing shock levels outside the apparatus would not have allowed this kind of learning and therefore was more suppressive when introduced into the apparatus. This may be related to the learned helplessness phenomenon, discussed in detail in chapter 9.

### Potential Problems Using Punishment

Since punishment is used so much, wisely or not, it is worthwhile to point out very specifically some pitfalls in its use.

1. *Make sure the punishment is punishing.* Punishment should be delivered promptly, whether in the form of a reprimand, a slap on the wrist, or withdrawal of privileges. The punishment must be associated with the act. In terms of the response definition, the punishment must be punishing. A slight word of discouragement which may stop one child from an activity may be completely ineffective with a different child. One may have to work at finding what is punishing for a particular individual. The punishment should not contain concealed rewards. For example, if a child is sent to his room as punishment, where he plays his stereo, watches TV, and phones his friends, the "punishment" is not likely to have much effect.

2. *Watch out for side effects of punishment.* Strong punishment may produce excessive emotional responses and/or escape behavior. These are minimized by careful response-contingent punishment, which is more effective and less disturbing than delayed or stimulus-contingent punishment. A good effect is that punishment may suppress undesirable behavior long enough for desirable behavior to occur to be rewarded. If a child spends all her class time fooling around or talking, she has little time to do things which are rewarded.

3. *Reinforce alternative behaviors.* The problem is to change behavior, not to be punishing. If desirable behaviors are rewarded at the same time that undesirable behaviors are punished, then the effects of punishment are likely to be more satisfactory. In fact, when alternative behaviors are rewarded punishment may not be necessary. If a child gets hold of a dangerous kitchen utensil to play with, the child may be praised for giving the utensil to the parent, who is at the same time giving him a toy to play with. The child can learn alternative behavior without punishment.

### SUMMARY

1. Instrumental escape learning refers to any situation where responses are reinforced by reducing the level of aversive stimulation. Such responses may or may not literally involve "running away." Almost any intense stimulus is potentially aversive.

2. Speed of escape is determined by such variables as amount and delay of reinforcement, but the *percentage* reduction of aversive stimulation is more

critical than the absolute amount of reduction. Incentive shift effects have been found with escape learning, just as with reward learning.

3. Drive and drive reduction theory accounts for much escape learning but fails to account for the *anticipation* of the amount of stimulus reduction shown by animals in escape learning situations. The concept of *anticipatory relaxation*, an incentive point of view, does account for such anticipatory responses.

4. Fear, an aversive emotional state or response, may be aroused by intense or painful unconditioned stimuli or by such specific stimulus patterns as snakes or insects. Fearful responses to such stimuli without prior learning might have evolved as an adaptive survival mechanism. Some fears are also related to direct changes in the nervous system, such as during illness.

5. Fears are readily conditioned in accordance with Pavlovian principles, but a fear of the unfamiliar also occurs. This depends on previously learned expectations, but is not classical conditioning.

6. *Phobias* are intense fears of specific stimuli, which are quickly acquired, difficult to eliminate, and often unrelated to objects which pose a real threat. Treatments for the elimination of phobias have involved extinction and counterconditioning procedures. Intense exposure to feared stimuli ("flooding") has also been effective in reducing or eliminating phobias, as clients discover their fears are unfounded.

7. *Avoidance behavior* consists of any response that prevents the occurrence of an anticipated aversive event. A major question is why animals or people continue avoiding, since they do not experience the aversive stimulus if they successfully avoid.

8. The most widely used interpretation of avoidance is a *two-process* (two-factor) *theory.* This says that organisms first learn to be *fearful* in the situation according to *classical conditioning* principles and then learn to avoid (prevent) the aversive stimulus according to *instrumental conditioning* principles. Neither process alone accounts for avoidance.

9. Fear is clearly important in the initial learning of avoidance responses, but is less clearly involved in their long-term maintenance. Fear and avoidance become *dissociated* during the course of avoidance learning. Avoidance responses may also undergo extinction without any marked reduction in fear.

10. The CS for avoidance generally has been considered important because it arouses fear, and because CS termination is reinforcing. Avoidance can be learned without any external stimulus to signal oncoming shock, however, and the CS may serve only as a cue to tell the organism *when* responding will prevent an aversive stimulus. In such situations, however, a fear stimulus from a completely different situation will increase the rate of avoidance responding.

11. *Cognitive* interpretations of avoidance say that organisms learn to expect that responding is *not* followed by shock and that non-responding *is* followed by shock. Since no-shock is preferred, organisms make the avoidance response.

12. *Punishment* involves the *inhibition* of responses by presenting aversive stimuli when such responses occur. As a practical matter, *whatever* stimuli suppress behavior may be considered punishers. Removal of some stimuli, such as withdrawing privileges, is also punishing.

13. *Response* factors are important in punishment, because a punisher may arouse responses which either compete with or *facilitate* a punished response. Punishment should arouse competing responses.

14. The *alternative response theory* says that punishment stimulates organisms to make some response other than the punished response, and this alternative response is reinforced. Punishment does not eliminate responses, it suppresses responses under particular circumstances.

15. *Stimulus* variables affecting power of punishment include *delay* between response and punishment, *intensity* of the punisher, and adaptation to the punishing stimulus.

16. Potential problems in using punishment are (1) making sure the punishing stimulus is in fact punishing, (2) making sure the side effects of punishment are not worse than the behavior being punished, and (3) reinforcing alternative behaviors.

# 8

# Frustration, Conflict, Anger, and Aggression

## FRUSTRATION

A student told me a story about a friend who was supposed to meet his wife at the airport before she left on a flight, but he was delayed and arrived at the airport too late. He thereupon beat in the hood of his car. This example indicates what we commonly mean by frustration: emotion aroused when an anticipated desirable goal is not attained. This leads to frustration, which in turn has some effect on behavior. Frustration is commonly considered an aversive state. As with other internal states we shall consider it as an *intervening variable* so that we can deal with it in objective terms.

### Definition

To define frustration as an intervening variable we have blocking of a goal as an antecedent condition and some response as a consequent condition.

| *Antecedent* | *Intervening Variable* | *Consequent* |
|---|---|---|
| Blocking of Goal Behavior → | Frustration → | Responses |
| | | (a) Emotional |
| | | (b) Behavioral |

Failing to reach the airport on time was the antecedent condition for our woebegone spouse, and beating in his car hood was the consequent. Had we *only* seen him beating in his car hood, we would have no firm justification for saying he was frustrated. Knowing that he had failed to reach his goal, however, we *are* justified in inferring frustration.

Several different consequent conditions might be used to define frustration, just as we define any emotion. Our friend might have *said* that he felt frustrated. Such verbal reports do not *always* mean that a person is actually frustrated, however. A person might use the term frustration to refer to any unhappy feeling without necessarily referring to a blocked goal. We might have used a *physiological* response as an indicator of frustration. If our friend's blood pressure had gone up, we might infer frustration.

Finally, we also had the *behavioral index*, his violent behavior toward his car.

Over the years, a number of specific response classes have been considered indicative of frustration. These include *aggressive behaviors, fixations* (rigid, unchanging behaviors), *regression* (reversion to more childlike modes of responding), more *vigorous behaviors, escape, avoidance,* and such *emotional* responses as crying. Much of the effort toward finding specific frustration responses was prompted by the *frustration-aggression hypothesis,* discussed in more detail later in this chapter. Briefly, the hypothesis says that frustration produces aggression: the searches for other responses were often attempts to prove or disprove that hypothesis (Lawson, 1965; Yates, 1962). Since responses to frustration are as likely to be as variable as responses to any other aversive condition, frustration is more profitably considered a general motivational condition, such as a *drive* (Brown & Farber, 1951), or an *aversive internal state*, which can be indexed by a variety of response measures.

Some authors have questioned the value of the frustration concept (Lawson, 1965), and contemporary texts devote relatively little space to it except for the specialized topics of frustration-aggression hypothesis or nonreward frustration. Frustration *is* an important concept, however, because it gives us conditions under which an aversive state is aroused when there are no aversive stimuli. Frustration grows out of positive expectations which are not fulfilled. To deny that this is important is to deny a large segment of human experience which most people consider important.

### Frustration as a Cue

Frustration has cue properties, just as fear does, but we need to distinguish between *frustration* and a frustrating *situation*. Frustration is the internal state which occurs when a goal is blocked. The frustrating situation is the condition in which that frustration occurs. This distinction is important because a particular behavior may occur in response to situational cues as well as frustration. For example, I once had a TV set that in its declining years had a very snowy screen. The temporary cure was to hit the set until the screen cleared. This usually worked and was cheaper than repairs. But how would a stranger viewing my behavior for the first time interpret it? She might conclude that in frustration I lashed out angrily at the source of my frustration. She would be interpreting my behavior in terms of an emotional state which she presumed to exist. Another interpretation, however, is that in a frustrating *situation* I hit the screen simply because that behavior had been rewarded in the past. The snowy screen (part of the situation) was the cue to which I was responding, not some emotional arousal. This interpretation does not require any motivational interpretation beyond the desire for a clear TV screen. Vigorous behavior in an apparently frustrating situation does not *always* mean strong frustration.

The internal state aroused by frustration may have cue properties, however, just as fear does. If I feel aroused in some frustrating circumstance, this feeling may cue me to behave in a certain way. It might warn me, for example, to control my temper and not do anything I might regret later.

In brief, then, when we analyze "frustration," we must look carefully at the nature of the situation and at the cue effects of frustration, as well as at the motivational effects.

**Motivational Effect of Frustration**

*Nonreward frustration.* Many years ago a psychologist named Tinklepaugh (1928) was training a monkey with standard monkey rewards, raisins and grapes, which the animal came to expect for its efforts. Tinklepaugh then substituted a piece of lettuce for the expected reward, and this obviously disturbed the animal. This observation has three important elements. First, the monkey had to learn to *expect* a particular reward. Second, the monkey got something *less attractive* than expected. Third, the change in reward produced a disturbance in the animal's behavior. Presumably, Tinklepaugh's monkey felt something like an upset student who has gotten a C after expecting an A. The antecedent condition for *nonreward frustration* is like the above, except that no expected reward at all is given. Amsel (1958; 1962) has most fully developed nonreward frustration theory, which he developed out of Hull's drive theory.

*Amsel's theory.* Assume that nonreward frustration is aversive and that situations in which it occurs will also become aversive and therefore tend to be escaped or avoided. Amsel considers that frustration has both drive and cue properties. As a *drive*, frustration should *energize* responses, an increase in frustration should be *punishing,* and a decrease in frustration should be *reinforcing.* As a *cue,* frustration may *evoke* responses or otherwise serve to *direct* behavior (which, recall, drive does not do according to Hull-Spence theory).

*Energizing effect of nonreward frustration.* Suppose we put an animal into a *double runway,* two separate runways strung together so that the goal box for the first runway is also the start box for the second runway. The animal runs in the first runway to get food in the first goal box, then when a door is opened, runs down the second runway to get food in the second goal box. The question is, After the animal has thoroughly learned the task, what will happen to running speed in the *second runway* if food is omitted in the *first goal box?* Frustration theory predicts the animal should run *faster* than usual because *nonreward in the first goal box is frustrating,* producing a higher level of drive, which should energize running in the second runway. And that is exactly what happens. The increase in running speed following nonreward is called the *frustration effect* (Amsel & Roussel, 1952). The animal does *not* run faster because it failed to get the food pellet in the first goal box and was therefore hungrier; control subjects that are *never* rewarded in the first goal box run *slower* in the second runway than frustrated animals (Wagner, 1963). Amsel proposed that during training an anticipatory goal response ($r_g$-$s_g$) is conditioned to apparatus cues. As $r_g$-$s_g$ becomes stronger, there is more frustration if reward is omitted. The frustration is a source of drive and hence

| START BOX 1 | RUNWAY 1 | GOAL 1 START 2 | RUNWAY 2 | GOAL BOX 2 |
|---|---|---|---|---|

**FIGURE 8-1.** Double runway apparatus for studying nonreward frustration. During training, the animal is rewarded in goal box 1 and goal box 2. In testing for frustration, reward is omitted in goal box 1 to determine the energizing effect of nonreward on running speed in runway 2.

the animal runs faster. The $r_g$-$s_g$ mechanism, of course, is the Hull-Spence equivalent of expectancy.

*Frustrative nonreward and extinction.* After an animal has learned to expect reward in the goal box, the animal is frustrated when the reward is omitted. The goal box becomes aversive when it becomes a signal for no reward, so the animal stops running to the goal box. Suppose, then, that one animal were trained with a large reward and another with a small reward. Which animal should extinguish faster? Since a large reward is a better *incentive,* we might expect the large-reward subject to run longer. Frustration theory says, however, that omission of a large reward should be more frustrating than omission of a small reward. The large-reward animal should extinguish faster than the small-reward animal, and indeed it does.

In similar fashion, when animals are shifted from a large to a small reward, the downshift is frustrating and the goal box becomes somewhat aversive. Running speed then drops (for a while at least) below that of animals continuously on small reward. Downshifted animals, of course, do continue to run because they are still being rewarded.

***Partial reinforcement effects.*** One of the more puzzling effects of rewards is that they have greater long-term effectiveness if they are *not* given for every response. Animals rewarded after every run in a runway or press of a lever (100% reinforcement) extinguish *faster* than animals rewarded only part of the time (partial reinforcement). This is called the *partial reinforcement extinction effect (PREE).* The obvious question is, How can a response rewarded part of the time be "stronger" than one rewarded all the time? We consider the problem in terms of frustration theory; more detailed accounts can be found in learning texts (e.g., Gordon, 1989).

According to frustration theory (Amsel, 1958), as we have seen, the shift from acquisition to extinction produces nonreward frustration and the animal stops running to the aversive goal box. With partially reinforced animals, the frustration interpretation is more complicated. During partial reinforcement training, the animal is frustrated on nonreinforced trials. The frustration has a *conditionable component,* $r_f$-$s_f$, which is analogous to the $r_g$-$s_g$ mechanism. That is, $r_f$-$s_f$ is a *fractional* component of the frustration response which can become conditioned to situational cues. Early in training, then, the partially reinforced animal runs more slowly than the 100%-reinforced animal because the partially reinforced animal has some anticipatory frustration (Wagner, 1963).

As frustration (and $r_f$ -$s_f$) occurs more often, however, $s_f$ becomes one of the stimuli to which running is conditioned. Eventually, instead of arousing avoidance of the goal box, $r_f$ -$s_f$ *facilitates* running: Apparatus Cues → ($r_f$ -$s_f$) → Running. As a consequence, when reward is omitted altogether the animal's performance does not suddenly fall apart, because performance has already been conditioned to frustration cues. Such an interpretation accounts for persistence of behavior in many situations. Some tennis players, for example, seem to thrive on emotional outburst and controversy. One interpretation for this is that their performance has become conditioned to the emotional arousal, and the emotional arousal is a "support stimulus" for their performance. In addition, of course, their motivational *arousal* may facilitate their performance. An "experienced" team also performs better "under pressure" because it has been in pressure situations before. The frustration cues ($r_f$-$s_f$) from tight situations become *conditioned* to performance rather than interfering with performance. This is like the partial reinforcement effect.

*Frustration and the small-trial PREE.*   By Amsel's account, anticipation of a goal ($r_g$-$s_g$) has to develop before there would be frustration, and $r_g$-$s_g$ was said to develop slowly. It was therefore a blow to the theory when it was found that the PREE could be obtained with only *two* acquisition trials, nonreinforced and reinforced versus two reinforced trials (McCain, 1966). Theoretical accounts of the PREE then turned to (a) a small-trial frustration effect, and (b) nonmotivational theories.

An important question to ask is whether stimuli associated with frustration do *in fact* become aversive. The answer to this is clearly yes. Daly (1974) demonstrated that rats frustrated by nonreward in the goal box learned faster to jump out of the goal box into an escape box than did control animals. Furthermore, (1) animals given 100% reinforcement during training learned to escape faster than animals with partial reinforcement, (2) animals given large rewards escaped faster than animals given small rewards, and (3) animals escaped faster after high-concentration sucrose rewards than low-sucrose rewards. In short, anticipation of greater reward leads to greater aversion than does anticipation of small reward.

Frustration theory does not say that *instrumental* responses are necessary for frustration, however. The only requirement is that the *expectation* of reward be frustrated. The frustration effects which follow instrumental responding should also be found after simply consuming food in a particular environment. As predicted, Daly found that after animals were directly placed into a goal box with food (but no running), then food was omitted, the animals learned to get out of the goal box faster than no-food control animals.

Brooks (1969) then argued that the small-trial PREE is better analyzed in terms of the frustration that develops during extinction (Daly's approach) than in terms of the conditioning of frustration during training (Amsel's approach). Brooks tested this by giving one group of animals six goal-box placements with a large reward (30 seconds' access to wet mash) and another group a small reward (one 45 mg food pellet). Half of each group got food on all trials and half on 50% of the trials. The 100%, large-reward group learned to escape faster when food was omitted than did the other three groups, which performed the same as a group never fed in the goal box. With large rewards there is indeed a partial-reinforcement frustration effect with a small number of trials.

Lest frustration theorists be too complacent, however, consider the following. We train animals in a *choice* apparatus, like a T-maze, with 100% reinforcement on one side and 50% on the other side. The animals eventually choose the 100% side every time (being forced, if necessary, to go to both sides equally often by closing the door to the preferred side). In extinction, the animals still choose the 100% side for many, many trials (Logan, 1968). This is *exactly opposite* what should happen according to frustration theory. In extinction, the 100% side should become more aversive than the 50% side and hence be chosen less often. It would appear that frustration theory does *not* apply here. For a variety of such reasons, *nonmotivational* accounts were developed to explain some "frustrative nonreward" effects.

### Nonmotivational Theories for "Frustrative" Nonreward

*Associative theory.*     Capaldi (e.g., 1967) proposed that following presentation of a reward, there is a *stimulus aftereffect* of the reward (Sr), a memory if you will. On trials when no reward is given, there is a different stimulus aftereffect (Sn). According to the theory, then, when the animal is put into the start box it remembers what happened following the last time it was in the start box. This memory (Sr or Sn) is conditioned to the running response on that trial *if* the response is rewarded. The exact predictions depend on the specific *pattern* of reward and nonreward trials, but we can readily see how the theory applies to the partial reinforcement extinction effect. In the following diagram, r and n refer to rewarded and nonrewarded trials.

|      | ACQUISITION | EXTINCTION |
|------|-------------|------------|
| 100% | r  r  r  r  r  r  r  r | n  n  n  n  n |
| 50%  | *n*  r  *n*  r  *n*  *n*  r  *n*  r  r | n  n  n  n  n |

With the 100% group, Sn never occurs during acquisition, so Sn is never conditioned to running. With the 50% group, however, Sn occurs and is followed by reward four out of five times in the above example. Therefore, in extinction the 50% group performs better. This would account for the PREE in single-response situations (like the straight runway) as well as the choice situations where the 100% side is preferred to the 50% side during extinction, where reward often follows nonreward. The predictions are more complicated in the latter situation because we would have to know the details of when the animals were forced to the nonpreferred side during acquisition.

*Inhibition theory.*   Staddon (1974) accounted for the nonreward frustration effect in the double runway as follows. In many operant conditioning situations, such as lever pressing, subjects show a *postreinforcement pause.* That is, they respond fairly regularly until they get the reward, then they stop responding for some period of time after the reward, and then start up again. Staddon suggests that when reward is omitted in the first goal box of the double runway the animal gives the appearance of more vigorous responding in the second runway because it does not show the postreinforcement pause.

## CONFLICT

Now let us turn to a special kind of frustration, where a goal is "blocked" by a *competing goal.* This is the classic conflict situation. Virtually all behavior involves some degree of conflict because we are always making choices among possible activities and goals. Some choices are so easily made that conflict is hardly noticeable, but in such situations as choice of a mate or a career the conflict is more severe and more emotion-arousing.

Conflict has long been considered a basic problem in neurotic behavior. In Freudian theory, for example, conflicts between the *id* (such biological "drives" as sex or aggression) and the *superego* (socialization) are particularly important. The goal of sexual gratification is blocked by the competing goal of social approval or fear of punishment. We shall not go into the psychoanalytic aspects of conflict in detail, but do note that clinical problems have long been a rich source of research ideas about conflict. The most dominant theory of conflict has been that of Neal Miller.

### Miller's Theory of Conflict

Miller and his associates (e.g., Dollard & Miller, 1941; Miller, 1959) have progressively developed the theory of conflict. Miller (1959) begins with six assumptions:

1.  The closer an organism is to a positive goal, the stronger the motivation to approach that goal. This is called an *approach gradient* (in Hull's theory, it was called a *goal gradient* and played an important role in much of Hull's theorizing).
2.  The closer an organism is to an aversive goal, the stronger the motivation to escape or avoid the goal. This is called an *avoidance gradient.*
3.  The avoidance gradient is *steeper* than the approach gradient. It drops off more rapidly as the organism is further from the goal.

4.  The level of either approach or avoidance gradients can be raised or lowered by appropriate manipulations of approach and avoidance motivation (such as changes in degree of hunger or level of fearfulness).

5.  Below the asymptote of learning, an increase in the number of reinforced trials will increase the strength of the response tendency which is reinforced (either approach or avoidance).

6.  When two incompatible responses are in conflict, the one with the stronger motivation (approach or avoidance) will occur.

The strength of approach or avoidance is a function of both *learning* and *motivation*, so Miller's concepts are more like Hull's excitatory potentials than just motivational concepts.

*Evidence for theory: Postulates 1–4.*   Judson Brown (1948) tested the first four assumptions. He tethered rats to a calibrated spring with a harness so he could record the strength of the rats' pull toward or away from a goal. Some animals were trained to run down an alleyway to food, then were stopped by the tether either "near" (30 cm) or "far" (170 cm) from the goal. The results were that:

1.  They pulled harder when they were in the near position.

2.  Other animals, shocked but not fed at the end of the runway, pulled away from the shock area harder when in the near position.

3.  The slope of the escape gradient was steeper between the two points than was that of the approach gradient. The results are shown in Figure 8–2 (a). The results are as predicted, but the gradients are not necessarily linear (it's just that two points can define only a linear function). The only real requirement of the theory, however, is that the gradients cross.

4.  Figure 8–2 (b) shows the results of testing the animals under strong versus weak avoidance. The overall gradient is lower with weak avoidance. Other animals, tested at 46 hours of deprivation, showed stronger approach than animals deprived for one hour. However, these animals were tested only at the near distance, so we can only assume the overall approach gradient was lower for one group than the other.

*Postulate 5.*   Kaufman and Miller (1949) supported the fifth assumption by showing that with more approach training trials the animals were more likely to go to the goal after having been shocked there.

*Postulate 6.*   The primary evidence for this is the fact of conflict resolution. That is, animals do ultimately approach or avoid.

Why is there a difference in the slope of approach and avoidance gradients? Miller (1959) suggested that hunger, which contributes to the approach motivation, is constant throughout the length of the alleyway. Incentive motivation is stronger as the animal is closer to the goal, but some stability is maintained by the internal deprivation cues. With avoidance, however, external cues are relatively more important; the goal box is more

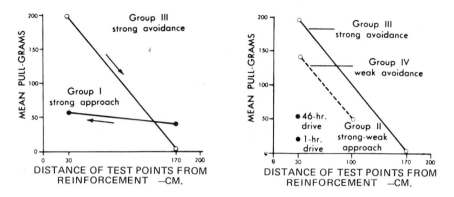

FIGURE 8-2.  (a) The approach gradient represents the mean force exerted by 46-hour motivated rats when restrained at two points in the alley. The avoidance gradient reveals the force exerted by rats in their efforts to avoid a region where strong shock has been given. Although the experimental points in this figure and in (b) have been joined by straight lines, no assumption is intended with respect to the linearity of the gradients. (b) This section illustrates the effect of reduced shock and reduced hunger upon the strengths of the avoidance and approach responses, respectively. (From Brown, 1948, p. 457 and 459. Copyright © 1948 by the American Psychological Association. Reprinted by permission.)

avoidance arousing than the start box. The farther the animal is from the source of the shock, the weaker the fear.

Miller's explanation is appealing, but raises questions. For example, it predicts that a stimulus generalization gradient under strong fear would be steeper than one obtained under weak fear. The evidence does not support this: Generalization gradients under strong fear are usually flatter (Kalish, 1969). Highly anxious people do not seem to discriminate as well between more and less fear-arousing situations as do less anxious individuals, and heart rate change with a strong shock UCS shows a flatter generalization gradient under high hunger than under low hunger. Hearst (1969) has found approach and avoidance gradients with a variety of slopes, depending on such details as number of test trials. Motivation then is a relevant variable in determining approach (or generalization) gradients, but not the only one.

### Types of Conflict

Psychologists generally distinguish four kinds of conflict, diagrammed in Figure 8-3, in terms of Miller's gradient theory.

1. *Approach-Approach.* Approach-approach conflict involves two discrete positive alternatives, A and B. As the organism moves toward A the tendency to approach A is even stronger and the tendency to approach B is less. Therefore the conflict is easily resolved. The fable of the jackass that starved to death between two bales of hay is charming but unlikely. What appears to be an approach-approach conflict may have avoidance elements, however. This produces the fourth kind of conflict we shall discuss.

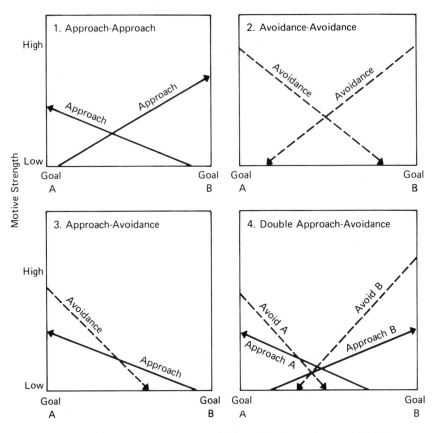

**FIGURE 8-3.** Four kinds of conflict in terms of Miller's gradient theory. See text for details.

2. *Avoidance-Avoidance.* Avoidance-avoidance conflict involves two aversive goals. As the organism moves away from one it necessarily moves toward the other, then is forced back toward the first, and so on. Such conflict gives rise to sayings such as "between the devil and the deep blue sea." If the organism has to stay in the situation, it should eventually become more or less immobile at the point of minimal aversive stimulation, where the two gradients intersect. This is commonly seen in the laboratory when an animal (for example, a rat) is shocked at either end of a runway and settles down in the middle.

   Given the chance to get away from such a totally disastrous situation, organisms will "leave the field," in Kurt Lewin's terms. This may involve physically escaping, but may also involve "psychological escape." Amnesia is often thought to have this motivational basis: A person in an intolerable situation may escape by "forgetting." Such forgetting is not consciously intentional, but nevertheless serves the purpose. Some people escape by sleeping, others by taking drugs. The ultimate escape is suicide.

3. *Approach-Avoidance.* Approach-avoidance conflict involves goals with both desirable and aversive features. As in Brown's experiment, an animal is trained to run down an alleyway to food, then the food container is wired so the animal gets shocked if it touches the food. This sets up the conflict. The animal then

vacillates in the runway because of its simultaneous motivation to approach and to avoid the same goal. At some distance from the goal, the approach motive is stronger, but as the animal approaches the goal the avoidance motive becomes stronger, and the animal reverses itself. The area in which vacillation occurs is the "conflict zone," the region in which the approach and avoidance gradients intersect.

Approach-avoidance conflicts have received considerable experimental attention because they seem to be most important. The individual is "bound" to the goal by the approach motive but prevented from reaching it by the avoidance motive. Usually, of course, the conflict is resolved in some way, and we must assume at least a temporary shift in the relative strengths of approach and avoidance so that the individual either goes all the way to the goal or so far away that the approach motivation is no longer effective.

4.  *Double Approach-Avoidance.* This conflict involves two goals, each having positive and negative features. This is common, because the choice of one goal often results in the loss of another, and this loss is a negative feature of the chosen goal. For example, you might have the choice of buying a large comfortable car that is expensive to maintain or a smaller, less comfortable car that costs less. To gain the good feature of one, you inevitably lose the good feature of the other. This type of conflict, perhaps better called *multiple approach-avoidance* because the alternatives may be more than two, is more typical of real-life situations but is also more difficult to analyze experimentally.

### Extensions of the Theory: Stimulus Similarity and Displacement.

Approach and avoidance gradients can be along the dimension of *spatial* distance from the goal, but they can also be along a dimension of *psychological distance,* such as temporal closeness (Fantino, 1987) or degree of similarity to the goal situation. If a person were in a situation similar, but not identical, to a previous conflict situation, what might she do? According to Miller's third postulate, the avoidance gradient is steeper than the approach gradient. In the similar situation, then, avoidance should decline more than approach, and the person should be relatively more likely to approach the goal.

Miller and Kraeling (1952) tested this deduction by first establishing an approach-avoidance conflict with rats in a white alleyway. The animals learned to run to food, then were shocked at the goal. They were then divided into three test groups: (1) tested in the original white training alley, (2) tested in a "dissimilar," narrower, gray alley, and (3) tested in a very different, even narrower, black alley. (Effects of alley color and width were controlled with other groups.) In the white alley, 23% of the animals reached the goal, as compared to 37% in the gray alley and 70% in the black alley. The prediction of weaker avoidance in the generalized alleys was thus confirmed.

Murray and Berkun (1955) suggested that the concept of *displacement* in psychoanalytic theory could also be translated into conflict theory. If an impulse arouses too much anxiety to be admitted into consciousness or to be expressed directly, then a conflict exists. For example, a man may hate his father but cannot admit this to himself, and therefore dreams of killing a policeman, who is similar to the father (an authority figure), but not identical. If avoidance decreases more rapidly than approach in a different situation, the individual should approach (attack) the "generalized" father (the policeman in the dream) more readily than the real father.

Murray and Berkun studied displacement in terms of spatial distance from the goal and stimulus generalization. After the usual food-shock training, tests were conducted in the training runway, but the animals could go through newly opened holes in the wall to an adjacent runway different from the training runway. As predicted, the animals tended to approach the goal partway in the training alley, then shift over to the next alley and approach nearer, then move into the third alley and approach the goal closer yet. The theory says that, as the animals approached the goal in the training alley, avoidance motivation increased until they sought escape into the less fearful adjacent alley. Avoidance motivation was then weaker until they moved closer to the goal, at which time avoidance motivation increased so much that they escaped into the third alley.

After the animals reached the goal in the *generalized* (dissimilar) alleys, they would also go all the way to the goal in the *original* alley. This suggested the effect we hope for in psychotherapy: Fear extinguished to the generalized alleyway when an animal was not shocked at the goal, much like a discussion of anxiety-arousing problems might reduce anxiety when a client is not punished by the therapist. An animal could then approach the original goal less fearfully, just as the client might approach his or her problems less fearfully outside the therapeutic situation.

Elder, Noblin, and Maher (1961) repeated the experiment above, but concluded that the *distance* from the original alley was the critical variable determining alley-switching, not color difference. This does not deny the displacement hypothesis, but raises questions about what generalization gradients are involved (i.e., stimulus similarity as compared to spatial distance).

## ANGER AND HOSTILITY

"Anger: emotional excitement induced by intense displeasure."
"Hostile: of or relating to an enemy; unfriendly." (Webster's *New Collegiate Dictionary*)

The frustration-aggression hypothesis says blocking a goal instigates the intention to harm someone. Many theorists believe that this is correct, however, only when the frustration produces *anger* or *hostility*. In this section we look more closely at anger as an emotion, and in the final section we look at aggressive behavior.

## The Conditions for Anger

In chapter 2 we saw that some emotion theorists heavily stress the importance of *cognitive appraisal* as a determinant of emotion. Anger is considered by some to be the emotion most susceptible to appraisal. In particular, it is thought that a person's anger in a frustrating situation depends on his or her interpretation of whether the goal-blocking was *justified* (Berkowitz, 1988; Averill, 1978; 1982; 1983). People become angry when they perceive that someone has unjustly or arbitrarily deprived them of some anticipated gratification. Pastore (1952), for example, presented research subjects with various frustration scenarios and asked them whether they would become angry. They reported they would not become angry if the thwarting were proper. A person might be disappointed at 12:15 if a store had closed at its usual 12:00 time and desirable refreshment could not be obtained. If admittance were refused at 11:55, however, one might become angry at this arbitrary frustration. Arbitrary frustrations produce more anger than justifiable or uncontrollable frustrations, but is arbitrariness a *necessary* condition for anger?

*Uncontrollable, nonarbitrary* frustrations can produce anger. In one study, research subjects imagining themselves caught in a traffic jam on the way to a job interview reported they would become very angry (Berkowitz, 1988). In another study, subjects overtly indicated hostile reactions toward a person who frustrated them by repeatedly misunderstanding and asking questions. Subjects did not show overt hostility toward a person said to be hard of hearing, who engaged in the same behaviors. Subsequently, however, subjects indicated disliking for the hearing-impaired person if they could do so privately (Burnstein & Worchel, 1962). In short, a nonarbitrary frustration produced hostility which was not publicly expressed.

Another interesting case is *competition*, where the very purpose is to frustrate the opponent, not letting him, her, or them win. Since such frustration is in the rules, it is not arbitrary. Nevertheless, competition can lead to anger and hostility. In a classic experiment by Sherif et al. (1961), summer campers were randomly put into two groups which were designated as competitive teams. Considerable hostility and overt aggression arose, which was reduced only by establishing *common goals* for both groups. For example, the two groups had to cooperate to get a stalled truck moving.

Berkowitz (1988) suggests that frustration/competition leads to aggressive actions only if *negative affect* is involved. The more intense the motivation to reach a goal, such as winning a major competition, the stronger the negative affect when that goal is in jeopardy, as we see in the animal research. It is important to distinguish between aggressiveness and *assertiveness*, however. We can compete assertively, without necessarily intending to *harm* someone (aggression). Anger and hostility would be more likely to develop, however, if a competitor were perceived as trying to hurt us. If a basketball player is perceived as trying to knock down an opponent, not simply trying to establish a position on the court, anger could readily arise (and frequently does).

### Anger Reduction

We often hear it said that holding in our anger is bad for our mental health, that we should *release* it, get it out. The "ventilationist" point of view holds that expressing anger is *cathartic,* that anger will be reduced faster if it is expressed. Holding anger in is said to be bad because we are stuck with the emotional arousal of anger, including autonomic arousal. Tavris (1983), however, argues that venting anger simply makes people angrier, raises the noise level of our lives, and does not do any particular good most of the time.

How fast anger subsides depends on many factors, and venting anger may indeed sustain or increase anger rather than reducing it. Hokanson (1970) found that male laboratory subjects intentionally angered by the experimenter tended to show a quicker drop in blood pressure if they responded in an angry manner, but that female subjects showed a more rapid drop if they responded in a conciliatory manner. Hokanson then went on to show that male subjects could be *taught* to respond in a more conciliatory manner and females in a more aggressive manner, and that blood pressure came down more quickly with the new mode of responding. Either angry *or* friendly responses could be "cathartic," if properly learned.

Tavris also argues that "talking out" anger does not reduce anger, it *rehearses* it. Couples who yell at each other usually get more angry, not less angry. In a study of aerospace engineers and technicians who had been laid off from their jobs, interview responses were compared with those of other employees who had voluntarily resigned. When fired employees targeted the company or a particular supervisor whom they could blame for their predicament they became more angry and hostile toward their target as a result of talking about the *target*. If they picked on a supervisor, they became more angry at the supervisor but not the company in general, and vice versa. Tavris suggests that getting angry is only cathartic if you get a sense of *control* from the anger, whether control of your own internal arousal or of the situation which was anger-provoking. The main points here are that anger is *not* an invariable result of frustration, anger may be lowered or raised by expressing anger, and the degree of anger we feel or express is in large part a *social construction*. That is, our anger is largely determined by the social context in which we have learned to respond to other people.

## AGGRESSION

### What Is Aggression?

No amount of definition seems to cover what everyone means by aggression. What has been called aggression ranges from attack and killing on the one hand to verbal descriptions of Rorschach inkblots on the other. Table

8-1 is a set of examples which may or may not be considered aggressive. Check the ones you think represent aggression. If you compare notes with someone else, the difficulty soon becomes obvious. For example, a definition including all *actual harm* would include Item 1 (Boy Scout) and Item 3 (flower pot) as well as Item 21 (hired killer). If actual harm and intent to harm are both considered necessary, then we eliminate Items 1 and 3, among others. If *intent alone* is deemed sufficient, even for a failed act (e.g., Item 2, assassin misses target), then we have yet another set of aggressive behaviors. If we exclude food-getting behavior (Item 4) or an act committed under someone else's orders (Item 6) the picture changes again. We conclude that no single circumstance can satisfactorily characterize everything that might be considered aggressive.

*Aggression and intent.*     Intent is a nebulous concept in the discussion of animal aggression but is widely accepted in definitions of human aggression. We may say that *aggressive behaviors are behaviors intended to do physical or psychological damage to someone.* Let us clarify this definition.

First, there is intent to harm. Did the defendant, with malice aforethought, intend to kill the victim? The jury's answer to that question is of vital interest to the defendant, but how can intention be determined?

**TABLE 8–1  Behaviors That Might Be Considered Aggressive.**

1. A Boy Scout helping an old lady across the street accidentally trips her and she sprains her ankle.
2. An assassin attempts to kill a presidential candidate but his shot misses.
3. A housewife knocks a flower pot off a fifth story window ledge and it hits a passerby.
4. A farmer kills a chicken for dinner.
5. In a debate, one person belittles another's qualifications.
6. A soldier presses a button that fires a nuclear missle and kills thousands of people he cannot even see.
7. A policeman trying to break up a riot hits a rioter on the head with a club and knocks him unconscious.
8. A cat stalks, catches, tosses around, and eventually kills a mouse.
9. A wife accuses her husband of having an affair and he retorts that after living with her anyone would have an affair.
10. A frightened boy, caught in the act of stealing and trying to escape, shoots his discoverer.
11. One child takes a toy away from another, making him cry.
12. A man unable to get into his locked car kicks in the side of the door.
13. A man pays 25¢ to beat an old car with an iron bar, which he does vigorously.
14. A football player blocks another player from behind (clipping) and breaks his leg.
15. A businessman hires a professional killer to "take care of" a business rival.
16. A woman carefully plots how she will kill her husband, then does so.
17. Two students get into a drunken brawl and one hits the other with a beer bottle.
18. A businessman works vigorously to improve his business and drive out the competition.
19. On the Rorschach inkblot test, a hospitalized mental patient is scored as being highly aggressive, although he has never actually harmed anyone.
20. A young boy talks a lot about how he is going to beat up others, but never does it.
21. A hired killer successfully completes his job.

Francis Irwin (1971) illustrated a way to determine intent with an episode from *Bullivant and the Lambs* (Compton-Burnett, 1949). The father of two young boys walks by a place in a garden where they are building a hutch, speaks with them, then continues walking on a path toward a footbridge over a deep ravine. The bridge had been so weakened by a storm the previous night that it would not support a man's weight, but this was not immediately visible. A warning sign had been posted, but the father (in the context of the story) concludes that his sons wanted him to die because they knew of the danger but did not tell him about it. Irwin analyzes the episode in terms of his criteria for intentional behavior, which were discussed in chapter 1. The father realized that the sons expected that (1) he would *not* be hurt if they told him of the danger, and (2) he *would* be hurt if they did not tell him, and they preferred (2) over (1)—his being hurt to his not being hurt. Intent is inferred from the choice of one act over another when the expected outcome of each act is known. In the list in Table 8-1, we assume that the Boy Scout does not expect that helping the old lady will harm her, so the unfortunate result is neither intentional nor aggressive. The man who employs an assassin, however, expects that this act will result in harm, and the employment is therefore an aggressive act.

The distinction between physical and psychological harm is straightforward. We may harm people by physically hitting them or by damaging their self-esteem. We make "cutting remarks," verbal barbs as ruthless as metal ones.

Much "aggression" research does not meet these definitional criteria, however. Tedeschi, Smith, and Brown (1974) even challenge the usefulness of intent as a research criterion because laboratory studies almost never establish aggressive intent in their subjects and frequently involve elaborate cover stories to seduce subjects into harmful behaviors. Laboratory subjects generally intend to carry out the experimenter's wishes, not to harm someone. This should be kept in mind while reading the pages that follow, as we explore stimulus-aroused aggression, instrumental aggression, and obedient aggression.

### Stimulus-Aroused Aggression

*The frustration-aggression hypothesis.*   Though Freud made the first modern statement that frustration leads to aggression, Dollard et al. (1939) developed a more testable theory which is illustrated by the following example. Four-year-old James hears the ice-cream truck bell and says he wants some ice cream. The following concepts come into play: (1) The bell *instigates* the response of trying to get ice cream. (2) A *goal-response* (such as eating the ice cream) *reduces the instigation to make the goal response.* (3) Prevention of the goal response produces *interference*; if we do not let James eat ice cream, this is interference. (4) Interference with the goal-directed response produces *frustration,* an internal state. (5) Frustration instigates *aggressive behavior* which is intended to harm someone. If the instigated aggressive behavior is itself interfered with, this is further instigation to aggressive behavior. (6) Aggressive behavior may be *inhibited,* particularly by fear of punishment. (7) Aggressive behavior may be *direct* (aimed at the source of the frustration) or *indirect* or *displaced.* Indirect aggression may involve a change in the *object* of aggression (perhaps a more vulnerable target than the direct object) or a change in the *form* of aggression (such as from physical to psychological). (8) According to the concept of *catharsis* (from the Greek word for cleansing or purging), aggressive acts are assumed to reduce further instigation to aggression.

*Criticisms of the hypothesis.* The first criticism of the hypothesis was that it simply is not always correct. Aggression has other causes, and frustration has other effects. A second difficulty is that the hypothesis seems to require two unseen processes: frustration and tendency to aggression, but without independent operations for each. If aggressive behavior occurs, we have to speculate that there was prior frustration. A frustrating situation however, may simply arouse an *aversive state,* without any behavior effects specific to frustration per se. We have already seen, for example, that whether people respond aggressively depends partly on whether they perceive that goal interference as justified. In any event, the frustration-aggression hypothesis has faded as a major theory in its own right, but elements of it are found in many discussions of aggression.

**Impulsive aggression.**   Berkowitz (e.g., 1974, 1988) maintains that environmental situations provoke impulsive attack behaviors. Most homicides, for example, are not premeditated, but are spontaneous and passionate, often arising from disagreements about relatively trivial matters. The threat of capital punishment has little deterrent value because in the heat of the moment the consequences of killing simply are not anticipated. A variety of stimulus events may facilitate, if not provoke, aggressive behaviors.

*Painful stimuli.* Painful stimuli frequently provoke escape and avoidance behaviors, but examples of attack are also well known. O'Kelly and Steckle (1939), observed in the laboratory that if two rats are put into a cage, with electric shock delivered through the floor, the rats will begin to attack each other. Fighting is more likely to occur if escape is not permitted, the confining space is small, and the shocks are frequent or intense. (Ulrich & Azrin, 1962).

Since it is possible under the right conditions to instigate such fighting every time animals are put together, could such "reflexive fighting" be conditioned to other stimuli? Vernon and Ulrich (1966) paired a sound with shock, but over hundreds of trials there was never more than about 50% fighting. The highly pugnacious Siamese fighting fish (*Betta splendens*), however, show more reliable conditioning of an aggressive display (e.g., Thompson &

Sturm, 1965). An interesting question is whether pain-induced aggression can be inhibited by *punishing* it. The Catch-22 is that a painful punishing stimulus might instigate *more* aggression, and exactly this happens with both rats and monkeys (Ulrich & Craine, 1964). Rats fight each other more if punished by shock, and monkeys bite at a ball more if they are punished with shock for shock-induced biting.

*Unpleasant environmental conditions. Crowding.* Proximity to other animals is one of the main precursors of fighting among either birds or mammals (Marler, 1966). This is particularly true among same-sex conspecifics, probably because they are the strongest competitors for resources and mates. Crowding among rats has produced disastrous consequences, including low birth rate, high infant mortality rate, homosexuality, heightened aggressiveness, and cannibalism (Calhoun, 1962).

Fortunately, human research does not bear out all the pessimistic implications of animal research. Some cities of very high population density (e.g., Hong Kong, Tokyo) have much less crime than cities of lower density. This indicates that the aversive consequences of crowding can be overridden or inhibited by social controls. Some indications of the aversive consequences of crowding, which *might* lead to more hostile behaviors, are the following (Bell, Fisher, & Loomis, 1978): (1) People working under crowded conditions report more discomfort, and males more so than females. (2) Males show increased physiological arousal under crowded conditions, but females do not. (3) People living under crowded conditions are less attracted to others, again more true for males than females. (4) People tend to withdraw from high density situations. (5) The greater the population density, as in an apartment building, the less likely people are to help each other. What makes crowding unpleasant? One possibility is that crowding produces a very high level of *arousal*, which is aversive. Another is that personal freedom is restricted and this reduced freedom is aversive. Freedom and control are discussed in detail in the next chapter.

*Weather conditions.* The weather provides a good example of a nonarbitrary source of aggressive acts; the weather is many things but it is not "unfair." Working under the dashboard of a car on a hot summer day, head upside down, glasses falling off, the perspiration flooding into one's eyes, can lead to frustration and hostility quite apart from any culpability of the weather. There is a phenomenon known as the "long hot summer effect," wherein crime rates are apparently higher during long sieges of hot weather. This has been used to account in part for urban riots (Carlsmith & Anderson, 1979), and such violent crimes as homicides and assaults (Anderson & Anderson, 1984). Laboratory studies have also indicated that high temperatures, smoke, and bad odors heighten aggressive activities (Berkowitz, 1983).

*Victims may provoke attack upon themselves.* Most murders are committed by people who know the victim well, the victim is often a relative, and the homicide is likely to have been preceded by an argument which escalated into a killing. The well-known popular singer, Marvin Gaye, was killed by his own father under such circumstances. In one study, a fourth of 600 homicides were at least partly provoked by the victim (Wolfgang, 1957). Toch (1970) also found from interviews with police, prison inmates, and from police records, that about 40% of violent sequences were initiated when an arresting officer notified a person of his arrest and was treated contemptuously. In some 27% of the cases, violence already existed that police action tended to inflame rather than dampen. The moral seems to be clear: One of the most effective ways to avoid being attacked is not to provoke attack on oneself. An argument for gun control is that even a robbery victim is less likely to get shot if he or she does not have a gun to provoke attack by an intruder. An acquaintance of the author's, a night manager of an all-night market, was killed when he picked up a gun and followed a robber out into the night.

This is about as close to suicide as you can get.

*The weapons effect.* Suppose you were asked to serve in an experiment studying physiological reactions to the stress produced by mild electric shocks. You and another subject are to evaluate each other's performance on a problem solving task by giving each other electric shocks. You get evaluated first. Seven shocks out of ten possible. Not very good. In your experimental room there is a telegraph key for delivering shocks to your partner, along with a rifle and a pistol left by a previous experimenter from an unrelated experiment. You deliver six shocks to your partner as evaluation of his performance.

You, of course, were in just one of a number of experimental conditions and your "partner" was really the experimenter's assistant. Your treatment was intended to anger you by giving you a large number of shocks and to provide aggression-arousing cues (the guns). Both of these factors were expected to make you more aggressive so that you would give more shocks than if you were less angry or did not have cues for aggressive behavior. Table 8–2 summarizes the results of this experiment by Berkowitz and Le Page (1967). Subjects getting seven shocks gave back more shocks than subjects getting

**TABLE 8-2   Mean Number of Shocks Given in Each Condition.**

|  | NUMBER OF SHOCKS RECEIVED BY THE SUBJECT | |
|---|---|---|
| CONDITION | 1 | 7 |
| Associated Weapons | 2.60 | 6.07 |
| Unassociated Weapons | 2.20 | 5.67 |
| No object | 3.07 | 4.67 |
| Badminton Rackets[a] | — | 4.60 |

[a]There was no one-shock group with badminton rackets.

From Berkowitz & Le Page, 1967, p. 205. Copyright © 1967 by the American Psychological Association. Reprinted by permission.

only one shock, supporting the anger-arousal part of the hypothesis. Subjects seeing the guns gave more shocks than those not seeing the guns, supporting the cue-arousal part of the hypothesis.

Berkowitz has spoken of this cue property in terms of classically conditioned aggressive responses. By prior association with anger, weapons become conditioned stimuli for anger. The anger then serves the twofold function of being a *cue* for making particular responses and of being a *drive* to intensify responses. Like fear or frustration, anger is a conditionable response with drive and cue properties. We must assume it is the *arousal* effect which is most critical here, however, for we can hardly assume that college students have learned to press a telegraph key when angry. In other situations, however, anger may be a more direct cue for a particular response. If I have previously learned to fire a gun while angry, sight of the weapon might be a conditioned stimulus to anger, and the anger might be a cue for firing the weapon. Diagrammatically:

Gun → Anger Response → Anger Stimulus → Firing Gun

Other factors in the situation, such as fear of retribution, would determine whether the gun will be fired.

Berkowitz and his associates have manipulated many variables which heighten aggressive responses toward the target (the fictitious other subject). For example, when the target was said to be a college boxer and subjects had been shown a boxing film, the target got more shocks. Subjects shown an exciting, but nonaggressive, track race did not give more shocks to the target. There is also evidence that generalized arousal may facilitate aggressive response, in line with Zillman's excitation-transfer theory, discussed in chapter 2. Thus, subjects frustrated when working a jigsaw puzzle subsequently delivered more shocks to the confederate (Geen & Berkowitz, 1967), a loud noise made subjects more aggressive (Geen & O'Neal, 1969), and a sex film led to more punishment of an antagonistic partner (Tannenbaum & Zillman, 1975). Finally, subjects seeing Kirk Douglas beaten up in a fight movie (*The Champion*), subsequently delivered more shocks to the confederate if told that the beating was *justified*, as if this produced some generalized justification for aggressive actions.

*Is the weapons effect an artifact?* Although the kind of research described above is dramatic, and obviously bears on such important questions as gun control and television violence, serious reservations have been raised about its meaning. First, in at least two sets of experiments the effects could not be repeated. Buss, Booker, and Buss (1972) reported five experiments in which neither firing guns nor the presence of guns enhanced shocking a confederate. Page and Sheidt (1971) could not reproduce the weapons effect, and suggested that the effect is due to an *experimenter demand to behave aggressively*. Given the situation, they suggest the subject does what he thinks he is *supposed* to do—act aggressively. Page and Sheidt report that subjects receiving seven shocks were no more angry than subjects getting one shock. On many occasions the author has outlined the experimental procedure to a class, and then asked how many shocks class members would give back after receiving one or seven shocks. The class estimates are very close to the results obtained with real subjects getting real shocks.

Berkowitz (1974) argued in defense that how weapons are *perceived* and *interpreted* by subjects is critical. If a subject thinks a gun is terrible and frightening, it might arouse more anxiety than aggression and even lead to *fewer* shocks being delivered. Granting the validity of this argument, it is difficult to see why the meaning should have been so different in Berkowitz's experiments than those reported from other laboratories.

*Aggression and coercive power.*    Tedeschi, Smith, and Brown (1974) view what is *called* human aggression as just another way people try to get what they want. When other methods fail, people threaten violence and sometimes back up the threat. Tedeschi et al. then suggest that the main problem is to determine conditions under which society *says* behavior is aggressive. Socially justified acts are not considered aggressive; unjustified ones are. No specific response is unambiguously aggressive, so researchers decide what they shall call aggressive.

The scientists' labelling of a particular behavior as aggressive may, however, ignore *negative reciprocity* and *equity*. Negative reciprocity is a social norm that gives a person the "right" retaliate for harm done. Equity is a social norm that says you can have an eye for an eye, but no more. Kane, Doerge, and Tedeschi (1973) illustrated this point by having subjects rate the aggressiveness of participants in various conditions of a hypothetical Berkowitz-type experiment. The result was that someone receiving seven shocks was not considered aggressive for giving back seven—that was perfectly equitable. Only if a person gave back more shocks than received was he considered aggressive. Since this never actually happened in the Berkowitz experiments, equity may have been demonstrated and not aggression.

Negative reciprocity and equity have considerable social importance, for if a person can change the meaning of his or her action, it may be judged nonaggressive. For example, German troops dressed as Polish soldiers "attacked" German installations along the Polish-German border in 1939. Hitler then "justified" the invasion of Poland as a countermeasure. Most of us try to make our actions *look* necessary or defensive so they will be *labelled* nonaggressive.

### Instrumental Aggression

Instrumental aggression refers to aggressive behavior done for some reward other than aggression itself. The prize fighter who fights for money engages in fisticuffs for a different reason than a jealous husband attacking his wife's lover. The difference is in intent. The husband intends to hurt the lover; the boxer has other goals. Research examples of instrumental aggression abound. Animals on an electric grid will fight each other if reinforced for doing so by turning off the shock. Human subjects praised for shocking another person in the Berkowitz-Le Page procedure deliver more shocks than subjects not praised for doing so (Geen & Pigg, 1970). Subjects rewarded for making hostile remarks are subsequently more punitive (Loew, 1967) and children rewarded for making hostile remarks select more aggressive toys to play with. Many illegal activities are also committed in the pursuit of other goals. Violent and nonviolent crimes are ways to get the money to support a drug addiction.

*Obedient aggression.* Many major atrocities have been well-documented: Nazi attempts to exterminate the Jews (12 million dead), the terrorism of the Stalinist regime (20 million estimated dead), Japanese atrocities in World War II, terrorist activities related to civil strife in Ireland, Israel, Pakistan, Chile, various African countries, and the My Lai massacre by Americans in Viet Nam. When such activities come to trial, however, it is very difficult to fix blame. It is often said that the "little guys" who pull the triggers are the scapegoats for the "big guys" who give the orders. But what are these little guys like that they follow such orders? Stanley Milgram (1974) made this question into a laboratory experiment.

How far, asked Milgram, will a normal person go in following repugnant orders? Using a good cross section of the adult population, not just college students, Milgram set up a situation where subjects were supposed to give a "learner" increasingly strong electric shocks every time the learner made a mistake in memorizing a list of words. The "learner," an experimental assistant, was a friendly, middle-aged man whom the subjects met prior to the experiment. The fake shock apparatus was clearly marked in 30 levels, ranging from 15 to 450 volts, and with such written labels as "Slight Shock" (15 to 60 volts), "Danger: Severe Shock" (375 to 420 volts), and "XXX" (435 to 450 volts). The learner followed a set routine: He was wrong about 75% of the time and complained of how painful the ever-increasing shocks were. The learner and subject were in different rooms. The subjects looked to the experimenter for guidance as they became unsure about what they were doing, but were told to continue and even to treat failure to respond as an error and to give another shock.

Before the experiment began, the anticipated results were rather innocuous. Milgram's students estimated that only about 3% of subjects would continue to shock the learner up to the maximum. In the very first experiment, however, *no subject stopped below 300 volts and 26 of 40 subjects went the limit to 450 volts.* Various checks indicated that the subjects really did believe they were delivering highly painful, perhaps dangerous, shocks to the learner. For example, subjects judged the intensity of the strongest shock as

13.4 on a 14 point scale. These results are astonishing in their suggestion of how easy it is to get one human to hurt another, especially since the subjects came from all walks of life, varied in age from 20 to 50 years, and (perhaps unlike college students) were likely to believe what they were told about their participation in "an experiment on learning and memory" conducted by Yale University.

Milgram replicated the above results, but also found some important modifying variables. For example, the closer the contact between subject and learner (complete isolation of the two, hearing the learner's voice, being in the same room, and touching), the less likely the subject was to give the strongest shock.

In another experiment (Sheridan & King, 1972), the learner was a puppy. The stated shock levels were highly exaggerated, but were sufficient to evoke obviously negative responses from the puppy. Most subjects, male or female, shocked the puppy all the way to the end of the scale.

The most serious criticism of the *experiments* is the possibility of experimenter demand; the subjects may have been aware of what they were *expected* to do. In one experiment subjects were read the method section of an "experimental proposal" for the Milgram experiment, clearly stating the shocks were not real (O'Leary, Willis, & Tomich, 1969). The subjects were then told to role play as if they were real subjects in the experiment. The results were virtually the same as Milgram's, supporting the experimenter demand interpretation. Strangely, however, the subjects also showed many of the same signs of tension as Milgram's subjects, as if they really thought the learner was being shocked. The validity of any of the above experimental results may be challenged, as with any experiment, but there is no argument about the reality of obedient aggression and its importance. It does seem clear that people do get themselves into situations where they feel compelled to carry out orders, because of their commitment or because of fear of punishment for not doing so, and do highly repugnant things. It is also possible that by shifting responsibility to someone who gives the orders to behave aggressively, fear of retaliation is reduced and some people may do things they have wanted to do anyway.

*Social learning and imitation.*    Social learning theory (e.g., Bandura, 1973) emphasizes all the possible sources of stimulation and reinforcement for behaviors that a social environment provides, but assigns special importance to *imitation* and *modeling*. A child sees an adult doing something ("modeling") and copies the behavior ("imitation"). Modeling and imitation become particularly important in terms of the role of television as an instigator or inhibitor of aggressive behaviors. It is well known that television is a source of *information* about aggressive activities, but it is less clear that television viewing is a sufficient cause for aggressive behaviors. Thus, a hoax following the story line of a television program was perpetrated on an airline. A bomb was said to be planted on an airliner and set to go off at any altitude less than 5,000 feet. The plane was rerouted to Denver, Colorado, which has an airport above 5,000 feet. Even more violent instances of imitation have been reported, such as dousing an innocent victim with gasoline and striking a match, after having seen such an act on television. Berkowitz (1984) has recorded many instances of epidemic violent behavior, apparently copied. One such example during the Viet Nam war was a brief flurry of self-directed aggression, setting oneself on fire in protest to the war. In all such examples, however, it is not clear whether the individual aggressors were *stimulated* to imitate aggressive acts when they would not have been aggressive otherwise, or whether they have simply been provided with *information* which helps them do something they were already motivated to do for other reasons.

Berkowitz (1984) argues that television (or other media events) can instill ideas into an audience which are then carried into action—the contagion of violence. He quotes Gabriel Tarde, a French sociologist writing in 1912, to the effect that "Epidemics of crime follow the line of the telegraph." Tarde reported that the infamous Jack the Ripper murders in London led to eight imitations in London itself, and others elsewhere. Berkowitz follows the *associative network* theory, which is discussed among theories of emotion in chapter 2. To reiterate briefly, memory is considered a series of *networks* which consist of *nodes* (representing thoughts, feelings, and actions) which are interconnected by *associative pathways*. When an aggressive idea is suggested by a violent movie, the idea *spreads* from its particular node to other nodes. The associative strength will be greater among aggressive nodes, so that other aggressive thoughts, feelings, or actions are more likely to occur. Thus, for example, subjects who constructed sentences out of aggressive words were more likely to give a negative evaluation to a person on the basis of a brief description than were subjects who made sentences from nonaggressive words (Wyer & Hartwick, 1980).

Berkowitz argues that one difficulty for imitation theory is that aggressive (or other) acts ought to be physically similar to the portrayed behavior (e.g., a knifing). But, most experiments record aggressive behaviors which are physically *different* from the behavior modeled. Associative network accounts for this by saying that portrayed violence would activate a node in an associative network, and that the spreading activation from this node could reach nodes for a number of *different* aggressive behaviors, not just the one depicted. This would mean, for example, that a subject in a laboratory, seeing a gun, would have the "gun node" activated. This would spread to other associated nodes, for example to a node for "hurting" something or someone. This could then facilitate pressing a button to deliver shocks. This explanation is more adequate to account for the weapons effect than the rather oversimplified classical conditioning interpretations used earlier.

This line of theory leads to another possibility, namely, what we see on television does not just activate a preexisting associative network, *it becomes part of the network*. Television violence then may become part of the reality of the viewer, so that the viewer "gets used to it" and thinks that the TV viewing *is* part of reality and should be treated that way. This is basically the argument used in connection with pornography and violence against women, that there is a kind of desensitization because it is accepted as reality. There does not appear to be much research evidence to support this view, however (Berkowitz, 1984).

In one of the classic studies of imitation of aggression, Bandura, Ross, and Ross (1963a) compared aggressive behaviors of nursery school children after the children observed aggressive behavior by live adults, a film of adults, or a film of cartoon characters (adults dressed in cat costumes). Control subjects were not shown the aggressive sequence. The groups were further subdivided according to whether models were the same or opposite sex of the child. The main aggressive behavior was hitting a three-foot-tall inflatable rubber doll. The model sat on the doll, hit it with a fist or mallet, threw it up in the air, and kicked it about the room. The model also said such things as "Sock him in the nose" or "Hit him down." Such specific behaviors by the model were intended to be behaviors which could clearly be identified as imitative on the part of the child. Each child was then mildly frustrated by first being allowed to play for a little while with an attractive toy and then being told that he or she could not play with it anymore. Toys in a different room, including a Bobo doll, could be played with, however. In each 5 seconds of a 20-minute test period, the child was scored for aggressive responses, a total of 240 possible scores. The response categories were imitative aggression, partially imitative aggression, mallet aggression, sitting on the doll, nonimitative aggression, and aggressive gun play (a gun was among the toys in the test room). The results are summarized in Table 8–3.

Certain results were clearcut: (1) Aggressive-model groups were more aggressive than the control group; (2) Boys were more aggressive than girls; (3) Girls were more aggressive with female models and boys more aggressive with male models; and (4) Live or film models, real people or cartoon characters, were equally effective models. In another study (Bandura et al., 1963b), children seeing an aggressive model rewarded were subsequently more aggressive than control subjects, and children observing the aggressive model punished were less aggressive. The children later identified the models as "good" (nonaggressive) or "bad" (aggressive), *but preferred the aggressive model when he succeeded but not if he failed.* Their reasoning was quite frank: The aggressive, rewarded model got what he wanted. Aggressive behavior was therefore viewed as a successful, instrumental behavior. It was a kind of coercive power.

**TABLE 8-3  Mean Aggression Scores for Subgroups of Experimental and Control Subjects.**

| RESPONSE CATEGORY | EXPERIMENTAL GROUPS | | | | | CONTROL GROUP |
| | REAL-LIFE AGGRESSIVE | | HUMAN FILM AGGRESSIVE | | CARTOON FILM –AGGRESSIVE | |
| | F MODEL | M MODEL | F MODEL | M MODEL | | |
| --- | --- | --- | --- | --- | --- | --- |
| Total aggression | | | | | | |
| Girls | 65.8 | 57.3 | 87.0 | 79.5 | 80.9 | 36.4 |
| Boys | 76.8 | 131.8 | 114.5 | 85.0 | 117.2 | 72.2 |
| Imitative aggression | | | | | | |
| Girls | 19.2 | 9.2 | 10.0 | 8.0 | 7.8 | 1.8 |
| Boys | 18.4 | 38.4 | 34.3 | 13.3 | 16.2 | 3.9 |
| Mallet aggression | | | | | | |
| Girls | 17.2 | 18.7 | 49.2 | 19.5 | 36.8 | 13.1 |
| Boys | 15.5 | 28.8 | 20.5 | 16.3 | 12.5 | 13.5 |
| Sits on Bobo Doll[a] | | | | | | |
| Girls | 10.4 | 5.6 | 10.3 | 4.5 | 15.3 | 3.3 |
| Boys | 1.3 | 0.7 | 7.7 | 0.0 | 5.6 | 0.6 |
| Nonimitative aggression | | | | | | |
| Girls | 27.6 | 24.9 | 24.0 | 34.3 | 27.5 | 17.8 |
| Boys | 35.5 | 48.6 | 46.8 | 31.8 | 71.8 | 40.4 |
| Aggressive gun play | | | | | | |
| Girls | 1.8 | 4.5 | 3.8 | 17.6 | 8.8 | 3.7 |
| Boys | 7.3 | 15.9 | 12.8 | 23.7 | 16.6 | 14.3 |

[a]This response category was not included in the total aggression score.

From Bandura, Ross, & Ross, 1963b, p. 6. Copyright © 1963 by the American Psychological Association. Reprinted by permission.

### Control of Aggression

*Catharsis versus social learning.*    Konrad Lorenz (1965), among others, has considered aggression to be instinctive, following the water-tank (hydraulic) model. Aggressive "energy" is said to well up inside the individual, like water in a tank, until it overflows into aggressive behavior spontaneously unless "drained off" harmlessly (catharsis). Lorenz has claimed that animals have instinctive inhibitions to aggression, so that a species does not kill itself off. Humans, on the other hand, (says Lorenz) do *not* have these inhibitions. Therefore, without some other outlet for the spontaneously building aggressive energy, humans will inevitably fight among themselves. Lorenz's solution is to provide alternative aggression outlets so that aggressive energy does not build up too much. Such *displacement* (indirect) activities as athletic events would presumably be cathartic because they would drain off aggressive energy harmlessly and hence reduce the likelihood of serious aggressive activity. This is the same as the ventilationist view of anger.

The alternative view from social learning theory, however, is exactly the opposite of the cathartic view. The learning view says that aggressive behavior occurs because it is rewarded and that successful aggression is *more likely* to occur again, not less likely. If either of these views were *entirely* correct, it would obviously be socially disastrous to try to control aggression on the basis of the *wrong* one, either instinct or social learning. It becomes critical then, to evaluate as best one can the evidence pro and con on these views. It is also possible that both views have some validity under particular circumstances. If so, the circumstances should be clarified.

The instinct model has not been taken seriously by either biologists or psychologists for many years (e.g., see Bandura, 1973). There is no known physiological mechanism by which there could be a buildup of instinctive energy as described by the model. Energy can be stored, of course, but it is in the form of fat or glycogen which is available for *all* behaviors, not just aggressive behaviors. As Scott (1971) pointed out, anger is aroused by *external stimuli*, not by some aggression-specific energy. Furthermore, internal arousal eventually dies out in the absence of further stimulation. It does not accumulate indefinitely, as the hydraulic model says. Neither is there real evidence that animals are kept from fighting by inhibitions which humans do not have. We saw earlier that either aggressive or nonaggressive responses may lead to a reduction of emotional arousal, depending on previous experience. Finally, in the face of such events as a 1964 soccer championship in Peru where fans got into a riot resulting in 300 deaths and 500 injuries, it is difficult to believe that vicarious participation in violence is cathartic. Indeed, fan violence is some of the most visible evidence against the cathartic view.

A comparison of the instinct and social learning views strongly favors the social learning view as an account of the great bulk of aggressive behavior.

In the case of impulsive aggression we do have noxious stimulation as a factor. Where aggression is preceded by anger, however, we have a social account of anger (that is, unjustified frustration). For instrumental aggression, we have aggressive behavior facilitated by reward and inhibited by fear of punishment.

*Biological factors.* (1) *Brain mechanisms.* In animal behavior, the limbic system and hypothalamus are particularly important for the arousal or modulation of aggressive behavior. *Stimulation* of some hypothalamic and midbrain areas produces attack behavior in animals, such as mouse-killing behavior by rats or cricket-killing behavior by mice. Stimulation of one part of the amygdala facilitates attack behavior, but the general function of the amygdala seems to be to modulate the effects of hypothalamic arousal. The septal area of the brain seems to work opposite the amygdala; septal stimulation has a calming effect, and septal lesions produce a more vicious animal. See Carlson (1987) for more details. It is important to realize in any discussion of brain mechanisms, however, that a change in a specific behavior following stimulation or lesion may result from indirect effects. For example, if we damage peripheral motor nerves so that an animal could not make aggressive movements we would not be likely to argue that we have influenced aggression except in a trivial way. If we damage a part of the brain which affects these same muscles, however, we are much more likely to speak (incorrectly) of a brain center for aggressive behavior.

In general, do we know enough about brain mechanisms to justify doing anything permanently to the brain when there might be serious side effects? In some cases the answer is clearly yes. We operate on the brain for tumors, for extremely severe epilepsy, or other physically definable pathologies where the benefits to the patient outweigh the potential risks. In the case of aggressive behaviors, where aggression (1) may be socially defined, (2) is often hard to identify as unambiguously aggressive, (3) is affected by noxious environmental events, as well as frustration, and (4) is heavily influenced by the specific ways in which an individual has learned to deal with situations, there seems to be little justification for surgical intervention (see also Valenstein, 1973).

(2) *Sex differences, hormones, and aggression.* In many species males are more aggressive than females. The hormonal basis for this (testosterone) is indicated by the fact that males are more aggressive during the mating season when male hormones are at their highest level and are least aggressive after castration (as with a gelding steer or horse).

There is also reported to be a disproportionate incidence of irritability and antisocial behavior of human females during menstrual and premenstrual periods. Possible reasons for this are lower progesterone levels, increase of the adrenal hormone *aldosterone*, low blood sugar level, and social learning (women may learn they are supposed to be irritable before or during their

periods). There is a host of individual, social, and biological factors all interacting which influence aggressive behaviors, and not any simple cause-effect
relationship.

*Television Viewing and Aggression.*    Because of great amount of exposure
to television, and the violence it portrays, much concern has been expressed
about TV as a contributor to real-life violence. There are individuals and
groups who claim that it is *obvious* that TV shows a massive amount of
violence and therefore produces an increase in violence outside the box.
Note that this is the social learning view, and that the cathartic view would
say that TV violence may protect society, not harm it. There certainly is no
dispute that there is a large amount of wanton killing, fighting, and property
damage shown on TV. We then have two questions to face. First, what data
are there to show that TV violence *is related* to real-life violence? And second,
if there is such a relationship, how do we *interpret* the data which show it? For
example, are the data *only* correlational? If there is a correlation between
viewing TV violence and real violence, there might be a causal relation
between the two or there might be some third factor influencing them both.

It does *not* appear that increased television viewing has *reduced* the
crime rate, as predicted by catharsis theory, and various experiments indicate
that children imitate what they have seen done by others. It is much less clear
how TV viewing ties into this. Survey studies cannot tell us much about
causes, and it is very hard to gain effective control over television viewing for
experimental purposes except in artificial situations where it is difficult to
generalize to real life. So let us look at some studies which give us at least a
flavor of what is involved.

*Correlational studies.* In one of the major studies (Eron, et al., 1972),
data relating TV viewing and aggressive behavior were collected for 427
children over a period of 10 years. In Grade 3, the original group of 875
children (every third grader in town) were judged by their peers as to how
aggressive they were. At the same time, data on other variables potentially
related to aggressive behavior of the children were collected from parents,
such as children's preferences in TV viewing. Each mother was asked the
child's three favorite TV shows, and these were given violence ratings based
on an independent judge's ratings of all the TV shows mentioned.

The 10-year follow-up data are referred to as Grade 13. At this time,
there were three measures of aggressiveness: peer ratings, subjects' self
reports, and a personality test. Other data, such as favorite programs, were
also collected by self reports. It is important to note that all the Grade 13
measures were obtained independently of the Grade 3 measures. The results
for boys are shown in Figure 8-4; the data for girls showed no significant
trends.

Figure 8-4 shows a *cross-lagged* correlation, a method for using correlational data to get at causal relations. First, there was a low (.21) but significant

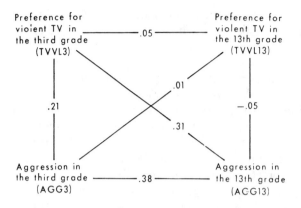

Preference for
violent TV in ———————— .05 ————————
the third grade
(TVVL3)

Preference for
violent TV in
the 13th grade
(TVVL13)

.01

.21

.31

−.05

Aggression in
the third grade ———————— .38 ————————
(AGG3)

Aggression in
the 13th grade
(ACGl3)

**FIGURE 8–4.** The correlations between a preference for violent television and peer-rated aggression for 211 boys over a 10-year-lag. (From Eron, Lefkowitz, Huesmann, and Walder, 1972, p. 257. Copyright ©1972 by the American Psychological Association. Reprinted by permission.)

relation between TV preference and aggressive behavior in Grade 3. This, of course, is ambiguous as regards causality. There was an even higher correlation between Grade 3 and Grade 13 aggressive behavior, which tells us only that the same people were violent ten years later. Two other correlations tell us more about the effect of TV viewing on violence: Grade 3 aggressiveness did *not* predict Grade 13 TV preference ($r = .01$), but Grade 3 TV preference did predict Grade 13 violence ($r = .31$). From this it appears that Grade 3 TV preference played a *causal* role in Grade 13 violence, but not the other way around. Television viewing habits are obviously not the only factor involved in Grade 13 aggression, since the correlations are not tremendously high, but it is remarkable that there are any significant correlations at all over a 10-year period. The data are, however, weakened by the lack of any relationship for the females. Reviewing all the published literature to date, Freedman (1984) concluded that there is a small but consistently positive correlation (somewhere between .10 and .20) between viewing TV violence and aggressiveness. This conclusion was based on research involving thousands of subjects, in several different countries. At the same time, it should be noted that this means that *only about 4% of the variation in aggressive behavior can be accounted for by variation in television viewing.* The most generous interpretation possible, based only on the *highest* of such correlations (on the order of .30), would account for only about 10% of the aggression variability in terms of TV viewing. This is not unimportant, but neither is it awe-inspiring.

*Field experiments.* These are studies in natural settings, with some degree of experimental control over television or movie viewing so that the effects of the kind or amount of viewing on behavior can be interpreted causally. Residential schools have been one of the more-used settings. Feshback and Singer (1971) did one such study, in which experimental subjects were allowed to watch violent programs over a period of six weeks while control subjects watched nonviolent programs. Measures of aggression were supervisors' ratings of fighting, teasing, breaking rules, and so on. The boys watching violent television were *less violent* at the end of six weeks than were those watching nonviolent television.

Interpretation of these results is subject to several caveats, however. First, the results held only in *institutional* settings, not in *boarding schools*. This at least challenges the generality of the results. Second, the institutional boys watching nonviolent television were *initially* more aggressive than were the boys watching violent television. When this initial difference is taken into account, the subsequent difference between the two groups dissipates. On the whole, in six out of seven of the research settings reported there was no positive relationship between violent TV viewing and aggressive behavior. In other studies of a similar nature (see Freedman, 1984, for detailed analyses and references), there were *at best* only a few modest relationships between TV viewing and aggressiveness found, most of the results being a mixed bag. Other reviewers have arrived at different conclusions from the data than did Freedman (Friedrich-Cofer & Huston, 1986), arguing that there is a more consistent relationship between violent TV viewing and aggressive behavior than Freedman's analysis would make it appear. This is a matter of *degree*, however, since the available data indicate that the relationship simply cannot be stronger than noted above (somewhere between $r = .10$ and $r = .20$).

Since the question of TV violence is also a question of public policy, it will be fought in the political arena as well as in the scientific arena. In such situations persuasiveness becomes as powerful a force as accuracy, and whoever is persuasive will have great impact on any policy decisions regarding TV content.

## SUMMARY

1. Frustration is commonly considered an aversive state which occurs when an anticipated desirable goal is not attained. Theoretically, we treat it as an intervening variable which has blocking of a goal as the antecedent condition and some emotional or behavioral event as the consequent condition. There are apparently no *unique* frustration responses.

2. Like fear, frustration may have both *cue* and *drive* properties. As a cue, frustration may help select or guide behavior; as a drive, frustration may energize behavior.

3. Frustration theory has been used to account for the superiority of *partial reinforcement* over continuous reinforcement for maintaining behavior during extinction. Frustration cues become conditioned to responses and help maintain behavior in the absence of reward.

4. The "better" (larger, tastier, etc.) the anticipated reward, the greater the frustration, and the more rapid the escape from frustrating situations.

5. *Conflict* is a special category of frustration, involving choices among incompatible responses so that achieving one goal precludes achieving another.

6.  The best developed *experimental* theory of conflict is that of Neal Miller. Miller assumes that the closer one is to a positive or negative goal, the stronger is the tendency to approach or avoid, respectively. These increasing tendencies are called *approach and avoidance gradients*, with the avoidance gradient being *steeper*.

7.  Four basic kinds of conflict are *approach-approach, avoidance-avoidance, approach-avoidance,* and *multiple approach-avoidance*. Most research has been done on approach-avoidance conflicts, where it is assumed that approach and avoidance gradients *intersect*. The point of intersection of the two gradients is the point of maximal conflict.

8.  Miller's theory has been extended to human clinical situations, with laboratory support. Animals may approach goals in situations similar, but not identical, to the training situation. This is similar to *displacement* in psychoanalytic theory.

9.  *Anger* is an emotion often thought to be aroused in situations where there is *arbitrary* blocking of a goal by someone. Anger may result in hostile actions toward others.

10. It is often said that we should *vent* our anger rather than hold it in because expressing the anger is *cathartic*, and expression of anger will reduce it faster. Another view, however, is that venting anger makes people angrier. Research suggests that anger and anger reduction are learned responses which can be changed with training.

11. Aggression is commonly defined in terms of *intent to do physical or psychological harm to someone*. No single circumstance satisfactorily characterizes every behavior that might be considered aggressive, however.

12. The *frustration-aggression hypothesis* states that frustration instigates aggression. Aggressive acts directed toward the blocking agent, or a substitute, are said to reduce the instigation to aggression. Reduction of the instigation is called *catharsis*. Direct aggressive acts may be inhibited by threat of punishment.

13. Aggressive behavior is often *impulsive*, arising from aversive environmental conditions, including bad social interactions. Aggressive acts may be facilitated by the presence of aggressive cues in the environment, such as weapons.

14. *Instrumental aggression* is harmful behavior rewarded by something other than the harm, such as a boxer fighting for pay, or people being obedient to orders.

15. Much aggressive behavior appears to be learned in imitation of others, and may often be a *power strategy* to get what one wants. A given behavior may not be interpreted as aggressive if it is perceived as *equitable reciprocation* for previous aggression.

16. Two major and opposing approaches to the control of aggression are (1) *catharsis theory*, which says that *vicarious* aggression will reduce the occurrence of truly harmful behavior, and (2) *social learning theory*, which says that social acceptance of aggressive acts rewards such acts, and that aggressive acts (vicarious or not) will lead to further aggression. Viewing violent TV shows seems to be only weakly related to actual aggressive behavior.

17. In lower animals there appear to be specific physiological mechanisms and brain locations related to aggressive behavior. In humans this is not so clearcut, due to the many possible causes of aggression.

# 9

# Anxiety, Stress, and Coping

Anxiety

Stress

Coping

Summary

## ANXIETY

Feelings of anxiety and despair are not new to modern man. Anxiety was described in Babylonian and Sumerian writings in the second and third millennia before Christ (McReynolds, 1980), is found in the writings of Homer, and is in the Christian Bible. Many psychologists attribute the beginnings of modern thought about anxiety, however, to the Danish philosopher Soren Kierkegaard (1813–1855; May 1950). Kierkegaard argued that man has the potential to be many different things, and these possibilities are his freedom. At the same time, this very confrontation with freedom, and the accompanying possibilities for failure and guilt, is his source of *dread* (anxiety). Indeed, the more creative a person is, the more possibilities she or he has and therefore the greater potential for anxiety. In this view, anxiety involves the inner conflict which arises from dealing with multiple possibilities. Anxiety is healthy if one moves through it to reach a higher level of development, but is unhealthy if one is "shut in" by it.

### Anxiety Versus Fear

Since the time of Sigmund Freud, anxiety and its reduction have been crucial concepts in clinical theory, whether psychoanalytic or behavioral, but there have been many views about the origins and nature of anxiety. One of Freud's best-known distinctions is between *objective anxiety* (what we would commonly call *fear*) and *neurotic anxiety*. Objective anxiety is directed toward some specific object, whereas neurotic anxiety is fear without a (recognized) cause. This distinction is widely accepted by psychologists. Freud also characterized neurotic anxiety as (1) out of proportion to the actual threat to the individual, (2) involving repression and conflict, and (3) involving defense mechanisms (projection, reaction formation, etc.). Most psychologists would agree that (1) Strong anxiety is an unpleasant emotional experience; (2) Anxiety is highly motivating, sometimes pushing people to extreme thoughts and behaviors to hold it down; and (3) Long periods of high anxiety and its attendant upheaval of the autonomic nervous system are bad for our health, producing so-called psychosomatic or stress disorders.

It is not always easy to maintain definitional distinctions, such as between fear and anxiety, however. The psychoanalyst may treat a phobia as the manifestation of a "deeper" anxiety which is to be understood by extensive verbal probing, whereas the behavior therapist may see the same phobia as a specific fear to be extinguished through the use of established learning theory principles. The fear/anxiety distinction is also difficult to maintain in animal research. We are hard put to say whether the laboratory rat is expressing "fear without a cause," so the fear/anxiety distinction is not very meaningful. Epstein (1967; 1986) has suggested a different distinction between fear and anxiety with humans. Anxiety, he says, is a qualitatively different experience than fear, and arises when we cannot cope with threat. An inability to cope with a threatening situation might be due to not recognizing the source of the threat. On the other hand, a soldier might specifically be afraid of mortar shells dropping around him, but also be anxious because he could do nothing about those falling shells. Anxiety in this view is not necessarily without a recognized cause. The critical element is ability to cope with a fearful situation. As we shall see, uncontrollable aversive events can also be produced in the animal laboratory, with adverse effects.

### Trait Versus State Anxiety

Anxiety research has also led to a distinction between *trait anxiety* (A-trait) and *state anxiety* (A-state). A-trait is a relatively enduring personality trait, a *disposition* to be anxious in many different situations, whereas A-state is the anxiety an individual experiences in a specific situation at a specific time (Cattell & Scheier, 1961; Spielberger, 1966; 1976). The two are commonly measured with the *State-Trait Anxiety Inventory* (STAI) (Spielberger, Gorsuch, & Lushene, 1970). It is often important to know whether a person is anxious all the time or is just anxious in some situations. Research has repeatedly shown that whether a person reports being anxious depends on the person, the situation he or she is in, and the type of "anxious" response being reported (Endler, Hunt, & Rosen, 1962). Endler, Hunt, and Rosen devised the *S-R Inventory of Anxiousness*, consisting of 11 different situations (such as starting on an auto trip or climbing on a mountain ledge) and 14 kinds of responses (such as heart beats faster, feels uneasy). A given person tends to rate himself or herself as more or less anxious according to the situation and the response. In practical terms, this implies that if anxiety is specific to situations and responses, then *treatments* may have to be equally specific. This, of course, has been the approach taken by behavior therapists.

### Physiology of Fear and Anxiety

It has long been known that fear and anxiety involve arousal of the sympathetic nervous system and related hormones. Recently, however, Gray (1982a, b) has proposed a theory which relates "anxious behavior" to specific brain locations and neurochemistry. Gray argues that there is a *behavioral inhibition system* (BIS), located in a *septal-hippocampal system* in the brain. In Gray's theory, activation of the BIS *is* anxiety.

Gray proposes that the BIS responds to several kinds of stimulus inputs with several kinds of response outputs, as follows:

| Input | Output |
|---|---|
| Signals of Punishment | Behavioral Inhibition |
| Signals of Nonreward | Increased Arousal |
| Novel Stimuli | Increased Attention |

When a person is engaged in some goal-oriented behavior, and faces threatening stimuli, frustrative nonreward, or unexpected stimuli, the BIS is activated. This activation inhibits the ongoing behavior and produces increased arousal, and the organism attends to the disruptive elements. Anxiety is experienced. Much of the evidence for Gray's theory is from research with *anti-anxiety* (tranquilizing) drugs. These drugs *reduce* each of the three kinds of responses above. Gray further suggests that these drugs reduce anxiety because they facilitate the effects of *gamma aminobutyric acid (GABA)*, a neurotransmitter.

Gray brings *cognitive* factors into the theory in the following manner. His theory says that an organism is continuously *comparing its plans for the future, its predicted outcomes of its present behavior, and stored information about the way the world works*. The septal-hippocampal system (part of the limbic system, and known to be involved in memory) serves as a *comparator*. It compares internal plans, predictions, and stored information with what is going on in the environment. As long as plans and expectations are being met, there is no anxiety and no behavioral inhibition. If, however, progress toward an expected outcome is interrupted by threat, frustration, or novel event, the BIS becomes active and anxiety is experienced.

### Cognition and Anxiety

In Gray's model, *signals* of punishment or nonreward are anxiety-provoking. The perceived threat, however, depends on the individual's *interpretation* or *appraisal* of signals in the environment. A person has to *know* that a particular signal means danger before he responds to it as a threatening stimulus. Research shows that clinical patients with anxiety neuroses express exaggerated thoughts about danger and exaggerated fear of the consequences of their behavior. They appraise life events as more dangerous and threatening than a more objective observer would (Beck & Rush, 1980).

## STRESS

### Early Stress Theory: The General Adaptation Syndrome

The concept of stress has subsumed much of the subject matter of frustration, conflict, and anxiety in recent years. This focus is largely due to the prodigious efforts of Hans Selye and his concept of the *general adaptation syndrome* (GAS). Selye (pronounced Sel-yea) considered the GAS to be common to many different "stress situations" and characterized it in three stages (Selye, 1956), which are summarized in Figure 9–1.

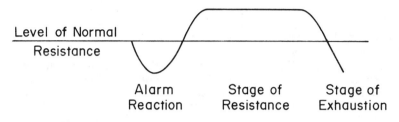

Level of Normal
Resistance

Alarm        Stage of        Stage of
Reaction     Resistance      Exhaustion

**FIGURE 9-1.** The time course of stress. (From *The Stress of Life* by Selye, ©1974 by McGraw Hill Book Co. Used with permission of publisher.)

1. *Alarm Reaction.* When an organism faces a *stressor*, such as disease, extreme temperature, or injury, the body shows an *alarm reaction,* such as a sudden drop in blood sugar level followed quickly by a counterresponse, such as an increase in blood sugar. Other typical changes are in blood pressure, heart rate, and release of adrenal hormones.

2. *Stage of Resistance.* The body now uses its resources to keep its physiology on a normal course during stress. Since the body has to work harder than usual to maintain itself, it is especially susceptible to the effects of additional stress. If this effortful resistance continues long enough, the body may "wear down" and go into the third stage.

3. *Stage of Exhaustion.* This stage, possibly life threatening, is characterized by *enlarged adrenal glands, shriveling of the thymus and lymph glands* (necessary to fight disease), and *gastrointestinal ulcers.* Other effects specific to particular stressors may also occur, but the three described here are widely found *regardless* of the source of the stressor. Hence the name "general adaptation syndrome."

A major advantage of the stress concept is that it provides medical and psychological researchers a common ground to work from. So-called *psychosomatic disorders,* illnesses sometimes said to be "in the head" and therefore not "real," make sense in terms of stress if we assume that stress has both psychological and physical origins. A great deal of research shows that this assumption is well founded, but also forces a more psychologically oriented definition of stress than that originally provided by Selye.

### Definitions of Stress

1. *Stimulus Definition.* We might define stress in terms of specific environmental (stimulus) conditions, such as loud noise or heat. These same conditions are not equally stressful for all individuals, however, so the stimulus definition has limited value.

2. *Response Definition.* Selye (1956, p. 55) said that "Stress is a state manifested by a syndrome," that a *pattern of symptoms* characterizes the emotional "fight-flight" reaction and leads to exhaustion. This is a response definition. We cannot use it to predict what situations will produce stress, however, and it

easily becomes a circular argument: "This must be a stressful situation because this person looks stressed." Experience tells us that some things produce stress, such as surgical anesthesia, pain, cold, or loss of blood, but this knowledge does not *define* stress for us.

3. *Interactive Definition.* To overcome the above difficulties, most psychologists define stress in terms of stimuli *and* responses, an *organism-environment interaction:* "Stress occurs when there is a substantial imbalance between the environmental demand and the response capability of the focal organism" (McGrath, 1970, p. 17).

The imbalance is partly subjective, depending on whether a person *perceives* that he or she can respond effectively to the environment, and whether it is *important* to do so. A person perfectly capable of responding effectively may not perceive that he or she can do so and is therefore "stressed." Conversely, a person may perceive that he or she is "invincible" and is therefore not stressed, even though objectively no more capable than the person who is stressed.

### Sources of Stress

As medical science has learned to control such killer diseases as tuberculosis and diphtheria, the importance of psychological stressors in such disorders has become more widely studied. Many health professionals recognize that the concept of a single cause for an illness is no longer adequate. Many different sources of stress, psychological and physical, precipitate illnesses ranging from hives to heart disease.

*Traumatic events.*    Being caught in a fire, being raped, witnessing a gory crime, or being held prisoner of war are examples of traumatic stressors. Even though a victim seems to be coping with the situation, a *delayed stress reaction* may appear weeks or months after the traumatic event has occurred. A victim may begin to feel depressed, have nightmares about the event, or have *flashbacks* and briefly relive the horror of the earlier experience. Such traumatic events are stressful but relatively rare.

*Recent life changes.*    Holmes and Rahe (1967) devised a scale to quantify the degree of stressfulness of many different life changes, as shown in Table 9-1. They suggested that the effects of life changes cumulate so that if the sum of the life changes exceeds 300 in a year, illness is more likely to occur. Such details are controversial for several reasons, however. First, all life changes do not mean the same thing to all people. One person's only divorce after 30 years of marriage would not mean the same thing as another's sixth divorce in six years. Second, some of the changes in the scale are themselves illnesses, and hence would probably contribute more to stress. Third, a person's score on the scale often depends on the memories of the person involved, and so may not be entirely reliable. Research also suggests that the

**TABLE 9-1   Life Change Events.**

| | LCU VALUES |
|---|---|
| FAMILY: | |
| Death of a spouse | 100 |
| Divorce | 73 |
| Marital separation | 65 |
| Death of close family member | 63 |
| Marriage | 50 |
| Marital reconciliation | 45 |
| Major change in health of family | 44 |
| Pregnancy | 40 |
| Addition of new family member | 39 |
| Major change in arguments with wife | 35 |
| Son or daughter leaving home | 29 |
| In-law troubles | 29 |
| Wife starting or ending work | 26 |
| Major change in family get-togethers | 15 |
| PERSONAL: | |
| Detention in jail | 63 |
| Major personal injury or illness | 53 |
| Sexual difficulties | 39 |
| Death of a close friend | 37 |
| Outstanding personal achievement | 28 |
| Start or end of formal schooling | 26 |
| Major change in living conditions | 25 |
| Major revision of personal habits | 24 |
| Changing to a new school | 20 |
| Change in residence | 20 |
| Major change in recreation | 19 |
| Major change in church activities | 19 |
| Major change in sleeping habits | 16 |
| Major change in eating habits | 15 |
| Vacation | 13 |
| Christmas | 12 |
| Minor violations of the law | 11 |
| WORK: | |
| Being fired from work | 47 |
| Retirement from work | 45 |
| Major business adjustment | 39 |
| Changing to different line of work | 36 |
| Major change in work responsibilities | 29 |
| Trouble with boss | 23 |
| Major change in working conditions | 20 |
| FINANCIAL: | |
| Major change in financial state | 38 |
| Mortgage or loan over $10,000 | 31 |
| Mortgage foreclosure | 30 |
| Mortgage or loan less than $10,000 | 17 |

From T.H. Holmes and R.H. Rahe (1967). The social readjustment rating scale. *Journal of Psychosomatic Research*, 11, 213–218. Copyright © 1967 by Pergamon Press. Used by permission.

negative events contribute to stress, not the positive ones. Details aside, however, life changes do contribute to stress.

*Hassles.* The stressfulness of such personal disasters as the loss of a loved one can hardly be overrated, but such disasters are not daily events. What most of us face most often is the stress of dealing with the hassles of everyday life (Lazarus, 1981). Many mothers, for example, may spend hours each week getting children to and from school, parties, and lessons, taking care of the family, and dealing with countless small family emergencies. As such hassles continue, stress increases and ability to cope with stress may go down. Long-term accumulation of small frustrations, hassles, and stress may occur in any occupation, for either men or women. People do lead lives of quiet desperation, and all their stresses may not be obvious to the outsider.

To fully understand why one person is more susceptible to stress than another, we have to explore individual differences in genetics, early life experiences, perceptions, and the relationships of all these to physical and psychological disorders. We shall limit ourselves to a few selected topics.

### Individual Differences in Susceptibility to Stress

The interactive definition of stress is a recognition of individual differences in susceptibility to stress. How do these individual differences arise? As we would expect, the evidence points to both genetic and learned differences.

*Genetic differences.* We need not discuss genetic differences in detail except to note that it has long been a practice in both applied and experimental settings to breed animals of very different temperaments. Some dogs (e.g., retrievers) are relatively unresponsive to stimulation, whereas others are highly excitable (e.g., Pekingese). In the laboratory, mice have been bred for high or low levels of emotional reactivity, indexed by measures of autonomic nervous system arousal and by such fearful behavior as crouching in a corner.

*Early experience.* Early experience may be either *prenatal* or *postnatal*. Early postnatal experiences have been emphasized by psychoanalysts from Freud on. A client's own recall of early infantile experience is not a reliable source of evidence, but many other supportive observations and research have been reported over the years. For example, infants in orphanages have had high incidence of health problems which are not due to poor health care but result from lack of stimulation in a dull and unchanging environment (Hunt, 1984). Laboratory research with animals also supports the conclusion that environmental stimulation in infancy is important to the general welfare of the individual.

According to psychoanalytic theory, early infantile trauma should produce later emotional disorders. Levine (1960) put this hypothesis to test with newborn rat pups. Contrary to expectation, he found that pups which were left entirely in the tender, loving care of their mothers were more anxious as adults in new situations than were pups which had been either "traumatized" by being shocked or handled a few minutes daily by the experimenter. Levine argued that the *stimulation* provided by either a mild shock or the handling facilitated later emotional stability. Subsequent evidence indicated that it might be that body cooling, which occurs when the infant is removed from the nest, is critical, but this possible change in stressors does little violence to the overall interpretation. It was also found that *escape learning is faster with nonhandled animals* but *avoidance learning is faster with handled animals.* This makes sense in terms of the kinds of behaviors required. Escape is usually a simple response, and the greater the fear arousal the faster the escape (as discussed in chapter 7). Avoidance, on the other hand, requires a more delicately timed response in the presence of a cue. Nonhandled animals might be *too emotional* to respond efficiently. Furthermore, the adrenalcorticosteroid levels of the nonhandled animals are slower to rise when shock is given and slower to fall when shock is terminated than the levels of shocked or handled animals. The autonomic responses of the nonhandled animals simply are not very efficient.

*Social Psychology of Rat Stress: Genetics-Experience Interactions.* Animals with the same genes may develop different degrees of emotionality in environments which differ in terms of social interactions. Denenberg (1963), for example, established emotional and nonemotional mother rats by Levine's procedure of differential early handling. He then reared children of emotional mothers with either emotional or nonemotional mothers, and did the same with children of nonemotional mothers. Birthing and parenting by emotional mothers produced the most emotional offspring, and birthing and parenting by nonemotional mothers produced the least emotional offspring, the other two combinations falling between. Thus, being born to an emotional mother was different than being born to a nonemotional mother. The fetus of the emotional mother may be "sensitized" by maternal adrenal hormones, for example. It was also found that the offspring of nonemotional mothers had a calming effect on an emotional foster mother, whereas offspring of emotional mothers had "upsetting" effects on a calm mother (Gray, 1971).

We thus have a combination of prenatal and postnatal factors which combine to determine emotionality and susceptibility to stress, without genetic differences. An infant which is "fearful" at birth may not be genetically so, and its emotionality may be exaggerated or reduced by subsequent social experiences.

### Emotional Conditioning

*Classical conditioning.*   Many emotional responses can be classically conditioned, and although there apparently are biological limits on the extent to which one stimulus can be paired with another to produce conditioning (see chapter 2), it appears that virtually any stimulus can be conditioned to some kind of response (e.g., Bykov, 1957; Razran, 1971). This means that stress responses can be conditioned to occur in situations where the original threat may never have occurred. For example, a person who has been punished by an authority figure as a child may experience anxiety in dealing with authority figures later in life.

*Instrumental conditioning of autonomic responses.*   For many years psychologists assumed that responses controlled by the autonomic nervous system could not be modified by rewarding or punishing their occurrence. For example, a person could not be taught to lower his heart rate by being rewarded for doing so. Initial reports of instrumental conditioning of autonomic responses were received with skepticism because alternative interpretations could readily account for apparent instrumental conditioning (Black, 1971). For example, skeletal responses to a CS might trigger unconditioned autonomic responses. Heart rate usually increases when we move about. Or, what appears to be instrumental conditioning may really be accidental classical conditioning. A stimulus preceding a reward might be classically conditioned to an autonomic response which is aroused when the reward is given. The autonomic response later occurs when the CS is presented, and not as a result of having been rewarded. The click of a food delivery mechanism might be conditioned to a change in heart rate, for example. Finally, and most difficult to rule out, is the possibility that the brain activities controlling skeletal movements might also control at least some autonomic activities. We know, for example, that the neurotransmitter *dopamine* is involved both in muscle activity and in the arousal of pleasure. In spite of these problems, the research has been intriguing because it is theoretically exciting and because it offered new possibilities for understanding and treating stress-related disorders.

*Instrumental autonomic conditioning with humans.* Kimmel and his associates reported the first instrumental autonomic conditioning studies with humans. Kimmel and Kimmel (1963) reinforced spontaneous GSR responses from subjects in a darkened room by briefly turning on a light. Over a conditioning session, subjects with reinforced GSRs increased the number of GSRs while control subjects did not. This appeared to be instrumental conditioning, but of course the subjects might have been moving a little, or even having exciting thoughts which aroused their GSRs. Subsequent experimenters have found a correlation between muscle action potentials and GSRs in such a situation, and others have not found any evidence of conditioning at all (Katkin, 1971). The human research has given little support to the notion of instrumental autonomic conditioning.

*Instrumental autonomic conditioning with animals.* To eliminate the problem of "unauthorized movements," researchers turned to the study of animals, using the arrow poison curare to temporarily paralyze subjects. DiCara and Miller (1968) reported that paralyzed rats could be trained to either increase or decrease their heart rate to avoid electric shock even when electrical recordings showed no muscle movements. Furthermore, since heart rate could be conditioned to go up or down, the results could not be due to just a conditioned arousal. Other experiments were equally dramatic. For example, it was reported that animals could learn to constrict the blood vessels in one ear but not the other.

The fly in the soup of instrumental autonomic conditioning turned out to be repeated failures to replicate the above results, in Miller's own lab or elsewhere, sometimes with literally hundreds of animals as subjects (Brenner, Eissenberg, & Middaugh, 1974; Roberts, Lacroix, & Wright, 1974). The status of instrumental autonomic conditioning is uncertain at best, and has received little attention in recent years. Interest has turned to *biofeedback*, which is discussed later in this chapter.

### Learned Helplessness, Control, and Stress

*Learned helplessness.* Some people are helpless and anxious in new situations, appearing to be at a loss to do anything. How does such helplessness come about? One theory is that organisms *learn that their behavior is ineffective and therefore do nothing.* Mowrer and Viek (1948) demonstrated an effect of helplessness in an experiment involving what they called *fear from a sense of helplessness.* Some subjects (laboratory rats) experienced a tone followed by an electric shock to the feet, which they could terminate by jumping off the floor. Other subjects could not end the shock by their own responses. The tone, a conditioned stimulus for fear, was then shown to be more punishing for the animals previously unable to escape the shock. Mowrer and Viek suggest that greater fear was produced because of the animals' helplessness in the shock situation.

Subsequent *learned helplessness* experiments show that prior experience with inescapable shock greatly interferes with later escape and avoidance learning (Overmier & Seligman, 1967; Seligman & Maier, 1967). Specifically, dogs previously shocked while in a harness would subsequently just sit and take shocks in a shuttle box, not even learning to escape from shock, much less avoid it. Figure 9–2 (Maier, Seligman, & Solomon, 1969) shows the escape latencies for "helpless" animals in the shuttle box compared to animals without earlier exposure to shock. Two-thirds of the 82 dogs given inescapable shock did not learn to escape from shock in the shuttle box, as compared

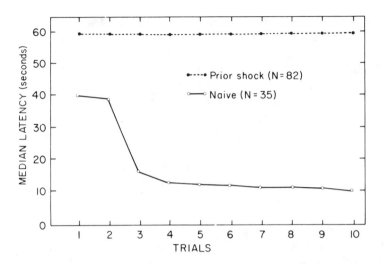

**FIGURE 9-2.**  The effects of inescapable shocks in the Pavlov harness on escape responding in the shuttle box. This figure shows that there is rapid escape learning by 35 naive dogs that received no shocks in the harness. In contrast, the median for 82 dogs that received inescapable shocks in the harness, prior to escape training in the shuttle box, shows failure to escape shock. The arbitrary failure criterion was 60 seconds a shock (a latency of 60 seconds after onset of the S+). (From Maier/Seligman/Solomon, "Pavlovian Fear Conditioning & Learned Helplessness," in PUNISHMENT AND AVERSIVE BEHAVIOR, Campbell/Church, eds., ©1969, p. 321. Reprinted by permission of Prentice Hall, Inc., Englewood Cliffs, New Jersey.

to only 6% of animals not shocked previously. An animal's lack of control over shock while in the harness is the critical event, since animals that are allowed to turn off the shock while in the harness later learn escape and avoidance responses without difficulty (Seligman & Maier, 1967). The learned helplessness effect is found with many species (cats, dogs, mice, monkeys, and humans), with several forms of aversive stimulation (electric shock, loud noise, forced swimming), and with different tasks (lever pressing, shuttle box avoidance, or, for humans, solving anagrams). It is therefore not just an isolated phenomenon.

*Learned helplessness in humans.* The procedures used to establish learned helplessness in laboratory animals quickly caught the attention of researchers interested in human clinical problems. Hiroto (1974) pointed out the similarity of the learned helplessness concept to that of *locus of control* (Rotter, 1966) and studied learned helplessness in subjects with high versus low external locus of control.[1] Using an analog of the animal procedures, Hiroto exposed his subjects to loud bursts of aversive noise. Some subjects could stop the noise by pushing a button, while others could not. Subjects could then move a knob to avoid a signalled noise, simulating the shuttle box.

---

[1] Locus of control refers to the extent to which a person believes that his or her success depends on his or her own actions (internal locus) or on outside forces or other people (external locus).

The subjects with previous uncontrollable noise learned to avoid more slowly and had more trials without responding at all. In addition, subjects with external locus of control performed more poorly than those with internal locus, and subjects led to believe that their success was due to chance did less well than those who believed that skill could be effective. Hiroto and Seligman (1975) subsequently reported similar results using solutions to anagram problems as the response. Other investigators have not always been able to replicate these results, but these experiments were important to the development of learned helplessness theory.

*Helplessness and depression.* Seligman (1975) proposed that learned helplessness might be the cause of depression, which he has referred to as the "common cold of psychiatric disorders." The difficulty with the helplessness interpretation for depression is that many individuals in a "helpless" situation do *not* become depressed, whereas many individuals who are not in "helpless" situations *do* become depressed. This suggests that differences in *perception of control* are important. Whether a situation is "helpless" depends on one's perception of the situation. This led to the *attributional theory of depression* (Abramson, Seligman, & Teasdale, 1978). The new theory was also intended to account for the observations that (a) lowered self-esteem is a common symptom of depression, (b) depressives frequently blame themselves for their failures, and (c) helplessness generalizes across many situations and times.

Attribution theory (Heider, 1958; and see chapter 11) is an account of how people search for *causes* for their own behavior or that of other people. A particular cause is *attributed* to some person, thing, or event. Within their theory, Abramson et al. defined the following three major *dimensions* of attribution which would be related to helplessness:

1.  *Internal versus external locus of control.* A particular event, such as success or failure at a job, is attributed to oneself (internal) or to some outside event (external), such as another person or to the difficulty of the job at which one succeeded or failed.
2.  *Stable versus unstable causes.* A stable cause is one which is enduring, such as a person's intellectual ability. An unstable cause is one which can vary from time to time, such as a person's motivation to study for an exam, or whether the questions on the exam happen to match what has been studied. Stable factors can be either internal or external.
3.  *Global versus specific.* An attribution may apply to a wide range of events or to a particular event. Thus, I might attribute my failure on an exam to such a global factor as "I always fail exams" or to some specific characteristic of this particular exam, such as, "I did not study for this exam."

Table 9-2 summarizes the above dimensions and the type of attributions which might occur in an academic setting involving *failure* on an examination. The attributional dimensions relate to depression as follows: (1) Lowered self-esteem occurs when a person attributes failure, which is a lack of control over the situation, to an *internal* dimension, such as lack of

**TABLE 9-2    The Attributional Model of Depression in Relation to Examination Failure.**

|  | INTERNAL | | EXTERNAL | |
| --- | --- | --- | --- | --- |
| DIMENSION | STABLE | UNSTABLE | STABLE | UNSTABLE |
| Global | I always fail examinations | I often don't study for exams | Exams are always too picky | I usually get the hard exam questions |
| Specific | This subject is too hard for me | I did not study for this exam | This exam was too hard | The questions on this exam weren't what I studied |

ability; (2) Attributing lack of control to *stable* factors produces a *generalized expectancy* of no control, thus extending helplessness and depression to other times and situations; and (3) *Global* attributions extend helplessness over situations, just as stability extends helplessness over time. The most helpless and depressing attribution should then be *an internal, stable, global attribution for lack of control (failure)*.

Seligman and his colleagues developed the *Attributional Style Questionnaire*, a self-report measure designed to score attributions in terms of the three attribution dimensions (Seligman, Abramson, Semmel, & von Bayer, 1979). As predicted, undergraduate students who were more depressed according to the Beck Depression Inventory (Beck, 1967) attributed bad outcomes more to internal, stable, and global factors than did the less-depressed students. Seligman and his colleagues argue that the depressive attributional style is a *cause* of depression, but attributional style may be more involved in the *maintenance* of depression after it has been initiated by some other factor (Munton, 1985). Robins (1988), noting the inconsistent conclusions about attributional style in previous reviews (Coyne & Gotlib, 1982; Hammen, 1985; Sweeney, Anderson, & Bailey, 1986) concluded that in studies where there were enough subjects to obtain significant results with a "medium size" difference between depressed and nondepressed groups, there were fairly consistent attributional differences between the groups. The question of causality is not yet answered, however.

The attribution model assumes, of course, that an individual has experienced negative life events so that depressive attributions can be made. The question is whether people with depressive attributional styles are more likely to become depressed after such events than are individuals with different attributional styles. Several studies of real-life negative events provide only modest support for the attributional style interpretation (Munton, 1985-86, p. 339). Feather and Barber (1983), for example, found that attributional style accounted for less than 10% of the variation in depression inventory scores of unemployed young Australians. The attribution model might be correct in the kinds of attributions important for depression, but data demonstrating the attribution-depression relationship are not very reliable (Munton, 1985–86).

### Stress and Control

The concept of control which is embodied in the learned helplessness research has been pursued with considerable success in other areas of research, with both human and animal subjects. The physiological effects of lack of control are especially noteworthy.

*Decisionmaking and ulcers.*   Folklore has it that the conflict of making decisions takes its toll through the ulcerated stomach if not the palpitating heart. Research has repeatedly shown, however, that *animals which do not have control over aversive events are the ones which develop ulcers* (Weiss, 1972, 1977). If two animals are simultaneously hooked up to an apparatus in such a way that only one of the animals controls the amount of shock received by both of them, the animal in charge does *not* develop ulcers.[2] The animal *without control* gets them. Figure 9–3 illustrates such an experimental arrangement.

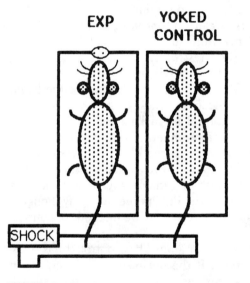

**FIGURE 9-3.**   Experimental arrangement for yoked-control procedure. Both animals receive shock through the tail simultaneously, but only the experimental animal (EXP) can turn off the shock for itself and for the control animal by pushing a button at the front of the apparatus. The control animal is helpless.

[2]A study by Brady (1958) on "executive monkeys" indicated that the decisionmaking monkey, the one who had to make responses in order to avoid shock for itself and for a control animal, developed ulcers. Flaws in this research were subsequently discovered, and it has not been replicated.

*Control in human research.*    In animal research it is relatively easy to say what we mean by control: An animal can or cannot terminate or postpone shock by its behavior. In human situations it can be more difficult to determine what constitutes control. Humans devise many methods to gain *what they perceive as control,* and perceived control is often the critical factor in stress.

Perceived control is not a simple idea, however; even learned helplessness may be a kind of control (Rothbaum, Weisz, & Snyder, 1982). The stereotypical southern belle of the *Gone With the Wind* genre tyrannizes others with her "helplessness" just as a baby tyrannizes its parents. Rothbaum et al. argue that people first try to *control events* (primary control) and, if this fails, they *adjust themselves to events* (secondary control), with much of life being a compromise between the two. Secondary control takes on many guises. *Predictive control* is achieved even in failure situations; failure becomes a predictable outcome and can be dealt with. *Illusory control* is achieved even in chance situations; a person may attribute chance outcomes to personal skill. Even the luck one might have at throwing dice becomes a kind of personal skill. *Vicarious control* can be gained by identifying with powerful others. The most intolerable situations, including prison camps, can be tolerable to a person who believes that God is on his or her side. *Interpretive control* can be gained if a person can find *meaning* in uncontrollable events, such as "This is a test of my faith, so I shall accept it." All these variations on control help alleviate the stressfulness of a situation.

Thompson (1981) sees meaning as the unifying element in many different kinds of control in aversive situations. She defines control as the belief that one can do something to reduce the aversiveness of an event. Meaning may affect a person's perception of control by making events seem more *endurable,* by interpreting bad events as forerunners of *future good events,* or by perceiving misfortune as a *part of some greater plan.* The lesson to be learned from the above citations of kinds of control would seem to be that methods of gaining control may be just as variable and idiosyncratic as methods of getting food or getting rid of pain. Put another way, any thoughts or behaviors which reduce stress are reinforced, and are methods of control.

*Predictability and control.*    If a person or animal has control, it has "mastery" or "power" over the environment. If the organism has power, it can *predict* the outcome of its actions because its expectancies are fulfilled. We may, then, ask whether *predictability alone* is sufficient to confer the *perception of control and thereby reduce stress* (Arthur, 1986; Fisher, 1984; Mineka & Henderson, 1985).

Considerable evidence shows that animals prefer to know that an aversive event is coming. Specifically, they prefer *signalled shock* to unsignalled shock. One interpretation for this is that the foreknowledge gives an animal a chance to *prepare* for the oncoming aversive event, such as by assuming a body posture which will make the shock less painful. Miller et al. (1983) found that animals preferred a strong, signalled shock to a weaker shock which was unsignalled. An information theory interpretation of this phenomenon says that even information about bad events is still information, and is reinforcing (see chapter 6 for more on rewards). In line with this interpretation, D'Amato and Safarjan (1979) found that animals preferred a situation where one signal predicted a long shock and a different signal predicted a brief shock, rather than signals which did not say which shock was coming. There are alternative interpretations for such phenomena (Mineka & Henderson, 1985), but the basic facts remain the same.

Research with humans (e.g., Miller & Managan, 1983) suggests that whether information about a forthcoming stressful medical procedure will reduce stress depends on how an individual typically copes with such situations. If a person's habitual style is to "blunt" the situation by distracting himself, then too much information may *not* alleviate stress. If a person uses the information to prepare for the forthcoming event, then it may alleviate stress. Weiss (1977) suggested that if an animal fails while attempting to control a predictable shock, the value of predictability is lost and stomach ulceration may occur just as it does in other uncontrollable shock experiments.

In summary, helplessness and control are important concepts related to the interactive definition of stress, which says that stress occurs when a person faces environmental challenges which he or she perceives cannot be met. A person may consider himself or herself unable to meet challenges because he or she is helpless and lacks the capacity to gain control.

### Type A Behavior and Stress

One of the most influential concepts in the study of stress and health has been that of the Type A behavior pattern (Friedman & Rosenman, 1974). The Type A "personality" is said to be characterized by *anger or hostility* and *excessive achievement striving.* These are manifest, for example, in easily aroused anger or irritation, doing everything as quickly as possible, being impatient with the slowness of others, and having a chronic sense of time urgency. The Type B behavior pattern, on the other hand, is defined by a *lack* of Type A characteristics. The interest in Type A is because Type A individuals are said to be more susceptible to coronary heart disease (CHD).

Early results from the *Western Collaborative Group Study,* one of the major research efforts examining Type A behavior and CHD, indicate that the *hostility* component of the Type A description is the only significant risk factor (Hecker, Chesney, Black, & Frautschi, 1988). Time orientation and achievement factors were not related to CHD. Interestingly, one of the Type A indicators ("self-aggrandizement") was *negatively correlated* with CHD, apparently serving as a kind of protective factor. These results are especially interesting because the data come from the first major *prospective* study in which Type A subjects were identified at the beginning of the study and were followed for eight-and-a-half years. Another recent study on over 2,000 cases of atherosclerosis found that Type A behavior predicted the severity of CHD only for subjects under 45 years of age. Between ages 46 and 55, Type A and Type B subjects were equivalent, and *over age 55 the Type B had more severe pathology* (Williams, Barefoot, Haney, Harrell, Blumental, Pryor, & Peterson, 1988).

To muddy the waters even further, another study reported that a measure of *neurotic hostility* was negatively correlated with coronary artery disease, but a measure of *nonneurotic hostility* was positively correlated with the disease (Siegman, Dembroski, & Ringle, 1987). In summary, it appears that nonneurotic hostility in younger patients may be a risk factor for CHD, but not for patients over 45 years of age, and that the total Type A complex is not a risk factor, only the hostility component. Obviously, we still have much to learn about hostility and heart disease.

### *Proposed mechanism of Type A heart disease.*

A commonly proposed mechanism for the development of cardiovascular disorder is that damage to the interior walls of arteries results from the stress of increased blood pressure or from circulating catecholamines, or both (Diamond, 1982). Lipoproteins accumulate at injury sites, eventually leading to occlusion of an artery, with either stroke (burst artery) or death of cardiac tissue as the blood supply is blocked off by *atherosclerotic plaques* (the fat deposits in the arteries). Since the Type A person is thought to be more physiologically reactive to stress situations, she or he is thought to be more susceptible to eventual cardiac disorder. During anger, for example, there is a greater output of noradrenaline, which in turn is correlated with diastolic blood pressure, a risk factor for CHD. Krantz and Manuck (1984) caution, however, that "[cardiac] ... reactivity *per se* should currently *not* be regarded as a proven risk factor" for cardiovascular disease (p. 435).

Until some other risk factor is found, however, autonomic reactivity is likely to remain a good candidate for cardiac risk because a number of kinds of data converge on that hypothesis. For example, Sherwood, Allen, Obrist, and Langer (1986) showed that subjects pressing a telegraph key to avoid shock took in more oxygen than the task itself required. This suggested that large amounts of oxygenated blood were getting into the tissues. This in turn produces a reflexive constriction of blood vessels, which increases blood pressure. This reflex response to control level of blood oxygen might in the long run lead to cardiovascular problems. The chronically angry or hostile person may be emotionally overresponsive to frustrating situations and more susceptible to cardiovascular disorders for the same reason (Diamond, 1982).

## Stress and the Environment

The concept of *environmental load* refers to the fact that different environments provide different amounts of *information* for a person to deal with (Mehrabian, 1976). A high-load environment is complex and changing, a low-load environment is simple and unchanging. A high load makes more demands on the individual, with greater chance of stress. Crowding and noise, among many other factors, add to environmental load.

*Crowding and stress.*    Animals and people tend to distance themselves from each other, maintaining *personal space,* which is often described as a "protective bubble" around the individual. Other individuals are kept at distances appropriate for certain kinds of activities, close for intimate activities, further away for business activities, and so on. A person moving too close to conduct business would be violating personal space, producing discomfort and stress. Personal space is said to be maintained for *protection* and for *communication* (Bell, Fisher, & Loomis, 1978).

We try to protect ourselves from overstimulation produced by too-close contact with others. Animal research is not always directly applicable to human situations, but certainly it influences our thinking. Therefore, we take note that animal populations are thought to rise and fall because population growth produces greater stress from excessive interanimal contact. Calhoun (1962) showed that if rodents are allowed unlimited food and water, but are limited in the amount of space they have to live and breed, the population will level off at a number well below the limit to which it could rise. There is a disastrous drop in birth rate, high infant mortality rate, homosexuality, greater aggressiveness, and cannibalism. A *behavioral sink* is established, usually around a food source, where there is a high density of animals and where many social problems occur. In the wild, these conditions can produce population decrements.

The communication function is that of sending a message that by maintaining a distance between ourselves and others we are *controlling* our space. Schmidt and Keating (1979) suggested that the term *crowding* is in fact a label we put on a situation when density results in a loss of personal control; a place becomes crowded when we perceive we are losing freedom because of the number of people. People with an external locus of control feel more crowded under given conditions than do people with an internal locus of control. The externals presumably are more responsive to crowding, as they are to other environmental factors. Studies in prisons also indicate that the greater the crowding, the higher the blood pressure and the greater the number of illnesses reported by inmates (Cox, Paulus, McCain, & Karlovac, 1982). Individuals in dense urban environments seem to maintain control partly by ignoring much of the environment, thereby reducing the amount of stimulation to be responded to. It is harder for prisoners to ignore each other.

A particularly poignant experiment on control was conducted by Rodin and Langer (1977) in a nursing home environment. Using standard institutional procedures as a baseline condition, a series of additional small responsibilities were given to the residents of one floor of the home. For example, they had more responsibility for room arrangements and had a houseplant to take care of if they wanted one. These residents then had a greater feeling of enjoyment in this environment than did residents who had less control over their lives.

*Noise and stress.*    About one American in three lives in a neighborhood so noisy that there is general annoyance and interference with communication (Cohen, Krantz, Evans, & Stokols, 1982). The noise comes from traffic, aircraft, construction, neighbors, children, pets, and so on. High-intensity noise can impair hearing and can also increase cardiovascular risk and produce disturbing psychological symptoms (Cohen & Weinstein, 1981). Laboratory research indicates that high-intensity noise narrows the focus of attention, reduces perceived control, and increases physiological arousal. In the *Los Angeles Noise Project,* Cohen et al. (1982) compared, over four years, the performance and blood pressure of children attending school near the Los Angeles International Airport with children at more distant points. Aircraft were taking off and landing an average of every two-and-a-half minutes during school hours, with peak noise intensities as high as 95 db. Mean systolic and diastolic pressures for the high-noise subjects were two to four points above the low-noise subjects, although still well within a normal range. The high-noise subjects were also poorer at solving puzzles than the low-noise subjects. The effects of the noisy environment were (to this reader, at least) surprisingly small, a testimonial perhaps to the resilience of children. Unwanted noise is nevertheless a great irritant to many people.

## COPING

### Nature of Coping

*Coping* refers to any way we may voluntarily try to control stress or anxiety in ourselves. Coping activities are *self-regulatory.* The individual *consciously* does something to deal with his or her own situation. Historically, psychologists have talked a great deal about *defense mechanisms* (such as repression, reaction formation, projection, and denial), whose function is also to reduce anxiety, but not consciously. Since defense mechanisms are described in standard texts for introductory or abnormal psychology, we shall look at approaches to coping which have received more attention in recent years.

One important aspect of newer approaches is that, in contrast to the classic mechanisms, there is no hint of "abnormality" in their use. In fact, there is increasing appreciation for a certain amount of folk wisdom. Consider the following "prescription" for a stress-free life:

1. Avoid fried meats, which angry up the blood.
2. If your stomach disputes you, lie down and pacify it with cool thoughts.
3. Keep the juices flowing by jangling around gently as you move.
4. Go very light on the vices, such as carrying on in society. The social ramble ain't restful.
5. Avoid running at all times.
6. Don't look back. Something might be gaining on you. (*Time*, June 15, 1953)

These rules are attributed to Satchel Paige, the legendary pitcher in the Negro major leagues. Paige broke into the "white" major leagues with the Cleveland Indians sometime between his forty-fifth and fifty-fifth years (he was never consistent about his birth date). His longevity might have been due to something besides his "rules," but their references to diet and relaxation have a modern ring to them.

### Classification of Coping Mechanisms

Folkman and Lazarus (1980) distinguished two kinds of coping. *Problem-focused* coping seeks to improve a stress situation by working on the cause of the stress, whether it be in the form of things, situations, or people. A person feeling the stress of overwork might try to reduce the workload, go on a vacation, use time more efficiently, and so on. *Emotion-focused (palliative)* coping activities do not change the situation, but instead make the person feel better. These might involve denying that there *is* a problem, engaging in vigorous exercise, or taking drugs or alcohol. Obviously, some emotion-focused behaviors may produce worse problems than those which initiated the coping. The effects of drugs, for example, might be worse than the job situation which led to taking drugs. As Monat and Lazarus (1985) also point out, people do not exclusively employ one form of coping response.

### Stress Management Techniques

Monat and Lazarus (1985) summarize a number of stress-management techniques in the following three broad categories.

1. *Changing environment and lifestyle.* The Satchel Paige "rules" largely fall into this category, which also includes such activities as time management, getting proper nutrition, exercising, stopping smoking and drinking, finding alternatives to frustrated goals, and so on. Many of the activities in this category are things that our grandmothers might have advised. In the more technical jargon of modern health psychology, many of these are *immunogenic behaviors*. That is, they *protect* us from the potential ravages of

too-severe stress. Other stress management techniques may be *pathogenic behaviors* (such as alcohol consumption or poor sleeping habits) which have ill effects.

2. *Changing personality or perceptions.* These might include such activities as assertiveness training (to achieve goals more successfully), thought stopping (not thinking about stress-provoking events), or modifying Type A behavior.

*Cognitive factors in coping.* As we have seen, theories of stress emphasize the importance of the *perception* of a situation as threatening. If two people are in a sinking boat, one may appraise the situation as dangerous (he cannot swim and believes the water to be deep) but the other appraises the situation as safe (he knows the water is only three feet deep). One way to cope with dangerous situations, then, is to *change our appraisals* of them. Throwing out the anchor would indicate the depth of the water and lead to a reappraisal of the situation.

*Lazarus's research on cognitive appraisal.* Lazarus (1968) recorded the GSR of subjects before and during a movie showing a primitive male puberty rite known as subcision, which consists of making several cuts on the underside of the initiate's penis. The movie uniformly produces emotional reactions in the viewers, with GSR peaks corresponding to each of the cuts. Lazarus asked whether different kinds of cognitive appraisals of the situation would diminish the emotional reactivity of different kinds of subjects. In one experiment, college students and relatively uneducated middle-management businessmen were compared. Three different soundtracks accompanied the otherwise silent film. In the first, there was no sound. In the second, the narrator said that the operation was not really unpleasant or painful and that the young man looked forward to it. In the third, a narrator described the scene objectively as just an interesting bit of anthropological data. The first narration involved the defense mechanism of *denial,* while the second involved the mechanism of *intellectualization.* Lazarus predicted that the college students would cope better (as indicated by lower GSR) by intellectualizing along with the soundtrack, but the businessmen would show less stress with the denial. The results came out as predicted. Another experiment showed that just presenting different introductions to the film was about as effective as narrations which continued throughout the film.

3. *Changing biological responses.* A person might try to control stress responses through the use of relaxation exercises, meditation, hypnosis, or biofeedback. The difference between this overall approach and those listed above is the emphasis on *directly* modifying the physiological responses to stress, without necessarily changing the stressful situation or the perception of it.

*Meditation.* There are many different forms of meditation (Ornstein, 1986), but the best-known in the United States is *transcendental meditation* (TM), a simplification of Zen Buddhism. Its primary *guru* (teacher) is Maharishi Mahesh Yogi. Under the guidance of a trained teacher, the initiate is given a *mantra*, a particular word or phrase that is said repeatedly. The mantra is a word or syllable, like "om," which has a soft rolling sound to it. The individual relaxes as much as possible in nondistracting conditions and concentrates on the mantra to the exclusion of other stimuli or thoughts.

Two 20-minute periods of meditation a day are claimed to make one happier, healthier, more loving, more energetic, and more able to use one's mind creatively. Many devotees are satisfied that they have indeed become better people through the use of TM, and quite possibly this is so. The question is whether TM does this and, if so, is there anything unique about it?

The TM movement makes extravagant claims for scientific validation (e.g., Bibliography, 1979). Evidence is claimed that TM decreases reaction time, improves problem solving, and contributes to better grades, reduced drug use and crime, greater emotional stability, reduced blood pressure, and so on. Much of the research is seriously flawed, however, because of *subject selection* and *lack of appropriate control conditions.*

TM research often involves comparisons of *experienced meditators* with *nonmeditators.* For example, Wallace, Dillbeck, Jacobe, and Harrington (1982, p. 57) reported that meditation "affects the aging of specific autonomic and sensory processes and thereby results in significantly younger biological ages in long-term meditators." The comparisons were among 11 people who did not meditate and 73 who were experienced meditators, with an average chronological age of 53 years for the two groups. Subsequent TM advertising used this research to support the claim that TM could *reverse* the aging process. It is impossible in this study, or any like it, to determine whether TM did anything at all. The group differences may reflect only that experienced meditators may have differed physically and psychologically from nonmeditators before they ever undertook meditation. In two experiments where all subjects volunteered in advance of the research and were randomly placed into experimental and control groups, TM did not produce any measurable personality change (Kline, Dockerty, & Farley, 1982) or improvement in several kinds of cognitive activity (Yuille & Sereda, 1980). The dropout rate in the latter study was over 40% in three months, indicating that a large proportion of TM initiates do not sustain their enthusiasm, and that experienced meditators are indeed a select group.

Second, assuming that some of the effects attributed to meditation are "real," what is it about meditation which produces these effects? The most obvious control condition is to have nonmeditators relax while meditators meditate. If the relaxation group shows the same changes as the meditating group, then we can attribute meditation effects to relaxation. There is no compelling evidence that meditation is associated with any unique physiological state. The effects of meditation are comparable to those produced by relaxation (Delmonte, 1984). Moreover, Holmes (1984) found that subjects who meditated showed just as strong somatic responses to stressful situations as did nonmeditators. Speech-anxious subjects assigned to a meditation condition did not show any lower heart rate during a subsequent speech than did subjects in three different control conditions (Kirsch & Henry, 1979).

In summary, meditation may be an especially effective way for some individuals to achieve relaxation, and it has some merit in that regard. Our existing knowledge does not show that TM (or any other form of meditation) produces a clearly different physiological state than other methods of achieving relaxation, however, and other relaxation techniques may be better for some people.

*Biofeedback.* Biofeedback refers to feedback information about any biological process. A stethoscope held to the chest provides biofeedback about our heart rate. Interest is generally centered on the electronic amplification of processes that are normally difficult to observe directly, however. Biofeedback instruments are amplifiers specialized to convert such physiological signals as skin temperature, blood pressure, heart rate, muscle tension, or EEG into readily identifiable visual or auditory stimuli which tell us what is happening. For example, a light may come on only when our brain is producing alpha waves, or a tone may change pitch upward or downward as muscle tension increases or decreases.

The therapeutic logic behind the use of biofeedback is generally that high levels of physiological activity are associated with tension (beta waves in the EEG, low skin resistance, high blood pressure and heart rate, and tense muscles). Biofeedback techniques can help us to learn what it feels like to relax by telling us when we relaxed even a tiny bit. Muscle tension, for example, often creeps up on us over a period of time so that we do not notice that we are getting tense; then suddenly we have headaches, muscle aches, or tics, or we grind our teeth. From electrodes placed on the appropriate muscles we can see or hear from the biofeedback instrument when there is an increase or decrease in tension. We may thereby learn to discriminate tension from relaxation and be able to control tension.

The initial wave of almost uncritical enthusiasm for biofeedback, related to interest in instrumental autonomic conditioning, has now subsided as the limitations of the technique have become apparent. Biofeedback works well for some kinds of problems, not so well for others. For example, it has been difficult to obtain reductions of heart rate or blood pressure of clinically significant magnitude that will last outside the laboratory setting. Ford (1982) concludes that the long-term (three months or more) effects for several disorders are as follows:

1. Raynaud's Disease[3]          70%
2. Vascular headache             70%
3. "Mixed" headache              60%

[3] A painful disorder of blood circulation in the hands characterized by extreme sensitivity to cold, resulting from vascular constrictions controlled by the autonomic nervous system.

| | |
|---|---|
| 4. Muscle headache | 50% or less |
| 5. Diastolic blood pressure | almost unaffected |
| 6. Irritable bowel syndrome | 50% |

The above percentages must be taken cautiously, since they usually refer to some degree of improvement in the specified percentage of patients treated in various studies, and frequently involve other treatments as well. What is clear is that biofeedback is far from 100% effective and the effectiveness it enjoys may often be due to a more general relaxation induced by the feedback technique.

## SUMMARY

1. Anxiety and fear are often distinguished in terms of a recognizable cause. Anxiety is an aversive state without a recognized cause, whereas fear does have an identifiable cause. Anxiety may also be considered an aversive state which occurs when the cause of fear cannot be controlled.

2. *Trait anxiety* is an enduring disposition to be anxious in many situations. *State anxiety* refers to anxiety aroused in a very specific situation.

3. Gray has proposed a theory which says that, when ongoing behaviors are interrupted by signals of punishment or nonreward, or by novel stimuli, activity in a *behavioral inhibition system* is aroused. This activity *is* anxiety, and produces inhibition of the ongoing behavior, increases physiological arousal, and increased attention to the threatening stimuli.

4. The *general adaptation syndrome* (GAS) is a physiological response to many kinds of environmental stressors. In the *stage of exhaustion* the organism's physiological defenses break down, and illness or death may ensue.

5. The *interactive definition* of stress says that stress occurs when the environment makes demands on the organism which the organism cannot meet. This definition accounts for individual differences in susceptibility to stress.

6. Stress may occur as a result of *traumatic events*, accumulated *life changes*, or accumulated daily *hassles*. Individual differences in susceptibility to stress depend on *genetics* and *early experiences*, both prenatal and postnatal. Early exposure to changing stimulation is important in developing resistance to stress. Emotional conditioning also occurs.

7. If an organism is repeatedly unable to be effective in its interactions with the environment, *learned helplessness* may result. This is a failure to respond, presumed to occur when the organism perceives that it has no *control* over the environment.

8. The *attributional theory of depression* says that human depression occurs when a person perceives that his/her failures are due to causes which are *internal* to the person, are *global* (occurring across many situations), and are *stable* across time.

9. Lack of control in aversive situations can produce such stress disorders as gastrointestinal ulcers. Humans develop many strategies for gaining *perceived control* in situations where there may be no real control. This helps to reduce the stressfulness of uncontrollable aversive events.

10. The anger/hostility component of the Type A behavior pattern appears to be related to coronary heart disease (CHD), but other aspects of Type A are not.

Anger and hostility are related to CHD in complex ways not yet understood, however.

11. A number of environmental events are stressful, including *noise* and *crowding*. Animals and people try to maintain a certain amount of *personal space* between themselves and others. This space *protects* the individual from overstimulation and *informs* others that the "owner" of the space is in control of the situation.

12. *Coping* refers to any way in which we more or less consciously try to control stress or anxiety in ourselves. *Problem-focused coping* seeks to change the cause of the stress. *Emotion-focused coping* tries to change the emotional response to the stressful situation.

13. Stress management techniques include changing the environment or one's lifestyle, changing one's perceptions (especially by reappraising the stressful situation), and changing biological responses (physiological arousal).

14. *Meditation* is a way of reducing physiological responsiveness by producing relaxation. There is little evidence that meditation does anything beyond producing general relaxation.

15. *Biofeedback* involves electronic amplification of physiological responses as a technique for learning how to control those responses. Biofeedback works best for relaxation of specific skeletal muscle groups, and disorders resulting from muscle tension. Feedback has not been found to be an effective procedure for reducing blood pressure.

# 10

# Cognitive Consistency

Thus far we have looked at motives which are closely related to arousal mechanisms in the brain, either the general arousal of the brainstem-thalamic system, or the hedonic arousal of the limbic system. In this chapter and the next we look at human motives which seem more divorced from the arousal structures and influenced more by social conditions and cognitive mechanisms. Such motives as need for consistency or achievement depend more on brain mechanisms in the neocortex. This is not to say that hunger or fear, for example, do not involve cortical processes. Neither is it to say that more social- or cognition-dependent motives are completely divorced from the arousal systems. It may well be, however, that such motives as need for achievement as we know it in humans could not develop without the neocortex which characterizes humans.

Earlier chapters covered the idea that *deviation from some norm* is motivating. For example, departure from an internal temperature of 98.6° F stimulates homeostatic mechanisms and behaviors to return temperature to "normal." Or, according to set point theory, when body weight drops below some value, a feeding mechanism is triggered. Or, departure from an optimal level of arousal may instigate activities to restore arousal to the optimal level. In each of these instances, temperature, weight, and arousal regulation, we can conceive of a thermostat-like mechanism which triggers appropriate activities to reduce the discrepancy between some ideal condition and an actual condition. This general approach is called *control theory* in engineering.

## CONTROL THEORY

Control theory is concerned with machines which engage in "purposive" behaviors aimed at some precisely defined goal (Hyland, 1988). Let us look at the example of a common thermostat more closely. We set the temperature at a point called the *reference criterion*, such as 72° F. A sensor in the thermostat detects the difference between the reference criterion and the room temperature by means of a device called a *comparator*. The *detected error* can be a temperature above or below the reference temperature at which the room is to be kept. The direction of the detected error determines the action taken by the system, whether a heating or cooling mechanism is turned on or off. As the error correction device (e.g., furnace or air conditioner) operates, new temperature signals go to the comparator. Eventually these *negative feedback signals* reduce the detected error to zero (room temperature = thermostat setting) and the system turns off. The "purpose" of the system is to keep the room temperature at a certain level, but the "purposefulness" is entirely within the physical properties of the system. Figure 10-1 illustrates the system. The generalized control system provides a framework for thinking about many motivational problems besides those

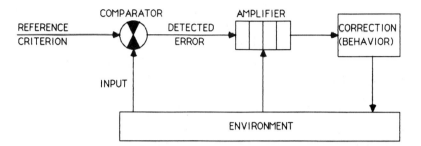

**FIGURE 10-1.**  Basic control system. Using the system as a thermostat, a reference criterion of some temperature would be set, such as 72°. A comparator within the thermostat would detect any error between the reference criterion and the surrounding environment, such as when the temperature drops too low. The error signal would be amplified so that corrective action (turning on the furnace) would occur.

which classically have been considered homeostatic. Among these are *cognitive inconsistencies.*

## COGNITIVE CONSISTENCY

There are two seemingly opposed views of inconsistency and change as motivational variables. The first is that inconsistency is aversive, and consistency is desirable. The second is that consistency (monotony) is aversive, and stimulus change is desirable. These views are not necessarily opposite and may in fact represent different points on some dimension, along the lines of arousal, for example. Either extreme inconsistency or extreme monotony may be aversive, but an intermediate degree of inconsistency may be tolerable and even sought.

Either consistency or inconsistency is in the eye of the beholder. One person may readily detect in unfolding events a consistent pattern that completely eludes someone else. Our concern, then, is with *consistency as perceived by an individual.* This is commonly called *cognitive consistency* and involves beliefs and thoughts as well as perception. We may say that inconsistency, or incongruity, exists when an event is perceived to be different from expectation. For example, a dog with wings would be incongruous only to a person who has already become familiar with dogs of the normal variety. In control theory terms, the familiar (expected) dog is a reference point and a comparator detects an "error," the difference between the expected and the observed dog. This triggers an internal arousal, along with attempts to deal with the incongruity. It is the motivating effect of incongruity as it produces striving for consistency which concerns us.

Stagner (1977) has pointed out that terms like dissonance, need achievement, and competence can also be put into such a framework. He says that an organism becomes more energetic whenever ". . . it encounters a discrepancy between current input and the established or preferred steady state with respect to that input" (1977, p. 107). Effort persists until the discrepancy has been removed. In this chapter, we look at some of the effects of incongruities at the biological level, at the individual level, and at the social level.

## A BIOLOGICAL MODEL: SOKOLOV

A Russian psychologist, E. N. Sokolov (1960), proposed a theory of attention based on the fact that responses to sensory inputs which normally arouse attention may *habituate* if presented frequently. For example, with repeated auditory stimulation by a tone of unvarying pitch, loudness, and duration, the response in the EEG declines. We have all experienced situations in which attention-getting stimuli, such as the noise of a large city, are unnoticed after a while. A sudden change in sound, even a silence, however, may immediately command our attention. Similarly, experimental subjects show an aroused EEG if just the pitch of the habituating tone is slightly changed.

At some level of the nervous system, there must be processing of such "unnoticed" stimulus inputs, however. Otherwise, we could not be strongly aroused by minor changes or cessation of stimulation. Sokolov's theory says that repetitious inputs are stored in the nervous system, and new inputs are each *compared* with the stored input. If input and storage are the same (and the input carries no biologically important information), then attention is not aroused. If an input signal is different from those previously stored, however, there is arousal of the EEG and of behavior, as well as other physiological activity (see Figure 10-2). Pavlov called such behavioral arousal the "orienting reflex." We "perk up" at a novel stimulus and are more prepared to cope with a threatening situation if necessary.

## AN INDIVIDUAL MODEL: TOTE

G. A. Miller, Galanter, and Pribram (1960) applied the incongruity notion to events ranging from neurological to social. Their basic unit for analysis was the TOTE unit. TOTE is the acronym for Test-Operate-Test-Exit. For example, suppose we want a nail hammered into a board and have some kind of plan of what we want. We look at the nail (Test) and see that it is not in the board. There is thus an incongruity between our plan and our image of how things are. We hit the nail with a hammer (Operate) and then look again (Test) to see if the nail and board are congruous with our plan. If our plan and the nail in the board coincide closely enough, the incongruity is gone and we turn to something else (Exit). Incongruity is thus a motivating force to keep us at the task until the incongruity is sufficiently diminished. The TOTE analysis is illustrated in Figure 10-3.

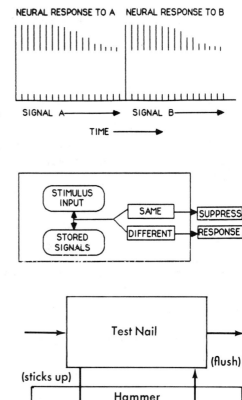

NEURAL RESPONSE TO A    NEURAL RESPONSE TO B

SIGNAL A ⟶    SIGNAL B ⟶

TIME ⟶

**FIGURE 10-2**
Sokolov model for habituation of orienting responses. The magnitude of neural responses to repetitious Signal A (such as a tone) gradually declines. If a new Signal, B, only slightly different from Signal A, is presented, there is once again a large response. According to Sokolov, stimulus inputs are compared with stored signals. If the stimuli are the same as the stored signals, there is suppression of responses to the stimuli. If the incoming stimulus is different from the stored signal, there is a neural response. The brain responds to changing stimulation..

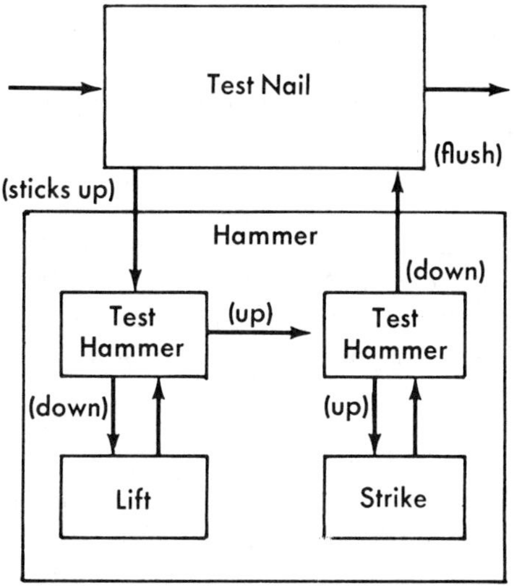

**FIGURE 10-3**
Test-Operate-Test-Exit (TOTE) model, illustrating a hierarchical plan for hammering a nail. The hammer and nail are both tested repeatedly until the nail is flush, at which time there is an exit to another nail or task. (From Miller, Galanter and Pribram, 1960. Used with permission of Holt, Rinehart, and Winston, Pub.).

TOTE units are hierarchical. For example, a building contractor has as one large TOTE unit the completion of an entire house. Along the way, however, there are numerous smaller TOTE units that require completion, such as laying the foundation, carpentry, plumbing, and so on. Each of these in turn has smaller TOTE units. In an overall plan, the completion of one TOTE unit leads to the start of the next. The importance of this theory was less in generating direct experiments than in casting many psychological problems into a cognitive frame of reference. The background of the authors (psycholinguist, experimental psychologist, and neuropsychologist) guaranteed that many problems and alternatives would be considered in the development of the model.

## A SOCIAL PERCEPTION MODEL: HEIDER

Suppose I like you and you like me, but we are in strong disagreement about a political candidate. We are in what Heider (1958) called a *state of imbalance.* If we agreed on the merits of the candidate, we would be in a state of *balance.* Imbalance is considered aversive, and we would therefore do something to reduce the imbalance. When "equilibrium" is restored, we are "satisfied." Imbalance is therefore like drive: Its presence initiates action and its reduction reinforces that action. There are a variety of cognitive or behavioral things one might do to reduce imbalance. For example, you might change your mind about the candidate, or about me, or about both of us. Or, you might avoid me until after the election. Imbalance is also perceived through the eyes of a particular individual and the problem is of *social perception,* not social conflict.

A simple state of perceived interpersonal imbalance can occur with just two people. If Frank likes Jane and Jane likes Frank, they both have a positive relation toward each other. If the affective sign of the relation is the same for both individuals (either positive or negative), the situation is balanced, and there is no "strain" to change it. A particularly interesting two-person case is unrequited love: One person has a strong positive sentiment for the other, but the second person is neutral or negative toward the first. It is here that we may see rapidly changing love-hate relationships. The individual whose positive sentiment is not returned may quickly come to be negative toward the second party, thus bringing the relationship back into balance. Since the problem is perceptual, there may be interesting "distortions." For example, Frank may like Jane and perceive that she does *not* like him, when in fact she does. Frank's perception of the situation, not the "real" state of affairs, determines the imbalance.

The more general case, however, to which most researchers have directed their attention is like our initial illustration. It involves a person (A), another person (B), and an entity (X), which may, for example, be an object, a third person, an idea, or an event. We have three possible pairs of relationships within an ABX *triad*: (1) AB, where A holds some affect toward B; (2) AX, where A holds some affect toward X, and (3) BX, where B holds some affect toward X.[1] A is the person whom, by definition, we are concerned with

[1]Heider also talks about *unit relations,* as well as affective relations. The affective relations are *sentiments,* the unit relations refer to the way things "go together" (through similarity or other perceptual or logical relations). Because of space limitations and our primary concern with motivation only the sentiment relations are discussed here. We are using the ABX symbolism popularized by Theodore Newcomb rather than the symbolism used by Heider.

at a particular time: it is A's perception of the relationships we are examining. Each of these three relationships can be positive or negative, and the general rule is that a triad is balanced if the algebraic product of the three is positive and imbalanced if the product is negative. This rule gives four balanced and four imbalanced triads, summarized in Table 10-1. Figure 10-4 illustrates two balanced and two imbalanced triads involving you (A), me (B), and the President of the United States (X).

Let us put Relationship 3 (balanced) and Relationship 6 (imbalanced) from Figure 10-4 into verbal form. In 3, you are A and have negative affect toward both me (B) and the President (X); since I like the President, the triad is balanced from the point of view of the focal person (A, who is you). If we were to shift the diagram so that I am the focal person, the situation might or might not remain balanced, depending on whether my attitude toward you were positive or negative. In Relationship 6, you have a negative attitude toward me, but we are both positive toward the President. By definition, this represents an imbalanced situation. In any real situation the valance sign ( + or − ) and intensity of affect would be determined by many factors (you might like some of the President's policies, but not others), and the degree of imbalance would in turn depend on these intensities as well as on signs. A mild imbalance would not produce much effort toward reducing the imbalance. We also assume that X is of interest or relevance to both A and B before

**TABLE 10-1    Balanced and Imbalanced Relationships with All Combinations of Positive and Negative AB, AX, and BX Relationships**

| | | BALANCED | | | | IMBALANCED | | |
|---|---|---|---|---|---|---|---|---|
| | | AB | AX | BX | | AB | AX | BX |
| | 1. | + | + | + | 5. | − | − | − |
| | 2. | + | − | − | 6. | − | + | + |
| | 3. | − | − | + | 7. | + | + | − |
| | 4. | − | + | − | 8. | + | − | + |

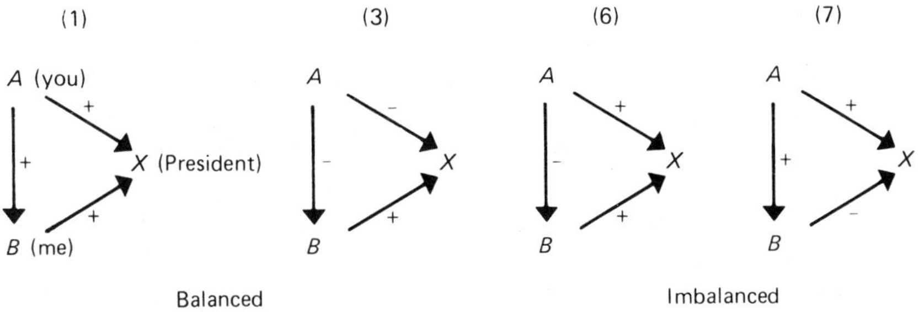

FIGURE 10-4.   Balanced triads (1 and 3) and imbalanced triads (6 and 7). See text and Table 10-1 for details.

there could be any imbalance. If neither A nor B was concerned about X one way or another, there would be no triad.

Although imbalance is generally considered undesirable, we can readily see, from the point of view of activation theory, for example, that some imbalance (like some activation or some frustration) often may be sought. Up to a point, we may enjoy political arguments with our friends.

Newcomb (1968) proposes that balanced relations 1 and 2 in Table 10-1 are in fact different from 3 and 4. Considerable research cited by Newcomb indicates that although 1 and 2 are desirable, 3, 4, 5, and 6 are all mildly undesirable, and 7 and 8 are the most undesirable. Newcomb, therefore, prefers to consider 1 and 2 balanced (pleasant), 3, 4, 5, and 6 nonbalanced (relatively neutral), and 7 and 8 imbalanced (unpleasant). The reason for this may be that negative relations are unpleasant, even though they may be balanced. Two people who do not like each other form a balanced situation, but neither may enjoy the situation. The evidence cited by Newcomb is not always consistent, but it does point up the fact that the logical relations (algebraic products) defining balance and imbalance do not necessarily coincide with the individual's perception of the situation or the affect he or she experiences.

## A COGNITIVE MODEL: FESTINGER'S COGNITIVE DISSONANCE THEORY

Heider's theory is generally accepted as the father of consistency theories, but the most influential has been Festinger's (1957) theory of cognitive dissonance. Dissonance is said to occur when two beliefs are incongruent, or if "the obverse of one element would follow from the other" (Festinger, 1957, p. 13). That is, there is cognitive dissonance if two beliefs lead to contradictory conclusions. Continuing to smoke is dissonant with the knowledge that smoking may lead to lung cancer. Cognitive dissonance, like imbalance, is considered a noxious state whose reduction is rewarding.

There are many possible ways of reducing dissonance but all involve a change in cognitions. We might add a new cognition ("the lung cancer research has produced ambiguous results") or alter existing ones ("cancer really isn't all that dangerous"). Note that the cognitions (beliefs) are important, not whether the beliefs are accurate. We might seek more information to try to reduce our dissonance, such as reading further on the problem of lung cancer. This could lead to the apocryphal outcome that "I read so much about lung cancer and smoking that I gave up reading." Facetious, perhaps, but not an entirely unreal possibility. We might, however, give up cigarettes as a means of reducing dissonance.

Dissonance, however, would not be the only factor determining whether we stopped smoking. Dissonance theory is not *all*-encompassing and

was never intended to be. Other desires and aversions might override dissonance and we might even engage in dissonance-*producing* activities. Group
pressure, for example, might push an adolescent into doing something that is
at odds with that young person's beliefs about himself or herself.

Let us now look at three kinds of dissonance experiments: (1) attitude
change in a free-choice situation, (2) attitude change in a forced-compliance
situation, and (3) dissonance and "primary drives." One of the strongest
points of the theory, Festinger has repeatedly argued, is that its predictions
are often not obvious, frequently being just the opposite of what an incentive
theory would predict.

### Attitude Change in the Free-Choice Situation

By *attitude*, we mean a positive or negative evaluation of some person,
object, or thing. By *attitude change*, we mean a change in either the sign
(from positive to negative, or vice versa) or intensity (weak positive to strong
positive, for example).

If we have a choice among attractive alternatives, we face conflict
because we stand to lose one alternative if we choose the other. If I choose to
buy a particular automobile, there may be dissonance because (1) I have
committed myself to a particular purchase, but (2) some other car might be a
better deal. The more important the decision or the more attractive the
alternative, the greater the potential dissonance aroused by the decision.

How would I reduce my dissonance? I might change my mind and
choose another alternative, but this would throw me back into the same
conflict. More likely, I might perceive the chosen alternative as *more attractive* and the unchosen alternative as *less attractive*. Such a change in perceived attractiveness ("spreading the alternatives") is perhaps the most common method of dissonance reduction in the free-choice situation (Insko &
Schopler, 1972). This is illustrated in an experiment by Brehm (1956), who
had subjects rate the desirability of a number of items (like a portable radio
and a desk lamp) for "consumer reactions." The subjects were then offered
whichever single item they would like to have. After the choice, they rated
the items again. The chosen items were now rated higher and the rejected
items lower.

An interesting question is whether the spreading occurs before or after
the decision is made. In the former case ("predecisional dissonance"), the
spreading would serve to help resolve the conflict so that a decision could be
made. This would not represent cognitive dissonance in the usual after-the-
fact way that dissonance is described, but the issue is not resolved (Insko &
Schopler, 1972).

Another procedure for facilitating postdecisional spreading might be to
seek information to support the decision. Having purchased my automobile, I
might keep a watchful eye on the newspaper ads for evidence that I really did

get a good deal. On the other hand, I might also *avoid* reading ads just so I could not find out I made a bad deal. Unfortunately, the theory does not tell us which is more likely to occur, and the research evidence for such postdecisional selective exposure to information is not strong.

## Attitude Change and Forced Compliance

One of the best-known dissonance experiments, often used as the prototype experiment for explaining and describing dissonance, is by Festinger and Carlsmith (1959). Their experiment involved *forced compliance* and *insufficient justification*. The situation was so structured that the subjects found it difficult not to do what the experimenter asked (forced compliance), but at the same time had little apparent reason for doing so (insufficient justification). The subjects were initially run through a very tedious task requiring them to turn pegs in holes. On completing the task, the subjects were asked if they would help persuade other persons to be subjects. This persuasion would involve telling the potential subjects that the task was interesting, or appealing in some way. The only other person was, in fact, a research assistant.

Half the real subjects were told they would receive a $20 retainer for their services, and the rest that they would receive $1. All subjects agreed to serve (indicating the power of the forced-compliance aspect). The critical measure of dissonance reduction was how the subjects evaluated the task after trying to persuade the assistant. It was independently ascertained that the task really was boring and the main assumption of the experiment was that making positive statements about the task would be discrepant with one's private evaluation. Incentive theory might say that the $20 subjects would view the task as more attractive, since it is associated with a large incentive. Receiving $20 should produce little dissonance, however, because $20 is "adequate justification" for making the discrepant statements. Therefore, according to dissonance theory, the subjects receiving $1 should show the most positive evaluation of the task. And, that is how the experiment turned out. As Festinger has commonly described the situation, "You come to love what you suffer for." The experiment is diagrammed in Figure 10-5.

As another example of such a forced-compliance experiment, A. R. Cohen, Brehm, and Fleming (1958) asked college students to write an essay supporting a view opposite their own opinion on a matter of current interest. Some students were given minimal reasons for engaging in the discrepant activity, but others were given many good reasons (such as helping the experimenter get his PhD). Again, subjects with minimal justification changed more favorably toward the view they had supported than did subjects with greater justification.

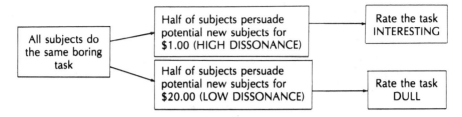
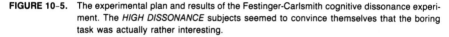

FIGURE 10-5.    The experimental plan and results of the Festinger-Carlsmith cognitive dissonance experiment. The *HIGH DISSONANCE* subjects seemed to convince themselves that the boring task was actually rather interesting.

### Dissonance and "Primary Drives"

Will a person committing himself or herself to something painful be less pained if there is little overt justification for the commitment? Zimbardo (1966) gave subjects in a "verbal learning" experiment electric shocks of a relatively high intensity. Half the subjects were then given the explicit choice of terminating the experiment or continuing. All continued. Of these, half received considerable justification for doing so (low dissonance), and half had minimal justification (high dissonance). The group without a choice was a control for continuing in the experiment without justification; of these, half the subjects got the same level shock in the second part of the experiment as in the first part (Hi-Hi), and half got a lower level (Hi-Mod). The most interesting measure was the change in galvanic skin response from before to after making the decision to continue. The results are summarized in Figure 10–6.

The Hi-Hi control group showed an increase in GSR, and the Hi-Mod group showed a decrease. The low-dissonance group also showed higher GSR. The GSR of the high-dissonance group, however, dropped as much as that of the Hi-Mod control group, for whom the shock level really was reduced. If we can believe the GSR, it appears that the shocks actually were less painful for subjects who made a commitment with minimal justification. We thus see an element of martyrdom: Commitment to a cause with little external justification may actually reduce the pain and suffering the martyr undergoes.

Mansson (quoted by Zimbardo, 1966, p. 918) posed a somewhat different question: "What happens when a thirsty person knows that he cannot drink for a longer period of time?" The subjects were made thirsty by eating saltine crackers with either peanut butter or a mixture of catsup, tabasco, and horseradish. They were then asked to commit themselves to going without water. The extreme levels of dissonance were to go without water for twenty-four hours with minimal justification (high dissonance) or four hours with much justification (low dissonance). Just prior to the anticipated deprivation

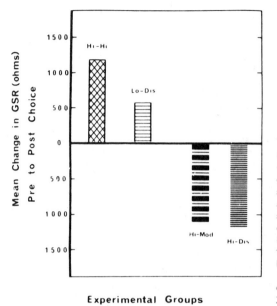

FIGURE 10-6
GSR changes for four experimental groups. Hi-Hi received a high level of shock in both phases of the experiment, and the Hi-Mod group had a reduction in shock level. Neither had a choice of continuing in the experiment. The Lo-Dis group had much verbal justification for continuing, and the Hi-Dis group had little justification. (From Zimbardo, 1966, p. 910. Reprinted by permission of N.Y. Academy of Sciences & P.G. Zimbardo.)

period, the subjects were allowed to drink water and, unknown to them, the amount was measured. The high-dissonance group drank an average of 128 ml, as compared to 155 ml for the low-dissonance group (estimated from Zimbardo, 1966, Figure 8, p. 918). The high-dissonance group seemed less thirsty after their commitment. Brehm (1962) reported similar results.

The implication of these studies is that if one has committed oneself to deprivation or pain with a small amount of justification, the degree of hunger, thirst, or pain is less. We do not know whether there is a reduced *need* for food or water, however, because these experiments have not provided enough detail to tell. Certainly the hypotheses being tested were intriguing, however, and the results suggest important cognitive factors in the basic motivational areas of hunger, thirst, and pain. In similar fashion, we might speculate that commitment to the priesthood and celibacy actually reduces sexual motivation.

### What Are the Necessary Conditions for Dissonance Arousal?

*The negative consequences of deception.* For a long time it has been clear that just attitude-behavior inconsistency *is not sufficient* to produce attitude change in the usual dissonance experiment setting. For example, Nel, Helmreich, and Aronson (1969) found that subjects giving counterattitudinal speeches to an audience only changed their own attitude if the audience was perceived as noncommittal with regard to the topic (legalization of marijuana). If the audience was perceived as either firmly for or against legalization, the speaker (the experimental subject) showed no attitude change. The argument, then, is that the subject must believe that he or she has had *an effect* on someone, and that this belief is annoying to the subject. The subject finds it unpleasant to believe that he has deceived someone and does what he or she can (attitude change) to reduce the unpleasantness.

*The importance of intent to deceive.*    Research has also consistently shown that subjects must perceive that they *freely chose to engage in behavior which contradicts their attitudes.* Going back to our earlier definition of intent, if a person perceives he has a choice between two actions, and knows the outcome of each, then the selection of either action is intentional. Applied to the dissonance situation, deception is intended if a person (a) perceives he has a choice between making a statement against his own attitude or not making such a statement, (b) knows the outcomes of these actions (that someone will or will not be deceived), and (c) chooses to make the counterattitudinal statement. If a person does not foresee the consequences of his possible actions, then intent is not present or can be denied. In this case, attitude change does not occur (Cooper & Fazio, 1984).

### Is Dissonance Actually Arousing?

If dissonance has drivelike arousal properties, then there should be evidence for such arousal besides just attitude change, some *independent* measure of arousal. Three lines of evidence are taken to support the existence of such arousal (Cooper & Fazio, 1984): (1) effects on simple versus complex tasks, (2) physiological measures, and (3) attribution effects, based on predictions from cognitive-arousal theory.

*Drivelike effects of dissonance on performance.*    According to Hull's drive theory (see chapter 3), high levels of drive should facilitate performance on simple, dominant responses but interfere with performance on more complex, nondominant responses. Several early studies indicated that high dissonance did have performance effects similar to those produced by, say, high anxiety (e.g., Cottrell & Wack, 1967; Waterman, 1969), but attitude changes were not demonstrated in the same experiments. Pallak and Pittman (1972) did report attitude change along with the drivelike effects, but the amount of evidence for both these occurring together is not great.

*Physiological measures of arousal.*    Cooper and Fazio (1984), almost 30 years after the introduction of dissonance theory, concluded that the physiological evidence for dissonance-produced arousal was at best ambiguous. However, using the standard procedure of having subjects write essays in opposition to their own attitudes, Croyle and Cooper (1983) found that only high-dissonance subjects (high-choice, counterattitudinal essay) showed elevated GSR levels immediately after writing their essay. Low-dissonance subjects (either low-choice and counterattitudinal essay, or high-choice and proattitudinal essay) showed briefer increments in GSR level than the high-dissonance group. Elkin and Leippe (1986) also found that a high-dissonance condition did produce a large GSR increment, but the GSR did *not go down* within five to seven minutes after the subjects had expressed their changed attitude. They argued that their data contradict dissonance theory because the theory says that dissonance arousal should be reduced by attitude change. Dissonance is supposedly an unpleasant state of tension (drive) which is reduced by bringing one's attitude into line with one's behavior.

The drive-reduction argument is not quite as simple as implied above, however, for three reasons. First, the dissonance reduction in the laboratory comes *after the attitude change.* Therefore, if the subjects engaged in dissonance-reducing attitude change *in the experiment* we would have to assume that they had *previously* been reinforced by dissonance reduction. Dissonance reduction in the laboratory could not account for the behavior which *precedes* the reduction. Second, if the subject had previously experienced dissonance reduction following attitude change outside the laboratory, then the subject would only have to *anticipate* that attitude change would be followed by arousal reduction in the laboratory. Arousal reduction in the laboratory would not have to occur *at all.* Third, while the GSR data is intriguing, and a step in the right direction, we have also seen (in chapter 3) that arousal cannot be equated with any specific physiological measure. Arousal can be separated into behavioral arousal, EEG arousal, and autonomic arousal. There is no indication as to which of these would be relevant to dissonance.

*Attribution and dissonance.*    Following the Schachter-Singer (1962) cognitive-arousal theory, it can be argued that dissonance-produced arousal should be subject to *cognitive labeling* the same as any other arousal. If the arousal is attributed to the dissonance, attitude change should occur. But, if the attribution is directed to some other source, attitude change should *not* occur. In support of the attribution hypothesis, Zanna and Cooper (1974) found that subjects given a placebo pill with the supposed side effect of producing tension did not show as much attitude change as did subjects given the placebo without this supposed side effect. The arousal was presumably attributed to the pill rather than to dissonance, so the subjects did not engage in dissonance-reducing behavior. Conversely, subjects under high dissonance conditions did not show attitude change if given phenobarbital, a central nervous system depressant (Cooper, Zanna, & Taves, 1978). Presumably, the drug reduced the dissonance-produced arousal, so there was no need for further dissonance-reducing activity. It was also found that attitude change was heightened by misattributing external arousal to dissonance. Subjects given a placebo containing amphetamine (which increases physiological arousal) showed greater attitude change than control subjects.

In summary, the evidence seems fairly convincing that experimental *procedures* for producing dissonance may also produce arousal of the GSR. But there is little compelling evidence that dissonance produces arousal and that attitude change is reinforced by dissonance reduction. The usual "dissonance" *procedures* may produce arousal, but for some reason other than dissonance per se. This is illustrated in Figure 10-7.

### Alternatives to Festinger's Theory

*Aronson's expectancy interpretation.*   Aronson (1968) suggested that dissonance does not occur with just any contradiction, but is specific to a violation of expectancies. Walking in the rain and not getting wet would create dissonance because walking in the rain arouses the expectancy of getting wet. According to Aronson dissonance is especially likely to occur in relation to one's self-concept. Aronson suggested that in the Festinger-Carlsmith experiment, for example, the dissonance was *not* just the result of telling someone the task was interesting when in fact it was boring. Rather, the dissonance resulted from the subjects' violation of their self-concepts. The individual who lies for $1 is doing something out of line with her concept of how she normally behaves. Aronson concluded that the strongest dissonance effects have been obtained in experiments where the self-concept was clearly involved.

**FIGURE 10-7A.**   Illustration of Cognitive Dissonance Theory. (1) Freely writing an essay counter to one's own attitude produces (2) dissonance between one's attitude and one's behavior. This dissonance is a state of aversive arousal. (3) To get rid of this unpleasant arousal, a person expresses an attitude more in favor of the essay topic than previously expressed. (4) The attitude change reduces the dissonance and arousal is therefore reduced.

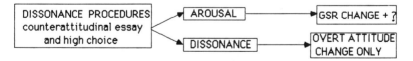

**FIGURE 10-7B.**   Alternatives to the Dissonance Theory. Dissonance procedures may produce arousal for some reason other than cognitive dissonance. The dissonance may lead to attitude change following self-perception, or as a means of better self-presentation, or for some other reason. Arousal may not be a link in the chain of events leading from dissonance procedures to overt attitude change.

*Bem's self-perception theory.*    Bem (1967, 1970) proposed to account for all the cognitive dissonance research with an essentially nonmotivational, Skinnerian approach. Rather than argue that subjects perform as they do because inconsistent cognitions are aversive, Bem proposed that the individual views his *own* behavior and the situation *just as he would view the behavior of another person in the same situation.* In the Festinger-Carlsmith experiment, suppose we could invisibly observe a college student offered $20 to lie to someone and then see him do it. We also see another student tell the same lie for a mere $1. What might we conclude? One reasonable interpretation would be that "For $20 the subject doesn't *have* to believe in what he's doing, but if he's doing it for a crummy dollar maybe he does believe it." Bem's interpretation is that the subject may look at his own behavior and draw the same conclusion.

Bem (1967) had subjects simply listen to tape-recorded descriptions of the Festinger-Carlsmith experiment (without hearing the actual results). Bem's subjects then rated the experimental task as they thought the Festinger-Carlsmith subjects would. There were three different conditions: the $1 inducement, the $20 inducement, and a control group with no inducement. Bem's subjects rated the task on a scale from − 5 (very dull) to + 5 (very interesting). Table 10-2 compares Bem's ratings with those from the original experiment. The absolute numerical values in the two experiments are different, but the trend of results is the same: The $1 group is more positive than either of the other groups in the experiment.

Bem (1970) argued with many experimental and "real-life" illustrations that our behavior often determines our attitudes, rather than the other way around. For example, factory workers who become shop stewards suddenly shift their attitudes to a more pro-labor position, while workers who are promoted to foreman shift suddenly in a pro-management direction. The proposition that we come to like (or believe) what we see ourselves do sounds intuitively backward, because we have all been brought up with the reverse notion, that our feelings determine our behavior. Note, however, that this belief is essentially the Cartesian dualistic interpretation of the mind-body relation discussed in chapter 1. That is, mind (attitudes, beliefs, etc.) causes

**TABLE 10-2    Comparison of Bem's (1967) Results With the Festinger-Carlsmith (1959) Results (See Text for Details)**

|  |  | EXPERIMENTAL CONDITION | |
| --- | --- | --- | --- |
| STUDY | CONTROL | $1 COMPENSATION | $20 COMPENSATION |
| Festinger-Carlsmith | −0.45 | +1.35 | −0.05 |
| Bem | −1.56 | +0.52 | −1.96 |

From D.J. Bem (1967). Self-perception: An alternative interpretation of cognitive dissonance phenomena. *Psychological Review, 74,* 183–200. Copyright © 1967 by the American Psychological Association. Used by permission.

behavior. Bem's position is that circumstances dictate behaviors, and that we infer our mental state, at least in part, from these circumstances and behaviors. An especially pernicious consequence of this argument is that people who confess to a crime may come to believe that they *are* guilty, and the freer the confession, the firmer the guilt feeling (Bem, 1970).

*Impression management.*    We can imagine that a subject in a dissonance experiment might not want to give the impression that he could be cheaply bought to engage in self-contradictory behavior, such as writing a counterattitudinal essay. To give the experimenter a more favorable impression, the subject might *report* a changed attitude more in line with his inconsistent behavior. The subject fibs a little about his attitude so that the experimenter will believe that he has actually developed the attitude he is now expressing. By this interpretation, there is no great moral dilemma, no unpleasantly overpowering state of arousal, and no attempt to figure out the discrepant behavior. One prediction from the impression-management hypothesis would be that if subjects thought the experimenter did not *know* they changed their attitude, or if they believed that the experimenter had a foolproof way to tell what their real attitude was, subjects should not show attitude change. Evidence for these hypotheses is ambiguous (Cooper & Fazio, 1984).

A potentially troublesome finding for the impression management interpretation is that subjects *do* appear to show increased arousal in the dissonance situation. If this arousal is actually related to their attitude change, then impression management theory would have to take this into account. Schlenker (1982) has proposed that the activity of selling oneself cheaply produces arousal because the subject wants to protect his or her self-esteem. Attitude change is one way to do this. This interpretation runs into some of the same problems as the dissonance-reduction interpretation. That is, if the arousal (social anxiety? guilt?) does not decrease after the changed attitude is expressed, what does arousal do? It may be that arousal does nothing at all. Arousal and impression management may in fact be parallel events, neither one causing the other. This could also be true of arousal and dissonance; the two might occur in parallel, but without causal significance for each other.

*Change in the motivational basis of dissonance.*    Greenwald and Ronis (1978) pointed out that there has been a drift in the nature of the motivational principle supposedly underlying cognitive dissonance. Initially, it was said that any two contradictory actions or beliefs were a source of dissonance. Then, inconsistency was said to be a major force only if the individual was *committed to behaving* in an inconsistent manner (Brehm & Cohen, 1962). Aronson (1968) then suggested that the *self-concept* was importantly involved. Wicklund and Brehm (1976) argued that dissonance reduction occurs only when the dissonant elements have been brought together through the *personal responsibility* of the individual who feels the dissonance. Impression management theorists argue that social anxiety is the motivating force. Greenwald and Ronis suggest that the more recent approaches are more akin to *ego-defensive actions,* as proposed by many personality theorists, than to dissonance and its reduction, as proposed by Festinger.

The increasing emphasis on the self-concept, suggest Greenwald and Ronis, is not bad. But, it may not really be dissonance, either. It is possible that the shift in focus has been due to a greater emphasis on those aspects of dissonance procedures which happen to overlap with ego-defensive activities. If the ego-defensive behaviors are particularly powerful (and the procedures for manipulating threat to the ego or self-esteem are strong) then these would in the "natural course of things" lead to a greater concern with them. The net effect may then be that dissonance theory in its original formulation has not been fully tested, because the predictions made by subsequent revisions simply are not relevant to the original statement.

In summary, cognitive dissonance theory has been a highly *fruitful* theory, generating much new research, controversy, and theory. The attitude change data generated by tests of the theory are often interpreted in other ways, and the theory is much less influential than it once was.

## A SOCIAL MODEL: CONFORMITY AND NONCONFORMITY

In a classic experiment, Solomon Asch (1951) had several subjects judge which of a set of lines matched the length of a standard line. All but one of the subjects were actually accomplices of the experimenter. The accomplices all made their judgments before the real subject made his, and on some occasions made obviously incorrect judgments. Under these circumstances the real subjects frequently went along with what they thought were the judgments of the other subjects. In other words, they took what the other subjects said as a *norm* and conformed to that norm. In fact, the real subjects often did not privately believe that the false answer was actually correct, but they publicly went along with it. They were concerned about the effects of being different from the norm, and their "error correction" procedure was to "go along."

In general, research shows a strong tendency for individuals to conform to whatever standards are set by their group. A person is rewarded for conformity and sanctioned for nonconformity. A group, like an individual, has goals, such as to maintain production or win a game. The group pressure for cooperation helps attain these goals, and the group, or its leader, provides rewards and punishments for individuals who do or do not "go along." Schacter (1951) found that individuals who consistently differed from a group in their attitudes were rejected by other group members. This can be severe punishment. The college freshman who dearly wants to become a member of a particular fraternity, for example, is not likely to deviate much from the norms of that group lest he not be invited. In terms of discrepancy, then, what we see are *group mechanisms* for keeping social behavior at an expected (reference) level. If individual behaviors depart from this, appropriate corrective actions are taken to bring the behavior back into line.

### Groupthink

An extreme case of conformity is when a group becomes so enthralled with an idea, no matter how divorced from reality, that it squelches all opposition to the idea. This is called *groupthink* (Janis, 1972). Three conditions which especially foster groupthink are strong group cohesiveness, isolation from other views, and endorsement of the policy decision by the group leader. Some of the characteristics of such a group are that there is *strong pressure* on group members (by each other) not to dissent, *self-censorship* of deviant ideas by members of the group, an *illusion of unanimity*, partly coming from the pressure to conform and the emergence of self-appointed *mind-guards*, members of the group who "protect" the others from inconsistent information and suppress views deviating from the consensus. Two prime examples are the Bay of Pigs invasion fiasco during the early days of the Kennedy administration and the Watergate affair during the Nixon administration. In both cases there were tight little White House groups working toward a certain goal, with strong rejection of anyone who did not conform. An equally powerful, but more recent example, is the PTL sex-and-money scandal under the administration of Jim Bakker. Bakker's inner circle provided a tight little conforming group which strongly rejected any deviation from its "party line."

## SOME GENERAL PROBLEMS FOR CONSISTENCY THEORIES

### The problem of increased arousal

One of the strongest arguments against homeostasis as the sole explanatory concept for all motivated behavior is that many behaviors seem to be tension-increasing, not tension-reducing. Arousal theory handled this problem by postulating an optimal level of arousal which people try to achieve. Since the optimal level is sometimes greater than one's level at the moment, arousal-increasing activities are sought. To some extent, within a control theory or consistency framework the arousal-increment problem theoretically can also be handled as follows. If I set myself a goal (or set up a plan), I work to bring reality into line with that plan. My "motivation" is to reduce the discrepancy between the plan and the way things are at the moment. If in the course of working toward my goal I should produce an increased level of arousal for myself, that is incidental to reducing the *larger* discrepancy. Recall that professional stunt performers are not sensation-seekers (Piet, 1987); they are workers who make their living doing dangerous activities and they do everything they can to reduce the danger. And, as Stagner (1977) noted, when Roald Amundsen set out for the South Pole he was not wearing his summer underwear and carrying a basket of fruit; he was very well prepared to protect himself as he carried out his plan. Hardship was necessary but otherwise incidental to the goal of reaching the pole.

### The problem of goal setting

The second problem, which is not at all handled easily by control theory, homeostatic theory, or discrepancy theories, is the question *Where do the goals come from?* Who sets the reference criterion? Who sets the thermostat? Who sets the plan against which an image is tested? Recall in chapter 1 that the distinction made between the *regulatory* and *purposive* approaches to motivation hinges precisely on this point. That is, the purposive approach is concerned with *which* goals we select, and the regulatory approach is concerned with returning to some *predefined* state (goal). The whole point of defining motivation as we did was that it seems to us that the question of goals is the prior question. Hyland (1988) finesses the problem by saying that goals are equivalent to reference criteria, but then simply says that the type of reference criterion does not affect the general operation of a control loop. Whether or not purpose precedes regulation, the question of purpose and choice of goals must be dealt with in any psychology of motivation.

### SUMMARY

1.  Departure from some norm is often motivating. In terms of *control theory*, a norm provides a *reference criterion*. Departure from the norm is detected by a *comparator*, and the *detected error* activates an *amplifier* which operates a mechanism to correct the detected error. This model applies to many aspects of motivated behavior, from temperature regulation to cognitive consistency.
2.  *Cognitive inconsistency* is perceived by an individual and may vary among individuals. It occurs when an event is perceived to be different from expectation.
3.  According to Sokolov's model of the *orienting reflex*, repetitious stimulus inputs may *habituate* and are not noticed after a while. A slight change in stimulus input arouses attention (the orienting reflex). The model says that incoming stimuli are compared with previous stimuli and are not responded to until a new stimulus is discrepant with the stored information.
4.  According to the TOTE (Test-Operate-Test-Exit) model, an *image* of the environment is compared with a *plan* of what we want to achieve. As long as the

image and the plan are discrepant (Test), we are motivated to act (Operate) to reduce the discrepancy. When the two are perceived to be in agreement (Test), we move ahead to some other plan (Exit).

5. Heider's *balance theory* concerns the consistency of relations among different people, a *social perception*. If A likes B, and B likes C, but A strongly dislikes C, there is an *imbalance* for A. Balance theory has been particularly concerned with *attitude change* as a way to restore balance.

6. *Cognitive dissonance* is said to occur when the same individual holds *contradictory beliefs*, or acts contrary to his or her beliefs. Dissonance is said to be aversive, and dissonance reduction is reinforcing.

7. In a typical dissonance experiment, subjects are subtly coerced to write essays against their own attitude regarding some topic (such as parking on campus). Subjects show attitude changes away from their original attitude if they believe that their inconsistent behavior has actually affected someone and if they believe they have chosen freely to engage in the counterattitudinal behavior.

8. Evidence that dissonance is actually arousing is slight, and mostly inferred from behavior. It has been shown that dissonance-arousing conditions produce an increased level of galvanic skin response, but not that the response goes down when subjects report their changed attitude. The arousal may not be causally related to reported attitude change.

9. Several alternative explanations for the results of dissonance experiments have been proposed. Bem's *self-perception theory* says that people infer their own attitudes the same way they infer the attitudes of other people, *by observing their own behavior*. According to *impression management theory*, subjects wish to maintain their self-esteem, therefore they report a changed attitude so that they will not appear to be easily swayed by the experimenter.

10. *Conformity* research shows the importance of dissonance reduction in social situations. When individuals fail to conform to group norms they may be ostracized; they may therefore conform to reduce the level of aversiveness of group reaction to their nonconformity.

11. *Groupthink* is an extreme example of conformity in which highly unrealistic goals may be maintained by a group because the group will hear only its own views and strongly reject any dissenting views.

# 11

# Achievement and Power

## ACHIEVEMENT MOTIVATION

An enduring practical question is how to get people to achieve more. We will consider whether there is a need for achievement which varies from person to person and which, under proper circumstances, might be learned.

### Definition of the Need for Achievement (n Ach)

We must first define achievement *motivation* independently of achievement *behavior*. Murray (1938, p. 80–81) defined need for achievement as a desire or tendency "to overcome obstacles, to exercise power, to strive to do something difficult as well and as quickly as possible." In his personality theory, n Ach was one of 20 manifest psychological needs (as distinct from such biological needs as hunger). Murray also devised the Thematic Apperception Test (TAT) as a means of studying personality and needs. This test consists of a series of pictures about which the individual tells a story to answer the questions: (1) What led up to the scene being depicted? (2) What is now happening in the scene? (3) How do the characters feel? (4) What will be the outcome? The relatively ambiguous pictures are supposed to evoke themes which will be characteristically different for different individuals.

Various scoring schemes for the stories are intended to detect themes indicative of the personality and needs of the individual telling the story. For example, one card shows a boy with a violin lying on a table in front of him while he looks into space. If the story is about a boy working hard to become a world-renowned violinist, the interpretation would be different from a story about a boy who is supposed to be practicing but who wants to be outside playing with his friends. The former story would indicate achievement, and the latter, affiliation. In the n Ach research, there are usually four pictures, with a time limit of five minutes for telling each story (Atkinson, 1958, McClelland et al., 1953). A more direct or objective test might seem better, but the fantasy measures have been successfully used for many years.

Need for achievement can presumably be *aroused*, but n Ach is not manipulated and controlled like hunger or thirst. Subjects who display high or low levels of n Ach in their stories are *selected* and then tested in achievement situations. Such tasks as simple arithmetic problems are done more rapidly by high n Ach individuals (McClelland, 1985). The obvious questions are, What produces higher n Ach? And, Why does n Ach lead to better performance?

### McClelland's Theory

McClelland et al. (1953) offered a hedonic interpretation of n Ach. Cues previously associated with hedonically positive events produce a particular rearousal of that affect. The individual partly experiences, as well as anticipates, a pleasurable outcome. If prior achievement situations have had good outcomes, an individual is more likely to engage in achievement behaviors. Conversely, if a person were punished for failing, a fear of failure could develop and there would be a motive to avoid failure.

Men with high n Ach tend to come from families in which achievement striving is emphasized, and young adults with high n Ach often report that their parents were not particularly warm individuals, who emphasized achievement rather than affiliation. In brief, the theory simply says that under appropriate conditions people will do what they have been rewarded for doing. If a competitive situation is a cue for rewarded achievement striving, then in competitive situations the individual will work harder.

### The Achieving Society

McClelland's interests broadened from laboratory tasks to social problems, and he tried to determine if n Ach was related to the rise and fall of cultures (McClelland, 1961). This idea was related to Max Weber's thesis in *The Protestant Ethic and the Spirit of Capitalism* ([1904] 1930), that the Protestant Revolution had infused a more vigorous spirit into both workers and entrepreneurs. What a society teaches its children about being independent was related to Protestantism on the one hand and social growth on the other. One advantage of the n Ach scoring system is that it can be applied to any written material, including old newspapers, books, or public records.

The Protestant Reformation was a liberation movement, a break from the authoritarianism of the Catholic church that led to a greater social, as well as ecclesiastical, freedom. Freedom also carries with it, however, a greater stress on individual responsibility and independence. Protestant individuals and countries should therefore show greater n Ach than Catholic individuals and countries. And, indeed, just as it had earlier been shown that boys separated from their fathers and forced to be more independent evidenced higher n Ach, so it was shown that Protestant families stressed independence earlier than Irish or Italian Catholic families of the same socioeconomic levels (McClelland, Rindlisbacher, & deCharms, 1955). Protestant children score higher on n Ach tests and Protestant countries are more advanced economically. The latter was shown by comparing such measures of economic development as per capita use of electricity and amount of shipping. Children's books have also been scored for achievement themes and related to economic growth. Between 1800 and 1850, for example, deCharms and Moeller (1962) found first an increase and then a decrease in number of patents per 100,000 people in the United States. This was closely paralleled by a rise and fall in achievement imagery in the children's books in the preceding 50 years, with a correlation of .79 between the two measures.

Individuals in "entrepreneurial" occupations should also have high n Ach scores. Occupation may have affected achievement scores rather than vice versa, but a longitudinal study avoids this ambiguity. McClelland (1965) found that 83% of Wesleyan graduates in entrepreneurial occupations 14 years after graduation had scored high n Ach when they were students, whereas only 21% of those in nonentrepreneurial occupations had high scores. Individuals with high n Ach are also more independent and less concerned with the feelings of others. McClelland came to view the "managerial type" in business as being a medium risk taker, wanting immediate feedback for his or her behavior, and working harder under conditions of achievement arousal. This type of person is not happy unless continually rewarded with success.

### Atkinson's Theory

John Atkinson (e.g., 1964) refined achievement theory. First, he put the theory into the framework of expectancy-value theory, following the orientations of Tolman and Kurt Lewin. Second, he emphasized the role of conflict, especially between n Ach and fear of failure.

*The tendency to success ($T_s$).* In Atkinson's theory the tendency to engage in achievement-oriented behaviors (tendency to success, or $T_s$) is a multiplicative function of (1) the *motivation* for success ($M_s$), which is the same as n Ach; (2) the *probability* of success ($P_s$); and (3) the *incentive value* of success ($I_s$). As a special assumption of the theory, it is postulated that $I_s$ is $1 - P_s$. That is, if the probability of success is very low, then the incentive value of success is very high, and vice versa. Other incentives are related to achievement, but other things being equal, the incentive value of success is important. The formula reads:

$$T_s = M_s \times P_s \times I_s$$

where $T_s$ = tendency to achieve success
$M_s$ = motive to success (n Ach)
$P_s$ = perceived probability of success
$I_s$ = incentive value of success, or $1 - P_s$

If any of the components is zero, then there will be no tendency to strive for success in a particular situation. The formula is, like the Hullian formula, multiplicative, and there is a crude analogy between concepts. Thus, $M_s$ is something like drive in that it is internal, $P_s$ is a learning component corresponding roughly to habit, and $I_s$ corresponds roughly to K. The parallel with Tolman is even closer, since $P_s$ is an expectancy and $I_s$ is a value.

There are obviously important differences from Hull, however, particularly with regard to $P_s$ and $I_s$. To illustrate, a reliable finding for high n Ach people is that they are *medium risk takers*. Given a choice of activities involving various probabilities of success, they tend to choose those that have a medium level of $P_s$. The Atkinson model accounts for this as follows: Since

$P_s$ can range from 0 to 1, $I_s$ can range from 1 to 0 because $I_s = 1 - P_s$. The maximum possible value of $P_s \times (1 - P_s)$ is obtained with $P_s = .50$. If $P_s = 90, 1 - P_s = .10$, and the product is .09. Similarly, if $P_s = .10$ and $1 - P_s = .90$, the product is .09. But if $P_s = .50$, the product is .25. Table 11-1 shows some worked examples of $T_s$ for various values of $M_s$ and $P_s$, and Figure 11-1 graphically illustrates the results.

For any value of $M_s$ except zero, $T_s$ is maximal at $P_s = .50$. With low values of $M_s$ the curve, as shown in Figure 11-1, is very shallow, but with increasing values of $M_s$, the curve is progressively steeper. With higher values of $M_s$, there is a greater tendency to choose tasks with a medium chance of success than either very easy or very difficult tasks. Part of the incentive value of a task lies in the potential attainment of risky success, some feeling of accomplishment that we may take to be pleasurable. For high n Ach ($M_s$) individuals, there is a strong desire to succeed, but success does not mean much if the job is too easy. Conversely, if the task is very difficult it has a high

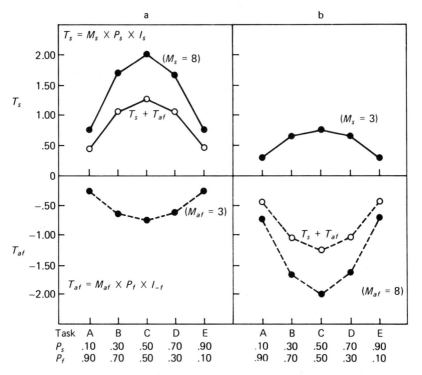

**FIGURE 11-1.** Illustrations of $T_s$ and $T_{af}$ and resultant tendencies to approach or avoid when $M_s$ = 3 or 8 and when $M_{af}$ = 3 or 8. In (a), the tendency to success is greater than the tendency to avoid failure, therefore, the resultant tendency, the algebraic summation of $T_s$ and $T_{af}$, is positive. In (b) the situation is just reversed, with the resultant tendency being negative. Note also that $T_s$ is a steeper function in (a) ($M_s$ = 8) than in (b) ($M_s$ = 3). This indicates why high n Ach individuals are medium-risk takers; medium probabilities of success produce much higher relative values of $T_s$ when $M_s$ is high.

**TABLE 11-1** Calculations of $T_s$ and $T_{af}$ for Five Different Difficulty Level Tasks and Different Values of $M_s$ and $M_{af}$.

| TASK | $P_S$ | $I_S$ | $T_S = M_S \times P_S \times I_S$ WHEN | | | $P_F$ | $I_{-F}$ | $T_{AF} = M_{AF} \times P_F \times I_{-F}$ WHEN | | |
|---|---|---|---|---|---|---|---|---|---|---|
| | | | $M_S = 1$ | $M_S = 3$ | $M_S = 8$ | | | $M_{AF} = 1$ | $M_{AF} = 3$ | $M_{AF} = 8$ |
| A | .90 | .10 | .09 | .27 | .72 | .10 | −.90 | −.09 | −.27 | −.72 |
| B | .70 | .30 | .21 | .63 | 1.68 | .30 | −.70 | −.21 | −.63 | −1.68 |
| C | .50 | .50 | .25 | .75 | 2.00 | .50 | −.50 | −.25 | −.75 | −2.00 |
| D | .30 | .70 | .21 | .63 | 1.68 | .70 | −.30 | −.21 | −.63 | −1.68 |
| E | .10 | .90 | .09 | .27 | .72 | .90 | −.10 | −.09 | −.27 | −.72 |

incentive value but little chance of succeeding and hence little chance of getting any feeling of accomplishment.

As one test of the theory, Atkinson (1958) told female subjects they were to compete for a prize of either $1.25 or $2.50. Four probabilities of winning were stated: $1/20$, $1/3$, $1/2$, and $3/4$. One task was to draw X's inside small circles for twenty minutes. The high-reward group performed better than the low-reward group, but performance declined for both groups when $P_s$ was said to be $3/4$ rather than $1/2$, confirming the prediction of an inverted-U function for performance with a higher probability of success.

**The tendency to avoid failure ($T_{af}$).**     Besides the "satisfaction" or "pride" that comes from success, there is "shame" from failure (tendency to avoid failure, or $T_{af}$). This negative affect presumably depends on one's previous experience with failure, whether one was punished or ridiculed. A multiplication formula is also used to determine the strength of the tendency to avoid failure. The components are (1) the *motive to avoid failure* ($M_{af}$), the fear of failure, commonly measured by a test anxiety questionnaire; (2) the *probability of failure* ($P_f$), which for any given task is $1 - P_s$; and (3) the *negative incentive value of failure* ($I_{-f}$) is $- (1 - P_f)$, which is the same as $-P_s$. If the probability of failure is .90, then $I_{-f}$ is $- (1 - .90) = -.10$. Since $P_s$ for this example is $1 - .90 = .10$, then $I_{-f} = -P_s = -.10$. The tendency to avoid failure is thus given by the formula:

$$T_{af} = M_{af} \times P_f \times I_{-f}$$

where   $T_{af}$ = the tendency to avoid failure
          $M_{af}$ = motive to avoid failure
           $P_f$ = probability of failure = $1 - P_s$
          $I_{-f}$ = negative incentive value of failure = $-P_s$

Table 11-1 and Figure 11-1 also show worked examples and a graphic illustration of the use of the formula. The formula says that if there is any motivation to avoid failure, there will be some tendency to avoid tasks that could potentially lead to failure. Furthermore, the maximum value of $T_{af}$ will also occur with medium-probability tasks. The logic is the same as with $T_s$. The maximum value of $P_f \times I_{-f}$ occurs when $P_f = .50$, but the product is a negative value. The tendency to avoid failure will be the strongest for tasks having a medium expectancy of failure — just the opposite of what is predicted for the individual with high n Ach. In everyday language, the person afraid of failing may choose a task which is so easy that he or she cannot fail or one which is so difficult that there is no shame in failing. A task of medium difficulty is too easy to fail and the shame too great, therefore it is avoided.

*The combination of $T_s$ and $T_{af}$.* The values of $I_s$, $P_f$, and $I_{-f}$ are all determined once we know the value of $P_s$. What differentiates $T_s$ and $T_{af}$, then, are the relative strengths of $M_s$ and $M_{af}$. The resolution of the conflict between $T_s$ and $T_{af}$ is then represented as follows:

$$T_s + T_{af} = (M_s \times P_s \times I_s) + (M_{af} \times P_f \times I_{-f})$$

Since $I_s$ is positive and $I_{-f}$ is negative, the sum can be positive ($T_s > T_{af}$), zero, or negative ($T_s < T_{af}$). In effect, then, if $M_s > M_{af}$, the individual should *choose* medium-probability tasks, but if $M_{af} > M_s$, the person should tend to *avoid* medium-probability tasks. The theory, then, resolves into being the same as any other conflict theory. (An addition to the formula, omitted here, is that there are other incentives besides $I_s$ and $I_f$). Atkinson's theory, with its special assumptions about positive and negative incentives for achievement, makes interesting and unique predictions, however. We shall illustrate these with task preference and level of aspiration.

*Task preference.* McClelland (1958) showed that high n Ach children preferred to toss a ring at a peg (the ringtoss game) from a medium distance, as compared to low n Ach children, who tended to choose either near or far distances. Atkinson and Litwin (1960) divided subjects into four groups of all combinations of high and low n Ach and high and low anxiety. They predicted that high $M_s$, low $M_{af}$ subjects would show the strongest tendency to choose medium distances in the ringtoss game and that high $M_{af}$, low $M_s$ subjects would avoid the middle range. The other two groups should fall between. The predictions were somewhat confirmed, as shown in Figure 11-2. The high $M_{af}$, low $M_s$ group tended to choose a middle range, but their preferences were spread across a wider range of distances than any other group. To obtain results exactly as predicted for the group where $M_{af} > M_s$ would depend on very exact measurements of $M_{af}$ and $M_s$. It may not really be in the present situation that $M_{af}$ was greater than $M_s$.

*Level of aspiration.* Suppose a high $M_s$ person chooses a task which he perceives to be of medium difficulty. By experimental prearrangement, he then either succeeds or fails. What difficulty level should he subsequently choose? One of the commonest results of such *level of aspiration* research is that people tend to change their goals realistically on the basis of experience (e.g., Lewin, Dembo, Festinger, & Sears, 1944). After failure, the goal is lowered; after success, it is raised. Atkinson's explanation is that after easy success, a person would perceive $P_s$ as higher than previously expected. He therefore sets the next goal higher because that would bring $P_s$ of this goal closer to his newly adjusted concept of a .50 goal. Conversely, if he failed he

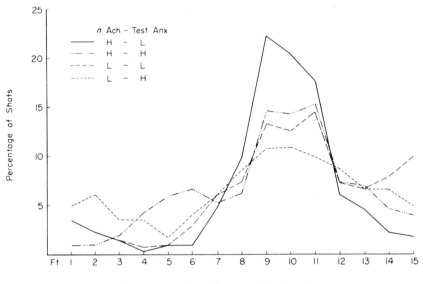

Distance from Target in Ring Toss Game

**FIGURE 11-2.** Percentage of shots taken from each distance by college men in a ring-toss game. Graph is smoothed according to the method of running averages, for S's classified as High or Low simultaneously in n Ach test anxiety, H-L (N = 13), H-H (N = 10), L-L (N = 9), L-H (N = 13). (From Atkinson and Litwin, 1960, p. 55. Copyright ©1960 by the American Psychological Association. Used with permission.)

would assume that $P_s$ was lower than he had expected, and hence choose a simpler task to bring $P_s$ up more nearly to .50. These are *typical shifts* in level-of-aspiration research.

There are sometimes peculiar *atypical shifts*, however. Some individuals *raise* their goals after failure and *lower* them after success. According to the theory, if $M_{af} > M_s$, then the individual should *avoid* medium-difficulty tasks. Now suppose a high $M_{af}$ subject is told he has a task where $P_s = .50$ and fails it. He may then believe that $P_s$ was *lower* than he initially thought, .35, for instance. An easier task would put him closer to $P_s = .50$, which should be aversive for him. He may therefore select a *more difficult task* (for example, where $P_s = .25$) than the one he failed at. Conversely, if successful at a task he believes to be $P_s = .50$, the subject may think the task was easier than he had believed, such as $P_s = .65$. Therefore, he would choose an even easier task next because he wants to keep away from the $P_s = .50$ task. Moulton (1965) actually got such results, for high $M_{af}$, low $M_s$ individuals, as well as showing that high $M_s$, low $M_{af}$ subjects and $M_s = M_{af}$ subjects made typical shifts more frequently. This is rather remarkable support for the theory.

*Does $I_s = (1 - P_s)$?* It is assumed that the probability and the positive incentive value of success are inversely related, and that a low value of $P_s$ should produce a positive affective experience. But what is the evidence for this? Feather (1967) set up an experiment where success and failure were rigged, and different subjects were told that the task had varying degrees of difficulty. If subjects believed success was due to skill, the degree of positive emotion was greater with increasing difficulty. But, if success was attributed to chance, there was only a slight change in emotion. There was also greater negative affect for skill-related failure than for chance-related failure. These results seem generally to support the idea that $P_s$ and $I_s$ are inversely related. The demonstration of hedonic differences related to success and failure do not tell us the nature of those differences, however. Weiner (1980) has argued that in achievement situations there are several possible sources of affect (such as generally feeling good or bad versus such specific emotions as pride and shame) and that detailed knowledge about such distinctions is necessary before we can really understand achievement motivation.

### Later Developments of Atkinson's Theory

The previous theory and data apply to *immediate* goals, but we all have *long-term* goals as well. The college student may momentarily face a particular exam, but the goal of passing this exam is related to the long-term goal of graduating. Obviously students take courses (perhaps required) which are above or below a perceived medium risk level because they have *future achievements* (such as graduation) and *external goals* (such as a job) to consider.

*Future orientation.*    Raynor (1974) proposed that *future* orientations intensify the overall level of $T_s$ in the *present* so that immediate and distant goals add together to affect achievement motivation. For example, the immediate goal of passing a course and the distant goal of graduating combine to influence how hard a student will work on a particular course. Future orientation is called *perceived instrumentality* because it is based on a person's perception of how instrumental a present behavior will be in achieving a long-term outcome. If graduation were not a goal, a student would be less likely to work hard on uninteresting or difficult courses. A complete analysis of future orientation also includes tendency to avoid future failure, such as failing to graduate. The specific equations for future orientation need not concern us here.

*External goals.*    Achievement theory was further advanced by Feather (1967), who also took such future *external* goals as money and a job into account. Given a specific future external goal (such as getting a particular job), the tendency to strive for this goal is the sum of present and future tendencies to strive for *success* (future orientation for success) and to strive for the external goal. Thus:

$$T_x = [T_s \text{ (immediate)} + T_s \text{ (distant)} + T_s \text{ (external)}] -$$
$$[T_{af} \text{ (immediate)} + T_{af} \text{ (distant)} + T_{af} \text{ (external)}];$$
where Tx is a specific goal in the future,
$T_s$ is tendency to success, and
$T_{af}$ is tendency to avoid failure.

Raynor (1970) tested the theory by looking at the effects of future orientation and achievement motivation on introductory psychology grades. Students rated the relevance and importance (the instrumentality) of their psychology course to their future goals, and were divided into those with high and low instrumentality for the course. Subjects were further divided into $M_s > M_{af}$ and $M_{af} > M_s$ groups. The course grades are shown in Table 11-2. As predicted, when $M_s > M_{af}$, higher perceived instrumentality enhanced performance (higher grades). This lent some support to the theory.

*Contingent path analysis.* It may have occurred to you that most long-term goals require many choices and many successes, not just the choice of a single goal. The student must pass a large number of courses, each with its own probability of success (whether for an A or just for passing). A *path* is a series of tasks, such as courses, which must be successfully completed. A *contingent path* is one where the probability of success for the whole path depends on success on *all* the tasks, such as having to pass all of one's courses in order to graduate. We now ask about how the choices among entire paths (such as the choice from among several majors), differ from choices of single goals.

Again, the maximal value of $T_s = P_s \times (1 - P)$ for a single goal occurs

**TABLE 11-2    Mean Grades in Introductory Psychology as a Function of Achievement-Related Motives and Perceived Instrumentality of the Course.**

|  | PERCEIVED INSTRUMENTALITY OF INTRODUCTORY PSYCHOLOGY | |
|  | LOW | HIGH |
| --- | --- | --- |
| Ms > Maf | 2.93 | 3.37 |
| Maf > Ms | 3.00 | 2.59 |

From J. O. Raynor (1970). Relationships between achievement-related motives, future orientation, and academic performances. *Journal of Personality and Social Psychology*, 15, 28–33. Copyright ©1970 by the American Psychological Association. Used by permission.

when $P_s$ = .50. But the probability of successfully completing *two* tasks where $P_s$ = .50 is only .25 (.50 × .50) and for three tasks is only .125 (.50 × .50 × .50). However success is defined, the probability drops off very rapidly in a contingent path when several steps are required. The path analysis tells us, then, that tasks with probabilities of success greater than .50 (e.g., .90) will be required to have reasonable values of $P_s$ for an entire path. The entire path is that which is *perceived* by the individual *before* entering the path, however, and this perception may change. What was initially perceived as an easy major, for example, may seem difficult after a couple of courses, and the whole path then is perceived differently. This may lead to a change of majors.

### Problems in Achievement Theory and Research

*Are women different from men?*   From the very beginning of McClelland's research, TAT scores have not predicted achievement performance for women. Consequently, most of the early research was done with males. Perhaps the type of pictures used in the tests or the definition of achievement were not appropriate for females. Taking a different approach, Horner (1968) speculated that females have a *motive to avoid success.* Some authors consider this to be equivalent to fear of failure, whereas others see it as a conflict between social stereotypes for female behavior and the actual behavior required for achievement. It has generally been men or boys, not women or girls, who are rewarded for being successfully competitive.

There *are* clearly demonstrated stereotypes for men and women around the world and both sexes ascribe to these about equally (Williams & Bennett, 1975; Williams & Best, 1982). For example, men are perceived to be more ambitious, assertive, confident, dominant, independent, logical, rational, steady, and unemotional, while women are seen as more affectionate, charming, emotional, fickle, frivolous, high-strung, nagging, rattle-brained, sentimental, talkative, and weak. As judged by a clinical psychologist, these stereotypes would be pathological if they described real people. Nevertheless, they represent how men and women *think* of others. Most people are *not* like stereotypes, and people do *not* describe *themselves* like the stereotypes, but deviations from the stereotypes for one's own sex may engender some anxiety and thus be avoided. The motivation to avoid deviations from stereotypes may occur equally in men and women.

Patty (1976) found that women high in "motivation to avoid success" (as measured by a standard technique developed by Horner) saw themselves as less affectionate than did women low in this motive. They also had low self-esteem, and the perception of being controlled by external events. They were career oriented, but aspired to "traditional female occupations." Their mothers were also in traditional occupations. Women low in motivation to avoid success, on the other hand, had mothers in "nontraditional" occupations and hence had a nonconforming role model. They may have rejected the stereotypic view and hence had no conflict about achievement. The general consensus now seems to be that there is no specific female motive to avoid success (Spence & Helmreich, 1983).

*Are fantasy measures of achievement reliable and valid?*   McClelland and his associates (1953) developed a complex scheme for scoring TAT pictures for achievement themes. Typically, four pictures were used with each subject. However, Entwisle (1972) found that scoring each picture as "1" or "0" for presence or absence of achievement theme correlated between .70 and .90 with the more complicated scoring. This means that the standard scoring schemes are little more refined than a four-item true-false test. This would account for the low estimates of test-retest reliability for TAT scoring of n Ach, correlations between .30 and .40. If reliability is so low, then it is surprising that n Ach scores ever predict actual performance. Atkinson (e.g., Atkinson, Bongort, & Price, 1978) has countered this line of criticism by a bold counterattack on traditional approaches to reliability. He argues, for example, that test-retest correlations may be low, but if test scores are split at the median into high and low groups, the same individuals tend to be in the high and low groups on retest. This is sufficient for *construct validity*.[1]

*Does the achievement literature show consistent results?*   Klinger (1966) found about as many published experiments on achievement motivation having statistically insignificant results as those with significant results. Even a close reading of research with positive results frequently leaves one with a little less confidence in the concept of n Ach than when one started. One possible explanation for the inconsistencies is that n Ach is a complex variable, not just a single dimension than can be measured by a single score. We shall return to this point.

*Is n Ach a motivational variable?*   It is widely assumed, dating back to Murray and McClelland's early work, that the TAT measures a *motivational disposition*. This is the degree to which an individual will show a particular motivational *state* under the appropriate circumstances. The motive must be *engaged* before it is effective (Klinger, 1966). The tendency to engage in achievement-oriented behaviors ($T_s$) does not occur unless achievement motivation ($M_s$) is aroused. There are several reasons for questioning whether n Ach is a motive at all, however.

First, n Ach scores correlate highly with verbal productivity (Entwisle,

[1]*Construct validity* refers to the capacity of a test to make predictions about research results, not just to *correlate* with some performance criterion. *Predictive validity* refers to the correlation between some present measure (such as an aptitude test) and some future criterion (such as performance at school or on the job).

1972). The number of words written per TAT story (verbal productivity) by ninth graders correlated more highly with school grades (about .35) than did the corresponding n Ach scores (about .25). Entwisle concluded that the modest relationship between n Ach scores and school performance result from the element of verbal productivity, which contributes both to the TAT score and to school performance. Second, subjects who demonstrate high *achievement imagery* in their TAT scores and high *achievement performance* in other situations may come from environments which stress achievement in a variety of ways (Klinger, 1966). Achievement imagery and performance may both be due to achievement arousal. That is to say, achievement imagery does not *cause* high achievement performance, they are simply correlated measures. This is illustrated as follows:

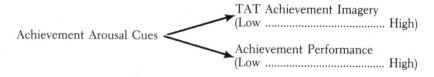

Another possibility, apparently more favored by Klinger, is that there may be an achievement motive, but that the *cue* value of achievement imagery has been neglected. We can illustrate this possibility as follows:

Achievement fantasy as a *cue* and achievement *motivation* both contribute to achievement performance. This looks remarkably like the Hullian formulation for the joint roles of drive and drive stimuli as determinants of performance, as discussed in chapter 5. In Hull's theory, the conditions for arousing drive also produce drive stimuli. Thus:

Achievement imagery sounds more complex than drive stimuli, but perhaps this is because we have impoverished ideas about drive stimuli. McClelland and Atkinson (1948) themselves showed that there was greater food imagery in food-deprived than nondeprived humans, and studies of starvation in humans have shown the same thing. Perhaps even the lowly rat has its fantasies of crackers and cheese.

### Multidimensional Nature of Achievement Motivation

Achievement motivation has several dimensions; it is not a single-dimensional variable as perhaps implied by the above discussion. We have already seen, for example, that some people strive for success because it is a positive goal; others strive for success because they fear the consequences of failure. Thus, one student might work hard in school because he really likes his courses and has fun with them, but another student might work equally hard because he fears the consequences of not getting good grades, such as not getting a good job or not getting into graduate school. For most students, need for achievement and fear of failure are probably mixed. A course may be enjoyable, but there is at least a twinge of anxiety about not doing well. Different approaches to achievement have provided insight into additional aspects of achievement, however.

Jackson, Ahmed, and Heapy (1976) postulated six distinct dimensions for achievement motivation: (1) status with experts; (2) acquisitiveness; (3) achievement via independence; (4) status with peers; (5) competitiveness; and (6) concern for excellence. They devised five different methods for measuring each of the six dimensions, resulting in thirty different scales. There were low correlations among different dimensions with all five measurement methods, but each of the five methods had high correlations *within* each of the dimensions. This is evidence that there are at least six achievement dimensions (more were not tested), which are reliable across different measurement scales. We may say that n Ach is a complex variable, and it is not sufficient to say that a particular person is at the "X percentile" in achievement motivation. Rather, we would need a *profile* of the individual, representing his or her location on each dimension of achievement motivation. We should then like to determine the conditions (situations, tasks, etc.) under which one dimension is more or less important than another.

### The Spence-Helmreich Model

Three particular dimensions of achievement motivation may seem familiar to the typical student (Spence & Helmreich, 1983). First, there is *satisfaction in work* itself, in a job well done. When a student writes a term paper she may well be concerned with the grade, but also with the satisfaction of having turned out a good piece of work. Second, there is a *sense of completion*, of satisfaction with getting a job done. Sometimes when we work at a job we simply are pleased that we get it done, not just relieved that the job is "finally finished." We are proud to have stayed the course. One of the reasons for running a marathon, such as in Boston or New York, is the satisfaction of simply having completed the 26-mile course. Third, there is a sense of *competitiveness*, enjoyment of competition and winning.

Spence and Helmreich (1983) devised a measure for these three aspects of achievement called the Work and Family Orientation Questionnaire (WOFO). This is an objectively scored questionnaire, shown in Table 11-3. (See Table 1-1, p. 42, of Spence & Helmreich, 1983). Men and women do not differ in the nature of their achievement motives as these are measured by the WOFO. Research in a rather impressive array of situations, ranging from grades in college to salaries in business organization consistently shows an interesting pattern of results. Grades and salaries are higher for people who have higher levels of motivation for work and mastery if they are low in competitiveness. If they are high in competitiveness, however, performance suffers. This is illustrated in Figure 11-3 (Spence & Helmreich, 1983). One possible explanation is that highly competitive people may focus so much on the competition, rather than doing a good job, that they perform less well than they would otherwise.

**TABLE 11-3  Items On Work, Mastery, and Competitiveness Scales of Work and Family Orientation Questionnaire**

Work

1. It is important for me to do my work as well as I can even if it isn't popular with my co-workers.
2. I find satisfaction in working as well as I can.
3. There is satisfaction in a job well done.
4. I find satisfaction in exceeding my previous performance even if I don't outperform others.
5. I like to work hard.
6. Part of my enjoyment in doing things is improving my past performance.

Mastery

1. I would rather do something at which I feel confident and relaxed than something which is challenging and difficult.
2. When a group I belong to plans an activity, I would rather direct it myself than just help outland have someone else organize it.
3. I would rather learn easy fun games than difficult thought games.
4. If I am not good at something, I would rather keep struggling to master it than move on to something I may be good at.
5. Once I undertake a task, I persist.
6. I prefer to work in situations that require a high level of skill.
7. I more often attempt tasks that I am not sure I can do than tasks that I believe I can do.
8. I like to be busy all the time.

Competitiveness

1. I enjoy working in situations involving competition with others.
2. It is important to me to perform better than others on a task.
3. I feel that winning is important in both work and games.
4. It annoys me when other people perform better than I do.
5. I try harder when I'm in competition with other people.

*Note:* Each item is accompanied by a 5-point rating scale ranging from "Strongly agree" to "Strongly disagree."

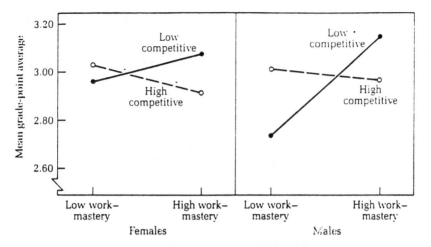

**FIGURE 11-3.** Mean grade-point averages in Low Competitive and High Competitive male and female undergraduate students. Work and Mastery are put together on the same horizontal axis because the effect of competitiveness is the same whether Low or High Work or How or High Mastery are compared. (From ACHIEVEMENT AND ACHIEVEMENT MOTIVES by J. T. Spence and R. L. Helmreich. Copyright ©1983 by W. H. Freeman and Company. Used by permission.)

## Attribution and Achievement

How do success and failure affect people's achievement motivation? Some people respond to failure by trying harder, others give up. One reason for such differences is that people may differ in what they see as the *causes* for success and failure. People who attribute failure to bad luck may respond differently in the future than do people who attribute failure to their own stupidity. The *attributional approach* to achievement motivation is concerned with just such questions. In chapters 2 and 9 are applications of attribution theory to emotion and depression. Here we look at attribution theory in the context of achievement.

*Nature of attribution theory.* Attribution theory is concerned with (1) the *causes* people find for their own behavior (or that of others) and (2) the *effects* of such attributions on emotion, motivation, and subsequent behaviors. The search for causal attributions is a cognitive process. We shall consider attribution theory in terms of *expectancy theory,* much like Rotter's (1954) approach, looking at four questions:

1. What do we mean by attribution?
2. Why do we make attributions?
3. How do we make attributions?
4. What are the effects of attributions on achievement-related motives, emotions, and behaviors?

*What do we mean by attribution?* Ellen notices that she feels tense and uncomfortable when Joyce is around. Ellen decides this is due to Joyce and hence attributes her discomfort to Joyce; she concludes that Joyce is the cause of her discomfort. *An attribution is an inference about causes.* We infer causes from events that we observe, including observations of our own feelings and behavior. We look for explanations of events (causes) by seeking *consistencies* in observations. Ellen perceived a consistency between Joyce's presence and her own feeling of discomfort, and thereby inferred that Joyce was the cause.

We relate attributions to expectancies as follows: An expectancy is a belief that one thing *will* follow from another; an attribution is a belief that one thing *has* followed from another. Thus:

Expectancy

Event A  ----------------------------------------------------------------- > > Event B

Attribution

Event A   < < ----------------------------------------------------------------- Event B

Expectancies and attributions are both inferences about relationships between events. Such events may be situations, behaviors, thoughts, or feelings. Expectancies and attributions both refer to correlations between events, but depending on our time frame we sometimes speak of expectancies and sometimes of attributions. Ellen will *expect* to feel uncomfortable if Joyce were present, and will *attribute* her discomfort to Joyce if Joyce is present.

Quantitatively, we may express expectancies and attributions as correlations. Expectancies can vary from $-1.00$ to $+1.00$. We may expect that Event B *will* follow from Event A (positive correlation), is unrelated to Event A (zero correlation), or will *not* follow from Event A (negative correlation). The strength of our expectation or belief is indicated by the size of the correlation.[2]

*Why do we make attributions?* Kelley (1967) suggested that people are motivated to obtain a *cognitive mastery* of the "causal structures" in their environment. They want to understand how their environment works. This is in line with one theory of rewards discussed in chapter 6, the idea that information is rewarding. Information about the environment is also tension reducing if we are in a situation where we do not know what to expect. The development of attributions fits readily into the information theory of reinforcement, or with a "need for cognition."

---

[2]The concept of dependent probability, which has the same absolute range of numbers (0 to 1.00) as correlation, expresses the same idea. To say that the probability of Event B following Event A is .50 is equivalent to saying there is a positive, but not perfect, correlation between the two events.

*How we make attributions: Covariation.* If an event occurs just one time, it is difficult to assign an unambiguous cause to that event. We cannot derive a reliable correlation between a single event and preceding events. In fact, however, people do jump to hasty conclusions with limited information, believing they know the cause of a one-time event. But more generally we infer causes when we have seen similar events occur consistently in similar circumstances. A football player who slips may attribute his "clumsiness" to wet ground because he knows from previous experiences that when the ground is wet he is more likely to slip.

We might also relate *several* possible causes with a particular event, technically known as *multiple correlation*. Any event or behavior is likely to have several events preceding the event in question. Our football player might be on wet ground, might be tired at the end of the game, might be running a play that happens to require a particularly difficult cut, and so on. What we are typically looking for is the most likely cause for a particular event. Three criteria are often imposed in order to define causation (Shaughnessy & Zeckmeister, 1985). First, there is *covariation* (correlation) between two events, Event B occurs following Event A, but not otherwise. Second, Event A *precedes* Event B. Third, other possible causes are *ruled out*. Given the difficulties of determining the causes of behaviors and emotions under controlled laboratory conditions, it is hardly surprising that people would have difficulty making accurate causal attributions in everyday life. What people respond to, however, is what they *perceive* to be causes, whether or not accurate in reality.

The discovery of a correlation, or a cause, between two events may be sought and rewarding in a motivational sense, but once achieved, an attribution may serve only as knowledge by which we guide our behavior. The attribution by itself does not necessarily motivate us to do things (Bem, 1972). We shall hereafter assume that, once achieved, attributions are informational cues which affect our emotions, motives, and behaviors. Before going on to the question of the effect of attributions, we need to look at some of the *kinds* of attributions which may be made.

**Locus of control.**   We saw in the discussion of learned helplessness that organisms without control over events may "give up" and not do anything in situations where they could actually be effective. Turned around, we can relate this to such concepts as *mastery, power,* and *competence.* Alfred Adler, once a follower of Freud, broke away from the master because he (Adler) believed that striving for personal control over one's own destiny was the most important form of motivation, not sex or aggression. A person without such a feeling of control had an *inferiority complex* and might overcompensate in his or her attempts to gain control. DeCharms (1968) described this in terms of *origins* and *pawns.* Some individuals feel they originate their own activities and are responsible for their own rewards and punishments. Others feel that, like chess pawns, they have little freedom of movement and that the freedom they do have is at the service of more powerful outside sources. These are subjective interpretations, however, and often depend on specific circumstances. In some situations we feel competent, and in other situations we feel helpless.

***Weiner's attributional theory of achievement.***    Weiner (1985) has presented the most detailed attributional theory of achievement motivation and emotion. This theory deals with the perceived causes of success and failure, the characteristics of causal thinking, and subsequent emotional experiences in relation to achievement behaviors.

*Perceived causes of success and failure.* There is a large number of *possible* causes for any specific success or failure. A relatively small number of causes appear repeatedly in relation to many situations, however. These may be *categorized* as follows:

> *Internal versus External.* A person may attribute success to himself, such as "I have a lot of ability and work hard." There is a common bias to attribute success to oneself ("I am clever"), but to attribute failure to outside factors ("The exam was too hard"). There is a phenomenon called the *fundamental attribution error,* which is the tendency to explain other people's actions in terms of internal causes and to explain one's own actions in terms of external causes. For example, "*He* fell down because he is clumsy" but "*I* fell down because the grass is slippery."
>
> *Stable versus Unstable.* A person might attribute success to ability (which is a relatively enduring characteristic) or to effort (which may be more fluctuating). Commonly ascribed stable and unstable external causes are *task difficulty* (stable) and *chance* (unstable). For example, "This is a very hard course" (task difficulty) or "I just didn't study the right things" (chance).
>
> *Controllable versus Uncontrollable.* Lack of trying and illness are both internal and unstable causes for failure, but there is an obvious difference between them. The former is controllable, but the latter is not. I might decide to try harder and overcome failure, but I cannot decide to overcome the flu. Effort is more controllable than illness.

Other, more specific attributions can be found for particular situations, but the above categories cut across considerable research.[3] In addition, detailed statistical analyses of the causes given by people to account for their actions have indicated that these categories are those used by real people, and are not just figments of attribution theorists' imaginations. Table 11-4 summarizes these attributions, with examples.

Given the above *structure* of causal relations, Weiner turns to the *dynamics* of perceived causality in terms of *expectancies* and *values*. Investiga-

---

[3]Weiner (1985) specifically excludes the specific-global dimension of attribution which Abramson et al. (1978) used in the attributional theory of learned helplessness. Weiner says (p. 554): "A general-specific property has not emerged in a single empirical investigation."

**TABLE 11–4   Summary of Causal Attribution Categories, Applied to Tennis**

|  | S = "I won because . . ." STABLE | F = I lost because . . ." UNSTABLE |
|---|---|---|
| | **CONTROLLABLE** | |
| *Internal* | Experience | Effort |
| | S: I'm well coached | S: I tried very hard |
| | F: I'm poorly coached | F: I didn't concentrate |
| *External* | Skill of others | Effort of others |
| | S: My opponent did not have lessons | S: My opponent didn't try |
| | F: My opponent had good coaching | F: My opponent really worked hard |
| | **UNCONTROLLABLE** | |
| *Internal* | Ability | Fatigue, mood, illness |
| | S: I'm a natural athlete | S: I really felt good |
| | F: I'm uncoordinated | F: I was too tired |
| *External* | Task Difficulty | Luck |
| | S: My opponents are poor | S: My serves went in |
| | F: Tennis is too hard | F: Line calls were bad |

tions of a number of different phenomena show how expectancies change according to prior successes or failures. In *level of aspiration* research, as we have seen, a *typical* change is that subjects will raise their standards for expected success after they have experienced success. Conversely, they lower their standards after failure (Lewin, Dembo, Festinger, & Sears, 1944). Research with gambling-type tasks, where nothing but chance is involved, shows what is called the *gambler's fallacy.* If a subject correctly calls "heads" in a 50:50 situation, he expects that tails is the more likely outcome on the next toss, even though the situation is still 50:50. On the other hand, after a brief run of luck, gamblers may believe they are on a hot streak and keep making the same bet. Weiner (1985) argues that the expectancy of success depends on the *stability* of the perceived cause of success. If a cause is perceived as stable, say ability to do a task well, then expectancy of success is greater than if the cause of success is perceived as unstable (good luck).

The next step in Weiner's theory is to examine emotional reactions to success and failure. In Tolman's theory of behavior (chapter 6), the tendency to engage in a particular behavior is jointly determined by the *expectancy* of achieving a particular goal and by the *incentive value* of the goal. Similarly, in Atkinson's theory, the tendency to engage in achievement activities is the product of the probability of success and the incentive value of success. Both of these approaches represent a class of theories known collectively as *expectancy-value theories.* The incentive value of a goal is considered in terms of what it *means* to a person, not just its "objective" value. For example, a person may spend hundreds of dollars on golfing equipment and lessons for the sake of winning a trophy worth $20. The importance of the trophy is emotional, not monetary.

Weiner then argues that each specific causal attribution has a *specific emotional consequence*, in addition to a more general positive or negative affective consequence. Future behaviors are then determined by the expectancy of a certain outcome and the specific emotional consequence of that outcome. An expected outcome might be *good* or *bad*, in general terms, but involve *pride* or *shame* in more specific terms. The exact relationship between such specific emotions and future behavior remains to be determined.

Attributions for success and failure are of interest, of course, to the extent that they will predict future achievement *behaviors*. There is evidence that particular attributions are related to need achievement scores. For example, Meyer (1973 cited in McClelland, 1985) found that high need for achievement subjects who performed better than they expected of themselves, attributed their performance to their own ability. Low need for achievement subjects, on the other hand, attributed unexpectedly good performance to something *outside* themselves and not to their own ability. Heckhausen (1975) reported that even though subjects high in need for achievement attributed failure to their own lack of effort, they did *not* subsequently show increased effort in another task. Thus, even though they had high need for achievement and believed that they had failed because they had not tried hard enough, they did not try harder on a subsequent task. Even though the attribution was as expected theoretically, the attribution did not relate to subsequent behavior. The most general conclusion which can be drawn about attributions and achievement, says McClelland (1985) is that high need for achievement subjects tend to attribute success to ability and failure to lack of effort, whereas subjects low in need for achievement tend to attribute failure to lack of ability. McClelland does *not* consider it to be empirically demonstrated that attributions for past performance will predict future achievement behavior very well.

### Is Control Always Sought?

One might conclude from the above discussion that control is always desirable and sought, but this is not necessarily so. Indeed, if a person does not care about having control, or cares but little, then uncontrollability should pose no threat and control might even be aversive and avoided. The first step in getting at such questions is to *measure* desire for control.

Burger and Cooper (1979) developed a *Desirability of Control Scale*, consisting of twenty items, such as "I try to avoid situations where someone else tells me what to do." The scale does not correlate with Rotter's locus of control scale, and apparently taps a characteristic different than perceived locus of control. Research with the scale has provided interesting results. For example, males generally have higher scores than females, which fits much data indicating that males are generally more aggressive and assertive than females. Burger and Cooper (1979) also showed that people with high desire for control are also more likely in ambiguous situations to perceive that they actually do have control. In a gambling game, for example, subjects who were given the *illusion of control* by letting them believe that their own actions determined the outcome of a random bet, actually began to bet higher stakes. Low desire-for-control subjects did not do this. A variety of subsequent experiments have extended such results, generally indicating differences between people high and low in desire of control. The implications of this line of research are very important for our understanding of control and related concepts (Burger, 1989).

## COMPETENCE AND POWER

The concepts of achievement motivation and control lead readily into the related topics of personal competence, as found in the concepts of *self-efficacy* and *power*.

### Self-Efficacy

Robert White (1957) argued that striving for *competence* is a major motive and that success produces feelings of *effectance*. Bandura (1977, 1982) proposed the concept of *self-efficacy*, which is the expectation that one can perform any particular action successfully. This is called an efficacy expectation, and people with greater perceived self-efficacy actually do perform better on many kinds of tasks. Efficacy is not just a matter of "will power," or determination to try harder, efficacy is established through successful experience. Bandura (1977) lists the following principles.

1. *Self-efficacy increases with personal accomplishment.* Perceived efficacy is greater if we have more accomplishments, and efficacy expectations generalize across situations. This is important because it means that efficacy training is possible.
2. *Self-efficacy can increase or decrease if we see others similar to ourselves succeeding or failing at a task.* This is important with regard to modeling as a method of teaching, suggesting that a model similar to the subject be used, such as one child modeling for another. If a person does try to imitate a model, the degree of perceived success is determined by the actual degree of success.
3. We can be *persuaded* that we are capable of coping with a difficult situation, but this breaks down if we actually fail in such situations. Persuasion may serve to get a person to try some activity, but must be followed by perceived success at the actual task.
4. *Emotional arousal can affect our feeling of self-efficacy.* If we are upset or overly anxious about some activity, such as giving a speech, we do not perceive our self-efficacy as high as when we are in a better mood. We may learn to use our emotion as a cue for lower self-efficacy, as in "I just cannot cope today," based on some particular emotional experience.

## Power

When we think of struggles between mighty nations, such as the United States and the Soviet Union, we usually think of "power politics." Who is going to dominate whom? When we think of politicians fighting for office, or business people fighting for control of an organization, we think of "power struggles." But striving for power, which we can think of as exerting control over other people, can be exercised in two-person groups as well as entire nations. Power struggles within and between families are major themes of novels and prime-time soap operas. Here we look at a few things psychologists have found in the study of power motivation in ordinary, everyday people.

*Measurement of power motivation.*    The most standard way to measure power motivation is similar to the scoring of imaginative stories for achievement. Winter (1973) developed a TAT scoring system for three categories of power imagery: (1) strong vigorous action that expresses power; (2) actions that arouse strong emotion in others; and (3) explicit concerns about reputation or position. Test-retest reliability is about the same as that obtained with scoring for achievement imagery (r = .45).

*Energizing effects of power motivation.*    It is assumed that, like achievement, power is a motive that has to be "engaged" by circumstances. Power is a latent motive until aroused. Steele (1977) examined the arousal of power motivation by having subjects write TAT stories after listening to tape recordings of either famous inspirational speeches or travelogues. Power scores were significantly higher after the inspirational speeches than before the speeches. (See also McClelland, 1985, p. 272.) Steele also obtained two different measures of arousal, a self-report of perceived arousal (Thayer, 1967), and amount of adrenaline in the urine. Both measures were significantly higher after the inspirational speeches than after the travelogue, with power scores and urinary adrenaline increase correlating +.71. This is an especially interesting finding because it seems to rule out experimenter demand effects. A person might report feeling more aroused after an inspirational speech because he thinks that he should be aroused under such circumstances, but it would seem more difficult to increase urinary adrenaline output on demand. Furthermore, adrenaline output was not correlated with achievement motivation scores obtained from the same subjects, which indicates that the speeches selectively aroused power motivation, not just any kind of motivation.

*Selective effects of power motivation.*    Power motivation may selectively tune us into power-related cues in the environment. McAdams and McClelland (1983) had subjects high and low in need for power listen to a tape recording of someone telling a story about a picture. The story had 15 power-related facts, 15 neutral facts, and 15 facts related to intimacy. Subjects high in need for power recalled a significantly greater proportion of power-related facts than neutral facts. Similarly, subjects high in need for power learned power-related stimulus materials faster than subjects low in need for power (McClelland, Davidson, Saron, & Floor, 1980).

*Power and aggressive behavior.*   Let us distinguish between *personal power* and *social power*. Personal power is considered to be more "primitive" than social power, and characterized by dominance over others. Social power is more subtle and has the aim of benefiting others. Persons high in these kinds of power might seek political office, but for the different reasons related to their kinds of power need—controlling or benefiting.

A high need for personal power is related to competitiveness and aggression. Men high in need for personal power have been found to do more fighting, drinking, gambling, and speeding than men low in need for personal power (McClelland, 1985). This is not true for women, however, possibly because women are taught to suppress aggressive tendencies more so than men. Such apparent socialization differences have also been found with men, however. Working-class men with high need for power have been found to be more aggressive than middle-class men with equivalent levels of power motivation. Middle-class men presumably have learned to suppress aggressive tendencies more than lower-class men.

*Power and other behaviors.*   People high in need for power act in such ways as to appear powerful. For example, they collect such symbols of power as *prestige possessions,* including certain types of cars and other material possessions (Winter, 1973). They are more likely to surround themselves with lesser known people who can be led, are more willing to take risks, and drink more. Power scores have actually been found to change with drinking, but the nature of the change depends on the type of power involved. Individuals high in personal power show progressively higher power scores with increased drinking. Individuals high in social power, on the other hand, show a decline in need-for-power scores when they drink heavily (Figure 11-4; McClelland, Davis, Kalin, & Wanner, 1971). Women, however, appear to respond differently to alcohol, feeling more friendly after drinking rather than more powerful (McClelland, 1985, p. 299).

Need for power may also express itself in what appear to be unusual occupational choices. For example, students high in need for power were most interested in teaching, psychology, ministry, business, and international diplomacy. Students low in need for power were more interested in government and politics, medicine, law, creative arts, and architecture. These seem like strange occupational preferences in relation to power, but when we think about it, there is a pattern. Teachers, psychologists, and ministers, for example, have occupations in which they normally exert considerable control over

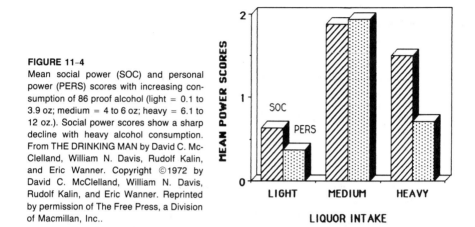

others in their day-to-day work. Politics, on the other hand, often does require much bargaining and compromise in order to get things done.

## SUMMARY

1. *Need for achievement* (n Ach) is defined as a desire or tendency "to overcome obstacles, to exercise power, to strive to do something difficult as well and as quickly as possible." Achievement need is commonly inferred from *achievement themes* in stories told by individuals about pictures. McClelland argued that achievement need develops out of previously rewarded achievement behavior, and the positive affect associated with achievement.

2. A more mathematical theory developed by Atkinson says that the tendency to engage in achievement behaviors (Ts) is the product of the motive for success (Ms = achievement need), the probability of success (Ps), and the incentive value of success (Is). Ps and Is are inversely related: Is = 1 − Ps. There is also a tendency to avoid failure (Taf), based on a fear of failure, thought to develop out of negative experiences in achievement situations. Ts and Taf are additive, with behavioral predictions based on which one is greater. Subsequent additions to the theory have been *external goals, future goals,* and sequential subgoals (called *paths*).

3. Problems with classic achievement theory have included questions of gender differences, the reliability of measures of achievement need, consistency of empirical results, and whether need achievement is a motivational variable at all.

4. Considerable evidence indicates that achievement is not a single dimension. Research by Spence and Helmreich has used the Work and Family Orientation Questionnaire (WOFO), which has achievement dimensions of *mastery, completion, and competitiveness.* A consistent pattern of results is that people high in competitiveness often do not perform as well as people who are less competitive.

5. *Attributional* approaches to achievement have tried to take individual differences in achievement motivation into account in terms of the attributions

people give for success or failure. Attributions are *explanations* people give for events.

6.  In Weiner's attributional theory there are three dimensions of attributions: (1) *internal versus external locus of control*, (2) *stable versus unstable factors*, and (3) *controllable versus uncontrollable factors*. It is assumed that each specific causal attribution for success or failure has particular emotional consequences, which in turn influence future achievement-oriented behaviors. Except for generally positive and negative emotional responses to success and failure, however, the relationship between specific emotions and achievement behaviors is speculative.

7.  There are individual differences in *desire for control*. People low in desire for control are not as affected by perceived loss of control as are people high in desire for control. Conversely, the "good effects" which accrue to people with control may not be so perceived by people with low desire for control.

8.  Bandura's theory of *self-efficacy* says that people who believe that their behavior will be more effective also perform more effectively. There are several ways to enhance self-efficacy, but *personal accomplishment* is the most powerful and enduring.

9.  *Power motivation* is defined as the desire to have control over others. It is measured by scoring imaginative stories for power imagery relating to strong, vigorous action, actions which arouse strong emotion in others and which demonstrate explicit concerns about reputation or position.

10. People high in need for power show increased internal arousal under conditions of arousal of the need. The degree of arousal is correlated with the level of power need. People with high need for power also tend to respond more selectively to environmental cues related to power, such as remembering power-related stimuli better.

11. *Personal power* is distinguished from *social power*, which is more altruistic. Men high in personal power tend to be aggressive and competitive, but women high in personal power are not. Socialization partly seems to determine such behaviors, since middle-class men are less aggressive than lower-class men with equal power scores.

# 12

# Interpersonal Attraction and Altruism

Across the spectrum of animal life, different species vary markedly in gregariousness. Ants and bees are almost invariably in large groups, but bears live a far more solitary existence. Some species of monkeys live in tribes, while individuals of other monkey species are nearly isolates. Humans are variable but on the whole are relatively social. The question for this chapter is, What attracts humans to each other?

We need to distinguish three different aspects of attraction. First, why do people *affiliate* with each other? People may affiliate for many reasons, not necessarily related to liking or loving. "Politics makes strange bedfellows" expresses directly the point that we may affiliate politically with people whom we might otherwise despise. Hopefully, we do affiliate with people we like or love, but liking and loving are not defining characteristics of affiliation. Liking and loving must also be distinguished. Such dictionary statements as "liking is a *fondness* for someone else" and that "loving involves *affection* or *passion*" point up a difference, but there is still disagreement about the similarities and differences between liking and loving. Is loving just a lot of liking, or are they two different processes? In this chapter we explore some of the *determinants* of affiliation, liking, and loving and describe how some *theories* account for these.

## AFFILIATION

### Measurement of Need for Affiliation

Individual differences in the *need for affiliation* (n Aff) have often been measured by the same general method for achievement or power. Subjects write fantasy stories about appropriate pictures, and the stories are scored in terms of affiliation themes (Boyatzis, 1973). The first step in using this approach is to show that relevant environmental conditions *arouse* n Aff, as measured with the fantasy scores. The second step is to determine the *validity* of n Aff by showing predictable performance differences between high and low n Aff subjects.

In an early study, Shipley and Veroff (1952) defined n Aff in terms of a need for security. They aroused n Aff in a group of fraternity members by having them rate each other on different personality characteristics, intended to make them think about interpersonal relations. A control group rated food preferences. Both groups then wrote their fantasy stories, in which statements indicating "concern about separation" were considered especially indicative of n Aff. As predicted, the experimental group wrote more such themes. Atkinson, Heyns, and Veroff (1954) used a similar arousal technique, but in their scoring emphasized themes related to seeking social acceptance. Again, the aroused subjects showed more such themes than control subjects. This raises the question whether there are possibly two different kinds of n Aff, *hope of affiliation* and *fear of rejection*, corresponding to *hope of success* and *fear of failure.* Boyatzis (1973) concluded that the TAT scoring procedures do not make the distinction well, and the issue of two different kinds of affiliation *as measured in this manner* is unsettled.

A number of studies provided evidence for the validity of n Aff scoring. In comparison to low n Aff subjects, high n Aff subjects (1) more accurately picked out faces from among briefly exposed stimuli (Atkinson & Walker, 1956); (2) more accurately described other people as those people described themselves, suggesting greater social sensitivity; (3) got better grades in courses taught by teachers judged to be warm and considerate (McKeachie, Lin, Milholland, & Issacson, (1966); and (4) got better grades in cooperatively structured groups than in competitively structured groups.

A further interesting finding is that there seems to be a *curvilinear* relationship between n Aff and performance. For example, persons with *moderate* levels of n Aff seem to be more effective managers. Those with low n Aff are too little concerned with interpersonal relationships to be effective, and those with high n Aff may let their concern for others interfere with getting the job done (Boyatzis, 1973). Research on leadership generally indicates the importance of a balance between "concern for people" and "concern for production," which may be best achieved by a person with a medium level n Aff.

### Determinants of Affiliation

*Biological factors.*    In evolutionary terms, the role of any individual is to perpetuate himself or herself by contributing to the gene pool of the species. The individual becomes "immortal" by putting a part of himself or herself into the gene pool. A rather startling fact is that we are each the offspring of millions of years of "perfect parentage," else we would not be here at all. We are the direct descendants of an unbroken line of parents who were attracted to each other at least long enough to mate. Sociobiology is "the application of evolutionary biology to the social behavior of animals, including *homo sapiens*" (Barash, 1978, p. 2). One particular area of sociobiological concern, *attachment behavior,* is especially relevant here.

Prolonged social isolation so frequently leads to loneliness and depression that these consequences often seem inevitable, and therefore biologically based. John Bowlby (1969) suggested that such *attachment behaviors* as clinging to the mother or acting distressed when the mother departs, are biologically based. According to Cairns (1979), however, the degree of the child's attachment at one age is not a good predictor of degree of attachment for the same child just a few months later. This suggests that attachment behaviors have a strong learning component. Species differences among monkeys are found for attachment behaviors, but such cross-species comparisons may not be relevant to individual differences *within the same species,* as with humans.

*Fear and anxiety.*   When we feel afraid we often want to be with some-one who might calm our fears. Even among laboratory rats the presence of another animal reduces the fearful behaviors of an animal that has been shocked in an experimental apparatus. One such fearful response is "crouch-ing in the corner," becoming very inactive. A previously shocked animal is more active if another animal is present, and more active yet if the other animal has itself *not* been shocked (Davitz & Mason, 1955). We can think of several ways that the presence of another person might reduce our respon-siveness to aversive situations. First, another person might serve as a "calm model," which the fearful person can imitate. Second, the companion may be a distraction, taking attention away from the fearful situation. Third, just the mere presence of another person might be fear-reducing, even if the other person does nothing (Epley, 1974).

Schachter (1959) studied fear and affiliation by threatening subjects with either strong or weak electric shock, and then giving them the choice of waiting for their punishment alone or with someone else. The strong-shock subjects did prefer to be with someone else, but it was not specifically demonstrated that this was fear-reducing. Wrightsman (1960), however, did report that his subjects were less afraid when waiting with someone else in a threatening situation. It has also been predicted, according to Hull's theory (chapter 3), that the presence of others should reduce *drive* (anxiety) and thereby facilitate performance on complex tasks and impair performance on simple tasks. The results have been ambiguous (Epley, 1974). This is not really surprising, however, since we have also seen that the presence of others may *increase* drive, the *social facilitation* effect (Zajonc, 1965). Harrison (1976) concluded that people might not want to affiliate in anxiety-arousing situa-tions if the presence of other people would lower their self-esteem. For example, an adult might not want others to watch him or her perform such an embarrassing act as drinking from a baby bottle. Affiliation and anxiety then may depend on the reasons for being anxious, not just the fact of being anxious.

*Other people as sources of assistance, stimulation, information, or self-evaluation.*

(1) We often need *assistance* from other people to achieve our goals and affiliate with others because of this need. The assistance that they give us may reinforce and maintain our affiliative behavior over long periods of time.

(2) Earlier we discussed the importance of *stimulus variation* as a source of arousal for optimal performance. What in fact is more variable, more full of surprises, or more stimulating than other people? Interesting people attract more friends or followers than boring people. There appears to be an optimal level of stimulation here also; a given person may be too stimulating for some people, too dull for others, and just right for somebody else.

(3) We have also seen that behavior is reinforced by new *information*. We read newspapers to get information, but other people also provide information or reduce uncertainty for us so we associate with them. Information may be important (world news) or trivial (gossip), but it is reinforcing and sought.

(4) We all need to evaluate ourselves, our opinions, our abilities, or our work from time to time. Lacking objective standards (such as for appearance), we often compare ourselves with other people. According to Festinger (1954) we make *social comparisons*, requiring affiliation, when we are uncertain about ourselves. We tend to seek normative information to judge ourselves from someone who is *similar* to us (in age, background, interest, experience, etc.) rather than someone who is very dissimilar. We seek information about the social norms which apply to us. Mills and Mintz (1972) used an interesting extension of cognitive arousal theory in connection with this aspect of affiliation. Subjects given caffeine, but misinformed about its arousing effects, chose more often to affiliate with other subjects than did subjects *not* given caffeine (not aroused) or subjects who were told about the caffeine effects (correctly understood what was happening to them). Presumably the misinformed subjects were uncertain about the source of their arousal and searched for the cause of the arousal by associating with other subjects in the same situation, whom they thought could help them evaluate their own condition.

*Freedom from internal constraints.*    Groups frequently restrain their members from doing certain things, but sometimes have just the opposite effect, reinforcing *uninhibited* behavior. Nude encounter groups and lynch mobs have in common that both support behaviors not usually acceptable. If an individual at a particular time is seeking freedom from self-imposed or typical group-imposed constraints, he or she may choose to affiliate with others even in so innocuous a situation as a party where the restraints can temporarily be discarded. We may become relatively anonymous and free of responsibility. Such *deindividuation* may temporarily be enjoyable, but Zimbardo (1969) suggests that after awhile *reindividuation* may become desirable; we want recognition by others.

## LIKING AND LOVING

### Different Views of Liking and Loving

The importance of interpersonal attraction in everyday matters can hardly be overstated. Walster and Walster (1976) put the situation bluntly: "A person who is liked by his comrades will amass enormous benefits; a person who is hated is in trouble" (p. 279). Not until the last twenty-five years, however, have psychological researchers done serious research on the topics of liking and loving, perhaps because the topic was considered too sensitive. Fortunately, there is now accumulating a respectable body of research and theory on interpersonal attraction. Let us look at some of the factors involved in attraction, and then get at the knottier problem of accounting theoretically for liking and loving.

### Determinants of Attraction

*Proximity.*    As the song says, "How can I ignore/the boy next door?" We are indeed more likely to become friends with people who are physically close to us. In dormitories, for example, people who are thrown together by the chance of alphabetical grouping are more likely to become friends with each other than with people who live further away in the dormitory (e.g., Newcomb, 1961; Priest & Sawyer, 1967; Segal, 1974). In the Segal study, for example, there was a very high correlation (.90) between liking a person and how close in the alphabet that person's name was to the rater's name. In purely practical terms, it takes less effort to interact and become friendly with people close by.

*Familiarity.*    The effects of familiarity are partly explained by the fact that when individuals live or work close to each other they can become more familiar with each other. We tend to like persons, objects, or even strange words in a foreign language better the more we have been exposed to them. Zajonc (1968) has given many examples of this *mere exposure effect*. For example, the "goodness" ratings of either fake Chinese characters or non-sense syllables increase regularly after zero, one, two, five, ten, and twenty-five exposures to these stimuli.

The mere exposure effect seems to run contrary to the adage that "familiarity breeds contempt." Indeed, we can all think of people whom we liked less after we got to know them better, but factors other than mere exposure are involved. For example, Burgess and Sales (1976) obtained the mere exposure effect with subjects who felt good about the overall experimental context, but not with subjects who disliked the experimental situation. It is not clear why this should be so, but one possibility is that when we are in a positive mood we tend to consider things generally better than if we are in a bad mood (see chapter 2). On a longer-term basis, other factors, such as the behavior of the other person we are thrown together with, affect liking. If another person's behavior were agreeable, we would expect increased liking with increased exposure, but we would expect disliking if the person were disagreeable. Stang (1974) suggested that simple exposure will increase liking (a) with individuals who are not very familiar to each other, (b) when exposure is moderate (so that boredom does not develop), and (c) when there is also exposure to a number of individuals for comparison.

*Physical attractiveness.*     Physical appearance is one of the most power-ful factors in interpersonal attraction. Research is relatively new, however, perhaps because physical attractiveness is such an "undemocratic" variable that psychologists have been reluctant to deal with it (Aronson, 1969). Physi-cal attractiveness draws preferential treatment from infancy through old age (Brehm, 1985). Attractive children are treated better in school; attractive adults are reprimanded less severely for transgressions and also receive more assistance and cooperation than less-attractive people. There are several possible explanations for such preferential treatment of attractive persons, however.

First, Brehm (1985) suggests that there is an *attractiveness stereotype,* an implicit personality theory wherein attractive people are assumed to have other virtues in addition to their appearance. Preferential treatment is thus perceived as their due. Second, attractive people *are* in fact more self-confident and have better mental health. This may result from being treated better by others and having more opportunity to be reinforced for social skills. Third, other people may wish to associate with attractive people because such an association enhances one's own self-image. Sigall and Landy (1973) found that a man seated with an attractive woman was evaluated more positively than when he was seated with an unattractive woman. In fact, he actually got negative evaluations when he was seated with the unattractive woman. Attractiveness may also simply be related to sexual arousal. This may be a poor basis for marriage if it is the only source of attraction, but it nevertheless occurs. Fortunately, perhaps, attractiveness seems to be a rela-tively more important factor in dating than in marrying (Stroebe, Insko, Thompson, & Layton, 1971). It is often said that physical attractiveness becomes less important in long-term relations, but Mathes (1975) found that over a series of five dates physical attractiveness was considered increasingly important. Five dates may not really constitute a "long-term" relationship, however.

In one of the early studies of attractiveness, Walster, Aronson, Abrahams, and Rottman (1966) arranged a "computer dance" for freshmen at the University of Minnesota. The actual pair assignment was random, except that women were all assigned taller men. At intermission, the subjects rated their partners on various characteristics, including physical attractiveness. At the original sign-up time, four experimenters also rated the subjects to provide an "objective" rating of attractiveness of each subject. About 10% of the least attractive females were later asked for dates by their partners at the dance, as compared to about a third of the most attractive females. These percentages are not overwhelming, but attractiveness was the best predictor available of who would be asked for a date later. The judges' ratings of attractiveness were not in high agreement, and this would tend to reduce the accuracy of predictions.

Physical attractiveness is a multidimensional variable, facial features being more important to some individuals, body characteristics to others, and so on. This inevitably leads to considerable individual differences in what is considered attractive. In fact, in the Walster et al. study, the attraction rating made by each male subject of his date was a better predictor of later dating than was the combined rating of the judges. Attractiveness is not uniquely a male concern, however, but may be expressed somewhat differently by males and females. Thus, Coombs and Kenkel (1966) found that males rated attractiveness more important *before* having a date with a particular girl. Women, on the other hand, had more complaints about the attractiveness of a date *afterwards*. Women, therefore, do not necessarily consider attractiveness as less important than men, women just express their interest in attractiveness somewhat differently than men do.

It is *not* true, however, that the physically most attractive member of the opposite sex is the one who will be most sought after or who will provide the best relationship. Rather, an important factor called the *matching principle* comes into play.

People tend to be attracted to others with similar physical characteristics, such as height and weight (Berscheid & Walster, 1969). The matching principle may work for somewhat complex reasons, however, A boy might *prefer* an exceptionally attractive girl, but if he is of medium attractiveness himself he might believe that she would not date him. The optimal choice, then, might be to choose a girl of medium attractiveness so that there is a good probability of a successful relationship. This is very similar to achievement theory, where the tendency to choose a particular activity (in this case, asking for a date) depends on the probability of success (Ps) and the incentive value of success (Is). A very attractive date could have a high incentive value, but the probability of success in getting a date with her may be perceived to be very low. Conversely, an unattractive date has a very low incentive value even though the perceived probability of success in getting a date is high. A man should then approach the most attractive woman that *he* could reasonably expect to date *him*.

In a study of the matching principle involving 120 couples with varying degrees of relationship (casual, serious, cohabiting, engaged/married), White (1980) found that couples more similar in attractiveness did stay together longer. There was a greater similarity of attractiveness (r = .63) between the engaged/married pairs than for the casually dating pairs (r = .18). In the casual and serious groups, the greater the dissimilarity, the more likely the couple was to break up during the time of the research (a school year). Part of the break-up was related to the desire of the more attractive member of a pair to have a relationship with someone else.

*Similarity.* We have heard it said that opposites attract, but people are not magnets, and this physical principle receives little support from research on interpersonal attraction. People who are *similar* are more likely to get together. Similarity refers to many different things, however, including attitudes, personality, physical characteristics, and reciprocity of behavior.

Research on *attitudinal similarity* indicates that the greater the percentage of topics on which two people have similar attitudes, the greater the liking (Byrne & Nelson, 1965). According to Schneider (1976), such attitudinal effects are not as strong in real-life situations as in research settings. The purpose of laboratory research, however, is precisely to separate out variables that are weaker in less well controlled situations, so this is not surprising. There are several general qualifications regarding similarity and liking which are worth noting, however (Sherrod, 1982): (1) Physical attractiveness overrides attitudinal similarity, at least for a first date; (2) If the similar individual is unattractive in some way, such as being emotionally disturbed or obnoxious, liking is *decreased*; (3) A *fear of rejection* by similar individuals may direct a person to dissimilar individuals who might be more accepting; and (4) A too-similar person may be rejected because an individual wishes to appear *unique*.

A kind of *personality* factor is found in the *need complementary hypothesis* (Winch, 1958). We might expect that opposites would attract because they fulfill the deficiencies of each other, but as noted above there is little support for this. For example, both dominant and submissive people prefer more dominant individuals as friends (Palmer & Byrne, 1970) and introverts and extraverts both prefer extraverts (Hendrick & Brown, 1971).

*Reciprocity.*     Finally, we are more prone to like others if we think they like us, which is the *reciprocity* principle (Peplau, 1982). Salespeople use this principle in face-to-face contacts, and large companies use it on a mass advertising basis ("Fly the friendly skies of United"). In laboratory discussion groups, subjects with low self-esteem are more prone to like the group if they believe the group likes them (Dittes, 1959). Subjects with high self-esteem, however, were less likely to be swayed by how they thought the group felt. A person can go too far in trying to attract others by expressing liking for them, however. Such *ingratiation* may work if it is perceived as sincere but have just the opposite effect, producing dislike, if perceived as a phony attempt to gain some advantage (Jones, 1964). What is perceived as "overdoing" praise or liking may depend very much on who is receiving the flattery, however. People starved for attention or praise may believe almost anything that will enhance their self-image, no matter how ingratiating or insincere.

### Theories of Liking and Loving

Let us now turn to theories of liking and loving which attempt to account for interpersonal attraction. Sternberg (1987) divides these into theories which consider liking and loving to be: (1) on a *quantitative continuum*, where loving is the equivalent of a lot of liking, (2) where loving and liking are *qualitatively* different, (3) where liking and loving are *overlapping sets,* with some similarities and some differences, and (4) where liking is a *subset* of loving, having some but not all the features of loving.

*Liking and loving as quantitative differences in level of attraction.*     According to *reinforcement theory,* John likes Mary if John experiences reward in the presence of Mary. Mary becomes a *secondary reinforcer* for John (Lott & Lott, 1974). Attraction can even develop accidentally if a particular person just happens to be present when rewards are received. In one study, for example, children came to like their *classmates* more if they were systematically rewarded by their teacher for various activities not directly related to their classmates. Their classmates just happened to be there (Lott & Lott, 1968). The opposite also happens; the messenger who delivers the bad news is seldom popular. Clore and Byrne (1974) suggested that a rewarding experience produces a positive emotional response which becomes attached to someone present at the time. This was related to Byrne's research on attraction and attitudinal similarity. The more similar the attitudes of two people the more they are reinforced by each other, hence the greater their attraction. A wide range of things may be reinforcing, including *intrinsic characteristics* of the other person (such as attractiveness, sense of humor, or intelligence) and *behaviors* of the other person (such as giving attention or other favors).

Social *exchange theory* (Rubin, 1973) uses terminology borrowed from the marketplace. As the name implies, exchange theory deals with mutually rewarding behaviors between people. Associating with another person involves *benefits* and *costs.* Positive attraction occurs when the anticipated benefits (rewards) are greater than the costs. Avoidance occurs when the costs exceed the benefits. A man and a woman may each have socially desirable qualities they can "trade off" to each other. A man gains more prestige by being seen with an attractive woman than an unattractive one, and attractive women are more likely to date or marry men of higher social status than their own. A physically less-attractive man can bring money, prestige, and power to the interpersonal bargaining table, as well as intellect, wit, and charm. Political power seems to be a universal bargaining commodity, as is the prestige of rock stars and athletes which can be traded for sexual favors.

*Equity theory* is a variation of social exchange theory. The distinguishing characteristic of equity theory is that a person in a relationship with someone else compares his or her *personal* ratio of costs to benefits with those of some *reference.* The standard terminology of equity theory is in term of inputs and outputs, where *input* (I) = *costs,* and *output* (O) = *benefits.* There are then three general possibilities for ratios:

1. Ip/Op = Ir/Or. In this case, the ratio of I/O for the person (p) in question is the *same* as that for the reference (r). Person p perceives there is *equity* between his or her inputs and outputs and those of the reference. The reference used may specifically be the other person in the relationship, some past relationship, or some abstract standard. When there is equity, there is satisfaction with the relationship. The major problem that arises, or course, is when there is *inequity*, as in the second case.

2. Ip/Op > Ir/Or. If person p perceives that he or she puts more into the relationship than the reference, but gets less out of it, there is a strain and the person will try to restore equity. Equity is a matter of perception, as well as reality, so it is important to change perceived equity. For example, if a woman feels that a man does not spend enough time with her, he may try to persuade her that his time is being used (such as working) to their mutual long-term benefit.

3. Ip/Op < Ir/Or. What happens in a relationship if a person feels that he or she is getting *more* than is equitable out of a relationship? Equity may be restored by putting more into the relationship, or by getting the other person to put *less* into the relationship.

These are just a few of the many predictions of equity theory, and the theory has received rather good support in research (e.g., Walster, Walster, & Berscheid, 1978).

*Cognitive consistency theory* (e.g., Festinger, 1957; Heider, 1958; Newcomb, 1968) can be applied to interpersonal attraction just as it is applied to interpersonal relationships of other kinds, as we saw in chapter 10 (Cognitive Consistency). Dissonance theory, for example, predicts that how we treat someone should affect our liking of them. If we treat an innocent person cruelly for no good reason, this should produce some dissonance between our behavior and our concept of ourself as a kind and honorable person. Paradoxically, then, we can develop a negative attitude toward someone whom we have "done wrong" because this change in attitude reduces the dissonance produced by the fact that we *have* done them wrong. Davis and Jones (1960) demonstrated this experimentally, but also found that the derogation of someone else did not occur if the subjects knew in advance that they could make amends to the other person (a laboratory assistant to whom they had read falsely negative evaluations). In this case, dissonance presumably did not develop. Even more paradoxically, the nicer we think we are the more we must derogate someone else, because of the greater dissonance. Conversely, we may come to have a more positive attitude toward a neutral person toward whom we have been unusually kind. We might also expect, however, that this positive effect would be less aversive and hence less attitude change could occur. The evidence is in fact weak (e.g., Berscheid & Walster, 1969; Schopler & Compere, 1971).

*Liking and loving as qualitatively different.*     *Clinical theory.* Some theories have always distinguished liking and loving as two different entities. Freud

(1938) looked upon love as a modified (sublimated) form of sexuality. That is, love occurs because sex is repressed. Maslow (1970) distinguished two kinds of love, D-Love and B-Love. D-Love (*deficiency love*) arises from lack of feelings of security and belongingness. B-Love (*being love*) comes from the desire for self-actualization. Other clinical theories have proposed other kinds of love, but in none of them is love generally considered as just a strong form of liking (Sternberg, 1987).

*Cognitive-arousal theory.* In his *Ars Amatoria (The Art of Love)*, a first-century how-to manual for romantic conquest, the Roman poet Ovid provided many helpful hints for would-be lovers. These involved grooming and behavior, as well as the suggestion that a good time to arouse passion in a woman was while watching gladiators fight in the arena. In modern times a football game or hockey match might suffice. A nineteenth-century German psychologist named Adolph Horwicz similarly proposed that any strong emotional arousal could facilitate love. The Ovid-Horwicz effect, until recently, was limited to empirical observation; it seemed to work. We now have cognitive-arousal theory to account for the effect (Walster, 1971; Patterson, 1976; Rubin, 1973).

Cognitive-arousal theory (Schacter & Singer, 1962; see chapter 2 in this book) says that emotional arousal is diffuse until labeled by the person experiencing the arousal. As discussed in chapter 2, exercise-induced arousal could be mistakenly attributed to sexual arousal. Along similar lines, Dutton and Aron (1974) found that a female who gathered information from males just after they crossed a high, swinging bridge was more likely to be contacted later than if she were at the end of a low, stable bridge. The swinging bridge presumably produced greater arousal, which was attributed to the female experimenter. It is also possible that there was a subject selection factor, so in a laboratory experiment Aron and Dutton randomly assigned males to high and low arousal conditions (threat of shock or no threat). Again, a female experimenter was more likely to be contacted later by subjects in the high arousal condition. White, Fishbein, and Rutstein (1981) found that an attractive person was rated as more attractive after two minutes of running in place than after 15 seconds. Similar results were obtained in a second experiment with both pleasant arousal (by a Steve Martin comedy clip) and unpleasant arousal (a grisly murder/mayhem clip). The authors conclude that type of arousal is irrelevant, again lending support to cognitive arousal theory.

Applied to passionate love, then, a person may be aroused for many reasons, but if a member of the opposite sex is present the arousal may be interpreted as love. Sexual arousal itself is readily interpreted as passionate because there are usually specific physiological-anatomical cues, but other sources of arousal (such as mild fear, frustration, excitement of an athletic contest, or exercise) may be labeled as love if a particular person happens along at the right time. Recall, from chapter 2, however, that there are many problems with cognitive-arousal theory, but that the less-sweeping *excitation transfer* theory holds up rather well.

Excitation transfer theory would say that if there is *already* some degree of sexual arousal that this may be *intensified* by additional arousal from an unrelated source. This line of theorizing explains a number of curious phenomena, why a "hard-to-get" person may be more attractive, for example. The apparently unobtainable person produces feelings of frustration, a form of arousal. This arousal may transfer to other feelings and be interpreted as heightened love. Even rejection, or discovering that the object of one's romantic inclination has another partner, may produce an emotional arousal that is interpreted as being even stronger love than existed before. Some people are "turned on" by a certain amount of "danger" in lovemaking (for example, having sex in locations where they might be caught or observed). This makes sense in terms of excitation-transfer theory.

Within the context of *evolutionary theory* we seek principles to account for love which would characterize many species, not just humans. Just as taste and smell influence attraction to food and aid individual (and species) survival, factors which increase interpersonal attraction also increase individual and species survival. Wilson (1981) proposed that love grows out of three instincts: (1) seeking protection from the environment by attachment to parents: (2) protection of infants by parents; and (3) sexual. This combination of presumably inborn features guarantees that attachments of individuals in a species will lead to procreation, infant protection, and species survival. These functions seem very different from those involved in liking.

*Liking and loving as overlapping sets. Rubin's theory of liking and loving.* Rubin (1970) distinguished liking as being based on *affection* and *respect*, whereas loving was said to be based on *attachment, caring,* and *intimacy.* One of the major contributions to this area of research was Rubin's incorporation of these concepts into two operational *measures* of liking and loving. On his scales, each of thirteen items is rated on a scale from "Not at all true" (1) to "Definitely true" (9). The "love scale" has such items as "If I were lonely, my first thought would be to seek (name) out." The "liking scale" has such items as "I have great confidence in (name)'s good judgment." As expected there is some correlation between the two scales (.56 for females and .36 for males), but not high enough to indicate the two scales are measuring exactly the same thing.

The validity of the scales was shown in several ways. The correlation between love scale score and simply *saying* that you are in love with somebody is .61 for women and .50 for men. In addition, loving and liking for one's romantic partner were higher than for one's same-sex friends. Other scales have since been developed (e.g., Lee, 1977; Levinger, Rands, & Talober, 1977; Steffen, McLaney, & Hustedt, 1982; Swensen, 1972) but the most important aspect of them all is the attempt to measure what so often has been considered the unmeasurable.

*Sternberg and Grajek's theory of overlapping bonds.* Sternberg and Grajek (1984) used complex statistical procedures to examine measures of liking and loving for one's lover, mother, father, sibling closest in age, and best friend of the same sex. Subjects were 35 men and 50 women ranging in age from 18 to 70 years. The major findings were that (1) love seemed to consist of three major components, called *intimacy, passion,* and *decision/commitment* (described more fully below) and (2) intimacy was involved in all the kinds of love relationships studied, but passion and decision/commitment varied. The authors concluded that love has a common core of the above elements, but the *experience* of love may differ depending on what other elements, or *bonds,* occur. Thus, the experience of love varies with the presence or absence of emotions other than passion, other thought processes besides decision/commitment, and motives other than love.

**Liking as a Subset of Loving.**     *Cluster theory.* Davis (1985) proposed that liking (friendship) consists of *enjoyment, mutual assistance, spontaneity, acceptance, trust, understanding,* and *confidence. Loving* consists of all elements of liking *plus* the elements of *passion, sexual desire, exclusiveness,* and *caring.* Davis's research indicates that spouses, lovers, and close friends do not differ much with regard to the elements of friendship. Spouses and lovers do differ from close friends, however, on the elements of loving, especially passion and caring.

*Triangular theory of liking and loving.* Sternberg (1986, 1987) has proposed what he calls the triangular theory of love, based on the three dimensions given above: (1) intimacy, (2) passion, (3) decision/commitment. *Intimacy* refers to feelings of *closeness* or *connectedness* between two people, including such factors as concern with the welfare of the loved one, mutual understanding, and sharing. *Passion* consists of the sources of arousal which we generally label as passion (emotional feelings and physical arousal). Sexual arousal is certainly a strong element, but such needs as for affiliation and self-actualization may also be involved. *Decision/commitment* refers to short-term and long-term elements. In the short term one person makes the *decision* that he or she loves another person. In the long term, one makes a *commitment* to maintain that love. The two do not necessarily go together; one can decide one is in love at the moment without making any long-term

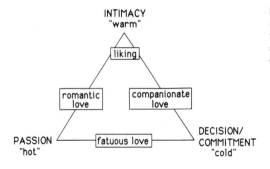

**FIGURE 12-1**

Sternberg's "triangular" theory of love. Different "types" of liking and loving relationships are defined by location with reference to the vertices of the triangle..

commitment. Likewise, one can make a long-term commitment (such as marriage) without necessarily deciding one is in love at the moment.

In simple form, the presence or absence of each of the above three components of love can result in eight possible combinations. In Sternberg's theory these are eight different kinds of liking or loving, as summarized in Table 12-1. Sternberg's names for each are also given.

Some brief descriptions of the eight types are as follows: (1) *Nonlove* means what the name implies, the absence of love (it is always a good idea to keep in mind that *zero* is a perfectly good mathematical quantity when describing something). (2) *Liking* is intimacy, without passion or commitment. Friendships can endure for decades without friends seeing each other for years at a time; love often is not so durable in this manner. (3) *Infatuated love* (infatuation) is a kind of love at first sight phenomenon, passion without intimacy or commitment (students always refer to this as the "one night stand"). (4) *Empty love* seems as vacuous as nonlove, but characterizes such social phenomena as arranged marriages, where there is commitment without intimacy or passion. It also characterizes a "burnt out marriage" or the end of some other long-term relation. (5) *Romantic love* has intimacy and passion, and is a kind of storybook love. There is stronger emotional bonding (intimacy) than with infatuated love, but not commitment. (6) *Companionate love* refers to a long-term, committed friendship. Such a friendship might characterize a marriage after the passion has died down. (7) *Fatuous love* is a combination of passion and decision/commitment, such as a whirlwind courtship and marriage. The commitment is based on passion rather than intimacy. (8) *Consummate love* represents a kind of ideal toward which we might strive, a kind of love to be found more in our dreams than in reality. And, if found, may be very hard to maintain.

**TABLE 12-1    Sternberg's Taxonomy of Kinds of Love Based on his Triangular Theory of Love**

| | COMPONENTS | | |
|---|---|---|---|
| KIND OF LOVE | INTIMACY | PASSION | DECISION/COMMITMENT |
| 1. Nonlove | 0 | 0 | 0 |
| 2. Liking | + | 0 | 0 |
| 3. Infatuated Love | 0 | + | 0 |
| 4. Empty Love | 0 | 0 | + |
| 5. Romantic Love | + | + | 0 |
| 6. Companionate Love | + | 0 | + |
| 7. Fatuous Love | 0 | + | + |
| 8. Consummate Love | + | + | + |

Note: + = component present; 0 = component absent. Most loving relationships fall somewhere between these "pure" types because the various components are present in various degrees, not in all-or-none fashion as indicated in the table. (After Sternberg, 1986, Table 2)

From R. J. Sternberg (1986). A triangular theory of love. *Psychological Review, 93,* 119–135. Copyright ©1986 by the American Psychological Association. Used by permission.

*Styles of love.* Hendrick and Hendrick (1986) distinguished six types or "styles" of love, and developed six corresponding scales for measuring each type.

The six styles, along with a sample scale item for each, are as follows:

1. *Eros.* Erotic love with strong physical preferences and commitment to the lover. Sample item: "My lover and I have the right physical 'chemistry' between us."
2. *Ludus.* Love is a game to be played with many partners. There is no great depth of feeling, and there is a manipulative quality to it. Many love relationships have a game-like quality, but are not as extreme as Ludus. Sample item: "I try to keep my lover uncertain about my commitment to him/her."
3. *Storge.* This is merging of love and friendship. It lacks the fiery quality of Eros and is more like companionate love. Sample item: "The best kind of love grows out of a long friendship."
4. *Pragma.* This style is rational and pragmatic, searching for the potential benefits and losses from the relationship. Love is planned. Sample item: "I try to plan my life carefully before choosing a lover."
5. *Mania.* This style is based on uncertainty about oneself and one's lover, greater concern with losing the lover than on positive aspects. Sample item: "I cannot relax if I suspect that my lover is with someone else."
6. *Agape.* A selfless, all-giving kind of love. Sample item: "I would rather suffer myself than let my lover suffer."

Research with the scales indicates that males tend to be more "ludic" (game-playing) than females but that females are somewhat more storgic, pragmatic, and manic than males. Males and females are about the same on Eros and Agape. Furthermore, individuals who score high on the Eros scale tend to have higher self-esteem, while those who score high on Mania tend to have lower self-esteem (Hendrick & Hendrick, 1986).

The range of theories, and of types of love within a theory, strongly indicate that love is not a single process which applies the same to all people in all situations. Love may mean different things to different people because there *are* different kinds of love masquerading under the same name. As the different types or styles of love are more clearly distinguished by research, we should better be able to understand the development of love and the relationship of love (or lack thereof) to other behaviors.

## ALTRUISM

Altruism, helping, and prosocial behavior are equivalent terms referring to behavior intended to benefit others without obvious benefit in return. Such behavior commonly characterizes people in love, but is broader than just that. The question we ask is, Under what conditions are people more or less likely to help someone else?

### Bystander Apathy

The single event which more than any other sparked interest in helping behavior was the 1964 case of Kitty Genovese. As she returned to her home in Queens (New York City) about 3:00 A.M. she was attacked and, over a half-hour period, was repeatedly stabbed, all the while screaming, and finally was killed. Thirty-eight neighbors watched the gory episode without so much as calling the police. The horror of this scene highlighted the dramatic *failure* of people to help a fellow person. An immediate interpretation was that "big city people" had become callous and indifferent to the plight of anyone else. At best, however, this is just one of many factors which determine when someone will help. We may divide these into characteristics of the situation, of the helper, and of the victim.

### Situational Influences

Latane and Darley (1970) argued that the presence of other bystanders makes it less likely that any one person will help. They staged elaborate "emergencies" in laboratories and public places, and observed bystander behavior. For example, they had smoke pour into a room where students were working, arranged for subjects to hear an apparent accident over an intercom, staged an epileptic seizure, and pulled a fake robbery in a liquor store (with the manager's permission). Their results consistently indicated that people were more likely to help if alone than if someone else were present. The proposed three complementary explanations for this:

1. *Audience inhibition.* If others are present we are slower to act because we are concerned about their evaluation of our behavior. Perhaps the smoke is not really an emergency and we would look foolish if we treated it as such.
2. *Social influence.* We watch others to see how they are acting. If *everyone* is trying to be "cool" and nonchalant, then a whole group may fool itself into believing there is no emergency.
3. *Diffusion of responsibility.* Psychologically, we may feel that if there is a single person present at an emergency it is more imperative to help. When more people are present there is less pressure for any single individual to help. Hence, nobody may act.

Latane and Darley found that a person alone would help someone about 95% of the time, but this dropped to 84% if someone else were present. The percentage dropped to 50 if another person present failed to respond to the emergency. Fortunately, people will help in the presence of others sometimes. Piliavin, Rodin, and Piliavin (1969) faked a collapse of a person on a subway train and found that 70% of the time bystanders helped immediately. The authors believed that this was because the emergency was unquestionable to the bystanders and there clearly was no one else to help except them.

The diffusion of responsibility phenomenon has subsequently been studied under the rubric of *social loafing* (Latane, 1981). The idea here is that people will generally work less hard if the work is shared than if working alone. For example, in a tug of war each individual on a team works less hard than if just one person on each team were pitted against one person on the other team.

**Costs and benefits of helping.**    In an informal way people weigh the relative costs and benefits of getting involved with any particular activity. The potential costs of intervening in a situation are inconvenience, unpleasantness, and possible danger. The costs of *not* helping may be feelings of guilt and possible scorn from others. Benefits of helping may be feeling greater self-esteem, praise from others, or thanks. Sometimes people do jump in and help without thinking at all, as did a bystander when a plane crashed into freezing waters in Washington, D.C. Research shows that:

- Bystanders are more likely to help someone neat and well-dressed than an apparent derelict or drunk or troublemaker.
- Bystanders are more likely to help someone with a cane rather than an apparent drunk carrying what appears to be a bottle in a brown bag.
- Bystanders are less likely to help if there is apparently some person more capable present (such as a person in a hospital uniform).

**Modeling.**    Bryan and Test (1967) had two disabled cars with women as drivers along the side of a busy street. Under one condition someone was helping the first woman driver, but under another condition not helping. Fifty-eight motorists stopped to help the second driver when they saw the first being aided, as compared to thirty-five when the first driver was not being aided. Similar results were obtained with people who saw another person donate to Salvation Army solicitors. If the model is *too* generous, however, potential donors might be scared off because they might be embarrassed by their own small contributions.

**The setting.**    Being a Good Samaritan may be discouraging for many reasons. Physicians may refrain from spontaneously helping accident victims for fear of malpractice suits. Within large cities there is also an element of trying to keep a certain amount of social distance between oneself and others. The hurried activity in a city may also make it more difficult to attract attention for help. Darley and Bateson (1973) found that if subjects were told to be someplace in a hurry they were less likely to stop and help someone in apparent difficulty. The subjects were theology students told to go to a lecture on Good Samaritanism!

*Severity of the emergency.*     Severity is not an overriding factor, else Kitty Genovese would have gotten help. The costs associated with helping seem particularly important in such situations. For example, in one study a bloodied victim was *less likely* than a nonbloodied victim to receive direct help. The bloodied victim did get more help indirectly, however, such as by a phone call.

### Characteristics of the Victim

A reputable looking victim has a better chance of getting help than a disreputable victim, but people are also more likely to help others who are like themselves. For example, in the early 1970's a "hippie-looking" person and a more conservative looking person solicited money from "hippies" and "straights" on the street. The person-on-the-street was more likely to help the solicitor who was more like himself or herself (Enswiller, Deaux, & Willits, 1971).

There is also the so-called *just world hypothesis,* which says that people bring their problems on themselves and they get what they deserve. Some people are unwilling to help others because they believe, rightly or wrongly, that people in trouble are getting what they deserve. The "just world" belief has strong implications for such social issues as welfare, and has certainly played a role in attitudes towards AIDS. Since AIDS has been more widespread among homosexuals and intravenous drug users sharing needles, there have been those (including public figures such as the Reverend Jerry Falwell) who have proclaimed the disease just retribution for a sinful life style.

Finally, the *norm of reciprocity* comes into play. If a person has given help to someone in the past, this "helping person" is more likely to get help in the future. Goranson and Berkowitz (1966) found that experimental subjects were more likely to help a laboratory supervisor if they believed the supervisor had previously volunteered to help them than if the supervisor had refused to help or if the help had been mandatory.

### Characteristics of the Helper

Several personal characteristics distinguish helpers from nonhelpers. Schwartz found that high scorers on his *Ascription of Responsibility Scale* (those who tended to ascribe responsibility to themselves rather than others) were more likely to take action in a fake emergency situation (Schwartz, 1968; Schwartz & Clausen, 1970). Similarly, people who feel *competent* are more likely to help, even if this feeling has only just been engendered in an experimental situation by success at an experimental task. Conversely, it has also been suggested that people with low self-esteem may be more likely to help if they can thereby raise their self-esteem. Finally, people are more generous if in a good mood (see chapter 2).

### Theories of Prosocial Behavior

*Freud's psychoanalytic theory.*   Freud divided personality into three parts — *id, ego,* and *superego.* The id refers to such "basic" drives as hunger, thirst, sex, and aggression. Superego is equivalent to "conscience." Ego is the rational part of the personality that tries to "referee" between the demands of the id for immediate gratification and the hesitancy on the part of the superego. These are not separately identifiable parts of the brain but are Freud's metaphorical way of looking at the mind. Our interest here is in superego, or conscience.

According to Freud, the superego develops as a child learns values (what is good and bad) from his or her parents and culture. These values are "internalized" and become part of the individual, serving as ideals and internal sources of reward and punishment. In a sense, the child develops a set of imaginary parents who, like Jiminy Cricket in *Pinocchio,* direct the child's behavior. If we do something we have learned is "wrong," we may be punished by feeling guilt and anxiety. If we do something that is "right" we are rewarded by feeling good. If certain ideals are strongly internalized we may, for example, do almost anything rather than lie or cheat. Martyrs appear to be people who would give up their lives rather than their ideals.

*Reinforcement theory.*   Reinforcement theory is similar to psychoanalytic theory, but reinforcement theorists would tend to emphasize reward and punishment for *specific* behaviors. Altruistic behavior would in this view occur only if it had been rewarded in the past. The anticipation of future rewards and punishments for helping (or not helping) are of course also important. Anticipations of punishment (inconvenience, possible danger) are weighed against possible rewards (being thanked, getting money, or intangible reward in the hereafter).

Moss and Page (1972) studied the effect of reward for helping on future helping. They approached passersby on the street and asked directions to a particular department store. The strangers were either rewarded with a smile and a thank you, were punished by being rudely told the direction did not make sense, or were left neutral (with just an "okay"). Farther down the street a female confederate dropped a small bag as the same passerby approached. Only 40% of the just-punished individuals picked up the bag for her, but 82% of the neutral subjects and 85% of the rewarded subjects did so. The rude response clearly had a detrimental effect, but the neutral subjects were about as helpful as the rewarded. Perhaps the simple acknowledgment of their previous help was sufficient reward to carry over.

*Kohlberg's theory of moral judgment.*   Kohlberg (1964) has proposed a theory of moral judgment which depends on the increasing ability of a child to understand complex situations. At the *preconventional* level, the child is primarily influenced by the consequences of his or her actions. That is, the child's behavior is determined by rewards and punishments, just as reinforcement theory says. The young child obeys adults because adults mete out punishment. At the *conventional* level, the older child becomes concerned with what others expect of him or her and tries to behave in a conventional way. This is a kind of conformity for the sake of conformity, having respect for authority because such respect is right and proper. At the *postconventional* level, which some adults never achieve, there is a mature level of conscience which is more influential than society's laws. The individual becomes concerned with moral values and the basis for laws. This level is important for any change in a system of justice. It does not represent a flagrant disregard of all of society's rules, but it is concerned with the basis of these rules and their moral correctness. For example, someone may intentionally break a law in order to test its constitutionality in court. Nonviolent methods of breaking the law as a matter of principle have been effective around the world, such as in bringing discriminatory laws to test in the civil rights activities starting in the 1960's.

***Latane and Darley's cognitive analysis.***    Latane and Darley (1970) approached the problem of helping behavior from a perception-cognition point of view. They suggest that the potential helper has to go through five steps.

1. You must *perceive* that something noteworthy is happening. If you do not hear gunshots, you are not going to rush to help someone who might be shot.
2. You must *interpret* what you have perceived. Having heard several loud sharp sounds, you might interpret them as gunshots or a car backfiring. Only if you interpret your perception as a real danger are you likely to help someone, otherwise you might appear foolish.
3. If you correctly interpret that someone needs help you must *decide* that it is *your responsibility* to help. If you think it is someone else's responsibility you may do nothing.
4. You must decide *what* to do. Should you call the police or fire department, take things into your own hands, or what?
5. You must actually *do* what you have decided is the best action.

Each of these five steps is influenced by many factors we have already discussed.

## SUMMARY

1. *Interpersonal attraction* can be divided into *affiliation, liking,* and *loving.*
2. Affiliation does not necessarily involve liking another. Reasons for affiliation may include *biological attachment, reduction of fear, assistance, stimulation, information,* and *self-evaluation.*

3. Determinants of attraction include *proximity, familiarity, physical attractiveness, similarity, and reciprocity.*

4. Theories of liking and loving can be categorized as: (1) liking and loving vary only *quantitatively,* (2) liking and loving are *qualitatively different,* (3) liking and loving share some common characteristics, and (4) liking consists of some of the characteristics of loving.

5. Views of loving being a "lot of liking" include: *reinforcement theory, social exchange theory, equity theory,* and *cognitive consistency theory.*

6. A major theory of liking and loving being different is cognitive-arousal theory, which says that we label arousal as love under certain circumstances.

7. Rubin's theory of liking and loving embodied some of the first attempts to measure liking and loving on quantitative scales.

8. Davis's *cluster theory* says that liking consists of such elements as enjoyment and acceptance, but loving consists of those elements *plus* passion, sexual desire, exclusiveness, and caring.

9. Sternberg's *triangular theory* says that love is based on the three dimensions of *intimacy, passion,* and *decision/commitment.* The relative amounts of each of these define eight different types of love.

10. *Altruism* (also called *prosocial behavior*) refers to behaviors intended to benefit others without obvious return benefit to oneself.

11. *Bystander apathy* is the *failure* of people to help others in emergencies. Important variables are the *presence of others, costs and benefits* of helping, characteristics of the *helper* and the *victim,* and situational factors.

12. *Psychoanalytic theory* says that people internalize social values which influence helping. *Reinforcement theory* says that people are altruistic if they have been rewarded for prosocial behavior in the past.

13. Kohlberg's *theory of moral judgment* assumes that people pass through various stages of moral development in sequence: *preconventional, conventional,* and *postconventional.*

14. Latane and Darley's *cognitive analysis* proposes that a person must *perceive* and *interpret* a situation as requiring help, *decide* that it is one's responsibility to help, decide *what* to do, and then *do* it.

# 13

# Applications of Motivation Theory

## JOB MOTIVATION AND SATISFACTION

### Orientation to Job Motivation

A common question from managers is "How can I motivate people to work harder?" We shall examine two aspects of motivation in industry: (1) motivation theory and research, and (2) job satisfaction. *Motivation theory* in business and industry is not unlike the more general theories discussed thus far; people are people at home or on the job. There is a considerable amount of specialized research on job motivation, however, which we can tap. *Job satisfaction* is commonly defined as a person's attitude, or emotional response, toward his or her job. Job satisfaction is thus a specialized application of attitude theory and research.

Historically, motivation "theory" in business was largely speculative, related to the perceived nature of humans. Such philosophical views as the following, accurate or not, have influenced managerial thinking about dealing with workers.

1. *Rational-economic man.* This view assumes that people are solely motivated by economic considerations and can make rational economic decisions. Workers are considered to be inherently lazy and will not work unless paid. Manipulation of wages and incentives should be sufficient to make them work. People are considered relatively interchangeable since they can be controlled by money.

2. *Social man.* The famous Hawthorne studies (Roethisberger & Dickinson, 1947) showed that such environmental conditions as lighting affected production far less than did such social factors as job satisfaction, social groupings, and conformity. The concept of social man developed from this, suggesting that workers are primarily motivated by social needs which are not met just by work. Workers may be more responsive to their peers than to their company.

3. *Self-actualizing man.* "According to the self-actualizing conception, man is seen as intrinsically motivated. . . . He takes pride in his work because it is *his* work" (Wrightsman, 1972, p. 510). Pride and satisfaction are not always possible in large amounts (as in menial labor), but where there is possibility for personal growth and accomplishment for the worker, a good leader will provide the opportunity.

4. *Complex man.* This view recognizes the variation in motives, emotions, experiences, and abilities of different people and that these *change over time*. New motives and new skills affect a worker's attitude about a job and how well the job can be handled. There is therefore *no single strategy* for dealing with all workers, and perhaps not even the same worker at different times.

*Theory X and Theory Y.* Douglas McGregor (1960) distinguished two approaches to management and the worker which he simply identified as Theory X and Theory Y, summarized by DuBrin (1980, p. 39) as follows:

- Theory X assumes that people dislike work and must be coerced, controlled, and directed toward organizational goals. Furthermore, most people prefer to be treated this way, so they can avoid responsibility.

- Theory Y, the integration of goals, emphasizes people's intrinsic interest in their work, their desire to be self-directing and to seek responsibility, and their capacity to be creative in solving business problems.

A marketing manager who believes in Theory X might try to motivate sales representatives as follows, again quoting DuBrin (p. 39):

> We have established sales quotas for each of you. Each year that your quota is reached, the company will pay for a five-day trip for you and your spouse. This will be in addition to your normal vacation . . . Sales representatives who are unable to meet their quotas for three consecutive quarters will probably not be invited back for a fourth quarter.

On the other hand, a Theory Y believer might say the following:

> You and your sales managers will get together on establishing sales quotas for each year. If you achieve your quotas, you will receive extra money. High performance in sales is one important factor in being considered for a management assignment. Another important part of your job besides selling is to keep our product-planning group informed about changes in consumer demand. Many of our new products in the past stemmed directly from the suggestions of sales representatives.

The newer views, departing from the economic man approach, have developed in part because research has shown that workers are indeed more complex than Theory X supposes. Unfortunately, it is still true that many employers believe that simply paying a person is sufficient to get the most there is to be gotten from a worker.

### Theories of Job Motivation

The previous philosophical approaches indicate different orientations to the questions of worker motivation, but are not articulated theories in any specific sense. We now look at more detailed theories.

*Herzberg's two-factor theory.* Frederick Herzberg (1968) suggested that some aspects of a job allow people to satisfy "higher level" needs, which he called *satisfiers* or *motivators*. He argued that people get and want more from their jobs than pay, such as recognition, responsibility, feelings of achievement, prestige, pleasure from social interactions, stimulation, and challenge. Some job elements are noticeable in their *absence*, however, and produce *dissatisfaction*. Such *dissatisfiers* tend to relate to annoying external conditions, such as company policy and its administration, supervision, working conditions, relations with others, status, and job security. Satisfaction of these needs is called *hygiene*. The heart of Herzberg's approach is that dissatisfaction may lower performance, but that hygienic measures will not markedly improve performance.

Herzberg repeatedly claimed that external incentives are *not* motivators. The distinction which Herzberg seemed to be trying to convey was between external rewards and intrinsic motivation. This distinction is certainly not unimportant, but since Herzberg did not make it clear, his resulting ideas were sometimes unusual. To argue that supervision is *not* motivating (whether by threat of firing or control of rewards) and that achievement, recognition, and responsibility *are* motivating simply flies in the face of any other major theoretical approach to motivation (e.g., see Locke, 1976). Achievement and recognition may be good motivators, but this is not equivalent to saying that supervisory practices or pay incentives have no role as motivators.

*Maslow's need hierarchy.*     Maslow's need hierarchy theory (e.g., Maslow, 1970) stratifies needs from the most basic biological to the most ethereal psychological: (1) *physiological* (such as hunger-thirst), (2) *safety and security,* (3) *love and belongingness,* (4) *self-esteem* (achievement, recognition), and (5) *self-actualization* (reaching one's highest potential). The essence of the theory is that needs lower in the hierarchy have to be at least partly fulfilled before those higher become active. As Maslow saw it, few individuals ever really reach the highest plateau, self-actualization, because of overconcern about lower-level needs, self-esteem, for example.

Maslow's theory seems to make sense in the industrial situation, where lower-level workers seem to be more motivated by money (needed for food and shelter) and are not much motivated to work creatively in their jobs. At higher levels, where income is sufficient to keep the wolf from the door, self-actualization seems more important. The theory is difficult to test, however, because in lower-level jobs there may be no *opportunity* for self-expression, and workers may seek other satisfactions outside the job. Research indicates that two "levels" of motivation are sufficient to account for work motivation. One level is the physiological-safey-belonging classification; the other is an esteem-achievement-actualization classification. This looks suspiciously like restatement of the external reward/intrinsic motivation distinction (e.g., see Steers & Porter, 1975; Landy & Trumbo, 1980).

*Expectancy theories.*     Expectancy theories are similar to Atkinson's achievement theory (chapter 11). They assume that a worker has information about the *probabilities* and *values* of success at various jobs or tasks, and uses this information to decide what choices will have the greatest *expected value* for him. Expected value (EV) is the product of probability (P) and value (V):

$$EV = P \times V$$

Suppose we have two alternatives for a business deal (or choices between jobs), A and B. Assume that A has a .80 probability of success with a

$20,000 payoff and B has a .20 probability of success, but the payoff is $50,000. With only this information, what is our best bet in the long run? Using the expected value approach we compare the two alternatives as follows:

$$EV(A) = .80 \times \$20,000 = \$16,000$$
$$EV(B) = .20 \times \$50,000 = \$10,000$$

The rational decision-maker should choose alternative A, which has the greater expected value. We can immediately see some complications, however. First, to what extent can we really know the probability of success? This is often a *subjective* judgment, and therefore we typically work with *subjective probabilities*. Second, to what extent are values other than money important, such as prestige or self-satisfaction? These are not easily quantifiable like money, so we deal with *subjective values*. In economics these are called *utilities* (and a great deal of economic theory has been devoted to finding ways of measuring utilities). We therefore end up with a measure called *subjective expected utility* (SEU):

SEU = Subjective Probability × Utility

***Vroom's valence-expectancy-instrumentality theory.***   The expectancy theory described above is a "generic" approach, common to all such theories. A more specific example is Vroom's (1964) theory, where expectancy is the perceived probability that a particular amount of *effort* will result in a particular outcome (such as higher pay or promotion or other goody). A worker might consider, "What are the chances I will get promoted if I work hard?" Based upon knowledge of the situation, the probability might be low, medium, or high. For example, a female in a male-dominated organization might consider the probability of advancement to be much lower than would a man in the same position. The second component of the expectancy is the *valence* (value) that some outcome (such as promotion) has for the worker. If a person does not value a promotion, we would not expect him or her to work hard for it. Putting this formulation into Vroom's terms we have Figure 13-1. This is the expectancy that work will lead to a certain level of *performance*, and that this performance will be *instrumental* in achieving the long-term goal (promo-

**FIGURE 13-1.**  Vroom's VIE model of job motivation and performance.

tion). If a person expects that hard work will *not* produce a high level of performance, or that high performance will *not* achieve the goal, the perceived instrumentality will be low and the person is not likely to work very hard.

*Equity theory.*   The author once listened to the complaint of a steel assembly worker about having to do some welding one day when the regular welder was sick. His complaint was not that he disliked welding or that it was more difficult or harder work than his regular job. Rather, he was dissatisfied because welders earn more than his job paid and he considered it unfair that he should be asked to weld but be paid at his own regular rate. This type of response is not readily explained by the previous theories, but is exactly what equity theory was designed to explain.

Equity theory (Adams, 1975) is a form of *discrepancy theory*, along the lines discussed in chapter 10 (cognitive consistency), and was discussed in chapter 12 (interpersonal attraction). To review quickly, the idea is that a person compares how hard he is working with what he is getting in return, and if he perceives a discrepancy he is unhappy. The discrepancy may be between the person's *internal* standard for what is equitable return for a certain amount of effort or it may be in *comparison* with some *external reference.* John may use George as a reference. George works a certain number of hours at a certain job and gets paid a certain amount. The ratio of his work/pay is John's reference. If John perceives that his own work/pay ratio is large compared to George's, this discrepancy produces an aversive emotional state in John, a degree of tension. How does John reduce this tension? He might slough off on his own work until he perceives that his return is proportionally the same as George's. Or, he might try to get a raise. Or, he might just complain and be rather unpleasant to be around.

Suppose that instead of John we have Joan getting the perceived low return for effort. What might she do? She might accept one of the traditional excuses for paying women less, such as "a man has a family to support." She might quit her job. She might ask for a raise. She might reduce her work output. She might file a complaint with the government under the Equal Pay Act or the Fair Employment Practices Act. In any event, neither John nor Joan is going to be a happy camper until there is some resolution to their perceived inequities.

What would happen if a person received *more* than he perceives that he deserves? There is some evidence that people will actually work harder, for awhile at least, apparently in order to restore equity. It does seem, however, that people adapt to the new level of return for their work so that it is no longer perceived as high, and work may drop back to where it had been previously.

The problems of research with equity theory in the industrial setting are that (1) pay is not the only outcome, as noted in the distinction between value and utility, and (2) the adequacy of the reference person that an individual compares himself or herself with is not always clear (Gibson, Ivancevich, & Donnelly, 1979, p. 117). There certainly is enough evidence from a variety of sources, however, to indicate that such discrepancies may indeed produce tension and disharmony (Landy & Trumbo, 1980).

*Behavior theory and goal setting.*   Any method of rewarding work or punishing nonwork (such as by firing a recalcitrant worker) is an application of instrumental (operant) conditioning to job motivation. The problem is that usually the people who use the application are not well versed in the details of this approach. A more sophisticated operant conditioning approach proceeds in three parts: (1) setting up environmental conditions to make particular behaviors more or less likely to occur. For example, working without interruption is easier if one's desk is not in a place that many people go by each day; (2) setting goals so the individual knows what performance is expected; and (3) reinforcing individuals for achieving those goals. Many questions still arise, however. Who will set the goals? How will reinforcement (feedback about success) be given?

*Emery Air Freight.* One of the best-documented cases of companywide adoption of these principles is the experience at the Emery Air Freight Company (Feeney, 1972). The problem was simple: Employees were using the wrong size cardboard cartons for shipping. Too-large cartons take up more space, which means fewer cartons per load and less profit. The "cure" for the problem was almost equally simple: Employees were *told* how to load cartons properly and were verbally reinforced for doing so. Improvement was immediate. Employees were also instructed to pay close attention to such details as the scheduling of pick-ups and deliveries, and goals were set for these. Again, performance improved markedly.

The "real" problem had been that the employees did not know exactly what they *should* be doing, nor what they *were* doing. They estimated they were about 90% efficient in their loading, whereas a quick check of the facts showed they were closer to 45% efficiency. Once it was determined where performance really was, and careful records were being kept, it was possible to institute rapid change at little expense. An initial investment of $5,000 in the program brought about improved efficiency ultimately worth millions of dollars.

*Locke's theory of goal setting.* Edwin Locke (e.g., 1968; Locke & Latham, 1984) has proposed two major principles of goal setting:

1.   Hard goals produce higher performance than easy goals.
2.   Specific goals produce higher performance than vague goals, such as "Do the best you can."

This is beautifully illustrated in a report by Latham and Baldes (1975).

The problem was that logging trucks were not being loaded nearly to capacity and more runs than necessary were being made by each truck. The solution was to tell each driver specifically to load his truck to 94% of the truck's legal weight, as compared to the approximately 60% average the drivers had been carrying. Figure 13-2 shows the result, a marked and sustained improvement. The drivers were given verbal praise for improving their load size, but they got no other reward and there was no special training for either drivers or supervisors.

Two additional principles in the application of goal-setting techniques should be adhered to, however. First, goals should be *attainable*. Specific goals should be difficult, not impossible. Research on United Fund campaigns illustrates this principle. When a goal of 20% increase over the previous year was set, productivity went up 25%. But a goal of 80% increase

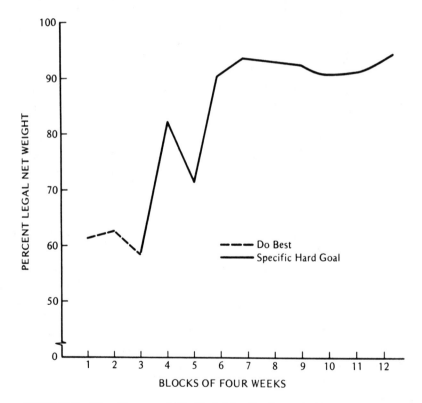

**FIGURE 13-2.**  When drivers were told to "do their best" loading trucks (dotted portion of curve), they only loaded them to about 60 percent of legal capacity. When given the specific instructions to loan them to 94 percent, however, there was an immediate and sustained increase in load size. (From Latham & Baldes, 1975. Used with permission. Copyright ©1975 by the American Psychological Association.)

resulted in only a 12% rise, and performance *declined* when the goal was doubled (Dessler, 1980). Second, goals should be *relevant* to the job at hand. A production supervisor should set goals for production, not sales. The goals should also be measured in objective and relevant terms, such as amount produced per unit time. There is also considerable value in *employee partici-pation* in goal setting. What a supervisor sees as an attainable goal may differ sharply from what an employee sees. Therefore, if supervisor and employee jointly set a goal which is satisfactory to both there is a greater chance of success because the goal is realistic and the employee is committed to trying to achieve the goal. Participation also increases job satisfaction.

### Job Satisfaction

Between 1935 and 1976 there were over 3,000 *published* studies of job satisfaction, an average of one every five days (Locke, 1976). Job satisfaction is considered so important because of the costs of dissatisfaction in employee turnover, absenteeism, and work performance. Turnover is one of the most expensive of personnel problems because of time and money lost in training workers over and over for the same jobs. The relationship between job satisfaction and absenteeism is somewhat difficult to document, but Smith (1977) cleverly did so. During a snowstorm in Chicago, job satisfaction pre-dicted rather well among a large number of managers who would or would not show up for work. Given a good excuse not to come to work, the less satisfied managers in a large corporation did not come to work, but better satisfied managers did. On the same day in New York City, where the weather was nice, job satisfaction did not predict absenteeism among compa-rable managers. It took the combination of environmental factors (storm) and personal factors (job satisfaction) to tease out the effect of job satisfaction on absenteeism.

*Meaning and measurement of job satisfaction.* Job satisfaction may be defined very simply as "the attitude one has toward his or her job" (McCor-mick & Ilgen, 1980, p. 303). An attitude is an emotional response toward something (in this case, a job), which can vary from positive to negative in any degree. Whatever might be said about attitudes in general applies to job satisfaction in particular. Thus, the measurement of job satisfaction, the relation of job satisfaction to behavior, and methods of improving job satisfac-tion are all special cases of the same problems raised about attitudes. Further-more, just as a job has many characteristics, so job satisfaction is necessarily a summation of worker attitudes about all these characteristics. Good and bad features of a job are balanced so that job satisfaction "on the whole" is relatively high or low. Table 13-1 shows a dozen dimensions of work which are related to job satisfaction.

**TABLE 13-1   Job Dimensions Typically Relevant to Job Satisfaction.**

| GENERAL CATEGORIES | SPECIFIC DIMENSION | DIMENSION DESCRIPTIONS |
|---|---|---|
| I. Events or Conditions | | |
| 1. Work | Work Itself | Includes intrinsic interest, variety, opportunity for learning, difficulty, amount, chances for success, control over work flow, etc. |
| 2. Rewards | Pay | Amount, fairness or equity, basis for pay, etc. |
| | Promotions | Opportunities for, basis of, fairness of, etc. |
| | Recognition | Praise, criticism, credit for work done, etc. |
| 3. Context of Work | Working Conditions | Hours, rest pauses, equipment, quality of the workspace, temperature, ventilation, location of plant, etc. |
| | Benefits | Pensions, medical and life insurance plans, annual leave, vacations, etc. |
| II. Agents | | |
| 1. Self | Self | Values, skills and abilities, etc. |
| 2. Others (In-Company) | Supervision | Supervisory style and influence, technical adequacy, administrative skills, etc. |
| | Co-Workers | Competence, friendliness, helpfulness, technical competence, etc. |
| 3. Others (Outside Company) | Customers | Technical competence, friendliness, etc. |
| | Family Members* | Supportiveness, knowledge of job, demands for time, etc. |
| | Others | Depending upon position, e.g. students, parents, voters |

*Not included in Locke's discussion.
Adapted from Locke, 1976, p. 1302. Copyright © 1980 by McCormick and Ilgen. Reprinted by permission of John Wiley & Sons, Inc.

*Job satisfaction and behavior.*    It is only partly true that "happy workers are good workers." The relationship between job satisfaction and performance is considerably less than perfect, and where such a correlation does exist, the cause may not be the one implied. For example, good performance may lead to high job satisfaction rather than the other way around. Lawler and Porter (1967) proposed that performance which leads to rewards produces satisfaction with the work and also produces the expectation that future performance will also lead to rewards. This is illustrated in Figure 13-3.

Several studies testing Lawler and Porter's model have indicated that there is greater job satisfaction when rewards are specifically related to job performance than when equal rewards are given but not specifically related

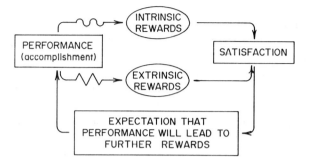

**FIGURE 13-3.** The Lawler-Porter model of job satisfaction, showing how performance leads to rewards and satisfaction and the expectation of future rewards. (From Lawler & Porter, 1967, Fig. 1. Figure slightly adapted by Dessler, 1980. Used with permission of Reston Publ. Co.)

to job performance. This suggests that job satisfaction comes with perceived *control* over events which produce success. Organizational attempts to "increase morale" by contrived programs may have some positive effects but do not necessarily lead to better performance since the "morale building events" are not related to performance.

### Theories of Job Satisfaction

Theories of job satisfaction involve motivational, emotional, and informational components, as do other attitude theories. The following three theories are illustrative.

*Instrumentality theory.* Job satisfaction is high to the extent that the job is instrumental in getting the worker what he or she values, or wants from the job. This might be pleasure in the work, security, prestige, money, short hours, autonomy, convenient location, or anything else considered valuable.

*Equity theory.* As discussed earlier, people generally want to get what they consider a fair (equitable) return for their behavior. This suggests there is greater job satisfaction if the worker perceives that the return for his or her work is equitable.

*The job characteristics model.* Hackman and Lawler (1971) defined six job attributes which might relate to job satisfaction: (1) *variety of work* on the job; (2) *autonomy* in doing work and making decisions; (3) *task identity*, doing a piece of work which can be clearly identified as the result of the worker's efforts; (4) receiving *performance feedback* about how well one is doing on the job; (5) *dealing with other people*; and (6) *friendship opportunities* on the job. Using a complex statistical procedure called *path analysis*, Hackman and Oldham (1976) found that the appropriate combinations of these factors did predict job satisfaction rather well.

Reith (1988) tested the generality of the Hackman-Oldham results by translating the model into academic terms. The basic assumption was that going to school is a student's job, and that all the elements which apply to satisfaction with other jobs would also apply to the classroom. Reith studied 180 students taking introductory psychology and found that measures of the combination of the various aspects of job satisfaction described above did correlate about .60 with course satisfaction. In fact, Reith's results were similar to those reported by Hackman and Oldham (1976), showing that job satisfaction can be fruitfully studied in academic settings. (One would not want to study job satisfaction exclusively in academia, but there is some value in being able to test theories in less formidable surroundings than unionized industries, and in applying models which might suggest improvements in academia.) Reith also found a significant relationship between degree of perceived equity in grading and course satisfaction.

## MOTIVATION IN SPORTS

### Why Do People Play Sports?

People engage in sports for many different reasons, just as they choose to participate in any other activity for different reasons. The following are some motivational factors.

*Arousal.*    The excitement produced by playing may make playful be-havior rewarding for its own sake. In chapter 3 we discussed the fact that people and animals may engage in activities which serve to increase their arousal, bringing them more nearly to an optimum level. Sports may bring a degree of *variety*, or *stimulus change*, into one's life. Thus, a person who works at a routine job all day may enjoy the change of pace and challenge provided by recreational activities.

*Achievement and competition.*    The pride of achievement may be sought in sports, as well as work. Similarly, competitiveness may also be experienced in sports.

*Self-expression.*    Sports can be a form of *self-expression* or *self-actualiza-tion* for some people in the same way that music, art, writing, or hobbies are vehicles for self-expression for other people (Weinberg, 1984).

*Social rewards.*    Many people enjoy sports because sports satisfy an affiliation motive through opportunity for interaction with others. A friendly softball game can be a family affair as much as a sports competition. A game of tennis may be played at a level below the capabilities of the players just in order to keep the game friendly, and to have a pleasant outing.

*Changes with age.*   As children get older, whether they turn to organized sports depends on the rewards gained from sports as compared to other activities, such as affiliation or achievement. After about age twelve, there is a marked decline in the numbers of boys and girls engaging in organized sport. One reason is that children perceive they are *not mastering* their particular sport and therefore do not find it rewarding (Roberts, 1984). At the same time, the other rewards are not strong enough to hold them since those rewards can be gained more easily elsewhere. This is unfortunate because slower-maturing children who are not the best of athletes in early adolescence may subsequently surpass the abilities of many of their earlier-maturing age mates (Roberts, 1984) and could enjoy sports activities later. Children who are attracted to a sport as a social event persist longer in the sport than those who are attracted to it because they believe they can get recognition by being good performers.

The extent to which a sport is rewarding for an individual depends partly on the goals that he or she sets. A mediocre athlete may play tennis regularly *if* the goal is to get some exercise, have a good time, and make a good shot now and then. Achievement theory (chapter 11) suggests that maximum enjoyment comes where there are about equal chances of winning or losing regardless of how well a person plays. In team or individual sports we usually put ourselves into competitions where we can have some successes but also risk failing. Without that risk the successes mean little.

### Motivational Factors Influencing Performance

We may use the entire spectrum of psychological principles to account for athletic performance, just as we would for any other behavior. We shall limit ourselves here to motivation/emotional factors.

*Social facilitation.*   If you have ever stood in front of an audience and been afraid or excited, you have an idea of the effect of an audience on athletic performance. An audience may be just another competitor or it may be a stadium full of people. Attempts to break track records invariably involve competition because runners run faster with competition, and a loud supportive audience is also an asset.

Audience effects depend on the type of activity, however. For well-learned or simple skills, an audience should improve performance. For complex or not well-learned skills, an audience may make performance worse (see chapter 3). Most observers were surprised that Boris Becker would win Wimbledon at age seventeen because they did not think he could stand the "centre court pressure." We may equate the pressure with social facilitation. But Becker had in fact been playing tournament tennis since he was about seven years old, was used to large audiences, and therefore was probably not as aroused as some other players his age might have been.

*Optimal levels of arousal.*    According to the Yerkes-Dodson law, the more complex the behavior, the lower the optimal level of motivation (chapter 3). Different activities in different sports require different complexities of behavior and should therefore have different optimal levels of arousal. A football coach might try to work his team into a passionate frenzy for a big game ("Win this one for the Gipper!"), but a golf coach would hardly do so. Golf requires delicately controlled movements, and golfers have to keep themselves calm.

Oxendine (1970) categorized different sports activities in terms of the amount of fine muscular control and judgment involved. Bowling, field goal kicking, skating, and tournament golf require delicate control, whereas weightlifting, sprinting, and football blocking and tackling do not require such control (quarterbacking probably does). Some research has supported the idea that activities requiring greater control have lower optimal levels of arousal. Golfers in three-day tournaments performed better with low levels of anxiety (Weinberg & Genuchi, 1980) but medium levels of anxiety were better for basketball (Sonstroem & Bernado, 1982). Klavora (1978) assessed the pregame anxiety levels of boys during a high school basketball season. Performance was determined by having coaches rate their players in terms of the players' customary levels of ability. Performance was found to be better with medium levels of anxiety.

Ideally, we would try to adjust the level of motivation for any particular athlete to the optimal level for his or her sport at a given time. Part of the art of coaching is to recognize when individual performers are not aroused enough or are too highly aroused. At the beginning of an important game, for example, players may be too highly aroused (too tense) and make errors, and the coach may call time out to calm down his players. Or, a team may be so confident of winning that the coach must work hard to get the team aroused to optimum performance. One of the most important motivational insights we can have about athletics, however, is that the *highest possible level of arousal is seldom the best level of arousal for maximum performance.*

*Self-regulation of arousal.*    Athletes themselves engage in various strategies to raise or lower their own arousal levels, just as people try to control their own anxiety or stress levels in other situations (chapter 9). Some athletes relax themselves with meditation before a contest, others engage in relaxation exercises. Some pray. During the 1988 World Series, Dodgers pitcher Orel Hershiser sang hymns to himself in the dugout. Good athletes commonly engage in *thought stopping,* tuning out thoughts which would be disruptive or anxiety arousing in relation to performance. For example, a golfer who just shot a double-bogey cannot afford to dwell on that thought as she or he continues to play, nor can a player who makes an error in the World Series. Among world-class athletes of similar ability in any sport, the small edge gained by psychological training may be the difference between an Olympic medal and oblivion.

### Aggression in Sports

Violent behavior is inherent in such contact sports as hockey and football, but is also frequent in such "noncontact" sports as basketball and soccer. We must distinguish between *assertiveness* and *aggressiveness*, however. In everyday conversation, people often *label* "trying hard" as being "aggressive," not using the term "aggressive" in the more precise sense of intending to harm someone. Two players diving to the floor for a loose basketball may be *called* aggressive when in fact they are being assertive. An injury resulting from the collision would be incidental to the assertiveness, an unintended harm. In contrast, intentional elbowing under the basket may be done to intimidate an opponent by hurting him. Such intimidation and other harmful activities become more acceptable if we blur the distinction between assertion and aggression. It is, of course, difficult for an observer to say when harmful behavior is in fact aggressive, so such behaviors are even more likely to pass unchallenged.

Why does truly aggressive behavior occur in sports? It does help win contests, but the story is somewhat more complicated. First of all, in many sports a certain degree of departure from the rules is allowed in order to maintain the flow of play. It is up to the referee(s) to keep play from getting out of hand. In important games, such as the NBA finals, referees are reluctant to "take the game out of the hands of the players" by too-frequent whistles. Under such conditions it is not uncommon for fights to erupt as players become frustrated. Furthermore, fans, coaches, and fellow players often reward individual violent behavior. It is often stated that hockey fans go more to see the fights than to see hockey. A hockey player on the bench may be expected to leap into a fight on the ice or be considered a coward or not a true team member if he fails to do so. Bench-emptying fights are not just a male prerogative. On January 15, 1986, the newspaper wire services reported brawls in a National Hockey League game and between two college women's basketball teams.

### Motivation for Watching Sports

The 1982 World Cup soccer match final drew an estimated 1.4 *billion* television viewers. Television advertising time during recent Superbowl games has sold for about $1 million a minute. One cable TV network (ESPN) devotes 24 hours a day to sports, and the major networks carry almost every sporting event of national interest. What is so attractive to viewers about sports?

*Basking in the reflected glory of the home team.*   Many viewers have a favorite team with which they can identify. When the "home team" wins, its fans feel proud and happy; when it loses, they are mightily unhappy. The depth of this feeling is shown by the harassment of coaches who lose too often, as if the fans themselves had been the losers. This may be true. The fans may have their self-esteem lowered if their team performs badly because they feel that losing somehow reflects on them. At the very least it does reflect on their ability to choose a winning team to support. The "national pride" of "winning" the Olympics and the "shame" of not winning highlights this whole phenomenon.

*Watching sports for arousal.* Many people go to sporting events because of the excitement of the crowd, the thrill of "being there." Sporting events, like movies, are also a *stimulus change,* a variation in the everyday routine of life and an opportunity for *affiliation* with one's friends.

*Sport as art.* Such events as gymnastics, diving, and figure skating are judged by artistic standards as well as athletic. In gymnastics there are required moves, demonstrating strength and balance, for example, but within these limits the ease and grace with which the moves are performed also determine the winner. Ballet movements and choreography have indeed become integral to gymnastics and figure skating. To a considerable extent, particular athletes gain a following because of the artistic manner in which they perform. A Michael Jordon slam dunk is a work of art by any standard.

*Fan aggression and mob behavior.* Chapter 8 presented two opposing views of the effects of observing violence: (1) Viewing is *cathartic* and reduces violence, and (2) Observed violence is a *model* which leads to more violence. Considerable evidence suggests the latter view is more correct. For example, fans were interviewed before and after the 1969 Army-Navy football game and the Army-Temple gymnastics meet held in the same month. There was a significant increase in reported hostility after the football game but not after the gymnastics meet, regardless of which team was supported (Goldstein & Arma, 1971). Similar results were found in a study of ice hockey and professional wrestling in contrast to swimming (Arma, Russel, & Sandelands, 1979). Such studies, along with casual observation, suggest that fan hostility increases with contact sports more than with noncontact sports. Player violence and fan violence may fuel each other. Soccer crowds have become so unruly on the European continent, especially when English teams are involved, that in 1985 several countries joined in a pact to reduce the violence. The critical incident was a riot between British and Italian fans in Belgium in which 41 people were killed.

How can we account for such violent behavior? One reason offered for the Belgian riot was that the English fans came from an economically depressed area. They had time on their hands, life was dull, and they were livening things up for themselves. It is generally conceded that the English fans went to Belgium "looking for trouble." We may then partly account for the riot in terms of the frustration-aggression hypothesis. Frustrated in their everyday lives, the fans became aggressive elsewhere.

There are other factors as well. The fans of one team may form a highly cohesive ingroup which rejects outsiders, producing an "us versus them" feeling which is frequently related to aggressive behavior (Sherif et al., 1961). Fans of one team reinforce each other for behavior which leads to trouble, such as shouting obscenities at opposing fans. It is also easier to be anonymous in a crowd, so the chances of being identified and caught for illegal behavior is reduced.

## MOTIVATION AND ADVERTISTING

### The Communication Model

One of the most frequently used psychological frameworks for advertising is the *communication model* of attitude change and persuasion (e.g., Faison, 1980; Petty & Cacioppo, 1984). Advertising, of course, is the attempt to persuade people to buy some product, commonly assuming that sales will be greater if attitudes toward the product are more positive. The model says, briefly, that the *source* of communication (sender) *encodes* an idea into a *message* which is transmitted to an *audience* (receiver) which *decodes* the message. Researchers have systematically studied characteristics of the source, message, and audience to determine what makes persuasive messages effective. We briefly outline some of the main findings of such research and then turn to the relevant motivational/emotional factors related to advertising.

1. The two most important *source characteristics* are *credibility* (a combination of trustworthiness and expertise) and *likability*.
2. *Message* characteristics are very complex, depending on the nature of the medium (e.g., visual, written, or oral), the type of arguments presented (one-sided versus two-sided), the order of presentation of arguments, and logical versus emotional appeals.
3. *Audience* characteristics include interest in and knowledge of the topic, and mood (which we may take to include motivational/emotional states in general).

### The Source

The primary purpose of appealing to motives in advertising is to attract *attention* to a product or to make a product more *favorable* (Petty & Cacioppo, 1984). Since the prospective audience is faced with literally hundreds of advertisements competing for attention, the advertiser's problem is to make his ad more attention-getting in some way. Other factors then determine whether a product will be purchased.

One method of increasing *apparent* source credibility is to have actors/actresses portray characters who symbolize credibility and honesty. The general assumption is that the *association* of the product with the credible or likable character will add credibility or likability to the product. This is simply classical conditioning at work. Thus, Robert Young, well-known to the TV audience for his portrayal of Marcus Welby, MD, advertised Maxwell House coffee. Similarly, "Four out of five doctors prefer . . . (fill in the name of your favorite across the counter medical product)." Joe Namath, a football hero and likable character, advertised popcorn poppers and pantyhose. General Mills puts famous athletes on the front of *Wheaties* packages. Perfumes, clothes, and other products have famous women associated with them, shoes are associated with athletes, and so on. Such ads have been considered most effective in changing viewer attitudes, however, under conditions where the viewer is not greatly involved with the product (Petty, Cacioppo, & Schumann, 1983). Pantyhose and popcorn poppers would seem to be in this category. Advertisements in recent years, however, have used such celebrities as James Garner and Ricardo Montalban to promote sales of automobiles, products which bear a hefty price tag and do have considerable consumer "involvement."

Research dating back to the 1950's (Hovland & Weiss, 1951) indicates that a source is more effective if s(he) argues *against* his or her own self-interest and does not appear to be trying to influence us. If the source puts on a "hard sell" too strongly, the audience may react against the message. If people believe they are being coerced or manipulated they tend to react negatively. Obviously, a person in an ad *is* trying to sell the product, but this can be softened in various ways. For example, the ad may show apparently unsolicited testimonials for the product, the source of the message apparently not trying to sell. (The viewer does not know how many people had to be filmed to get one unsolicited testimonial, of course). Such "soft sells" may avoid reactance, however.

### The Message

Sex in advertising is a time-honored way to attract attention to the ad. Semi-clad buxom females are associated with everything from shoes to motorcycles. The "Maidenform woman" and her brassieres have been around for years, but more recently ads for blue jeans and undershorts have drawn attention to other parts of the anatomy. Sex does not necessarily have a favorable result in advertising, however. In a study where different versions of the same ad showed different amounts of clothing on the model (female) it was found that explicit nudity lowered the perceived quality of either body oil or ratchet sets (Peterson & Kerin, 1977). A more modest but still sexy model enhanced body oil but not ratchet sets. Thus, moderately sexy advertisements may enhance products where an attractive body is relevant to the ad (such as body oil) but not if it is irrelevant (such as with tool kits). The Maidenform woman, of course, wears the relevant product, and rounded derrieres are covered by the denim product advertised. Too-explicit sexual advertising may arouse negative responses from viewers, regardless of the product. What is considered *too* explicit by the viewing audience, however, does change with the times, and this has to be judged by continual research.

*Fear arousal.* Traders in persuasive messages have long debated the value of negative emotional appeals in advertising. It would appear, for example, that health products could be sold more effectively if a certain amount of fear were introduced into the product advertising. The difficulties in doing this, however, are made obvious by the relative ineffectiveness of the Surgeon General's warnings on cigarette packages to cut down on cigarette consumption. Fear of lung cancer seems not to deter a great percentage of smokers. To the extent that fear arousal is effective, two fairly simple rules may be followed (Secord & Backman, 1974):

1. *"Action instructions" (what to do) are not very effective without any fear arousal at all, but a small amount of arousal is about as effective as a large amount.* Very strong fear arousal may, indeed, produce a defensive reaction such that the viewer puts the whole issue out of his or her mind. Faison (1980, p. 244) describes an audience reaction test to two different toothpaste commercials. One of them simple showed that a person using Brand X for a long time had few cavities. The other showed acid dripping on a tooth, the tooth disintegrating before the viewers' eyes. The product name associated with this fearsome scene was less well remembered than with the more mundane scene, apparently because the scene was so aversive that the viewers tuned out the name of the product.

2. *Fear arousal is more effective if the action proposed is something that will reduce the fear.* An effective tire advertisement showed a woman on a lonely road gazing at a flat tire on her car. The caption said, "When there's no man around, Goodyear should be" (Kleppner, 1977). Two aspects of this ad are important. First, there is a small amount of fear arousal about the consequences of not having good tires. Second, there is something suggested that the viewer can do, that is, buy Goodyear tires. Fear arousal without instructions on how to reduce fear is just fear arousal.

### The Audience

The motivational state of the consumer audience may determine the effectiveness of an advertisement. For example, an ad for a cold remedy is much less likely to influence your purchase if you do not have a cold. But, if you have a sniffly cold in the middle of winter, a TV commercial with a well-known actor extolling the virtues of a cold medicine may be very effective.

### Subliminal Advertising

Every few years the question arises whether persuasive techniques, including advertising, can be effective without people being aware of them. This is known as *subliminal perception* and *subliminal advertising*, perception of stimuli below the threshold for conscious awareness. One of the most notorious claims came in 1957 when a theatre manager said he had flashed slides saying BUY POPCORN on the screen during the showing of a film. Supposedly the slide presentations were so brief that the audience was not consciously aware of them. He claimed a dramatic increase in popcorn sales as a result. The spectre of such powerful mind control caused something of a furor, and bills making subliminal advertising illegal were even introduced into Congress. A number of good experimental psychologists also went to their laboratories to research the subject, with the result that no one could substantiate the original claims. For example, subjects "subliminally" subjected to the word "Beef" did not subsequently choose beef in preference to other meat sandwiches (Byrne, 1959). In a field study, local TV stations participated by sending out messages in the manner described for the "buy popcorn" report. Telephone surveys taken immediately afterwards showed no effect of these messages on any kind of viewer behavior. Research on this topic so repeatedly came up dry that Dixon (1971) was prompted to say that he knew of no evidence to support the "buy popcorn" effect. There has been no evidence for the effect since then, either.

Actually, psychologists had been researching the topics of perception and persuasion for many years prior to the popcorn claim, and there was no reason to believe that so-called subliminal (below-threshold) messages should have been effective. First, whether or not *consciously* perceived, a message would have to get through the eyes and into the nervous system in order to affect behavior. It is doubtful such messages could be received with brief flashes of a slide mixed in with thousands of other unrelated movie frames. Second, even if the signal did reach the nervous system, there is no reason to expect that a viewer should perform like a robot to go out and buy anything. Although we may perceive some messages via stimuli of near-threshold intensity or duration, such effects are difficult-to-achieve laboratory phenomena obtained under very restricted conditions — if at all (e.g., Öhman, 1985; see chapter 2). The most recent claims of any behavioral effects of such messages, by Silverman and his students (e.g., Silverman, 1982) have been severely challenged on grounds of weak methodology and the failure of other researchers to reproduce the phenomena (Balay & Shevrin, 1988). The general conclusion to be reached about subliminal advertising is that it is truly a subliminal phenomenon.

## SUMMARY

1. *Job motivation* refers to those motivational variables that influence worker productivity. *Job satisfaction* refers to worker attitudes (positive or negative) toward the job.
2. Many "theories" of worker behavior have been more philosophical than scientific. McGregor distinguished two broadly different approaches to worker mo-

tivation. *Theory X*, representing traditional views, assumes that workers dislike work and have to be coerced to do it. *Theory Y*, a more modern view, emphasizes that workers want self-satisfaction from work, which includes responsibility and autonomy.

3. Maslow's *need hierarchy theory* distinguishes *physiological, safety, belongingness, self-esteem, and self-actualization* needs. The latter become more dominant when the former have been satisfied. Research evidence only supports a two-level approach, however (combining the first three and last two needs into two separate groupings).

4. *Expectancy theories,* much like achievement theory, emphasizes workers' perceptions of the probabilities and values of successfully completing some job. *Instrumentality theory* emphasizes the importance of workers' perceptions that a given behavior will be instrumental in obtaining a desired goal.

5. *Equity theory* emphasizes workers' desires to get an equitable return for work done. What is considered equitable may be based on some internal standard or on some external reference, such as what another worker gets for doing similar work. Perceived inequity produces tension, which a worker may try to reduce by working less hard, trying to get more money, etc.

6. *Goal setting theory* emphasizes setting *high* (but reasonable) and *specific* goals, and giving feedback about whether these goals are being achieved.

7. Job *satisfaction* is only partly related to job *productivity*. Performance which leads to rewards produces satisfaction, which leads to the expectation that future performance will also lead to rewards. Job satisfaction alone does not increase productivity greatly.

8. Theories accounting for job satisfaction include *instrumentality theory, equity theory*, and the *job characteristics* theory.

9. The motivation for engaging in sports activities is much the same as for other activities: to provide *arousal, achievement* and *competition, self expression,* and *social rewards* such as affiliation. After about age twelve, there is a sharp decline in participation in organized sports as children see that they are not mastering their sport.

10. An important problem for competitors is to achieve the *optimal level of motivation* for a sport. The optimal level of arousal varies with the kind of sport (e.g. golf has a lower optimal level than football) and some athletes learn to effectively increase or decrease their own arousal levels.

11. Player *aggression* in sports may occur as the result of *frustration* or *pain* which occur during the course of play (stimulus aroused aggression), and because players and fans *reinforce* aggressive behavior, which is instrumental to winning.

12. Some of the reasons people *watch* sports are: they feel good if the team they identify with is successful, the excitement of the contest, and the contest provides opportunity for affiliation with others. Fan aggression more severe than player aggression is sometimes stimulated by athletic contests.

13. A framework for encompassing many aspects of advertising is the *communication model*, which looks upon persuasive communications from the points of view of a *source*, a *message*, and an *audience*.

14. The two most important source characteristics are *credibility* and *likability*. Advertisers try to capitalize on these by using as sources people who give the appearance of credibility or who are popular celebrities. A source is also consid-

ered to be more effective if (s)he does not appear to be trying to influence us too heavily.

15. A major emotional content of advertising messages is sexual, but research suggests that moderate sexuality which is relevant to the product advertised is most effective. Too-explicit nudity or sexual connotations for irrelevant products may backfire and engender negative attitudes toward an ad.

16. Some fear arousal in advertising may be effective if accompanied by instructions about what to do to reduce the threat which produces the fear. Overly strong fear arousal may simple cause the audience to tune out the message.

17. The motivational state or mood of an audience modifies the effect of an advertising message. A person with a cold is more likely to pay attention to cold remedy ads.

18. Claims have been made that *subliminal advertising* is a powerful tool. There is virtually no evidence, however, that advertising messages below the level of conscious awareness have any unique influence on consumer behavior. Subliminal perception phenomena are difficult to demonstrate under controlled laboratory conditions, even without trying to influence other behavior.

# Epilogue

The first edition of *Motivation* concluded with a brief epilogue about where motivation theory and research seemed to be headed at the time (1978). In outline form, the following were suggested:

1.  Motivation is becoming more *cognitive*.
2.  Motivation is becoming more *biological*.
3.  There is increasing interest in the interactions of cognitive, social, and physiological determinants of behavior.
4.  The problem of "motivational" vs. "associative" interpretations of behavior will continue to be a theoretical issue.
5.  Approach and avoidance behaviors, and related concepts, are likely to remain at the core of motivation theory.
6.  It may well be that there are behaviors which can be accounted for *without using motivational concepts*. Some responses may be direct responses to stimuli, perhaps habitual responses, which occur in the absence of a "relevant" motivational state.

These trends seem generally to have held, but now, twelve years later, there are additional refinements of these trends, as well as some new ones.

1.  *The role of cognition in motivation/emotion remains a central issue.* The Zajonc-Lazarus controversy highlighted some of the major issues involved in the

question of whether emotion is primary or is secondary to appraisal. In particular, the arguments forced the question of what we *mean* by appraisal, whether appraisals are necessarily *conscious,* for example.

Other examples of the concern with cognition are the continued interest in attributional approaches to emotion and motivation. Cognitive-arousal theory seems to have been overplayed (all emotion is *not* just general arousal plus an attribution), but there is little doubt that appraisals can modify emotions. The question is, under what conditions and to what extent is such modification possible? In a general sense, we may ask to what extent attributions about the causes of arousal, or of success or failure, lead to emotional changes (e.g. depression or happiness), and affect future behaviors. The role of attributions is empirically less settled than preliminary theoretical statements might sometimes suggest.

2. *The importance of biological factors continues to be appreciated.* The large number of neurotransmitters and neurohormones discoverd during the past few years provides a continual challenge to determine how such neurochemicals may relate to motivational and emotional phenomena and even to usurp more "traditional" behavioral theories. Addictive behaviors, for example, have become more understandable in biochemical terms. Similarly, studies of histamine, serotonin, bombesin, cholecystokinin, and other neurochemicals have greatly modified our thinking about hunger, thirst, and other homeostatic problems.

Biological limits on motivational/emotional phenomena become increasingly apparent. The difficulties of generalizing across species about the specific mechanisms for feeding onset and termination, for example, have resulted in greater concern with ecological principles in feeding. More "macro" approaches, such as optimal foraging theory and behavioral economics, are attempts to deal with such problems.

3. *Emotion theory and research have expanded at a particularly high rate,* both as an independent field and in relation to motivation. Research has been increasingly concerned with the relation of emotional expression to emotional experience, with emphasis on underlying neural structures (including hemispheric differences). The question of how many emotions there are, and how they are to be described, remains an issue. Discovery of the roles of dopamine in relation to natural rewards, electrical self-stimulation of the brain, feeding behavior, drug addictions, and affect provides a good example of the convergence of a number of discrete motivational/emotional phenomena on a common emotional mechanism. We may expect to discover other such "core" mechanisms.

4. *Research and theory on stress, coping, and the self-regulation of internal states has greatly intensified.* Social, cognitive, and biological interactions are emphasized. For example, *social* conditions which an *individual perceives* he can (or cannot) control may influence *immune* responses. The search for psychological mediators of stress (e.g. personality variables) no doubt will continue. Personality "typing" (e.g. Type A or the Hardy personality) will probably contribute less to our understanding, however, than will historically more basic and better understood psychological concepts, such as frustration, anger, and neuroticism. Perceived control has become a central concept for understanding anxiety and stress. How one responds emotionally to lack of control (e.g., angrily or giving up) may be an important factor in stress disorders.

# References

ABRAMSON, L. Y., SELIGMAN, M. E. P., & TEASDALE, J. (1978). Learned helplessness in humans: Critique and reformulation. *Journal of Abnormal Psychology, 87,* 49-74.

ADAMETZ, J. H. (1959). Rate of recovery of functioning in cats with rostral reticular lesions. *Journal of Neurosurgery, 16,* 85-98.

ADAMS, J. S. (1975). Inequity in social exchange. In R. M. Steers & L. W. Porter (Eds.), *Motivation and work behavior.* New York: McGraw-Hill.

AMSEL, A. (1958). The role of frustrative nonreward in noncontinuous reward situations. *Psychological Bulletin, 55,* 102-119.

AMSEL, A. (1962). Frustrative nonreward in partial reinforcement and discrimination learning: Some recent history and a theoretical extension. *Psychological Review, 69,* 306-328.

AMSEL, A. (1968). Secondary reinforcement and frustration. *Psychological Bulletin, 69,* 278.

AMSEL, A., & ROUSSEL, J. (1952). Motivational properties of frustration: I. Effect on running response of the addition of frustration to the motivational complex. *Journal of Experimental Psychology, 43,* 363-368.

ANAND, B. K., CHHINA, G. S., & SINGH, B. (1962). Effect of glucose on the activity of hypothalamic "feeding centers." *Science, 138,* 597-598.

ANDERSON, C., & ANDERSON, D. (1984). Ambient temperature and violent crimes: Tests of the linear and curvilinear hypotheses. *Journal of Personality and Social Psychology, 46,* 91-97.

ANDERSON, R., MANOOGIAN, S., & REZNICK, S. (1976). The undermining and enhancing of intrinsic motivation in preschool children. *Journal of Personality and Social Psychology, 34,* 915-922.

ANDERSSON, B. (1952). Polydipsia caused by intrahypothalamic injections of hypertonic NaCl solutions. *Experientia, 8,* 157-158.

ANGER, D. (1963). The role of temporal discrimination in the reinforcement of Sidman avoidance behavior. *Journal of the Experimental Analysis of Behavior, 6,* 477-506.

ARMA, R., RUSSELL, G., & SANDELANDS, M. (1979). Effects of the hostility of spectators on viewing aggressive sports. *Social Psychology Quarterly, 42,* 274-279.

ARNOLD, M. B. (1970). *Feelings and emotions.* The Loyola Symposium. New York: Academic Press.

ARONSON, E. (1968). Dissonance theory: Progress and problems. In R. P. Abelson, E. Aronson, W. J. McGuire, T. M. Newcomb, M. J. Rosenberg, & P. H. Tannenbaum (Eds.), *Theories of cognitive consistency: A sourcebook.* Chicago: Rand McNally.

ARONSON, E. (1969). Some antecedents of interpersonal attraction. In W. J. Arnold & D. Levine (Eds.), *Nebraska symposium on motivation* (Vol. 7, pp. 143-178). Lincoln: University of Nebraska Press.

ARTHUR, A. Z. (1986). Stress of predictable and unpredictable shock. *Psychological Bulletin, 100,* 379-383.

ASCH, S. (1951). Effects of group pressure upon the modification and distortion of judgment. In Z. H. Guetzkokw (Ed.), *Groups, leadership, and men.* Pittsburgh: Carnegie.

ASERINSKY, E., & KLEITMAN, N. (1953). Regularly occurring periods of eye motility and concomitant phenomena during sleep. *Science, 118,* 273.

ASHIDA, S. (1969). The effects of deprivation and post-deprivation on the heart rate of rats. *Psychonomic Society, 14,* 123-124.

ATKINSON, J. W. (1958). *Motives in fantasy, action, and society.* New York: D. Van Nostrand.

ATKINSON, J. W. (1964). *An introduction to motivation.* New York: D. Van Nostrand.

ATKINSON, J. W., & BIRCH, D. (1970). *The dynamics of action.* New York: Wiley.

ATKINSON, J. W., & BIRCH, D. (1978). *Introduction to motivation* (2nd ed.). New York: D. Van Nostrand.

ATKINSON, J. W., BONGORT, K., & PRICE, L. H. (1977). Explorations using computer simulation to comprehend TAT measurement of motivation. *Motivation and Emotion, 1,* 1-27.

ATKINSON, J. W., HEYNS, R. W., & VEROFF, J. (1954). The effect of experimental arousal of the affiliation motive on thematic apperception. *Journal of Abnormal and Social Psychology, 49,* 405-410.

ATKINSON, J. W., & LITWIN, G. H. (1960). Achievement motive and test anxiety conceived as motive to approach success and motive to avoid failure. *Journal of Abnormal and Social Psychology, 60,* 52-63.

ATKINSON, J. W., & WALKER, E. L. (1956). The affiliation motive and perceptual sensitivity to faces. *Journal of Abnormal and Social Psychology, 53,* 38-41.

AVERILL, J. (1978). Anger. In H. E. Howe & R. A. Dienstbier (Eds.), *Nebraska Symposium on Motivation: 1978.* Lincoln: University of Nebraska Press.

AVERILL, J. (1982). *Anger and aggression: An essay on emotion.* New York: Springer-Verlag.

AVERILL, J. (1983). Studies on anger and aggression: Implications for theories of emotion. *American Psychologist, 38,* 1145-1160.

AZRIN, N. H. & HOLZ, W. C. (1966). Punishment. In W. K. Honig (Ed.), *Operant behavior: Areas of research and application.* New York: Appleton-Century-Crofts.

BAILEY, C. J. (1955). The effectiveness of drives as cues. *Journal of Comparative and Physiological Psychology, 48,* 183-187.

BALAY, J., & SHEVRIN, H. (1988). The subliminal psychodynamic activation method: A critical review. *American Psychologist, 43,* 161-174.

BANDURA, A. (1973). *Aggression: A social learning analysis.* Englewood Cliffs, NJ: Prentice-Hall, Inc.

BANDURA, A. (1977). Self-efficacy: Toward a unifying theory of behavioral change. *Psychological Review, 84,* 191-215.

BANDURA, A. (1982). Self-efficacy mechanism in human agency. *American Psychologist, 37,* 122–147.

BANDURA, A., ROSS, D., & ROSS, S. A. (1963a). A comparative test of the status envy, social power, and secondary reinforcement theories of identificatory learning. *Journal of Abnormal and Social Psychology, 67,* 527–534.

BANDURA, A., ROSS, D., & ROSS, S. A. (1963b). Imitation of film-mediated aggressive models. *Journal of Abnormal and Social Psychology, 66,* 3–11.

BARASH, D. P. (1978). *Sociobiology and behavior.* New York: Elsevier.

BAREFOOT, J. C., & STRAUB, R. B. (1971). Opportunity for information search and the effect of false heart rate feedback. *Journal of Personality and Social Psychology, 17,* 154–157.

BEACH, F. A. (1942). Analysis of factors involved in the arousal, maintenance, and manifestation of sexual excitement in male animals. *Psychosomatic Medicine, 4,* 173–198.

BEACH, F. A. (1969). Locks and beagles. *American Psychologist, 24,* 971–989.

BEAMER, W., BERMONT, G., & CLEGG, M. (1969). Copulatory behavior of the ram, *Ovis aries.* II. Factors affecting copulatory satiety. *Animal Behavior, 17,* 706–711.

BECK, A. T. (1967). *Depression: Clinical, experimental and theoretical aspects.* New York: Harper and Row.

BECK, A. T., & RUSH, A. J. (1980). A cognitive model of anxiety formation and anxiety reduction. In C. D. Spielberger & I. W. Sarason (Eds.), *Stress and anxiety* (Vol. 10, pp. 349–365.).

BECK, R. C. (1961). On secondary reinforcement and shock termination. *Psychological Bulletin, 58,* 28–45.

BECK, R. C. (1962). The rat's adaptation to a 33.5-hour water deprivation schedule. *Journal of Comparative and Physiological Psychology, 55,* 646–648.

BECK, R. C. (1964). Some effects of restricted water intake on consummatory behavior in the rat. In M. J. Wayner (Ed.), *Thirst.* Oxford: Pergamon.

BECK, R. C. (1967). Clearance of ingested sucrose solutions from the stomach and intestines of the rat. *Journal of Comparative and Physiological Psychology, 64,* 243–249.

BECK, R. C. (1979). Roles of taste and learning in water regulation. Commentary on Toates: Homeostasis and drinking. *The Brain and Behavioral Sciences, 2,* 102–103.

BECK, R. C. (1983). *Motivation: Theories and principles* (2nd ed.). Englewood Cliffs, NJ: Prentice-Hall, Inc.

BECK, R. C., & BIDWELL, L. D. (1974). Incentive properties of sucrose and saccharin under different deprivation conditions. *Learning and Motivation, 5,* 328–335.

BECK, R. C., & ELLIS, V. T. (1966). Sucrose reinforcement thresholds for hungry, thirsty, and non-deprived rats. *Psychonomic Society, 4,* 199–200.

BECK, R. C., GIBSON, C., ELLIOT, W., SIMMONS, C., MATTESON, N., & McDANIEL, L. (1988). False physiological feedback and emotion. *Motivation and Emotion, 12,* 217–236.

BECK, R. C., & MEINRATH, A. (1978). *Some physiological variables related to incentive motivation.* Paper presented at the 86th Annual Convention of the American Psychological Association, Toronto, Canada.

BECK, R. C., NASH, R., VIERNSTEIN, L., & GORDON, L. (1972). Sucrose preferences of hungry and thirsty rats as a function of duration of presentation of test solutions. *Journals of Comparative and Physiological Psychology, 78,* 40–50.

BECK, R. C., SELF, J. L., & CARTER, D. J. (1965). Sucrose preference thresholds for satiated and water-deprived rats. *Psychological Reports, 16,* 901–905.

BELANGER, D., & FELDMAN, S. N. (1962). Effects of water deprivation upon heart rate and instrumental activity in the rat. *Journal of Comparative and Physiological Psychology, 55,* 220–225.

BELL, P. A., FISHER, J. D., & LOOMIS, R. J. (1978). *Environmental psychology.* Philadelphia: W. B. Saunders.

BELL, R. W., NOAH, J. C., & DAVIS, J. R., JR. (1965). Interactive effects of shock intensity and delay of reinforcement on escape conditioning. *Psychonomic Science, 3*, 505–506.

BELLOWS, R. T. (1939). Time factors in water drinking in dogs. *American Journal of Physiology, 125*, 87–97.

BEM, D. J. (1967). Self-perception: An alternative interpretation of cognitive dissonance phenomena. *Psychological Review, 74*, 183–200.

BEM, D. J. (1970). *Beliefs, attitudes, and human affairs.* Monterey, CA: Brooks/Cole.

BEM, D. J. (1972). Self-perception theory. In L. Berkowitz (Ed.), *Advances in experimental social psychology* (Vol. 6). New York: Academic.

BENTHAM, J. (1936). The principles of morals and legislation. In E. A. Burtt (Ed.), *The English philosophers from Bacon to Mill.* New York: Modern Library. (Original work published 1789)

BERKELEY, G. (1939). Principles of human knowledge. In E. A. Burtt (Ed.), *The English philosophers from Bacon to Mill.* New York: Modern Library. (Original work published 1710).

BERKOWITZ, L. (1974). Some determinants of impulsive aggression: Role of mediated associations with reinforcements for aggression. *Psychological Review, 81*, 165–176.

BERKOWITZ, L. (1983). Aversively stimulated aggression: Some parallels and differences in research with animals and humans. *American Psychologist, 38*, 1135–1144.

BERKOWITZ, L. (1984). Some effects of thoughts on anti- and prosocial influences of media events: A cognitive-neoassociation analysis. *Psychological Bulletin, 95*, 410–427.

BERKOWITZ, L. (1988). Frustrations, appraisals, and aversively stimulated aggression. *Aggressive Behavior, 14*(1), 3–11.

BERKOWITZ, L., & LE PAGE, A. (1967). Weapons as aggression-eliciting stimuli. *Journal of Personality and Social Psychology, 7*, 202–207.

BERLYNE, D. E. (1960). *Conflict, arousal, and curiosity.* New York: McGraw-Hill.

BERLYNE, D. E. (1971). *Aesthetics and psychobiology.* New York: Appleton-Century-Crofts.

BERNARD, C. (1957). *An introduction to the study of experimental medicine* (H. C. Greene, Trans.). New York: Dover. (Original work published 1865)

BERSCHEID, E., & WALSTER, E. H. (1969). *Interpersonal attraction.* Reading, MA: Addison-Wesley.

BERSCHEID, E., & WALSTER, E. H. (1974). A little bit about love. In T. L. Huston (Ed.), *Foundations of interpersonal attraction.* New York: Academic.

BEXTON, W. H., HERON, W., & SCOTT, T. H. (1954). Effects of decreased variation in the sensory environment. *Canadian Journal of Psychology, 8*, 70–76.

BINDRA, D. (1969). The interrelated mechanisms of reinforcement and motivation, and the nature of their influence on response. In W. J. Arnold & D. Levine (Eds.), *Nebraska symposium on motivation.* Lincoln: University of Nebraska Press.

BINDRA, D. (1978). How adaptive behavior is produced: A perceptual-motivational alternative to response-reinforcement. *The Behavioral and Brain Sciences, 1*, 41–91.

BINDRA, D., & PALFAI, T. (1967). Nature of positive and negative incentive-motivational effects on general activity. *Journal of Comparative and Physiological Psychology, 52*, 165–166.

BITTERMAN, M. E. (1967). Learning in animals. In H. Helson & W. Bevan (Eds.), *Contemporary approaches to psychology.* New York: Van Nostrand.

BLACK, A. H. (1971). Autonomic aversive conditioning in intrahuman subjects. In F. R. Brush (Ed.), *Aversive conditioning and learning.* New York: Academic.

BLACK, A. H., CARLSON, N. J., & SOLOMON, R. L. (1962). Exploratory studies of the conditioning of autonomic responses on curarized dogs. *Psychological Monographs, 76*, (Whole No. 548).

BLACK, R. W. (1965). On the combination of drive and incentive motivation. *Psychological Review, 72*, 310–317.

BLACK, R. W. (1969). Incentive motivation and the parameters of reward in instrumental conditioning. In W. J. Arnold & D. Levine (Eds.), *Nebraska symposium on motivation.* Lincoln: University of Nebraska Press.

BLANEY, P. H. (1986). Affect and memory: A review. *Psychology Bulletin, 99,* 229–246.

BOLLES, R. C. (1962). The readiness to eat and drink: The effect of deprivation conditions. *Journal of Comparative and Physiological Psychology, 55,* 230–234.

BOLLES, R. C. (1963). A failure to find evidence of the estrus cycle in the rat's activity level. *Psychological Bulletin, 12,* 530.

BOLLES, R. C. (1967). *Theory of motivation.* New York: Harper & Row.

BOLLES, R. C. (1970). Species-specific defense reactions and avoidance learning. *Psychological Review, 71,* 32–48.

BOLLES, R. C. (1972). Reinforcement, expectancy, and learning. *Psychological Review, 79,* 394–409.

BOLLES, R. C. (1975). *Theory of motivation* (2nd ed.). New York: Harper & Row.

BOLLES, R. C., GROSSEN, N. E., HARGRAVE, G. E., & DUNCAN, P. M. (1970). Effects of conditioned appetitive stimuli on the acquisition and extinction of a runway response. *Journal of Experimental Psychology, 85,* 138–140.

BOLLES, R. C., & MOOT, S. A. (1972). Derived motives. *Annual Review of Psychology, 23,* 51–72.

BOULZE, D., MONTASTRUC, P., & CABANAC, M. (1983). Water intake, pleasure and water intake in humans. *Physiology and Behavior, 30,* 97–102.

BOWER, G. H. (1981). Mood and memory. *American Psychologist, 36,* 129–148.

BOWER, G. H., FOWLER, H., & TRAPOLD, M. A. (1959). Escape learning as a function of amount of shock reduction. *Journal of Experimental Psychology, 58,* 482–484.

BOWER, G. H., McLEAN, J., & MEACHAM, J. (1966). Value of knowing when reinforcement is due. *Journal of Comparative and Physiological Psychology, 62,* 183–192.

BOWER, G. H., GILLIGAN, S. G., & MONTEIRO, K. P. (1981). Selectivity of learning caused by affective states. *Journal of Experimental Psychology: General, 110,* 451–473.

BOWLBY, J. (1969). *Attachment and loss. Vol. 1. Attachment.* London: Hogarth.

BOYATZIS, R. E. (1973). Affiliation motivation. In D. C. McClelland & R. S. Steel (Eds.), *Human motivation: A book of readings.* Morristown, NJ: General Learning Press.

BRADY, J. V. (1958). Ulcers in "executive" monkeys. *Scientific American, 199,* 95–100.

BRALA, P. M., & HAGEN, P. M. (1983). Effects of sweetness perception and caloric value of a preload on short term intake. *Physiology and Behavior, 30,* 1–9.

BREHM, J. W. (1956). Post-decision changes in the desirability of alternatives. *Journal of Abnormal and Social Psychology, 52,* 384–389.

BREHM, J. W. (1962). Motivational effects of cognitive dissonance. *Nebraska symposium on motivation.* Lincoln: University of Nebraska Press.

BREHM, J. W., & COHEN, A. R. (1962). *Explorations in cognitive dissonance.* New York: Wiley.

BREHM, S. S. (1985). *Intimate relationships.* New York: Random House.

BRENNER, J., EISSENBERG, E., & MIDDAUGH, S. (1974). Respiratory and somatomotor factors associated with operant conditioning of cardiovascular responses in curarized rats. In P. A. Obrist, A. H. Black, J. Brenner, & L. V. DiCara (Eds.), *Cardiovascular psychophysiology.* Chicago: Aldine.

BRIDGMAN, P. W. (1927). *The logic of modern physics.* New York: Macmillan.

BRILLHART, C. A. (1975). *The relationship between heart rate, activity, and bar pressing with varying levels of sucrose incentive.* Unpublished master's thesis, Wake Forest University, Winston-Salem, NC.

BROADHURST, P. L. (1957). Emotionality and the Yerkes-Dodson Law. *Journal of Experimental Psychology, 54,* 345–352.

BROGDEN, W. J., LIPMAN, E. A., & CULLER, E. (1938). The role of incentive in conditioning and learning. *American Journal of Psychology, 51,* 109–117.

BROOKS, C. I. (1969). Frustration to nonreward following limited reward experience. *Journal of Experimental Psychology, 81,* 403–405.

BROWN, J. S. (1948). Gradients of approach and avoidance responses and their relation to level of motivation. *Journal of Comparative and Physiological Psychology, 41*, 451–465.

BROWN, J. S. (1961). *The motivation of behavior.* New York: McGraw-Hill.

BROWN, J. S., & FARBER, I. E. (1951). Emotions conceptualized as intervening variables—With suggestions toward a theory of frustration. *Psychological Bulletin, 48*, 465–495.

BROWN, J. S., KALISH, H. I., & FARBER, I. E. (1951). Conditioned fear as revealed by magnitude of startle response to an auditory stimulus. *Journal of Experimental Psychology, 41*, 317–328.

BRYAN, J. H., & TEST, M. A. (1967). Models and helping: Naturalistic studies in aiding behavior. *Journal of Personality and Social Psychology, 6*, 400–407.

BUCK, R. (1985). Prime theory: An integrated view of motivation and emotion. *Psychological Review, 92*, 389–413.

BUCK, R. (1985). *The communication of emotion.* New York: Guilford Press.

BUGELSKI, B. R. (1938). Extinction with and without sub-goal reinforcement. *Journal of Comparative Psychology, 26*, 121–133.

BUGELSKI, B. R. (1956). *The psychology of learning.* New York: Holt, Rinehart, and Winston.

BURGER, J. (1989). Negative reactions to increases in perceived personal control. *Journal of Personality and Social Psychology, 56*, 246–256.

BURGER, J. M. (1980). *Effectance motivation and the overjustification effect.* Unpublished doctoral dissertation. University of Missouri-Columbia.

BURGER, J. M., & ARKIN, R. M. (1980). Prediction, control and learned helplessness. *Journal of Personality and Social Psychology, 38*, 482–491.

BURGER, J. M., & COOPER, H. M. (1979). The desirability of control. *Motivation and Emotion, 3*, 381–393.

BURGESS, T. D. G., & SALES, S. M. (1971). Attitudinal effects of "mere exposure": A reevaluation. *Journal of Experimental Social Psychology, 7*, 461–472.

BURNSTEIN, E., & WORCHEL, P. (1962). Arbitrariness of frustration and its consequences for aggression in a social situation. *Journal of Personality, 30*, 528–541.

BUSS, A. H., BOOKER, A., & BUSS, E. (1972). Firing a weapon and aggression. *Journal of Personality and Social Psychology, 22*, 296–302.

BYKOV, K. M. (1957). *The cerebral cortex and the internal organs* (W. H. Gantt, Trans. and Ed.). New York: Chemical Publishing.

BYRNE, D. (1974). *An introduction to psychology* (2nd ed.). Englewood Cliffs, NJ: Prentice-Hall.

BYRNE, D., & NELSON, D. (1965). Attraction as a linear function of proportion of positive reinforcements. *Journal of Personality and Social Psychology, 1*, 659–663.

CACIOPPO, J. T., & PETTY, R. E. (1982). The need for cognition. *Journal of Personality and Social Psychology, 42*, 116–131.

CACIOPPO, J., PETTY, R., LOSCH, M., & KIN, H. (1986). Electromyographic activity over facial muscle regions can differentiate the valence and intensity of affective reactions. *Journal of Personality and Social Psychology, 50*(2), 260–268.

CAIRNS, R. B. (1979). *Social development.* San Francisco: Freeman.

CALHOUN, J. B. (1962). Population density and social pathology. *Scientific American, 206*, 139–148.

CAMP, D. S., RAYMOND, G. A., & CHURCH, R. M. (1967). Temporal relationship between response and punishment. *Journal of Experimental Psychology, 74*, 114–123.

CAMPBELL, B. A. (1964). Theory and research on the effects of water deprivation on random activity in the rat. In M. J. Wayner (Ed.), *Thirst.* Oxford: Pergamon.

CAMPBELL, B. A., & CHURCH, R. M. (1969). *Punishment and aversive behavior.* New York: Appleton-Century-Crofts.

CAMPBELL, B. A., & CICALA, G. A. (1962). Studies of water deprivation in rats as a function of age. *Journal of Comparative and Physiological Psychology, 55,* 763–768.

CAMPBELL, B. A., & KRAELING, D. (1953). Response strengths as a function of drive level and amount of drive reduction. *Journal of Experimental Psychology, 45,* 97–101.

CAMPBELL, B. A., & MASTERSON, F. A. (1969). Psychophysics of punishment. In B. A. Campbell & R. M. Church (Eds.), *Punishment and aversive behavior.* New York: Appleton-Century-Crofts.

CAMPBELL, B. A., SMITH, N. F., MISANIN, J. R., & JAYNES, J. (1966). Species differences in activity during hunger and thirst. *Journal of Comparative and Physiological Psychology, 61,* 123–127.

CANNON, W. B. (1927). The James–Lange theory of emotions: A critical examination and an alternative theory. *American Journal of Psychology, 39,* 106–124.

CANNON, W. B. (1934). Hunger and thirst. In C. Murchison (Ed.), *Handbook of general experimental psychology.* Worcester, MA: Clark University Press.

CANNON, W. B. (1939). *Bodily changes in pain, hunger, fear and rage: An account of recent researches into the function of emotional excitement* (2nd ed.). New York: Appleton-Century-Crofts.

CANNON, W. B. (1939). *The wisdom of the body.* New York: Norton.

CANTOR, J. R., ZILLMAN, D., & BRYANT, J. (1975). Enhancement of experienced sexual arousal in response to erotic stimuli through misattribution of unrelated residual excitation. *Journal of Personality and Social Psychology, 32,* 69–75.

CAPALDI, E. D., & DAVIDSON, T. L. (1979). Control of instrumental behavior by deprivation stimuli. *Journal of Experimental Psychology: Animal Behavior Processes, 5,* 355–367.

CAPALDI, E. D. & MYERS, D. E. (1982). Taste preferences as a function of food deprivation during original taste exposure. *Animal learning and behavior, 10,* 211–219.

CAPALDI, E. D., VIVIEROS, D. M., & DAVIDSON, T. L. (1981). Deprivation stimulus intensity and incentive factors in the control of instrumental responding. *Journal of Experimental Psychology: Animal Behavior Processes, 7,* 140–149.

CAPALDI, E. J. (1967). A sequential hypothesis of instrumental learning. In K. W. Spence & J. T. Spence (Eds.), *The psychology of learning and motivation* (Vol. 1). New York: Academic.

CARACO, T., MARTINDALE, S., & WHITTAM, T. S. (1980). An empirical demonstration of risk-sensitive foraging preferences. *Animal Behavior, 28,* 820–830.

CARLSMITH, J. M., & ANDERSON, C. A. (1979). Ambient temperature and the occurrence of collective violence: A new analysis. *Journal of Personality and Social Psychology, 37,* 337–344.

CARLSON, N. R. (1980). *Physiology of behavior* (2nd ed.). Boston: Allyn & Bacon.

CARLSON, N. R. (1987). *Physiology of behavior* (3rd ed.). Boston: Allyn & Bacon.

CARR, H. A. (1925). *Psychology, a study of mental activity.* New York: Longmans.

CATTELL, R. B., & SCHEIER, I. (1961). *The meaning and measurement of neuroticism and anxiety.* New York: Wiley.

CHURCH, R. M. (1969). Response suppression. In B. A. Campbell & R. M. Church (Eds.), *Punishment and aversive behavior.* New York: Appleton-Century-Crofts.

CHWALISZ, K., DIENER, E., & GALLAGHER, D. (1988). Autonomic arousal and emotional experience: Evidence from the spinal cord injured. *Journal of Personality and Social Psychology, 54,* 820–828.

CLARK, M. S., & ISEN, A. (1982). Toward understanding the relationship between feeling states and social behavior. In A. Hastorf & A. Isen (Eds.), *Cognitive social psychology* (pp. 73–108). Amsterdam: Elsevier North-Holland.

CLORE, G. L., & BYRNE, D. (1974). A reinforcement-affect model of attraction. In T. C. Houston (Ed.), *Foundations of interpersonal attraction,* New York: Academic Press.

COHEN, A. R., BREHM, J. W., & FLEMING, W. H. (1958). Attitude change and justification for compliance. *Journal of Abnormal and Social Psychology, 56,* 276–278.

COHEN, P. S., & TOKIEDA, F. (1972). Sucrose-water preference reversal in the water-deprived rat. *Journal of Comparative and Physiological Psychology, 79,* 254–258.

COHEN, S., KRANTZ, D. S., EVANS, G. W., & STOKOLS, D. (1982). Community noise, behavior, and health: The Los Angeles noise project. In A. Baum & J. Singer (Eds.), *Advances in environmental psychology* (Vol. 4: Environment and Health). Hillsdale, NJ: Lawrence Erlbaum Associates.

COHEN, S., & WEINSTEIN, N. (1981). Nonauditory effects of noise on behavior and health. *Journal of Social Issues, 37,* 36–70.

COLLET, L., & DUCLAUX, R. (1986). Hemispheric lateralizations of emotions: Absence of electrophysiological arguments. *Physiology and Behavior, 40,* 215–220.

COLLIER, G., HIRSCH, E., & HAMLIN, P. (1972). The ecological determinants of reinforcement. *Physiology and Behavior, 9,* 705–716.

COLLIER, G., KANAREK, R., HIRSCH, E., & MARWINE, A. (1976). Environmental determinants of feeding behavior or how to turn a rat into a tiger. In M. H. Siegel & H. P. Zeigler (Eds.), *Psychological research: The inside story.* New York: Harper & Row.

COLLIER, G., & MYERS, L. (1961). The loci of reinforcement. *Journal of Experimental Psychology, 61,* 57–66.

COMPTON-BURNETT, I. (1949). *Bullivant and the lambs.* New York: Knopf.

COOMBS, R. H., & KENKEL, W. F. (1966). Sex differences in dating aspirations and satisfaction with computer-selected partners. *Journal of Marriage, 28,* 62–66.

COOPER, J., & FAZIO, R. H. (1984). A new look at dissonance theory. In L. Berkowitz (Ed.), *Advances in experimental social psychology* (Vol. 17, pp. 229–266). New York: Academic Press.

COOPER, J., ZANNA, M. P., & TAVES, P. A. (1978). Arousal as a necessary condition for attitude change following induced compliance. *Journal of Personality and Social Psychology, 36,* 1101–1106.

CORBETT, S. W., & KEESEY, R. E. (1982). Energy balance of rats with lateral hypothalamic lesions. *American Journal of Physiology, 242,* 273–279.

CORBIT, J. D. (1969). Osmotic thirst: Theoretical and experimental analysis. *Journal of Comparative and Physiological Psychology, 67,* 3–14.

COTTRELL, N. B., & WACK, D. C. (1967). The energizing effect of cognitive dissonance on dominant and subordinate responses. *Journal of Personality and Social Psychology, 16,* 132–138.

COX, V. C., PAULUS, P. B., MCCAIN, G., & KARLOVAC, M. (1982). The relationship between crowding and health. In A. Baum & J. E. Singer (Eds.), *Advances in environmental psychology, Vol. 4: Environment and health.* Hillsdale, NJ: Lawrence Erlbaum Associates, Publishers.

COYNE, J. C., & GOTLIEB, I. H. (1983). The role of cognition in depression: A critical appraisal. *Psychological Bulletin, 94,* 472–505.

CRAWFORD, M. (1977). Brief "response prevention" in a novel place can facilitate avoidance extinction. *Learning and Motivation, 8,* 39–53.

CRESPI, L. P. (1942). Quantitative variation of incentive and performance in the white rat. *American Journal of Psychology, 55,* 457–517.

CRESPI, L. P. (1944). Amount of reinforcement and level of performance. *Psychological Review, 51,* 341–357.

CROYLE, R. T., & COOPER, J. (1983). Dissonance arousal: Physiological evidence. *Journal of Personality and Social Psychology, 45,* 782–791.

CSIKSZENTMIHALYI, M. (1978). Intrinsic rewards and emergent motivation. In M. Lepper & D. Greene (Eds.), *The hidden costs of reward.* New York: Lawrence Erlbaum Associates, Inc.

DACKIS, C. A., & GOLD, M. S. (1985). New concepts in cocaine addiction: The dopamine depletion hypothesis. *Neuroscience and Neurobehavioral Reviews, 9,* 469-477.

DALY, H. B. (1974). Reinforcing properties of escape from frustration aroused in various learning situations. In G. H. Bower (Ed.), *The psychology of learning and motivation* (Vol. 8). New York: Academic.

DARLEY, J. M., & BATESON, C. D. (1973). From Jerusalem to Jericho: A study of situational and dispositional variables in helping behavior. *Journal of Personality and Social Psychology, 27,* 100-108.

DARWIN, C. R. (1936). *The origin of the species.* Modern Library, No. G 27. New York: Random House. (Original work published 1859)

DARWIN, C. R. (1965). *The expression of the emotions in man and animals.* London: Murray. (Original work published 1872)

DASHIELL, J. F. (1925). A quantitative demonstration of animal drive. *Journal of Comparative and Physiological Psychology, 5,* 205-208.

DAVIS, J. D., & MILLER, N. E. (1963). Fear and pain: Their effect on self-injection of amobarbital sodium by rats. *Science, 141,* 1286-1287.

DAVIS, K. E. (1985, February). Near and dear: Friendship and love compared. *Psychology Today,* pp. 23-30.

DAVIS, K. E., & JONES, E. E. (1960). Changes in interpersonal perception as a means of reducing cognitive dissonance. *Journal of Abnormal and Social Psychology, 61,* 402-410.

DAVIS, M. (1986). Pharmacological and anatomical analysis of fear conditioning using the fear-potentiated startle paradigm. *Behavioral Neuroscience, 100*(6), 814-824.

DAVIS, M., & ASTRACHAN, D. I. (1978). Conditioned fear and startle magnitude. *Journal of Experimental Psychology: Animal Behavior Processes, 4,* 95-103.

DAVITZ, J. R. (1955). Reinforcement of fear at the beginning and end of shock. *Journal of Comparative and Physiological Psychology, 48,* 152-155.

DAVITZ, J. R. (1970). A dictionary and grammar of emotion. In M. L. Arnold (Ed.), *Feelings and emotions: The Loyola symposium.* New York: Academic Press.

DAVITZ, J. R., & MASON, D. J. (1955). Socially facilitated reduction of a fear response in rats. *Journal of Comparative and Physiological Psychology, 48,* 149-151.

DECHARMS, R. (1968). *Personal causation: The internal affective determinants of behavior.* New York: Academic.

DECHARMS, R., & MOELLER, G. H. (1962). Values expressed in children's readers: 1800-1950. *Journal of Abnormal and Social Psychology, 64,* 136-142.

DECI, E. L. (1975). *Intrinsic motivation.* New York: Plenum.

DECI, E. L. (1978). Applications of research on the effects of rewards. In M. Lepper & D. Greene (Eds.), *The hidden cost of reward.* New York: Lawrence Erlbaum Associates, Inc.

DECI, E. L. (1980). *The psychology of self-determination.* Lexington, MA: D. C. Heath and Company.

DECI, E. L., & RYAN, R. M. (1985). *Intrinsic motivation and self-determination in human behavior.* New York: Plenum Press.

DELGADO, J. M. R., ROBERTS, W. W., & MILLER, N. E. (1954). Learning motivated by electrical stimulation of the brain. *American Journal of Physiology, 179,* 587-593.

DELMONTE, M. M. (1984). Biochemical indices associated with meditation practice: A literature review. *Neuroscience and Biobehavioral Reviews, 9,* 557-561.

DEMBER, W., & RICHMAN, C. L. (1989). *Spontaneous alternation behavior.* New York: Springer-Verlag.

DEMBER, W. M. (1965). The new look in motivation. *American Scientist, 53,* 409-427.

DEMBER, W. M., & EARL, R. W. (1957). Analysis of exploratory, manipulatory, and curiosity behaviors. *Psychological Review, 64*, 91–96.

DEMENT, W., & KLEITMAN, N. (1957). Cyclic variations in EEG during sleep and their relation to eye movements, body motility, and dreaming. *Electroencephalography and Clinical Neurophysiology, 9*, 673–690.

DENENBERG, V. H. (1963). Early experience and emotional development. *Scientific American, 208*, 138–146.

DENNY, M. R. (1971). Relaxation theory and experiments. In F. R. Brush (Ed.), *Aversive conditioning and learning.* New York: Academic.

DENNY, M. R., & ADELMAN, H. M. (1955). Elicitation theory: I. An analysis of two typical learning situations. *Psychological Review, 62*, 290–296.

DESCARTES, R. (1892). Les passions l'ame. In H. A. P. Torrey (Tr.), *The philosophy of Descartes in extracts from his writings.* New York: Holt. (Original work published in 1650)

DESSLER, G. (1980). *Human behavior: Improving performance at work.* Reston, VA: Reston Publishing Company.

DEUTSCH, J. A., & HARDY, W. T. (1977). Cholecystokinin produces bait shyness in rats. *Nature, 266*, 196.

DIAMOND, E. (1982). The role of anger and hostility in essential hypertension and coronary heart disease. *Psychological Bulletin, 92*(2), 410–433.

DiCARA, L. V., & MILLER, N. E. (1968). Changes in heart rate instrumentally learned by curarized rats as avoidance responses. *Journal of Comparative and Physiological Psychology, 65*, 8–12.

DITTES, J. E. (1959). Attractiveness of a group as a function of self-esteem and acceptance by group. *Journal of Abnormal and Social Psychology, 59*, 77–82.

DIXON, N. F. (1971). *Subliminal perception: The nature of a controversy.* London: McGraw-Hill.

DOLLARD, J., DOOB, L., MILLER, N. E., MOWRER, O. H., & SEARS, R. (1939). *Frustration and aggression.* New Haven, CT: Yale University Press.

DOLLARD, J., & MILLER, N. E. (1941). *Social learning and imitation.* New Haven, CT: Yale University Press.

DuBRIN, A. J. (1980). *Effective business psychology.* Reston, VA: Reston Publishing Company.

DuCHARME, R. (1966). Physical activity and deactivation: Abatement of cardiac rhythm during the course of instrumental activity. *Canadian Journal of Psychology, 20*, 445–454.

DUFFY, E. (1934). Emotion: An example of the need for reorientation in psychology. *Psychological Review, 41*, 184–198.

DUFFY, E. (1962). *Activation and behavior.* New York: Wiley.

DUNCAN, G. M. (TR.). (1890). *The philosophical works of Leibnitz.* New Haven, CT: Yale.

DUNHAM, P. J. (1971). Punishment: Method and theory. *Psychological Review, 78*, 58–70.

DUTTON, D. G., & ARON, A. P. (1974). Some evidence for heightened sexual attraction under conditions of high anxiety. *Journal of Personality and Social Psychology, 30*, 570–577.

EGGER, M. D., & MILLER, N. E. (1962). Secondary reinforcement in rats as a function of information value and reliability of the stimulus. *Journal of Experimental Psychology, 64*, 97–104.

EGGER, M. D., & MILLER, N. E. (1963). When is a reward reinforcing? An experimental study of the information hypothesis. *Journal of Comparative and Physiological Psychology, 56*, 132–137.

EIBL-EIBESFELDT, I. (1975). *Ethology: The biology of behavior* (2nd ed., E. Klinghammer, Trans.). New York: Holt, Rinehart and Winston.

EICH, J. E. (1980). The cue-dependent nature of state-dependent retrieval. *Memory and Cognition, 8*, 157–173.

EIFERT, G. H., CRAILL, L., CAREY, E., & O'CONNOR, C. (1988). Affect modification through evaluative conditioning with music. *Behavior Research and Therapy, 26,* 321–330.

EISMAN, E. (1966). Effects of deprivation and consummatory activity on heart rate. *Journal of Comparative and Physiological Psychology, 62,* 71–75.

EKMAN, P., & FRIESEN, W. V. (1971). Constants across cultures in the face and emotion. *Journal of Personality and Social Psychology, 17,* 124–129.

EKMAN, P., & FRIESEN, W. V. (1975). *Unmasking the face.* Englewood Cliffs, NJ: Prentice-Hall, Inc.

EKMAN, P. H., & FRIESEN, W. V. (1978). *The facial action coding system (FACS): A technique for the measurement of facial action.* Palo Alto, CA: Consulting Psychologists Press.

EKMAN, P., & FRIESEN, W. V. (1986). A new pancultural facial expression of emotion. *Motivation and Emotion, 10,* 159–168.

EKMAN, P., & OSTER, H. (1979). Facial expressions of emotion. In M. R. Rosenzwerg and L. W. Porter (Eds.), *Annual review of psychology.* Palo Alto, CA: Annual Reviews, Inc.

ELDER, T., NOBLIN, C. D., & MAHER, B. A. (1961). The extinction of fear as a function of distance versus dissimilarity from the original conflict situation. *Journal of Abnormal and Social Psychology, 64,* 97–112.

ELKIN, R. A., & LEIPPE, M. R. (1986). Physiological arousal, dissonance, and attitude change: Evidence for a dissonance-arousal link and a "don't remind me effect." *Journal of Personality and Social Psychology, 51*(1), 55–65.

ELLIOTT, R. (1975). Heart rate, activity, and activation in rats. *Psychophysiology, 12,* 298–305.

ELLIS, H. C., THOMAS, R. L., McFARLAND, D., & LANE, W. L. (1985). Emotional mood states and retrieval in episodic memory. *Journal of Experimental Psychology: Learning, Memory, and Cognition, 11,* 363–370.

ENDLER, N. S., & HUNT, J. McV. (1966). Sources of behavioral variance as measured by the S-R inventory of anxiousness. *Psychological Bulletin, 65,* 336–346.

ENDLER, N. S., HUNT, J. McV., & ROSENSTEIN, A. J. (1962). An S-R inventory of anxiousness. *Psychological Monographs, 76,* (Whole No. 536).

ENSCORE, S. D., MONK, D. L., KOZUB, F. J., & BLICK, K. A. (1976). Establishment of a secondary drive based on thirst: A replication. *Journal of General Psychology, 94,* 193–197.

ENSWILLER, T., DEAUX, K., & WILLITS, J. E. (1971). Similarity, sex, and requests for small favors. *Journal of Applied Psychology, 1,* 284–291.

ENTWISLE, D. R. (1972). To dispel fantasies about fantasy-based measures of achievement motivation. *Psychological Bulletin, 77,* 377–391.

EPLEY, S. W. (1974). Reduction of the behavioral effects of aversive stimulation by the presence of companions. *Psychological Bulletin, 81,* 271–283.

EPSTEIN, A. N. (1967). Oropharyngeal factors in feeding and drinking. In C. F. Code (Ed.), *Handbook of physiology* (Section 6. Alimentary canal. Vol. 1). Washington, DC: American Physiological Society.

EPSTEIN, A. N. (1971). The lateral hypothalamic syndrome: Its implications for the physiological psychology of hunger and thirst. In E. Stellar & J. M. Sprague (Eds.), *Progress in physiological psychology.* New York: Academic.

EPSTEIN, A. N. (1982). Instinct and motivation as explanations for complex behavior. In D. W. Pfaff (Ed.), *The physiological mechanisms of motivation.* New York: Springer-Verlag.

EPSTEIN, A. N., & TEITELBAUM, P. (1962). Regulation of food intake in the absence of taste, smell, and other oropharyngeal sensations. *Journal of Comparative and Physiological Psychology, 55,* 753–759.

EPSTEIN, S. (1967). Toward a unified theory of anxiety. In B. Maher (Ed.), *Progress in experimental personality research.* New York: Academic.

EPSTEIN, S. (1986). Anxiety, arousal, and the self-concept. In C. Spielberger & I. G. Sarason (Eds.), *Stress and anxiety. Vol. 10: A sourcebook of theory and research*. Washington: Hemisphere.

ERON, L. D., LEFKOWITZ, M. M., HUESMANN, L. R., & WALDER, L. Q. (1972). Does television violence cause aggression? *American Psychologist, 27*, 253–263.

ESTES, W. K. (1958). Stimulus-response theory of drive. In M. R. Jones (Ed.), *Nebraska symposium on motivation*. Lincoln: University of Nebraska Press.

ESTES, W. K., & SKINNER, B. F. (1941). Some quantitative properties of anxiety. *Journal of Experimental Psychology, 29*, 390–400.

ETTINGER, R. H., THOMPSON, S., & STADDON, J. E. R. (1986). Cholecystokinin, diet palatability, and feeding regulation in rats. *Physiology and Behavior, 36*, 801–809.

FAISON, E. W. (1980). *Advertising: A behavioral approach for managers*. New York: John Wiley & Sons.

FALK, J. L. (1961). The behavior regulation of water-electrolyte balance. In M. R. Jones (Ed.), *Nebraska symposium on motivation*. Lincoln: University of Nebraska Press.

FALK, J. L. (1969). Conditions producing psychogenic polydipsia in animals. *Animals of the New York Academy of Sciences, 157*, 569–593.

FANTINO, E. (1987). Operant conditioning simulations of foraging and the delay-reduction hypothesis. In A. Kamil, J. Krebs, & H. Pulliam (Eds.), *Foraging behavior*. New York: Plenum.

FARLEY, F. (1986, May). The big T in personality. *Psychology Today*, pp. 46–50.

FEATHER, N. T. (1967). Valence of outcome and expectation of success in relation to task difficulty and perceived locus of control. *Journal of Personality and Social Psychology, 7*, 372–386.

FEATHER, N. T., & BARBOR, J. G. (1983). Depressive reactions and unemployment. *Journal of Abnormal Psychology, 92*, 185–195.

FEENEY, E. J. (1972). Performance audit, feedback, and positive reinforcement. *Training and Development Journal, 26*, 8–13.

FERNANDEZ, A., & GLENBERG, A. M. (1985). Changing environmental context does not reliably affect memory. *Memory and Cognition, 13*, 333–345.

FESHBACH, S., & SINGER, R. D. (1971). *Television and aggression: an experimental field study*. San Francisco: Jossey-Bass.

FESTINGER, L. (1954). A theory of social comparison processes. *Human Relations, 7*, 117–140.

FESTINGER, L. (1957). *A theory of cognitive dissonance*. Evanston, IL: Row, Peterson.

FESTINGER, L., & CARLSMITH, J. M. (1959). Cognitive consequences of forced compliance. *Journal of Abnormal and Social Psychology, 58*, 203–210.

FINGER, F. W. (1965). Effect of food deprivation on running-wheel activity in naive rats. *Psychological Reports, 16*, 753–757.

FINGER, F. L., REID, L. S., & WEASNER, M. H. (1957). The effect of reinforcement upon activity during cyclic food deprivation. *Journal of Comparative and Physiological Psychology, 50*, 495–498.

FISHER, A. E. (1964). Chemical stimulation of the brain. *Scientific American, 210*, 60–68.

FISHER, S. (1984). *Stress and the perception of control*. Hillsdale, NJ: Lawrence Erlbaum Associates Publishers.

FITZSIMMONS, J. T. (1972). Thirst. *Psychological Review, 52*, 468–561.

FITZSIMMONS, J. T., & LEMAGNEN, J. (1969). Eating as a regulatory control of drinking in the rat. *Journal of Comparative and Physiological Psychology, 67*, 273–283.

FLAHERTY, C. F. (1982). Incentive contrast: A review of behavioral changes following shifts in reward. *Animal Learning and Behavior, 19*, 409–440.

FOA, E. B., & KOZAK, M. J. (1986). Emotional processing of fear: Exposure to corrective information. *Psychological Bulletin, 99*, 20–35.

FOLKMAN, S., & LAZARUS, R. S. (1980). An analysis of coping in a middle-aged community sample. *Journal of Health and Social Behavior, 21*, 219–239.

FORD, M. R. (1982). Biofeedback treatment for headaches, Raynaud's disease, essential hypertension, and irritable bowel syndrome: A review of the long-term follow-up literature. *Biofeedback and Self-Regulation, 7*, 521–536.

FOWLER, H., & MILLER, N. E. (1963). Facilitation and inhibition of runway performance by hind- and forepaw shock of various intensities. *Journal of Comparative and Physiological Psychology, 56*, 801–805.

FOWLER, H., & TRAPOLD, M. A. (1962). Escape performance as a function of delay of reinforcement. *Journal of Experimental Psychology, 63*, 464–467.

FOWLES, D. (1983). Motivational effects on heart rate and electrodermal activity: Implications for research on personality and psychopathology. *Journal of Research in Personality, 17*, 48–71.

FREEDMAN, J. L. (1984). Effect of television violence on aggressiveness. *Psychological Bulletin, 96*, 227–246.

FREUD, S. (1935). *A general introduction to psycho-analysis.* New York: Liveright. (Original work published 1920)

FREUD, S. (1938). *The basic writings of Sigmund Freud.* [Ed. A. A. Brill]. New York: Random House, Inc.

FRIEDMAN, M., & ROSENMAN, R. H. (1974). *Type A behavior and your heart.* New York: Alfred A. Knopf.

FRIEDMAN, M. L. (1978). Hyperphagia in rats with experimental diabetes mellitus: A response to a decreased supply of utilizable fuels. *Journal of Comparative and Physiological Psychology, 92*, 109–117.

FRIEDMAN, M. L., & STRICKER, E. M. (1976). The physiological psychology of hunger: A physiological perspective. *Psychological Review, 83*, 409–431.

FRIEDRICH-COFER, L., & HUSTON, A. C. (1986). Television violence and aggression: The debate continues. *Psychological Bulletin, 100*, 364–371.

FUHRER, M., & BAER, P. E. (1965). Differential classical conditioning: Verbalization of stimulus contingencies. *Science, 150*, 1479–1481.

GALEF, B. G., JR. (1971). Social effects in the weaning of the domestic rat pups. *Journal of Comparative and Physiological Psychology, 75*, 358–362.

GALEF, B. G., JR., & HENDERSON, P. W. (1972). Mother's milk: A determinant of the feeding preferences of weaning rat pups. *Journal of Comparative and Physiological Psychology, 78*, 213–219.

GALLAGHER, J. E., & ASH, M. (1978). Sexual imprinting: The stability of mate preference in Japanese quail (cotnurnix cotnurnix japonica). *Animal Learning and Behavior, 6*, 363–365.

GALLISTEL, C. R., SHIZGAL, P., & YEOMANS, J. S. (1981). A portrait of the substrate for self-stimulation. *Psychological Review, 88*, 228–273.

GARCIA, J., & ERVIN, R. R. (1968). Gustatory visceral and telereceptor cutaneous conditioning— Adaptation in external and internal milieus. *Communications in Behavioral Biology, 1* (Part A), 389–415.

GARNER, W. R., HAKE, H. W., & ERIKSEN, C. W. (1956). Operationalism and the concept of perception. *Psychological Review, 63*, 149–159.

GAZZANIGA, M. S. (1967). The split brain in man. *Scientific American, 217*, 24–29.

GEEN, R. G., & BERKOWITZ, L. (1967). Some conditions facilitating the occurrence of aggression after the observation of violence. *Journal of Personality, 35*, 666–667.

GEEN, R. G., & O'NEAL, E. C. (1969). Activation of cue-elicited aggression by general arousal. *Journal of Personality and Social Psychology, 11*, 289–292.

GEEN, R. G., & PIGG, R. (1970). Acquisition of an aggressive response and its generalization to verbal behavior. *Journal of Personality and Social Psychology, 15*, 165–170.

GHENT, L. (1957). Some effects of deprivation on eating and drinking behavior. *Journal of Comparative and Physiological Psychology, 50,* 172–176.

GIBSON, J. L., IVANCEVICH, J. M., & DONNELLY, J. H. (1979). *Organization: Behavior, structure, processes.* Dallas: Irwin-Dorsey.

GILMAN, A. (1937). The relation between blood osmotic pressure, fluid distribution, and voluntary water intake. *American Journal of Physiology, 120,* 323–328.

GLADUE, B. A., GREEN, R., HELLMAN, R. E. (1984). Neuroendocrine response to estrogen and sexual orientation. *Science, 225,* 1496–1499.

GLICKMAN, S. E., & SCHIFF, B. B. (1967). A biological theory of reinforcement. *Psychological Review, 74,* 81–109.

GOLD, R. M. (1967). Aphagia and adipsia following unilateral and bilaterally asymmetrical lesions in rats. *Physiology and Behavior, 2,* 211–220.

GOLDSTEIN, J., & ARMA, R. (1971). Effect of observing athletic contests on hostility. *Sociometry, 54,* 83–91.

GORANSON, R., & BERKOWITZ, L. (1966). Reciprocity and responsibility reactions to prior help. *Journal of Personality and Social Psychology, 3,* 227–232.

GORDON, W. C. (1989). *Learning.* Belmont, CA: Wadsworth.

GRAFF, H., & STELLAR, E. (1962). Hyperphagia, obesity, and finickiness. *Journal of Comparative and Physiological Psychology, 55,* 418–424.

GRAY, J. (1971). *The psychology of fear and stress.* New York: McGraw-Hill.

GRAY, J. A. (1982a). *The neuropsychology of anxiety: An enquiry into the the functions of the septo-hippocampal system.* Oxford: Oxford University Press.

GRAY, J. A. (1982b). Precis of "The neuropsychology of anxiety: An enquiry into the functions of the septo-hippocampal system." *The Behavioral and Brain Sciences, 5,* 469–534.

GRAY, R. D. (1987). Faith and foraging: A critique of the "paradigm argument from design." In A. Kamil, J. Krebs, & H. Pulliam (Eds.), *Foraging behavior.* New York: Plenum.

GREENWALD, A. G., & RONIS, D. L. (1978). Twenty years of cognitive dissonance: Case study of the evolution of a theory. *Psychological Review, 85,* 53–57.

GREGORY, E., ENGLE, K., & PFAFF, D. (1975). Male hamster preference for odors of female hamster vaginal discharges: Studies of experiential and hormonal determinants. *Journal of Comparative and Physiological Psychology, 89,* 442–446.

GRICE, G. R., & DAVIS, J. D. (1957). Effect of irrelevant thirst motivation on a response learned with food reward. *Journal of Experimental Psychology, 53,* 347–352.

GROSSMAN, S. P. (1962). Direct adrenergic and cholinergic stimulation of hypothalamic mechanisms. *American Journal of Physiology, 202,* 872–882.

GROSSMAN, S. P. (1975). Role of the hypothalamus in the regulation of food and water intake. *Psychological Review, 82,* 200–224.

GROSSMAN, S. P. (1979). The biology of motivation. *Annual Review of Psychology, 30,* 209–242.

GUERIN, B., & INNES, J. M. (1984). Explanations of social facilitation: A review. *Current Psychological Research and Reviews, 3,* 32–52.

GUTHRIE, E. R. (1952). *The psychology of learning* (rev. ed.). New York: Harper & Row.

GUTTMAN, N. (1953). Operant conditioning, extinction, and periodic reinforcement in relation to concentration of sucrose used as reinforcing agent. *Journal of Experimental Psychology, 46,* 213–224.

GUTTMAN, N. (1954). Equal-reinforcement values for sucrose and glucose solutions compared with equal-sweetness values. *Journal of Comparative and Physiological Psychology, 47,* 358–361.

HACKMAN, J. R., & LAWLER, E. E. (1971). Employee reactions to job characteristics. *Journal of Applied Psychology, 55,* 259–286.

HACKMAN, J. R., & OLDHAM, G. R. (1976). Motivation through the design of work: Test of a theory. *Organizational Behavior and Human Performance, 16,* 250–279.

HAHN, W. W., STERN, J., & McDONALD, D. (1962). Effects of water deprivation and bar pressing activity on heart rate of the male albino rat. *Journal of Comparative and Physiological Psychology, 55,* 786–790.

HALL, J. F. (1958). The influence of learning in activity wheel behavior. *Journal of Genetic Psychology, 92,* 121–125.

HAMMEN, C. L. (1985). Predicting depression: A cognitive-behavior perspective. In P. C. Kendall (Ed.), *Advances in cognitive-behavioral research and therapy* (Vol. 4, pp. 30–71). New York: Academic Press.

HARLOW, H. F. (1953). Mice, monkeys, men, and motives. *Psychological Review, 60,* 23–32.

HARRIS, L. J., CLAY, J., HARGREAVES, F. J., & WARD, A. (1933). Appetite and choice of diet: The ability of the vitamin B deficient rat to discriminate between diets containing and lacking the vitamin. *Proceedings of the Royal Society, London, 113*(Serial B), 161–190.

HARRISON, A. A. (1976). *Individuals and groups.* Monterey, CA: Brooks/Cole.

HATTON, G. I., & ALMLI, C. R. (1967). Learned and unlearned components of the rat's adaptation to water deprivation. *Psychonomic Society, 9,* 583–584.

HEARST, E. (1969). Aversive conditioning and the external stimulus. In B. A. Campbell & R. M. Church (Eds.), *Punishment and aversive behavior.* New York: Appleton-Century-Crofts.

HEBB, D. O. (1946). On the nature of fear. *Psychological Review, 53,* 259–276.

HEBB, D. O. (1949). *The organization of behavior.* New York: Wiley.

HEBB, D. O. (1955). Drives and the CNS (conceptual nervous system). *Psychological Review, 62,* 243–254.

HECKER, M. H., CHESNEY, M. A., BLACK, G. W., & FRAUTSCHI, N. (1988). Coronary-prone behaviors in the Western Collaborative Group Study. *Psychosomatic Medicine, 50,* 153–164.

HECKHAUSEN, H. (1975). *Effort expenditure, aspiration level and self-evaluation before and after unexpected performance shifts.* Cited in McClelland (1985).

HEIDER, F. (1958). *The psychology of interpersonal relations.* New York: Wiley.

HENDRICK, C., & BROWN, S. R. (1971). Introversion, extroversion, and interpersonal attraction. *Journal of Personality and Social Psychology, 20,* 31–36.

HENDRICK, C., & HENDRICK, S. (1986). A theory and method of love. *Journal of Comparative and Physiological Psychology, 50,* 392–402.

HENDRY, D. P. (ED.). (1969). *Conditioned reinforcement.* Homewood, IL: Dorsey.

HERRNSTEIN, R. J. (1969). Method and theory in the study of avoidance. *Psychological Review, 76,* 49–69.

HERZBERG, F. (1968). One more time: How do you motivate employees? *Harvard Business Review,* January-February.

HESS, E. H. (1962). Ethology: An approach toward the complete analysis of behavior. In R. Brown, E. Galanter, E. H. Hess, & G. Mandler (Eds.), *New directions in psychology.* New York: Holt, Rinehart and Winston.

HINDE, R. A., THORPE, W. H., & VINCE, M. A. (1956). The following response in young coots and moorhens. *Behaviour, 9,* 214–242.

HIROTO, D. S. (1974). Locus of control and learned helplessness. *Journal of Experimental Psychology, 102*(2), 187–193.

HIROTO, D. S., & SELIGMAN, M. E. P. (1975). Generality of learned helplessness in man. *Journal of Comparative and Physiological Psychology, 31,* 211–217.

HOEBEL, B. G. (1969). Feeding and self-stimulation. *Neural Regulation of Food and Water Intake. Annals of the New York Academy of Sciences, 157,* 758–778.

HOEBEL, B. G. (1971). Feeding: Neural control of intake. In V. E. Hall, A. C. Giese, & R. Sonnenschein (Eds.), *Annual review of psychology* (Vol. 33). Palo Alto, CA: Annual Reviews.

HOFFMAN, H. S., & FLESHLER, M. (1962). The course of emotionality in the development of avoidance. *Journal of Experimental Psychology, 64,* 288–294.

HOHMANN, G. W. (1966). Some effects on spinal cord lesions on experienced emotional feelings. *Psychophysiology, 3,* 143–156.

HOKANSON, J. E. (1970). Psychophysiological evaluation of the catharsis hypothesis. In E. I. Megargee & J. E. Hokanson (Eds.), *The dynamics of aggression.* New York: Harper & Row.

HOLMAN, G. L. (1969). Intragastric reinforcement effect. *Journal of Comparative and Physiological Psychology, 69,* 432–441.

HOLMES, D. S. (1984). Meditation and somatic arousal reduction: A review of the experimental evidence. *American Psychologist, 39,* 1–10.

HOLMES, T. H., & RAHE, R. H. (1967). The social readjustment rating scale. *Journal of Psychosomatic Research, 11,* 213–218.

HORNER, M. (1968). *Sex differences in achievement motivation and performance in competitive and noncompetitive situations.* Unpublished doctoral dissertation, University of Michigan.

HOVLAND, C., & WEISS, W. (1957). The influence of source credibility on communication effectiveness. *Public Opinion Quarterly, 15,* 635–650.

HULL, C. L. (1943). *Principles of behavior.* New York: Appleton-Century-Crofts.

HULL, C. L. (1952). *A behavior system.* New Haven, CT: Yale University Press.

HULL, C. L., & HOVLAND, C. I., ROSS, R. T., HALL, M., PERKINS, D. T., & FITCH, F. B. (1940). *Mathematico-deductive theory of rote learning.* New Haven, CT: Yale University Press.

HUME, D. (1939). An enquiry concerning human understanding. In E. A. Burtt (Ed.), *The English philosophers from Bacon to Mill.* New York: Random House (Modern Library). (Original work published 1748)

HUNT, H. F., & BRADY, J. V. (1955). Some effects of punishment and intercurrent "anxiety" on a simple operant. *Journal of Comparative and Physiological Psychology, 48,* 305–310.

HUNT, J. McV. (1965). Intrinsic motivation and its role in psychological development. In D. Levine (Ed.), *Nebraska symposium on motivation.* Lincoln: University of Nebraska Press.

HUNT, J. McV. (1984). The role of early experience in the development of intelligence and personality. In N. Endler & J. M. Hunt (Eds.), *Personality and the behavior disorders* (2nd ed.). New York: John Wiley and Sons.

HURSH, S. R. (1984). Behavioral economics. *Journal of Experimental Analysis of Behavior, 42,* 435–452.

HYLAND, M. (1988). Motivational control theory: An integrated framework. *Journal of Personality and Social Psychology, 55,* 542–551.

INSKO, C. A., & SCHOPLER, J. (1972). *Experimental social psychology.* New York: Academic.

IRWIN, F. W. (1971). *Intentional behavior and motivation: A cognitive theory.* Philadelphia: Lippincott.

ISEN, A. (1984). Toward understanding the role of affect in cognition. In R. S. Wyer & T. K. Srull (Eds.), *Handbook of social cognition* (Vol. 3, pp. 179–236). Hillsdale, NJ: Erlbaum.

IZARD, C. E. (1971). *The face of emotion.* New York: Appleton.

IZARD, C. E. (1977). *Human emotions.* New York: Plenum Press.

JACKSON, D. N., AHMED, S. A., & HEAPY, N. A. (1976). Is achievement a unitary construct? *Journal of Research in Personality, 10,* 1–21.

JACOBS, H. L. (1964). Observations on the ontogeny of saccharin preference in the neonate rat. *Psychonomic Society, 1,* 105–106.

JACOBS, H. L., & SHARMA, K. N. (1969). Taste versus calories: Sensory and metabolic signals in the control of food intake. *Neural Regulation of Food and Water Intake. Annals of the New York Academy of Sciences, 157,* 1084–1125.

JACOBS, L., BERSCHEID, E., & WALSTER, E. (1971). Self-esteem and attraction. *Journal of Personality and Social Psychology, 17,* 84–91.

JAMES, W. (1884). What is an emotion? *Mind, 9,* 188–205.

JAMES, W. (1890). *Principles of psychology.* New York: Holt.

JANIS, I., MAHL, G. F., KAGAN, J., & HOLT, R. R. (1969). *Personality.* New York: Harcourt Brace Jovanovich.

JANIS, I. L. (1972). *Victims of groupthink.* Boston: Houghton-Mifflin.

JOHNSON, D. F., & COLLIER, F. H. (1987). Caloric regulation and patterns of food choice in a patchy environment: The value and cost of alternative foods. *Physiology and Behavior, 39,* 351–359.

JONES, E. E. (1964). *Ingratiation.* New York: Appleton-Century-Crofts.

JONES, H. E., & JONES, M. C. (1928). A study of fear. *Childhood Education, 5,* 136–143.

JONES, M. C. (1924). The elimination of children's fears. *Journal of Experimental Psychology, 7,* 382–390.

JOUVET, M. (1967). The states of sleep. *Scientific American, 216,* 62–72.

KALAT, J. (1988). *Biological psychology* (3rd ed.). Belmont, CA: Wadsworth Publishing Company.

KALISH, H. I. (1954). Strength of fear as a function of the number of acquisition and extinction trails. *Journal of Experimental Psychology, 47,* 1–9.

KALISH, H. I. (1969). Stimulus generalization. In M. Marx (Ed.), *Learning processes.* New York: Macmillan.

KAMIL, A. C., KREBS, J. R., & PULLIAM, H. R. (EDS.). (1987). *Foraging behavior.* New York: Plenum.

KAMIN, L. J. (1956). The effects of termination of the CS and avoidance of the US on avoidance learning. *Journal of Comparative and Physiological Psychology, 49,* 420–424.

KAMIN, L. J., BRINER, C. J., & BLACK, A. H. (1963). Conditioned suppression as a monitor of fear of the CS in the course of avoidance learning. *Journal of Comparative and Physiological Psychology, 56,* 497–501.

KANE, T. R., DOERGE, P., & TEDESCHI, J. T. (1973). When is intentional harm-doing perceived as aggressive? A naive reappraisal of the Berkowitz aggression paradigm. *Proceedings of the 81st Annual Convention of the American Psychological Association,* Montreal, Canada, 8, 113–114. Washington, DC: American Psychological Association.

KATKIN, E. S. (1971). *Instrumental autonomic conditioning.* New York: General Learning Press.

KAUFMAN, E. L., & MILLER, N. E. (1949). Effect of number of reinforcements on strength of approach in an approach-avoidance conflict. *Journal of Comparative and Physiological Psychology, 42,* 65–74.

KEESEY, R. E., & POWLEY, T. L. (1986). The regulation of body weight. *Annual Review of Psychology, 37,* 109–133.

KELLEY, H. H. (1967). Attribution theory in social psychology. In D. Levine (Ed.), *Nebraska symposium on motivation.* Lincoln: University of Nebraska Press.

KIMMEL, E., & KIMMEL, H. D. (1963). A replication of operant conditioning of the GSR. *Journal of Experimental Psychology, 65,* 212–213.

KINSEY, A. C., POMEROY, W. B., & MARTIN, C. E. (1948). *Sexual behavior in the human male.* Philadelphia: Saunders.

KINSEY, A. C., POMEROY, W. B., MARTIN, C. E., & GEBHARD, P. (1953). *Sexual behavior in the human female*. Philadelphia: Saunders.

KIRSCH, I., & HENRY, D. (1979). Self-desensitization and meditation in the reduction of public speaking anxiety. *Journal of Consulting and Clinical Psychology, 47*, 536–541.

KISSILEFF, H. R. (1973). Nonhomeostatic controls of drinking. In A. N. Epstein, H. R. Kissileff, & E. Stellar (Eds.), *The neuropsychology of thirst: New findings and advances in concepts*. Washington, DC: Winston.

KLAVORA, P. (1978). An attempt to derive inverted-U curves based on the relationship between anxiety and athletic performance. In D. M. Landers & R. W. Christina (Eds.), *Psychology of motor behavior and sport—1977*. Champaign, IL: Human Kinetics.

KLEPPNER, O. (1977). *Advertising procedure* (6th ed). Englewood Cliffs, NJ: Prentice-Hall.

KLINE, K. S., DOCKERTY, E. M., & FARLEY, F. H. (1982). Transcendental meditation, self-actualization, and global personality. *The Journal of General Psychology, 106*, 3–8.

KLINGER, E. (1966). Fantasy need achievement. *Psychological Bulletin, 66*, 291–306.

KLINGER, E. (1975). Consequences of commitment to and disengagement from incentives. *Psychological Review, 82*, 1–25.

KLINGER, E. (1977). *Meaning and void: Inner experience and the incentives in people's lives*. Minneapolis: University of Minnesota Press.

KLUGER, M. J., & ROTTENBERG, B. A. (1979). Fever and reduced iron: Their interaction as a host defense response to bacterial infection. *Science, 203*, 374–376.

KLUVER, H., & BUCY, P. C. (1937). Psychic blindness and other symptoms following bilateral temporal lobectomy in rhesus monkeys. *American Journal of Physiology, 119*, 352–353.

KOHLBERG, L. (1964). Development of moral character and moral ideology. In M. L. Hoffman & L. W. Hoffman (Eds.), *Review of child development research* (Vol. 1). New York: Russell Sage Foundation.

KRAELING, D. (1961). Analysis of amount of reward as a variable in learning. *Journal of Comparative and Physiological Psychology, 54*, 560–564.

KRALEY, F. S., SIMANSKY, K. J., COOGAN, L. A., & TRATTNER, M. S. (1985). Histamine and serotonin independently elicit drinking the rat. *Physiology and Behavior, 34*, 963–967.

KRALY, S. F. (1984). Physiology of drinking elicited by eating. *Psychological Review, 91*(4), 478–490.

KRANTZ, D. S., & MANUCK, S. B. (1984). Acute psychophysiologic reactivity and risk of cardiovascular disease: A review and methodological critique. *Psychological Bulletin, 96*, 435–464.

KRAUT, R. E., & JOHNSTON, R. E. (1979). Social and emotional messages of smiling: An ethological approach. *Journal of Personality and Social Psychology, 37*, 1539–1553.

KRECH, D., CRUTCHFIELD, R. & LIVSON, N. (1970) *Elements of psychology*. New York: Alfred A. Knopf.

KRIECKHAUS, E. E., & WOLF, G. (1968). Acquisition of sodium by rats: Interaction of innate mechanisms and latent learning. *Journal of Comparative and Physiological Psychology, 65*, 197–201.

KRUGLANSKI, A. (1978). Endogeneous attribution and intrinsic motivation. In M. R. Leppen & D. Greene (Eds.), *The hidden costs of reward*. Hillsdale, NJ: Erlbaum.

KURTZ, K. H., & SIEGAL, A. (1966). Conditioned fear and magnitude of startle response: A replication and extension. *Journal of Comparative and Physiological Psychology, 62*, 8–14.

KUTSCHER, C. (1964). Some physiological correlates of adaptation to a water deprivation schedule. In M. J. Wayner (Ed.), *Thirst*. Oxford: Pergamon.

LACEY, J. I. (1962). Somatic response patterning and stress: Some revisions of activation theory. In M. H. Appley & R. Trumbull (Eds.), *Psychological stress: Issues in research*. Englewood Cliffs, NJ: Prentice-Hall.

LACEY, J. I., KAGAN, J., LACEY, B. C., & MOSS, H. A. (1963). The visceral level: Situational determinants and behavioral correlates of autonomic response. In P. Knapp (Ed.), *Expression of the emotions in man*. New York: International Universities Press.

LACEY, J. I., & LACEY, B. C. (1970). Some automatic-central nervous system interrelationships. In P. Black (Ed.), *Physiological correlates of emotion*. New York: Academic.

LAIRD, J. D. (1974). Self-attribution of emotion: The effects of expressive behavior on the quality of emotional experience. *Journal of Personality and Social Psychology, 29,* 475–486.

LANDY, F. J., & TRUMBO, D. H. (1980). *Psychology of work behavior*. Homewood, IL: The Dorsey Press.

LANGE, G. C. (1885). *Om sinds bivogelser*. Copenhagen.

LASHLEY, K. S. (1938). Experimental analysis of instinctive behavior. *Psychological Review, 45,* 445–471.

LASHLEY, K. (1950). In search of the engram. *Symposium of the Society of Experimental Biology, 4,* 454–582.

LATANE, B. (1981). The psychology of social impact. *American Psychologist, 36,* 343–356.

LATANE, B., & DARLEY, J. M. (1970). *The unresponsive bystander: Why doesn't he help?* New York: Appleton-Century-Crofts.

LATHAM, G. P., & BALDES, J. J. (1975). The "practical significance" in Locke's theory of goal setting. *Journal of Applied Psychology, 60,* 122–124.

LAWLER, E. E., & PORTER, L. W. (1967). The effects of performance on job satisfaction. *Industrial Relations, 20,* 20–28.

LAWLESS, H. T. (1987). Gustatory psychophysics. In T. E. Finger & W. L. Silver (Eds.), *Neurobiology of taste and smell*. New York: Wiley Interscience.

LAWSON, R. (1965). *Frustration: The development of a scientific concept*. New York: Macmillan.

LAZARUS, R. S. (1968). Emotion and adaptation: Conceptual and empirical relations In E. J. Arnold (Ed.), *Nebraska symposium on motivation*. Lincoln, NE: University of Nebraska Press.

LAZARUS, R. S. (1981). Little hassles can be dangerous to your health. *Psychology Today, 15,* 58–61.

LAZARUS, R. S. (1984). On the primacy of cognition. *American Psychologist, 39*(2), 124–129.

LAZARUS, R. S., & FOLKMAN, S. (1984). *Stress, appraisal, and coping*. New York: McGraw-Hill.

LEA, S. E. G. (1978). The psychology of economics of demand. *Psychological Bulletin, 85,* 441–466.

LEAF, R. C. (1964). Avoidance response evocation as a function of prior discriminative fear conditioning under curare. *Journal of Comparative and Physiological Psychology, 58,* 446–449.

LEATON, R. N., & BORSZCZ, B. (1985). Potentiated startle: Its relation to freezing and shock intensity in rats. *Journal of Experimental Psychology: Animal Behavior Processes, 11*(3), 421–428.

LEE, J. A. (1977). A typology of styles of loving. *Personality and Social Psychology Bulletin, 3,* 173–182.

LEEPER, R. (1935). The role of motivation in learning: A study of the phenomenon of differential motivational control of the utilization of habits. *Journal of Genetic Psychology, 46,* 3–40.

LEPPER, M., & GREENE, D. (1978). *The hidden cost of reward*. New York: Lawrence Erlbaum Associates, Inc.

LEVENTHAL, H., & TOMARKEN, A. (1986). Emotion: Today's problems. *Annual Review of Psychology, 37,* 565–610.

LEVINE, S. (1960). Stimulation in infancy. *Scientific American, 202,* 80–86.

LEVINGER, G., RANDS, M., & TALOBER, R. (1977). *The assessment of involvement and rewardingness in close and casual pair relationships* (National Science Foundation Tech. Dept. DIC). Amherst: University of Massachusetts.

LEWIN, K., DEMBO, T., FESTINGER, L., & SEARS, P. S. (1944). Level of aspiration. In J. McV. Hunt (Ed.), *Personality and the behavior disorders*. New York: Ronald Press.

LINDSLEY, D. B. (1950). Emotions and the electroencephalogram. In M. L. Reymert (Ed.), *Feelings and emotions: The mooseheart symposium*. New York: McGraw-Hill.

LINDSLEY, D. B. (1951). Emotion. In S. S. Stevens (Ed.), *Handbook of experimental psychology*. New York: Wiley.

LINDSLEY, D. B., SCHREINER, L. H., KNOWLES, W. B., & MAGOUN, H. W. (1950). Behavioral and EEG changes following chronic brain stem lesions in the cat. *Electroencephalography and Clinical Neurophysiology, 2*, 483–498.

LIPPSITT, L., REILLY, B. M., BUTCHER, M. J., & GREENWOOD, M. M. (1976). The stability and interrelationships of newborn sucking and heart rate. *Developmental Psychobiology, 9*, 305–310.

LOCKE, E. A. (1968). Toward a theory of task motivation and incentives. *Organizational Behavior and Human Performance, 3*, 157–189.

LOCKE, E. A. (1976). Nature and causes of job satisfaction. In M. Dunnette (Ed.), *Handbook of industrial and organizational psychology*. New York: Rand-McNally.

LOCKE, E. A., & LATHAM, G. P. (1984). *Goal setting: A motivational technique that works!* Englewood Cliffs, NJ: Prentice-Hall, Inc.

LOEW, C. A. (1967). Acquisition of a hostile attitude and its relationship to aggressive behavior. *Journal of Personality and Social Psychology, 5*, 335–341.

LOGAN, F. A. (1960). *Incentive*. New Haven, CT: Yale University Press.

LOGAN, F. A. (1965). Decision making by rats: Delay versus amount of reward. *Journal of Comparative and Physiological Psychology, 59*, 1–12.

LOGAN, F. A. (1968). Incentive theory and changes in reward. In G. H. Bower (Ed.), *The psychology of learning and motivation* (Vol. 2). New York: Academic.

LoLORDO, V. M. (1969). Positive conditioned reinforcement from aversive situations. *Psychological Bulletin, 72*, 193–203.

LORENZ, K. (1966). *On aggression*. New York: Harcourt Brace Jovanovich.

LOTT, A. J., & LOTT, B. E. (1974). The role of reward in the foundation of positive interpersonal attitudes. In T. C. Huston (Ed.), *Foundations of interpersonal attraction*. New York: Academic Press.

LOTT, D. F. (1967). Secondary reinforcement and frustration: A conceptual paradox. *Psychological Bulletin, 67*, 197–198.

MacCORQUODALE, K., & MEEHL, P. E. (1954). Edward C. Tolman. In W. Estes, S. Koch, K. MacCorquodale, P. E. Meehl, C. G. Mueller, W. N. Schoenfeld, & W. S. Verplanck (Eds.), *Modern learning theory*. New York: Appleton-Century-Crofts.

MAGOUN, H. W. (1954). The ascending reticular system and wakefulness. In J. F. Delafresnaye (Ed.), *Brain mechanisms and consciousness*. Blackwell: Oxford.

MAIER, S. F., SELIGMAN, M. E. P., & SOLOMON, R. L. (1969). Pavlovian fear conditioning and learned helplessness: Effects on escape and avoidance behavior of (a) the CS-UCS contingency and (b) the independence of UCS and voluntary responding. In B. A. Campbell & R. M. Church (Eds.), *Punishment and aversive behavior*. New York: Appleton-Century-Crofts.

MALMO, R. B. (1959). Activation: A neuropsychological dimension. *Psychological Review, 66*, 367–386.

MALMO, R. B. (1975). *Our emotions, needs, and our archaic brain*. New York: Holt, Rinehart and Winston.

MANDLER, G. (1962). Emotions. In T. M. Newcomb (Ed.), *New directions in psychology*. New York: Holt, Rinehart and Winston.

MANDLER, G. (1975). *Mind and emotion*. New York: Wiley.

MANSSON, H. H. (1966). The cognitive control of thirst motivation: A dissonance approach. Unpublished doctoral dissertation, New York University. Cited in P. G. Zimbardo. The cognitive control of motivation. *Transactions of the New York Academy of Sciences*, Series II, 28, 902–922.

MARLER, P. (1976). On animal aggression: The roles of strangeness and familiarity. *American Psychologist, 31*, 239–246.

MARSHALL, G. D., & ZIMBARDO, P. G. (1979). Affective consequences of inadequately explained physiological arousal. *Journal of Personality and Social Psychology, 37*, 970–988.

MASLACH, C. (1979). Negative emotional biasing of unexplained arousal. *Journal of Personality and Social Psychology, 37*, 953–969.

MASLOW, A. H. (1970). *Motivation and personality* (2nd ed.). New York: Harper & Row.

MASSERMAN, J. H. (1943). *Behavior and neurosis*. Chicago: University of Chicago Press.

MASTERS, W. H., & JOHNSON, V. (1966) *Human sexual response*. Boston: Little, Brown.

MATHES (1975). The effects of physical attractiveness and anxiety on heterosexual attraction over a series of five encounters. *Journal of Marriage and the Family, 37*, 769–774.

MATHIEU, M. (1973). Effects of overtraining and high activation on bar pressing of rats tested under water deprivation. *Journal of Comparative and Physiological Psychology, 85*, 353–360.

MATSUMOTO, D. (1987). The role of facial response in the experience of emotion: More methodological problems and a meta-analysis. *Journal of Personality and Social Psychology, 52*(4), 769–774.

MATTES, R. D. (1987). Sensory influences on food intake and utilization in humans. *Human Nutrition: Applied Nutrition, 41A*, 77–95.

MATTES, R. D., & MELA, D. J. (1986). Relationships between and among selected measures of sweet-taste preference and dietary intake. *Chemical Senses, 11*, 523–539.

MAY, R. (1950). *The meaning of anxiety*. New York: Ronald Press.

MCADAMS, D. P., & MCCLELLAND, D. C. (1983). *Social motives and memory*. Unpublished manuscript, Harvard University, Department of Psychology and Social Relations. Cited in McClelland (1985, p. 279).

MCALLISTER, W. R., & MCALLISTER, D. E. (1971). Behavioral measurement of conditioned fear. In F. R. Brush (Ed.), *Aversive conditioning and learning*. New York: Academic.

MCCAIN, G. (1966). Partial reinforcement effects following a small number of acquisition trials. *Psychonomic Monograph Supplements, 1*, 251–270.

MCCLEARY, R. A. (1953). Taste and post–ingestion factors in specific-hunger behavior. *Journal of Comparative and Physiological Psychology, 46*, 411–421.

MCCLEARY, R. A., & LAZARUS, R. S. (1949). Autonomic discrimination without awareness: An interim report. *Journal of Personality, 18*, 171–179.

MCCLELLAND, D. (1985). *Human motivation*. New York: Scott-Freeman.

MCCLELLAND, D. C. (1958). Risk-taking in children with high and low need for achievement. In J. W. Atkinson (Ed.), *Motives in fantasy, action, and society*. Princeton: Van Nostrand.

MCCLELLAND, D. C. (1961). *The achieving society*. Princeton: Van Nostrand.

MCCLELLAND, D. C. (1965). N achievement and entrepreneurship: A longitudinal study. *Journal of Personality and Social Psychology, 1*, 389–392.

MCCLELLAND, D. C., & ATKINSON, J. W. (1948). The projective expression of needs. I. The effect of different intensities of the hunger drive on perception. *Journal of Personality, 25*, 205–232.

McClelland, D. C., Atkinson, J. W., Clark, R. A., & Lowell, E. L. (1953). *The achievement motive.* New York: Appleton-Century-Crofts.

McClelland, D. C., Davidson, R., Saron, C., & Floor, E. (1980). The need for power, brain norepinephrine turnover, and learning. *Biological Psychology, 10,* 93–102.

McClelland, D. C., Davis, W. W., Kalin, R., & Wanner, E. (1972). *The drinking man: Alcohol and human motivation.* New York: Free Press.

McClelland, D. C., Rindlisbacher, A., & DeCharms, R. C. (1955). Religious and other sources of parental attitudes toward independence training. In D. C. McClelland (Ed.), *Studies in motivation.* New York: Appleton-Century-Crofts.

McCormick, D. A., & Thompson, R. F. (1984). Cerebellum: Essential involvement in the classically conditioned eyelid response. *Science, 223,* 296–299.

McCormick, E. J., & Ilgen, D. R. (1980). *Industrial psychology* (7th ed). Englewood Cliffs, NJ: Prentice-Hall.

McGinnies, E. (1949). Emotionality and perceptual defense. *Psychological Review, 56,* 244–251.

McGrath, J. E. (1970). *Social and psychological factors in stress.* New York: Holt, Rinehart and Winston.

McGregor, D. (1960). *The human side of enterprise.* New York: McGraw-Hill.

McKeachie, W. J., Lin, Y., Milholland, J., & Issacson, R. (1966). Student affiliation motives, teacher warmth, and academic achievement. *Journal of Personality and Social Psychology, 4,* 457–461.

McNally, R. J. (1987). Preparedness and phobias: A review. *Psychological Bulletin, 101,* 283–303.

McReynolds, P. (1986). Changing conceptions of anxiety: A historical review and proposed integration. In C. Spielberger & J. W. Sarason (Eds.), *Stress and Anxiety* (Vol. 10). New York: Hemisphere Publishing Corporation.

Meehl, P. E. (1950). On the circularity of the law of effect. *Psychological Bulletin, 47,* 52–75.

Mehrabian, A. (1976). *Public spaces and private places.* New York: Basic Books.

Mendelson, J., & Chillag, D. (1970). Tongue cooling: A new reward for thirsty rodents. *Science, 170,* 1418–1421.

Meryman, J. J. (1961). *Magnitude of startle response as a function of hunger and fear.* Unpublished master's thesis, State University of Iowa. Cited by Brown, 1961.

Meyer, W. U. (1973). *Leistungsmotiv and ursachenerklarung von Erfolg and Misserfolg.* Stuttgart: Klett.

Michaels, R. R., Huber, M. J., & McCann, D. S. (1976). Evaluation of Transcendental Meditation as a method of reducing stress. *Science, 192,* 1242–1244.

Milgram, S. (1974). *Obedience to authority: An experimental view.* New York: Harper & Row.

Miller, G. A., Galanter, E., & Pribram, K. H. (1960). *Plans and the structure of behavior.* New York: Holt, Rinehart and Winston.

Miller, N. E. (1948). Studies of fear as an acquirable drive: I. Fear as motivation and fear-reduction as reinforcement in the learning of new responses. *Journal of Experimental Psychology, 38,* 89–101.

Miller, N. E. (1951a). Comments on multi-process conceptions of learning. *Psychological Review, 58,* 375–381.

Miller, N. E. (1951b). Learnable drives and rewards. In S. S. Stevens (Ed.), *Handbook of experimental psychology.* New York: Wiley.

Miller, N. E. (1959). Liberalization of basic S-R concepts: Extensions to conflict behavior, motivation and social learning. In S. Koch (Ed.), *Psychology: A study of a science* (Vol. 2). New York: McGraw-Hill.

Miller, N. E. (1960). Learning resistance to pain and fear: Effects of overlearning, exposure, and rewarded exposure in context. *Journal of Experimental Psychology, 60,* 137–145.

MILLER, N. E., & DOLLARD, J. (1950). *Personality and psychotherapy.* New York: McGraw Hill.

MILLER, N. E., & KESSEN, M. L. (1952). Reward effects of food via stomach fistula compared with those of food via mouth. *Journal of Comparative and Physiological Psychology, 45,* 555-564.

MILLER, N. E., & KRAELING, D. (1952). Displacement: Greater generalization of approach than avoidance in a generalized approach-avoidance conflict. *Journal of Experimental Psychology, 43,* 217-221.

MILLER, R. R., GRECO, C., VIGORITO, M., & MARLIN, N. A. (1983). Signaled tailshock is perceived as similar to a stronger unsignaled tailshock: Implications for a functional analysis of classical conditioning. *Journal of Experimental Psychology: Animal Behavior Processes, 9,* 105-131.

MILLER, S. M., & MANGAN, C. E. (1983). Interacting effects of information and coping style in adapting to gynecologic stress: Should the doctor tell all? *Journal of Personality and Social Psychology, 45,* 223-236.

MILLS, J., & MINTZ, P. M. (1972). Effect of unexplained arousal on affiliation. *Journal of Personality and Social Psychology, 24,* 11-13.

MINEKA, S. (1979). The role of fear in theories of avoidance learning, flooding, and extinction. *Psychological Bulletin, 5,* 985-1010.

MINEKA, S., & HENDERSON, R. W. (1985). Controllability and predictability in acquired motivation. *Annual Review of Psychology, 36,* 495-529.

MONAT, A., & LAZARUS, R. S. (1985). Stress and coping—some current issues and controversies. In A. Monat & R. Lazarus (Eds.), *Stress and coping* (2nd ed.). New York: Columbia University Press.

MONEY, J. (1987). Sin, sickness, or status: Homosexual gender identity and psychoneuroendocrinology. *American Psychologist, 42,* 284-299.

MONEY, J., & EHRHARDT, A. (1972). *Man & woman, boy & girl.* Baltimore: Johns Hopkins University Press.

MONTGOMERY, K. C. (1953). The effect of hunger and thirst drives upon exploratory behavior. *Journal of Comparative and Physiological Psychology, 46,* 315-319.

MOOK, D. G. (1963). Oral and post-ingestional determinants of the intake of various solutions in rats with esophageal fistulas. *Journal of Comparative and Physiological Psychology, 56,* 645-659.

MOOK, D. G., BRANE, J. A., GONDER-FREDERICK, L., & WHITT, J. A. (1986). Satieties and cross-satieties for three diets in the rat. *Physiology and Behavior, 36,* 887-895.

MORGAN, C. T. (1943). *Physiological psychology.* New York: McGraw-Hill.

MORGAN, C. T. (1959). Physiological theory of drive. In S. Koch (Ed.), *Psychology: A study of science* (Vol. 1). New York: McGraw-Hill.

MORGANE, P. J. (1964). Limbic-hypothalamic-midbrain interaction in thirst and thirst motivated behavior. In M. J. Wayner (Ed.), *Thirst.* Oxford: Pergamon.

MORRIS, C. W. (1938). Foundations of the theory of signs. In O. Neurath, R. Carnap, & C. Morris (Eds.), *International encyclopedia of unified science* (Vol. 1). Chicago: University of Chicago Press.

MORRISON, A. R. (1983). A window on the sleeping brain. *Scientific American, 248*(4), 94-102.

MORUZZI, G., & MAGOUN, H. W. (1949). Brain stem and reticular formation and activation of the EEG. *Electroencephalography and Clinical Neurophysiology, 1,* 455-473.

MOSCOVITCH, A., & LoLORDO, V. M. (1968). Role of safety in the Pavlovian backward fear conditioning procedure. *Journal of Comparative and Physiological Psychology, 66,* 673-678.

MOSS, M. K., & PAGE, R. A. (1972). Reinforcement and helping behavior. *Journal of Applied Social Psychology, 2,* 360-371.

MOULTON, R. W. (1965). Effects of success and failure on level of aspiration as related to achievement motives. *Journal of Personality and Social Psychology, 1,* 399–406.

MOWRER, O. H. (1939). A stimulus-response analysis of anxiety and its role as a reinforcing agent. *Psychological Review, 46,* 553–564.

MOWRER, O. H. (1960). *Learning theory and behavior.* New York: Wiley.

MOWRER, O. H., & AIKEN, E. G. (1954). Contiguity vs. drive-reduction in conditioned fear: Temporal variations in conditioned and unconditioned stimulus. *American Journal of Psychology, 67,* 26–38.

MOWRER, O. H., & LAMOREAUX, R. R. (1946). Fear as an intervening variable in avoidance conditioning. *Journal of Comparative Psychology, 39,* 29–50.

MOWRER, O. H., & SOLOMON, L. N. (1954). Contiguity vs. drive-reduction in conditioned fear: The proximity and abruptness of drive-reduction. *American Journal of Psychology, 67,* 15–25.

MOWRER, O. H., & VIEK, P. (1948). An experimental analogue of fear from a sense of helplessness. *Journal of Abnormal and Social Psychology, 83,* 193–200.

MUNTON, A. G. (1985–1986). Learned helplessness, attribution theory, and the nature of cognitions: A critical evaluation. *Current Psychological Research and Reviews,* Winter, 331–348.

MURRAY, E. J., & BERKUN, M. M. (1955). Displacement as a function of conflict. *Journal of Abnormal and Social Psychology, 51,* 47–56.

MURRAY, H. A. (1938). *Explorations in personality.* New York: Oxford University Press.

NEISS, R. (1988). Reconceptualizing arousal: Psychobiological states in motor performance. *Psychological Bulletin, 103,* 345–366.

NEL, E., HELMREICH, R., & ARONSON, E. (1969). Opinion change in the advocate as a function of the persuasibility of the audience: A clarification of the meaning of dissonance. *Journal of Personality and Social Psychology, 12,* 117–124.

NEWCOMB, T. M. (1961). *The acquaintance process.* New York: Holt, Rinehart and Winston.

NEWCOMB, T. (1968). Interpersonal balance. In R. P. Abelson, E. Aronson, W. J. McGuire, T. M. Newcomb, M. J. Rosenberg, & P. H. Tannenbaum (Eds.), *Theories of cognitive consistency: A sourcebook.* Chicago: Rand McNally.

NICHOLAIDIS, S. (1968). Responses des unites osmosensibles hypothalamiques aux stimulations saliens at aqueuses de la langue. *Competes rendus hebdomadaires des seances de l'academie des sciences,* Series C, 267, 2352–2355.

NISBETT, R. E. (1972). Hunger, obesity, and the ventromedial hypothalamus. *Psychological Review, 79,* 433–453.

NOTZ, W. W. (1975). Work motivation and the negative effects of extrinsic rewards: A review with implications for theory and practice. *American Psychologist, 9,* 844–891.

NOVIN, D. (1962). The relation between electrical conductivity of brain tissue and thirst in the rat. *Journal of Comparative and Physiological Psychology, 55,* 145–154.

OBRIST, P. A. (1976). The cardiovascular-behavioral interaction—As it appears today. *Psychophysiology, 13,* 95–107.

OBRIST, P. A. (1981). *Cardiovascular psychophysiology: A perspective.* New York: Plenum Press.

ÖHMAN, A. (1986). Face the beast and fear the face: Animal and social fears as prototypes for evolutionary analyses of emotion. *Psychophysiology, 23*(2), 123–145.

O'KELLY, L. I., & BECK, R. C. (1960). Water regulation in the rat: III. The artificial control of thirst with stomach loads of water and sodium chloride. *Psychological Monographs, 74*(13, Whole No. 500).

O'KELLY, L. I., HATTON, G., TUCKER, L., & WESTALL, D. (1965). Water regulation in the rat: Heart rate as a function of hydration, anesthesia, and association with reinforcement. *Journal of Comparative and Physiological Psychology, 59,* 159–165.

O'KELLY, L. I., & STECKLE, L. C. (1939). A note on long-enduring emotional responses in the rat. *Journal of Psychology, 8,* 125–131.

OLDS, J. (1956). Pleasure centers in the brain. *Scientific American, 195,* 105–116.

OLDS, J. (1958). Satiation effects in self-stimulation of the brain. *Journal of Comparative and Physiological Psychology, 51,* 675–678.

OLDS, J. (1961). Differential effects of drive and drugs on self-stimulation at different brain sites. In D. E. Sheer (Ed.), *Electrical stimulation of the brain.* Austin: University of Texas Press.

OLDS, J., & MILNER, P. (1954). Positive reinforcement produced by electrical stimulation of the septal area and other regions of the rat brain. *Journal of Comparative and Physiological Psychology, 47,* 419–427.

O'LEARY, C. J., WILLIS, F. N., & TOMICH, E. (1969). Conformity under deceptive and nondeceptive techniques. *Sociological Quarterly,* Winter, 87–93.

OOMURA, Y., KIMURA, K., OOYAMA, H., MAENO, T., IKI, M., & KUNIYOSHI, M. (1964). Reciprocal activities of the ventromedial and lateral hypothalamic areas of cats. *Science, 143,* 484–485.

ORNSTEIN, R. (1986). *The psychology of consciousness.* New York: Penguin.

OSGOOD, C. E. (1950). Can Tolman's theory of learning handle avoidance training? *Psychological Review, 57,* 133–137.

OSGOOD, C. E., SUCI, G. J., & TANNENBAUM, P. H. (1957). *The measurement of meaning.* Urbana: University of Illinois Press.

OVERMIER, J. B., & LAWRY, J. A. (1979). Pavlovian conditioning and the mediation of behavior. In G. H. Bower (Ed.), *The psychology of learning and motivation* (Vol. 13). New York: Academic Press.

OVERMIER, J. B., & SELIGMAN, M. E. P. (1967). Effects of inescapable shock upon subsequent escape and avoidance responding. *Journal of Comparative and Physiological Psychology, 63,* 28–33.

OXENDINE, J. B. (1970). Emotional arousal and motor performance. *Quest, 13,* 23–32.

PAGE, H. A. (1955). The facilitation of experimental extinction by response prevention as a function of the acquisition of a new response. *Journal of Comparative and Physiological Psychology, 48,* 14–16.

PAGE, M. M., & SCHEIDT, R. J. (1971). The elusive weapons effect: Demand awareness, evaluation apprehension, and slightly sophisticated subjects. *Journal of Personality and Social Psychology, 20,* 304–318.

PALLAK, M. S., & PITTMAN, T. S. (1972). General motivational effects of dissonance arousal. *Journal of Personality and Social Psychology, 21,* 349–358.

PALMER, J., & BYRNE, D. (1970). Attraction toward dominant and submissive strangers: Similarity versus complementarity. *Journal of Experimental Research in Psychology, 4,* 108–115.

PAPEZ, J. W. (1937). A proposed mechanism of emotion. *Archives of Neurology and Psychiatry, 38,* 725–743.

PARKINSON, B. (1985). Emotional effects of false autonomic feedback. *Psychological Bulletin, 98*(3), 471–494.

PARKINSON, B., MANSTEAD, A. S. R. (1981). An examination of the roles played by meaning of feedback and attention to feedback in the "Valins effect." *Journal of Personality and Social Psychology, 40,* 239–245.

PASTORE, N. (1952). The role of arbitrariness in the frustration-aggression hypothesis. *Journal of Abnormal and Social Psychology, 57,* 728–731.

PATTERSON, M. L. (1976). An arousal model for interpersonal intimacy. *Psychological Review, 83,* 235–245.

PATTY, R. A. (1976). Motive to avoid success and instructional set. *Sex Roles, 2,* 81–83.

PENFIELD, W. & JASPER, H. H. (1954). Epilepsy and the functional anatomy of the brain. Boston: Little Brown.

PEPLAU, L. A. (1982). Interpersonal attraction. In D. Sherrod (Ed.), *Social psychology.* New York: Random House.

PEPPER, S. (1959). A neural-identity theory of mind. In S. Hook (Ed.), *Dimensions of mind.* New York: Collier.

PERIN, C. T. (1942). Behavioral potentiality as a joint function of the amount of training and the degree of hunger at the time of extinction. *Journal of Experimental Psychology, 30,* 93–113.

PETERSON, R. A., & KERIN, R. A. (1977). The female role in advertising: Some experimental evidence. *Journal of Marketing, 41,* 59–63.

PETTY, R. E., & CACIOPPO, J. T. (1984). Motivational factors in consumer response to advertisements. In R. G. Geen, W. W. Beatty, & R. M. Arkin (Eds.), *Human motivation.* New York: Allyn and Bacon.

PETTY, R. E., CACIOPPO, J. T., & SCHUMANN, D. (1983). Central and peripheral routes to advertising effectiveness: The moderating role of involvement. *Journal of Consumer Research, 10,* 135–146.

PFAFF, D. (ED.) (1982). *The physiological mechanisms of motivation.* New York: Springer-Verlag.

PFAFFMANN, C. (1960). The pleasures of sensation. *Psychological Review, 67,* 253–268.

PFAFFMANN, C., & BARE, J. K. (1950). Gustatory nerve discharges in normal and adrenalectomized rats. *Journal of Comparative and Physiological Psychology, 43,* 320–324.

PIET, S. (1987). What motivates stunt men? *Motivation and Emotion, 11*(2), 195–213.

PILIAVIN, I., RODIN, J., & PILIAVIN, J. (1969). Good Samaritanism: An underground phenomenon? *Journal of Personality and Social Psychology, 13,* 289–299.

PLUTCHIK, R. (1980). *Emotion: A psychoevolutionary synthesis.* New York: Harper & Row.

POPPER, K. R. (1959). *The logic of scientific discovery.* New York: Harper & Row.

POSTMAN, L. (1947). The history and present status of the law of effect. *Psychological Bulletin, 44,* 489–563.

POSTMAN, L., BRONSON, W., & GROPPER, G. L. (1953). Is there a mechanism of perceptual defense? *Journal of Abnormal and Social Psychology, 48,* 215–224.

POWLEY, T. L. (1977). The ventromedial hypothalamic syndrome, satiety, and a cephalic phase hypothesis. *Psychological Review, 84,* 89–126.

POWLEY, T. L., & KEESEY, R. E. (1970). Relationship of body weight to the lateral hypothalamic feeding syndrome. *Journal of Comparative and Physiological Psychology, 70,* 25–36.

PREMACK, D. (1959). Toward empirical behavioral laws: I. Positive reinforcement. *Psychological Review, 66,* 219–233.

PREMACK, D. (1971). Catching up with common sense or two sides of a generalization: Reinforcement and punishment. In R. Glaser (Ed.), *The nature of reinforcement.* New York: Academic.

PRIEST, R. F., & SAWYER, J. (1967). Proximity and peership: Bases of balance in interpersonal attraction. *American Journal of Sociology, 7,* 21027.

PRITCHARD, R. M. (1961). Stabilized images on the retina. *Scientific American, 204,* 72–78.

PURETO, A., DEUTSCH, J. A., MOLINA, F., & ROLL, P. L. (1976). Rapid discrimination of rewarding nutrient by the upper gastrointestinal tract. *Science, 192,* 485–486.

RAMIREZ, I., & FULLER, J. L. (1976). Genetic influence on water and sweetened water consumption in mice. *Physiology and Behavior, 16,* 163–168.

RANSON, S. W., FISCHER, C., & INGRAM, W. R. (1938). The hypothalamicohypophyseal mechanism in diabetes insipidus. Paper read before Association for Research in Nervous and Mental Diseases, December 1936. In *The pituitary gland.* Baltimore, MD: Williams and Wilkins.

RAY, O. (1963). The effects of tranquilizers on positively and negatively motivated behavior in rats. *Psychopharmacologia, 4,* 326–342.

RAYNOR, J. O. (1970). Relationships between achievement-related motives, future orientation, and academic performance. *Journal of Personality and Social Psychology, 15,* 28–33.

RAYNOR, J. O. (1974). Motivation and career striving. In J. W. Atkinson & J. O. Raynor (Eds.), *Motivation and achievement*. Washington, DC: Winston (Halsted Press/Wiley).

RAZRAN, G. (1961). The observable unconscious and the inferable conscious in current Soviet psychophysiology: Interoceptive conditioning, semantic conditioning, and the orienting reflex. *Psychological Review, 68*, 81–147.

REISEN, A. H. (1961). Stimulation as a requirement for growth and function in behavioral development. In D. W. Fiske & J. R. Maddi (Eds.), *Functions of varied experiences*. Homewood, IL: Dorsey.

REISENZEIN, R. (1983). The Schachter theory of emotion: Two decades later. *Psychological Bulletin, 94*, 239–264.

REITH, J. (1988). *Job satisfaction parallels in higher education*. Unpublished master's thesis, Wake Forest University, Winston-Salem, NC.

RESCORLA, R. A. (1967). Pavlovian conditioning and its proper control procedure. *Psychological Review, 74*, 71–80.

RESCORLA, R. A. (1969). Establishment of a positive reinforcer through contrast with shock. *Journal of Comparative and Physiological Psychology, 67*, 260–263.

RESCORLA, R. A. (1987). A Pavlovian analysis of goal-directed behavior. *American Psychologist, 42*, 119–129.

RESCORLA, R. A., & SOLOMON, R. L. (1967). Two-process learning theory: Relationships between Pavlovian conditioning and instrumental learning. *Psychological Review, 74*, 151–182.

REVUSKY, S. H. (1967). Hunger level during food consumption: Effects on subsequent preferences. *Psychonomic Science, 7*, 109–110.

REVUSKY, S. H. (1968). Effects of thirst level during consumption of flavored water on subsequent preference. *Journal of Comparative and Physiological Psychology, 66*, 777-779.

REVUSKY, S. H., & GARCIA, J. (1970). Learned associations over long delays. In C. H. Bower & J. T. Spence (Eds.), *The psychology of learning and motivation: Advances in research and theory* (Vol. 4). New York: Academic.

RICHMAN, C. L., DEMBER, W., & KIM, P. (Winter 1986–87). Spontaneous alternation behavior in animals: A review. *Current Psychological Research and Reviews, 5*, 358–391.

RICHTER, C. P. (1936). Increased salt appetite in adrenalectomized rats. *American Journal of Physiology, 115*, 155–161.

RIMM, D. C., & MASTERS, J. C. (1979). *Behavior therapy: Techniques and empirical findings* (2nd ed.). New York: Academic Press.

RINN, W. (1984). The neuropsychology of facial expression: A review of the neurological and psychological mechanisms for producing facial expressions. *Psychological Bulletin, 95*(1), 52–77.

ROBERTS, G. C. (1984). Toward a new theory of motivation in sport: The role of perceived ability. In R. M. Silva & R. S. Weinberg (Eds.), *Psychological foundations of sport*. Champaign, IL: Human Kinetics Publishers, Inc.

ROBERTS, L. E. (1974). Comparative psychophysiology of the electrodermal and cardiac control systems. In P. A. Obrist, A. H. Black, J. Brener, & L. V. DiCara (Eds.), *Cardiovascular psychophysiology*. Chicago: Aldine.

ROBERTS, L. E., LACROIX, J. M., & WRIGHT, M. (1974). Comparative studies of operant electrodermal and heart rate conditioning in curarized rats. In P. A. Obrist, A. H. Black, J. Brener, & L. V. DiCara (Eds.), *Cardiovascular psychophysiology*. Chicago: Aldine.

ROBBINS, D. (1969). Effect of duration of water reinforcement on running behavior and consummatory activity. *Journal of Comparative and Physiological Psychology, 69*, 311–316.

ROBINS, C. J. (1988). Attributions and depression: Why is the literature so inconsistent? *Journal of Personality and Social Psychology, 54*(5), 880–889.

RODGERS, W. L., EPSTEIN, A. N., & TEITELBAUM, P. (1965). Lateral hypothalamic aphagia: Motor failure or motivational deficit? *American Journal of Physiology, 208*, 334–342.

RODIN, J. (1981). Current status of the internal-external hypothesis for obesity: What went wrong? *American Psychologist, 36,* 361–372.

RODIN, J., & LANGER, E. J. (1977). Long-term effects of control-relevant intervention with the institutionalized aged. *Journal of Personality and Social Psychology, 35,* 897–902.

ROETHLISBERGER, F. J. & DICKSON, W. J. (1947)). *Management and the worker.* Cambridge, Mass.: Harvard Univ. Press.

ROLLS, E. T., ROLLS, B. J., & ROWE, E. A. (1983). Sensory-specific and motivation-specific satiety for the sight and taste of food and water in man. *Physiology and Behavior, 30,* 185–192.

ROTHBAUM, F., WEISZ, J. R., & SNYDER, S. S. (1982). Changing the world and changing the self: A two process model of perceived control. *Journal of Personality and Social Psychology, 42,* 5–37.

ROTTER, J. B. (1954). *Social learning and clinical psychology.* Englewood Cliffs, NJ: Prentice-Hall.

ROTTER, J. B. (1966). Generalized expectancies for internal versus external control of reinforcement. *Psychological Monographs, 80*(Whole No. 609).

ROUTTENBERG, A. (1968). The two-arousal hypothesis: Reticular formation and limbic system. *Psychological Review, 75,* 51–80.

ROZIN, P., & KALAT, J. W. (1971). Specific hungers and poison avoidance as adaptive specializations of learning. *Psychological Review, 78,* 459–486.

ROZIN, P., & SCHILLER, D. (1980). The nature and acquisition of a preference for chili peppers by humans. *Motivation and Emotion, 4,* 77–101.

RUBIN, Z. (1970). Measurement of romantic love. *Journal of Personality and Social Psychology, 16,* 265–273.

RUBIN, Z. (1973). *Liking and loving.* New York: Holt, Rinehart and Winston.

RUSSELL, J. A. (1979). Affective space is bipolar. *Journal of Personality and Social Psychology, 37,* 345–356.

RUSSELL, J. A. (1980). A circumplex model of affect. *Journal of Personality and Social Psychology, 39,* 1161–1178.

RUSSELL, J. A., & BULLOCK, M. (1985). Multidimensional scaling of emotional facial expressions: Similarity from preschoolers to adults. *Journal of Personality and Social Psychology, 48,* 1290–1298.

RUSSELL, J. A., & MEHRABIAN, A. (1977). Evidence for a three-factor theory of emotions. *Journal of Research in Psychology, 11,* 273–294.

RYLE, G. (1949). *The concept of mind.* New York: Barnes & Noble.

SATINOFF, E. (1983). A reevaluation of the concept of the homeostatic organization of temperature regulation. In E. Satinoff & P. Teitelbaum (Eds.), *Handbook of behavioral neurobiology* (Vol. 6). New York: Plenum.

SCHACHTER, S. (1951). Deviation, rejection, and communication. *Journal of Abnormal and Social Psychology, 46,* 190–207.

SCHACHTER, S. (1959). *The psychology of affiliation.* Palo Alto, CA: Stanford University Press.

SCHACHTER, S. (1971a). *Emotion, obesity, and crime.* New York: Academic.

SCHACHTER, S. (1971b). Some extraordinary facts about obese humans and rats. *American Psychologist, 26,* 129–144.

SCHACHTER, S., & SINGER, J. E. (1962). Cognitive, social, and physiological determinants of emotional state. *Psychological Review, 69,* 379–399.

SCHEIN, M. W., & HALE, E. R. (1965). Stimuli eliciting sexual behavior. In J. Beach (Ed.), *Sex and behavior.* New York: John Wiley and Sons.

SCHIFFMAN, S. S., & ENGELHARD, H. H., III. (1976). Taste of dipeptides. *Physiology and Behavior, 17,* 523–535.

SCHLENKER, B. (1982). Translating actions into attitudes: An identity analytic approach to the explanation of social conduct. In L. Berkowitz (Ed.), *Advances in experimental social psychology* (Vol. 15). New York: Academic Press.

SCHLOSBERG, H. (1954). Three dimensions of emotion. *Psychological Review, 61,* 81–88.

SCHMIDT, D. E., & KEATING, J. P. (1979). Human crowding and personal control: An integration of the research. *Psychological Bulletin, 86,* 680–700.

SCHMIDT, H., JR., STEWART, A. L., & PEREZ, V. J. (1967). Learned reduction of drinking latency. *Journal of Genetic Psychology, 111,* 219–225.

SCHNEIDER, D. J. (1976) *Social psychology.* Reading, MA: Addison-Wesley.

SCHOPLER, J., & COMPERE, J. S. (1971). Effects of being kind or harsh to another on liking. *Journal of Personality and Social Psychology, 20,* 155–159.

SCHWARTZ, S. (1968). Words, deeds, and the perception of consequences and responsibility in action situations. *Journal of Personality and Social Psychology, 10,* 232–242.

SCHWARTZ, S., & CLAUSEN, G. T. (1970). Responsibility, norms, and helping in an emergency. *Journal of Personality and Social Psychology, 16,* 299–310.

SCLAFANI, A., & NISSENBAUM, J. W. (1987). Taste preference thresholds for polycose, maltose, and sucrose in rats. *Neuroscience and Biobehavioral Reviews, 11,* 181–185.

SCOTT, J. P. (1971). Theoretical issues concerning the origin and causes of fighting. In B. E. Eleftheriou & J. P. Scott (Eds.), *The physiology of aggression and defeat.* New York: Plenum.

SECORD, P. F. & BACKMAN, C. W. (1974). *Social psychology.* New York: McGraw-Hill.

SEGAL, M. W. (1974). Alphabet and attraction: An unobtrusive measure of the effect of propinquity in a field setting. *Journal of Personality and Social Psychology, 30,* 654–657.

SELIGMAN, M. E. P. (1970). On the generality of the laws of learning. *Psychological Review, 77,* 406–418.

SELIGMAN, M. E. P. (1971). Phobias and preparedness. *Behavior Therapy, 2,* 307–320.

SELIGMAN, M. E. P. (1975). *Helplessness: On depression, development and death.* San Francisco: W. H. Freeman.

SELIGMAN, M. E. P., ABRAMSON, L. Y., SEMMEL, A., & VON BAYER, C. (1979). Depressive attributional style. *Journal of Abnormal Psychology, 88,* 242–247.

SELIGMAN, M. E. P., & JOHNSTON, J. C. (1973). A cognitive theory of avoidance learning. In F. J. McGurgan & D. B. Lumsden (Eds.), *Contemporary approaches to conditioning and learning.* Washington, DC: Winston.

SELIGMAN, M. E. P., & MAIER, S. F. (1967). Failure to escape traumatic shock. *Journal of Experimental Psychology, 74,* 1–9.

SELYE, H. (1956). *The stress of life.* New York: McGraw-Hill.

SETA, J. J., CRISSON, J. E., SETA, C. E., & WANG, M. A. (in press). Task performance and perceptions of anxiety: Averaging and summation in an evaluative setting. *Journal of Personality and Social Psychology.*

SHARMA, K. N., ANAND, B. K., DUA, S., & SINGH, B. (1961). Role of stomach in regulation of activities of hypothalamic feeding centers. *American Journal of Physiology, 201,* 593–598.

SHAUGHNESSY, J. J., & ZECKMEISTER, E. B. (1985). *Research methods in psychology.* New York: Alfred A. Knopf.

SHEFFIELD, F. D. (1948). Avoidance training and the contiguity principle. *Journal of Comparative and Physiological Psychology, 41,* 165–177.

SHEFFIELD, F. D. (1966). New evidence on the drive-induction theory of reinforcement. In R. N. Haber (Ed.), *Current research in motivation.* New York: Holt, Rinehart and Winston.

SHEFFIELD, F. D., & ROBY, T. B. (1950). Reward value of a non-nutritive sweet taste. *Journal of Comparative and Physiological Psychology, 43,* 471–481.

SHEFFIELD, F. D., WULFF, J. J., & BACKER, R. (1951). Reward value of copulation without sex drive reduction. *Journal of Comparative and Physiological Psychology, 44,* 3–8.

SHERIDAN, C. L., & KING, R. G. (1972). Obedience to authority with an authentic victim. *Proceedings, Eightieth annual convention, American Psychological Association,* Honolulu, 165–166. Washington, DC: American Psychological Association.

SHERIF, M., HARVEY, O. J., WHITE, B., HOOD, W., & SHERIF, C. (1961). *Intergroup conflict and cooperation: The robber's cave experiment.* Norman, OK: Institute of Group Relations, University of Oklahoma.

SHERROD, D. (1982). *Social psychology.* New York: Random House.

SHERWOOD, A., ALLEN, M. T., OBRIST, P. A., & LANGER, A. W. (1986). Evaluation of beta-adrenergic influences on cardiovascular and metabolic adjustments to physical and psychological stress. *Psychophysiology, 23*(1), 89–104.

SHIPLEY, T. E., & VEROFF, J. (1952). A projective measure of need for affiliation. *Journal of Experimental Psychology, 43,* 349–356.

SIDMAN, M. (1962). Reduction of shock frequency as reinforcement for avoidance behavior. *Journal of the Experimental Analysis of Behavior, 5,* 247–257.

SIDMAN, M. (1966). Avoidance behavior. In W. K. Honig (Ed.), *Operant behavior: Areas of research and application.* New York: Appleton-Century-Crofts.

SIEGEL, P. S., & MILBY, J. B. (1969). Secondary reinforcement in relation to shock termination. *Psychological Bulletin, 72,* 146–156.

SIEGMAN, A. W., DEMBROSKI, T. M., & RINGLE, N. (1987). Components of hostility and the severity of coronary artery disease. *Psychosomatic Medicine, 49,* 127–135.

SIGALL, H., & LANDY, D. (1973). Radiating beauty: Effects of having a physically attractive partner on person perception. *Journal of Personality and Social Psychology, 28,* 218–224.

SILVERMAN, L. (1982, May). Mommy and I are one. *Psychology Today,* pp. 24–36.

SKINNER, B. F. (1938). *The behavior of organisms.* New York: Appleton-Century-Crofts.

SKINNER, B. F. (1948). *Walden II.* New York: MacMillan.

SMITH, F. J. (1977). Work attitudes as predictors of attendance on a specific day. *Journal of Applied Psychology, 62,* 16–19.

SOKOLOV, E. N. (1960). Neuronal models of the orienting reflex. In M. A. B. Brazier (Ed.), *The central nervous system and behavior: Transaction of the third conference.* New York: Josiah Macy, Jr., Foundation.

SOLOMON, R. L. (1980). The opponent-process theory of acquired motivation: The costs of pleasure and the benefits of pain. *American Psychologist, 35,* 691–712.

SOLOMON, R. L., & CORBIT, J. D. (1974). An opponent-process theory of motivation: I. Temporal dynamics of affect. *Psychological Review, 81,* 119–145.

SOLOMON, R. L., & TURNER, L. H. (1962). Discriminative classical conditioning in dogs paralyzed by curare can later control discriminative avoidance responses in the normal state. *Psychological Review, 69,* 202–219.

SOLOMON, R. L., & WYNNE, L. C. (1950). Avoidance conditioning in normal dogs and in dogs deprived of normal autonomic functioning. *American Psychologist, 5,* 264.

SOLOMON, R. L., & WYNNE, L. C. (1954). Traumatic avoidance learning: The principles of anxiety conservation and partial irreversibility. *Psychological Review, 61,* 353–385.

SONSTROEM, R. J. (1984). An overview of anxiety in sport. In J. M. Silva & R. S. Weinberg (Eds.), *Psychological foundations of sport.* Champaign, IL: Human Kinetics.

SONSTROEM, R. J., & BERNADO, P. B. (1982). Intraindividual pregame state anxiety and basketball performance: A re-examination of the inverted-U curve. *Journal of Sport Psychology, 4,* 235–245.

SPENCE, J., & HELMREICH, R. (1983). Types of achievement and achievement-related motives and rewards. In J. Spence (Ed.), *Achievement and achievement motives.* San Francisco: W. H. Freeman.

SPENCE, K. W. (1956). *Behavior theory and conditioning.* New Haven, CT: Yale University Press.

SPENCE, K. W., & TAYLOR, J. (1951). Anxiety and strength of the U.S. as a determinant of eyelid conditioning. *Journal of Experimental Psychology, 42,* 183–188.

SPIELBERGER, C. D. (1966). Theory and research on anxiety. In C. D. Spielberger (Ed.), *Anxiety and behavior.* New York: Academic.

SPIELBERGER, C. D. (1976). The nature and measurement of anxiety. In C. D. Spielberger & R. Diaz-Guerrero (Eds.), *Cross-cultural anxiety.* Washington, DC: Hemisphere.

SPIELBERGER, C. D., GORSUCH, R. L., & LUSHENE, R. F. (1970). *Manual for the State-Trait Anxiety Inventory.* Palo Alto, CA: Consulting Psychologists Press.

SPRAGUE, J. M., CHAMBERS, W. W., & STELLAR, E. (1961). Attentive, affective, and adaptive behavior in the cat. *Science, 133,* 165-173.

STADDON, J. E. R. (1974). Temporal control, attention, and memory. *Psychological Review, 81,* 375-391.

STAGNER, R. (1977). Homeostasis, discrepancy, and motivation. *Motivation and Emotion, 1,* 103-137.

STANG, D. J. (1974). Methodological factors in mere exposure research. *Psychological Bulletin, 81,* 1014-1025.

STARR, M. D., & MINEKA, S. (1977). Determinants of fear over the course of avoidance learning. *Learning and Motivation, 8,* 332-350.

STAVELY, H. E., JR. (1966). Effect of escape duration and shock intensity on the acquisition and extinction of an escape response. *Journal of Experimental Psychology, 72,* 698-703.

STEELE, R. S. (1977). Power motivation, activation, and inspirational speeches. *Journal of Personality, 45,* 53-64.

STEERS, R. M., & PORTER, L. W. (1975). *Motivation and work behavior.* New York: McGraw-Hill

STEFFEN, J. J., MCLANEY, M. A., & HUSTEDT, T. K. (1982). *The development of a scale of limerence.* Paper presented at the annual convention of the American Psychological Association, Washington, DC.

STEGGERDA, F. R. (1941). Observations on the water intake in an adult man with dysfunctioning salivary glands. *American Journal of Psychology, 132,* 517-521.

STELLAR, E. (1954). The physiology of motivation. *Psychological Review, 61,* 5-22.

STELLAR, J. R., & STELLAR, E. (1985). *The neurobiology of motivation and reward.* New York: Springer-Verlag.

STEPHENS, D. W., & KREBS, J. R. (1986). *Foraging theory.* Princeton: Princeton University Press.

STERN, R. M., BOTTO, R. W., & HERRICK, C. D. (1972). Behavioral and physiological effects of false heart rate feedback: A replication and extension. *Psychophysiology, 9,* 21-29.

STERNBERG, R. J. (1986). A triangular theory of love. *Psychological Review, 93,* 119-135.

STERNBERG, R. J. (1987). Liking versus loving: A comparative evaluation of theories. *Psychological Bulletin, 102,* 331-345.

STERNBERG, R. J., & GRAJEK, S. (1984). The nature of love. *Journal of Personality and Social Psychology, 47,* 312-329.

STORMS, M. D. (1983a). *Development of sexual orientation.* Washington, DC: Office of Social and Ethical Responsibility, American Psychological Association.

STORMS, M. D. (1983b). A theory of erotic orientation development. *Psychological Review, 88,* 340-353.

STORMS, M. D., & NISBETT, R. E. (1970). Insomnia and the attribution process. *Journal of Personality and Social Psychology, 16,* 319-328.

STROEBE, W. C., INSKO, A., THOMPSON, V. D., & LAYTON, B. D. (1971). Effects of physical attractiveness, attitude similarity, and sex on various aspects of interpersonal attraction. *Journal of Personality and Social Psychology, 18,* 79-91.

SULLIVAN, M., & BRENDER, W. (1986). Facial electromyography: A measure of affective processes during sexual arousal. *Psychophysiology, 23*(2), 182-188.

SUTTERER, J. R., & BECK, R. C. (1970). Human responses to stimuli associated with shock onset and termination. *Journal of Experimental Research in Personality, 4,* 163-170.

SWEENEY, P. D., ANDERSON, K., & BAILEY, S. (1986). Attributional style in depression: A meta-analytic review. *Journal of Personality and Social Psychology, 50,* 947-991.

SWENSON, C. H. (1972). The behavior of love. In H. A. Otto (Ed.), *Love today*. New York: Associations Press.

TANG, M., & COLLIER, G. (1971). Effect of successive deprivations and recoveries on the level of instrumental performance in the rat. *Journal of Comparative and Physiological Psychology, 74*, 108–114.

TANNENBAUM, P. H., & ZILLMANN, D. (1975). Emotional arousal in the facilitation of aggression through communication. In L. Berkowitz (Ed.), *Advances in experimental social psychology* (Vol. 8). New York: Academic.

TAVRIS, C. (1983). *Anger: The misunderstood emotion*. New York: Simon & Schuster.

TAYLOR, J. A. (1953). A personality scale of manifest anxiety. *Journal of Abnormal and Social Psychology, 48*, 285–290.

TAYLOR, S. E., & FISKE, S. T. (1978). Salience, attention, and attribution: Top of the head phenomena. In L. Berkowitz (Ed.), *Advances in experimental social psychology* (Vol. 11). New York: Academic Press.

TEDESCHI, J. T., SMITH, R. B., III., & BROWN, R. C., JR. (1974). A reinterpretation of research on aggression. *Psychological Bulletin, 81*, 540–562.

TEITELBAUM, P. (1961). Disturbances in feeding and drinking behavior after hypothalamic lesions. In M. R. Jones (Ed.), *Nebraska symposium on motivation*. Lincoln: University of Nebraska Press.

TEITELBAUM, P. (1971). The encephalization of hunger. In E. Stellar & J. M. Sprague (Eds.), *Progress in physiological psychology*. New York: Academic.

TEITELBAUM, P., & CYTAWA, J. (1965). Spreading depression and recovery from lateral hypothalamic damage. *Science, 147*, 61–63.

TEITELBAUM, P., & EPSTEIN, A. N. (1962). The lateral hypothalamic syndrome: Recovery of feeding and drinking after lateral hypothalamic lesions. *Psychological Review, 69*, 74–90.

THAYER, R. C. (1978). Toward a psychological theory of multidimensional activation (arousal). *Motivation and Emotion, 2*, 1–34.

THAYER, R. E. (1967). Measurement of activation through self-report. *Psychological Reports, 20*, 663–678.

THISTLEWAITE, D. (1951). A critical review of latent learning and related experiments. *Psychological Bulletin, 48*, 97–129.

THOMPSON, S. C. (1981). Will it hurt less if I control it?: A complex answer to a simple question. *Psychological Bulletin, 90*, 89–101.

THOMPSON, T. I., & STURM, T. (1965). Visual reinforcer color and operant behavior in the Siamese fighting fish. *Journal of Experimental Analysis of Behavior, 8*, 341–344.

THORNDIKE, E. L. (1932). *The fundamentals of learning*. New York: Columbia University Press.

TINKLEPAUGH, O. L. (1928). An experimental study of representative factors in monkeys. *Journal of Comparative Psychology, 8*, 197–236.

TOATES, F. M. (1979). Homeostasis and drinking. *The Behavioral and Brain Sciences, 2*, 95–139.

TOCH, H. (1970). The social psychology of violence. Division 8 invited address, American Psychological Association Meeting, New York, September, 1966. Reprinted in E. I. Megargee & J. E. Hokanson (Eds.), *The dynamics of aggression: Individual, group and international analyses*. New York: Harper & Row.

TOLMAN, E. C. (1932). *Purposive behavior in animals and men*. New York: Appleton-Century-Crofts.

TOLMAN, E. C. (1938). The determiners of behavior at a choice point. *Psychological Review, 45*, 1–41.

TOLMAN, E. C. (1948). Cognitive maps in rats and men. *Psychological Review, 55*, 189–208.

TOLMAN, E. C. (1959). Principles of purposive behavior. In S. Koch (Ed.), *Psychology: A study of a science* (Vol. 2). New York: McGraw-Hill.

TOLMAN, E. C., & HONZIK, C. H. (1930). Degrees of hunger; reward and nonreward; and maze learning in rats. *University of California Publications in Psychology, 4,* 241–256.

TOMKINS, S. (1962). *Affect, imagery, and consciousness: The positive affects* (Vol. 1). New York: Springer.

TOMKINS, S. (1981). The quest for primary motives: Biography and autobiography of an idea. *Journal of Personality and Social Psychology, 41,* 306–329.

TOULMIN, S. (1953). *The philosophy of science—An introduction.* London: Hutchinson.

TOURANGEAU, R., & ELLSWORTH, P. (1979). The role of facial response in the experience of emotion. *Journal of Personality and Social Psychology, 37,* 1519–1531.

TOWBIN, E. J. (1949). Gastric distention as a factor in the satiation of thirst in esophagustomized dogs. *American Journal of Physiology, 159,* 533–541.

TREIT, D., SPETCH, M. L., & DEUTSCH, J. A. (1983). Variety in the flavor of food enhances eating in the rat: A controlled demonstration. *Physiology and Behavior, 30,* 207–211.

TRIPPLET, N. (1897). The dynamogenic factors in pacemaking and competition. *American Journal of Psychology, 9,* 507–533.

TROWILL, J. A., PANKSEPP, J., & GANDELMAN, R. (1969). An incentive model of rewarding brain stimulation. *Psychological Review, 76,* 264–281.

TUCKER, D. M. (1981). Lateral brain function, emotion, and conceptualization. *Psychological Bulletin, 89,* 19–46.

TURNER, M. B. (1967). *Philosophy and the science of behavior.* New York: Appleton-Century-Crofts.

ULRICH, R. E., & AZRIN, N. H. (1962). Reflexive fighting in response to aversive stimulation. *Journal of the Experimental Analysis of Behavior, 5,* 511–520.

ULRICH, R. E., & CRAINE, W. H. (1964). Behavior: Persistence of shock-induced aggression. *Science, 143,* 971–973.

VALENSTEIN, E. (1973). *Brain control: A critical examination of brain stimulation and psychosurgery.* New York: Wiley.

VALENSTEIN, E. S., COX, V. C., & KAKOLEWSKI, J. W. (1970). Re-examination of the role of the hypothalamus in motivation. *Psychological Review, 77,* 16–31.

VALENSTIEN, E. S., KAKOLEWSKI, J., & COX, V. C. (1967). Sex differences in taste preference for glucose and saccharin solutions. *Science, 156,* 942–943.

VALENTINE, C. W. (1930). The innate bases of fear. *Journal of Genetic Psychology, 37,* 394–419.

VALINS, S. (1966). Cognitive effects of false heart-rate feedback. *Journal of Personality and Social Psychology, 4,* 400–408.

VALINS, S. (1970). The perception and labeling of bodily changes as determinants of emotional behavior. In P. Black (Ed.), *Physiological correlates of emotion.* New York: Academic.

VERNON, W., & ULRICH, R. E. (1966). Classical conditioning of pain-elicited aggression. *Science, 152,* 668–669.

VEROFF, J. (1957). Development and validation of projective measures of power motivation. *Journal of Abnormal and Social Psychology, 54,* 1–8.

VERPLANCK, W. S., & HAYES, J. R. (1953). Eating and drinking as a function of maintenance schedule. *Journal of Comparative and Physiological Psychology, 46,* 327–333.

VERTES, R. M. (1986). A life-sustaining function for REM sleep: A theory. *Neuroscience and Biobehavioral Reviews, 10,* 371–376.

VORSTEG, R. H. (1974). Operant reinforcement theory and determinism. *Behaviorism, 2,* 108–119.

VROOM, V. H. (1964). *Work and motivation.* New York: Wiley.

WAGNER, A. R. (1963). Conditioned frustration as a learned drive. *Journal of Experimental Psychology, 66,* 142–148.

WALLACE, R. K., DILLBECK, M., JACOBE, E., & HARRINGTON, B. (1982). The effects of Transcendental Meditation and the TM-Sidhi program on the aging process. *International Journal of Neuroscience, 16,* 53–58.

WALSTER, E. (1971). Passionate love. In B. Murstein (Ed.), *Theories of attraction and love.* New York: Springer.

WALSTER, E., ARONSON, E., ABRAHAMS, D., & ROTTMAN, L. (1966). Importance of physical attractiveness in dating behavior. *Journal of Personality and Social Psychology, 4,* 508–516.

WALSTER, E., & WALSTER, G. W. (1976). Interpersonal attraction. In B. Seidenberg & A. Snadowsky (Eds.), *Social psychology.* New York: The Free Press.

WARDEN, C. J. (1931). *Animal motivation: Experimental studies on the albino rat.* New York: Columbia University Press.

WARREN, R. M., & PFAFFMANN, C. (1958). Early experience and taste aversion. *Journal of Comparative and Physiological Psychology, 52,* 263–266.

WATERMAN, C. K. (1969). The facilitating and interfering effects of cognitive dissonance on simple and complex paired associates learning tasks. *Journal of Experimental Social Psychology, 5,* 31–42.

WATSON, J. B. (1924). *Psychology from the standpoint of a behaviorist.* Philadelphia: Lippincott.

WATSON, J. B., & RAYNER, R. (1920). Conditioned emotional reactions, *Journal of Experimental Psychology, 3,* 1–14.

WEBER, M. (1930). *The protestant ethic and the spirit of capitalism.* (T. Parsons, Trans.). New York: Scribner. (Original work published 1904)

WEINBERG, R. S. (1984). The relationship between extrinsic rewards and intrinsic motivation in sports. In R. M. Silva & R. S. Weinberg (Eds.), *Psychological foundations of sport.* Champaign, IL: Human Kinetics Publishers, Inc.

WEINBERG, R. S., & GENUCHI, M. (1980). Relationship between competitive train anxiety, state anxiety, and golf performance: A field study. *Journal of Sport Psychology, 2,* 148–154.

WEINER, B. (1980). *Human motivation.* New York: Holt, Rinehart and Winston.

WEINER, B. (1985). An attributional theory of achievement motivation and emotion. *Psychological Review, 92,* 548–573.

WEISS, J. M. (1972). Psychological factors in stress and disease. *Scientific American, 226,* 104–113.

WEISS, J. M. (1977). Psychological and behavioral influences on gastrointestinal lesions in animal models. In J. Maser & M. E. P. Seligman (Eds.), *Psychopathology: Experimental models* (pp. 232–269). San Francisco: Freeman.

WEISS, R. F., & MILLER, F. G. (1971). The drive theory of social facilitation. *Psychological Review, 78,* 44–57.

WERBOFF, J., DUANE, D., & COHEN, B. D. (1964). Extinction of conditioned avoidance and heart rate responses in rats. *Journal of Psychosomatic Research, 8,* 29–33.

WHALEN, R. E. (1966). Sexual motivation. *Psychological Review, 73,* 151–163.

WHITE, G. L. (1980). Physical attractiveness and courtship progress. *Journal of Personality and Social Psychology, 39,* 660–668.

WHITE, G. L., FISHBEIN, E., & RUTSTEIN, J. (1981). Passionate love: The misattribution of arousal. *Journal of Personality and Social Psychology, 41,* 56–62.

WHITE, N. M. (1986). Control of sensorimotor function by dopaminergic nigrostriatal neurons: Influence on eating and drinking. *Neuroscience and Biobehavioral Reviews, 10,* 15–36.

WHITE, R. W. (1959). Motivation reconsidered: The concept of competence. *Psychological Review, 66,* 297–333.

WICKLUND, R. A., & BREHM, J. W. (1976). *Perspectives on cognitive dissonance.* Hillsdale, NJ: Erlbaum.

WIKE, E. L. (1966). *Secondary reinforcement: Selected experiments.* New York: Harper & Row.

WILCOXIN, H. C., DRAGOIN, W. B., & KRAL, P. A. (1971). Illness-induced aversions in rat and quail: Relative salience of visual and gustatory cues. *Science, 171,* 826–828.

WILLIAMS, D. R., & TEITELBAUM, P. (1956). Control of drinking by means of an operant conditioning technique. *Science, 124,* 1294–1296.

WILLIAMS, J. E., & BENNETT, S. M. (1975). The definition of sex stereotypes via the Adjective Check List. *Sex Roles, 1,* 327–337.

WILLIAMS, J. E., & BEST, D. L. (1982). *Measuring sex stereotypes: A thirty-nation study.* Beverly Hills, CA: Sage Publications.

WILLIAMS, R. A. (1968). Effects of repeated food deprivations and repeated feeding tests on feeding behavior. *Journal of Comparative and Physiological Psychology, 65,* 222–226.

WILLIAMS, R. B., BAREFOOT, J. C., HANEY, T. L., HARRELL, F. E., BLUMENTHAL, J. A., PRYOR, D. B., & PETERSON, B. (1988). Type A behavior and angiographically documented coronary atherosclerosis in a sample of 2,289 patients. *Psychosomatic Medicine, 50,* 139–152.

WILSON, G. (1981). *The Coolidge effect: An evolutionary account of human sexuality.* New York: William Morrow.

WINCH, R. F. (1958). *Mate selection: A study of complementary needs.* New York: Harper & Row.

WINTER, D. G. (1973). *The power motive.* New York: Free Press.

WOLF, A. V. (1958). *Thirst: Physiology of the urge to drink and problems of water lack.* Springfield, IL: Thomas.

WOLFGANG, M. E. (1957). Victim-precipitated criminal homicide. *Journal of Criminal Law, Criminology, and Police Science, 48,* 1–11.

WOLPE, J., & RACHMAN, S. (1960). Psychoanalytic "evidence": A critique based on Freud's case of Little Hans. *Journal of Nervous and Mental Disease, 131,* 135–148.

WONG, R. (1976). *Motivation: A biobehavioral analysis of consummatory activities.* New York: Macmillan.

WONG, R. (1979). Experiential and circadian influences on drinking: Commentary on Toates: Homeostasis and drinking. *The Behavioral and Brain Sciences, 2,* 123.

WOODS, P. J. (1967). Performance changes in escape conditioning following shifts in the magnitude of reinforcement. *Journal of Experimental Psychology, 75,* 487–491.

WOODS, P. J., DAVIDSON, E. H., & PETERS, R. J., JR. (1964). Instrumental escape conditioning in water tank: Effects of variations in drive stimulus intensity and reinforcement magnitude. *Journal of Comparative and Physiological Psychology, 57,* 466–470.

WOODWORTH, R. S., & SCHLOSBERG, H. (1954). *Experimental psychology* (rev. ed.). New York: Holt, Rinehart and Winston.

WRIGHT, J. H. (1965). Test for a learned drive based on the hunger drive. *Journal of Experimental Psychology, 70,* 580–584.

WRIGHTSMAN, L. S. (1972). *Social psychology in the 70's.* Monterey, CA: Brooks/Cole.

WRIGHTSMAN, L. S., JR. (1960). Effects of waiting with others on changes in level of felt anxiety. *Journal of Abnormal and Social Psychology, 61,* 216–222.

WUNDT, W. (1902). *Outlines of psychology* (2nd ed., C. H. Judd, Trans.). Leipzig: Engelmann.

WYCKOFF, L. B., SIDOWSKI, J., & CHAMBLISS, D. J. (1958). An experimental study of the relationship between secondary reinforcing and cue effects of a stimulus. *Journal of Comparative and Physiological Psychology, 51,* 103–109.

WYER, R., & HARTWICK, J. (1980). The role of information retrieval and conditional inference processes in belief formation and change. In L. Berkowitz (Ed.), *Advances in experimental social psychology* (Vol. 13, pp. 243–284). New York: Academic Press.

WYRWICKA, W., & DOBRZECKA, C. (1960). Relationship between feeding and satiation centers of the hypothalamus. *Science, 132,* 805–806.

YATES, A. J. (1962). *Frustration and conflict.* New York: Wiley.

YERKES, R. M., & DODSON, J. D. (1908). The relation of strength of stimulus to rapidity of habit-formation. *Journal of Comparative and Neurological Psychology, 18,* 459–482.

YOUNG, P. T. (1959). The role of affective processes in learning and motivation. *Psychological Review, 66,* 104–125.

YOUNG, P. T. (1961). *Motivation and emotion: A survey of the determinants of human and animal activity.* New York: Wiley.

YOUNG, P. T. (1968). Evaluation and preferences in behavioral development. *Psychological Review, 75,* 222–241.

YUILLE, J. C., & SEREDA, L. (1980). Positive effects of mediation: A limited generalization? *Journal of Applied Psychology, 65,* 333–340.

ZAJONC, R. B. (1965). Social facilitation. *Science, 149,* 269–274.

ZAJONC, R. B. (1968). Attitudinal effects of mere exposure. *Journal of Personality and Social Psychology Monograph Supplements, 9,* (2, Pt. 2), 1–27.

ZAJONC, R. B. (1984). On the primacy of affect. *American Psychologist, 39*(2), 117–123.

ZAJONC, R. B., & SALES, S. M. (1966). Social facilitation of dominant and subordinate responses. *Journal of Experimental and Social Psychology, 2,* 160–168.

ZANNA, M. P., & COOPER, J. (1974). Dissonance and the pill: An attribution approach to studying the arousal properties of dissonance. *Journal of Personality and Social Psychology, 29,* 703–709.

ZEAMAN, D. (1949). Response latency as a function of the amount of reinforcement. *Journal of Experimental Psychology, 39,* 466–483.

ZILLMAN, D. (1978). Attribution and misattribution of excitatory reactions. In J. H. Harvey, W. J. Ickes, & R. F. Kidd, (Eds.), *New directions in attribution research* (Vol. 2, pp. 355–368). Hillsdale, NJ: Erlbaum.

ZIMBARDO, P. G. (1966). The cognitive control of motivation. *Transactions of the New York Academic of Sciences,* Series II, 28, 902–922.

ZIMBARDO, P. G. (1969). The human choice: Individualization, reason, and order versus deindividuation, impulse, and chaos. In W. Arnold & M. Levine (Eds.), *Nebraska symposium on motivation.* Lincoln: University of Nebraska Press.

ZIMMERMAN, D. W. (1957). Durable secondary reinforcement: Method and theory. *Psychological Review, 64,* 373–383.

ZIMMERMAN, D. W. (1959). Sustained performance in rats based on secondary reinforcement. *Journal of Comparative and Physiological Psychology, 52,* 353–358.

ZUCKERMAN, M. (1979). *Sensation seeking: Beyond the optimal level of arousal.* Hillsdale, NJ: Lawrence Erlbaum Associates, Publishers.

ZUCKERMAN, M. (1984). Sensation-seeking: A comparative approach to a human trait. *Behavioral and Brain Sciences, 7,* 413–434.

ZUCKERMAN, M., EYSENCK, S., & EYSENCK, H. J. (1978). Sensation seeking in England and American: Cross-cultural, age, and sex comparisons. *Journal of Consulting and Clinical Psychology, 46,* 139–149.

ZUGER, D. (1976). Monozygotic twins discordant for homosexuality: Report of a pair and significance of the phenomenon. *Comprehensive Psychiatry, 17,* 661–669.

# Author Index

Gladue, B. A.,  141
Glenberg, A. M.,  61
Glickman, S. E.,  154
Gold, M. S.,  148, 149
Gold, R. M.,  109
Goldstein, J.,  354
Gonder-Frederick, L.,  115
Goranson, R.,  335
Gordon, L.,  125
Gordon, W. C.,  83, 214
Gorsuch, R. L.,  225
Gotlieb, I. H.,  256
Graff, H.,  111
Grajek, S.,  329
Gray, J.,  192, 251
Gray, J. A.,  199, 245, 246, 267
Gray, R. D.,  119, 120
Green, R.,  141
Greene, D.,  181
Greenwald, A. G.,  285, 286
Greenwood, M. M.,  96
Gregory, E.,  137
Grice, G. R.,  78
Gropper, G. L.,  13
Grossen, N. E.,  178
Grossman, S. P.,  109, 111
Guerrin, B.,  81
Guthrie, E. R.,  20
Guttman, N.,  163, 164

**Hackman, J. R.,  349, 350**
Hagen, P. M.,  115
Hahn, W. W.,  96
Hake, H. W.,  12
Hall, J. F.,  77
Hall, M.,  16
Hamlin, P.,  118
Hammen, C. L.,  256
Haney, T. L.,  260
Hardy, W. T.,  114
Hargrave, G. E.,  178
Hargreaves, F. J.,  116
Harlow, H. F.,  157
Harrell, F. E.,  260
Harrington, B.,  265
Harris, L. J.,  116
Harrison, A. A.,  320
Hartwick, J.,  284
Hatton, G.,  95
Hatton, G. I.,  127
Hayes, J. R.,  78
Heapy, N. A.,  304
Hearts, E.,  219
Hebb, D. O.,  71, 87, 90, 91, 93, 192, 193
Hecker, M. H.,  259
Heckhausen, H.,  311
Heider, F.,  255, 274, 276, 327
Hellman, R. E.,  141

Helmreich, R.,  280, 302, 304, 305, 306, 315
Henderson, P. W.,  117, 157
Henderson, R. W.,  258, 259
Hendrick, C.,  325, 332
Hendrick, S.,  332
Hendry, D. P.,  160
Henry, D.,  266
Heron, W.,  91
Herrick, C. D.,  55
Herrnstein, R. J.,  201
Herzberg, F.,  341, 342
Hess, E. H.,  71
Heyns, R. W.,  318
Hinde, R. A.,  71
Hiroto, D. S.,  254, 255
Hirsch, E.,  118
Hoebel, B. G.,  108. 146
Hoffman, H. S.,  196, 198
Hohmann, G. W.,  34
Hokanson, J. E.,  224
Holman, G. L.,  156
Holmes, D. S.,  265
Holmes, T. H.,  248, 249
Holz, W. C.,  206
Honzik, C. H.,  165, 166
Horner, M.,  301
Hovland, C. I.,  16, 356
Huesmann, L. R.,  240
Hull, C. L.,  14, 15, 16, 20, 72, 73, 74, 75, 76, 77, 78, 81, 91, 103, 153, 155, 166, 167, 168, 169, 170, 171, 172, 173, 174, 185, 213, 214, 217, 218, 281, 293, 303, 320
Hume, D.,  5, 16
Hunt, H. F.,  205
Hunt, J. McV.,  92, 245, 250
Hustedt, T. K.,  329
Huston, A. C.,  241
Hyland, M.,  280, 288

**Iki, M.,  111**
Ilgen, D. R.,  347, 348
Ingram, W. R.,  123
Innes, J. M.,  81
Insko, A.,  323
Insko, C. A.,  277
Irwin, F. W.,  24, 25, 203, 226
Isen, A.,  49, 58, 59
Issacson, R.,  319
Ivancevich, J. M.,  345
Izard, C. E.,  40, 44

**Jackson, D. N.,  304**
Jacobe, E.,  265
Jacobs, H. L.,  118, 157
James. W.,  18, 19, 31, 32, 34, 44, 63, 66, 67
Janis, I. L.,  287

# Subject Index